The
New Testament

---

with the
Joseph Smith Translation

Includes:

All Textual Changes made by
the Prophet Joseph Smith

and

The Four Gospels
in Chronological Harmony and Parallel Columns

Compiled by

Steven J. Hite and Julie M. Hite

Published by

The Veritas Group
Orem, Utah

The New Testament with the
Joseph Smith Translation
(4th edition)

Copyright 1996, 1995, 1994, 1992, 1989
by Steven J. and Julie M. Hite

Published by:
The Veritas Group
560 South 500 East
Orem, UT 84097
801-224-2903

Additional copies may be ordered
from the above address

DEDICATION

To Our Children

Melissa
Rachel
David
Shelley
Laurie

INTRODUCTION

In Doctrine and Covenants 45:60-61, 73:3-4, and 76:15, Joseph Smith was commanded by the Lord to "translate" the Bible. While the meaning of "translate" might initially seem obvious, there are actually several interesting and viable possibilities. Dr. Robert L. Millet, Dean of Religious Education at Brigham Young University, has described three perspectives for how one can view Joseph Smith's "translation" (1985, p. 43). He proposes that Joseph's "translation" could be:

1) Inspired prophetic commentary; and/or,

2) Harmonization of the themes, accounts and theologies in the Biblical text with Joseph's progressing understanding of truth, focused by his continuing revelations from the Lord; and/or,

3) Restoration by Joseph of text originally included in the Bible, but lost or changed through centuries of textual transmission and cross-language rendering.

Each of these three possibilities should be especially interesting to Latter-day Saints. Whether a given change represents one or more of these three possibilities, "new" ways of reading the text, and therefrom new insights, are possible.

The Joseph Smith Translation (JST)

After purchasing an 1828 edition of the King James Version (KJV) Bible from E. B. Grandin, the Prophet Joseph Smith spent 16 years, virtually to the time of his martyrdom, following the Lord's commandment to translate. This enormous effort produced changes in over 4,000 verses of the text of the KJV Bible. The marked Bible and accompanying manuscripts produced by Joseph in the translation process were, following his death, left in the private possession of Emma Hale Smith. Later in her life, she donated the manuscript to the Reorganized Church of Jesus Christ of Latter Day Saints (RLDS). The manuscript has remained in their possession to the present time.

For a substantial period of time, access for LDS scholars to the Bible and manuscripts of Joseph's work was very limited. This limited access created some feelings of caution on the part of LDS students of the scriptures concerning the accuracy of the JST texts being published by the RLDS church (such as the *Inspired Bible*). However, since Robert J. Matthews, former Dean of BYU Religious Education, was given full access to the Bible and manuscripts in the 1960's, no serious doubt has survived in the LDS scholarly community that the Joseph Smith Translation, as represented in RLDS publications, is fundamentally reliable and complete when compared to Joseph's original work.

Previous JST Integrations

The numerous past efforts at integrating the JST have produced very different and interesting texts. For example, in 1970 the Herald Press in Independence, Missouri published a comprehensive parallel text of all JST variations against the King James version. The exclusion of non-modified verses, although understandable due to space limitations, makes this text strictly a reference work, rather than a study text. The changes are available in context of the verse, but the verse is not available in the context of the full chapter, or even the surrounding verses. Additionally, the book does not highlight the additions or deletions, leaving the reader to compare verses word by word to determine where the changes have been made.

An interesting problem associated with the Herald Press book was described by Robert Matthews (1971): "Some variant readings that are given are not actually revisions. Differences are due to the use of different editions of the King James Version rather than to deliberate revision by the Prophet Joseph." Matthews points out that the Herald Press did not take into account the fact that KJV Bibles published in England and the United States in the early 1800's sometimes differed in their use of articles, pronouns and the spelling of some words.

In fact, in the course of this compilation, nine such mistakes[1] were uncovered by a word by word comparison of the Herald Press JST text of the Four Gospels against both an American and English 1828 version of the KJV, and the 1981 LDS version of the KJV[2].

The main limitation to *all* of the previous attempts at integrating the JST text is the lack of full context. Perhaps the main barrier to any complete integration is the fact that the actual mechanics (such as which JST words were meant as replacements for which specific KJV words) are nearly impossible to establish[3]. However, it is possible to construct the integration so that the text can be read either as it normally would as KJV text (without the JST changes), or as it would with Joseph's translation, without having to assert the actual mechanical process. This compilation has approached the integration of the JST texts in this fashion.

Integration of the Joseph Smith Translation

The organization of this text was done in such a way as to maximize the ability of the reader to use the current LDS version scriptures, with their extensive footnotes and topical guide references. Specifically, the changes in the numbering of verses made by Joseph Smith in his translation were not represented in this text so that readers could more easily find the passage in the current LDS version scriptures.

In generating the most reasonably reliable text, both in relation to the JST alterations and the paralleling of the text, this project made use of a number of generally available publications[4]. The microfilm copy of the JST manuscripts, in possession of the Harold B. Lee Library at BYU was also consulted when conflicts between sources were encountered. In instances where two sources

---

[1] In Matthew 27:13, Mark 1:6, 2:25, 11:8, Luke 4:33, 5:24, 11:32, 16:23, and John 13:5, the Herald Press text indicated JST corrections that were actually only variations between the American and English 1828 versions and/or more recent editions such as the 1981 LDS version scriptures.

[2] Although comparison of these versions also demonstrated differences in punctuation, no attempt was made at reconciling these deviations in this text outside of those embedded in the JST revisions. The reason for this is found in the fact that punctuation is, itself, largely absent (in the modern sense of punctuation) in original biblical texts and is subject to deviation between versions, editions and printings. The choice was made, for practical terms, therefore, to note only punctuation that Joseph made, and not become engaged in establishing one edition's punctuation over another as authoritative.

[3] Personal communication received from Dr. Richard P. Howard in 1989, as Church Historian and head of the Archives of the RLDS Church.

[4] See the bibliography at the end of this book.

conflicted, precedence was always given to the most original source (usually the microfilm version). All changes in spelling, words, phrases and verses made by the Prophet Joseph Smith were included in this work (from one letter to multiple verses).

The Four Gospels

Even the youngest of Christians can name the authors of the four Gospels in order: Matthew, Mark, Luke and John. These four names flow naturally and create in our minds a mental picture of the scriptures that we have come to love and cherish. The stories of Jesus and his apostles, the miracles, the atonement, and other spiritually significant events are summoned to our minds each time we recite the names of these sacred books.

We are so familiar with these first four books that it is hard to imagine that they ever have been, or even could be, arranged any other way. The presentation of the Gospels that we now know and appreciate, is, however, the product of a long historical process. The fact that not all of the Gospels were written simultaneously should give us the first clue that the order and structure of early Christian scriptures was quite different than our current collection.

Although there were many transitions in both the form and content of the Gospels in the early Christian church, perhaps the first of major interest to the approach we have used in this volume occurred in about AD 170. Tatian, an Assyrian Christian, created a continuous narrative (harmony) using all four Gospels (Bruce, p. 23). This version of the Gospels, known as the *Diatessaron*, was probably compiled in Rome using the Greek language. The Assyrian Christians used this version of the Gospels as their "authorized" version until the fifth century, AD.

The rearrangement of the individual four books of the Gospels into a variety of formats has continued ever since, including: unified continuous; chronologized continuous; separate parallel; separate, chronologized parallel; separate books, etc. All of these arrangements of the basic Gospels texts share a common goal: a better understanding of the life, ministry, and teachings of the Saviour and his Apostles. Some formats (especially a parallel comparison of the individual books) seek further to provide insight into the unique contributions and character of the four authors.

By far, most of the changes made in the new Testament by Joseph Smith are found in the four gospels. The tremendous possibilities that lie in integrating the parallel format with the changes made by the prophet Joseph Smith are clear. With Joseph's textual changes to the four gospels available in parallel form, we can broaden our perspective by exploring important questions, such as:

    1) Are the changes Joseph made in harmony with the writing style and characteristics of the original authors?

    2) Was Joseph consistent in making changes across the stories and teachings represented in more than one of the Gospels?

    3) Are there significant doctrinal implications in the Joseph Smith Translation when compared to the King James Version?

It is our hope that this text will be useful in the study of the life of the Christ and the Gospel, as illustrated both by the original authors of the New Testament and, under specific commandment of the Lord, the Prophet Joseph.

Description of Text Format

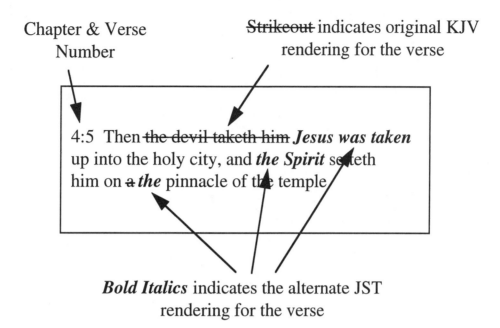

Chapter & Verse Number

~~Strikeout~~ indicates original KJV rendering for the verse

4:5 Then ~~the devil taketh him~~ ***Jesus was taken*** up into the holy city, and ***the Spirit*** setteth him on ~~a~~ ***the*** pinnacle of the temple,

Bold Italics indicates the alternate JST rendering for the verse

Joseph Smith Translation

When reading the text, if the reader were to ignore the words ~~marked by the strikeout line~~, and include the words that are ***bolded and italicized***, the reading of the passage would be that of the complete JST, i.e.:

> c4v5 Then ***Jesus was taken*** up into the holy city, and ***the Spirit*** setteth him on ***the*** pinnacle of the temple,

King James Version

Reversing that process to include the words ~~marked by the strikeout line~~, and ignore the words that are ***bolded and italicized***, would render the text as the regular KJV, i.e.:

> c4v5 Then ~~the devil taketh him~~ up into the holy city, and setteth him on ~~a~~ pinnacle of the temple,

This provides a practical way of comparing how the JST might impact the reading of a particular section. In many cases the impact is quite dramatic, as in the full account of the fast and temptation of Christ (see section C-4 in this volume) of which this example verse is a part.

TABLE OF CONTENTS

E. The Galilean Ministry (cont.)

E. The Galilean Ministry (cont.)

F. THE LATER JUDEAN MINISTRY 105

F. The Later Judean Ministry (cont.)

G. THE PEREAN MINISTRY 131

G. The Perean Ministry (cont.)

H. THE WEEK OF THE ATONEMENT 157

H. The Week of the Atonement (cont.)

H. The Week of the Atonement (cont.)

I. HIS RESURRECTION AND MINISTRY 215

The
New Testament

---

with the
Joseph Smith Translation

Section I

The Four Gospels

in
Parallel Columns
and
Chronological Harmony

SECTION A: INTRODUCTORY COMMENTS BY THE GOSPEL WRITERS

MATTHEW	MARK	LUKE	JOHN

A-1. MARK'S INTRODUCTION

1:1 The beginning of the gospel of Jesus Christ, the Son of God;

A-2. LUKE'S PREFACE

1:1 ~~Forasmuch as~~ *As I am a messenger of Jesus Christ, and knowing that* many have taken in hand to set forth in order a declaration of those things which are most surely believed among us,

1:2 Even as they delivered them unto us, ~~which~~ *who* from the beginning were eyewitnesses, and ministers of the word;

1:3 It seemed good to me also, having had perfect understanding of all things from the very first, to write unto thee in order, most excellent Theophilus,

1:4 That thou mightest know the certainty of those things, wherein thou hast been instructed.

A-3. THE TESTIMONY OF JOHN

1:1 In the beginning was the *gospel preached through the Son. And the gospel was the* ~~W~~word, and the ~~W~~word was with ~~God, and the Word was God.~~ *the Son, and the Son was with God, and the Son was of God.*

1:2 The same was in the beginning with God.

1:3 All things were made by him; and without him was not any thing made ~~that~~ *which* was made.

1:4 In him was ~~life~~ *the gospel; and the gospel was the life,* and the life was the light of men.

1:5 And the light shineth in ~~darkness~~ *the world*; and the ~~darkness comprehended~~ *world perceiveth* it not.

1:6 There was a man sent from God, whose name was John.

1:7 The same came *into the world* for a witness, to bear witness of the Light, *to bear record of the gospel through the Son, unto all,* that ~~all men~~ through him *men* might believe.

1:8 He was not that Light, but ~~was sent~~ *came* to bear witness of that Light.

1:9 ~~That~~ *Which* was the true Light, which lighteth every man ~~that~~ *who* cometh into the world.

1:10 *Even the Son of God.* He *who* was in the world, and the world was made by him, and the world knew him not.

1:11 He came unto his own, and his own received him not.

1:12 But as many as received him, to them gave he power to become the sons of God, ~~even~~ *only* to them ~~that~~ *who* believe on his name:

1:13 ~~Which were~~ *He was* born, not of blood, nor of the will of the flesh, nor of the will of man, but of God.

1:14 And the *same* ~~W~~*w*ord was made flesh, and dwelt among us, (and we beheld his glory, the glory as of the ~~o~~*O*nly ~~b~~*B*egotten of the Father,) full of grace and truth.

1:15 John ~~bare~~ *bear* witness of him, and cried, saying, This ~~was~~ *is* he of whom I spake, He ~~that~~ *who* cometh after me is preferred before me: for he was before me.

1:16 *For in the beginning was the Word, even the Son, who is made flesh, and sent unto us by the will of the Father. And as many as believe on his name shall receive of his fulness.* And of his fulness have all we received, ~~and grace for grace~~ *even immortality and eternal life, through his grace.*

1:17 For the law was given ~~by~~ *through* Moses, but ~~grace~~ *life* and truth came ~~by~~ *through* Jesus Christ. *For the law was after a carnal commandment, to the administration of death; but the gospel was after the power of an endless life, through Jesus Christ, the Only Begotten Son, who is in the bosom of the Father.*

1:18 *And* No man hath seen God at any time; ~~the only begotten Son, which is in the bosom of the Father, he hath declared him~~ *except he hath borne record of the Son; for except it is through him no man can be saved.*

MATTHEW	MARK	LUKE	JOHN

B-1. ANNUNCIATION TO ZACHARIAS

1:5 There was in the days of Herod, the king of ~~Judaea~~ Judea, a certain priest named Zacharias, of the course of Abia: and his wife ~~was~~ *being* of the daughters of Aaron, and her name ~~was Elisabeth~~ Elizabeth,

1:6 ~~And they~~ were both righteous before God, walking in all the commandments and ordinances of the Lord blameless.

1:7 And they had no child, ~~because that Elisabeth~~ Elizabeth was barren, and they ~~both were now~~ *were both* well stricken in years.

1:8 ~~And it came to pass, that~~ *And* while he executed the priest's office before God in the order of his ~~course~~ *priesthood*,

1:9 According to the ~~custom of the priest's office~~ *law*, his lot was to burn incense when he went into the temple of the Lord.

1:10 ~~And~~ the whole multitude of the people were praying without at the time of incense.

1:11 And there appeared unto him an angel of the Lord standing on the right side of the altar of incense.

1:12 And when Zacharias saw ~~him~~ *the angel*, he was troubled, and fear fell upon him.

1:13 But the angel said unto him, Fear not, Zacharias: for thy prayer is heard; and thy wife Elisabeth shall bear thee a son, and thou shalt call his name John.

1:14 ~~And~~ thou shalt have joy and gladness; and many shall rejoice at his birth.

1:15 For he shall be great in the sight of the Lord, and shall drink neither wine nor strong drink; and he shall be filled with the Holy Ghost, even from his mother's womb.

1:16 And many of the children of Israel shall he turn to the Lord their God.

1:17 And he shall go before ~~him~~ *the Lord* in the spirit and power of Elias, to turn the hearts of the fathers to the children, and the disobedient to the wisdom of the just; to make ready a people prepared for the Lord.

1:18 And Zacharias said unto the angel, Whereby shall I know this? for I am an old man, and my wife *is* well stricken in years.

1:19 And the angel answering said unto him, I am Gabriel, ~~that~~ *who* stand in the presence of God; and am sent to speak unto thee, and to ~~shew~~ *show* thee these glad tidings.

1:20 And, behold, thou shalt be dumb, and not able to speak, until the day that these things shall be

MATTHEW	MARK	LUKE	JOHN

performed, because thou believest not my words, which shall be fulfilled in their season.

1:21 And the people waited for Zacharias, and marvelled that he tarried so long in the temple.

1:22 And when he came out, he could not speak unto them: and they perceived that he had seen a vision in the temple: for he beckoned unto them, and remained speechless.

1:23 And ~~it came to pass, that,~~ as soon as the days of his ministration were accomplished, he departed to his own house.

B-2. ELISABETH'S SECLUSION

1:24 And after those days his wife Elisabeth conceived, and hid herself five months, saying,

1:25 Thus hath the Lord dealt with me in the days wherein he looked on me, to take away my reproach *from* among men.

B-3. ANNUNCIATION TO MARY

1:26 And in the sixth month the angel Gabriel was sent from God unto a city of Galilee, named Nazareth,

1:27 To a virgin espoused to a man whose name was Joseph, of the house of David; and the virgin's name was Mary.

1:28 And the angel came in unto her, and said, Hail, thou *virgin,* ~~that~~ *who* art highly ~~favoured~~ *favored of the Lord,* the Lord is with thee: *for thou art chosen and* blessed ~~art thou~~ among women.

1:29 And when she saw ~~him~~ *the angel,* she was troubled at his saying, and ~~cast~~ *pondered* in her mind what manner of salutation this should be.

1:30 And the angel said unto her, Fear not, Mary: for thou hast found favour with God.

1:31 And, behold, thou shalt conceive ~~in thy womb,~~ and bring forth a son, and ~~shalt~~ *shall* call his name JESUS.

1:32 He shall be great, and shall be called the Son of the Highest: and the Lord God shall give unto him the throne of his father David:

1:33 And he shall reign over the house of Jacob for ever; and of his kingdom there shall be no end.

1:34 Then said Mary unto the angel, How ~~shall~~ *can* this be~~, seeing I know not a man~~?

1:35 And the angel answered and said unto her, ~~The Holy Ghost shall come upon thee, and the power of~~

MATTHEW	MARK	LUKE	JOHN

the ~~Highest shall overshadow thee:~~ *Of the Holy Ghost, and the power of the Highest.* t*T*herefore also that holy ~~thing which~~ *child that* shall be born of thee shall be called the Son of God.

1:36   And, behold, thy cousin ~~Elisabeth~~ *Elizabeth*, she hath also conceived a son in her old age: and this is the sixth month with her, who was called barren.

1:37   For with God nothing ~~shall~~ *can* be impossible.

1:38   And Mary said, Behold the handmaid of the Lord; be it unto me according to thy word. And the angel departed from her.

B-4. MARY VISITS ELISABETH

1:39   And ~~Mary arose~~ in those days, ~~and~~ *Mary* went into the hill country with haste, into a city of Juda;

1:40   And entered into the house of Zacharias, and saluted Elisabeth.

1:41   And it came to pass, that, when Elisabeth heard the salutation of Mary, the babe leaped in her womb; and Elisabeth was filled with the Holy Ghost:

1:42   And she spake out with a loud voice, and said, Blessed art thou among women, and blessed is the fruit of thy womb.

1:43   And ~~whence is this to me~~ *why is it, that this blessing is upon me*, that the mother of my Lord should come to me?

1:44   For, lo, as soon as the voice of thy salutation sounded in mine ears, the babe leaped in my womb for joy.

1:45   And blessed ~~is she that~~ *art thou who* believed: for ~~there shall be a performance of those things which were told her from the Lord~~ *those things which were told thee by the angel of the Lord, shall be fulfilled.*

1:46   And Mary said, My soul doth magnify the Lord,

1:47   And my spirit ~~hath~~ rejoice*dth* in God my ~~Saviour~~ *Savior*.

1:48   For he hath regarded the low estate of his handmaiden: for, behold, from henceforth all generations shall call me blessed.

1:49   For he ~~that~~ *who* is mighty hath done to me great things; and ~~holy is his~~ *I will magnify his holy* name.

1:50   ~~And~~ *For* his mercy ~~is on them that~~ *on those who* fear him from generation to generation.

1:51   He hath ~~shewed~~ *showed* strength with his arm; he hath scattered the proud in the imagination of their hearts.

MATTHEW	MARK	LUKE	JOHN

1:52 He hath put down the mighty from their *high* seats, and exalted them of low degree.

1:53 He hath filled the hungry with good things; ~~and~~ *but* the rich he hath sent empty away.

1:54 He hath ~~holpen~~ *helped* his servant Israel, in remembrance of ~~his~~ mercy;

1:55 As he spake to our fathers, to Abraham, and to his seed for ever.

B-5. JOHN THE BAPTIST IS BORN

1:57 *And* Now ~~Elisabeth's~~ *Elizabeth's* full time came that she should be delivered; and she brought forth a son.

1:58 And her ~~neighbours~~ *neighbors* and her cousins heard how the Lord had ~~shewed~~ *showed* great mercy ~~upon~~ *unto* her; and they rejoiced with her.

1:59 And it came to pass, that on the eighth day they came to circumcise the child; and they called him Zacharias, after the name of his father.

1:60 And his mother answered and said, Not so; but he shall be called John.

1:61 And they said unto her, There is none of thy kindred that is called by this name.

1:62 And they made signs to his father, *and asked him* how he would have him called.

1:63 And he asked for a writing table, and wrote, saying, His name is John. And they *all* marvelled ~~all~~.

1:64 And his mouth was opened immediately, and ~~his tongue loosed, and~~ he spake *with his tongue*, and praised God.

B-6. ZACHARIAS' PROPHECY

1:67 And his father Zacharias was filled with the Holy Ghost, and prophesied, saying,

1:68 Blessed be the Lord God of Israel; for he hath visited and redeemed his people,

1:69 And hath raised up an horn of salvation for us in the house of his servant David;

1:70 As he spake by the mouth of his holy prophets, ~~which have been~~ *ever* since the world began:

1:71 That we should be saved from our enemies, and from the hand of all ~~that~~ *those who* hate us;

1:72 To perform the mercy promised to our fathers, and to remember his holy covenant;

1:73 The oath which he sware to our father Abraham,

1:74 That he would grant unto us, that we being delivered out of the

MATTHEW	MARK	LUKE	JOHN

LUKE

hand of our enemies might serve him without fear,

1:75   In holiness and righteousness before him, all the days of our ~~life~~ *lives*.

1:76   And thou, child, shalt be called the prophet of the Highest: for thou shalt go before the face of the Lord to prepare his ways;

1:77   To give knowledge of salvation unto his people by *baptism for* the remission of their sins,

1:78   Through the tender mercy of our God; whereby the dayspring from on high hath visited us,

1:79   To give light to them ~~that~~ *who* sit in darkness and ~~in~~ the shadow of death, to guide our feet into the way of peace.

1:65   And fear came on all ~~that~~ *who* dwelt round about them: and all these sayings were noised abroad throughout all the hill country of ~~Judaea~~ *Judea*.

1:66   And all they that heard them laid them up in their hearts, saying, What manner of child shall this be! And the hand of the Lord was with him.

B-7. MARY'S RETURN TO NAZARETH

LUKE

1:56   And Mary abode with ~~her~~ *Elizabeth* about three months, and returned to her own house.

B-8. ANNUNCIATION TO JOSEPH

MATTHEW

1:18   Now, *as it is written,* the birth of Jesus Christ was on this wise: ~~When as~~ *After* his mother Mary was espoused to Joseph, before they came together, she was found with child of the Holy Ghost.

1:19   Then Joseph her husband, being a just man, and not willing to make her a publick example, was minded to put her away privily.

1:20   But while he thought on these things, behold, the angel of the Lord appeared unto him in a ~~dream~~ *vision*, saying, Joseph, thou son of David, fear not to take unto thee Mary thy wife: for that which is conceived in her is of the Holy Ghost.

1:21   And she shall bring forth a son, and thou shalt call his name JESUS: for he shall save his people from their sins.

1:22   Now ~~all~~ this ~~was done~~ *took place*, that ~~it~~ *all things* might be fulfilled, which ~~was~~ *were* spoken of the Lord, by the ~~prophet~~ *prophets*, saying,

1:23   Behold, a virgin shall be with child, and shall bring forth a son, and they shall call his name

MATTHEW	MARK	LUKE	JOHN

Emmanuel, which being interpreted is, God with us.

1:24 Then Joseph ~~being raised from sleep~~ , *awaking out of his vision,* did as the angel of the Lord had bidden him, and took unto him his wife:

1:25(a) And knew her not ~~till~~ *until* she had brought forth her firstborn son:

B-9. CAESAR'S TAX

2:1 And it came to pass in those days, that there went out a decree from Caesar Augustus, that all ~~the world~~ *his empire* should be taxed.

2:2 (~~And~~ this *same* taxing was ~~first made~~ when Cyrenius was governor of Syria.)

2:3 And all went to be taxed, every one ~~into~~ his own city.

B-10. BETHLEHEM - CHRIST'S BIRTH

2:4 And Joseph also went up from Galilee, out of the city of Nazareth, into Judaea, unto the city of David, which is called Bethlehem; (because he was of the house and lineage of David:)

2:5 To be taxed with Mary his espoused wife, *she* being great with child.

2:6 And so it was, that, while they were there, the days were accomplished that she should be delivered.

2:7 And she brought forth her firstborn son, and wrapped him in swaddling clothes, and laid him in a manger; because there was ~~no~~ *none to give* room for them in the inn*s*.

B-11. THE SHEPHERDS AND THE ANGELS

2:8 And there were in the same country shepherds abiding in the field, keeping watch over their flock*s* by night.

2:9 And, lo, ~~the~~ *an* angel of the Lord ~~came upon~~ *appeared unto* them, and the glory of the Lord shone round about them: and they were sore afraid.

2:10 ~~And~~ *But* the angel said unto them, Fear not: for, behold, I bring you good tidings of great joy, which shall be to all people.

2:11 For unto you is born this day in the city of David a ~~Saviour, which~~ *Savior, who* is Christ the Lord.

2:12 ~~And this shall be a sign unto you;~~ *And this is the way* Ye shall find the babe, *he is* wrapped in

MATTHEW	MARK	LUKE	JOHN

swaddling clothes, **and is** lying in a manger.

2:13 And suddenly there was with the angel a multitude of the heavenly host praising God, and saying,

2:14 Glory to God in the highest, and on earth peace, good will to~~ward~~ men.

2:15 And it came to pass, ~~as~~ *when* the angels were gone away from them into heaven, the shepherds said one to another, Let us now go even unto Bethlehem, and see this thing which is come to pass, which the Lord ha~~th~~*s* made known unto us.

2:16 And they came with haste, and found Mary, and Joseph, and the babe lying in a manger.

2:17 And when they had seen ~~it~~, they made known abroad the saying which was told them concerning this child.

2:18 ~~And~~ all they ~~that~~ *who* heard it wondered at those things which were told them by the shepherds.

2:19 But Mary kept all these things, and pondered them in her heart.

2:20 And the shepherds returned, glorifying and praising God for all the things ~~that~~ *which* they had heard and seen, as ~~it was told~~ *they were manifested* unto them.

B-12. CIRCUMCISION AND NAMING OF JESUS

1:25(b) and ~~he~~ *they* called his name JESUS.

2:21 And when eight days were accomplished for the circumcising of the child, his name was called JESUS, which was so named of the angel before he was conceived ~~in the womb~~.

B-13. THE GENEALOGIES OF JESUS

1:1 The book of the generation of Jesus Christ, the son of David, the son of Abraham.

1:2 Abraham begat Isaac; and Isaac begat Jacob; and Jacob begat Judas and his brethren;

1:3 And Judas begat Phares and Zara of Thamar; and Phares begat Esrom; and Esrom begat Aram;

1:4 And Aram begat Aminadab; and Aminadab begat Naasson; and Naasson begat Salmon;

1:5 And Salmon begat Booz of Rachab; and Booz begat Obed of Ruth; and Obed begat Jesse;

1:6 And Jesse begat David the king; and David the king begat Solomon of her ~~that had been the wife~~ *whom David had taken* of Urias;

MATTHEW	MARK	LUKE	JOHN

1:7 And Solomon begat Roboam; and Roboam begat Abia; and Abia begat Asa;

1:8 And Asa begat Josaphat; and Josaphat begat Joram; and Joram begat Ozias;

1:9 And Ozias begat Joatham; and Joatham begat Achaz; and Achaz begat Ezekias;

1:10 And Ezekias begat Manasses; and Manasses begat Amon; and Amon begat Josias;

1:11 And Josias begat Jechonias and his brethren, about the time they were carried away to Babylon:

1:12 And after they were brought to Babylon, Jechonias begat Salathiel; and Salathiel begat Zorobabel;

1:13 And Zorobabel begat Abiud; and Abiud begat Eliakim; and Eliakim begat Azor;

1:14 And Azor begat Sadoc; and Sadoc begat Achim; and Achim begat Eliud;

1:15 And Eliud begat Eleazar; and Eleazar begat Matthan; and Matthan begat Jacob;

1:16 And Jacob begat Joseph the husband of Mary, of whom was born Jesus, *as the prophets have written,* who is called Christ.

3:23(b) being (as was supposed *of the world*) the son of Joseph, ~~which was the son~~ *who was from the loins* of Heli,

3:24 ~~Which was the son~~ *who was from the loins* of Matthat, ~~which~~ *who* was the son of Levi, ~~which was the son~~ *who was a descendant* of Melchi, ~~which was the son~~ *and* of Janna, ~~which was the son~~ *and* of Joseph,

3:25 ~~Which was the son~~ *and* of Mattathias, ~~which was the son~~ *and* of Amos, ~~which was the son~~ *and* of Naum, ~~which was the son~~ *and* of Esli, ~~which was the son~~ *and* of Nagge,

3:26 ~~Which was the son~~ *And* of Maath, ~~which was the son~~ *and* of Mattathias, ~~which was the son~~ *and* of Semei, ~~which was the son~~ *and* of Joseph, ~~which was the son~~ *and* of Juda,

3:27 ~~Which was the son~~ *and* of Joanna, ~~which was the son~~ *and* of Rhesa, ~~which was the son~~ *and* of Zorobabel, ~~which was the son~~ *and* of Salathiel, ~~which~~ *who* was the son of Neri,

3:28 ~~Which was the son~~ *Who was a descendant* of Melchi, ~~which was the son~~ *and* of Addi, ~~which was the son~~ *and* of Cosam, ~~which was the son~~ *and* of Elmodam, ~~which was the son~~ *and* of Er,

3:29 ~~Which was the son~~ *And* of Jose, ~~which was the son~~ *and* of

MATTHEW	MARK	LUKE	JOHN

Eliezer, ~~which was the son~~ *and* of ~~Jorim~~ *Joram*, ~~which was the son~~ *and* of Matthat, ~~which was the son~~ *and* of Levi,

3:30 ~~Which was the son~~ *And* of Simeon, ~~which was the son~~ *and* of Juda, ~~which was the son~~ *and* of Joseph, ~~which was the son~~ *and* of Jonan, ~~which was the son~~ *and* of Eliakim,

3:31 ~~Which was the son~~ *And* of Melea, ~~which was the son~~ *and* of Menan, ~~which was the son~~ *and* of Mattatha, ~~which was the son~~ *and* of Nathan, ~~which was the son~~ *and* of David,

3:32 ~~Which was the son~~ *And* of Jesse, ~~which was the son~~ *and* of Obed, ~~which was the son~~ *and* of Booz, ~~which was the son~~ *and* of Salmon, ~~which was the son~~ *and* of Naasson,

3:33 ~~Which was the son~~ *And* of Aminadab, ~~which was the son~~ *and* of Aram, ~~which was the son~~ *and* of Esrom, ~~which was the son~~ *and* of Phares, ~~which was the son~~ *and* of Juda,

3:34 ~~Which was the son~~ *And* of Jacob, ~~which was the son~~ *and* of Isaac, ~~which was the son~~ *and* of Abraham, ~~which was the son~~ *and* of Thara, ~~which was the son~~ *and* of Nachor,

3:35 ~~Which was the son~~ *And* of Saruch, ~~which was the son~~ *and* of Ragau, ~~which was the son~~ *and* of Phalec, ~~which was the son~~ *and* of Heber, ~~which was the son~~ *and* of Sala,

3:36 ~~Which was the son~~ *And* of Cainan, ~~which was the son~~ *and* of Arphaxad, ~~which was the son~~ *and* of ~~Sem~~ *Shem*, ~~which was the son~~ *and* of Noe, ~~which was the son~~ *and* of Lamech,

3:37 ~~Which was the son~~ *And* of Mathusala, ~~which was the son~~ *and* of Enoch, ~~which was the son~~ *and* of Jared, ~~which was the son~~ *and* of Maleleel, ~~which was the son~~ *and* of Cainan,

3:38 ~~Which was the son~~ *And* of Enos, ~~which was the son~~ *and* of Seth, ~~which was the son~~ *and* of Adam, ~~which was the son of God~~ *who was formed of God, and the first man upon the earth*.

1:17 So all the generations from Abraham to David ~~are~~ *were* fourteen generations; and from David until the carrying away into Babylon ~~are~~ *, were* fourteen generations; and from the carrying away into Babylon ~~unto~~ *until* Christ ~~are~~ *, were* fourteen generations.

MATTHEW	MARK	LUKE	JOHN

B-14. JESUS PRESENTED IN THE TEMPLE

2:22 And when the days of her purification according to the law of Moses were accomplished, they brought him to Jerusalem, to present him to the Lord;

2:23 (As it is written in the law of the Lord, Every male ~~that~~ *which* openeth the womb shall be called holy to the Lord;)

2:24 And to offer a sacrifice according to that which is ~~said~~ *written* in the law of the Lord, A pair of turtledoves, or two young pigeons.

2:25 And, behold, there was a man ~~in~~ *at* Jerusalem, whose name was Simeon; and the same man was just and devout, waiting for the consolation of Israel: and the Holy Ghost was upon him.

2:26 And it was revealed unto him by the Holy Ghost, that he should not see death, before he had seen the Lord's Christ.

2:27 And he came by the Spirit into the temple: and when the parents brought in the child, *even* Jesus, to do for him after the custom of the law,

2:28 Then took he him up in his arms, and blessed God, and said,

2:29 Lord, now lettest ~~thou~~ thy servant depart in peace, according to thy word:

2:30 For mine eyes have seen thy salvation,

2:31 Which thou hast prepared before the face of all people;

2:32 A light to lighten the Gentiles, and the glory of thy people Israel.

2:33 And Joseph and ~~his mother~~ *Mary* marvelled at those things which were spoken of ~~him~~ *the child*.

2:34 And Simeon blessed them, and said unto Mary ~~his mother~~, Behold, this child is set for the fall and rising again of many in Israel; and for a sign which shall be spoken against;

2:35 (Yea, a sword shall pierce through *him to the wounding of* ~~thy~~ *thine* own soul also,) that the thoughts of many hearts may be revealed.

2:36 And there was one Anna, a prophetess, the daughter of Phanuel, of the tribe of A*sher*: she was of a great age, and had lived with ~~an~~ husband *only* seven years ~~from her virginity~~ , *whom she married in her youth*;

2:37 And she ~~was~~ *lived* a widow ~~of~~ about fourscore and four years, ~~which~~ *who* departed not from the temple, but served God with fastings and prayers night and day.

2:38 And she coming in that instant gave thanks likewise unto the

MATTHEW	MARK	LUKE	JOHN

Lord, and spake of him to all ~~them that~~ *those who* looked for redemption in Jerusalem.
2:39(a)   And when they had performed all things according to the law of the Lord,

---

B-15. VISIT OF THE WISE MEN

2:1   Now when Jesus was born in Bethlehem of Judaea in the days of Herod the king, behold, there came wise men from the east to Jerusalem,

2:2   Saying, Where is ~~he~~ *the child* that is born ~~King~~ *, the Messiah* of the Jews? for we have seen his star in the east, and ~~are~~ *have* come to worship him.

2:3   When Herod the king had heard ~~these things~~ *of the child*, he was troubled, and all Jerusalem with him.

2:4   And when he had gathered all the chief priests and scribes of the people together, he demanded of them *, saying, where is the place that is written of by the prophets, in which* Christ should be ~~born.~~*? For he greatly feared, yet he believed not the prophets.*

2:5   And they said unto him, *It is written by the prophets, that he should be born* In Bethlehem of ~~Judaea~~ *Judea*: for thus ~~it is written by the prophet~~ *have they said,*

2:6   *The word of the Lord came unto us, saying,* And thou Bethlehem, *which lieth* in the land of ~~Juda~~ *Judea, in thee shall be born a prince, which* art not the least among the princes of ~~Juda~~ *Judea*: for out of thee shall come ~~a Governor~~ *the Messiah*, ~~that~~ *who* shall ~~rule~~ *save* my people Israel.

2:7   Then Herod, when he had ~~privily~~ called the wise men *privily*, inquired of them diligently what time the star appeared.

2:8   And he sent them to Bethlehem, and said, Go and search diligently for the young child; and when ye have found ~~him~~ *the child*, bring me word again, that I may come and worship him also.

2:9   When they had heard the king, they departed; and, lo, the star, which they saw in the east, went before them, ~~till~~ *until* it came and stood over where the young child was.

2:10   When they saw the star, they rejoiced with exceeding great joy.

2:11   And when they were come into the house, they saw the young child with Mary his mother, and fell down, and worshipped him: and when they had opened their

MATTHEW	MARK	LUKE	JOHN

treasures, they presented unto him gifts; gold, and frankincense, and myrrh.

2:12 And being warned of God in a dream that they should not return to Herod, they departed into their own country another way.

B-16. FLIGHT INTO EGYPT

2:13 And when they were departed, behold, the angel of the Lord appearethd to Joseph in a dream *vision*, saying, Arise, and take the young child and his mother, and flee into Egypt, and be *tarry* thou there until I bring thee word: for Herod will seek the young child to destroy him.

2:14 When *And then* he arose, he *and* took the young child and his *the child's* mother by night, and departed into Egypt:

2:15 And was there until the death of Herod: that it might be fulfilled which was spoken of the Lord by the prophet, saying, Out of Egypt have I called my son.

B-17. SLAUGHTER OF CHILDREN

2:16 Then Herod, when he saw that he was mocked of the wise men, was exceeding wroth, and sent forth, and slew all the children that were in Bethlehem, and in all the coasts thereof, from two years old and under, according to the time which he had diligently enquired of the wise men.

2:17 Then was fulfilled that which was spoken by Jeremy *Jeremiah* the prophet, saying,

2:18 In Rama*h* was there *was* a voice heard, lamentation, and weeping, and great mourning, Rachel weeping for *the loss of* her children, and would not be comforted, because they are *were* not.

B-18. RETURN TO NAZARETH FROM EGYPT

2:19 But when Herod was dead, behold, an angel of the Lord appeareth *appeared* in a dream *vision* to Joseph in Egypt,

2:20 Saying, Arise, and take the young child and his mother, and go into the land of Israel: for they are dead which *who* sought the young child's life.

2:21 And he arose, and took the young child and his mother, and came into the land of Israel.

MATTHEW	MARK	LUKE	JOHN

MATTHEW

2:22 But when he heard that Archelaus did reign in ~~Judaea~~ *Judea* in the ~~room~~ *stead* of his father Herod, he was afraid to go thither: *but,* notwithstanding, being warned of God in a ~~dream~~ *vision,* he ~~turned aside~~ *went* into the *eastern* parts of Galilee:
2:23(a) And he came and dwelt in a city called Nazareth: that it might be fulfilled which was spoken by the prophets, He shall be called a Nazarene.

LUKE

2:39(b) they returned into Galilee, to their own city Nazareth.

B-19. JESUS AS A CHILD

LUKE

2:40 And the child grew, and waxed strong in spirit, *being* filled with wisdom: and the grace of God was upon him.

B-20. THE BOY JESUS AT THE TEMPLE: AGE TWELVE

LUKE

2:41 Now his parents went to Jerusalem every year at the feast of the passover.
2:42 And when he was twelve years old, they went up to Jerusalem after the custom ~~of~~ *, to* the feast.
2:43 And when they had fulfilled the days, as they returned, the child Jesus tarried behind in Jerusalem; and Joseph and his mother knew not ~~of it~~ *that he tarried*.
2:44 But they, supposing him to have been in the company, went a day's journey; and they sought him among ~~their kinsfolk~~ *his kindred* and acquaintance.
2:45 And when they found him not, they turned back again to Jerusalem, seeking him.
2:46 And it came to pass, ~~that~~ after three days they found him in the temple, sitting in the midst of the doctors, ~~both hearing them, and asking them questions~~ *and they were hearing him, and asking him questions.*
2:47 And all ~~that~~ *who* heard him were astonished at his understanding and answers.
2:48 And when ~~they~~ *his parents* saw him, they were amazed: and his mother said unto him, Son, why hast thou thus dealt with us? behold, thy father and I have sought thee sorrowing.
2:49 And he said unto them, ~~How~~ *why* is it that ye sought me? ~~wist~~ *Knew* ye not that I must be about my Father's business?
2:50 And they understood not the saying which he spake unto them.
2:51 And he went down with them, and came to Nazareth, and was subject unto them: ~~but~~ *and* his mother kept all these sayings in her heart.

MATTHEW	MARK	LUKE	JOHN

B-21. JESUS AS A YOUNG MAN

2:23(b)   And it came to pass that Jesus grew up with his brethren,

2:52 And Jesus increased in wisdom and stature, and in favour with God and man.

and waxed strong, and waited upon the Lord for the time of his ministry to come. And he served under his father, and he spake not as other men, neither could he be taught; for he needed not that any man should teach him. And after many years, the hour of his ministry drew nigh.

B-22. JOHN THE BAPTIST'S PREPARATION

1:80 And the child grew, and waxed strong in spirit, and was in the deserts ~~till~~ *until* the day of his ~~shewing~~ *showing* unto Israel.

MATTHEW	MARK	LUKE	JOHN

C-1. BACKGROUND OF JOHN'S MINISTRY

| | | 3:1 Now in the fifteenth year of the reign of Tiberius Caesar, Pontius Pilate being governor of ~~Judaea~~ *Judea*, and Herod being tetrarch of Galilee, and his brother Philip tetrarch of Ituraea and of the region of Trachonitis, and Lysanias the tetrarch of Abilene, 3:2 Annas and Caiaphas being the high priests, *Now in this same year* the word of God came unto John the son of Zacharias in the wilderness. | |

C-2. THE PREACHING OF JOHN THE BAPTIST

3:1 *And* In those days came John the Baptist, preaching in the wilderness of ~~Judaea~~ *Judea*,
3:2 And saying, Repent ye: for the kingdom of heaven is at hand.
3:3 For ~~this is~~ *I am* he ~~that~~ *who* was spoken of by the prophet Esaias, saying,

The voice of one crying in the wilderness, Prepare ye the way of the Lord, *and* make his paths straight.

1:4 John did baptize in the wilderness, and preach the baptism of repentance for the remission of sins.

1:2 As it is written in the prophets,

Behold, I send my messenger before thy face, which shall prepare thy way before thee.
1:3 The voice of one crying in the wilderness, Prepare ye the way of the Lord, make his paths straight.

3:3 And he came into all the country about Jordan, preaching the baptism of repentance for the remission of sins;

3:4 As it is written in the book of the ~~words of~~ *prophet* Esaias ~~the prophet~~, *and these are the words,* saying,

The voice of one crying in the wilderness, Prepare ye the way of the Lord, *and* make his paths straight.
3:5 *For behold, and lo, he shall come, as it is written in the book of the prophets, to take away the sins of the world, and to bring salvation unto the heathen nations, to gather together those who are lost, who are of the sheepfold of Israel; Yea, even the dispersed and afflicted; and also to prepare the way, and make possible the preaching of the gospel unto the Gentiles; And to be a light unto all who sit in darkness, unto the uttermost parts of the earth; to bring to pass the resurrection from the dead, and to ascend up on high, to dwell on the right hand of the Father, Until the fullness of time, and the law and the testimony shall be sealed, and the keys of the kingdom shall be delivered up again unto the Father; To administer justice unto all; to come down in judgment upon all, and to convince all the ungodly of their ungodly deeds, which they have commited; and all this in the day that he shall come; For it is a day of power; yea, Every valley shall be filled, and every mountain and hill shall be brought low; and the crooked shall be made straight, and the rough ways shall be made smooth;*

MATTHEW	MARK	LUKE	JOHN

3:4 And the same John had his raiment of camel's hair, and a leathern girdle about his loins; and his ~~meat~~ *food* was locusts and wild honey.

3:5 Then went out to him Jerusalem, and all ~~Judaea~~ *Judea*, and all the region round about Jordan,

3:6 And *many* were baptized of him in Jordan, confessing their sins.

3:7 But when he saw many of the Pharisees and Sadducees come to his baptism,

he said unto them,

O generation of vipers, who hath warned you to flee from the wrath to come?

3:8 *Why is it that ye receive not the preaching of him whom God hath sent? If ye receive not this in your hearts, ye receive not me; and if ye receive not me, ye receive not him of whom I am sent to bear record; and for your sins ye have no cloak. Repent, therefore, and* Bring forth ~~therefore~~ fruits meet for repentance:

3:9 And think not to say within yourselves, ~~We have Abraham to our father:~~ *We are the children of Abraham, and we only have power to bring seed unto our father Abraham;*

for I say unto you, that God is able of these stones to raise up children unto Abraham.

3:10 And now also the axe is laid unto the root of the trees: therefore every tree which bringeth not forth good fruit ~~is~~ *, shall be* hewn down, and cast into the fire.

1:6 And John was clothed with camel's hair, and with a girdle of a skin about his loins;
and he did eat locusts and wild honey;

1:5 And there went out unto him all the land of ~~Judaea~~ *Judea*, and they of Jerusalem,

and *many* were ~~all~~ baptized of him in the river ~~of~~ Jordan, confessing their sins.

3:6 And all flesh shall see the salvation of God.

3:7 Then *John* said ~~he~~ to the multitude that came forth to be baptized of him,
crying against them with a loud voice, saying
O generation of vipers, who hath warned you to flee from the wrath to come?

3:8 Bring forth therefore fruits worthy of repentance,
and begin not to say within yourselves, ~~We have Abraham to~~ *Abraham is* our father:

we have kept the commandments of God, and none can inherit the promises but the children of Abraham;
for I say unto you, That God is able of these stones to raise up children unto Abraham.

3:9 And now also the axe is laid unto the root of the trees: every tree therefore which bringeth not forth good fruit ~~is~~ *shall be* hewn down, and cast into the fire.

3:10 And the people asked him, saying, What shall we do then?

3:11 He answere~~th~~*d* and sai~~th~~*d* unto them, He that hath two coats, let him impart to him that hath none; and he that hath meat, let him do likewise.

3:12 Then came also publicans to be baptized, and said unto him, Master, what shall we do?

3:13 And he said unto them, Exact no more than that which is appointed *unto* you. *For it is well known unto you, Theophilus, that after the manner of the Jews, and according to the custom of their law in receiving money into the treasury, that out of the*

MATTHEW	MARK	LUKE	JOHN

abundance which was received, was appointed unto the poor, every man his portion; And after this manner did the publicans also, wherefore John said unto them, Exact no more than that which is appointed you.

3:14 And the soldiers likewise demanded of him, saying, And what shall we do? And he said unto them, Do violence to no man, neither accuse any falsely; and be content with your wages.

3:15 And as the people were in expectation, and all men mused in their hearts of John, whether he were the Christ, or not;

3:11 I indeed baptize you with water ~~unto~~ *upon your* repentance: ~~but he that~~ *and when he of whom I bear record* cometh ~~after me~~ , *who* is mightier than I, whose shoes I am not worthy to bear, *(or whose place I am not able to fill,) as I said,*
I indeed baptize you before he cometh, that when he cometh he ~~shall~~ *may* baptize you with the Holy Ghost, and ~~with~~ fire.
3:12 *And it is he of whom I shall bear record,* Whose fan ~~is~~ *shall be* in his hand, and he will thoroughly purge his floor, and gather his wheat into the garner; but *in the fulness of his own time* he will burn up the chaff with unquenchable fire.
Thus came John, preaching and baptizing in the river of Jordan; bearing record, that he who was coming after him had power to baptize with the Holy Ghost and fire.

1:7a And preached, saying,

There cometh one mightier than I after me, the latchet of whose shoes I am not worthy to stoop down and unloose.
1:8 I indeed have baptized you with water: but he shall *not only* baptize you with *water, but with fire, and* the Holy Ghost.

3:16 John answered, saying unto ~~them~~ all, I indeed baptize you with water;

but *there cometh* one mightier than I ~~cometh~~, the latchet of whose shoes I am not worthy to unloose:

he shall baptize you with the Holy Ghost and with fire:

3:17 Whose fan is in his hand, and he will throughly purge his floor, and will gather the wheat into his garner; but the chaff he will burn with fire unquenchable.

3:18 And many other things in his exhortation preached he unto the people.

C-3. JOHN BAPTIZES JESUS

3:13 *And* Then cometh Jesus from Galilee to Jordan unto John, to be baptized of him.
3:14 But John ~~forbad~~ *refused* him, saying, I have need to be baptized of thee, and *why* comest thou to me?
3:15 And Jesus answering said unto him, Suffer ~~it to be so now:~~ *me to be baptized of thee,* for thus it becometh us to fulfil all righteousness. Then he suffered him. *And John went down into the water and baptized him.*

1:9 And it came to pass in those days, that Jesus came from Nazareth of Galilee,

and was baptized of John in Jordan.

3:21 Now when all the people were baptized, it came to pass, that Jesus also *came unto John;*

and being baptized *of him*, and praying,

MATTHEW	MARK	LUKE	JOHN

3:16 And Jesus, when he was baptized, went up straightway out of the water: and *John saw, and* lo, the heavens were opened unto him, and he saw the Spirit of God descending like a dove, and lighting upon ~~him~~ *Jesus*:

3:17 And lo, *he heard* a voice from heaven, saying, This is my beloved Son, in whom I am well pleased. *Hear ye him.*

1:10 And straightway coming up out of the water,

he saw the heavens opened,

and the Spirit like a dove descending upon him:

1:11 And there came a voice from heaven, saying, Thou art my beloved Son, in whom I am well pleased.
And John bare record of it.

the heaven was opened,

3:22 And the Holy Ghost descended in ~~a~~ bodily shape like a dove upon him,
and a voice came from heaven, which said, Thou art my beloved Son; in thee I am well pleased.

3:23(a) And Jesus himself began to be about thirty years of age, *having lived with his father,*

C-4. THE TEMPTATION OF JESUS

4:1 Then was Jesus led up of the Spirit into the wilderness to be ~~tempted of the devil~~ *with God.*

4:2 And when he had fasted forty days and forty nights, *and had communed with God,* he was afterward an hungered, *and was left to be tempted of the devil.*

4:3 And when the tempter came to him, he said, If thou be the Son of God, command that these stones be made bread.
4:4 But ~~he~~ *Jesus* answered and said, It is written, Man shall not live by bread alone, but by every word that proceedeth out of the mouth of God.
4:5 Then ~~the devil taketh him~~ *Jesus was taken* up into the holy city, and *the Spirit* setteth him on ~~a~~ *the* pinnacle of the temple,
4:6 ~~And saith~~ *Then the devil came* unto him *and said,* If thou be the Son of God, cast thyself down: for it is written, He shall give his angels charge concerning thee:

and in their hands they shall bear thee up, lest at any time thou dash thy foot against a stone.
4:7 Jesus said unto him, It is written again, Thou shalt not tempt the Lord thy God.
4:8 *And* Again, ~~the devil~~ *Jesus was in the Spirit, and it* taketh him up into an exceeding high mountain, and ~~sheweth~~ *showeth* him all the kingdoms of the world, and the glory of them;
4:9 And ~~saith unto him~~ *the devil came unto him again, and said,* All these things will I give *unto* thee,

if thou wilt fall down and worship me.

1:12 And immediately the Spirit ~~driveth~~ *took* him into the wilderness.

1:13(a) And he was there in the wilderness forty days,

~~tempted of~~ Satan *seeking to tempt him*; and was with the wild beasts;

4:1 And Jesus being full of the Holy Ghost returned from Jordan, and was led by the Spirit into the wilderness,
4:2 ~~Being forty days tempted of the devil~~ *And after forty days,*

the devil came unto him, to tempt him. And in those days he did eat nothing: and when they were ended, he afterward*s* hungered.
4:3 And the devil said unto him, If thou be the Son of God, command this stone that it be made bread.
4:4 And Jesus answered him, saying, It is written, That man shall not live by bread alone, but by every word of God.

4:9 And ~~he~~ *the Spirit* brought him to Jerusalem, and set him on a pinnacle of the temple,

and the devil came unto him and said unto him, If thou be the Son of God, cast thyself down from hence:
4:10 For it is written, He shall give his angels charge over thee, to keep thee:
4:11 And in ~~their~~ *his* hands they shall bear thee up, lest at any time thou dash thy foot against a stone.
4:12 And Jesus answering said unto him, It is ~~said~~ *written*, Thou shalt not tempt the Lord thy God.
4:5 And the ~~devil,~~ *Spirit* tak~~ing~~*eth* him up into an high mountain, ~~shewed unto him~~ *and he beheld* all the kingdoms of the world in a moment of time.

4:6 And the devil *came unto him, and* said unto him, All this power will I give thee, and the glory of them: for ~~that is~~ *they are* delivered unto me; and to whomsoever I will I give ~~it~~ *them*.
4:7 If thou therefore wilt worship me, all shall be thine.

MATTHEW	MARK	LUKE	JOHN
4:10 Then saith Jesus unto him, Get thee hence, Satan: for it is written, Thou shalt worship the Lord thy God, and him only shalt thou serve. 4:11 Then the devil leaveth him,		4:8 And Jesus answered and said unto him, Get thee behind me, Satan: for it is written, Thou shalt worship the Lord thy God, and him only shalt thou serve. 4:13 And when the devil had ended all the temptation, he departed from him for a season.	
and, behold, angels came and ministered unto him.	1:13(b) and the angels ministered unto him.		

C-5. JOHN TESTIFIES OF JESUS

1:19 And this is the record of John, when the Jews sent priests and Levites from Jerusalem to ask him, Who art thou?

1:20 And he confessed, and denied not *that he was Elias*; but confessed, *saying,* I am not the Christ.

1:21 And they asked him, What then? Art thou Elias? And he saith, I am not. *saying, How then art thou Elias? And he said, I am not that Elias who was to restore all things. And they asked him, saying,* Art thou that prophet? And he answered, No.

1:22 Then said they unto him, Who art thou? that we may give an answer to them that sent us. What sayest thou of thyself?

1:23 He said, I am the voice of one crying in the wilderness, Make straight the way of the Lord, as said the prophet Esaias.

1:24 And they which *who* were sent were of the Pharisees.

1:25 And they asked him, and said unto him, Why baptizest thou then, if thou be not that *the* Christ, nor Elias *who was to restore all things*, neither that prophet?

1:26 John answered them, saying, I baptize with water: but there standeth one among you, whom ye know not;

1:27 He it is *of whom I bear record. He is that prophet, even Elias,* who coming after me is preferred before me, whose shoe's latchet I am not worthy to unloose, *or whose place I am not able to fill; for he shall baptize, not only with water, but with fire, and with the Holy Ghost.*

1:28 These things were done in Bethabara beyond Jordan, where John was baptizing. (see after verse 34)

1:29 The next day John seeth Jesus coming unto him, and saith*d,* Behold the Lamb of God, which *who* taketh away the sin of the world.

1:30 *And John bare record of him unto the people, saying,* This

MATTHEW	MARK	LUKE	JOHN

is he of whom I said, After me cometh a man ~~which~~ *who* is preferred before me: for he was before me.

1:31 And I knew him ~~not:~~ ~~but~~ *and* that he should be made manifest to Israel, therefore am I come baptizing with water.

1:32 And John bare record, saying, ***When he was baptized of me,*** I saw the Spirit descending from heaven like a dove, and it abode upon him.

1:33 And I knew him ~~not:~~ ~~but he that~~ *for he who* sent me to baptize with water, the same said unto me, Upon whom thou shalt see the Spirit descending, and remaining on him, the same is he ~~which~~ *who* baptizeth with the Holy Ghost.

1:34 And I saw, and bare record that this is the Son of God.

1:28 These things were done in Bethabara, beyond Jordan, where John was baptizing. (*verse order changed by JST*)

C-6. THE CALLING OF ANDREW, SIMON, PHILIP AND NATHANIEL

1:35 Again the next day after John stood, and two of his disciples;

1:36 And looking upon Jesus as he walked, he saith, Behold the Lamb of God!

1:37 And the two disciples heard him speak, and they followed Jesus.

1:38 Then Jesus turned, and saw them following *him*, and sai~~th~~*d* unto them, What seek ye? They ~~said~~ *say* unto him, Rabbi, (which is to say, being interpreted, Master,) where dwellest thou?

1:39 He sai~~th~~*d* unto them, Come and see. ***And*** They came and saw where he dwelt, and abode with him that day: for it was about the tenth hour.

1:40 One of the two ~~which~~ *who* heard John ~~speak~~, and followed ~~him~~ *Jesus*, was Andrew, Simon Peter's brother.

1:41 He first findeth his own brother Simon, and saith unto him, We have found the Messias, which is, being interpreted, the Christ.

1:42 And he brought him to Jesus. And when Jesus beheld him, he said, Thou art Simon the son of Jona: thou shalt be called Cephas, which is by interpretation, ~~A stone~~ *a seer, or a stone.* ***And they were fishermen. And they straightway left all, and followed Jesus.***

1:43 The day following Jesus would go forth into Galilee, and findeth Philip, and saith unto him, Follow me.

MATTHEW	MARK	LUKE	JOHN

JOHN

1:44 Now Philip was ~~of~~ *at* Bethsaida, the city of Andrew and Peter.

1:45 Philip findeth Nathanael, and saith unto him, We have found him, of whom Moses in the law, and the prophets, did write, Jesus of Nazareth, the son of Joseph.

1:46 And Nathanael said unto him, Can there any good thing come out of Nazareth? Philip saith unto him, Come and see.

1:47 Jesus saw Nathanael coming to him, and saith of him, Behold an Israelite indeed, in whom is no guile!

1:48 Nathanael sai~~th~~d unto him, Whence knowest thou me? Jesus ~~answered and~~ *answering* said unto him, Before ~~that~~ Philip called thee, when thou wast under the fig tree, I saw thee.

1:49 Nathanael answered and saith unto him, Rabbi, thou art the Son of God; thou art the King of Israel.

1:50 Jesus answered and said unto him, Because I said unto thee, I saw thee under the fig tree, believest thou? thou shalt see greater things than these.

1:51 And he saith unto him, Verily, verily, I say unto you, Hereafter ye shall see heaven open, and the angels of God ascending and descending upon the Son of man.

C-7. FIRST MIRACLE: THE MARRIAGE IN CANA

2:1 And *on* the third day *of the week* there was a marriage in Cana of Galilee; and the mother of Jesus was there:

2:2 And ~~both~~ Jesus was called, and his disciples, to the marriage.

2:3 And when they wanted wine, ~~the mother of Jesus saith~~ *his mother said* unto him, They have no wine.

2:4 Jesus sai~~th~~d unto her, Woman, what ~~have I to do with thee?~~ *wilt thou have me do for thee? that I will do; for* mine hour is not yet come.

2:5 His mother sai~~th~~d unto the servants, Whatsoever he saith unto you, *see that ye* do it.

2:6 ~~And~~ there were set there six waterpots of stone, after the manner of the purifying of the Jews, containing two or three firkins apiece.

2:7 Jesus saith unto them, Fill the waterpots with water. And they filled them up to the brim.

2:8 And he sai~~th~~d ~~unto them~~, Draw out now, and bear unto the governor of the feast. And they bare ~~it~~ *unto him*.

MATTHEW	MARK	LUKE	JOHN

2:9 When the ~~ruler~~ *governor* of the feast had tasted the water ~~that~~ *which* was made wine, ~~and~~ *he* knew not whence it was: (but the servants ~~which~~ *who* drew the water knew;) the governor of the feast called the bridegroom,

2:10 And saith unto him, Every man at the beginning doth set forth good wine; and when men have well drunk, then that which is worse: but thou hast kept the good wine until now.

2:11 This beginning of miracles did Jesus in Cana of Galilee, and manifested forth his glory; and ~~his disciples believed on him~~ *the faith of his disciples was strengthened in him*.

C-8. JESUS GOES TO CAPERNAUM

2:12 After this he went down to Capernaum, he, and his mother, and his brethren, and his disciples: and they continued there not many days.

MATTHEW	MARK	LUKE	JOHN

D-1. JESUS CLEANSES THE TEMPLE

2:13 And the Jews' passover was at hand, and Jesus went up to Jerusalem,

2:14 And found in the temple those ~~that~~ *who* sold oxen and sheep and doves, and the changers of money sitting:

2:15 And when he had made a scourge of small cords, he drove them all out of the temple, and the sheep, and the oxen; and poured out the changers' money, and overthrew the tables;

2:16 And said unto them ~~that~~ *who* sold doves, Take these things hence; make not my Father's house ~~an~~ house of merchandise.

2:17 And his disciples remembered that it was written, The zeal of ~~thine~~ *thy* house hath eaten me up.

2:18 Then ~~answered~~ *spake* the Jews and said unto him, What sign ~~shewest~~ *showest* thou unto us, seeing ~~that~~ thou doest these things?

2:19 Jesus answered and said unto them, Destroy this temple, and in three days I will raise it up.

2:20 Then said the Jews, Forty and six years was this temple in building, and wilt thou rear it up in three days?

2:21 But he spake of the temple of his body.

2:22 When therefore he was risen from the dead, his disciples remembered that he had said this unto them; and they ~~believed~~ *remembered* the ~~s~~Scripture, and the word which Jesus had said *unto them*.

D-2. JESUS ATTENDS PASSOVER

2:23 Now when he was in Jerusalem at the passover, ~~in~~ *on* the feast day, many believed ~~in~~ *on* his name, when they saw the miracles which he did.

2:24 But Jesus did not commit himself unto them, because he knew all ~~men~~ *things*,

2:25 And needed not that any should testify of man: for he knew what was in man.

D-3. NICODEMUS VISITS JESUS AT NIGHT

3:1 There was a man of the Pharisees, named Nicodemus, a ruler of the Jews:

3:2 The same came to Jesus by night, and said unto him, Rabbi, we know that thou art a teacher come from God: for no man can do

MATTHEW	MARK	LUKE	JOHN

these miracles ~~that~~ *which* thou doest, except God be with him.

3:3 Jesus answered and said unto him, Verily, verily, I say unto thee, Except a man be born again, he cannot see the kingdom of God.

3:4 Nicodemus saith unto him, How can a man be born when he is old? can he enter the second time into his mother's womb, and be born?

3:5 Jesus answered, Verily, verily, I say unto thee, Except a man be born of water and ~~of~~ the Spirit, he cannot enter into the kingdom of God.

3:6 That which is born of the flesh is flesh; and that which is born of the Spirit is spirit.

3:7 Marvel not that I said unto thee, Ye must be born again.

3:8 The wind bloweth where it listeth, and thou hearest the sound thereof, but canst not tell whence it cometh, and whither it goeth: so is every one ~~that~~ *who* is born of the Spirit.

3:9 Nicodemus answered and said unto him, How can these things be?

3:10 Jesus answered and said ~~unto him~~, Art thou a master of Israel, and knowest not these things?

3:11 Verily, verily, I say unto thee, We speak that we do know, and testify that we have seen; and ye receive not our witness.

3:12 If I have told you earthly things, and ye believe not, how shall ye believe, if I tell you ~~of~~ heavenly things?

3:13 ~~And~~ *I tell you,* no man hath ascended up to heaven, but he ~~that~~ *who* came down from heaven, ~~even~~ the Son of ~~m~~*M*an ~~which~~ *who* is in heaven.

3:14 And as Moses lifted up the serpent in the wilderness, even so must the Son of man be lifted up:

3:15 That whosoever believeth ~~in~~ *on* him should not perish, but have eternal life.

3:16 For God so loved the world, that he gave his ~~o~~*O*nly ~~b~~*B*egotten Son, that whosoever believeth ~~in~~ *on* him should not perish, but have everlasting life.

3:17 For God sent not his Son into the world to condemn the world; but that the world through him might be saved.

3:18 He ~~that~~ *who* believeth on him is not condemned: but he ~~that~~ *who* believeth not is condemned already, because he hath not believed ~~in~~ *on* the name of the only begotten Son of God, *which was before preached by the mouth of the holy prophets; for they testified of me.*

MATTHEW	MARK	LUKE	JOHN

3:19 And this is the condemnation, that light is come into the world, and men ~~loved~~ *love* darkness rather than light, because their deeds ~~were~~ *are* evil.

3:20 For every one ~~that~~ *who* doeth evil hateth the light, neither cometh to the light, lest his deeds should be reproved.

3:21 But he ~~that doeth~~ *who loveth* truth cometh to the light, that his deeds may be made manifest, ~~that they are wrought in God~~ *And he who obeyeth the truth, the works which he doeth they are of God*.

D-4. JOHN'S MINISTRY AND FURTHER TESTIMONY OF CHRIST

3:22 After these things came Jesus and his disciples into the land of ~~Judaea~~ *Judea*; and there he tarried with them, and baptized.

3:23 And John also was baptizing in Aenon near to Salim, because there was much water there: and they came, and were baptized.

3:24 For John was not yet cast into prison.

3:25 Then there arose a question between some of John's disciples and the Jews about purifying.

3:26 And they came unto John, and said unto him, Rabbi, he ~~that~~ *who* was with thee beyond Jordan, to whom thou ~~barest~~ *bearest* witness, behold, the same baptizeth, and ~~all men~~ *he receiveth of all people who* come ~~un~~to him.

3:27 John answered and said, A man can receive nothing, except it be given him from heaven.

3:28 Ye yourselves bear me witness, that I said, I am not the Christ, but that I am sent before him.

3:29 He ~~that~~ *who* hath the bride is the bridegroom: but the friend of the bridegroom, ~~which~~ *who* standeth and heareth him, rejoiceth greatly because of the bridegroom's voice: this my joy therefore is fulfilled.

3:30 He must increase, but I must decrease.

3:31 He ~~that~~ *who* cometh from above is above all: he ~~that~~ *who* is of the earth is earthly, and speaketh of the earth: he ~~that~~ *who* cometh from heaven is above all.

3:32 And what he hath seen and heard, that he testifieth; and ~~no man~~ *but few men* receiveth his testimony.

3:33 He ~~that~~ *who* hath received his testimony hath set to his seal that God is true.

3:34 For he whom God hath sent speaketh the words of God: for God giveth *him* not the Spirit by

MATTHEW	MARK	LUKE	JOHN
			measure unto him *for he dwelleth in him, even the fulness.*
			3:35 The Father loveth the Son, and hath given all things into his hand.
			3:36 *And* He ~~that~~ *who* believeth on the Son hath everlasting life; *and shall receive of his fulness:* ~~and he that~~ *But he who* believeth not the Son shall not ~~see life; but~~ *receive of his fulness; for* the wrath of God ~~abideth~~ *is up*on him.

D-5. HEROD IMPRISONS JOHN THE BAPTIST

MATTHEW	MARK	LUKE	JOHN
14:3 For Herod had laid hold on John, and bound him, and put him in prison for Herodias' sake, his brother Philip's wife.	6:17 For Herod himself had sent forth and laid hold upon John, and bound him in prison for Herodias' sake, his brother Philip's wife: for he had married her.	3:19 But Herod the tetrarch, being reproved ~~by~~ *of* him for Herodias his brother Philip's wife, and for all the evils which Herod had done,	
14:4 For John said unto him, It is not lawful for thee to have her.	6:18 For John had said unto Herod, It is not lawful for thee to have thy brother's wife.		
	6:19 Therefore Herodias had a quarrel against him, and would have killed him; but she could not:		
	6:20 For Herod feared John, knowing that he was a just man and ~~an~~ holy *man, and one who feared God*, and observed *to worship* him; and when he heard him, he did many things *for him*, and heard him gladly.		
14:5 And when he would have put him to death, he feared the multitude, because they counted him as a prophet.			
		3:20 Added yet this above all, that he shut up John in prison.	

D-6. RETURN TO GALILEE

MATTHEW	MARK	LUKE	JOHN
			4:1 When therefore ~~the Lord knew how~~ the Pharisees had heard that Jesus made and baptized more disciples than John, *they sought more diligently some means that they might put him to death, for many received John as a prophet, but they believed not on Jesus.*
			4:2 (~~Though Jesus~~ *Now the Lord knew this, though* he himself baptized not *so many as* ~~but~~ his disciples, *For he suffered them for an example, preferring one another.*)
4:12 *And* Now ~~when~~ Jesus ~~had heard~~ *knew* that John was cast into prison, *and* he *sent angels, and, behold, they came and ministered unto him.*	1:14 Now after that John was put in prison,		
And Jesus departed into Galilee;	Jesus came into Galilee, preaching the gospel of the kingdom of God,	4:14 And Jesus returned in the power of the Spirit into Galilee: and there went out a fame of him through all the region round about.	4:3 *And* He left ~~Judaea~~ *Judea*, and departed again into Galilee.

D-7. SAMARITAN WOMAN AT JACOB'S WELL

4:4 And ~~he~~ *said unto his disciples, I* must needs go through Samaria.

4:5 Then *he* cometh ~~he~~ to ~~a~~ *the* city of Samaria, which is called Sychar, near to the parcel of ground ~~that~~ *which* Jacob gave to his son Joseph~~.~~ *;*

4:6 ~~Now~~ *the place where* Jacob's well was ~~there~~. ~~Jesus therefore, being wearied~~ *Now Jesus being weary* with his journey, *it being about the sixth hour,* sat ~~thus~~ *down* on the well: ~~and it was about the sixth hour.~~

4:7 *And* There ~~cometh~~ *came* a woman of Samaria to draw water: Jesus sai~~th~~*d* unto her, Give me to drink.

4:8 (~~For~~ *Now* his disciples were gone away ~~unto~~ *into* the city to buy meat.)

4:9 ~~Then saith the woman of Samaria~~ *Wherefore he being alone, the woman of Samaria said* unto him, How is it that thou, being a Jew, askest drink of me, ~~which~~ *who* am a woman of Samaria? ~~for~~ the Jews have no dealings with the Samaritans.

4:10 Jesus answered and said unto her, If thou knewest the gift of God, and who it is that saith to thee, Give me to drink; thou wouldest have asked of him, and he would have given thee living water.

4:11 The woman saith unto him, Sir, thou hast nothing to draw with, and the well is deep: from whence then hast thou that living water?

4:12 Art thou greater than our father Jacob, ~~which~~ *who* gave us the well, and drank thereof himself, and his children, and his cattle?

4:13 Jesus answered and said unto her, Whosoever ~~drinketh~~ *shall drink* of this ~~water~~ *well* shall thirst again:

4:14 But whosoever drinketh of the water ~~that~~ *which* I shall give him shall never thirst; but the water that I shall give him shall be in him a well of water springing up into everlasting life.

4:15 The woman sai~~th~~*d* unto him, Sir, give me *of* this water, that I thirst not, neither come hither to draw.

4:16 Jesus saith unto her, Go, call thy husband, and come hither.

4:17 The woman answered and said, I have no husband. Jesus said unto her, Thou hast well said, I have no husband:

4:18 For thou hast had five husbands; and he whom thou now hast is not thy husband: in that saidst thou truly.

MATTHEW	MARK	LUKE	JOHN

4:19 The woman saith unto him, Sir, I perceive that thou art a prophet.

4:20 Our fathers worshipped in this mountain; and ye say, that in Jerusalem is the place where men ought to worship.

4:21 Jesus saith unto her, Woman, believe me, the hour cometh, when ye shall neither in this mountain, nor yet at Jerusalem, worship the Father.

4:22 Ye worship ye know not what: we know what we worship: ~~for~~ *and* salvation is of the Jews.

4:23 ~~But~~ *And* the hour cometh, and now is, when the true worshippers shall worship the Father in spirit and in truth: for the Father seeketh such to worship him.

4:24 ~~God is a Spirit~~ *For unto such hath God promised his Spirit*: and they ~~that~~ *who* worship him must worship him in spirit and in truth.

4:25 The woman sai~~th~~*d* unto him, I know that Messias cometh, ~~which~~ *who* is called Christ: when he is come, he will tell us all things.

4:26 Jesus sai~~th~~*d* unto her, I ~~that~~ *who* speak unto thee am ~~he~~ *the Messias*.

4:27 And upon this came his disciples, and marvelled that he talked with the woman: yet no man said, What seekest thou? or, Why talkest thou with her?

4:28 The woman then left her waterpot, and went her way into the city, and saith to the men,

4:29 Come, see a man, ~~which~~ *who* told me all things that ~~ever I did~~ *I have ever done*: is not this the Christ?

4:30 Then they went out of the city, and came unto him.

4:31 In the mean ~~while~~ *time* his disciples prayed him, saying, Master, eat.

4:32 But he said unto them, I have meat to eat that ye know not of.

4:33 Therefore said the disciples one to another, Hath any man brought him ~~ought~~ *meat* to eat?

4:34 Jesus sai~~th~~*d* unto them, My meat is to do the will of him ~~that~~ *who* sent me, and to finish his work.

4:35 Say not ye, There are yet four months, ~~and~~ then cometh harvest? behold, I say unto you, Lift up your eyes, and look on the fields; for they are white already to harvest.

4:36 And he ~~that~~ *who* reapeth receiveth wages, and gathereth fruit unto life eternal: that both he ~~that~~

MATTHEW	MARK	LUKE	JOHN

who soweth and he ~~that~~ *who* reapeth may rejoice together.

4:37 And herein is that saying true, One soweth, and another reapeth.

4:38 I *have* sent you to reap that whereon ye bestowed no ~~labour~~ *labor*: ~~other men~~ *the prophets have labored* ~~laboured~~, and ye ~~are~~ *have* entered into their ~~labours~~ *labors*.

4:39 And many of the Samaritans of that city believed on him for the saying of the woman, ~~which~~ *who* testified, He told me all that ~~ever I did~~ *I have ever done*.

4:40 So when the Samaritans were come unto him, they besought him that he would tarry with them: and he abode there two days.

4:41 And many more believed because of his own word;

4:42 And said unto the woman, Now we believe not because of thy saying: ~~for~~ we have heard ~~him~~ *for* ourselves, and know that this is indeed the Christ, the ~~Saviour~~ *Savior* of the world.

MATTHEW	MARK	LUKE	JOHN

E-1. JESUS GOES TO GALILEE

MATTHEW	MARK	LUKE	JOHN
			4:43 Now after two days he departed thence, and went into Galilee.
			4:44 For Jesus himself testified, that a prophet hath no ~~honour~~ *honor* in his own country.
			4:45 Then when he ~~was~~ *had* come into Galilee,
		4:15 And he taught in their synagogues, being glorified of all *who believed on his name*.	
			the Galilaeans received him, having seen all the things ~~that~~ *which* he did at Jerusalem at the feast: for they also went unto the feast.

E-2. NOBELMAN'S SON IS HEALED

MATTHEW	MARK	LUKE	JOHN
			4:46 So Jesus came again into Cana of Galilee, where he made the water wine. And there was a certain nobleman, whose son was sick at Capernaum.
			4:47 When he heard that Jesus was come out of ~~Judaea~~ *Judea* into Galilee, he went unto him, and besought him that he would come down, and heal his son: for he was at the point of death.
			4:48 Then said Jesus unto him, Except ye see signs and wonders, ye will not believe.
			4:49 The nobleman sai~~th~~*d* unto him, Sir, come down ~~ere~~ *before* my child die.
			4:50 Jesus sai~~th~~*d* unto him, Go thy way; thy son liveth. And the man believed the word ~~that~~ *which* Jesus had spoken unto him, and he went his way.
			4:51 And as he was now going down *to his house*, his servants met him, and ~~told him~~ *spake*, saying, Thy son liveth.
			4:52 Then inquired he of them the hour when he began to amend. And they said unto him, Yesterday at the seventh hour the fever left him.
			4:53 So the father knew that ~~it was at~~ *his son was healed in* the same hour, in the which Jesus said unto him, Thy son liveth: and himself believed, and his whole house.
			4:54 This ~~is again~~ *being* the second miracle ~~that~~ *which* Jesus ~~did~~ *had done*, when he ~~was~~ *had* come out of ~~Judaea~~ *Judea* into Galilee.

E-3. JESUS REJECTED AT NAZARETH

4:16 And he came to Nazareth, where he had been brought up: and, as his custom was, he went into the synagogue on the sabbath day, and stood up ~~for~~ to read.

4:17 And there was delivered unto him the book of the prophet Esaias. And when he had opened the book, he found the place where it was written,

4:18 The sSpirit of the Lord is upon me, because he hath anointed me to preach the gospel to the poor; he hath sent me to heal the brokenhearted, to preach deliverance to the captives, and *the* recovering of sight to the blind, to set at liberty them that are bruised,

4:19 To preach the acceptable year of the Lord.

4:20 And he closed the book, and he gave it again to the minister, and *he* sat down. And the eyes of all ~~them that~~ *those who* were in the synagogue were fastened on him.

4:21 And he began to say unto them, This day is this sScripture fulfilled in your ears.

4:22 And all bare him witness, and wondered at the gracious words which proceeded out of his mouth. And they said, Is not this Joseph's son?

4:23 And he said unto them, Ye will surely say unto me this proverb, Physician, heal thyself: whatsoever we have heard *was* done in Capernaum, do also here in thy country.

4:24 And he said, Verily I say unto you, No prophet is accepted in his own country.

4:25 But I tell you ~~of a~~ *the* truth, many widows were in Israel in the days of Elias, when the heaven was shut up three years and six months, ~~when~~ *and* great famine was throughout all the land;

4:26 But unto none of them was Elias sent, save unto Sarepta, ~~a city~~ of Sidon, unto a woman that was a widow.

4:27 And many lepers were in Israel in the time of Eliseus the prophet; and none of them ~~was~~ *were* cleansed, ~~saving~~ *save* Naaman the Syrian.

4:28 And all they in the synagogue, when they heard these things, were filled with wrath,

4:29 And rose up, and thrust him out of the city, and led him unto the brow of the hill whereon their city was built, that they might cast him down headlong.

4:30 But he passing through the midst of them went his way,

MATTHEW	MARK	LUKE	JOHN

E-4. JOURNEY TO CAPERNAUM

4:13 And leaving Nazareth, *in Zebulun,* he came and dwelt in Capernaum, which is upon the sea coast, in the borders of ~~Zabulon and~~ Nephthalim:
4:14 That it might be fulfilled which was spoken by Esaias the prophet, saying,
4:15 The land of ~~Zabulon~~ *Zebulun,* and the land of Nephthalim, ~~by~~ *in* the way of the sea, beyond Jordan, Galilee of the Gentiles;
4:16 The people which sat in darkness saw *a* great light; and *un*to them ~~which~~ *that* sat in the region and shadow of death , light is sprung up.
4:17 From that time Jesus began to preach, and to say,

Repent: for the kingdom of heaven is at hand.

1:15 And saying,
The time is fulfilled, and the kingdom of God is at hand: repent ye, and believe the gospel.

E-5. PETER, ANDREW, JAMES AND JOHN: FISHERS OF MEN

4:18 And Jesus, walking by the sea of Galilee, saw two brethren, Simon called Peter, and Andrew his brother, casting a net into the sea: for they were fishers.

1:16 Now as he walked by the sea of Galilee, he saw
Simon and Andrew his brother casting a net into the sea: for they were fishers.

5:1 And it came to pass, ~~that,~~ as the people pressed upon him to hear the word of God, he stood by the lake of Gennesaret,
5:2 And saw two ships standing ~~by~~ *on* the lake: but the fishermen were gone out of them, and were ~~washing~~ *wetting* their nets.
5:3 And he entered into one of the ships, which was Simon's, and prayed him that he would thrust out a little from the land. And he sat down, and taught the people out of the ship.
5:4 Now when he had ~~left~~ *done* speaking, he said ~~un~~to Simon, Launch out into the deep, and let down your nets for a draught.
5:5 And Simon answering said unto him, Master, we have toiled all the night, and have taken nothing: nevertheless at thy word I will let down the net.
5:6 And when they had ~~this~~ done *this*, they ~~inclosed~~ *enclosed* a great multitude of fishes: and their net brake.
5:7 And they beckoned unto their partners, ~~which~~ *who* were in the other ship, that they should come and help them. And they came, and filled both the ships, so that they began to sink.

MATTHEW	MARK	LUKE	JOHN
		5:8 When Simon Peter saw ~~it~~ *the multitude of fishes*, he fell down at Jesus' knees, saying, Depart from me; for I am a sinful man, O Lord. 5:9 For he was astonished, and all ~~that~~ *who* were with him, at the draught of the fishes which they had taken: 5:10 And so ~~was~~ *were* also James, and John, the sons of Zebedee, ~~which~~ *who* were partners with Simon. And Jesus said unto Simon,	
4:19 And he sai~~th~~d unto them, *I am he of whom it is written by the prophets;* Follow me, and I will make you fishers of men.	1:17 And Jesus said unto them, Come ye after me, and I will make you to become fishers of men.	Fear not; from henceforth, *for* thou shalt catch men. 5:11 And when they had brought their ships to land,	
4:20 And they, *believing on his words,* ~~straightway~~ left their net~~s~~, and *straightway* followed him. 4:21 And going on from thence, he saw other two brethren, James ~~the son of Zebedee~~, and John his brother, *the sons of Zebedee,* in a ship with Zebedee their father, mending their net~~s~~; and he called them. 4:22 And they immediately left ~~the ship and~~ their father *in the ship*, and followed him.	1:18 And straightway they forsook their nets, and followed him. 1:19 And when he had gone a little farther thence, he saw James the son of Zebedee, and John his brother, who also were in the ship mending their nets. 1:20 And ~~straightway~~ he called them: and *straightway* they left their father Zebedee in the ship with the hired servants, and went after him.	they forsook all, and followed him.	

E-6. JESUS TEACHES WITH POWER AND AUTHORITY

MATTHEW	MARK	LUKE	JOHN
	1:21 And they went into Capernaum; and straightway on the ~~s~~*S*abbath day he entered into the synagogue, and taught. 1:22 And they were astonished at his doctrine: for he taught them as one that had authority, and not as the scribes.	4:31 And came down to Capernaum, a city of Galilee, and taught them on the sabbath days. 4:32 And they were astonished at his doctrine: for his word*s* ~~was~~ *were* with power.	

E-7. AN UNCLEAN SPIRIT CAST OUT

MATTHEW	MARK	LUKE	JOHN
	1:23 And there was in their synagogue a man with an unclean spirit; and he cried out, 1:24 Saying, Let us alone; what have we to do with thee, thou Jesus of Nazareth? art thou come to destroy us? I know thee who thou art, the Holy One of God. 1:25 And Jesus rebuked him, saying, Hold thy peace, and come out of him. 1:26 And when the unclean spirit had torn him, and cried with a loud voice, he came out of him. 1:27 And they were all amazed, insomuch that they questioned among themselves, saying, What thing is this? what new doctrine is this?	4:33 And in the synagogue there was a man, ~~which~~ *who* had a spirit of an unclean devil, and cried out with a loud voice, 4:34 Saying, Let us alone; what have we to do with thee, ~~thou~~ Jesus of Nazareth? art thou come to destroy us? I know thee who thou art; the Holy One of God. 4:35 ~~And~~ Jesus rebuked him, saying, Hold thy peace, and come out of him. And when the devil had thrown him in the midst, he came out of him, and hurt him not. 4:36 And they were all amazed, and spake among themselves, saying, What a word is this!	

MATTHEW	MARK	LUKE	JOHN

| | for with authority commandeth he even the unclean spirits, and they do obey him.
1:28 And immediately his fame spread abroad throughout all the region round about Galilee. | for with authority and power he commandeth the unclean spirits, and they come out.
4:37 And the fame of him went out in~~to~~ every place ~~of the country~~ round about. | |

E-8. PETER'S MOTHER-IN-LAW IS HEALED

MATTHEW	MARK	LUKE	JOHN
8:14 And when Jesus was come into Peter's house, he saw his wife's mother laid, and sick of a fever.	1:29 And forthwith, when they were come out of the synagogue, they entered into the house of Simon and Andrew, with James and John. 1:30 ~~But~~ *And* Simon's wife's mother lay sick of a fever, and ~~anon they tell him of~~ *they besought him for* her.	4:38 And he arose, *and went* out of the synagogue, and entered into Simon's house. And Simon's wife's mother was taken with a great fever; and they besought him for *to heal* her.	
8:15 And he touched her hand, and the fever left her: and she arose, and ministered unto them.	1:31 And he came and took her by the hand, and lifted her up; and immediately the fever left her, and she *came and* ministered unto them.	4:39 And he stood over her, and rebuked the fever; and it left her: and immediately she arose and ministered unto them.	
8:16 *Now* When the eve*ning* was come, they brought unto him many that were possessed with devils:	1:32 And at ~~even, when the sun did set~~ *evening after sunset*, they brought unto him all that were diseased, and them that were possessed with devils. 1:33 And all the city was gathered together at the door.	4:40 Now when the sun was setting, all they ~~that~~ *who* had any sick with divers diseases brought them unto him;	
and he cast out the *evil* spirits with ~~his~~ *the* word, and healed all that were sick:	1:34 And he healed many that were sick of divers diseases, and cast out many devils;	and he laid his hands on every one of them, and healed them. 4:41 And devils also came out of many, crying out, and saying, Thou art Christ the Son of God. And he rebuking them suffered them not to speak: for they knew that he was Christ.	
	and suffered not the devils to speak, because they knew him.		
8:17 That it might be fulfilled which was spoken by Esaias the prophet, saying, Himself took our infirmities, and bare our sicknesses.			

E-9. JESUS PREACHES AND HEALS IN GALILEE

MATTHEW	MARK	LUKE	JOHN
	1:35 And in the morning, rising up a great while before day, he went out, and departed into a solitary place, and there prayed. 1:36 And Simon and they that were with him followed after him. 1:37 And when they had found him, they said unto him, All men seek for thee.	4:42 And when it was day, he departed and went into a ~~desert~~ *solitary* place: and the people sought him, and came unto him,	
	1:38 And he said unto them, Let us go into the next towns, that I may preach there also: for therefore came I forth.	and ~~stayed~~ *desired* him, that he should not depart from them. 4:43 ~~And~~ *But* he said unto them, I must preach the kingdom of God to other cities also: for therefore am I sent.	
4:23 And Jesus went about all Galilee, teaching in their synagogues, and preaching the gospel of the kingdom, and healing all manner of sickness and all manner of disease*s* among the	1:39 And he preached in their synagogues throughout all Galilee, and cast out devils.	4:44 And he preached in the synagogues of Galilee.	

MATTHEW	MARK	LUKE	JOHN

people *which believed on his name*.

4:24 And his fame went throughout all Syria: and they brought unto him all sick people that were taken with divers diseases and torments, and those ~~which~~ *who* were possessed with devils, and those ~~which~~ *who* were lunatick, and those that had the palsy; and he healed them.

4:25 And there followed him great multitudes of people from Galilee, and ~~from~~ Decapolis, and ~~from~~ Jerusalem, and ~~from Judaea~~ *Judea*, and ~~from~~ beyond Jordan.

E-10. A LEPER IS CLEANSED

8:2 And, behold, there came a leper ~~and worshipped~~ *worshipping* him, saying,
Lord, if thou wilt, thou canst make me clean.

8:3 And Jesus put forth his hand, and touched him, saying,
I will; be thou clean.

And immediately his leprosy was cleansed.

8:4 And Jesus ~~saith~~d unto him, See thou tell no man;
but go thy way, ~~shew~~ *show* thyself to the priest,
and offer the gift that Moses commanded, for a testimony unto them.

1:40 And there came a leper to him, beseeching him, and kneeling down to him, ~~and saying unto him~~ *said*, If thou wilt, thou canst make me clean.
1:41 And Jesus, moved with compassion, put forth his hand, and touched him, and ~~saith~~d unto him, I will; be thou clean.
1:42 And as soon as he had spoken, immediately the leprosy departed from him, and he was cleansed.
1:43 And he straitly charged him, and forthwith sent him away;
1:44 And saith unto him, See thou say nothing to any man: but go thy way, ~~shew~~ *show* thyself to the priest,
and offer for thy cleansing those things which Moses commanded, for a testimony unto them.
1:45 But he went out, and began to publish it much, and to blaze abroad the matter,

insomuch that Jesus could no more openly enter into the city, but was without in ~~desert~~ *solitary* places:

and they came to him from every quarter.

5:12 And it came to pass, when he was in a certain city,
behold a man full of leprosy: who seeing Jesus fell on his face, and besought him, saying,
Lord, if thou wilt, thou canst make me clean.

5:13 And he put forth his hand, and touched him, saying, I will: be thou clean.

And immediately the leprosy departed from him.

5:14 And he charged him to tell no man:
but *said unto him,*

go, and ~~shew~~ *show* thyself to the priest*s*,
and offer for thy cleansing, according as Moses commanded, for a testimony unto them.
5:15 But so much the more went there a fame abroad of him:

and great multitudes came together to hear, and to be healed by him of their infirmities.

5:16 And he withdrew himself into the wilderness, and prayed.

E-11. JESUS HEALS A MAN WITH THE PALSY

2:1 And again he entered into Capernaum, after ~~some~~ *many* days; and it was noised that he was in the house.

5:17 And it came to pass on a certain day, as he was teaching, that there were Pharisees and doctors of the law sitting by, ~~which~~ *who* were come out of every town of Galilee, and ~~Judaea~~ *Judea*, and

LUKE: Jerusalem: and the power of the Lord was present to heal them.

MARK 2:2 And straightway many were gathered together, insomuch that there was no room to receive ~~them~~ *the multitude*, no, not so much as about the door: and he preached the word unto them.

MATTHEW 9:2 And, behold, they brought to him a man sick of the palsy, lying on a bed:

MARK 2:3 And they come unto him, bringing one sick of the palsy, which was borne of four *persons*.

LUKE 5:18 And, behold, men brought in a bed a man ~~which~~ *who* was taken with a palsy: and they sought ~~means~~ to bring him in, and to lay him before ~~him~~ *Jesus*.

MARK 2:4 And when they could not come nigh unto him for the press,

they uncovered the roof where he was: and when they had broken it up, they let down the bed wherein the sick of the palsy lay.

LUKE 5:19 And when they *found that they* could not ~~find by what way they might~~ bring him in ~~because of~~ *for* the multitude, they went upon the housetop, and let him down through the tiling with his couch into the midst before Jesus.

MATTHEW and Jesus ~~seeing~~ *knowing* their faith said unto the sick of the palsy; Son, be of good cheer; thy sins be forgiven thee*; go thy way and sin no more*.

MARK 2:5 When Jesus saw their faith, he said unto the sick of the palsy,

Son, thy sins be forgiven thee.

LUKE 5:20 ~~And when~~ *Now* he saw their faith, ~~he~~ *and* said unto ~~him,~~ *the* ~~M~~*m*an, thy sins are forgiven thee.

MATTHEW 9:3 And, behold, certain of the scribes said within themselves,

This man blasphemeth.

MARK 2:6 But there were certain of the scribes sitting there, and reasoning in their hearts,

MARK 2:7 Why doth this man thus speak blasphemies? who can forgive sins but God only?

LUKE 5:21 And the scribes and ~~the~~ Pharisees began to reason, saying,

Who is this ~~which~~ *that* speaketh blasphemies? Who can forgive sins, but God alone?

MATTHEW 9:4 And Jesus knowing their thoughts said,

Wherefore *is it that ye* think ~~ye~~ evil in your hearts?

MARK 2:8 And immediately when Jesus perceived in his spirit that they so reasoned within themselves, he said unto them, Why reason ye these things in your hearts?

LUKE 5:22 But ~~when~~ Jesus perceived their thoughts, ~~he answering~~ *and he* said unto them, What reason ye in your hearts?

MATTHEW 9:5 For ~~whether~~ is *it not* easier, to say, Thy sins be forgiven thee; ~~or~~ *than* to say, Arise, and walk?

MARK 2:9 ~~Whether~~ is it *not* easier to say to the sick of the palsy, Thy sins be forgiven thee; ~~or~~ *than* to say, Arise, and take up thy bed, and walk?

LUKE 5:23 ~~Whether is easier, to say, Thy sins be forgiven thee; or to say, Rise up and walk?~~ *Does it require more power to forgive sins than to make the sick rise up and walk?*

MATTHEW 9:6 But *I said this* that ye may know that the Son of man hath power on earth to forgive sins, (then ~~saith he~~ *Jesus said un*to the sick of the palsy,) Arise, take up thy bed, and go unto ~~thine~~ *thy* house.

MARK 2:10 But that ye may know that the Son of man hath power on earth to forgive sins, (he sai~~th~~*d* to the sick of the palsy,)

LUKE 5:24 But that ye may know that the Son of ~~m~~*M*an hath power upon earth to forgive sins, *I said it. And* (he said unto the sick of the palsy,)

MARK 2:11 I say unto thee, Arise, and take up thy bed, and go thy way into thine house.

LUKE I say unto thee, Arise, and take up thy couch, and go ~~into thine~~ *unto thy* house.

MATTHEW 9:7 And he *immediately* arose, and departed to his house.

MARK 2:12 And immediately he arose, took up the bed, and went forth before them all;

LUKE 5:25 And immediately he rose up before them, and took up that whereon he lay, and departed to his own house, glorifying God.

MATTHEW 9:8 But when the multitudes saw it, they marvelled, and glorified God, ~~which~~ *who* had given such power unto men.

MARK insomuch that they were all amazed, and *many* glorified God, saying, We never saw ~~it on this fashion~~ *the power of God after this manner*.

LUKE 5:26 And they were all amazed, and they glorified God, and were filled with fear, saying, We have seen strange things to day.

MATTHEW	MARK	LUKE	JOHN

E-12. MATTHEW IS CALLED

Mark

2:13 And ~~he~~ *Jesus* went forth again by the sea side; and all the multitude resorted unto him, and he taught them.

Matthew

9:9 And as Jesus passed forth from thence, he saw a man, named Matthew, sitting at the ~~receipt of custom:~~ *place where they received tribute, as was customary in those days,*
and he sai~~th~~*d* unto him, Follow me. And he arose, and followed him.

Mark

2:14 And as he passed by, he saw Levi the son of Alphaeus sitting at the ~~receipt of custom~~ *place where they receive tribute, as was customary in those days*,

and *he* said unto him, Follow me. And he arose and followed him.

Luke

5:27 And after these things he went forth, and saw a publican, named Levi, sitting at the ~~receipt of~~ *place where they received* custom:

and he said unto him, Follow me.
5:28 And he left all, rose up, and followed him.

E-13. THE CALL FOR SINNERS TO REPENT

Matthew

9:10 And it came to pass, as Jesus sat at meat in the house, behold, many publicans and sinners came and sat down with him and *with* his disciples.

9:11 And when the Pharisees saw ~~it~~ *them*, they said unto his disciples,
Why eateth your Master with publicans and sinners?

9:12 But when Jesus heard ~~that~~ *them*, he said unto them, They that be whole need not a physician, but they that are sick.
9:13 But go ye and learn what ~~that~~ *this* meaneth, I will have mercy, and not sacrifice:
for I am not come to call the righteous, but sinners to repentance.

Mark

2:15 And it came to pass, that, as Jesus sat at meat in his house, many publicans and sinners sat also together with ~~Jesus~~ *him* and his disciples: for there were many, and they followed him.
2:16 And when the scribes and Pharisees saw him eat with publicans and sinners, they said unto his disciples, How is it that he eateth and drinketh with publicans and sinners?
2:17 When Jesus heard ~~it~~ *this*, he sai~~th~~*d* unto them, They that are whole have no need of the physician, but they that are sick:

I came not to call the righteous, but sinners to repentance.

Luke

5:29 And Levi made him a great feast in his own house: and there was a great company of publicans and of others that sat down with them.

5:30 But ~~their~~ *the* scribes and Pharisees murmured against his disciples, saying,
Why do ye eat and drink with publicans and sinners?

5:31 ~~And~~ Jesus answering said unto them, They that are whole need not a physician; but they that are sick.

5:32 I came not to call the righteous, but sinners to repentance.

E-14. NEW WINE INTO NEW BOTTLES: JESUS AND THE LAW

Matthew

9:14 ~~Then~~ *And while he was thus teaching, there* came to him the disciples of John, saying,

Why do we and the Pharisees fast oft, but thy disciples fast not?

9:15 And Jesus said unto them, Can the children of the bridechamber mourn, as long as the bridegroom is with them?

but the days will come, when the bridegroom shall be taken from them, and then shall they fast.

9:16 *Then said the Pharisees unto him, Why will ye not receive us with our baptism, seeing we keep the whole law? But Jesus said unto them, Ye keep not the law. If ye had kept the law, ye would have received me, for I am*

Mark

2:18 And *they came and said unto him,* the disciples of John and of the Pharisees used to fast: and ~~they come and say unto him,~~ Why do the disciples of John and of the Pharisees fast, but thy disciples fast not?

2:19 And Jesus said unto them, Can the children of the bridechamber fast, while the bridegroom is with them? as long as they have the bridegroom with them, they cannot fast.
2:20 But the days will come, when the bridegroom shall be taken away from them, and then shall they fast in those days.

Luke

5:33 And they said unto him,

Why do the disciples of John fast often, and make prayers, and likewise the disciples of the Pharisees; but thine eat and drink?
5:34 And he said unto them, Can ye make the children of the bridechamber fast, while the bridegroom is with them?

5:35 But the days will come, when the bridegroom shall be taken away from them, and then shall they fast in those days.

MATTHEW	MARK	LUKE	JOHN

he who gave the law. I receive not you with your baptism, because it profiteth nothing. For when that which is new is come, the old is ready to be put away.

For No man putteth a piece of new cloth ~~unto~~ *on* an old garment, for that which is put in to fill it up taketh from the garment, and the rent is made worse.

9:17 Neither do men put new wine into old bottles: else the bottles break, and the wine runneth out, and the bottles perish:

but they put new wine into new bottles, and both are preserved.

2:21 No man also seweth a piece of new cloth on an old garment: else the new piece that filled it up taketh away from the old, and the rent is made worse.

2:22 And no man putteth new wine into old bottles: else the new wine doth burst the bottles, and the wine is spilled, and the bottles will be marred:

but new wine must be put into new bottles.

5:36 And he spake also a parable unto them; No man putteth a piece of ~~a new garment~~ *new cloth* upon an old *garment*; if ~~otherwise~~ *so*, then ~~both~~ the new maketh a rent, and ~~the piece that was taken out of the new~~ agreeth not with the old.

5:37 And no man putteth new wine into old bottles; else the new wine will burst the bottles, and be spilled, and the bottles shall perish.

5:38 But new wine must be put into new bottles; and both are preserved.

5:39 No man also having ~~drunk~~ *drank* old wine ~~straightway~~ desireth new: for he saith, The old is better.

E-15. JESUS AGAIN ATTENDS PASSOVER AT JERUSALEM

5:1 After this there was a feast of the Jews; and Jesus went up to Jerusalem.

E-16. JESUS HEALS ON THE SABBATH

5:2 Now there is at Jerusalem by the sheep market a pool, which is called in the Hebrew tongue Bethesda, having five porches.

5:3 In these *porches* lay a great ~~multitude of~~ *many* impotent folk, of blind, halt, withered, waiting for the moving of the water.

5:4 For an angel went down at a certain season into the pool, and troubled the water: whosoever then first after the troubling of the water stepped in was made whole of whatsoever disease he had.

5:5 And a certain man was there, ~~which~~ *who* had an infirmity thirty and eight years.

5:6 ~~When~~ *And* Jesus saw him lie, and knew that he had been now a long time ~~in that case~~ *afflicted*, *and* he sait~~h~~*d* unto him, Wilt thou be made whole?

5:7 The impotent man answered him, Sir, I have no man, when the water is troubled, to put me into the pool: but while I am coming, another steppeth down before me.

5:8 Jesus saith unto him, Rise, take up thy bed, and walk.

5:9 And immediately the man was made whole, and took up his bed, and walked: and ~~on the same day was the sabbath~~ *on the Sabbath day*.

5:10 The Jews therefore said unto him ~~that~~ *who* was cured, It is the

MATTHEW	MARK	LUKE	JOHN

sSabbath day: it is not lawful for thee to carry thy bed.

5:11 He answered them, He ~~that~~ *who* made me whole, ~~the same~~ said unto me, Take up thy bed, and walk.

5:12 Then ~~asked~~ *answered* they him, *saying,* What man is ~~that which~~ *he who* said unto thee, Take up thy bed, and walk?

5:13 And he that was healed ~~wist~~ *knew* not who it was: for Jesus had conveyed himself away, a multitude being in ~~that~~ *the* place.

5:14 Afterward Jesus findeth him in the temple, and said unto him, Behold, thou art made whole: sin no more, lest a worse thing come unto thee.

5:15 The man departed, and told the Jews that it was Jesus, ~~which~~ *who* had made him whole.

5:16 And therefore did the Jews persecute Jesus, and sought to slay him, because he had done these things on the sabbath day.

E-17. JESUS DOES ONLY THE WORKS OF HIS FATHER

5:17 But Jesus answered them, My Father worketh hitherto, and I work.

5:18 Therefore the Jews sought the more to kill him, because he *had* not only ~~had~~ broken the sSabbath, but said also that God was his Father, making himself equal with God.

5:19 Then answered Jesus and said unto them, Verily, verily, I say unto you, The Son can do nothing of himself, but what he seeth the Father do: for what things soever he doeth, these also doeth the Son likewise.

5:20 For the Father loveth the Son, and sheweth him all things that himself doeth: and he will shew him greater works than these, that ye may marvel.

5:21 For as the Father raiseth up the dead, and quickeneth them; even so the Son quickeneth whom he will.

5:22 For the Father judgeth no man, but hath committed all judgment unto the Son:

5:23 That all ~~men~~ should ~~honour~~ *honor* the Son, even as they ~~honour~~ *honor* the Father. He ~~that~~ *who* ~~honoureth~~ *honoreth* not the Son ~~honoureth~~ *honoreth* not the Father ~~which~~ *who* hath sent him.

5:24 Verily, verily, I say unto you, He ~~that~~ *who* heareth my word, and believeth on him ~~that~~ *who* sent me, hath everlasting life, and shall not come into condemnation; but is passed from death unto life.

MATTHEW	MARK	LUKE	JOHN

5:25 Verily, verily, I say unto you, The hour is coming, and now is, when the dead shall hear the voice of the Son of God: and they ~~that~~ *who* hear shall live.

5:26 For as the Father hath life in himself; so hath he given to the Son to have life in himself;

5:27 And hath given him authority to execute judgment also, because he is the Son of man.

5:28 Marvel not at this: for the hour is coming, in the which all ~~that~~ *who* are in the graves shall hear his voice,

5:29 And shall come forth; they ~~that~~ *who* have done good, ~~unto~~ *in* the resurrection of ~~life~~ *the just*; and they ~~that~~ *who* have done evil, ~~unto~~ *in* the resurrection of ~~damnation~~ *the unjust*.

5:30 ~~I can of mine own self do nothing;~~ *And shall be judged of the Son of Man. For* as I hear, I judge: and my judgment is just; *For I can of mine own self do nothing;* because I seek not mine own will, but the will of the Father ~~which~~ *who* hath sent me.

5:31 *Therefore* If I bear witness of myself, my witness is ~~not~~ true.

5:32 *For I am not alone,* There is another ~~that~~ *who* beareth witness of me; and I know that the ~~witness which he witnesseth~~ *testimony which he giveth* of me is true.

5:33 Ye sent unto John, and he bare witness *also* unto the truth.

5:34 ~~But I receive not testimony from man, but~~ *And he received not his testimony of man, but of God, and ye yourselves say that he is a prophet, therefore ye ought to receive his testimony.* ~~t~~*T*hese things I say, that ye might be saved

5:35 He was a burning and a shining light: and ye were willing for a season to rejoice in his light.

5:36 But I have *a* greater witness than ~~that~~ *the testimony* of John: for the works which the Father hath given me to finish, the same works that I do, bear witness of me, that the Father hath sent me.

5:37 And the Father himself, ~~which hath~~ *who* sent me, hath borne witness of me. *And verily I testify unto you, that* Ye have ~~neither~~ *never* heard his voice at any time, nor seen his shape.

5:38 ~~And~~ *For* ye have not his word abiding in you: ~~for~~ *and him* whom he hath sent, ~~him~~ ye believe not.

5:39 Search the scriptures; for in them ye think ye have eternal life: and they are they which testify of me.

5:40 And ye will not come to me, that ye might have life*, lest ye should honor me.*

MATTHEW	MARK	LUKE	JOHN

5:41 I receive not honour from men.

5:42 But I know you, that ye have not the love of God in you.

5:43 I am come in my Father's name, and ye receive me not: if another shall come in his own name, him ye will receive.

5:44 How can ye believe, ~~which receive~~ *who seek* ~~honour~~ *honor* one of another, and seek not the ~~honour that~~ *honor which* cometh from God only?

5:45 Do not think that I will accuse you to the Father: there is ~~one that~~ *Moses who* accuseth you, ~~even Moses,~~ in whom ye trust.

5:46 For had ye believed Moses, ye would have believed me: for he wrote of me.

5:47 But if ye believe not his writings, how shall ye believe my words?

E-18. JESUS: LORD OF THE SABBATH

12:1 At that time Jesus went on the sabbath day through the corn; and his disciples were an hungred, and began to pluck the ears of corn, and to eat.

12:2 But when the Pharisees saw ~~it~~ *them*, they said unto him, Behold, thy disciples do that which is not lawful to do upon the ~~s~~Sabbath day.

12:3 But he said unto them, Have ye not read what David did, when he was an hungered, and they that were with him;

12:4 How he entered into the house of God, and did eat the shewbread, which was not lawful for him to eat, neither for them ~~which~~ *that* were with him, but only for the priests?

12:5 Or have ye not read in the law, how that on the ~~s~~Sabbath days the priests in the temple profane the ~~s~~Sabbath, and *ye say they* are blameless?

12:6 But I say unto you, That in this place is one greater than the temple.

12:7 But if ye had known what this meaneth, I will have mercy, and not sacrifice, ye would not have condemned the guiltless.

2:23 And it came to pass, that he went through the corn fields on the ~~s~~Sabbath day; and his disciples began, as they went, to pluck the ears of corn.

2:24 And the Pharisees said unto him, Behold, why do ~~they~~ *thy disciples* on the ~~s~~Sabbath day that which is not lawful?

2:25 And he said unto them, Have ye never read what David did, when he had need, and was an hungered, he, and they ~~that~~ *who* were with him?

2:26 How he went into the house of God in the days of Abiathar the high priest, and did eat the shewbread, which is not lawful to eat but for the priests, and gave also to them which were with him?

2:27 And he said unto them, The ~~s~~Sabbath was made for man, and not man for the ~~s~~Sabbath: *Wherefore the Sabbath was given unto man for a day of rest; and also that man should glorify God, and not that man should not eat; For the Son of Man made the Sabbath day,*

6:1 And it came to pass on the second sabbath after the first, that he went through the corn fields; and his disciples plucked the ears of corn, and did eat, rubbing them in their hands.

6:2 And certain of the Pharisees said unto them, Why do ye that which is not lawful to do on the sabbath days?

6:3 And Jesus answering them said, Have ye not read so much as this, what David did, when *he* himself was an hungered, and they ~~which~~ *who* were with him;

6:4 How he went into the house of God, and did take and eat the shewbread, and gave also to them ~~that~~ *who* were with him; which it is not lawful to eat but for the priests alone?

MATTHEW	MARK	LUKE	JOHN

12:8   For the Son of m*M*an is Lord even of the s*S*abbath ~~day~~.

2:28   Therefore the Son of m*M*an is Lord also of the s*S*abbath.

6:5   And he said unto them, That the Son of man is Lord also of the sabbath.

E-19. MAN'S WITHERED HAND HEALED ON THE SABBATH

12:9   And when he was departed thence,

he went into their synagogue*s*:

12:10   And, behold, there was a man which had ~~his~~ *a withered* hand ~~withered~~.

And they asked him, saying, Is it lawful to heal on the s*S*abbath days? that they might accuse him.

12:11   And he said unto them,

What man shall there be among you, that shall have one sheep, and if it fall into a pit on the s*S*abbath day, will he not lay hold on it, and lift it out?
12:12   How much then is a man better than a sheep? Wherefore it is lawful to do well on the s*S*abbath days.

12:13   Then sai~~th~~*d* he to the man, Stretch forth ~~thine~~ *thy* hand. And he stretched it forth; and it was restored whole, like ~~as~~ *unto* the other.
12:14   Then the Pharisees went out,

and held a council against him, how they might destroy him.

3:1   And he entered again into the synagogue;
and there was a man there which had a withered hand.

3:2   And they watched him~~,~~ *to see* whether he would heal him on the s*S*abbath day;

that they might accuse him.

3:3   And he sai~~th~~*d* unto the man which had the withered hand, Stand forth.

3:4   And he sai~~th~~*d* unto them, Is it lawful to do good on the s*S*abbath days, or to do evil? to save life, or to kill? But they held their peace.

3:5   And when he had looked round about on them with anger, being grieved for the hardness of their hearts,
he sai~~th~~*d* unto the man,
Stretch forth thine hand. And he stretched ~~it~~ out *his hand*: and his hand was restored whole as the other.
3:6   And the Pharisees went forth,

and straightway took counsel with the Herodians against him, how they might destroy him.

6:6   And it came to pass also on another sabbath,
that he entered into the synagogue and taught:
and there was a man whose right hand was withered.

6:7   And the scribes and Pharisees watched him, whether he would heal on the sabbath day;

that they might find an accusation against him.
6:8   But he knew their thoughts, and said to the man ~~which~~ *who* had the withered hand,
Rise up, and stand forth in the midst.
And he arose and stood forth.
6:9   Then said Jesus unto them, I will ask you one thing; Is it lawful on the s*S*abbath days to do good, or to do evil? to save life, or to destroy ~~it~~?

6:10   And looking round about upon them all,

he said unto the man,
Stretch forth thy hand. And he did so: and his hand was restored whole as the other.

6:11   And they were filled with madness;
and communed one with another what they might do to Jesus.

MATTHEW	MARK	LUKE	JOHN

E-20. JESUS AMONG THE MULTITUDES

12:15 But ~~when~~ Jesus knew ~~it~~ *when they took counsel, and* he withdrew himself from thence:

and great multitudes followed him,

3:7 But Jesus withdrew himself with his disciples to the sea: and a great multitude from Galilee followed him, and from ~~Judaea~~ *Judea,*

3:8 And from Jerusalem, and from ~~Idumaea~~ *Idumea,* and from beyond Jordan; and they about Tyre and Sidon, a great multitude, when they had heard what great things he did, came unto him.

and he healed ~~them all~~ *their sick;*

3:9 And he spake ***un***to his disciples, that a small ship should wait on him because of the multitude, lest they should throng him.
3:10 For he had healed many; insomuch that they pressed upon him for to touch him~~, a~~. *A*s many as had plagues ~~.~~
3:11 And unclean spirits, when they saw him, fell down before him, and cried, saying, Thou art the Son of God.

12:16 And charged them that they should not make him known:

3:12 And he straitly charged them that they should not make him known.

12:17 That it might be fulfilled which was spoken by Esaias the prophet, saying,
12:18 Behold my servant, whom I have chosen; my beloved, in whom my soul is well pleased: I will put my ~~s~~*S*pirit upon him, and he shall ~~shew~~ *show* judgment to the Gentiles.
12:19 He shall not strive, nor cry; neither shall any man hear his voice in the streets.
12:20 A bruised reed shall he not break, and smoking flax shall he not quench, till he send forth judgment unto victory.
12:21 And in his name shall the Gentiles trust.

E-21. THE TWELVE APOSTLES CALLED AND ORDAINED

3:13 And he goeth up into a mountain,

and calleth ~~unto him~~ whom he would: and they came unto him.
3:14 And he ordained twelve, that they should be with him, and that he might send them forth to preach,
3:15 And to have power to heal sicknesses, and to cast out devils:

6:12 And it came to pass in those days, that he went out into a mountain to pray, and continued all night in prayer to God.
6:13 And when it was day, he called ~~unto him~~ his disciples:

and of them he chose twelve, whom also he named apostles;

10:2 Now the names of the twelve apostles are these;

MATTHEW	MARK	LUKE	JOHN
The first, Simon, who is called Peter, and Andrew his brother; James the son of Zebedee, and John his brother;	3:16 And Simon he surnamed Peter; 3:17 And James the son of Zebedee, and John the brother of James; and he surnamed them Boanerges, which is, The sons of thunder:	6:14 Simon, (whom he also named Peter,) and Andrew his brother, James and John,	
10:3 Philip, and Bartholomew; Thomas, and Matthew the publican; James the son of Alphaeus, and Lebbaeus, whose surname was Thaddaeus; 10:4 Simon the Canaanite, and	3:18 And Andrew, and Philip, and Bartholomew, and Matthew, and Thomas, and James the son of Alphaeus, and Thaddaeus, and Simon the Canaanite,	Philip and Bartholomew, 6:15 Matthew and Thomas, James the son of Alphaeus, and Simon called Zelotes, 6:16 And Judas the brother of James,	
Judas Iscariot, who also betrayed him.	3:19(a) And Judas Iscariot, which also betrayed him:	and Judas Iscariot, which *who* also was the traitor.	

E-22a. THE SERMON ON THE MOUNT -- THE BEATITUDES

LUKE

6:17 And he came down with them, and stood in the plain, and the company of his disciples, and a great multitude of people out of all Judaea *Judea* and Jerusalem, and from the sea coasts of Tyre and Sidon, which *who* came to hear him, and to be healed of their diseases;
6:18 And they that *who* were vexed with unclean spirits: and they were healed.
6:19 And the whole multitude sought to touch him: for there went virtue out of him, and healed them all.

MATTHEW

5:1 And *Jesus,* seeing the multitudes, he went up into a mountain: and when he was set *down*, his disciples came unto him:

LUKE

6:20 And he lifted up his eyes on his disciples, and said,

MATTHEW

5:2 And he opened his mouth, and taught them, saying, *Blessed are they who shall believe on me; and again, more blessed are they who shall believe on your words, when ye shall testify that ye have seen me and that I am. Yea, blessed are they who shall believe on your words, and come down into the depth of humility, and be baptized in my name; for they shall be visited with fire and the Holy Ghost, and shall receive a remission of their sins.*
5:3 *Yea,* Blessed are the poor in spirit *who come unto me;*: for theirs is the kingdom of heaven.

LUKE

Blessed be ye *are the* poor: for yours *theirs* is the kingdom of God.

Blessed are ye that *they who* weep now: for ye *they* shall laugh.

MATTHEW

5:4 *And again,* Blessed are they that mourn: for they shall be comforted.
5:5 *And* Blessed are the meek: for they shall inherit the earth.

MATTHEW	MARK	LUKE	JOHN

MATTHEW

5:6 *And* Blessed are *all* they ~~which~~ *that* do hunger and thirst after righteousness: for they shall be filled *with the Holy Ghost*.

5:7 *And* Blessed are the merciful: for they shall obtain mercy.

5:8 *And* Blessed are *all* the pure in heart: for they shall see God.

5:9 *And* Blessed are *all* the peacemakers: for they shall be called the children of God.

5:10 Blessed are *all* they ~~which~~ *that* are persecuted for ~~righteousness'~~ *my name's* sake: for theirs is the kingdom of heaven.

5:11 *And* Blessed are ye, when men shall revile you, and persecute you, and shall say all manner of evil against you falsely, for my sake.

5:12 ~~Rejoice~~ *For ye shall have great joy*, and be exceeding glad: for great ~~is~~ *shall be* your reward in heaven: for so persecuted they the prophets which were before you.

LUKE

6:21 Blessed are ~~ye that~~ *they who* hunger now: for ~~ye~~ *they* shall be filled.

6:22 Blessed are ye, when men shall hate you, and when they shall separate you from ~~their company~~ *among them*, and shall reproach you, and cast out your name as evil, for the Son of ~~m~~*M*an's sake.

6:23 Rejoice ye in that day, and leap for joy: for, behold, your reward ~~is~~ *shall be* great in heaven: for in the like manner did their fathers unto the prophets.

6:24 But woe unto you that are rich! for ye have received your consolation.

6:25 Woe unto you ~~that~~ *who* are full! for ye shall hunger. Woe unto you ~~that~~ *who* laugh now! for ye shall mourn and weep.

6:26 Woe unto you, when all men shall speak well of you! for so did their fathers to the false prophets.

E-22b. THE SERMON ON THE MOUNT -- THE SAVOUR OF SALT

5:13 ~~Ye are~~ *Verily, verily, I say unto you, I give unto you to be* the salt of the earth: but if the salt ~~have lost his savour~~ *shall lose its savor*, wherewith shall ~~it~~ *the earth* be salted? ~~it is~~ *The salt shall* thenceforth *be* good for nothing, but to be cast out, and to be trodden under foot of men.

E-22c. THE SERMON ON THE MOUNT -- THE LIGHT OF THE WORLD

5:14 ~~Ye are~~ *Verily, verily, I say unto you, I give unto you to be* the light of the world. A city that is set on ~~an~~ hill cannot be hid.

5:15 ~~Neither~~ *Behold,* do men light a candle, and put it under a bushel~~,~~*?* *Nay,* but on a candlestick; and it giveth light ~~un~~to all that are in the house.

5:16 *Therefore,* Let your light so shine before ~~men~~ *this world*, that they may see your good works, and glorify your Father ~~which~~ *who* is in heaven.

| MATTHEW | MARK | LUKE | JOHN |

E-22d. THE SERMON ON THE MOUNT -- FULFILLING THE LAW RIGHTEOUSLY

5:17 Think not that I am come to destroy the law, or the prophets: I am not come to destroy, but to fulfil.

5:18 For verily I say unto you, T̶i̶l̶l̶ heaven and earth *must* pass *away, but* one jot or one tittle shall in no wise pass from the law, t̶i̶l̶l̶ *until* all be fulfilled.

5:19 Whosoever therefore shall break one of these least commandments, and shall teach men so *to do*, he shall b̶e̶ ̶c̶a̶l̶l̶e̶d̶ ̶t̶h̶e̶ l̶e̶a̶s̶t̶ *in no wise be saved* in the kingdom of heaven: but whosoever shall do and teach t̶h̶e̶m̶ *these commandments of the law until it be fulfilled*, the same shall be called great, *and shall be saved* in the kingdom of heaven.

5:20 For I say unto you, T̶h̶a̶t̶ except your righteousness shall exceed t̶h̶e̶ ̶r̶i̶g̶h̶t̶e̶o̶u̶s̶n̶e̶s̶s̶ *that* of the scribes and Pharisees, ye shall in no case enter into the kingdom of heaven.

5:21 Ye have heard that it w̶a̶s̶ *hath been* said by them of old time *that*, Thou shalt not kill; and whosoever shall kill shall be in danger of the judgment *of God*:

5:22 But I say unto you, That whosoever is angry with his brother w̶i̶t̶h̶o̶u̶t̶ ̶a̶ ̶c̶a̶u̶s̶e̶ shall be in danger of t̶h̶e̶ *his* judgment: and whosoever shall say to his brother, Raca, *or Rabcha,* shall be in danger of the council: b̶u̶t̶ *and* whosoever shall say *to his brother*, Thou fool, shall be in danger of hell fire.

5:23 Therefore if *ye shall come unto me, or shall desire to come unto me, or if* thou bring thy gift to the altar, and there rememberest that thy brother hath ought against thee;

5:24 Leave t̶h̶e̶r̶e̶ *thou* thy gift before the altar, and go thy way;̶ *unto thy brother, and* first be reconciled to thy brother, and then come and offer thy gift.

5:25 Agree with thine adversary quickly, whiles thou art in the way with him; lest at any time t̶h̶e̶ *thine* adversary deliver thee to the judge, and the judge deliver thee to the officer, and thou be cast into prison.

5:26 Verily I say unto thee, Thou shalt by no means come out thence, t̶i̶l̶l̶ *until* thou hast paid the uttermost farthing.

5:27 Y̶e̶ ̶h̶a̶v̶e̶ ̶h̶e̶a̶r̶d̶ ̶t̶h̶a̶t̶ ̶i̶t̶ ̶w̶a̶s̶ s̶a̶i̶d̶ *Behold, it was written* by them of old time, Thou shalt not commit adultery:

5:28 But I say unto you, That whosoever looketh on a woman to lust after her hath committed adultery with her already in his heart. *Behold, I give unto you a commandment, that ye suffer none of these things to enter into your heart, for it is better that ye deny yourselves of these things, where in ye will take up your cross, than ye should be cast into hell.*

5:29 ~~And~~ *Wherefore,* if thy right eye offend thee, pluck it out, and cast it from thee: for it is profitable for thee that one of thy members should perish, and not that thy whole body should be cast into hell.

5:30 ~~And~~ *Or* if thy right hand offend thee, cut if off, and cast it from thee: for it is profitable for thee that one of thy members should perish, and not that thy whole body should be cast into hell. *And now this I speak, a parable concerning your sins; wherefore, cast them from you, that ye may not be hewn down and cast into the fire.*

5:31 It hath been ~~said~~ *written that*, Whosoever shall put away his wife, let him give her a writing of divorcement:

5:32 ~~But~~ *Verily, verily,* I say unto you, That whosoever shall put away his wife, saving for the cause of fornication, causeth her to commit adultery: and whosoever shall marry her that is divorced committeth adultery.

5:33 Again, ~~ye have heard that it hath been said~~ *it hath been written* by them of old time, Thou shalt not forswear thyself, but shalt perform unto the Lord thine oaths:

5:34 But I say unto you, Swear not at all; neither by heaven; for it is God's throne:

5:35 Nor by the earth; for it is his footstool: neither by Jerusalem; for it is the city of the great King.

5:36 Neither shalt thou swear by thy head, because thou canst not make one hair white or black.

5:37 But let your communication be, Yea, yea; Nay, nay: for whatsoever is more than these cometh of evil.

5:38 Ye have heard that it hath been said, An eye for an eye, and a tooth for a tooth:

5:39 But I say unto you, That ye resist not evil: but whosoever shall smite thee on thy right cheek, turn to him the other also.

5:40 And if any man will sue thee at the law, and take away thy coat,

6:29 And unto him ~~that~~ *who* smiteth thee on the ~~one~~ cheek offer also the other; *or, in other words, it is better to offer the other, than to revile again.*

MATTHEW	MARK	LUKE	JOHN

let him have it, and if he sue thee again, let him have thy cloke also.

and him ~~that~~ *who* taketh away thy cloke forbid not to take thy coat also.
6:30 *For it is better that thou suffer thine enemy to take these things, than to contend with him. Verily I say unto you, Your heavenly Father who seeth in secret, shall bring that wicked one into judgment.*

5:41 And whosoever shall compel thee to go a mile, *go with him a mile; and whosoever shall compel thee to go with him twain, thou shalt* go with him twain.
5:42 Give to him that asketh thee, and from him that would borrow of thee turn not thou away.

Therefore, Give to every man ~~that~~ *who* asketh of thee; and of him ~~that~~ *who* taketh away thy goods ask them not again.
6:31 And as ye would that men should do to you, do ye also to them likewise.

5:43 Ye have heard that it hath been said, Thou shalt love thy ~~neighbour~~ *neighbor*, and hate thine enemy.
5:44 But I say unto you, Love your enemies, bless them that curse you, do good to them that hate you, and pray for them which despitefully use you, and persecute you;

6:27 But I say unto you ~~which~~ *who* hear *my words*, Love your enemies, do good to them ~~which~~ *who* hate you,
6:28 Bless them ~~that~~ *who* curse you, and pray for them ~~which~~ *who* despitefully use you *and persecute you.*

5:45 That ye may be the children of your Father ~~which~~ *who* is in heaven: for he maketh his sun to rise on the evil and on the good, and sendeth rain on the just and on the unjust.
5:46 For if ye love *only* them which love you, what reward have ~~ye~~ *you*? do not even the publicans the same?

6:32 For if ye love them *only* ~~which~~ *who* love you, what ~~thank have ye~~ *reward have you*? for sinners also ~~love those that love them~~ *do even the same.*

5:47 And if ye salute your brethren only, what do ye more than others? do not even the publicans ~~so~~ *the same*?

6:33 ~~And if ye do good to them which do good to you, what thank have ye? for sinners also do even the same.~~
6:34 And if ye lend to them of whom ye hope to receive, what ~~thank~~ *reward* have ~~ye~~ *you*? for sinners also lend to sinners, to receive as much again.
6:35 But love ye your enemies, and do good, and lend, hoping for nothing again; and your reward shall be great, and ye shall be the children of the Highest: for he is kind unto the unthankful and to the evil.
6:36 Be ye therefore merciful, as your Father also is merciful.

5:48 ~~Be ye therefore~~ *Ye are therefore commanded to be* perfect, even as your Father which is in heaven is perfect.

E-22e. THE SERMON ON THE MOUNT -- THE LORD'S PRAYER

6:1 *And it came to pass that, as Jesus taught his disciples, he said unto them,* Take heed that ye do not your alms before men, to be seen of them: otherwise ye have no reward of your Father ~~which~~ *who* is in heaven.

6:2 Therefore when thou doest ~~thine~~ alms, do not sound a trumpet before thee, as the hypocrites do in the synagogues and in the streets, that they may have glory of men. Verily I say unto you, They have their reward.

6:3 But when thou doest alms, let ~~not thy left hand know~~ *it be unto thee as thy left hand not knowing* what thy right hand doeth:

6:4 That thine alms may be in secret: and thy Father ~~which~~ *who* seeth in secret himself shall reward thee openly.

6:5 And when thou prayest, thou shalt not be as the hypocrites ~~are~~: for they love to pray standing in the synagogues and in the corners of the streets, that they may be seen of men~~.~~ *; For* Verily I say unto you, They have their reward.

6:6 But thou, when thou prayest, enter into thy closet, and when thou hast shut ~~thy~~ *the* door, pray to thy Father ~~which~~ *who* is in secret; and thy Father ~~which~~ *who* seeth in secret shall reward thee openly.

6:7 But when ye pray, use not vain repetitions, as the ~~heathen~~ *hypocrites* do: for they think that they shall be heard for their much speaking.

6:8 ~~Be not ye therefore~~ *Therefore be ye not* like unto them: for your Father knoweth what things ye have need of, before ye ask him.

6:9 *Therefore* After this manner ~~therefore pray ye~~ *shall ye pray, saying,* Our Father ~~which~~ *who* art in heaven, Hallowed be thy name.

6:10 Thy kingdom come. Thy will be done ~~in~~ *on* earth, as it is *done* in heaven.

6:11 Give us this day our daily bread.

6:12 And forgive us our ~~debts~~ *trespasses*, as we forgive ~~our debtors~~ *those who trespass against us*.

6:13 And ~~lead~~ *suffer* us not *to be led* into temptation, but deliver us from evil: For thine is the kingdom, and the power, and the glory, ~~for~~ *forever and* ever. Amen.

6:14 For if ye forgive men their trespasses, *who trespass against you,* your heavenly Father will also forgive you:

6:15 But if ye forgive not men their trespasses, neither will your *heavenly* Father forgive *you* your trespasses.

6:16 Moreover when ye fast, be not, as the hypocrites, of a sad countenance: for they disfigure their faces, that they may appear unto men to fast. Verily I say unto you, They have their reward.

6:17 But thou, when thou fastest, anoint thine head, and wash thy face;

6:18 That thou appear not unto men to fast, but unto thy Father ~~which~~ *who* is in secret: and thy Father, ~~which~~ *who* seeth in secret, shall reward thee openly.

6:19 Lay not up for yourselves treasures upon earth, where moth and rust doth corrupt, and where thieves break through and steal:

6:20 But lay up for yourselves treasures in heaven, where neither moth nor rust doth corrupt, and where thieves do not break through nor steal:

6:21 For where your treasure is, there will your heart be also.

6:22 The light of the body is the eye: if therefore thine eye be single *to the glory of God*, thy whole body shall be full of light.

6:23 But if thine eye be evil, thy whole body shall be full of darkness. If therefore the light ~~that~~ *which* is in thee be darkness, how great ~~is~~ *shall* that darkness *be.* ‡

6:24 No man can serve two masters: for either he will hate the one, and love the other; or else he will hold to the one, and despise the other. Ye cannot serve God and ~~m~~*M*ammon.

6:25 *And, again, I say unto you, go ye into the world, and care not for the world; for the world will hate you, and will persecute you, and will turn you out of their synagogues. Nevertheless, ye shall go forth from house to house, teaching the people; and I will go before you. And your heavenly Father will provide for you, whatsoever things ye need for food, what ye shall eat; and for raiment, what ye shall wear or put on.* Therefore I say unto you, Take no thought for your life, what ye shall eat, or what ye shall drink; nor yet for your body, what ye shall put on. Is not the life more than meat, and the body than raiment?

6:26 Behold the fowls of the air: for they sow not, neither do they reap, nor gather into barns; yet your heavenly Father feedeth them. Are ye not much better than they? *How much more will he not feed*

MATTHEW	**MARK**	**LUKE**	**JOHN**

you? Wherefore take no thought for these things, but keep my commandments wherewith I have commanded you.

6:27 *For* Which of you by taking thought can add one cubit unto his stature?

6:28 And why take ye thought for raiment? Consider the lilies of the field, how they grow; they toil not, neither do they spin:

6:29 And yet I say unto you, That even Solomon in all his glory was not arrayed like one of these.

6:30 ~~Wherefore~~ *Therefore*, if God so clothe the grass of the field, which to day is, and to morrow is cast into the oven, ~~shall he not much more clothe you,~~ *how much more will he not provide for you,* ~~O ye~~ *if ye are not* of little faith?

6:31 Therefore take no thought, saying, What shall we eat? or, What shall we drink? or, Wherewithal shall we be clothed?

6:32 ~~(For~~ *Why is it that ye murmer among yourselves, saying, We cannot obey thy word because ye have not all these things, and seek to excuse yourselves, saying that,* after all these things do the Gentiles seek~~).~~ ~~for~~ *Behold, I say unto you, that* your heavenly Father knoweth that ye have need of all these things.

6:33 *Wherefore, seek not the things of this world* But seek ye first *to build up* the kingdom of God, and *to establish* his righteousness; and all these things shall be added unto you.

6:34 Take therefore no thought for the morrow: for the morrow shall take thought for the things of itself. Sufficient unto the day ~~is~~ *shall be* the evil thereof.

E-22f. THE SERMON ON THE MOUNT -- JUDGE WITH RIGHTEOUS JUDGEMENT

7:1 *Now these are the words which Jesus taught his disciples that they should say unto the people.*
Judge not *unrighteously*, that ye be not judged*; but judge righteous judgement*.

6:37 Judge not, and ye shall not be judged: condemn not, and ye shall not be condemned: forgive, and ye shall be forgiven:

6:38 Give, and it shall be given unto you; good measure, pressed down, and shaken together, and running over, shall men give into your bosom.

7:2 For with what judgment ye *shall* judge, ye shall be judged:

MATTHEW	MARK	LUKE	JOHN

and with what measure ye mete, it shall be measured to you again.

For with the same measure that ye mete withal it shall be measured to you again.

6:39 And he spake a parable unto them, Can the blind lead the blind? shall they not both fall into the ditch?

6:40 ~~The~~ *A* disciple is not above his master: but every one that is perfect shall be as his master.

6:41 And why beholdest thou the mote ~~that~~ *which* is in thy brother's eye, but perceivest not the beam that is in thine own eye?

7:3 And *again, ye shall say unto them,* why *is it that thou* beholdest ~~thou~~ the mote that is in thy brother's eye, but considerest not the beam that is in thine own eye?

7:4 Or how wilt thou say to thy brother,
Let me pull out the mote out of thine eye; and ~~, behold,~~ *canst not behold* a beam ~~is~~ in thine own eye?

And Jesus said unto his disciples, Beholdest thou the scribes, and the Pharisees, and the Priests, and the Levites? They teach in their synagogues, but do not observe the law, nor the commandments; and all have gone out of the way, and are under sin. Go thou and say unto them, Why teach ye men the law and the commandments, when ye yourselves are the children of corruption?

7:5 ~~Thou hypocrite~~ *Say unto them, Ye hypocrites,* first cast out the beam out of thine own eye; and then shalt thou see clearly to cast out the mote out of thy brother's eye.

7:6 ~~Give not~~ *Go ye into the world, saying unto all, Repent, for the kingdom of heaven has come nigh unto you. And the mysteries of the kingdom ye shall keep within yourselves; for it is not meet to give* that which is holy unto the dogs, neither cast ye your pearls ~~before~~ *unto* swine, lest they trample them under their feet ~~, and~~ *. For the world cannot receive that which ye, yourselves, are not able to bear; wherefore ye shall not give your pearls unto them, lest they* turn again and rend you.

7:7 *Say unto them, Ask of God;* Ask, and it shall be given you; seek, and ye shall find; knock, and it shall be opened unto you:

7:8 For every one that asketh receiveth; and he that seeketh findeth; and *un*to him that knocketh it shall be opened.

7:9 *And then said his disciples unto him, they will say unto us, We ourselves are righteous, and need not that any man should teach us. God, we know, heard Moses and some of the prophets; but us he will not hear. And they will say, We have the law for our*

6:42 ~~Either~~ *Again,* how canst thou say to thy brother, ~~Brother,~~ let me pull out the mote that is in thine eye, when thou thyself beholdest not the beam ~~that~~ *which* is in thine own eye?

Thou hypocrite,
cast out first the beam out of thine own eye,
and then shalt thou see clearly to pull out the mote ~~that~~ *which* is in thy brother's eye.

MATTHEW	MARK	LUKE	JOHN

salvation, and that is sufficient for us. Then Jesus answered, and said unto his disciples, thus shall ye say unto them, What man among you, having a son, and he shall be standing out, and shall say, Father, open thy house that I may come in and sup with thee, will not say, Come in, my son; for mine is thine, and thine is mine?
Or what man is there ~~of~~ *among* you, who~~m~~ if his son ask bread, will ~~he~~ give him a stone?
7:10 Or if he ask a fish, will he give him a serpent?
7:11 If ye then, being evil, know how to give good gifts unto your children, how much more shall your Father ~~which~~ *who* is in heaven give good things to them that ask him?
7:12 Therefore all things whatsoever ye would that men should do to you, do ye even so to them: for this is the law and the prophets.
7:13 *Repent, therefore, and* Enter ye in at the strait gate: for wide is the gate, and broad is the way, that leadeth to destruction, and many there be ~~which~~ *who* go in thereat:
7:14 Because strait is the gate, and narrow is the way, ~~which~~ *that* leadeth unto life, and few there be that find it.

E-22g. THE SERMON ON THE MOUNT -- GOOD FRUITS

7:15 *And, again,* Beware of false prophets, ~~which~~ *who* come to you in sheep's clothing, but inwardly they are ravening wolves.
7:16 Ye shall know them by their fruits.
For Do men gather grapes of thorns, or figs of thistles?

7:17 Even so every good tree bringeth forth good fruit; but a corrupt tree bringeth forth evil fruit.
7:18 A good tree cannot bring forth evil fruit, neither can a corrupt tree bring forth good fruit.
7:19 Every tree that bringeth not forth good fruit is hewn down, and cast into the fire.
7:20 Wherefore by their fruits ye shall know them.

6:44 For every tree is known by his own fruit.
For of thorns men do not gather figs, nor of a bramble bush gather they grapes.
6:43 For a good tree bringeth not forth corrupt fruit; neither doth a corrupt tree bring forth good fruit.

6:45 A good man out of the good treasure of his heart bringeth forth that which is good; and an evil man out of the evil treasure of his heart bringeth forth that which is evil: for of the abundance of the heart his mouth speaketh.
6:46 And why call ye me, Lord, Lord, and do not the things which I say?

MATTHEW	MARK	LUKE	JOHN

7:21 *Verily I say unto you, it is* Not every one that saith unto me, Lord, Lord, *that* shall enter into the kingdom of heaven; but he that doeth the will of my Father ~~which~~ *who* is in heaven. *For the day soon cometh, that men shall come before me to judgment, to be judged according to their works.*
7:22 *And* Many will say to me in that day, Lord, Lord, have we not prophesied in thy name? and in thy name ~~have~~ cast out devils? and in thy name done many wonderful works?
7:23 And then will I ~~profess unto them~~ *say,* ~~I never knew you:~~ *Ye never knew me;* depart from me, ye that work iniquity.
7:24 Therefore whosoever heareth these sayings of mine, and doeth them,

I will liken him unto a wise man, ~~which~~ *who* built his house upon a rock:
7:25 And the rain*s* descended, and the floods came, and the winds blew, and beat upon that house; and it fell not: for it was founded upon a rock.
7:26 And every one that heareth these sayings of mine, and doeth them not, shall be likened unto a foolish man, ~~which~~ *who* built his house upon the sand:
7:27 And the rain*s* descended, and the floods came, and the winds blew, and beat upon that house; and it fell: and great was the fall of it.
7:28 And it came to pass, when Jesus had ended these sayings *with his disciples*, the people were astonished at his doctrine:
7:29 For he taught them as one having authority *from God*, and not as *having authority from* the scribes.

6:47 Whosoever cometh to me, and heareth my sayings, and doeth them,
I will shew you to whom he is like:
6:48 He is like a man which built an house, and digged deep, and laid the foundation on a rock:
and when the flood arose, the stream beat vehemently upon that house, and could not shake it: for it was founded upon a rock.

6:49 But he that heareth, and doeth not,
is like a man that without a foundation built an house upon the earth;
against which the stream did beat vehemently, and immediately it fell; and the ruin of that house was great.

E-23. JESUS HEALS CENTURION'S SERVANT AT CAPERNAUM

8:1 *And* When ~~he~~ *Jesus* was come down from the mountain, great multitudes followed him.

8:5 And when Jesus was entered into Capernaum,
there came unto him a centurion,

beseeching him,

7:1 Now when he had ended all ~~his~~ *these* sayings in the audience of the people, he entered into Capernaum.
7:2 And a certain centurion's servant, who was dear unto him, was sick, and ready to die.
7:3 And when he heard of Jesus, he sent unto him the elders of the Jews, beseeching him that he would come and heal his servant.

MATTHEW	MARK	LUKE	JOHN

8:6 And saying, Lord, my servant lieth at home sick of the palsy, grievously tormented.

8:7 And Jesus sait*hd* unto him, I will come and heal him.

8:8 The centurion answered and said, Lord, I am not worthy that thou shouldest come under my roof:

but speak the word only, and my servant shall be healed.
8:9 For I am a man under authority, having soldiers under me: and I say to this man, Go, and he goeth; and to another, Come, and he cometh; and to my servant, Do this, and he doeth it.
8:10 ~~When Jesus heard it, he marvelled, and~~ *And when they that followed him, heard this, they marvelled.*
And when Jesus heard this,

he said to them that followed, Verily I say unto you, I have not found so great faith, no, not in Israel.
8:11 And I say unto you, That many shall come from the east and *the* west, and shall sit down with Abraham, and Isaac, and Jacob, in the kingdom of heaven.
8:12 But the children of the ~~kingdom~~ *wicked one* shall be cast out into outer darkness: there shall be weeping and gnashing of teeth.
8:13 And Jesus said unto the centurion, Go thy way; and as thou hast believed, so be it done unto thee. And his servant was healed in the selfsame hour.

7:4 And when they came to Jesus, they besought him instantly, saying,

That he was worthy for whom he should do this:
7:5 For he loveth our nation, and he hath built us a synagogue.

7:6 Then Jesus went with them. And when he was now not far from the house, the centurion sent friends to him, saying unto him, Lord, trouble not thyself: for I am not worthy that thou shouldest enter under my roof:
7:7 Wherefore neither thought I myself worthy to come unto thee: but say ~~in a~~ *the* word, and my servant shall be healed.
7:8 For I also am a man set under authority, having under me soldiers, and I say unto one, Go, and he goeth; and to another, Come, and he cometh; and to my servant, Do this, and he doeth it.

7:9 When Jesus heard these things, he marvelled at him, and turned him about, and said unto the people ~~that~~ *who* followed him, I say unto you, I have not found so great faith, no, not in Israel.

7:10 And they ~~that~~ *who* were sent, returning to the house, found the servant whole ~~that~~ *who* had been sick.

E-24. A WIDOW'S SON RAISED FROM THE DEAD

7:11 And it came to pass the day after, that he went into a city called Nain; and many of his disciples went with him, and much people.
7:12 Now when he came nigh to the gate of the city, behold, there was a dead man carried out, the only son of his mother, and she was a widow: and ~~much~~ *many* people of the city ~~was~~ *were* with her.

MATTHEW	MARK	LUKE	JOHN

LUKE

7:13 And ~~when~~ *now* the Lord saw her, ~~he~~ *and* had compassion on her, and *he* said unto her, Weep not.

7:14 And he came and touched the bier: and they ~~that~~ *who* bare ~~him~~ *it* stood still. And he said, Young man, I say unto thee, Arise.

7:15 And he ~~that~~ *who* was dead sat up, and began to speak. And he delivered him to his mother.

7:16 And there came a fear on all: and they glorified God, saying, That a great prophet is risen up among us; and, That God hath visited his people.

7:17 And this rumour of him went forth throughout all Judaea, and throughout all the region round about.

E-25. MESSENGERS SENT TO JESUS FROM JOHN

MATTHEW

11:2 Now when John had heard in the prison the works of Christ,

he sent two of his disciples,

11:3 And said unto him, Art thou he *of whom it is written in the prophets* that *he* should come, or do we look for another?

11:4 Jesus answered and said unto them, Go and ~~shew~~ *tell* John again *of* those things which ye do hear and see:

11:5 *How* The blind receive their sight, and the lame walk, *and* the lepers are cleansed, and the deaf hear, *and* the dead are raised up, and the poor have the gospel preached *un*to them.

11:6 And blessed is ~~he~~ *John, and* whosoever shall not be offended in me.

LUKE

7:18 And the disciples of John shewed him of all these things.

7:19 And John calling ~~unto him~~ two of his disciples sent them to Jesus, saying, Art thou he that should come? or look we for another?

7:20 When the men were come unto him, they said, John Baptist hath sent us unto thee, saying, Art thou he ~~that~~ *who* should come?

or look we for another?

7:21 And in that same hour he cured many of ~~their~~ infirmities and plagues, and of evil spirits; and unto many ~~that were~~ blind he gave sight.

7:22 Then Jesus answering said unto them, Go your way, and tell John what things ye have seen and heard;

how that the blind see, the lame walk, the lepers are cleansed, the deaf hear, the dead are raised, *and* to the poor the gospel is preached.

7:23 And blessed ~~is he~~ *are they*, whos~~oever~~ shall not be offended in me.

MATTHEW	MARK	LUKE	JOHN

E-26. JESUS TESTIFIES OF JOHN

11:7 And as they departed, Jesus began to say unto the multitudes concerning John,

What went ye out into the wilderness to see? *Was it* A reed shaken with the wind? *And they answered him, No.*
11:8 *And he said,* But what went ye out for to see? *Was it* A man clothed in soft raiment? behold, they that wear soft clothing are in kings' *king's* houses.
11:9 But what went ye out for to see? A prophet? yea, I say unto you, and more than a prophet.

11:10 For this is he, *the one* of whom it is written, Behold, I send my messenger before thy face, which shall prepare thy way before thee.
11:11 Verily I say unto you, Among them that are born of women there hath not risen a greater than John the Baptist: notwithstanding he that is least in the kingdom of heaven is greater than he.
11:12 And from the days of John the Baptist until now the kingdom of heaven suffereth violence, and the violent take it by force.
11:13 *But the days will come, when the violent shall have no power;* For all the prophets and the law prophesied *that it should be thus* until John.
11:14 *Yea, as many as have prophesied have foretold of these days.* And if ye will receive it, this is *verily, he was the* Elias, which *who* was for to come *and prepare all things.*
11:15 He that hath ears to hear, let him hear.

11:16 But whereunto shall I liken this generation?

It is like unto children sitting in the markets, and calling unto their fellows,
11:17 And saying, We have piped unto you, and ye have not danced; we have mourned unto *for* you, and ye have not lamented.
11:18 For John came neither eating nor drinking, and they say,

7:24 And when the messengers of John were departed, he began to speak unto the people concerning John,
What went ye out into the wilderness for to see? A reed shaken with the wind?

7:25 But what went ye out for to see? *Or* A man clothed in soft raiment? Behold, they which *who* are gorgeously apparelled, and live delicately, are in kings' courts.
7:26 But what went ye out for to see? A prophet? Yea, I say unto you, and much more than a prophet.
7:27 This is he *the one*, of whom it is written, Behold, I send my messenger before thy face, which *who* shall prepare thy way before thee.
7:28 For I say unto you, Among those that *who* are born of women there is not a greater prophet than John the Baptist: but he that *who* is least in the kingdom of God is greater than he.

7:29 And all the people that *who* heard him, and the publicans, justified God, being baptized with the baptism of John.
7:30 But the Pharisees and lawyers rejected the counsel of God against themselves, being not *being* baptized of him.
7:31 And the Lord said, Whereunto then shall I liken the men of this generation? and to what are they like?
7:32 They are like unto children sitting in the marketplace, and calling one to another, and saying, We have piped unto *for* you, and ye have not danced; we have mourned to *for* you, and ye have not wept.
7:33 For John the Baptist came neither eating bread nor drinking

MATTHEW	MARK	LUKE	JOHN

He hath a devil.

11:19 The Son of ~~m~~Man came eating and drinking, and they say, Behold a man gluttonous, and a winebibber, a friend of publicans and sinners.

But *I say unto you,* wisdom is justified of her children.

wine; and ye say, He hath a devil.

7:34 The Son of man is come eating and drinking; and ye say, Behold a gluttonous man, and a winebibber, a friend of publicans and sinners!

7:35 But wisdom is justified of all her children.

E-27. JESUS' FEET ANOINTED WITH OIL

7:36 And one of the Pharisees desired him that he would eat with him. And he went into the Pharisee's house, and sat down to meat.

7:37 And, behold, a woman in the city, ~~which~~ *who* was a sinner, when she knew that Jesus sat at meat in the Pharisee's house, brought an alabaster box of ointment,

7:38 And stood at his feet ~~behind him~~ weeping, and began to wash his feet with tears, and did wipe them with the hairs of her head, and kissed his feet, and anointed them with ~~the~~ ointment.

7:39 Now when the Pharisee ~~which~~ *who* had bidden him saw ~~it~~ *this*, he spake within himself, saying, This man, if he were a prophet, would have known who ~~and~~ *, or* what manner of woman this is ~~that~~ *who* toucheth him: for she is a sinner.

7:40 And Jesus answering said unto him, Simon, I have somewhat to say unto thee. And he sai~~th~~*d*, Master, say on.

7:41 *And Jesus said,* There was a certain creditor ~~which~~ *who* had two debtors: the one owed five hundred pence, and the other fifty.

7:42 And when *he found* they had nothing to pay, he frankly forgave them both. Tell me therefore, which of them will love him most?

7:43 Simon answered and said, I suppose ~~that he,~~ *the man* to whom he forgave most. And he said unto him, Thou hast rightly judged.

7:44 And he turned to the woman, and said unto Simon, Seest thou this woman? I entered into ~~thine~~ *thy* house, thou gavest me no water for my feet: but she hath washed my feet with tears, and wiped them with the hairs of her head.

7:45 Thou gavest me no kiss: but this woman since the time I came in hath not ceased to kiss my feet.

7:46 My head with oil thou didst not anoint: but this woman hath anointed my feet with ointment.

7:47 Wherefore I say unto thee, Her sins, which are many, are forgiven; for she loved much: but to whom little is forgiven, the same loveth little.

MATTHEW	MARK	LUKE	JOHN

7:48 And he said unto her, Thy sins are forgiven.
7:49 And they that sat at meat with him began to say within themselves, Who is this that forgiveth sins also?
7:50 And he said to the woman, Thy faith hath saved thee; go in peace.

E-28. PREACHES IN GALILEE WITH THE TWELVE

8:1 And it came to pass afterward, that he went throughout every city and village, preaching and shewing *showing* the glad tidings of the kingdom of God: and the twelve *who were ordained of him,* were with him,
8:2 And certain women, which *who* had been healed of evil spirits and infirmities, Mary called Magdalene, out of whom went seven devils,
8:3 And Joanna the wife of Chuza Herod's steward, and Susanna, and many others, which ministered unto him of *with* their substance.

E-29. JESUS AND BEELZEBUB

3:19(b) and they went into an house.
3:20 And the multitude cometh together again, so that they could not so much as eat bread.
3:21 And when his friends heard of it *him speak*, they went out to lay hold on him: for they said, He is beside himself.

12:22 Then was brought unto him one possessed with a devil, blind, and dumb: and he healed him, insomuch that the blind and dumb both spake and saw.
12:23 And all the people were amazed, and said, Is not this the sSon of David?
12:24 But when the Pharisees heard it *that he had cast out the devil*, they said, This fellow *man* doth not cast out devils, but by Beelzebub the prince of the devils.
12:25 And Jesus knew their thoughts, and said unto them,

3:22 And the scribes which came down from Jerusalem said,
He hath Beelzebub, and by the prince of the devils casteth , he *casteth* out devils.
3:23 *Now Jesus knew this,* And he called them unto him, and said unto them in parables, How can Satan cast out Satan?
3:24 And if a kingdom be divided against itself, *how can* that kingdom cannot stand.

Every kingdom divided against itself is brought to desolation; and every city or house divided against itself shall not stand:

3:25 And if a house be divided against itself, that house cannot stand.

12:26 And if Satan cast out Satan, he is divided against himself; how shall then *shall* his kingdom stand?

3:26 And if Satan rise up against himself, and be divided, he cannot stand, but *speedily* hath an end.

MATTHEW	MARK	LUKE	JOHN

12:27 And if I by Beelzebub cast out devils, by whom do your children cast ~~them~~ out *devils*? therefore they shall be your judges.
12:28 But if I cast out devils by the Spirit of God, then the kingdom of God is come unto you. *For they also cast out devils by the Spirit of God, for unto them is given power over devils, that they may cast them out.*
12:29 Or else how can one enter into a strong man's house, and spoil his goods, except he first bind the strong man? and then he will spoil his house.
12:30 He that is not with me is against me; and he that gathereth not with me scattereth abroad.

3:27 No man can enter into a strong man's house, and spoil his goods, except he will first bind the strong man; and then he will spoil his house.

E-30. NO FORGIVENESS FOR BLASPHEMY AGAINST HOLY GHOST

12:31 Wherefore I say unto you, All manner of sin and blasphemy shall be forgiven unto men *who receive me and repent*:

but the blasphemy against the Holy Ghost, *it* shall not be forgiven unto men.

12:32 And whosoever speaketh a word against the Son of ~~m~~*M*an, it shall be forgiven him: but whosoever speaketh against the Holy Ghost, it shall not be forgiven him, neither in this world, neither in the world to come.
12:33 Either make the tree good, and his fruit good; or else make the tree corrupt, and his fruit corrupt: for the tree is known by his fruit.
12:34 *And Jesus said,* O ye generation of vipers, how can ye, being evil, speak good things? for out of the abundance of the heart the mouth speaketh.
12:35 A good man out of the good treasure of the heart bringeth forth good things: and an evil man out of the evil treasure bringeth forth evil things.
12:36 ~~But~~ *And again* I say unto you, That every idle word that men shall speak, they shall give account thereof in the day of judgment.

3:28 *And then came certain men unto him, accusing him, saying Why do ye receive sinners, seeing thou makest thyself the Son of God. But he answered them and said,* Verily I say unto you, All sins *which men have committed, when they repent,* shall be forgiven ~~unto the sons of men~~ *them; for I came to preach repentance unto the sons of men.* And blasphemies wherewith soever they shall blaspheme *shall be forgiven them that come unto me and do the works which they see me do.*
3:29 But *there is a sin which shall not be forgiven.* He that shall blaspheme against the Holy Ghost hath never forgiveness, but is in danger of *being cut down out of the world. And they shall inherit* eternal damnation:

MATTHEW	MARK	LUKE	JOHN

12:37 For by thy words thou shalt be justified, and by thy words thou shalt be condemned.

	3:30 *And this he said unto them* Because they said, He hath an unclean spirit.		

E-31. JESUS DISCUSSES SIGNS

12:38 Then certain of the scribes and of the Pharisees answered, saying, Master, we would see a sign from thee.

12:39 But he answered and said unto them, An evil and adulterous generation seeketh after a sign; and there shall no sign be given to it, but the sign of the prophet Jonas:

12:40 For as Jonas was three days and three nights in the whale's belly; so shall the Son of mM*an* be three days and three nights in the heart of the earth.

12:41 The men of Nineveh shall rise in judgment with this generation, and shall condemn it: because they repented at the preaching of Jonas; and, *ye* behold, a greater than Jonas is here.

12:42 The queen of the south shall rise up in the *day of* judgment with this generation, and shall condemn it: for she came from the uttermost parts of the earth to hear the wisdom of Solomon; and, *ye* behold, a greater than Solomon is here.

12:43 *Then came some of the scribes and said unto him, Master, it is written that, Every sin shall be forgiven; but ye say, Whosoever speaketh against the Holy Ghost shall not be forgiven. And they asked him, saying, how can these things be? And he said unto them,* When the unclean spirit is gone out of a man, he walketh through dry places, seeking rest, and findeth none*; but when a man speaketh against the Holy Ghost,*

12:44 Then he saith, I will return into my house from whence I came out; and when he is come, he findeth it *him* empty, swept, and garnished*; for the good spirit leaveth him unto himself.*

12:45 Then goeth he *the evil spirit*, and taketh with himself seven other spirits more wicked than himself, and they enter in and dwell there: and the last state *end* of that man is worse than the first. Even so shall it be also unto this wicked generation.

MATTHEW	MARK	LUKE	JOHN

E-32. JESUS' MOTHER AND BRETHREN SEEK HIM

12:46 *And* While he yet talked to the people,

behold, his mother and his brethren stood without, desiring to speak with him.

12:47 Then one said unto him, Behold, thy mother and thy brethren stand without, desiring to speak with thee.

12:48 But he answered and said unto ~~him~~ *the man* that told him, Who is my mother? and who are my brethren?
12:49 And he stretched forth his hand toward his disciples, and said, Behold my mother and my brethren!
12:50 ~~For~~ *And he gave them charge concerning her, saying, I go my way, for my Father hath sent me. And* whosoever shall do the will of my Father which is in heaven, the same is my brother, and sister, and mother.

3:31 *While he was yet with them, and while he was yet speaking,* There came then *some* his brethren and his mother, and, standing without, sent unto him, calling *unto* him.

3:32 And the multitude sat about him, and they said unto him, Behold, thy mother and thy brethren without seek for thee.

3:33 And he answered them, saying, Who is my mother, or *who are* my brethren?

3:34 And he looked round about on them which sat about him, and said, Behold my mother and my brethren!

3:35 For whosoever shall do the will of God, the same is my brother, and my sister, and mother.

8:19 Then came to him his mother and his brethren, and could not ~~come at him for the press~~ *speak to him for the multitude*.
8:20 And ~~it was told him by certain which said~~ *some who stood by, said unto him*, Thy mother and thy brethren stand without, desiring to see thee.

8:21 And he answered and said unto them,

My mother and my brethren are ~~these which~~ *those who* hear the word of God, and do it.

E-33. PARABLE OF THE SOWER

13:1 *And it came to pass* the same day went Jesus out of the house, and sat by the sea side.
13:2 And great multitudes were gathered together unto him, so that he went into a ship, and sat; and the whole multitude stood on the shore.
13:3 And he spake many things unto them in parables, saying,

Behold, a sower went forth to sow;

13:4 And when he sowed, some seeds fell by the way side, and the fowls came and devoured them up:

13:5 Some fell upon stony places, where they had not much earth: and forthwith they sprung up, ~~because they had no deepness of earth:~~

13:6 And when the sun was up, they were scorched, *because they had no deepness of earth*;
and because they had no root, they withered away.
13:7 And some fell among thorns; and the thorns sprung up, and choked them:
13:8 But other*s* fell into good ground, and brought forth fruit, some an hundredfold, some sixtyfold, some thirtyfold.

4:1 And he began again to teach by the sea side:

and there was gathered unto him a great multitude, so that he entered into a ship, and sat in the sea; and the whole multitude was by the sea on the land.
4:2 And he taught them many things by parables, and *he* said unto them in his doctrine,
4:3 Hearken; Behold, there went out a sower to sow:
4:4 And it came to pass, as he sowed, some fell by the way side, and the fowls of the air came and devoured it up.
4:5 And some fell on stony ground, where it had not much earth; and immediately it sprang up, because it had no depth of earth:
4:6 But when the sun was up, it was scorched;

and because it had no root, it withered away.
4:7 And some fell among thorns, and the thorns grew up, and choked it, and it yielded no fruit.
4:8 And other *seed* fell on good ground, and did yield fruit that sprang up and increased; and brought forth, some thirty-*fold*, and some sixty, and some an hundred.

8:4 And when much people were gathered together, and were come to him out of every city,

he spake by a parable, *saying*:

8:5 A sower went out to sow his seed:
and as he sowed, some fell by the way side; and it was trodden down, and the fowls of the air devoured it.
8:6 And some fell upon a rock; and as soon as it was sprung up, it withered away, because it lacked moisture.

8:7 And some fell among thorns; and the thorns sprang up with it, and choked it.
8:8 And others fell on good ground, and sprang up, and bare fruit an hundredfold.

MATTHEW	MARK	LUKE	JOHN

MATTHEW

13:9 Who hath ears to hear, let him hear.

13:10 ~~And~~ *Then* the disciples came, and said unto him, Why speakest thou unto them in parables?

13:11 He answered and said unto them, Because it is given unto you to know the mysteries of the kingdom of heaven,
but to them it is not given.

13:12 For whosoever ~~hath~~ *receiveth*, to him shall be given, and he shall have more abundance: but whosoever ~~hath not~~ *continueth not to receive*, from him shall be taken away even that he hath.
13:13 Therefore speak I to them in parables: because they seeing see not; and hearing they hear not, neither do they understand.
13:14 And in them is fulfilled the prophecy of Esaias *concerning them*, which saith, By hearing ye shall hear, and shall not understand; and seeing ye shall see, and shall not perceive:
13:15 For this people's heart is waxed gross, and their ears are dull of hearing, and their eyes they have closed;
lest at any time they should see with their eyes, and hear with their ears, and should understand with their heart*s*, and should be converted, and I should heal them.
13:16 But blessed are your eyes, for they see: and your ears, for they hear. *And blessed are you because these things are come unto you, that you might understand them.*
13:17 ~~For~~ *And* verily I say unto you, ~~That many prophets and righteous men~~ *many righteous prophets* have desired to see ~~those things~~ *these days* which ~~ye~~ *you* see, and have not seen them; and to hear ~~those things~~ *that* which ~~ye~~ *you* hear, and have not heard ~~them~~.

13:18 Hear ye therefore the parable of the sower.

13:19 When any one heareth the word of the kingdom, and understandeth ~~it~~ not,
then cometh the wicked one, and catcheth away that which was sown in his heart.
This is he which received seed by the way side.

MARK

4:9 And he said unto them, He that hath ears to hear, let him hear.

4:10 And when he was alone *with the twelve*, *and they that believed in him*, they that were about him with the twelve asked of him the parable.
4:11 And he said unto them, Unto you it is given to know the mystery of the kingdom of God:

but unto them that are without, all these things are done in parables:

4:12 That seeing they may see, and not perceive; and hearing they may hear, and not understand;

lest at any time

they should be converted, and their sins should be forgiven them.

4:13 And he said unto them, Know ye not this parable? and how then will ye know all parables?

4:14 The sower soweth the word.

4:15 And these are they by the way side, where the word is sown; but when they have heard,

Satan cometh immediately, and taketh away the word that was sown in their hearts.

LUKE

And when he had said these things, he cried, He ~~that~~ *who* hath ears to hear, let him hear.
8:9 And his disciples asked him, saying, What might this parable be?

8:10 And he said, Unto you it is given to know the mysteries of the kingdom of God:

but to others in parables;

that seeing they might not see, and hearing they might not understand.

8:11 Now the parable is this:

The seed is the word of God.
8:12 ~~Those~~ *That which fell* by the way side are they ~~that~~ *who* hear;

~~then cometh~~ *and* the devil *cometh*, and taketh away the word out of their hearts,

MATTHEW

13:20 But he that received the seed into stony places, the same is he that heareth the word, and ~~anon~~ *readily* with joy receiveth it;

13:21 Yet ~~hath~~ he *hath* not root in himself, ~~but dureth~~ *and endureth but* for a while: for when tribulation or persecution ariseth because of the word, by and by he is offended.

13:22 He also ~~that~~ *who* received seed among the thorns is he that heareth the word;

and the care of this world, and the deceitfulness of riches,

choke the word, and he becometh unfruitful.

13:23 But he that received seed into the good ground is he that heareth the word, and understandeth ~~it~~ *and endureth*; which also beareth fruit, and bringeth forth, some an hundredfold, some sixty, some thirty.

MARK

4:16 And these are they likewise which ~~are sown~~ *receive the word* on stony ground; who, when they have heard the word, immediately receive it with gladness;

4:17 And have no root in themselves, and so endure but for a time: *and* afterward, when affliction or persecution ariseth for the word's sake, immediately they are offended.

4:18 And these are they ~~which are sown~~ *who receive the word* among thorns; such as hear the word,

4:19 And the cares of this world, and the deceitfulness of riches, and the lusts of other things entering in, choke the word, and it becometh unfruitful.

4:20 And these are they ~~which are sown~~ *who receive the word* on good ground; such as hear the word, and receive it, and bring forth fruit, some thirty-fold, some sixty, and some an hundred.

4:21 And he said unto them, Is a candle brought to be put under a bushel, or under a bed? and not to be set on a candlestick? *I say unto you, Nay;*

4:22 For there is nothing hid, which shall not be manifested; neither was any thing kept secret, but that it should *in due time* come abroad.

4:23 If any man have ears to hear, let him hear.

4:24 And he said unto them, Take heed what ye hear: *for* with what measure ye mete, it shall be measured to you: and unto you that ~~hear~~ *continue to receive,* shall more be given.

4:25 For he that ~~hath~~ *receiveth*, to him shall be given: ~~and~~ *but* he that ~~hath not~~ *continueth not to receive*, from him shall be taken even that which he hath.

LUKE

lest they should believe and be saved.

8:13 ~~They~~ *That which fell* on the rock are they, ~~which~~ *who*, when they hear, receive the word with joy;

and ~~these~~ *they* have no root, ~~which~~ *but* for a while believe, and in *a* time of temptation fall away.

8:14 And that which fell among thorns are they, ~~which~~ *who*, when they have heard, go forth,

and are choked with cares and riches and pleasures of ~~this~~ life, and bring no fruit to perfection.

8:15 But that *which fell* on the good ground are they, ~~which~~ *who receive the word* in an honest and good heart, having heard the word, keep ~~it~~ *what they hear*, and bring forth fruit with patience.

8:16 *For* No man, when he hath lighted a candle, covereth it with a vessel, or putteth it under a bed; but setteth it on a candlestick, that they ~~which~~ *who* enter in may see the light.

8:17 For nothing is secret, ~~that~~ *which* shall not be made manifest; neither ~~any thing~~ hid, ~~that~~ *which* shall not be *made* known and ~~come~~ *go* abroad.

8:18 Take heed therefore how ye hear:

for whosoever ~~hath~~ *receiveth*, to him shall be given; and whosoever ~~hath~~ *receiveth* not, from him shall be taken even that which he seemeth to have.

MATTHEW	MARK	LUKE	JOHN

E-34. PARABLE OF THE SEED

4:26 And he said, So is the kingdom of God, as if a man should cast seed into the ground;
4:27 And should sleep, and rise night and day, and the seed should spring and grow up, he knoweth not how.
4:28 For the earth bringeth forth fruit of herself; first the blade, then the ear, after that the full corn in the ear.
4:29 But when the fruit is brought forth, immediately he putteth in the sickle, because the harvest is come.

E-35. PARABLE OF WHEAT AND TARES

13:24 Another parable put he forth unto them, saying, The kingdom of heaven is likened unto a man which sowed good seed in his field:
13:25 But while ~~men~~ *he* slept, his enemy came and sowed tares among the wheat, and went his way.
13:26 But when the blade ~~was~~ sprung up, and brought forth fruit, then appeared the tares also.
13:27 So the servants of the householder came and said unto him, Sir, didst not thou sow good seed in thy field? ~~from~~ whence then hath it tares?
13:28 He said unto them, An enemy hath done this. *And* The servants said unto him, Wilt thou then that we go and gather them up?
13:29 But he said, Nay; lest while ye gather up the tares, ye root up also the wheat with them.
13:30 Let both grow together until the harvest: and in the time of harvest I will say to the reapers, Gather ye together first the ~~tares, and bind them in bundles to burn them: but gather the wheat into my barn~~ *wheat into my barn; and the tares are bound in bundles to be burned.*

E-36. PARABLES OF MUSTARD SEED AND LEAVEN

13:31 *And* Another parable put he forth unto them, saying,

4:30 And he said, Whereunto shall ~~we~~ *I* liken the kingdom of God? or with what comparison shall we compare it?

The kingdom of heaven is like to a grain of mustard seed, which a man took, and sowed in his field:
13:32 Which indeed is the least of all seeds:
but when it is grown, it is the

4:31 It is like a grain of mustard seed, which, when it is sown in the earth,
is less than all the seeds that be in the earth:
4:32 But when it is sown, it

MATTHEW	MARK	LUKE	JOHN

greatest among herbs, and becometh a tree,

so that the birds of the air come and lodge in the branches thereof.
13:33 Another parable spake he unto them; The kingdom of heaven is like unto leaven, which a woman took, and hid in three measures of meal, till the whole was leavened.
13:34 All these things spake Jesus unto the multitude in parables;

groweth up, and becometh greater than all herbs, and shooteth out great branches;
so that the fowls of the air may lodge under the shadow of it.

4:33 And with many such parables spake he the word unto them, as they were able to hear it *bare,*
4:34 But without a parable spake he not unto them:

and without a parable spake he not unto them:
13:35 That it might be fulfilled which was spoken by the prophet, saying, I will open my mouth in parables; I will utter things which have been kept secret from the foundation of the world.

and when they were alone, he expounded all things to his disciples.

E-37. EXPLANATION OF THE WHEAT AND TARES

13:36 Then Jesus sent the multitude away, and went into the house: and his disciples came unto him, saying, Declare unto us the parable of the tares of the field.
13:37 He answered and said unto them, He that soweth the good seed is the Son of man;
13:38 The field is the world; the good seed are the children of the kingdom; but the tares are the children of the wicked one;
13:39 The enemy that sowed them is the devil; the harvest is the end of the world, *or the destruction of the wicked*; and the reapers are the angels, *or the messengers sent of heaven*.
13:40 As therefore the tares are gathered and burned in the fire; so shall it be in the end of this world *or the destruction of the wicked*.
13:41 The Son of man shall send forth his angels, *For in that day, before the Son of Man shall come, he shall send forth his angels and messengers of heaven.* and they shall gather out of his kingdom all things that offend, and them which do iniquity;
13:42 And shall cast them into a furnace of fire *among the wicked: and* there shall be wailing and gnashing of teeth, *for the world shall be burned with fire*.
13:43 Then shall the righteous shine forth as the sun in the kingdom of their Father. Who hath ears to hear, let him hear.

MATTHEW	MARK	LUKE	JOHN

E-38. PARABLES CONCERNING THE KINGDOM OF HEAVEN

13:44 Again, the kingdom of heaven is like unto *a* treasure hid in a field; the which *And* when a man hath found *a treasure which is hid*, he hideth, and *secureth it, and, straightway* for joy thereof goeth and selleth all that he hath, and buyeth that field.

13:45 *And* Again, the kingdom of heaven is like unto a merchant man, seeking goodly pearls:

13:46 Who, when he had found one pearl of great price, *he* went and sold all that he had, and bought it.

13:47 Again, the kingdom of heaven is like unto a net, that was cast into the sea, and gathered of every kind:

13:48 Which, when it was full, they drew to shore, and sat down, and gathered the good into vessels, but cast the bad away.

13:49 So shall it be at the end of the world, *and the world is the children of the wicked*: the angels shall come forth, and sever the wicked from among the just,

13:50 And shall cast them into the furnace of fire *out into the world to be burned*: there shall be wailing and gnashing of teeth.

13:51 *Then* Jesus saithd unto them, Have ye understood all these things? They say unto him, Yea, Lord.

13:52 Then said he unto them, Therefore every scribe which is *well* instructed unto *in the things of* the kingdom of heaven is like unto a man that is an householder*; a man, therefore*, which bringeth forth out of his treasure things *that which is* new and old.

13:53 And it came to pass, that when Jesus had finished these parables, he departed thence.

E-39. JESUS CALMS THE STORM AT SEA

MATTHEW

8:18 Now when Jesus saw great multitudes about him, he gave commandment to depart unto the other side *of the sea*.

8:23 And when he was entered into a ship, his disciples followed *came unto* him.

MARK

4:35 And the same day, when the even was come, he saithd unto them, Let us pass over unto the other side.

4:36 And when they had sent away the multitude, they took him even as he was in the ship.

And there were also with him other little ships.

LUKE

8:22 Now it came to pass on a certain day, that he went into a ship with his disciples: and he said unto them, Let us go over unto the other side of the lake. And they launched forth.

8:23 But as they sailed he fell asleep:

MATTHEW | MARK | LUKE | JOHN

MATTHEW

8:24 And, behold, there arose a great tempest in the sea, insomuch that the ship was covered with the waves:

but he was asleep.
8:25 And his disciples came *un*to him, and awoke him, saying, Lord, save us: *else* we perish.

8:26(b) Then he arose, and rebuked the winds and the sea;

and there was a great calm.
8:26(a) And he sait*hd* unto them, Why are ye fearful, O ye of little faith?
8:27 But the men marvelled, saying,
What manner of man is this, that even the winds and the sea obey him!

MARK

4:37 And there arose a great storm of wind, and the waves beat *over* into the ship, ~~so that it was now full.~~

4:38 And he was in the hinder part of the ship, asleep on a pillow: and they ~~awake~~ *awoke* him, and ~~say~~ *said* unto him, Master, carest thou not that we perish?

4:39 And he arose, and rebuked the wind, and said unto the sea, Peace, be still. And the wind ceased, and there was a great calm.
4:40 And he said unto them, Why are ye so fearful? how is it that ye have no faith?
4:41 And they feared exceedingly, and said one to another,
What manner of man is this, that even the wind and the sea obey him?

LUKE

and there came down a storm of wind on the lake; and

they were filled with ~~water~~ *fear*, and were in ~~jeopardy~~ *danger*.

8:24 And they came to him, and awoke him, saying, Master, master, we perish.
Then he arose, and rebuked the wind and the raging of the wate*r*s: and they ceased, and there was a calm.
8:25 And he said unto them, Where is your faith?

And they being afraid wondered, saying one to another,
What manner of man is this! for he commandeth even the winds and wate*r*s, and they obey him.

E-40. JESUS CASTS OUT LEGION OF DEVILS INTO SWINE

MATTHEW

8:28 And when he was come to the other side into the country of the Gergesenes,

there met him ~~two~~ *a man* possessed with devils, coming out of the tombs,

exceeding fierce, so that no man ~~might~~ *could* pass ~~by~~ that way.

8:29 And, behold, ~~they~~ *he* cried out, saying, What have we to do with thee, Jesus, thou Son of God?

art thou come hither to torment us before the time?

MARK

5:1 And they came over unto the other side of the sea, into the country of the Gadarenes.
5:2 And when he was come out of the ship, immediately there met him out of the tombs a man with an unclean spirit,

5:3 Who had ~~his~~ *been* dwelling among the tombs; and no man could bind him, no, not with chains:
5:4 Because that he had been often bound with fetters and chains, and the chains had been plucked asunder by him, and the fetters broken in pieces: neither could any man tame him.

5:5 And always, night and day, he was in the mountains, and in the tombs, crying, and cutting himself with stones.
5:6 But when he saw Jesus afar off, he ran and worshipped him,
5:7 And cried with a loud voice, and said, What have I to do with thee, Jesus, thou Son of the most high God?
I adjure thee by God, that thou torment me not.
5:8 For he said unto him, Come out of the man, ~~thou~~ unclean spirit.

LUKE

8:26 And they arrived at the country of the Gadarenes, which is over against Galilee.
8:27 And when he went forth to land, there met him out of the city a certain man, which had devils *for a* long time,
and *and he would* ~~ware~~ *wear* no clothes, neither abode in ~~any~~ *a* house, but in the tombs.

8:29(b) For oftentimes it had caught him: and he was kept bound with chains and in fetters; and he brake the bands, and was driven of the devil into the wilderness.)

8:28 When he saw Jesus,

he cried out, and fell down before him, and with a loud voice said, What have I to do with thee, Jesus, thou Son of God most high?
I beseech thee, torment me not.

8:29(a) (For he had commanded the unclean spirit to come out of the man.

MATTHEW	MARK	LUKE	JOHN

MARK

5:9 And he ~~asked him, What is~~ *commanded him saying, declare* thy name? And he answered, saying, My name is Legion: for we are many.
5:10 And he besought him much that he would not send them away out of the country.

LUKE

8:30 And Jesus asked him, saying, What is thy name? And he said, Legion: because many devils were entered into him.

MATTHEW

8:30 And there was a good way off from them ~~an~~ herd of many swine feeding.
8:31 So the devils besought him, saying, If thou cast us out, suffer us to go ~~away~~ into the herd of swine.
8:32 And he said unto them, Go.

MARK

5:11 Now there was there nigh unto the mountains a great herd of swine feeding.
5:12 And all the devils besought him, saying, Send us into the swine, that we may enter into them.
5:13 And forthwith Jesus gave them leave.

LUKE

8:32 And there was there ~~an~~ herd of many swine feeding on the mountain:
and they besought him that he would suffer them to enter into ~~them.~~ *the swine,*

And he suffered them.
8:31 And they besought him also, that he would not command them to go out into the deep. *And he said unto them, Come out of the man.* *(verse order changed by JST)*
8:33 Then went the devils out of the man, and entered into the swine: and the herd ran violently down a steep place into the lake, and were choked.

MATTHEW

And when they were come out, they went into the herd of swine: and, behold, the whole herd of swine ran violently down a steep place into the sea, and perished in the waters.
8:33 And they that kept them fled, and went their ~~ways~~ into the city, and told every thing *which took place*, and what was befallen ~~to~~ the possessed of the devils.
8:34 And, behold, the whole city came out to meet Jesus: and when they saw him,

MARK

And the unclean spirits went out, and entered into the swine: and the herd ran violently down a steep place into the sea, (they were about two thousand;) and were choked in the sea.
5:14 And they that fed the swine fled, and told ~~it~~ *the people* in the city, and in the country, *all that was done unto the swine*.

And they went out to see what it was that was done.
5:15 And they ~~come~~ *came* to Jesus, and ~~see~~ *saw* him that was possessed with the devil, and had the ~~l~~Legion, sitting, and clothed, and in his right mind: and they were afraid.
5:16 And they that saw ~~it~~ *the miracle,* told them *that came out,* how it befell ~~to~~ him that was possessed with the devil, *and how the devil was cast out,* and ~~also~~ concerning the swine.

LUKE

8:34 When they ~~that~~ *who* fed ~~them~~ *the swine* saw what was done, they fled, and went and told ~~it~~ *the people* in the city and in the country.
8:35 Then they went out to see what was done;
and came to Jesus, and found the man, out of whom the devils were departed, sitting at the feet of Jesus, clothed, and in his right mind: and they were afraid.

8:36 They also ~~which~~ *who* saw ~~it~~ *the miracle* told them by what means he ~~that~~ *who* was possessed of the devils was healed.

8:37 Then the whole multitude of the country of the ~~Gadarenes~~ *Gardarenes* round about besought ~~him~~ *Jesus* to depart from them; for they were taken with great fear: and ~~he~~ *Jesus* went up into the ship, and returned back again.
8:38 Now the man out of whom the devils were departed besought him that he might be with him:

but Jesus sent him away, saying,

8:39 Return to thine own house, and ~~shew~~ *show* how great things God hath done unto thee.

And he went his way, and published throughout the whole city how great things Jesus had done unto him.

MATTHEW

they besought him that he would depart out of their coasts.

MARK

5:17 And they began *immediately* to pray him to depart out of their coasts.

5:18 And when he was come into the ship,
he that had been possessed with the devil, *spoke to Jesus, and* prayed him that he might be with him.
5:19 Howbeit Jesus suffered him not, but sai~~th~~*d* unto him,
Go home to thy friends, and tell them how great things the Lord hath done for thee, and hath had compassion on thee.
5:20 And he departed, and began to publish in Decapolis how great things Jesus had done for him: and all ~~men~~ *that heard him* did marvel.

MATTHEW	MARK	LUKE	JOHN

E-41. THE RETURN TO CAPERNAUM

9:1 And he *Jesus* entered into a ship, and passed over,

and came into his own city.

5:21 And when Jesus was *had* passed over again by ship unto the other side,

much people gathered unto him: and he was nigh unto the sea.

8:40 And it came to pass, that, when Jesus was returned,

the people gladly received him: for they were all waiting for him.

E-42. JAIRUS SEEKS JESUS

9:18 While he spake these things unto them, behold, there came a certain ruler,
and worshipped him,

saying, My daughter is even now dead *dying*:

but come and lay thy hand upon her, and she shall live.

9:19 And Jesus arose, and followed him, and so did *also* his disciples*, and much people thronged him*.

5:22 And, behold, there cometh one of the rulers of the synagogue, Jairus by name;
and when he saw him, he fell at his feet,
5:23 And besought him greatly,

saying, My little daughter lieth at the point of death:

I pray thee, come and lay thy hands on her, that she may be healed; and she shall live.
5:24 And Jesus *he* went with him; and much people followed him, and thronged him.

8:41 And, behold, there came a man named Jairus, and he was a ruler of the synagogue:
and he fell down at Jesus' feet,

and besought him that he would come into his house:
8:42 For he had one *an* only daughter, about twelve years of age, and she lay a dying.

But as he went the people thronged him.

E-43. WOMAN TOUCHES JESUS AND IS HEALED

9:20 And, behold, a woman, which was diseased with an issue of blood twelve years,

came behind him, and touched the hem of his garment:
9:21 For she said within herself, If I may but touch his garment, I shall be whole.

9:22 But Jesus turned him about, and when he saw her,

5:25 And a certain woman, which had an issue of blood twelve years,

5:26 And had suffered many things of many physicians, and had spent all that she had, and was nothing bettered, but rather grew worse,
5:27 When she had heard of Jesus, *she* came in the press behind, and touched his garment.

5:28 For she said, If I may touch but his clothes, I shall be whole.

5:29 And straightway the fountain of her blood was dried up; and she felt in her body that she was healed of that plague.
5:30 And Jesus, immediately knowing in himself that virtue had gone out of him, turned him about in the press,
and said, Who touched my clothes?

5:31 And his disciples said unto him, Thou seest the multitude thronging thee, and sayest thou, Who touched me?
5:32 And he looked round about to see her that had done this thing.
5:33 But the woman fearing and trembling, knowing what was done in her, came and fell down before him, and told him all the truth.

8:43 And a woman having an issue of blood twelve years,

which *who* had spent all her living upon physicians, neither could be healed of any,

8:44 Came behind him *Jesus*, and touched the border of his garment:

and immediately her issue of blood stanched *staunched*.

8:46 And Jesus said, Somebody *Some one* hath touched me: for I perceive that virtue is gone out of me.
8:45 And Jesus said, Who touched me?
When all denied,
Peter and they that *who* were with him said, Master, the multitude throng thee and press *upon* thee, and sayest thou, Who touched me?

8:47 And when the woman saw *found* that she was not hid, she came trembling, and falling down before him, she declared unto him

MATTHEW	MARK	LUKE	JOHN

		before all the people for what cause she had touched him and how she was healed immediately.	
he said, Daughter, be of good comfort; thy faith hath made thee whole.	5:34 And he said unto her, Daughter, thy faith hath made thee whole; go in peace, and be whole of thy plague.	8:48 And he said unto her, Daughter, be of good comfort: thy faith hath made thee whole; go in peace.	
And the woman was made whole from that hour.			

E-44. JAIRUS' DAUGHTER RAISED

	5:35 While he yet spake, there came from the ruler of the synagogue's house ~~certain which~~ *a man who* said, Thy daughter is dead: why troublest thou the Master any further?	8:49 While he yet spake, there cometh one from the ruler of the synagogue's house, saying to him, Thy daughter is dead; trouble not the Master.	
	5:36 As soon as *he spake,* Jesus heard the word that was spoken, ~~he saith~~ *and said* unto the ruler of the synagogue, Be not afraid, only believe.	8:50 ~~But when Jesus heard it, he answered him, saying~~ *But Jesus heard him, and he said unto the ruler of the synagogue,* Fear not: believe only, and she shall be made whole.	
	5:37 And he suffered no man to follow him, save Peter, and James, and John the brother of James.	8:51 And when he came into the house, he suffered no man to go in, save Peter, and James, and John, and the father and the mother of the maiden.	
9:23 And when Jesus came into the ruler's house, and saw the minstrels and the people making a noise,	5:38 And he cometh to the house of the ruler of the synagogue, and seeth the tumult, and them that wept and wailed greatly.		
9:24 He said unto them, Give place: for the maid is not dead, but sleepeth. And they laughed him to scorn.	5:39 And when he was come in, he sai~~th~~*d* unto them, Why make ye this ado, and weep? the damsel is not dead, but sleepeth. 5:40 And they laughed him to scorn.	8:52 And all wept, and bewailed her: but he said, Weep not; she is not dead, but sleepeth.	
9:25 But when the people were put forth, he went in,	But when he had put them all out, he taketh the father and the mother of the damsel, and them that were with him, and entereth in where the damsel was lying.	8:53 And they laughed him to scorn, knowing that she was dead. 8:54 And he put them all out,	
and took her by the hand,	5:41 And he took the damsel by the hand, and said unto her, Talitha cumi; which is, being interpreted, Damsel, I say unto thee, arise.	and took her by the hand, and *he* called, saying,	
and the maid arose.	5:42 And straightway the damsel arose, and walked; for she was ~~of the age of~~ twelve years *old.* And they were astonished with a great astonishment.	Maid, arise. 8:55(a) And her spirit came again, and she arose straightway:	
	5:43 And he charged them straitly that no man should know it; and commanded that something should be given her to eat.	8:56 And her parents were astonished: but he charged them that they should tell no man what was done. 8:55(b) and he commanded to give her meat.	
9:26 And the fame ~~hereof~~ *of Jesus* went abroad into all that land.			

E-45. TWO BLIND MEN HEALED

9:27 And when Jesus departed thence, two blind men followed him, crying, and saying, *Jesus,* Thou Son of David, have mercy on us.

9:28 And when he was come into the house, the blind men came to him: and Jesus saithd unto them, Believe ye that I am able to do this? They said unto him, Yea, Lord.

9:29 Then touched he their eyes, saying, According to your faith be it unto you.

9:30 And their eyes were opened; and ~~Jesus~~ straitly *he* charged them, saying, *Keep my commandments and* See *ye tell no man in this place,* that no man know it.

9:31 But they, when they were departed, spread abroad his fame in all that country.

E-46. DEVIL CAST OUT OF DUMB MAN

9:32 *And* As they went out, behold, they brought to him a dumb man possessed with a devil.

9:33 And when the devil was cast out, the dumb *man* spake: and the multitudes marvelled, saying, It was never so seen in Israel.

9:34 But the Pharisees said, He casteth out *the* devils through the prince of the devils.

E-47. REJECTED AT NAZARETH AGAIN

13:54 And when he was come into his own country,

he taught them in their synagogue*s*, insomuch that they were astonished, and said,

Whence hath this ~~man~~ *Jesus* this wisdom,

and these mighty works?

13:55 Is not this the carpenter's son? is not his mother called Mary? and his brethren, James, and Joses, and Simon, and Judas?

13:56 And his sisters, are they not all with us? Whence then hath this man all these things?

13:57 And they were offended ~~in~~ *at* him. But Jesus said unto them, A prophet is not without ~~honour~~ *honor,* save in his own country, and in his own house.

6:1 And he went out from thence, and came into his own country;

and his disciples follow him.

6:2 And when the ~~s~~*S*abbath day was come, he began to teach in the synagogue: and many hearing ~~him~~ were astonished *at his words,* saying,

From whence hath this man these things? and what wisdom is this ~~which~~ *that* is given unto him, that even such mighty works are wrought by his hands?

6:3 Is not this the carpenter, the son of Mary, the brother of James, and Joses, and of Juda, and Simon?

and are not his sisters here with us?

And they were offended at him.

6:4 But Jesus said unto them, A prophet is not without ~~honour~~ *honor,* ~~but~~ *save* in his own country, and among his own kin, and in his own house.

MATTHEW	MARK	LUKE	JOHN

13:58 And he did not many mighty works there because of their unbelief.

6:5 And he could there do no mighty work *there*,

save that he laid his hands upon a few sick folk, and *they were* healed ~~them~~.
6:6(a) And he marvelled because of their unbelief.

E-48. TOURS GALILEE AGAIN

9:35 And Jesus went about all the cities and villages, teaching in their synagogues, and preaching the gospel of the kingdom, and healing every sickness and ~~every~~ disease among the people.
9:36 But when he saw the multitudes, he was moved with compassion on them, because they fainted, and were scattered abroad, as sheep having no shepherd.
9:37 Then sai~~th~~d he unto his disciples, The harvest truly is plenteous, but the labourers are few;
9:38 Pray ye therefore the Lord of the harvest, that he will send forth ~~labourers~~ *laborers* into his harvest.

6:6(b) And he went round about the villages, teaching.

E-49. SENDS OUT THE TWELVE APOSTLES

10:1 And when he had called unto him his twelve disciples,

he gave them power ~~against~~ *over* unclean spirits, to cast them out, and to heal all manner of sickness and all manner of disease.

6:7 And he called ~~unto him~~ the twelve, and began to send them forth by two and two;
and gave them power over unclean spirits;

9:1 Then he called his twelve disciples together,

and *he* gave them power and authority over all devils, and to cure diseases.

9:2 And he sent them to preach the kingdom of God, and to heal the sick.

10:5 These twelve Jesus sent forth, and commanded them, saying, Go not into the way of the Gentiles, and *enter ye not* into any city of the Samaritans ~~enter ye not~~:
10:6 But ~~go~~ rather *go* to the lost sheep of the house of Israel.
10:7 And as ye go, preach, saying, The kingdom of heaven is at hand.
10:8 Heal the sick, cleanse the lepers, raise the dead, cast out devils: freely ye have received, freely give.
10:9 Provide neither gold, nor silver, nor brass in your purses,
10:10 Nor scrip for your journey, neither two coats, neither shoes, nor yet staves:

for the workman is worthy of his meat.

6:8 And commanded them that they should take nothing for their journey, save a staff only; no scrip, n*o*r bread, n*o*r money in their purse:
6:9 But *should* be shod with sandals; and not ~~put on~~ *take* two coats.

9:3 And he said unto them, Take nothing for your journey, neither staves, nor scrip, neither bread, neither money; neither have two coats apiece.

MATTHEW	MARK	LUKE	JOHN

10:11 And into whatsoever city or town ye shall enter, inquire *enquire* who in it is worthy;
and there abide till ye go thence.
10:12 And when ye come into an house, salute it.
10:13 And if the house be worthy, let your peace come upon it: but if it be not worthy, let your peace return to you.
10:14 And whosoever shall not receive you, nor hear your words, when ye depart out of that house or city, shake off the dust of your feet *for a testimony against them*.
10:15 *And,* Verily I say unto you, It shall be more tolerable for the land of Sodom and Gomorrha *Gomorrah* in the day of judgment, than for that city.
10:16 Behold, I send you forth as sheep in the midst of wolves: be ye therefore wise as serpents *servants*, and *as* harmless as doves.
10:17 But beware of men: for they will deliver you up to the councils, and they will scourge you in their synagogues;
10:18 And ye shall be brought before governors and kings for my sake, for a testimony against them and the Gentiles.
10:19 But when they deliver you up, take no thought how or what ye shall speak: for it shall be given you in that same hour what ye shall speak.
10:20 For it is not ye that speak, but the Spirit of your Father which speaketh in you.
10:21 And the brother shall deliver up the brother to death, and the father the child: and the children shall rise up against their parents, and cause them to be put to death.
10:22 And ye shall be hated of all men *the world* for my name's sake: but he that endureth to the end shall be saved.
10:23 But when they persecute you in this *one* city, flee ye into another: for verily I say unto you, Ye shall not have gone over the cities of Israel, till the Son of mM*an* be come.
10:24 *Remember,* The disciple is not above his master, nor the servant above his lord.
10:25 It is enough for *that* the disciple that he be as his master, and the servant as his lord. If they have called the master of the house Beelzebub, how much more shall they call them of his household?
10:26 Fear them not therefore: for there is nothing covered, that shall not be revealed; and hid, that shall not be known.
10:27 What I tell you in darkness,

6:10 And he said unto them, In what place soever *whatsoever place* ye enter into an house, there abide till ye depart from that place.

6:11 And whosoever shall not receive you, nor hear you, when ye depart thence, shake off the dust under *of* your feet for a testimony against them.
Verily I say unto you,
It shall be more tolerable for Sodom and Gomorrha in the day of judgment, than for that city.

9:4 And *into* whatsoever house ye enter into, there abide, and thence depart *until ye depart thence*.

9:5 And whosoever will not receive you, when ye go out of that city, shake off the very dust from your feet for a testimony against them.

MATTHEW	MARK	LUKE	JOHN

that ~~speak~~ *preach* ye in light: and what ye hear in the ear, ~~that~~ preach ye upon the housetops.

10:28 And fear not them ~~which~~ *who are able to* kill the body, but are not able to kill the soul: but rather fear him which is able to destroy both soul and body in hell.

10:29 Are not two sparrows sold for a farthing? and one of them shall not fall on the ground without your Father *knoweth it*.

10:30 ~~But~~ *And* the very hairs of your head are all numbered.

10:31 Fear ye not therefore, ye are of more value than many sparrows.

10:32 Whosoever therefore shall confess me before men, him will I confess also before my Father ~~which~~ *who* is in heaven.

10:33 But whosoever shall deny me before men, him will I also deny before my Father ~~which~~ *who* is in heaven.

10:34 Think not that I am come to send peace on earth: I came not to send peace, but a sword.

10:35 For I am come to set a man at variance against his father, and the daughter against her mother, and the daughter in law against her mother in law.

10:36 And a man's foes shall be they of his own household.

10:37 He ~~that~~ *who* loveth father or mother more than me is not worthy of me: and he ~~that~~ *who* loveth son or daughter more than me is not worthy of me.

10:38 And he ~~that~~ *who* taketh not his cross, and followeth after me, is not worthy of me.

10:39 He ~~that findeth~~ *who seeketh to save* his life shall lose it: and he ~~that~~ *who* loseth his life for my sake shall find it.

10:40 He ~~that~~ *who* receiveth you receiveth me, and he ~~that~~ *who* receiveth me receiveth him ~~that~~ *who* sent me.

10:41 He that receiveth a prophet in the name of a prophet shall receive a prophet's reward; ~~and~~ he that receiveth a righteous man in the name of a righteous man shall receive a righteous man's reward.

10:42 And whosoever shall give to drink unto one of these little ones a cup of cold water only in the name of a disciple, verily I say unto you, he shall in no wise lose his reward.

6:12 And they went out, and preached that men should repent.

6:13 And they cast out many devils, and anointed with oil many that were sick, and *they were* healed ~~them~~.

9:6 And they departed, and went through the towns, preaching the gospel,

and healing every where.

E-50. JESUS PREACHES IN GALILEE

11:1 And it came to pass, when Jesus had made an end of commanding his twelve disciples, he departed thence to teach and to preach in their cities.

E-51. DEATH OF JOHN THE BAPTIST

MATTHEW

14:6 But when Herod's birthday was kept,

the daughter of Herodias danced before them,
and pleased Herod.

14:7 Whereupon he promised with an oath to give her ~~whatsoever~~ *whatever* she would ask.

14:8 And she, being before instructed of her mother,

said,
Give me here John Baptist's head in a charger.

14:9 And the king was sorry: nevertheless for the oath's sake, and them which sat with him at meat, he commanded it to be given ~~her~~.
14:10 And he sent,

and beheaded John in the prison.
14:11 And his head was brought in a charger, and given to the damsel: and she brought it to her mother.
14:12 And his disciples came, and took up the body, and buried it,

and went and told Jesus.

MARK

6:21 ~~And when a convenient day was come, that Herod on his birthday made a supper to~~ *But when Herod's birth-day was come, he made a supper for his* his lords, high captains, and chief ~~estates~~ *priests* of Galilee;
6:22 And when the daughter of ~~the said~~ Herodias came in, and danced, and pleased Herod and them that sat with him, the king said unto the damsel, Ask of me whatsoever thou wilt, and I will give it thee.
6:23 And he sware unto her, Whatsoever thou shalt ask of me, I will give it thee,
unto the half of my kingdom.
6:24 And she went forth, and said unto her mother, What shall I ask? And she said, The head of John the Baptist.

6:25 And she came in straightway with haste unto the king, and asked, saying,
I will that thou give me by and by in a charger the head of John the Baptist.
6:26 And the king was exceeding sorry; ~~yet~~ *but* for his oath's sake, and for their sakes which sat with him, he would not reject her.

6:27 And immediately the king sent an executioner, and commanded his head to be brought: and he went and beheaded him in the prison,
6:28 And brought his head in a charger, and gave it to the damsel: and the damsel gave it to her mother.
6:29 And when ~~his~~ *John's* disciples heard of it, they came and took up his corpse, and laid it in a tomb.

MATTHEW	MARK	LUKE	JOHN

E-52. RETURN OF THE TWELVE APOSTLES

MATTHEW	MARK	LUKE	JOHN
	6:30 ~~And~~ *Now* the apostles gathered themselves together unto Jesus, and told him all things, both what they had done, and what they had taught.	9:10 And the apostles, when they ~~were~~ returned, told ~~him~~ *Jesus* all that they had done.	
14:13 When Jesus heard ~~of it~~ *that John was beheaded*,			
	6:31 And he said unto them, Come ye yourselves apart into a ~~desert~~ *solitary* place, and rest a while: for there were many coming and going, and they had no leisure, *not* so much as to eat.		
he departed thence by ship into a desert place apart:	6:32 And they departed into a ~~desert~~ *solitary* place by ship privately.	And he took them, and went aside privately into a ~~desert~~ *solitary* place belonging to the city called Bethsaida.	6:1 After these things Jesus went over the sea of Galilee, which is the sea of Tiberias.
	6:33 And the people saw them departing, and many knew ~~him~~ *Jesus*,		
and when the people had heard ~~thereof~~ *of him*, they followed him on foot out of the cities.	and ran afoot thither out of all cities, and ~~outwent~~ *out-ran* them, and came together unto him.	9:11(a) And the people, when they knew it, followed him:	6:2 And a great multitude followed him, because they saw his miracles which he did on them that were diseased.

E-53. JESUS FEEDS THE FIVE THOUSAND

MATTHEW	MARK	LUKE	JOHN
			6:3 And Jesus went up into a mountain, and there he sat with his disciples.
			6:4 And the passover, a feast of the Jews, was nigh.
14:14 And Jesus went forth, and saw a great multitude, and was moved with compassion towards them,	6:34 And Jesus, when he came out, saw much people, and was moved with compassion toward them, because they were as sheep not having a shepherd:		6:5 When Jesus then lifted up his eyes, and saw a great company come unto him,
	and he began to teach them many things.	9:11(b) and he received them, and spake unto them of the kingdom of God, and healed them ~~that~~ *who* had need of healing.	
and he healed their sick.			
14:15 And when it was evening, his disciples came to him, saying,	6:35 And when the day was now far spent, his disciples came unto him, and said,	9:12 And when the day began to wear away, then came the twelve, and said unto him,	
This is a desert place, and the time is now past;	This is a ~~desert~~ *solitary* place, and now the time ~~is far passed~~ *for departure is come*:		
send the multitude away, that they may go into the villages, and buy themselves victuals.	6:36 Send them away, that they may go into the country round about, and into the villages, and buy themselves bread: for they have nothing to eat.	Send the multitude away, that they may go into the towns and country round about, and lodge, and get victuals: for we are here in a ~~desert~~ *solitary* place.	
14:16 But Jesus said unto them, They need not depart; give ye them to eat.	6:37 *And* He answered and said unto them, Give ye them to eat.	9:13 But he said unto them, Give ye them to eat.	
	And they say unto him, Shall we go and buy two hundred pennyworth of bread, and give them to eat?		
			he saith unto Philip, Whence shall we buy bread, that these may eat? 6:6 And this he said to prove him:

MATTHEW	MARK	LUKE	JOHN
			for he himself knew what he would do.
			6:7 Philip answered him, Two hundred pennyworth of bread is not sufficient for them, that every one of them may take a little.
	6:38 He sai~~thd~~ unto them, How many loaves have ye? go and see.		
			6:8 One of his disciples, Andrew, Simon Peter's brother, saith unto him,
14:17 And they say unto him, We have here but five loaves, and two fishes.	And when they knew, they say, Five, and two fishes.	And they said, We have ~~no more~~ but five loaves and two fishes; *and except we should go and buy meat, we can provide no more food* for all this ~~people~~ *multitude*.	6:9 There is a lad here, which hath five barley loaves, and two small fishes: but what are they among so many?
		9:14 For they were *in number* about five thousand men.	6:10(b) in number about five thousand.
14:18 He said, Bring them hither to me.			
14:19 And he commanded the multitude to sit down on the grass,	6:39 And he commanded them to make all sit down by companies upon the green grass.	And ~~he~~ *Jesus* said ~~un~~to his disciples, Make them sit down by fifties in a company.	6:10(a) And Jesus said, Make the men sit down.
	6:40 And they sat down in ranks, by hundreds, and by fifties.	9:15 And they did so, and made them all sit down.	Now there was much grass in the place. So the men sat down,
and *he* took the five loaves, and the two fishes, and looking up to heaven, he blessed, and brake,	6:41 And when he had taken the five loaves and ~~the~~ two fishes, he looked up to heaven, and blessed, and brake the loaves,	9:16 Then he took the five loaves and the two fishes, and looking up to heaven, he blessed them, and brake,	6:11 And Jesus took the loaves; and when he had given thanks,
and gave the loaves to ~~his~~ *the* disciples, and the disciples to the multitude.	and gave ~~them~~ to his disciples to set before ~~them~~ *the multitude*; and the two fishes divided he among them all.	and gave to the disciples to set before the multitude.	he distributed to the disciples, and the disciples to them that were set down; and likewise of the fishes as much as they would.
14:20 And they did all eat, and were filled:	6:42 And they did all eat, and were filled.	9:17 And they did eat, and were all filled:	6:12 When they ~~were filled~~ *had eaten and were satisfied*, he said unto his disciples, Gather up the fragments that remain, that nothing be lost.
and they took up of the fragments that remained twelve baskets full.	6:43 And they took up twelve baskets full of the fragments, and of the fishes.	and there was taken up of fragments ~~that~~ *which* remained ~~to them~~ twelve baskets.	6:13 Therefore they gathered them together, and filled twelve baskets with the fragments of the five barley loaves, which remained over and above unto them that had eaten.
14:21 And they that had eaten were about five thousand men, beside*s* women and children.	6:44 And they that did eat of the loaves were about five thousand men.		
			6:14 Then those men, when they had seen the miracle that Jesus did, said, This is of a truth that prophet that should come into the world.

E-54. JESUS AVOIDS BEING MADE A KING

MATTHEW	MARK	LUKE	JOHN
			6:15 When Jesus therefore perceived that they would come and take him by force, to make him a king,
14:22 And straightway Jesus constrained his disciples to get into a ship, and to go before him unto the other side, while he sent the multitudes away.	6:45 And straightway he constrained his disciples to get into the ship, and to go to the other side before *him,* unto Bethsaida, while he sent away the people.		
14:23 And when he had sent the multitudes away, he went up into a mountain apart to pray: and when the evening was come, he was there alone.	6:46 And when he had sent them away, he departed into a mountain to pray.		he departed again into a mountain himself alone.

MATTHEW	MARK	LUKE	JOHN

E-55. JESUS WALKS ON THE WATER

			6:16 And when even was now come, his disciples went down unto the sea,
			6:17 And entered into a ship, and went over the sea toward Capernaum. And it was now dark, and Jesus was not come to them.
	6:47 And when even was come, the ship was in the midst of the sea, and he alone on the land.		6:18 And the sea arose by reason of a great wind that blew.
14:24 But the ship was now in the midst of the sea, tossed with *the* waves: for the wind was contrary.	6:48 And he saw them toiling in rowing; for the wind was contrary unto them:		
			6:19 So when they had rowed about five and twenty or thirty furlongs,
14:25 And in the fourth watch of the night Jesus went unto them, walking on the sea.	and about the fourth watch of the night he cometh unto them, walking upon the sea, ~~and~~ *as if he* would have passed by them.		
14:26 And when the disciples saw him walking on the sea, they were troubled, saying, It is a spirit; and they cried out for fear.	6:49 ~~But~~ *And* when they saw him walking upon the sea, they supposed it had been a spirit, and cried out: 6:50 For they all saw him, and were troubled.		they see Jesus walking on the sea, and drawing nigh unto the ship: and they were afraid.
14:27 But straightway Jesus spake unto them, saying, Be of good cheer; it is I; be not afraid. 14:28 And Peter answered him and said, Lord, if it be thou, bid me come unto thee on the water. 14:29 And he said, Come. And when Peter was come down out of the ship, he walked on the water, to go to Jesus. 14:30 But when he saw the wind boisterous, he was afraid; and beginning to sink, he cried, saying, Lord, save me. 14:31 And immediately Jesus stretched forth his hand, and caught him, and said unto him, O thou of little faith, wherefore didst thou doubt?	And immediately he talked with them, and sai~~d~~*th* unto them, Be of good cheer: it is I; be not afraid.		6:20 But he saith unto them, It is I; be not afraid.
14:32 And when they were come into the ship, the wind ceased.	6:51 And he went up unto them into the ship; and the wind ceased:		6:21 Then they willingly received him into the ship: and immediately the ship was at the land whither they went.
	and they were sore amazed in themselves beyond measure, and wondered. 6:52 For they considered not ~~the miracle~~ of the loaves: for their heart*s* ~~was~~ *were* hardened.		
14:33 Then they that were in the ship came and worshipped him, saying, Of a truth thou art the Son of God.			

MATTHEW	MARK	LUKE	JOHN

E-56. JESUS HEALS PEOPLE OF GENNESARET

14:34 And when they were gone over, they came into the land of Gennesaret.

14:35 And when the men of that place had knowledge of him, they sent out into all that country round about, and brought unto him all that were diseased;

14:36 And besought him that they might only touch the hem of his garment: and as many as touched were made perfectly whole.

6:53 And when they had passed over, they came into the land of Gennesaret, and drew to the shore.
6:54 And when they were come out of the ship, straightway ~~they~~ *the people* knew him,
6:55 And ran through that whole region round about, and began to carry about in beds those that were sick, where they heard he was.
6:56 And whithersoever he entered, into villages, or cities, or country, they laid the sick in the streets, and besought him that they might touch if it were but the border of his garment: and as many as touched him were made whole.

E-57. JESUS IS THE BREAD OF LIFE

6:22 The day following, when the people which stood on the other side of the sea saw that there was none other boat there, save that one whereinto his disciples were entered, and that Jesus went not with his disciples into the boat, but that his disciples were gone away alone;
6:23 (Howbeit there came other boats from Tiberias nigh unto the place where they did eat bread, after that the Lord had given thanks:)
6:24 When the people therefore saw that Jesus was not there, neither his disciples, they also took shipping, and came to Capernaum, seeking for Jesus.
6:25 And when they had found him on the other side of the sea, they said unto him, Rabbi, ~~when~~ *how* camest thou hither?
6:26 Jesus answered them and said, Verily, verily, I say unto you, Ye seek me, not *because ye desire to keep my sayings, neither* because ye saw the miracles, but because ye did eat of the loaves, and were filled.
6:27 Labour not for the meat which perisheth, but for that meat which endureth unto everlasting life, which the Son of ~~m~~*M*an ~~shall~~ *hath power to* give unto you: for him hath God the Father sealed.
6:28 Then said they unto him, What shall we do, that we might work the works of God?
6:29 Jesus answered and said unto them, This is the work of God, that ye believe on him whom he hath sent.
6:30 They said therefore unto him, What sign shewest thou then,

that we may see, and believe thee? what dost thou work?

6:31 Our fathers did eat manna in the desert; as it is written, He gave them bread from heaven to eat.

6:32 Then Jesus said unto them, Verily, verily, I say unto you, Moses gave you not that bread from heaven; but my Father giveth you the true bread from heaven.

6:33 For the bread of God is he which cometh down from heaven, and giveth life unto the world.

6:34 Then said they unto him, Lord, evermore give us this bread.

6:35 And Jesus said unto them, I am the bread of life: he that cometh to me shall never hunger; and he that believeth on me shall never thirst.

6:36 But I said unto you, That ye also have seen me, and believe not.

6:37 All that the Father giveth me shall come to me; and him that cometh to me I will in no wise cast out.

6:38 For I came down from heaven, not to do mine own will, but the will of him that sent me.

6:39 And this is the Father's will which hath sent me, that of all which he hath given me I should lose nothing, but should raise it up again at the last day.

6:40 And this is the will of him that sent me, that every one which seeth the Son, and believeth on him, may have everlasting life: and I will raise him up *in the resurrection of the just* at the last day.

6:41 The Jews then murmured at him, because he said, I am the bread which came down from heaven.

6:42 And they said, Is not this Jesus, the son of Joseph, whose father and mother we know? how is it then that he saith, I came down from heaven?

6:43 Jesus therefore answered and said unto them, Murmur not among yourselves.

6:44 No man can come to me, except ~~the Father which hath sent me draw him: and~~ *he doeth the will of my Father who hath sent me. And this is the will of him who hath sent me, that ye receive the Son; for the Father beareth record of him; and he who receiveth the testimony, and doeth the will of him who sent me,* I will raise him up ~~him up at the last day~~ *in the resurrection of the just.*

6:45 *For* It is written in the prophets, And ~~they~~ *these* shall ~~be~~ all *be* taught of God. Every man therefore that hath heard, and hath learned of the Father, cometh unto me.

6:46 Not that any man hath seen the Father, save he which is of God, he hath seen the Father.

6:47 Verily, verily, I say unto you, He that believeth on me hath everlasting life.

6:48 I am that bread of life.

6:50 This is the bread which cometh down from heaven, that a man may eat thereof, and not die.

6:49 Your fathers did eat manna in the wilderness, and are dead.

6:51 *But* I am the living bread which came down from heaven: if any man eat of this bread, he shall live for ever: and the bread that I will give is my flesh, which I will give for the life of the world.

6:52 The Jews therefore strove among themselves, saying, How can this man give us his flesh to eat?

6:53 Then Jesus said unto them, Verily, verily, I say unto you, Except ye eat the flesh of the Son of man, and drink his blood, ye have no life in you.

6:54 Whoso eateth my flesh, and drinketh my blood, hath eternal life; and I will raise him up *in the resurrection of the just* at the last day.

6:55 For my flesh is meat indeed, and my blood is drink indeed.

6:56 He that eateth my flesh, and drinketh my blood, dwelleth in me, and I in him.

6:57 As the living Father hath sent me, and I live by the Father: so he that eateth me, even he shall live by me.

6:58 This is that bread which came down from heaven: not as your fathers did eat manna, and are dead: he that eateth of this bread shall live for ever.

6:59 These things said he in the synagogue, as he taught in Capernaum.

E-58. JESUS IS REJECTED BY MANY

6:60 Many therefore of his disciples, when they had heard this, said, This is an hard saying; who can hear it?

6:61 When Jesus knew in himself that his disciples murmured at it, he said unto them, Doth this offend you?

6:62 What and if ye shall see the Son of man ascend up where he was before?

6:63 It is the spirit that quickeneth; the flesh profiteth nothing: the words that I speak unto you, they are spirit, and they are life.

MATTHEW	MARK	LUKE	JOHN

JOHN

6:64 But there are some of you that believe not. For Jesus knew from the beginning who they were that believed not, and who should betray him.

6:65 And he said, Therefore said I unto you, that no man can come unto me, except ~~it were given unto him of my Father~~ *he doeth the will of my Father who hath sent me*.

6:66 From that time many of his disciples went back, and walked no more with him.

6:67 Then said Jesus unto the twelve, Will ye also go away?

6:68 Then Simon Peter answered him, Lord, to whom shall we go? thou hast the words of eternal life.

6:69 And we believe and are sure that thou art that Christ, the Son of the living God.

6:70 Jesus answered them, Have not I chosen you twelve, and one of you is a devil?

6:71 He spake of Judas Iscariot the son of Simon: for he it was that should betray him, being one of the twelve.

E-59. JEWS SEEK TO KILL JESUS

JOHN

7:1 After these things Jesus walked in Galilee: for he would not walk in Jewry, because the Jews sought to kill him.

E-60. CLEANLINESS: CONFLICT WITH SCRIBES AND PHARISEES

MATTHEW

15:1 Then came to Jesus scribes and Pharisees, which were of Jerusalem,

saying,

15:2 Why do thy disciples transgress the tradition of the elders? for they wash not their hands when they eat bread.

15:7 *O* Ye hypocrites, well did Esaias prophesy of you, saying,

15:8 This people draw~~eth~~ nigh unto me with their mouth, and ~~honoureth~~ *honoreth* me with their

MARK

7:1 Then came together unto him the Pharisees, and certain of the scribes, which came from Jerusalem.

7:2 And when they saw some of his disciples eat bread with defiled, that is to say, with unwashen, hands, they found fault.

7:3 For the Pharisees, and all the Jews, except they wash ~~their~~ hands oft, eat not, holding the tradition of the elders.

7:4 And when they come from the market, except they wash *their bodies*, they eat not. And many other things there be, which they have received to hold, as the washing of cups, and pots, ~~brasen~~ *brazen* vessels, and of tables.

7:5 ~~Then~~ *And* the Pharisees and scribes asked him, Why walk not thy disciples according to the tradition*s* of the elders, but eat bread with unwashen hands?

7:6 He answered and said unto them, Well hath ~~Esaias~~ *Isaiah* prophesied of you hypocrites, as it is written, This people ~~honoureth~~ *honoreth* me with their lips, but their heart is far from me.

lips; but their heart is far from me.
15:9 But in vain they do worship me, teaching ~~for~~ *the* doctrines *and* the commandments of men.

7:7 Howbeit in vain do they worship me, teaching ~~for~~ *the* doctrines ~~the~~ *and* commandments of men.

7:8 For laying aside the commandment of God, ye hold the tradition of men, ~~as~~ the washing of pots and *of* cups: and many other such like things ye do.

15:3 But he answered and said unto them, Why do ye also transgress the commandment of God by your tradition?

7:9 And he said unto them, ~~Full well~~ *Yea, altogether* ye reject the commandment of God, that ye may keep your own tradition.

7:10 *Full well is it written of you, by the prophets whom ye have rejected. They testified these things of a truth and their blood shall be upon you. Ye have kept not the ordinances of God;* For Moses said, ~~Honour~~ *Honor* thy father and thy mother; and, Whoso curseth father or mother, let him die the death *of the transgressor, as it is written in your law; but ye keep not the law*:

15:4 For God commanded, saying, Honour thy father and mother: and, He that curseth father or mother, let him die the death *which Moses shall appoint*.

15:5 But ye say, Whosoever shall say to ~~his~~ father or ~~his~~ mother, ~~It is a gift,~~ by whatsoever thou mightest be profited by me, *it is a gift from me*;

7:11 ~~But~~ ye say, If a man shall say to his father or mother, ~~It is~~ Corban, that is to say, a gift, by whatsoever thou mightest be profited by me; he ~~shall be free~~ *is of age*.

15:6 And ~~honour~~ *honor* not his father or his mother, ~~he shall be free~~ *it is well*.
Thus have ye made the commandment of God of none effect by your tradition.

7:12 And ye suffer him no more to do ~~ought~~ *aught* for his father or his mother;

7:13 Making the word of God of none effect through your tradition, which ye have delivered: and many such like things do ye.

15:10 And he called the multitude, and said unto them, Hear, and understand:

7:14 And when he had called all the people ~~unto him~~, he said unto them, Hearken unto me every one ~~of you~~, and understand:

15:11 Not that which goeth into the mouth defileth a man;

7:15 There is nothing from without ~~a man~~, that entering into ~~him~~ *a man,* can defile him, *which is food*: but the things which come out of him, those are they that defile the man, *that proceedeth forth out of the heart*.

but that which cometh out of the mouth, this defileth ~~a~~ *the* man.

7:16 If any man have ears to hear, let him hear.

7:17 And when he was entered into the house from *among* the people,

15:12 Then came his disciples, and said unto him, Knowest thou that the Pharisees were offended, after they heard this saying?
15:13 But he answered and said, Every plant, which my heavenly Father hath not planted, shall be rooted up.
15:14 Let them alone: they be blind leaders of the blind. And if the blind lead the blind, both shall fall into the ditch.
15:15 Then answered Peter and said unto him, Declare unto us this parable.

his disciples asked him concerning the parable.

MATTHEW	MARK	LUKE	JOHN

15:16 And Jesus said, Are ye also yet without understanding?

15:17 Do ~~not~~ ye *not* yet understand, that whatsoever entereth in at the mouth goeth into the belly,

and is cast out into the draught?

15:18 But those things which proceed out of the mouth come forth from the heart; and they defile the man.

15:19 For out of the heart proceed evil thoughts, murders, adulteries, fornications, thefts, false witness, blasphemies:

15:20 These are the things which defile a man:
but to eat with unwashen hands defileth not a man.

7:18 And he sai~~th~~*d* unto them, Are ye ~~so~~ without understanding also? Do ye not perceive, that whatsoever thing from without entereth into the man, ~~it~~ cannot defile him;

7:19 Because it entereth not into his heart, but into the belly, and goeth out into the draught, purging all meats?

7:20 And he said, That which cometh out of ~~the~~ *a* man, ~~that~~ defileth the man.

7:21 For from within, out of the heart of men, proceed evil thoughts, adulteries, fornications, murders,

7:22 Thefts, covetousness, wickedness, deceit, lasciviousness, an evil eye, blasphemy, pride, foolishness:

7:23 All these evil things come from within, and defile the man.

E-61. A GENTILE'S DAUGHTER IS HEALED

15:21 Then Jesus went thence, and departed into the coasts of Tyre and Sidon.

15:22 And, behold, a woman of Canaan came out of the same coasts,

and cried unto him, saying, Have mercy on me, O Lord, thou Son of David; my daughter is grievously vexed with a devil.

15:23 But he answered her not a word. And his disciples came and besought him, saying, Send her away; for she crieth after us.

15:24 ~~But~~ he answered ~~and said~~, I am not sent but unto the lost sheep of the house of Israel.

15:25 Then came she and worshipped him, saying, Lord, help me.

15:26 But he answered and said,

It is not meet to take the children's bread, and to cast it to dogs.

7:24 And from thence he arose, and went into the borders of Tyre and Sidon, and entered into a~~n~~ house, and would ~~have no man know it: but he could not be hid.~~ *that no man should come unto him. But he could not deny them; for he had compassion upon all men.*

7:25 For a ~~certain~~ woman,

whose young daughter had an unclean spirit, heard of him, and came and fell at his feet:

7:26 The woman was a Greek, a Syrophenician by nation; and she besought him that he would cast forth the devil out of her daughter.

7:27 But Jesus said unto her, Let the children *of the kingdom* first be filled:
for it is not meet to take the children's bread, and to cast it unto the dogs.

MATTHEW	MARK	LUKE	JOHN

15:27 And she said, Truth, Lord: yet the dogs eat ~~of~~ the crumbs ~~which~~ *that* fall from ~~their masters'~~ *the master's* table.

15:28 Then Jesus answered and said unto her, O woman, great is thy faith: be it unto thee even as thou wilt.

And her daughter was made whole from that very hour.

7:28 And she answered and said unto him, Yes, Lord: *thou sayest truly,* yet the dogs under the table eat of the children's crumbs.

7:29 And he said unto her,

For this saying go thy way; the devil is gone out of thy daughter.

7:30 And when she was come to her house, she found *that* the devil *had* gone out, and her daughter *was* laid upon the bed.

E-62. HEALS MANY AT SEA OF GALILEE

15:29 And Jesus departed from thence, and came nigh unto the sea of Galilee;

and went up into a mountain, and sat down there.

15:30 And great multitudes came unto him, having with them ~~those that were~~ *some* lame, blind, dumb, maimed, and many others, and cast them down at Jesus' feet; and he healed them:

7:31 And again, departing from the coasts of Tyre and Sidon, he came unto the sea of Galilee, through the midst of the coasts of Decapolis.

7:32 And they ~~bring~~ *brought* unto him one that was deaf, and had an impediment in his speech; and they ~~beseech~~ *besought* him to put his hand upon him.

7:33 And he took him aside from the multitude, and put his fingers into his ears, and he spit, and touched his tongue;

7:34 And looking up to heaven, he sighed, and sai~~th~~*d* unto him, Ephphatha, that is, Be opened.

7:35 And straightway his ears were opened, and the string of his tongue was loosed, and he spake plain.

7:36 And he charged them that they should tell no man: but the more he charged them, so much the more a great deal they published ~~it~~ *him*;

15:31 Insomuch that the multitude wondered, when they saw the dumb to speak, the maimed to be whole, the lame to walk, and the blind to see:

and they glorified the God of Israel.

7:37 And were beyond measure astonished, saying, He hath done all things well: he maketh both the deaf to hear, and the dumb to speak.

MATTHEW	MARK	LUKE	JOHN

E-63. JESUS FEEDS THE FOUR THOUSAND

15:32   Then Jesus called his disciples ~~unto him,~~ and said,

I have compassion on the multitude, because they continue with me now three days, and have nothing to eat:
and I will not send them away fasting, lest they faint in the way.

15:33   And his disciples say unto him, Whence should we have so much bread in the wilderness, as to fill so great a multitude?

15:34   And Jesus sai~~th~~*d* unto them, How many loaves have ye? And they said, Seven, and a few little fishes.
15:35   And he commanded the multitude to sit down on the ground.
15:36   And he took the seven loaves and the fishes, and gave thanks, and brake ~~them~~ *the bread*, and gave to his disciples, and the disciples to the multitude.

15:37   And they did all eat, and were filled: and they took up of the broken meat ~~that was left~~ seven baskets full.
15:38   And they that did eat were four thousand men, beside*s* women and children.

8:1   In those days the multitude being very great, and having nothing to eat, Jesus called his disciples ~~unto him~~, and sai~~th~~*d* unto them,
8:2   I have compassion on the multitude, because they have now been with me three days, and have nothing to eat:
8:3   And if I send them away fasting to their own houses, they will faint by the way: for divers of them came from *a*far.
8:4   And his disciples answered him, From whence can a man satisfy these ~~men~~ *, so great a multitude,* with bread here in the wilderness?
8:5   And he asked them, How many loaves have ye?
And they said, Seven.

8:6   And he commanded the people to sit down on the ground:

and he took the seven loaves, and gave thanks, and brake, and gave to his disciples to set before ~~them~~ *the people*; and they did set them before the people.
8:7   And they had a few small fishes: and he blessed *them*, and commanded to set them also before ~~them~~ *the people, that they should eat*.
8:8   So they did eat, and were filled: and they took up of the broken ~~meat~~ *bread* that was left seven baskets.
8:9   And they that had eaten were about four thousand:

and he sent them away.

E-64. JESUS AT MAGDALA

15:39   And he sent away the multitude, and took ship, and came into the coasts of Magdala,

8:10   And straightway he entered into a ship with his disciples,
and came into the parts of Dalmanutha.

E-65. FURTHER DISCOURSE ON SIGNS

16:1   The Pharisees also with the Sadducees came, and tempting *Jesus,* desired him that he would ~~shew~~ *show* them a sign from heaven.
16:2   *And* He answered and said unto them, When it is evening, ye say, ~~It will be fair weather~~ *the weather is fair*, for the sky is red.
16:3   And in the morning *ye say*, ~~It will be foul weather~~ *the weather is foul* to day: for the sky is red

8:11   And the Pharisees came forth, and began to question with him, seeking of him a sign from heaven, tempting him.

MATTHEW

and ~~lowring~~ *lowering*. O ~~ye~~ hypocrites, ye can discern the face of the sky; but ~~can ye not discern~~ *ye cannot tell* the signs of the times?

16:4   A wicked and adulterous generation seeketh after a sign; and there shall no sign be given unto it, but the sign of the prophet Jonas.

And he left them, and departed.

MARK

8:12   And he sighed deeply in his spirit, and sai~~th~~*d*, Why doth this generation seek after a sign? verily I say unto you,

There shall no sign be given unto this generation, *save the sign of the prophet Jonah; for as Jonah was three days and three nights in the whale's belly, so likewise shall the Son of Man be buried in the bowels of the earth.*

8:13   And he left them, and entering into the ship again, *he* departed to the other side.

E-66. THE LEAVEN OF THE PHARISEES

MATTHEW

16:5   And when his disciples were come to the other side, they had forgotten to take bread.

16:6   Then Jesus said unto them, Take heed and beware of the leaven of the Pharisees and of the Sadducees.
16:7   And they reasoned among themselves, saying, ~~It is~~ *he said this* because we have taken no bread.
16:8   ~~Which when Jesus perceived,~~ *And when they reasoned among themselves, Jesus perceived it; and* he said unto them, O ye of little faith, why reason ye among yourselves, because ye have brought no bread?
16:9   Do ye not yet understand,

neither remember the five loaves of the five thousand, and how many baskets ye took up?

16:10   Neither the seven loaves of the four thousand, and how many baskets ye took up?

16:11   How is it that ye do not understand that I spake ~~it not to~~ *not unto* you concerning bread, that ye should beware of the leaven of the Pharisees and of the Sadducees?
16:12   Then understood they how that he bade them not beware of the leaven of bread, but of the doctrine of the Pharisees and of the Sadducees.

MARK

8:14   Now the ~~disciples~~ *multitude* had forgotten to take bread, neither had they in the ship with them more than one loaf.
8:15   And he charged them, saying, Take heed, *and* beware of the leaven of the Pharisees, and ~~of~~ the leaven of Herod.
8:16   And they reasoned among themselves, saying, ~~It is~~ *He hath said this,* because we have no bread.
8:17   And when *they said this among themselves,* Jesus knew it, *and* he sai~~th~~*d* unto them,

Why reason ye, because ye have no bread?

perceive ye not yet, neither understand *ye*? ~~have ye your heart~~ *are your hearts* yet hardened?
8:18   Having eyes, see ye not? and having ears, hear ye not? and do ye not remember?
8:19   When I brake the five loaves among *the* five thousand, how many baskets full of fragments took ye up?
They say unto him, Twelve.
8:20   And when the seven among *the* four thousand, how many baskets full of fragments took ye up? And they said, Seven.
8:21   And he said unto them, How is it that ye do not understand?

MATTHEW	MARK	LUKE	JOHN

E-67. THE HEALING OF A BLIND MAN

	MARK		
	8:22 And he cometh to Bethsaida; and they bring a blind man unto him, and besought him to touch him.		

8:23 And he took the blind man by the hand, and led him out of the town; and when he had spit *up*on his eyes, and put his hands upon him, he asked him if he saw ~~ought.~~ *aught?*

8:24 And he looked up, and said, I see men as trees, walking.

8:25 After that he put his hands again upon his eyes, and made him look up: and he was restored, and saw every man clearly.

8:26 And he sent him away to his house, saying, Neither go into the town, nor tell ~~it~~ *what is done,* to any in the town.

E-68. HEROD'S OPINION OF JESUS: JOHN THE BAPTIST RISEN FROM THE DEAD

MATTHEW	MARK	LUKE	JOHN
14:1 At that time Herod the tetrarch heard of the fame of Jesus,	6:14 And ~~k~~*K*ing Herod heard of ~~him~~ *Jesus*; (for his name was spread abroad:)	9:7 Now Herod the tetrarch heard of all that was done by ~~him~~: *Jesus;* and he was perplexed, because that it was said of some, that John was risen from the dead;	
14:2 And said unto his servants, This is John the Baptist; he is risen from the dead; and therefore mighty works do ~~shew~~ *show* forth themselves in him.	and he said, That John the Baptist was risen from the dead, and therefore mighty works do ~~shew~~ *show* forth themselves in him.		
	6:15 Others said, That it is Elias. And others said, That it is a prophet, or as one of the prophets. 6:16 But when Herod heard ~~thereof~~ *of him*, he said, It is John, whom I beheaded: he is risen from the dead.	9:8 And of some, that Elias had appeared; and of others, that one of the old prophets was risen again.	
		9:9 And Herod said, John have I beheaded: but who is this, of whom I hear such things? And he desired to see him.	

E-69. PETER TESTIFIES THAT JESUS IS THE CHRIST

MATTHEW	MARK	LUKE	JOHN
16:13 *And* When Jesus came into the coasts of Caesarea Philippi, he asked his disciples, saying, Whom do men say that I the Son of ~~m~~*M*an am?	8:27 And Jesus went out, and his disciples, into the towns of Caesarea Philippi: and by the way he asked his disciples, saying unto them, Whom do men say that I am?	9:18 And it came to pass, ~~as he was alone praying, his disciples were with him: and~~ *as he went alone with his disciples to pray,* he asked them, saying, Whom say the people that I am?	
16:14 And they said, Some say ~~that thou art~~ John the Baptist: some, Elias; and others, Jeremias, or one of the prophets.	8:28 And they answered, John the Baptist: but some say, Elias; and others, One of the prophets.	9:19 They answering said, *some say,* John the Baptist; but ~~some~~ *others* say, Elias; and others ~~say,~~ that one of the old prophets is risen again.	
16:15 He saith*d* unto them, But whom say ye that I am? 16:16 And Simon Peter answered and said, Thou art the Christ, the Son of the living God. 16:17 And Jesus answered and said unto him, Blessed art thou,	8:29 And he saith*d* unto them, But whom say ye that I am? And Peter answere~~th~~*d* and saith*d* unto him, Thou art the Christ, *the Son of the living God*.	9:20 He said unto them, But who~~m~~ say ye that I am? Peter answering said, The Christ, *the Son* of God.	

MATTHEW	MARK	LUKE	JOHN

Simon Barjona: for flesh and blood hath not revealed ~~it~~ *this* unto thee, but my Father ~~which~~ *who* is in heaven.

16:18 And I say also unto thee, That thou art Peter, and upon this rock I will build my church; and the gates of hell shall not prevail against it.

16:19 And I will give unto thee the keys of the kingdom of heaven: and whatsoever thou shalt bind on earth shall be bound in heaven: and whatsoever thou shalt loose on earth shall be loosed in heaven.

16:20 Then charged he his disciples that they should tell no man that he was Jesus the Christ.

8:30 And he charged them that they should tell no man of him.

9:21 And he straitly charged them, and commanded them to tell no man ~~that thing~~ *of him*;

E-70. JESUS FORETELLS HIS DEATH AND RESURRECTION

16:21 From that time forth began Jesus to ~~shew~~ *show* unto his disciples, how that he must go ~~unto~~ Jerusalem, and suffer many things of the elders and chief priests and scribes, and be killed, and be raised again the third day.

16:22 Then Peter took him, and began to rebuke him, saying, Be it far from thee, Lord: this shall not be *done* unto thee.

16:23 But he turned, and said unto Peter,

Get thee behind me, Satan: thou art an offence unto me: for thou savourest not the things that be of God, but those that be of men.

16:24 Then said Jesus unto his disciples,
If any man will come after me, let him deny himself, and take up his cross, and follow me.

16:25 *And now for a man to take up his cross, is to deny himself all ungodliness, and every worldly lust, and keep my commandments. Break not my commandments for to save your lives;* For whosoever will save his life *in this world*, shall lose it *in the world to come.*

and whosoever will lose his life *in this world,* for my sake shall find it *in the world to come.*

16:26 *Therefore, forsake the world, and save your souls;*
For what is a man profited, if he shall gain the whole world, and lose his own soul?

8:31 And he began to teach them, that the Son of ~~m~~*M*an must suffer many things, and be rejected of the elders, and ~~of~~ the chief priests, and scribes, and be killed, and after three days rise again.

8:32 And he spake that saying openly. And Peter took him, and began to rebuke him.

8:33 But when he had turned about and looked *up*on his disciples, he rebuked Peter, saying, Get thee behind me, Satan: for thou ~~savourest~~ *savorest* not the things that be of God, but the things that be of ~~men~~ *man*.

8:34 And when he had called the people ~~unto him~~ with his disciples also, he said unto them,
Whosoever will come after me, let him deny himself, and take up his cross, and follow me.

8:35 For whosoever will save his life shall lose it;

or whosoever will save his life, shall be willing to lay it down for my sake; and if he is not willing to lay it down for my sake, he shall lose it. But whosoever shall *be willing to* lose his life for my sake, and the ~~gospel's~~ *gospel*, the same shall save it.

8:36 For what shall it profit a man, if he shall gain the whole world, and lose his own soul?

9:22 Saying, The Son of man must suffer many things, and be rejected of the elders and chief priests and scribes, and be slain, and be raised the third day.

9:23 And he said to them all,
If any man will come after me, let him deny himself, and take up his cross daily, and follow me.

9:24 For whosoever will save his life ~~shall~~, *must be willing to* lose it *for my sake*:

~~but~~ *and* whosoever will *be willing to* lose his life for my sake, the same shall save it.

9:25 For what ~~is a man advantaged,~~ *doth it profit a man* if he gain the whole world, and *yet he receive him not whom God hath ordained, and he* ~~lose himself,~~

MATTHEW	MARK	LUKE	JOHN
		lose his own soul, ~~or be cast away~~ and he himself be a castaway?	
	8:37 Or what shall a man give in exchange for his soul?		
	8:38 *Therefore deny yourselves of these, and be not ashamed of me.* Whosoever ~~therefore~~ shall be ashamed of me and of my words in this adulterous and sinful generation;	9:26 For whosoever shall be ashamed of me and of my words,	
~~or what shall a man give in exchange for his soul?~~	of him also shall the Son of ~~m~~*M*an be ashamed, when he cometh in the glory of his Father with the holy angels.	of him shall the Son of ~~m~~*M*an be ashamed, when he shall come in his own ~~glory, and in his Father's, and of~~ *kingdom, clothed in the glory of his Father, with* the holy angels.	
16:27 For the Son of ~~m~~*M*an shall come in the glory of his Father with his angels;			
and then he shall reward every man according to his works.			
	And they shall not have part in that resurrection when he cometh. For verily I say unto you, That he shall come; and he that layeth down his life for my sake and the gospel's shall come with him, and shall be clothed with his glory in the cloud, on the right hand of the Son of Man.		
	9:1 And he said unto them *again*, Verily I say unto you, That there be some of them that stand here, which shall not taste of death, till they have seen the kingdom of God come with power.		
16:28 Verily I say unto you, There be some standing here, which shall not taste of death, till they see the Son of ~~m~~*M*an coming in his kingdom.		9:27 ~~But~~ *Verily,* I tell you of a truth, there ~~be~~ *are* some standing here, ~~which~~ *who* shall not taste of death, ~~till~~ *until* they see the kingdom of God *coming in power*.	

E-71. THE TRANSFIGURATION

MATTHEW	MARK	LUKE	JOHN
17:1 And after six days Jesus taketh Peter, James, and John his brother,	9:2 And after six days Jesus taketh ~~with him~~ Peter, and James, and John, *who asked him many questions concerning his sayings;* and *Jesus* leadeth them up into ~~an~~ high mountain apart by themselves:	9:28 And it came to pass ~~about an~~ eight days after these sayings, *that* he took Peter and John and James, and went up into a mountain to pray.	
and bringeth them up into an high mountain apart,			
17:2 And was transfigured before them: and his face did shine as the sun, and his raiment was white as the light.	and he was transfigured before them.	9:29 And as he prayed, the fashion of his countenance was ~~altered~~ *changed*,	
	9:3 And his raiment became shining, exceeding white as snow; so *white* as no fuller on earth ~~can white~~ *could whiten* them.	and his raiment ~~was~~ *became* white and ~~glistering~~ *glittering*.	
17:3 And, behold, there appeared unto them Moses and Elias talking with him.	9:4 And there appeared unto them Elias with Moses, *or in other words, John the Baptist and Moses*: and they were talking with Jesus.	9:30 And, behold, there *came and* talked with him two men, ~~which were~~ *even* Moses and Elias:	
		9:31 Who appeared in glory, and spake of his ~~decease~~ *death, and also his resurrection,* which he should accomplish at Jerusalem.	
		9:32 But Peter and they ~~that~~ *who* were with him were heavy with sleep: and when they were awake, they saw his glory, and the two men ~~that~~ *who* stood with him.	
		9:33 And ~~it came to pass, as they~~ *after the two men* departed from him, Peter said unto Jesus, Master, it is good for us to be here: ~~and~~ let us make three tabernacles; one for thee, and one for Moses, and one for Elias: not knowing what he said.	
17:4 Then answered Peter, and said unto Jesus, Lord, it is good for us to be here: if thou wilt, let us make here three tabernacles; one for thee, ~~and~~ one for Moses, and one for Elias.	9:5 And Peter answered and said to Jesus, Master, it is good for us to be here: and let us make three tabernacles; one for thee, and one for Moses, and one for Elias.		

MATTHEW	MARK	LUKE	JOHN

MARK

9:6 For he ~~wist~~ *knew* not what to say; for they were sore afraid.
9:7 And there was a cloud that overshadowed them:

MATTHEW

17:5 While he yet spake, behold, a bright cloud overshadowed them:

LUKE

9:34 While he thus spake, there came a cloud, and overshadowed them *all*: and they feared as they entered into the cloud.

MATTHEW

and behold a voice out of the cloud, which said, This is my beloved Son, in whom I am well pleased; hear ye him.
17:6 And when the disciples heard ~~it~~ *the voice*, they fell on their fac*es*, and were sore afraid.
17:7 And Jesus came and touched them, and said, Arise, and be not afraid.
17:8 And when they had lifted up their eyes,

they saw no man, save Jesus only.

17:9 And as they came down from the mountain, Jesus charged them, saying, Tell the vision to no man, until the Son of man be risen again from the dead.

MARK

and a voice came out of the cloud, saying, This is my beloved Son: hear him.

9:8 And suddenly, when they had looked round about *with great astonishment*,
they saw no man any more, save Jesus only with themselves. *And immediately they departed.*
9:9 And as they came down from the mountain, he charged them that they should tell no man what things they had seen, till the Son of ~~m~~*M*an ~~were~~ *was* risen from the dead.
9:10 And they kept that saying with themselves,

questioning one with another what the rising from the dead should mean.

LUKE

9:35 And there came a voice out of the cloud, saying, This is my beloved Son: hear him.

9:36 And when the voice was past,

Jesus was found alone.

And ~~they kept it~~ *these things they kept* close, and *they* told no man in those days any of those things which they had seen.

MATTHEW

17:10 And his disciples asked him, saying, Why then say the scribes that Elias must first come?
17:11 And Jesus answered and said unto them, Elias truly shall first come, and restore all things, *as the prophets have written.*

17:12 ~~But~~ *And again* I say unto you, That Elias ~~is~~ *has* come already, *concerning whom it is written, Behold, I will send my messenger, and he shall prepare the way before me*~~,~~ *;* and they knew him not, ~~but~~ *and* have done unto him whatsoever they listed.

Likewise shall also the Son of man suffer of them.

17:13 *But I say unto you, Who is Elias? Behold, this is Elias, whom I send to prepare the way before me.* Then the disciples understood that he spake unto them of John the Baptist, *and also of another who should come and restore all things, as it is written by the prophets.*

MARK

9:11 And they asked him, saying, Why say the scribes that Elias must first come?
9:12 And he answered and told them, *saying,* Elias verily cometh first, and ~~restoreth~~ *prepareth* all things; *and teacheth you of the prophets;* ~~and~~ how it is written of the Son of ~~m~~*M*an, that he must suffer many things, and be set at ~~nought~~ *naught*.
9:13 ~~But~~ *Again* I say unto you, That Elias is indeed come,

~~and~~ *but* they have done unto him whatsoever they listed, *and even* as it is written of him.

and he bore record of me, and they received him not.

Verily this was Elias.

E-72. THE HEALING OF A DEMONIC BOY

LUKE

9:37 And it came to pass, that on the next day, when they were come down from the hill,
much people met him.

MATTHEW

17:14 And when they were come to the multitude,

MARK

9:14 And when he came to ~~his~~ *the* disciples, he saw a great multitude about them, and the scribes questioning with them.
9:15 And straightway all the people, when they beheld him, were greatly amazed, and running to him saluted him.
9:16 And ~~he~~ *Jesus* asked the scribes, What question*ed* ye with them?
9:17 And one of the multitude answered and said, Master, I have brought unto thee my son, ~~which~~ *who* hath a dumb spirit *that is a devil*;

LUKE

9:38 And, behold, a man of the company cried out, saying,

Master, I beseech thee, look upon my son: for he is mine only child.

MATTHEW

there came to him a certain man, kneeling down to him, and saying,

17:15 Lord, have mercy on my son: for he is lunati~~ck~~, and sore vexed: for ofttimes he falleth into the fire, and oft into the water.

MARK

9:18 And ~~wheresoever he taketh~~ *when he seizeth* him, he teareth him: and he foameth, and gnasheth with his teeth, and pineth away:

LUKE

9:39 And, lo, a spirit taketh him, and he suddenly crieth out; and it teareth him that he foameth ~~again~~, and bruising him hardly departeth from him.
9:40 And I besought thy disciples to cast him out; and they could not.

MATTHEW

17:16 And I brought him to thy disciples, and they could not cure him.
17:17 Then Jesus answered and said, O faithless and perverse generation, how long shall I be with you? how long shall I suffer you? bring him hither to me.

MARK

and I spake to thy disciples that they ~~should~~ *might* cast him out; and they could not.

9:19 ~~He answereth~~ *Jesus spake unto* him, and sai~~th~~*d*, O faithless generation, how long shall I be with you? how long shall I suffer you? bring him unto me.
9:20 And they brought him unto ~~him~~ *Jesus*:

and when ~~he~~ *the man* saw him, ~~straightway the spirit tare him~~ *immediately he was torn by the spirit*; and he fell on the ground, and wallowed foaming.
9:21 And ~~he~~ *Jesus* asked his father, How long *a time* is it ~~ago~~ since this came unto him? And ~~he~~ *his father* said, ~~Of~~ *When* a child.
9:22 And ofttimes it hath cast him into the fire, and into the waters, to destroy him: but if thou canst ~~do any thing~~, *I ask thee to* have compassion on us, and help us.
9:23 Jesus said unto him, If thou ~~canst believe, all things are~~ *wilt believe all things I shall say unto you, this is* possible to him that believeth.
9:24 And ~~straightway~~ *immediately* the father of the child cried out,

LUKE

9:41 And Jesus answering said, O faithless and perverse generation, how long shall I be with you, and suffer you?
Bring thy son hither.

9:42 And as he was ~~yet a~~ coming,

the devil threw him down, and tare him *again*.

MATTHEW	MARK	LUKE	JOHN
	and said with tears, Lord, I believe; help thou mine unbelief.		
	9:25 When Jesus saw that the people came running together,		
17:18 And Jesus rebuked the devil;	he rebuked the foul spirit, saying unto him, Thou dumb and deaf spirit, I charge thee, *to* come out of him, and enter no more into him.	And Jesus rebuked the unclean spirit,	
and he departed out of him:	9:26 And the *Now the dumb and deaf* spirit cried, and rent him sore, and came out of him: and he was as one dead; insomuch that many said, He is dead.		
and the child was cured from that very hour.	9:27 But Jesus took him by the hand, and lifted him up; and he arose.	and healed the child, and delivered him again to his father.	
		9:43(a) And they were all amazed at the mighty power of God.	
17:19 Then came the disciples to Jesus apart, and said, Why could not we cast him out?	9:28 And when he *Jesus* was come into the house, his disciples asked him privately, Why could not we cast him out?		
17:20 And Jesus said unto them, Because of your unbelief: for verily I say unto you, If ye have faith as a grain of mustard seed, ye shall say unto this mountain, Remove hence to yonder place; and it shall remove; and nothing shall be impossible unto you.	9:29 And he said unto them,		
17:21 Howbeit this kind goeth not out but by prayer and fasting.	This kind can come forth by nothing, but by prayer and fasting.		

E-73. HIS DEATH AND RESURRECTION AGAIN FORETOLD

MATTHEW	MARK	LUKE	JOHN
	9:30 And they departed thence, and passed through Galilee *privately*;		
17:22 And while they abode in Galilee,			
	and *for* he would not that any man should know it.		
		9:43(b) But while they wondered every one at all things which Jesus did,	
Jesus said unto them,	9:31 For *And* he taught his disciples, and said unto them,	he said unto his disciples,	
		9:44 Let these sayings sink down into your ears *hearts*:	
The Son of mMan shall be betrayed into the hands of men:	The Son of mMan is delivered into the hands of men,	for the Son of mMan shall be delivered into the hands of men.	
17:23 And they shall kill him, and the third day he shall be raised again.	and they shall kill him; and after that he is killed, he shall rise the third day.		
And they were exceeding sorry.			
	9:32 But they understood not that saying,	9:45 But they understood not this saying, and it was hid from them, that they perceived it not: and they feared to ask him of that saying.	
	and were afraid to ask him.		

E-74. TRIBUTE MONEY

MATTHEW

17:24 And when they were come to Capernaum, they that received tribute ~~money~~ came to Peter, and said, Doth not your master pay tribute?
17:25 He sai~~th~~*d*, ~~Yes~~ *Yea*. And when he was come into the house, Jesus ~~prevented~~ *rebuked* him, saying, What thinkest thou, Simon? of whom do the kings of the earth take custom or tribute? of their own children, or of strangers?
17:26 Peter sai~~th~~*d* unto him, Of strangers. Jesus sai~~th~~*d* unto him, Then are the children free.
17:27 Notwithstanding, lest we should offend them, go thou to the sea, and cast ~~an~~ *a* hook, and take up the fish that first cometh up; and when thou hast opened his mouth, thou shalt find a piece of money: that take, and give unto them for me and thee.

MARK

9:33(a) And he came to Capernaum:

E-75. JESUS TEACHES ON HUMILITY, SERVICE AND FORGIVENESS

MATTHEW

18:1 At the same time came the disciples unto Jesus, saying, Who is the greatest in the kingdom of heaven?

MARK

9:33(b) and being in the house

he asked them, ~~What~~ *why* was it that ye disputed among yourselves by the way?
9:34 But they held their peace*, being afraid*: for by the way they had disputed among themselves, who ~~should be~~ *was* the greatest *among them*.

LUKE

9:46 Then there arose a reasoning among them, ~~which~~ *who* of them should be greatest.

9:47 And Jesus, perceiving the thought*s* of their heart*s*,

MATTHEW

18:2 And Jesus called a little child unto him, and set him in the midst of them,

LUKE

took a child, and set him ~~by him~~ *in the midst*,

MARK

9:35 ~~And he~~ *Now Jesus* sat down, and called the twelve, and sai~~th~~*d* unto them, If any man desire to be first, the same shall be last of all, and servant of all.
9:36 And he took a child, and ~~set him~~ *sat* in the midst of them: and when he had taken ~~him~~ *the child* in his arms,
he said unto them,

LUKE

9:48 And said unto them,

MATTHEW

18:3 And said, Verily I say unto you, Except ye be converted, and become as little children, ye shall not enter into the kingdom of heaven.
18:4 Whosoever therefore shall humble himself as this little child, the same is greatest in the kingdom of heaven.
18:5 And whoso shall receive one such little child in my name receiveth me.

MARK

9:37 Whosoever shall ~~receive one of such children in my name,~~ *humble himself like one of these children, and* receiveth me, ye

LUKE

Whosoever shall receive this child in my name receiveth me: and whosoever shall receive me receiveth him ~~that~~ *who* sent me:

shall receive in my name: and whosoever shall receive me, receiveth not me *only*, but him that sent me, *even the Father*.

9:38 And John ~~answered~~ *spake unto* him, saying, Master, we saw one casting out devils in thy name, and he followeth not us: and we forbad him, because he ~~followeth~~ *followed* not us.
9:39 But Jesus said, Forbid him not: for there is no man which shall do a miracle in my name, that can ~~lightly~~ speak evil of me.
9:40 For he that is not against us is on our part.
9:41 ~~For~~ *And* whosoever shall give you a cup of water to drink in my name, because ye belong to Christ, verily I say unto you, he shall not lose his reward.
9:42 And whosoever shall offend one of these little ones that believe in me, it is better for him that a millstone were hanged about his neck, and he were cast into the sea.

for he ~~that~~ *who* is least among you all, the same shall be great.
9:49 And John ~~answered~~ *spake* and said, Master, we saw one casting out devils in thy name;

and we forbad*e* him, because he followeth not with us.
9:50 And Jesus said unto him, Forbid ~~him~~ not *any*:

for he ~~that~~ *who* is not against us is for us.

18:6 But whoso shall offend one of these little ones which believe in me, it were better for him that a millstone were hanged about his neck, and ~~that~~ he were drowned in the depth of the sea.
18:7 Woe unto the world because of offences! for it must needs be that offences come; but woe to that man by whom the offence cometh!
18:8 Wherefore if thy hand or thy foot offend thee, cut ~~them~~ *it* off, and cast ~~them~~ *it* from thee:

9:43 ~~And~~ *Therefore,* if thy hand offend thee, cut it off:
or if thy brother offend thee and confess not and forsake not, he shall be cut off.
It is better for thee to enter into life maimed, than having two hands to go into hell,

for it is better for thee to enter into life halt or maimed, rather than having two hands or two feet to be cast into everlasting fire.

For it is better for thee to enter into life without thy brother, than for thee and thy brother to be cast into hell, into the fire that never shall be quenched:
9:44 Where their worm dieth not, and the fire is not quenched.
9:45 And *again,* if thy foot offend thee, cut it off: *for he that is thy standard, by whom thou walkest, if he become a transgressor, he shall be cut off.* it is better for thee to enter halt into life, than having two feet to be cast into hell, into the fire that never shall be quenched:
9:46 ~~Where their worm dieth not, and the fire is not quenched.~~
9:47 *Therefore, let every man stand or fall, by himself, and not for another; or not trusting another. Seek unto my father, and it shall be done in that very moment what ye shall ask, if ye ask in faith, believing that ye shall receive.*

MATTHEW	MARK	LUKE	JOHN

18:9 And if thine eye offend thee,

And if thine eye *which seeth for thee, him that is appointed to watch over thee to show thee light, become a transgressor and* offend thee,

pluck it out, and cast it from thee: it is better for thee to enter into life with one eye, rather than having two eyes to be cast into hell fire. *And a man's hand is his friend, and his foot, also; and a man's eye, are they of his own household.*

pluck ~~it~~ *him* out: it is better for thee to enter into the kingdom of God with one eye, than having two eyes to be cast into hell fire:

9:48 *For it is better that thyself should be saved, than to be cast into hell with thy brother,* Where their worm dieth not, and *where* the fire is not quenched.
9:49 For every one shall be salted with fire, and every sacrifice shall be salted with salt.
9:50 ~~Salt is~~ *But the salt must be* good: ~~but~~ *For* if the salt have lost his saltness, wherewith will ye season it? *(the sacrifice;) therefore it must needs be that ye* Have salt in yourselves, and have peace one with another.

18:10 Take heed that ye despise not one of these little ones; for I say unto you, That in heaven their angels do always behold the face of my Father ~~which~~ *who* is in heaven.
18:11 For the Son of man is come to save that which was lost. *And to call sinners to repentance; but these little ones have no need of repentance, and I will save them.*
18:12 How think ye? if a man have ~~an~~ hundred sheep, and one of them be gone astray, doth he not leave the ninety and nine, and goeth into the mountains, and seeketh that which is gone astray?
18:13 And if so be that he find it, verily I say unto you, he rejoiceth more ~~of that sheep~~ *over that which is lost*, than ~~of~~ *over* the ninety and nine which went not astray.
18:14 Even so it is not the will of your Father which is in heaven, that one of these little ones should perish.
18:15 Moreover if thy brother shall trespass against thee, go and tell him his fault between thee and him alone: if he shall hear thee, thou hast gained thy brother.
18:16 But if he will not hear thee, then take with thee one or two more, that in the mouth of two or three witnesses every word may be established.
18:17 And if he shall neglect to hear them, tell it unto the church: but if he neglect to hear the church, let him be unto thee as an heathen man and a publican.
18:18 Verily I say unto you,

MATTHEW	MARK	LUKE	JOHN

Whatsoever ye shall bind on earth shall be bound in heaven: and whatsoever ye shall loose on earth shall be loosed in heaven.

18:19 Again I say unto you, That if two of you shall agree on earth as touching any thing that they shall ask, *that they may not ask amiss,* it shall be done for them of my Father which is in heaven.

18:20 For where two or three are gathered together in my name, there am I in the midst of them.

18:21 Then came Peter to him, and said, Lord, how oft shall my brother sin against me, and I forgive him? till seven times?

18:22 Jesus sai~~th~~*d* unto him, I say not unto thee, Until seven times: but, Until seventy times seven.

18:23 Therefore is the kingdom of heaven likened unto a certain king, ~~which~~ *who* would take account of his servants.

18:24 And when he had begun to reckon, one was brought unto him, ~~which~~ *who* owed him ten thousand talents.

18:25 But forasmuch as he had not to pay, his lord commanded him to be sold, and his wife, and children, and all that he had, and payment to be made.

18:26 *And* The servant ~~therefore fell down, and worshipped~~ *besought* him, saying, Lord, have patience with me, and I will pay thee all.

18:27 Then the lord of that servant was moved with compassion, and loosed him, and forgave him the debt. *The servant, therefore, fell down and worshipped him.*

18:28 But the same servant went out, and found one of his fellowservants, which owed him an hundred pence: and he laid hands on him, and took him by the throat, saying, Pay me that thou owest.

18:29 And his fellowservant fell down at his feet, and besought him, saying, Have patience with me, and I will pay thee all.

18:30 And he would not: but went and cast him into prison, till he should pay the debt.

18:31 So when his fellowservants saw what was done, they were very sorry, and came and told unto their lord all that was done.

18:32 Then his lord, after that he had called him, said unto him, O thou wicked servant, I forgave thee all that debt, because thou desiredst me:

18:33 Shouldest not thou also have had compassion on thy fellowservant, even as I had pity on thee?

MATTHEW	MARK	LUKE	JOHN

18:34 And his lord was wroth, and delivered him to the tormentors, till he should pay all that was due unto him.

18:35 So likewise shall my heavenly Father do also unto you, if ye from your hearts forgive not every one his brother their trespasses.

E-76. JESUS SENDS OUT THE SEVENTY

10:1 After these things the Lord appointed other seventy also, and sent them two and two before his face into every city and place, ~~whither~~ *where* he himself would come.

10:2 ~~Therefore said he~~ *And he said* unto them, The harvest truly is great, but the ~~labourers are~~ *laborers* few: pray ye therefore the Lord of the harvest, that he would send forth ~~labourers~~ *laborers* into his harvest.

10:3 Go your ways: behold, I send you forth as lambs among wolves.

10:4 Carry neither purse, nor scrip, nor shoes: ~~and salute no man~~ *nor salute any man* by the way.

10:5 And into whatsoever house ye enter, first say, Peace ~~be~~ to this house.

10:6 And if the son of peace be there, your peace shall rest upon it: if not, it shall turn to you again.

10:7 And ~~in the same house~~ *into whatsoever house they receive you,* remain, eating and drinking such things as they give: for the ~~labourer~~ *laborer* is worthy of his hire. Go not from house to house.

10:8 And into whatsoever city ye enter, and they receive you, eat such things as are set before you:

10:9 And heal the sick that are therein, and say ~~unto them~~, The kingdom of God is come nigh unto you.

10:10 But into whatsoever city ye enter, and they receive you not, go your ways out into the streets of the same, and say,

10:11 Even the very dust of your city, which cleaveth on us, we do wipe off against you: notwithstanding be ~~ye~~ sure of this, that the kingdom of God is come nigh unto you.

10:12 But I say unto you, that it shall be more tolerable in ~~that~~ *the* day *of judgment* for Sodom, than for that city.

11:20 Then began he to upbraid the cities wherein most of his mighty works were done, because they repented not:

11:21 Woe unto thee, Chorazin!

10:13 *Then began he to upbraid the people in every city wherein his mighty works were done, who received him not, saying,*
Woe unto thee, Chorazin! woe

MATTHEW	MARK	LUKE	JOHN

woe unto thee, Bethsaida! for if the mighty works, which were done in you, had been done in Tyre and Sidon, they would have repented long ~~ago~~ *since* in sackcloth and ashes.

11:22 But I say unto you, It shall be more tolerable for Tyre and Sidon at the day of judgment, than for you.

11:23 And thou, Capernaum, which art exalted unto heaven, shalt be brought down to hell: for if the mighty works, which have been done in thee, had been done in Sodom, it would have remained until this day.

11:24 But I say unto you, ~~That~~ it shall be more tolerable for the land of Sodom in the day of judgment, than for thee.

unto thee, Bethsaida! for if the mighty works had been done in Tyre and Sidon, which have been done in you, they ~~had a great while ago~~ *would have* repented, sitting in sackcloth and ashes.

10:14 But it shall be more tolerable for Tyre and Sidon ~~at the~~ *in the day of* judgment, than for you.

10:15 And thou, Capernaum, which art exalted to heaven, ~~shalt~~ *shall* be thrust down to hell.

10:16 *And he said unto his disciples,* He that heareth you heareth me; and he that despiseth you despiseth me; and he that despiseth me despiseth him ~~that~~ *who* sent me.

MATTHEW	MARK	LUKE	JOHN

F-1. JESUS ENTREATED TO GO TO THE FEAST OF THE TABERNACLES

7:2 Now the Jews' feast of tabernacles was at hand.

7:3 His brethren therefore said unto him, Depart hence, and go into ~~Judaea~~ *Judea*, that thy disciples *there* also may see the works that thou doest.

7:4 For there is no man that doeth any thing in secret, ~~and~~ *but* he himself seeketh to be known openly. If thou do these things, ~~shew~~ *show* thyself to the world.

7:5 For neither did his brethren believe in him.

7:6 Then Jesus said unto them, My time is not yet come: but your time is alway ready.

7:7 The world cannot hate you; but me it hateth, because I testify of it, that the works thereof are evil.

7:8 Go ye up unto this feast: I go not up yet unto this feast; for my time is not yet full come.

7:9 When he had said these words unto them, he ~~abode~~ *continued* still in Galilee.

F-2. JESUS SECRETLY ATTENDS THE FEAST

9:51 And it came to pass, when the time was come that he should be received up, he stedfastly set his face to go to Jerusalem,

7:10 But ~~when~~ *after* his brethren were gone up, then went he also up unto the feast, not openly, but as it were in secret.

9:52 And sent messengers before his face: and they went, and entered into a village of the Samaritans, to make ready for him.

9:53 And ~~they did~~ *the Samaritans would* not receive him, because his face was *turned* as though he would go to Jerusalem.

9:54 And when his disciples James and John saw ~~this~~ *that they would not receive him*, they said, Lord, wilt thou that we command fire to come down from heaven, and consume them, even as Elias did?

9:55 But he turned, and rebuked them, and said, Ye know not what manner of spirit ye are of.

9:56 For the Son of man is not come to destroy men's lives, but to save them. And they went to another village.

MATTHEW	MARK	LUKE	JOHN

F-3. SACRIFICE REQUIRED TO FOLLOW JESUS

8:19 And a certain scribe came *unto him*, and said ~~unto him~~, Master, I will follow thee whithersoever thou goest.

8:20 And Jesus sait~~h~~d unto him, The foxes have holes, and the birds of the air have nests; but the Son of ~~m~~*M*an hath not where to lay his head.

8:21 And another of his disciples said unto him, Lord, suffer me first to go and bury my father.

8:22 But Jesus said unto him, Follow me; and let the dead bury their dead.

9:57 And it came to pass, ~~that,~~ as they went in the way, a certain man said unto him, Lord, I will follow thee whithersoever thou goest.

9:58 And Jesus said unto him, *the* Foxes have holes, and *the* birds of the air have nests; but the Son of ~~m~~*M*an hath not where to lay his head.

9:59 And he said unto another, Follow me. But he said, Lord, suffer me first to go and bury my father.

9:60 Jesus said unto him, Let the dead bury their dead: but go thou and preach the kingdom of God.

9:61 And another also said, Lord, I will follow thee; but let me first go bid them farewell, ~~which~~ *who* are ~~at home~~ at my house.

9:62 And Jesus said unto him, No man, having put his hand to the plough, and looking back, is fit for the kingdom of God.

F-4. CROWDS AT THE FEAST DISCUSS JESUS

7:11 Then the Jews sought him at the feast, and said, Where is he?

7:12 And there was much murmuring among the people concerning him: for some said, He is a good man: others said, Nay; but he deceiveth the people.

7:13 Howbeit no man spake openly of him for fear of the Jews.

F-5. JESUS TEACHES AT THE TEMPLE

7:14 Now about the midst of the feast Jesus went up into the temple, and taught.

7:15 And the Jews marvelled, saying, How knoweth this man letters, having never learned?

7:16 Jesus answered them, and said, My doctrine is not mine, but his that sent me.

7:17 If any man will do his will, he shall know of the doctrine, whether it be of God, or whether I speak of myself.

7:18 He that speaketh of himself seeketh his own glory: but he that seeketh his glory that sent him, the same is true, and no unrighteousness is in him.

7:19 Did not Moses give you the law, and yet none of you keepeth the law? Why go ye about to kill me?

7:20 The people answered and said, Thou hast a devil: who goeth about to kill thee?

7:21 Jesus answered and said unto

MATTHEW	MARK	LUKE	JOHN

them, I have done one work, and ye all marvel.

7:22 Moses therefore gave unto you circumcision; (not because it is of Moses, but of the fathers;) and ye on the sabbath day circumcise a man.

7:23 If a man on the sabbath day receive circumcision, that the law of Moses should not be broken; are ye angry at me, because I have made a man every whit whole on the sabbath day?

7:24 Judge not according to ~~the appearance~~ *your traditions*, but judge righteous judgment.

7:25 Then said some of them of Jerusalem, Is not this he, whom they seek to kill?

7:26 But, lo, he speaketh boldly, and they say nothing unto him. Do the rulers know indeed that this is the very Christ?

7:27 Howbeit we know this man whence he is: but when Christ cometh, no man knoweth whence he is.

7:28 Then cried Jesus in the temple as he taught, saying, Ye both know me, and ye know whence I am: and I am not come of myself, but he that sent me is true, whom ye know not.

7:29 But I know him: for I am from him, and he hath sent me.

7:30 Then they sought to take him: but no man laid hands on him, because his hour was not yet come.

7:31 And many of the people believed on him, and said, When Christ cometh, will he do more miracles than these which this man hath done?

7:32 The Pharisees heard that the people murmured such things concerning him; and the Pharisees and the chief priests sent officers to take him.

7:33 Then said Jesus unto them, Yet a little while ~~am~~ I *am* with you, and then I go unto him that sent me.

7:34 Ye shall seek me, and shall not find me: and where I am, thither ye cannot come.

7:35 Then said the Jews among themselves, Whither will he go, that we shall not find him? will he go unto the dispersed among the Gentiles, and teach the Gentiles?

7:36 What manner of saying is this that he said, Ye shall seek me, and shall not find me: and where I am, thither ye cannot come?

MATTHEW	MARK	LUKE	JOHN

F-6. CROWDS DEBATE ABOUT JESUS

7:37 In the last day, that great day of the feast, Jesus stood and cried, saying, If any man thirst, let him come unto me, and drink.

7:38 He that believeth on me, as the scripture hath said, out of his belly shall flow rivers of living water.

7:39 (But this spake he of the Spirit, which they that believe on him should receive: for the Holy Ghost was ~~not yet given; because that Jesus was not yet glorified~~ *promised unto them who believe, after that Jesus was glorified*.)

7:40 Many of the people therefore, when they heard this saying, said, Of a truth this is the Prophet.

7:41 Others said, This is the Christ. But some said, Shall Christ come out of Galilee?

7:42 Hath not the scripture said, That Christ cometh of the seed of David, and out of the town of Bethlehem, where David was?

7:43 So there was a division among the people because of him.

7:44 And some of them would have taken him; but no man laid hands on him.

7:45 Then came the officers to the chief priests and Pharisees; and they said unto them, Why have ye not brought him?

7:46 The officers answered, Never man spake like this man.

7:47 Then answered them the Pharisees, Are ye also deceived?

7:48 Have any of the rulers or of the Pharisees believed on him?

7:49 But this people who knoweth not the law are cursed.

7:50 Nicodemus saith unto them, (he that came to Jesus by night, being one of them,)

7:51 Doth our law judge any man, before it hear him, and know what he doeth?

7:52 They answered and said unto him, Art thou also of Galilee? Search, and look: for out of Galilee ariseth no prophet.

7:53 And every man went unto his own house.

F-7. WOMAN CAUGHT IN ADULTERY

8:1 *And* Jesus went unto the mount of Olives.

8:2 ~~And~~ early in the morning he came again into the temple, and all the people came unto him; and he sat down, and taught them.

8:3 And the scribes and Pharisees brought unto him a woman taken in adultery; and when they had set her in the midst *of the people*,

8:4 They say unto him, Master, this woman was taken in adultery, in the very act.

8:5 Now Moses in the law commanded us, that such should be stoned: but what sayest thou?

8:6 This they said, tempting him, that they might have to accuse him. But Jesus stooped down, and with his finger wrote on the ground, as though he heard them not.

8:7 So when they continued asking him, he lifted up himself, and said unto them, He that is without sin among you, let him first cast a stone at her.

8:8 And again he stooped down, and wrote on the ground.

8:9 And they which heard it, being convicted by their own conscience, went out one by one, beginning at the eldest, even unto the last: and Jesus was left alone, and the woman standing in the midst *of the temple*.

8:10 When Jesus had ~~lifted~~ *raised* up himself, and saw none ~~but the woman~~ *of her accusers, and the woman standing*, he said unto her, Woman, where are those thine accusers? hath no man condemned thee?

8:11 She said, No man, Lord. And Jesus said unto her, Neither do I condemn thee: go, and sin no more. *And the woman glorified God from that hour, and believed on his name.*

F-8. JESUS TESTIFIES OF HIMSELF

8:12 Then spake Jesus again unto them, saying, I am the light of the world: he that followeth me shall not walk in darkness, but shall have the light of life.

8:13 The Pharisees therefore said unto him, Thou bearest record of thyself; thy record is not true.

8:14 Jesus answered and said unto them, Though I bear record of myself, yet my record is true: for I know whence I came, and whither I go; but ye cannot tell whence I come, and whither I go.

8:15 Ye judge after the flesh; I judge no man.

8:16 And yet if I judge, my judgment is true: for I am not alone, but I and the Father that sent me.

8:17 It is also written in your law, that the testimony of two men is true.

8:18 I am one that bear witness of myself, and the Father that sent me

MATTHEW	MARK	LUKE	JOHN

beareth witness of me.

8:19 Then said they unto him, Where is thy Father? Jesus answered, Ye neither know me, nor my Father: if ye had known me, ye should have known my Father also.

8:20 These words spake Jesus in the treasury, as he taught in the temple: and no man laid hands on him; for his hour was not yet come.

8:21 Then said Jesus again unto them, I go my way, and ye shall seek me, and shall die in your sins: whither I go, ye cannot come.

8:22 Then said the Jews, Will he kill himself? because he saith, Whither I go, ye cannot come.

8:23 And he said unto them, Ye are from beneath; I am from above: ye are of this world; I am not of this world.

8:24 I said therefore unto you, that ye shall die in your sins: for if ye believe not that I am he, ye shall die in your sins.

8:25 Then said they unto him, Who art thou? And Jesus saith unto them, Even the same that I said unto you from the beginning.

8:26 I have many things to say and to judge of you: but he that sent me is true; and I speak to the world those things which I have heard of him.

8:27 They understood not that he spake to them of the Father.

8:28 Then said Jesus unto them, When ye have lifted up the Son of man, then shall ye know that I am he, and that I do nothing of myself; but as my Father hath taught me, I speak these things.

8:29 And he that sent me is with me: the Father hath not left me alone; for I do always those things that please him.

8:30 As he spake these words, many believed on him.

F-9. WHO IS ABRAHAM'S SEED?

8:31 Then said Jesus to those Jews which believed on him, If ye continue in my word, then are ye my disciples indeed;

8:32 And ye shall know the truth, and the truth shall make you free.

8:33 They answered him, We be Abraham's seed, and were never in bondage to any man: how sayest thou, Ye shall be made free?

8:34 Jesus answered them, Verily, verily, I say unto you, Whosoever committeth sin is the servant of sin.

8:35 And the servant abideth not in the house for ever: but the Son abideth ever.

MATTHEW	MARK	LUKE	JOHN

8:36 If the Son therefore shall make you free, ye shall be free indeed.

8:37 I know that ye are Abraham's seed; but ye seek to kill me, because my word hath no place in you.

8:38 I speak that which I have seen with my Father: and ye do that which ye have seen with your father.

8:39 They answered and said unto him, Abraham is our father. Jesus saith unto them, If ye were Abraham's children, ye would do the works of Abraham.

8:40 But now ye seek to kill me, a man that hath told you the truth, which I have heard of God: this did not Abraham.

8:41 Ye do the deeds of your father. Then said they to him, We be not born of fornication; we have one Father, even God.

8:42 Jesus said unto them, If God were your Father, ye would love me: for I proceeded forth and came from God; neither came I of myself, but he sent me.

8:43 Why do ye not understand my speech? even because ye cannot ~~hear~~ *bear* my word.

8:44 Ye are of your father the devil, and the lusts of your father ye will do. He was a murderer from the beginning, and abode not in the truth, because there is no truth in him. When he speaketh a lie, he speaketh of his own: for he is a liar, and the father of it.

8:45 And because I tell you the truth, ye believe me not.

8:46 Which of you convinceth me of sin? And if I say the truth, why do ye not believe me?

8:47 He that is of God ~~heareth~~ *receiveth* God's words: ye therefore ~~hear~~ *receive* them not, because ye are not of God.

8:48 Then answered the Jews, and said unto him, Say we not well that thou art a Samaritan, and hast a devil?

8:49 Jesus answered, I have not a devil; but I honour my Father, and ye do dishonour me.

8:50 And I seek not mine own glory: there is one that seeketh and judgeth.

8:51 Verily, verily, I say unto you, If a man keep my saying, he shall never see death.

8:52 Then said the Jews unto him, Now we know that thou hast a devil. Abraham is dead, and the prophets; and thou sayest, If a man keep my saying, he shall never taste of death.

8:53 Art thou greater than our father Abraham, which is dead?

MATTHEW	MARK	LUKE	JOHN

and the prophets are dead: whom makest thou thyself?

8:54 Jesus answered, If I honour myself, my honour is nothing: it is my Father that honoureth me; of whom ye say, that he is your God:

8:55 Yet ye have not known him; but I know him: and if I should say, I know him not, I shall be a liar like unto you: but I know him, and keep his saying.

8:56 Your father Abraham rejoiced to see my day: and he saw it, and was glad.

8:57 Then said the Jews unto him, Thou art not yet fifty years old, and hast thou seen Abraham?

8:58 Jesus said unto them, Verily, verily, I say unto you, Before Abraham was, I am.

8:59 Then took they up stones to cast at him: but Jesus hid himself, and went out of the temple, going through the midst of them, and so passed by.

F-10. JESUS HEALS A MAN BLIND SINCE BIRTH

9:1 And as Jesus passed by, he saw a man which was blind from his birth.

9:2 And his disciples asked him, saying, Master, who did sin, this man, or his parents, that he was born blind?

9:3 Jesus answered, Neither hath this man sinned, nor his parents: but that the works of God should be made manifest in him.

9:4 I must work the works of him that sent me, while ~~it is day: the night cometh, when no man can work~~ *I am with you; the time cometh when I shall have finished my work, then I go unto the Father*.

9:5 As long as I am in the world, I am the light of the world.

9:6 When he had thus spoken, he spat on the ground, and made clay of the spittle, and he anointed the eyes of the blind man with the clay,

9:7 And said unto him, Go, wash in the pool of Siloam, (which is by interpretation, Sent.) He went his way therefore, and washed, and came seeing.

9:8 The ~~neighbours~~ *neighbors* therefore, and they which before had seen him that he was blind, said, Is not this he that sat and begged?

9:9 Some said, This is he: others said, He is like him: but he said, I am he.

9:10 Therefore said they unto him, How were thine eyes opened?

9:11 He answered and said, A man that is called Jesus made clay,

MATTHEW	MARK	LUKE	JOHN

and anointed mine eyes, and said unto me, Go to the pool of Siloam, and wash: and I went and washed, and I received sight.

9:12 Then said they unto him, Where is he? He said, I know not.

9:13 *And* They brought *him who had been blind* to the Pharisees ~~him that aforetime was blind~~.

9:14 And it was the sabbath day when Jesus made the clay, and opened his eyes.

9:15 Then again the Pharisees also asked him how he had received his sight. He said unto them, He put clay upon mine eyes, and I washed, and do see.

9:16 Therefore said some of the Pharisees, This man is not of God, because he keepeth not the sabbath day. Others said, How can a man that is a sinner do such miracles? And there was a division among them.

9:17 They say unto the blind man again, What sayest thou of him, ~~that he~~ *who* hath opened thine eyes? He said, He is a prophet.

9:18 But the Jews did not believe concerning him, that he had been blind, and received his sight, until they called the parents of him that had received his sight.

9:19 And they asked them, saying, Is this your son, who ye say was born blind? how then doth he now see?

9:20 His parents answered them and said, We know that this is our son, and that he was born blind:

9:21 But by what means he now seeth, we know not; or who hath opened his eyes, we know not: he is of age; ask him: he shall speak for himself.

9:22 These words spake his parents, because they feared the Jews: for the Jews had agreed already, that if any man did confess that he was Christ, he should be put out of the synagogue.

9:23 Therefore said his parents, He is of age; ask him.

9:24 Then again called they the man that was blind, and said unto him, Give God the praise: we know that this man is a sinner.

9:25 He answered and said, Whether he be a sinner or no, I know not: one thing I know, that, whereas I was blind, now I see.

9:26 Then said they to him again, What did he to thee? how opened he thine eyes?

9:27 He answered them, I have told you already, and ye did not ~~hear~~ *believe*: wherefore would ye ~~hear it~~ *believe if I should tell you* again? ~~will ye also~~ *And would you* be his disciples?

MATTHEW	MARK	LUKE	JOHN

9:28 Then they reviled him, and said, Thou art his disciple; but we are Moses' disciples.

9:29 We know that God spake unto Moses: as for this ~~fellow~~ *man*, we know not from whence he is.

9:30 The man answered and said unto them, Why herein is a marvellous thing, that ye know not from whence he is, and yet he hath opened mine eyes.

9:31 Now we know that God heareth not sinners: but if any man be a worshipper of God, and doeth his will, him he heareth.

9:32 Since the world began was it not heard that any man opened the eyes of one that was born blind, *except he be of God*.

9:33 If this man were not of God, he could do nothing.

9:34 They answered and said unto him, Thou wast altogether born in sins, and dost thou teach us? And they cast him out.

9:35 Jesus heard that they had cast him out; and when he had found him, he said unto him, Dost thou believe on the Son of God?

9:36 He answered and said, Who is he, Lord, that I might believe on him?

9:37 And Jesus said unto him, Thou hast both seen him, and it is he that talketh with thee.

9:38 And he said, Lord, I believe. And he worshipped him.

9:39 And Jesus said, For judgment I am come into this world, that they which see not might see; and that they which see might be made blind.

9:40 And some of the Pharisees which were with him heard these words, and said unto him, Are we blind also?

9:41 Jesus said unto them, If ye were blind, ye should have no sin: but now ye say, We see; therefore your sin remaineth.

F-11. JESUS IS THE GOOD SHEPHERD

10:1 Verily, verily, I say unto you, He that entereth not by the door into the sheepfold, but climbeth up some other way, the same is a thief and a robber.

10:2 But he that entereth in by the door is the shepherd of the sheep.

10:3 To him the porter openeth; and the sheep hear his voice: and he calleth his own sheep by name, and leadeth them out.

10:4 And when he putteth forth his own sheep, he goeth before them, and the sheep follow him: for they know his voice.

10:5 And a stranger will they not

MATTHEW	MARK	LUKE	JOHN

follow, but will flee from him: for they know not the voice of strangers.

10:6 This parable spake Jesus unto them: but they understood not what things they were which he spake unto them.

10:7 Then said Jesus unto them again, Verily, verily, I say unto you, I am the door of the sheep*fold*.

10:8 All that ever came before me *who testified not of me* are thieves and robbers: but the sheep did not hear them.

10:9 I am the door: by me if any man enter in, he shall be saved, and shall go in and out, and find pasture.

10:10 The thief cometh not, but for to steal, and to kill, and to destroy: I am come that they might have life, and that they might have it more abundantly.

10:11 I am the good shepherd: the good shepherd giveth his life for ~~the~~ *his* sheep.

10:12 ~~But he that is an hireling, and not the shepherd~~ *And the shepherd is not as a hireling*, whose own the sheep are not, *who* seeth the wolf coming, and leaveth the sheep, and fleeth: and the wolf catcheth ~~them,~~ *the sheep* and scattereth ~~the sheep~~ *them*.

10:14 *For* I am the good shepherd, and know my sheep, and am known of mine.

10:13 ~~The~~ *But he who is a* hireling fleeth, because he is ~~an~~ hireling, and careth not for the sheep. (*verse 13 & 14 order changed by JST*)

10:15 As the Father knoweth me, even so know I the Father: and I lay down my life for the sheep.

10:16 And other sheep I have, which are not of this fold: them also I must bring, and they shall hear my voice; and there shall be one fold, and one shepherd.

10:17 Therefore doth my Father love me, because I lay down my life, that I might take it again.

10:18 No man taketh it from me, but I lay it down of myself. I have power to lay it down, and I have power to take it again. This commandment have I received of my Father.

10:19 There was a division therefore again among the Jews for these sayings.

10:20 And many of them said, He hath a devil, and is mad; why hear ye him?

10:21 Others said, These are not the words of him that hath a devil. Can a devil open the eyes of the blind?

F-12. PARABLE OF THE GOOD SAMARITAN

10:25 And, behold, a certain lawyer stood up, and tempted him, saying, Master, what shall I do to inherit eternal life?

10:26 He said unto him, What is written in the law? how readest thou?

10:27 And he answering said, Thou shalt love the Lord thy God with all thy heart, and with all thy soul, and with all thy strength, and with all thy mind; and thy ~~neighbour~~ *neighbor* as thyself.

10:28 And he said unto him, Thou hast answered right: this do, and thou shalt live.

10:29 But he, willing to justify himself, said unto Jesus, And who is my ~~neighbour~~ *neighbor*?

10:30 And Jesus answering said, A certain man went down from Jerusalem to Jericho, and fell among thieves, ~~which~~ *who* stripped him of his raiment, and wounded him, and departed, leaving him half dead.

10:31 And by chance there came down a certain priest that way: and when he saw him, he passed by on the other side *of the way*.

10:32 And likewise a Levite, when he was at the place, came and looked *up*on him, and passed by on the other side *of the way; for they desired in their hearts that it might not be known that they had seen him*.

10:33 But a certain Samaritan, as he journeyed, came where he was: and when he saw him, he had compassion on him,

10:34 And went to him, and bound up his wounds, pouring in oil and wine, and set him on his own beast, and brought him to an inn, and took care of him.

10:35 And on the morrow when he departed, he took ~~out two pence~~ *money*, and gave ~~them~~ to the host, and said unto him, Take care of him; and whatsoever thou spendest more, when I come again, I will repay thee.

10:36 ~~Which~~ *Who* now of these three, thinkest thou, was ~~neighbour~~ *neighbor* unto him that fell among the thieves?

10:37 And he said, He ~~that shewed~~ *who showed* mercy on him. Then said Jesus unto him, Go, and do ~~thou~~ likewise.

MATTHEW	MARK	LUKE	JOHN

F-13. MARY AND MARTHA

10:38 Now it came to pass, as they went, ~~that he~~ *they* entered into a certain village: and a certain woman named Martha received him into her house.

10:39 And she had a sister called Mary, which also sat at Jesus' feet, and heard his word*s*.

10:40 But Martha was cumbered about much serving, and came to him, and said, Lord, dost thou not care that my sister hath left me to serve alone? bid her therefore that she help me.

10:41 And Jesus answered and said unto her, Martha, Martha, thou art careful and troubled about many things:

10:42 But one thing is needful: and Mary hath chosen that good part, which shall not be taken away from her.

F-14. THE LORD'S PRAYER

11:1 And it came to pass, ~~that, as he~~ *as Jesus* was praying in a certain place, when he ceased, one of his disciples said unto him, Lord, teach us to pray, as John also taught his disciples.

11:2 And he said unto them, When ye pray, say, Our Father ~~which~~ *who* art in heaven, Hallowed be thy name. Thy kingdom come. Thy will be done, as in heaven, so in earth.

11:3 Give us day by day our daily bread.

11:4 And forgive us our sins; for we also forgive every one that is indebted to us. And ~~lead us not into~~ *let us not be led unto* temptation; but deliver us from evil. *For thine is the kingdom and power. Amen.*

11:5 And he said unto them, *Your heavenly Father will not fail to give unto you whatsoever ye ask of him. And he spake a parable, saying,* Which of you shall have a friend, and shall go unto him at midnight, and say unto him, Friend, lend me three loaves;

11:6 For a friend of mine *has come to me* in his journey ~~is come to me~~, and I have nothing to set before him?

11:7 And he from within shall answer and say, Trouble me not: the door is now shut, and my children are with me in bed; I cannot rise and give thee.

11:8 I say unto you, Though he will not rise and give him, because he is his friend, yet because of his importunity he will rise and give him as many as he needeth.

11:9 And I say unto you, Ask, and it shall be given you; seek, and ye shall find; knock, and it shall be opened unto you.

11:10 For every one ~~that~~ *who* asketh receiveth; and he that seeketh findeth; and to him that knocketh it shall be opened.

11:11 If a son shall ask bread of any of you ~~that~~ *who* is a father, will he give him a stone? or if ~~he ask~~ a fish, will he for a fish give him a serpent?

11:12 Or if he shall ask an egg, will he offer him a scorpion?

11:13 If ye then, being evil, know how to give good gifts unto your children: how much more shall your heavenly Father give *good gifts, through* the Holy Spirit to them ~~that~~ *who* ask him?

F-15. ACCUSED AGAIN OF CASTING OUT DEVILS BY BEELZEBUB

11:14 And he was casting ~~out~~ a devil *out of a man*, and ~~it~~ *he* was dumb. And it came to pass, when the devil was gone out, the dumb spake; and the people wondered.

11:15 But some of them said, He casteth out devils through Beelzebub the chief of the devils.

11:16 And others, tempting ~~him~~, sought of him a sign from heaven.

11:17 But he, knowing their thoughts, said unto them, Every kingdom divided against itself is brought to desolation; and a house divided ~~against a house~~ *cannot stand, but* falleth.

11:18 If Satan also be divided against himself, how ~~shall~~ *can* his kingdom stand? *I say this,* because ~~ye~~ *you* say that I cast out devils through Beelzebub.

11:19 And if I by Beelzebub cast out devils, by whom do your sons cast ~~them~~ out *devils*? therefore shall they be your judges.

11:20 But if I with the finger of God cast out devils, no doubt the kingdom of God is come upon you.

11:21 When a strong man armed keepeth his palace, his goods are in peace:

11:22 But when a stronger than he shall come upon him, and overcome him, he taketh from him all his armour wherein he trusted, and divideth his ~~spoils~~ *goods*.

11:23 He that is not with me is against me: and he ~~that~~ *who* gathereth not with me scattereth.

11:24 When the unclean spirit is gone out of a man, ~~he~~ *it* walketh through dry places, seeking rest;

and finding none, ~~he~~ *it* saith, I will return unto ~~my~~ *mine* house whence I came out.

11:25 And when ~~he~~ *it* cometh, ~~he~~ *it* findeth ~~it~~ *the house* swept and garnished.

11:26 Then goeth ~~he~~ *the evil spirit*, and taketh ~~to him~~ seven other spirits more wicked than himself; and they enter in, and dwell there: and the last ~~state~~ *end* of that man is worse than the first.

11:27 And it came to pass, as he spake these things, a certain woman of the company lifted up her voice, and said unto him, Blessed is the womb ~~that~~ *which* bare thee, and the paps which thou hast sucked.

11:28 ~~But~~ *And* he said, Yea ~~rather~~, *and* blessed are *all* they ~~that~~ *who* hear the word of God, and keep it.

11:29 ~~And~~ when the people were gathered thick together, he began to say, This is an evil generation: they seek a sign; and there shall no sign be given ~~it~~ *them*, but the sign of Jonas the prophet.

11:30 For as Jonas was a sign unto the Ninevites, so *also* shall ~~also~~ the Son of ~~m~~*M*an be to this generation.

11:31 The queen of the south shall rise up in the *day of* judgment with the men of this generation, and condemn them: for she came from the utmost parts of the earth to hear the wisdom of Solomon; and, behold, a greater than Solomon is here.

11:32 The men of ~~Nineve~~ *Nineveh* shall rise up in the *day of* judgment with this generation, and shall condemn it: for they repented at the preaching of Jonas; and, behold, a greater than Jonas is here.

11:33 No man, when he hath lighted a candle, putteth it in a secret place, neither under a bushel, but on a candlestick, that they ~~which~~ *who* come in may see the light.

11:34 The light of the body is the eye: therefore when thine eye is single, thy whole body also is full of light; but when thine eye is evil, thy body also is full of darkness.

11:35 Take heed therefore that the light which is in thee be not darkness.

11:36 If thy whole body therefore ~~be~~ *is* full of light, having no part dark, the whole shall be full of light, as when the bright shining of a candle *lighteneth a room and* doth give ~~thee~~ *the* light *in all the room*.

F-16. REBUKES PHARISEES, SCRIBES AND LAWYERS FOR HYPOCRISY

11:37 And as he spake, a certain Pharisee besought him to dine with him: and he went in, and sat down to meat.

11:38 And when the Pharisee saw ~~it~~ *him*, he marvelled that he had not first washed before dinner.

11:39 And the Lord said unto him, Now do ~~ye~~ *you* Pharisees make clean the outside of the cup and the platter; but your inward part is full of ravening and wickedness.

11:40 ~~Ye~~ *O* fools, did not he ~~that~~ *who* made that which is without make that which is within also?

11:41 But *if ye would* rather give alms of such things as ye have; and, ~~behold, all things are clean unto you~~ *observe to do all things which I have commanded you, then would your inner parts be clean also*.

11:42 But *I say unto you,* woe *be* unto you, Pharisees! for ye tithe mint and rue and all manner of herbs, and pass over judgment and the love of God: these ought ye to have done, and not to leave the other undone.

11:43 Woe unto you, Pharisees! for ye love the uppermost seats in the synagogues, and greetings in the markets.

11:44 Woe unto you, scribes and Pharisees, hypocrites! for ye are as graves which appear not, and the men ~~that~~ *who* walk over ~~them~~ are not aware of them.

11:45 Then answered one of the lawyers, and said unto him, Master, thus saying thou reproachest us also.

11:46 And he said, Woe unto you ~~also, ye~~ lawyers*, also*! for ye lade men with burdens grievous to be borne, and ye yourselves touch not the burdens with one of your fingers.

11:47 Woe unto you! for ~~ye~~ *you* build the sepulchres of the prophets, and your fathers killed them.

11:48 Truly ye bear witness that ye allow the deeds of your fathers: for they indeed killed them, and ye build their sepulchres.

11:49 Therefore also said the wisdom of God, I will send them prophets and apostles, and some of them they shall slay and persecute:

11:50 That the blood of all the prophets, which was shed from the foundation of the world, may be required of this generation;

11:51 From the blood of Abel unto the blood of Zacharias, ~~which~~ *who* perished between the altar and

MATTHEW	MARK	LUKE	JOHN

the temple: verily I say unto you, It shall be required of this generation.

11:52 Woe unto you, lawyers! for ye have taken away the key of knowledge, *the fulness of the scriptures*: ye entered not in yourselves *into the kingdom*, and them that *those who* were entering in ye hindered.

11:53 And as he said these things unto them, the scribes and the Pharisees began to *be angry, and to* urge him vehemently, and *endeavoring* to provoke him to speak of many things:

11:54 Laying wait for him, and seeking to catch something out of his mouth, that they might accuse him.

F-17. WARNS TO BEWARE OF THE PHARISEES

12:1 In the mean time, when there were gathered together an innumerable multitude of people, insomuch that they trode one upon another, he began to say unto his disciples first of all, Beware ye of the leaven of the Pharisees, which is hypocrisy.

12:2 For there is nothing covered, that *which* shall not be revealed; neither hid, that *which* shall not be known.

12:3 Therefore whatsoever ye have spoken in darkness shall be heard in the light; and that which ye have spoken in the ear in closets shall be proclaimed upon the housetops.

12:4 And I say unto you my friends, Be not afraid of them that *who* kill the body, and after that have no more that they can do.

12:5 But I will forewarn you whom ye shall fear: Fear him, which *who* after he hath killed hath power to cast into hell; yea, I say unto you, Fear him.

12:6 Are not five sparrows sold for two farthings, and not one of them is forgotten before God?

12:7 But even the very hairs of your head are all numbered. Fear not therefore: ye are of more value than many sparrows.

12:8 Also I say unto you, Whosoever shall confess me before men, him shall the Son of man also confess before the angels of God:

12:9 But he that *who* denieth me before men, shall be denied before the angels of God.

12:10 *Now his disciples knew that he said this, because they had spoken evil against him before the people; for they were afraid to confess him before men. And they reasoned among themselves, saying, He knoweth our hearts, and he speaketh to our condemnation, and we shall not be forgiven. But he answered them, and said unto them,* ~~And~~ whosoever shall speak a word against the Son of ~~m~~*M*an, *and repenteth,* it shall be forgiven him: but unto him ~~that~~ *who* blasphemeth against the Holy Ghost, it shall not be forgiven *him*.

12:11 And *again I say unto you,* ~~when~~ they *shall* bring you unto the synagogues, and ~~unto~~ *before* magistrates, and powers, *When they do this,* take ye no thought how or what thing ye shall answer, or what ye shall say:

12:12 For the Holy Ghost shall teach you in the same hour what ye ought to say.

F-18. PARABLE OF THE RICH FOOL

12:13 And one of the company said unto him, Master, speak to my brother, that he divide the inheritance with me.

12:14 And he said unto him, Man, who made me a judge or a divider over you?

12:15 And he said unto them, Take heed, and beware of covetousness: for a man's life consisteth not in the abundance of the things which he possesseth.

12:16 And he spake a parable unto them, saying, The ground of a certain rich man brought forth plentifully:

12:17 And he thought within himself, saying, What shall I do, because I have no room where to bestow my fruits?

12:18 And he said, This will I do: I will pull down my barns, and build greater; and there will I bestow all my fruits and my goods.

12:19 And I will say to my soul, Soul, thou hast much goods laid up for many years; take thine ease, eat, drink, and be merry.

12:20 But God said unto him, Thou fool, this night thy soul shall be required of thee: then whose shall those things be, which thou hast provided?

12:21 So ~~is he that~~ *shall it be with him who* layeth up treasure for himself, and is not rich toward God.

F-19. DISCIPLES TO SEEK FIRST THE KINGDOM OF GOD

12:22 And he said unto his disciples, Therefore I say unto you, Take no thought for your life, what ye shall eat; neither for the body,

MATTHEW	MARK	LUKE	JOHN

what ye shall put on.

12:23 *For* The life is more than meat, and the body ~~is more~~ than raiment.

12:24 Consider the ravens: for they neither sow nor reap; which neither have storehouse nor barn; ~~and~~ *nevertheless* God feedeth them: ~~how much more~~ are ye *not* better than the fowls?

12:25 And ~~which~~ *who* of you ~~with~~ *by* taking thought can add to his stature one cubit?

12:26 If ye then be not able to do that ~~thing~~ which is least, why take ye thought for the rest?

12:27 Consider the lilies how they grow: they toil not, they spin not; and yet I say unto you, that Solomon in all his glory was not arrayed like one of these.

12:28 If then God so clothe the grass, which is to day in the field, and to morrow is cast ~~into~~ the oven; how much more will he ~~clothe~~ *provide for* you, ~~O ye~~ *if ye are not* of little faith?

12:29 ~~And~~ *Therefore,* seek not ye what ye shall eat, or what ye shall drink, neither be ye of doubtful mind.

12:30 For all these things do the nations of the world seek after: and your Father *who is in heaven,* knoweth that ye have need of these things. *And ye are sent unto them to be their ministers, and the laborer is worthy of his hire; for the law saith, That a man shall not muzzle the ox that treadeth out the corn.*

12:31 ~~But rather~~ *Therefore* seek ye *to bring forth* the kingdom of God; and all these things shall be added unto you.

12:32 Fear not, little flock; for it is your Father's good pleasure to give you the kingdom.

12:33 *This he spake unto his disciples, saying,* Sell that ye have, and give alms; provide *not for* yourselves bags which wax ~~not~~ old, *but rather* a treasure in the heavens that faileth not, where no thief approacheth, neither moth corrupteth.

12:34 For where your treasure is, there will your heart be also.

F-20. COUNSELS TO ALWAYS BE PREPARED FOR THE SECOND COMING

12:35 Let your loins be girded about, and *have* your lights burning;

12:36 ~~And~~ *That* ye yourselves *may be* like unto men ~~that~~ *who* wait for their ‖Lord, when he will return from the wedding; that when he cometh and knocketh, they may open unto him immediately.

MATTHEW	MARK	LUKE	JOHN

12:37 *Verily, I say unto you,* Blessed are those servants, whom the ~~l~~Lord when he cometh shall find watching: ~~verily I say unto you, that~~ *for* he shall gird himself, and make them to sit down to meat, and will come forth and serve them.

12:38 ~~And if~~ *For, behold, he cometh in the first watch of the night, and he shall also come in the second watch, and again he shall come in the third watch. And verily I say unto you, He hath already come, as it is written of him; and again when* he shall come in the second watch, or come in the third watch, ~~and find them so,~~ blessed are those servants *when he cometh, that he shall find so doing; For the Lord of those servants shall gird himself, and make them to sit down to meat, and will come forth and serve them. And now, verily I say these things unto you, that ye may know this, that the coming of the Lord is as a thief in the night. And it is like unto a man who is an householder, who, if he watcheth not his goods, the thief cometh in an hour of which he is not aware, and taketh his goods, and divideth them among his fellows.*

12:39 ~~And this know, that~~ *And they said among themselves,* if the goodman of the house had known what hour the thief would come, he would have watched, and not have suffered his house to be broken through *and the loss of his goods.*

12:40 *And he said unto them, Verily I say unto you,* Be ye therefore ready also: for the Son of ~~m~~*M*an cometh at an hour when ye think not.

12:41 Then Peter said unto him, Lord, speakest thou this parable unto us, or ~~even~~ *un*to all?

12:42 And the Lord said, ~~Who then is that faithful and wise steward,~~ *I speak unto those* whom the Lord shall make rulers over his household, to give ~~them~~ *his children* their portion of meat in due season~~?~~ . *And they said, Who then is that faithful and wise servant? And the Lord said unto them, It is that servant who watcheth, to impart his portion of meat in due season.*

12:43 Blessed ~~is~~ *be* that servant, whom his ~~l~~Lord ~~when he cometh~~ shall find, *when he cometh,* so doing.

12:44 Of a truth I say unto you, that he will make him ruler over all that he hath.

12:45 But ~~and if that servant~~ *the evil servant is he who is not found watching. And if that servant is*

MATTHEW	MARK	LUKE	JOHN

not found watching, he will say in his heart, My ~~l~~Lord delayeth his coming; and shall begin to beat the menservants and maidens, and to eat and drink, and to be drunken;

12:46 The ~~l~~Lord of that servant will come in a day ~~when~~ he looketh not for ~~him~~, and at an hour when he is not aware, and will cut him ~~in sunder~~ *down*, and will appoint him his portion with the unbelievers.

12:47 And that servant, ~~which~~ *who* knew his ~~l~~Lord's will, and prepared not ~~himself~~ *for his Lord's coming*, neither did according to his will, shall be beaten with many stripes.

12:48 But he that knew not *his Lord's will*, and did commit things worthy of stripes, shall be beaten with few ~~stripes~~. For unto whomsoever much is given, of him shall ~~be~~ much *be* required: and to whom ~~men have~~ *the Lord has* committed much, of him ~~they~~ will *men* ask the more.

12:49 *For they are not well pleased with the Lord's doings; therefore* I am come to send fire on the earth; and what *is it to you,* ~~will I if~~ *if I will that* it be already kindled?

12:50 But I have a baptism to be baptized with; and how am I ~~straitened till~~ *straightened until* it be accomplished!

12:51 Suppose ye that I am come to give peace on earth? I tell you, Nay; but rather division:

12:52 For from henceforth there shall be five in one house divided, three against two, and two against three.

12:53 The father shall be divided against the son, and the son against the father; the mother against the daughter, and the daughter against the mother; the mother in law against her daughter in law, and the daughter in law against her mother in law.

12:54 And he said also *un*to the people, When ye see a cloud rise out of the west, ~~straightway~~ ye say *straightway*, There cometh a shower; and so it is.

12:55 And when ~~ye see~~ the south wind blow*s*, ye say, There will be heat; and it cometh to pass.

12:56 ~~Ye~~ *O* hypocrites, ye can discern the face of the sky and of the earth; but how is it that ye do not discern this time?

12:57 Yea, and why even of yourselves judge ye not what is right?

12:58 ~~When thou goest with thine adversary to the magistrate, as thou art in the way,~~ *Why goest thou to thine adversary for a magistrate, when thou art in the way with thine enemy?* *Why not* give diligence that thou mayest be delivered from him; lest he hale thee to the judge, and the judge deliver thee to the officer, and the officer cast thee into prison.

12:59 I tell thee, thou shalt not depart thence, till thou hast paid the very last mite.

F-21. CALL TO REPENTANCE

13:1 *And* There were present at that ~~season~~ *time,* some ~~that told~~ *who spake unto* him of the ~~Galilaeans~~ *Galileans*, whose blood Pilate had mingled with their sacrifices.

13:2 And Jesus ~~answering~~ said unto them, Suppose ye that these ~~Galilaeans~~ *Galileans* were sinners above all the ~~Galilaeans~~ *Galileans*, because they suffered such things?

13:3 I tell you, Nay: but, except ye repent, ye shall all likewise perish.

13:4 Or those eighteen, upon whom the tower in Siloam fell, and slew them, think ye that they were sinners above all men ~~that~~ *who* dwelt in Jerusalem?

13:5 I tell you, Nay: but, except ye repent, ye shall all likewise perish.

F-22. PARABLE OF THE BARREN FIG TREE

13:6 He spake also this parable; A certain *husband*man had a fig tree planted in ~~his~~ *the* vineyard; ~~and~~ he came and sought fruit thereon, and found none.

13:7 Then said he unto the dresser of his vineyard, Behold, these three years I come seeking fruit on this fig tree, and find none: cut it down; why cumbereth it the ground?

13:8 And he answering said unto him, Lord, let it alone this year also, till I shall dig about it, and dung it:

13:9 And if it bear fruit, ~~well~~ *the tree is saved*: and if not, ~~then~~ after that thou shalt cut it down. *And many other parables spake he unto the people.*

F-23. A WOMAN IS HEALED ON THE SABBATH

13:10 And *after this, as* he was teaching in one of the synagogues on the ~~s~~*S*abbath.

13:11 ~~And,~~ behold, there was a woman ~~which~~ *who* had a spirit of infirmity eighteen years, and was bowed together, and could in no

MATTHEW	MARK	LUKE	JOHN

wise ~~lift up herself~~ *straighten up*.

13:12 And when Jesus saw her, he called ~~her to him,~~ and said unto her, Woman, thou art loosed from thine ~~infirmity~~ *infirmities*.

13:13 And he laid ~~his~~ hands on her: and immediately she was made straight, and glorified God.

13:14 And the ruler of the synagogue ~~answered~~ *was filled* with indignation, because that Jesus had healed on the ~~s~~*S*abbath day, and said unto the people, There are six days in which men ought to work: in them therefore come and be healed, and not on the ~~s~~*S*abbath day.

13:15 The Lord then ~~answered~~ *said unto* him, ~~and said, Thou~~ *O* hypocrite, doth not each one of you on the ~~s~~*S*abbath loose his ox or his ass from the stall, and lead him away to watering?

13:16 And ought not this woman, being a daughter of Abraham, whom Satan hath bound, lo, these eighteen years, be loosed from this bond on the sabbath day?

13:17 And when he had said these things, all his adversaries were ashamed: and all ~~the people~~ *his disciples* rejoiced for all the glorious things ~~that~~ *which* were done by him.

F-24. PARABLE OF THE MUSTARD SEED AND LEAVEN

13:18 Then said he, Unto what is the kingdom of God like? and whereunto shall I resemble it?

13:19 It is like a grain of mustard seed, which a man took, and cast into his garden; and it grew, and waxed a great tree; and the fowls of the air lodged in the branches of it.

13:20 And again he said, Whereunto shall I liken the kingdom of God?

13:21 It is like leaven, which a woman took and hid in three measures of meal, till the whole was leavened.

F-25. THE SEVENTY RETURN

10:17 And the seventy returned again with joy, saying, Lord, even the devils are subject ~~un~~to us through thy name.

10:18 And he said unto them, ~~I beheld Satan~~ as lightning fall*eth* from heaven*, I beheld Satan also falling*.

10:19 Behold, I *will* give unto you power ~~to tread on~~ *over* serpents and scorpions, and over all the power of the enemy: and nothing shall by any

MATTHEW	MARK	LUKE	JOHN

means hurt you.
10:20   Notwithstanding in this rejoice not, that the spirits are subject unto you; but rather rejoice, because your names are written in heaven.

11:25   *And* At that time*, there came a voice out of heaven, and* Jesus answered and said,
I thank thee, O Father, Lord of heaven and earth, because thou hast hid these things from the wise and prudent, and hast revealed them unto babes.

10:21   In that hour Jesus rejoiced in spirit, and said, I thank thee, O Father, Lord of heaven and earth, that thou hast hid these things from ~~the~~ *them who think they are* wise and prudent, and hast revealed them unto babes:
even so, Father; for so it seemed good in thy sight.

11:26   Even so, Father: for so it seemed good in thy sight.
11:27   All things are delivered unto me of my Father: and no man knoweth the Son, but the Father; neither knoweth any man the Father, save the Son, and ~~he to whomsoever the Son will reveal him~~ *they to whom the Son will reveal himself; they shall see the Father also*.

10:22   All things are delivered to me of my Father: and no man knoweth ~~who the Son is, but the Father; and who the Father is, but the Son, and he~~ *that the Son is the Father, and the Father is the Son, but him* to whom the Son will reveal ~~him~~ *it*.

10:23   And he turned him unto his disciples, and said privately, Blessed are the eyes which see the things that ye see:
10:24   For I tell you, that many prophets and kings have desired to see those things which ye see, and have not seen them; and to hear those things which ye hear, and have not heard them.

F-26. FOLLOW JESUS AND FIND REST

11:28   *Then spake Jesus, saying,*
Come unto me, all ye that ~~labour~~ *labor* and are heavy laden, and I will give you rest.
11:29   Take my yoke upon you, and learn of me; for I am meek and lowly in heart: and ye shall find rest unto your souls.
11:30   For my yoke is easy, and my burden is light.

F-27. THE FEAST OF DEDICATION IN JERUSALEM

10:22 And it was at Jerusalem the feast of the dedication, and it was winter.

10:23 And Jesus walked in the temple in Solomon's porch.

10:24 Then came the Jews round about him, and said unto him, How long dost thou make us to doubt? If thou be the Christ, tell us plainly.

10:25 Jesus answered them, I told you, and ye believed not: the works that I do in my Father's name, they bear witness of me.

10:26 But ye believe not, because ye are not of my sheep, as I said unto you.

10:27 My sheep hear my voice, and I know them, and they follow me:

10:28 And I give unto them eternal life; and they shall never perish, neither shall any man pluck them out of my hand.

10:29 My Father, which gave them me, is greater than all; and no man is able to pluck them out of my Father's hand.

10:30 I and my Father are one.

10:31 Then the Jews took up stones again to stone him.

10:32 Jesus answered them, Many good works have I shewed you from my Father; for which of those works do ye stone me?

10:33 The Jews answered him, saying, For a good work we stone thee not; but for blasphemy; and because that thou, being a man, makest thyself God.

10:34 Jesus answered them, Is it not written in your law, I said, Ye are gods?

10:35 If he called them gods, unto whom the word of God came, and the scripture cannot be broken;

10:36 Say ye of him, whom the Father hath sanctified, and sent into the world, Thou blasphemest; because I said, I am the Son of God?

10:37 If I do not the works of my Father, believe me not.

10:38 But if I do, though ye believe not me, believe the works: that ye may know, and believe, that the Father is in me, and I in him.

10:39(a) Therefore they sought again to take him:

MATTHEW	MARK	LUKE	JOHN

F-28. JESUS GOES ACROSS JORDAN TO ESCAPE THE JEWS

10:39(b)   but he escaped out of their hand,

10:40   And went away again beyond Jordan into the place where John at first baptized; and there he abode.

10:41   And many resorted unto him, and said, John did no miracle: but all things that John spake of this man were true.

10:42   And many believed on him there.

MATTHEW	MARK	LUKE	JOHN

G-1. TEACHINGS AT JERUSALEM

13:22 And he went through the cities and villages, teaching, and journeying toward Jerusalem.

G-2. THE FIRST SHALL BE LAST AND THE LAST SHALL BE FIRST

13:23 ~~Then~~ *And there* said one unto him, Lord, are there few *only* that be saved? And he ~~said unto them~~ *answered him, and said,*

13:24 Strive to enter in at the strait gate: for ~~many,~~ I say unto you, ~~will~~ *many shall* seek to enter in, and shall not be able*; for the Lord shall not always strive with man.*

13:25 *Therefore* When once the ~~master~~ *Lord* of the ~~house~~ *kingdom* is risen up, and hath shut ~~to~~ the door *of the kingdom*, ~~and ye begin to~~ *then ye shall* stand without, and ~~to~~ knock at the door, saying, Lord, Lord, open unto us; ~~and he~~ *But the Lord* shall answer and say unto you, ~~I know you not~~ *I will not receive you, for ye know not from* whence ye are.

13:26 Then shall ye begin to say, We have eaten and drunk in thy presence, and thou hast taught in our streets.

13:27 But he shall say, I tell you, ~~I know you not~~ *ye know not from* whence ye are; depart from me, all ~~ye~~ workers of iniquity.

13:28 There shall be weeping and gnashing of teeth *among you*, when ye shall see Abraham, and Isaac, and Jacob, and all the prophets, in the kingdom of God, and you ~~yourselves~~ *are* thrust out.

13:29 And *verily I say unto you,* they shall come from the east, and ~~from~~ the west, and from the north, and ~~from~~ the south, and shall sit down in the kingdom of God.

13:30 And, behold, there are last which shall be first, and there are first which shall be last, *and shall be saved therein*.

G-3. THE LAMENT OVER JERUSALEM

13:31 ~~The same day there came~~ *And as he was thus teaching there came to him* certain of the Pharisees, saying unto him, Get thee out, and depart hence: for Herod will kill thee.

13:32 And he said unto them, Go ye, and tell ~~that fox~~ *Herod*, Behold, I cast out devils, and ~~I~~ do cures to day and to morrow, and the third day I shall be perfected.

13:33 Nevertheless I must walk to

MATTHEW	MARK	LUKE	JOHN

day, and to morrow, and the ~~day following~~ *third day*: for it cannot be that a prophet perish out of Jerusalem.

13:34 *This he spake, signifying of his death. And in this very hour he began to weep over Jerusalem, saying,* O Jerusalem, Jerusalem, ~~which~~ *thou who* killest the prophets, and stonest them ~~that~~ *who* are sent unto thee; how often would I have gathered thy children together, as a hen doth gather her brood under her wings, and ye would not!

13:35 Behold, your house is left unto you desolate: and verily I say unto you, Ye shall not ~~see me, until~~ *know me, until ye have received from the hand of the Lord a just recompense for all your sins; until* the time come when ye shall say, Blessed is he ~~that~~ *who* cometh in the name of the Lord.

G-4. A MAN WITH DROPSY HEALED ON THE SABBATH

14:1 And it came to pass, as he went into the house of one of the chief Pharisees to eat bread on the sabbath day, that they watched him.

14:2 And, behold, there was a certain man before him ~~which~~ *who* had the dropsy.

14:3 And Jesus ~~answering~~ spake unto the lawyers and Pharisees, saying, Is it lawful to heal on the ~~s~~Sabbath day?

14:4 And they held their peace. And he took ~~him~~ *the man*, and healed him, and let him go;

14:5 And ~~answered them, saying~~ *spake unto them again, saying*, Which of you shall have an ass or an ox fallen into a pit, and will not straightway pull him out on the ~~s~~Sabbath day?

14:6 And they could not answer him ~~again~~ to these things.

G-5. PARABLE OF THE WEDDING FEAST

14:7 And he put forth a parable *unto them concerning* those ~~which~~ *who* were bidden *to a wedding*, ~~when he marked~~ *for he knew* how they chose out the chief rooms; *and exalted themselves one above another; wherefore he spake unto them,* saying ~~unto them~~ ,

14:8 When thou art bidden of any man to a wedding, sit not down in the highest room; lest a more honourable man than thou be bidden of him;

14:9 And he ~~that~~ *who* bade thee, ~~and~~ *with* him *who is more honorable,* come and say to thee,

Give this man place; and thou begin with shame to take the lowest room.

14:10 But when thou art bidden, go and sit down in the lowest room; that when he ~~that~~ *who* bade thee cometh, he may say unto thee, Friend, go up higher: then shalt thou have ~~worship~~ *honor of God,* in the presence of them ~~that~~ *who* sit at meat with thee.

14:11 For whosoever exalteth himself shall be abased; and he ~~that~~ *who* humbleth himself shall be exalted.

G-6. PARABLE OF THE GREAT SUPPER

14:12 Then said he also ~~to him that bade him~~ *concerning him who bade to the wedding*, When thou makest a dinner or a supper, call not thy friends, nor thy brethren, neither thy kinsmen, nor ~~thy~~ rich ~~neighbours~~ *neighbors*; lest they also bid thee again, and a recompence be made thee.

14:13 But when thou makest a feast, call the poor, the maimed, the lame, the blind:

14:14 And thou shalt be blessed; for they cannot recompense thee: for thou shalt be recompensed at the resurrection of the just.

14:15 And when one of them ~~that~~ *who* sat at meat with him heard these things, he said unto him, Blessed is he ~~that~~ *who* shall eat bread in the kingdom of God.

14:16 Then said he unto him, A certain man made a great supper, and bade many:

14:17 And sent his servant at supper time to say to them ~~that~~ *who* were bidden, Come; for all things are now ready.

14:18 And they all with one consent began to make excuse. The first said unto him, I have bought a piece of ground, and I must needs go and see it: I pray thee have me excused.

14:19 And another said, I have bought five yoke of oxen, and I go to prove them: I pray thee have me excused.

14:20 And another said, I have married a wife, ~~and~~ therefore I cannot come.

14:21 So that servant came, and ~~shewed~~ *showed* his lord these things. Then the master of the house being angry said to his servant, Go out quickly into the streets and lanes of the city, and bring ~~in~~ hither the poor, and the maimed, ~~and~~ the halt, and the blind.

14:22 And the servant said, Lord,

MATTHEW	MARK	LUKE	JOHN

it is done as thou hast commanded, and yet there is room.

14:23 And the ~~l~~Lord said unto ~~the~~ *his* servant, Go out into the highways and hedges, and compel ~~them~~ *men* to come in, that my house may be filled.

14:24 For I say unto you, That none of those men ~~which~~ *who* were bidden shall taste of my supper.

G-7. DISCOURSE ON SACRIFICE

14:25 *And when he had finished these sayings, he departed thence,* And there went great multitudes with him: and he turned, and said unto them,

14:26 If any man come to me, and hate not his father, and mother, and wife, and children, and brethren, and sisters, *or husband,* yea, and his own life also, *or in other words, is afraid to lay down his life for my sake,* ~~he~~ cannot be my disciple.

14:27 And whosoever doth not bear his cross, and come after me, cannot be my disciple.

14:28 *Wherefore, settle this in your hearts, that ye will do the things which I shall teach and command you.* For which of you, intending to build a tower, sitteth not down first, and counteth the cost, whether he have ~~sufficient~~ *money* to finish ~~it~~ *his work*?

14:29 Lest ~~haply~~*, unhappily,* after he ~~hath~~ *has* laid the foundation, and is not able to finish ~~it~~ *his work*, all ~~that~~ *who* behold ~~it~~ begin to mock him,

14:30 Saying, This man began to build, and was not able to finish. *And this he said, signifying there should not any man follow him, unless he was able to continue; saying,*

14:31 Or what king, going to make war against another king, sitteth not down first, and consulteth whether he be able with ten thousand to meet him that cometh against him with twenty thousand?

14:32 Or else, while the other is yet a great way off, he sendeth an ambassage, and desireth conditions of peace.

14:33 So likewise, whosoever ~~he be~~ of you that forsaketh not all that he hath, he cannot be my disciple.

14:34 ~~Salt is~~ *Then certain of them came to him, saying Good Master, we have Moses and the prophets, and whosoever shall live by them, shall he not have life? And Jesus answered saying, Ye know not Moses, neither the*

MATTHEW	MARK	LUKE	JOHN

prophets; for if ye had known them, ye would have believed on me; for to this intent they were written. For I am sent that ye might have life. Therefore I will liken it unto that salt which is good: but if the salt ~~have~~ *has* lost ~~his savour~~ *its savor,* wherewith shall it be seasoned?

14:35 It is neither fit for the land, nor yet for the dunghill; ~~but~~ men cast it out. He ~~that~~ *who* hath ears to hear, let him hear. *These things he said, signifying that which was written, verily must all be fulfilled.*

G-8. PARABLE OF THE LOST SHEEP

15:1 Then drew near unto him ~~all~~ *many of* the publicans and sinners ~~for~~ to hear him.

15:2 And the Pharisees and scribes murmured, saying, This man receiveth sinners, and eateth with them.

15:3 And he spake this parable unto them, saying,

15:4 What man of you, having ~~an~~ hundred sheep, if he lose one of them, doth not leave the ninety and nine ~~in the wilderness,~~ and go *into the wilderness* after that which is lost, until he find it?

15:5 And when he hath found it, he layeth it on his shoulders, rejoicing.

15:6 And when he cometh home, he calleth together his friends and neighbours, ~~saying~~ *and saith* unto them, Rejoice with me; for I have found my sheep which was lost.

15:7 I say unto you, that likewise joy shall be in heaven over one sinner that repenteth, more than over ninety and nine just persons, ~~which~~ *who* need no repentance.

G-9. PARABLE OF THE LOST COIN

15:8 Either what woman having ten pieces of silver, if she lose one piece, doth not light a candle, and sweep the house, and seek diligently till she find it?

15:9 And when she hath found it, she ~~calleth~~ *called* her friends and ~~her neighbours~~ *neighbors* together, saying, Rejoice with me; for I have found the piece which I had lost.

15:10 Likewise, I say unto you, there is joy in the presence of the angels of God over one sinner ~~that~~ *who* repenteth.

G-10. PARABLE OF THE PRODIGAL SON

15:11 And he said, A certain man had two sons:

15:12 And the younger of them said to his father, Father, give me the portion of goods ~~that~~ *which* falleth to me. And he divided unto them his living.

15:13 And not many days after the younger son gathered all together, and took his journey into a far country, and there wasted his substance with riotous living.

15:14 And when he had spent all, there arose a mighty famine in that land; and he began to be in want.

15:15 And he went and joined himself to a citizen of that country; and he sent him into his fields to feed swine.

15:16 And he would fain have filled his belly with the husks ~~that~~ *which* the swine did eat: and no man gave unto him.

15:17 And when he came to himself, he said, How many hired servants of my father's have bread enough and to spare, and I perish with hunger!

15:18 I will arise and go to my father, and will say unto him, Father, I have sinned against heaven, and before thee,

15:19 And am no more worthy to be called thy son: make me as one of thy hired servants.

15:20 And he arose, and came to his father. But when he was yet a great way off, his father saw him, and had compassion, and ran, and fell on his neck, and kissed him.

15:21 And the son said unto him, Father, I have sinned against heaven, and in thy sight, and am no more worthy to be called thy son.

15:22 But the father said *un*to his servants, Bring forth the best robe, and put it on him; and put a ring on his ~~hand~~ *finger*, and shoes on his feet:

15:23 And bring hither the fatted calf, and kill it; and let us eat, and be merry:

15:24 For this my son was dead, and is alive again; he was lost, and is found. And they began to be merry.

15:25 Now his elder son was in the field: and as he came and drew nigh to the house, he heard musick and dancing.

15:26 And he called one of the servants, and asked what these things meant.

15:27 And he said unto him, Thy brother is come; and thy father hath killed the fatted calf, because he hath received him safe and sound.

MATTHEW	MARK	LUKE	JOHN

15:28 And he was angry, and would not go in: therefore came his father out, and intreated him.

15:29 And he answering said to his father, Lo, these many years do I serve thee, neither transgressed I at any time thy commandment: and ~~yet~~ thou never gavest me a kid, that I might make merry with my friends:

15:30 But as soon as this thy son was come, ~~which~~ *who* hath devoured thy living with harlots, thou hast killed for him the fatted calf.

15:31 And he said unto him, Son, thou art ever with me, and all that I have is thine.

15:32 It was meet that we should make merry, and be glad: for this thy brother was dead, and is alive again; and was lost, and is found.

G-11. PARABLE OF THE UNJUST STEWARD

16:1 And he said also unto his disciples, There was a certain rich man, ~~which~~ *who* had a steward; and the same was accused unto him that he had wasted his goods.

16:2 And he called him, and said unto him, How is it that I hear this of thee? give an account of thy stewardship; for thou mayest be no longer steward.

16:3 Then the steward said within himself, What shall I do? for my lord taketh away from me the stewardship: I cannot dig; to beg I am ashamed.

16:4 I am resolved what to do, that, when I am put out of the stewardship, they may receive me into their houses.

16:5 So he called every one of his lord's debtors ~~unto him~~, and said unto the first, How much owest thou unto my lord?

16:6 And he said, An hundred measures of oil. And he said unto him, Take thy bill, and sit down quickly, and write fifty.

16:7 Then said he to another, And how much owest thou? And he said, An hundred measures of wheat. And he said unto him, Take thy bill, and write fourscore.

16:8 And the lord commended the unjust steward, because he had done wisely: for the children of this world are *wiser* in their generation ~~wiser~~ than the children of light.

16:9 And I say unto you, Make to yourselves friends of the mammon of unrighteousness; that, when ye fail, they may receive you into everlasting habitations.

16:10 He ~~that~~ *who* is faithful in that which is least is faithful also in

MATTHEW	MARK	LUKE	JOHN

much: and he ~~that~~ *who* is unjust in the least is *also* unjust ~~also~~ in much.

16:11   If therefore ye have not been faithful in the unrighteous mammon, who will commit to your trust the true riches?

16:12   And if ye have not been faithful in that which is another man's, who shall give *unto* you that which is your own?

16:13   No servant can serve two masters: for either he will hate the one, and love the other; or else he will hold to the one, and despise the other.   Ye cannot serve God and mammon.

G-12.   THE PHARASEES AND THEIR HYPOCRISY

16:14   And the Pharisees also, who were covetous, heard all these things: and they derided him.

16:15   And he said unto them, Ye are they ~~which~~ *who* justify yourselves before men; but God knoweth your hearts: for that which is highly esteemed among men is abomination in the sight of God.

16:16   *And they said unto him, we have* The law and the prophets ~~were until John:~~ ; *but as for this man we will not receive him to be our ruler; for he maketh himself to be a judge over us. Then said Jesus unto them, The law and the prophets testify of me; yea, and all the prophets who have written, even until John, have foretold of these days.*   Since that time the kingdom of God is preached, and every man *who seeketh truth* presseth into it.

16:17   And it is easier for heaven and earth to pass, than *for* one tittle of the law to fail.

16:18   *And why teach ye the law, and deny that which is written; and condemn him whom the Father hath sent to fulfill the law, that ye might all be redeemed? O fools! for you have said in your hearts, There is no God. And you pervert the right way; and the kingdom of heaven suffereth violence of you; and you persecute the meek; and in your violence you seek to destroy the kingdom; and ye take the children of the kingdom by force. Woe unto you, ye adulterers!   And they reviled him again, being angry for the saying, that they were adulterers. But he continued, saying,* Whosoever putteth away his wife, and marrieth another, committeth adultery: and whosoever marrieth her that is put away from her husband committeth adultery.

G-13. THE RICH MAN AND LAZARUS

16:19 *Verily I say unto you, I will liken you unto the rich man. For* There was a certain rich man, ~~which~~ *who* was clothed in purple and fine linen, and fared sumptuously every day:

16:20 And there was a certain beggar named Lazarus, ~~which~~ *who* was laid at his gate, full of sores,

16:21 And desiring to be fed with the crumbs which fell from the rich man's table: moreover the dogs came and licked his sores.

16:22 And it came to pass, that the beggar died, and was carried ~~by~~ *of* the angels into Abraham's bosom: the rich man also died, and was buried;

16:23 And in hell he lift up his eyes, being in torments, and ~~seeth~~ *saw* Abraham afar off, and Lazarus in his bosom.

16:24 And he cried and said, Father Abraham, have mercy on me, and send Lazarus, that he may dip the tip of his finger in water, and cool my tongue; for I am tormented in this flame.

16:25 But Abraham said, Son, remember that thou in thy lifetime receivedst thy good things, and likewise Lazarus evil things: but now he is comforted, and thou art tormented.

16:26 And besides all this, between us and you there is a great gulf fixed: so that they ~~which~~ *who* would pass from hence to you cannot; neither can they pass to us, that would come from thence.

16:27 Then he said, I pray thee therefore, father, that thou wouldest send him to my father's house:

16:28 For I have five brethren; that he may testify unto them, lest they also come into this place of torment.

16:29 Abraham sai~~th~~*d* unto him, They have Moses and the prophets; let them hear them.

16:30 And he said, Nay, father Abraham: but if one went unto them from the dead, they will repent.

16:31 And he said unto him, If they hear not Moses and the prophets, neither will they be persuaded, though one ~~rose~~ *should rise* from the dead.

MATTHEW	MARK	LUKE	JOHN

G-14. DISCOURSE ON OFFENSE, FORGIVENESS AND FAITH

17:1   Then said he unto the disciples, It is impossible but that offences will come: but woe ~~unto~~ him, through whom they come!

17:2   It were better for him that a millstone were hanged about his neck, and he cast into the sea, than that he should offend one of these little ones.

17:3   Take heed to yourselves: If ~~thy~~ *your* brother trespass against thee, rebuke him; and if he repent, forgive him.

17:4   And if he trespass against ~~thee~~ *you* seven times in a day, and seven times in a day turn ~~again~~ to ~~thee~~ *you again*, saying, I repent; ~~thou~~ *you* shalt forgive him.

17:5   And the apostles said unto ~~the Lord~~ *him, Lord*, Increase our faith.

17:6   And the Lord said, If ~~ye~~ *you* had faith as a grain of mustard seed, ~~ye~~ *you* might say unto this ~~sycamine~~ *sycamore* tree, Be thou plucked up by the root*s*, and be thou planted in the sea; and it should obey you.

17:7   But ~~which~~ *who* of you, having a servant plowing or feeding cattle, will say unto him ~~by and by,~~ when he is come from the field, Go and sit down to meat?

17:8   ~~And~~ will *he* not rather say unto him, Make ready wherewith I may sup, and gird ~~thyself~~ *yourself*, and serve me, till I have eaten and drunken; and afterward, *by and by, you shall* ~~thou shalt~~ eat and drink?

17:9   Doth he thank that servant because he ~~did~~ *doeth* the things ~~that~~ *which* were commanded him? I ~~trow not~~ *say unto you, Nay*.

17:10   So likewise ye, when ye shall have done all those things which are commanded you, say, We are unprofitable servants: we have done that which was *no more than* our duty to do.

G-15. LAZARUS IS RAISED FROM THE DEAD

11:1   Now a certain man was sick, ~~named~~ *whose name was* Lazarus, of *the town of* Bethany, ~~the town of Mary and her sister Martha~~.

11:2   ~~(It was that~~ *And* Mary, ~~which~~ *his sister, who* anointed the Lord with ointment, and wiped his feet with her hair, *lived with her sister Martha, in* whose *house her* brother Lazarus was sick.~~)~~

11:3   Therefore his sisters sent unto him, saying, Lord, behold, he whom thou lovest is sick.

11:4   *And* When Jesus heard ~~that~~

MATTHEW	MARK	LUKE	JOHN

he was sick, he said, This sickness is not unto death, but for the glory of God, that the Son of God might be glorified thereby.

11:5 Now Jesus loved Martha, and her sister, and Lazarus.

11:6 ~~When he had heard therefore that he was sick, he abode two days still~~ *And Jesus tarried two days, after he heard that Lazarus was sick,* in the same place where he was.

11:7 ~~Then~~ after that ~~saith he to~~ *he said unto* his disciples, Let us go into ~~Judaea~~ *Judea* again.

11:8 *But* His disciples ~~say~~ *said* unto him, Master, the Jews of late sought to stone thee; and goest thou thither again?

11:9 Jesus answered, Are there not twelve hours in the day? If any man walk in the day, he stumbleth not, because he seeth the light of this world.

11:10 But if a man walk in the night, he stumbleth, because there is no light in him.

11:11 These things said he: and after that he saith unto them, Our friend Lazarus sleepeth; but I go, that I may awake him out of sleep.

11:12 Then said his disciples, Lord, if he sleep, he shall do well.

11:13 Howbeit Jesus spake of his death: but they thought that he had spoken of taking of rest in sleep.

11:14 Then said Jesus unto them plainly, Lazarus is dead.

11:15 And I am glad for your sakes that I was not there, to the intent ye may believe; nevertheless let us go unto him.

11:16 Then said Thomas, which is called Didymus, unto his fellow disciples, Let us also go, that we may die with him*; for they feared lest the Jews should take Jesus and put him to death, for as yet they did not understand the power of God*.

11:17 ~~Then~~ *And* when Jesus came *to Bethany, to Martha's house,* ~~he found that he had lain~~ *Lazarus had already been* in the grave four days ~~already~~ .

11:18 Now Bethany was nigh unto Jerusalem, about fifteen furlongs off:

11:19 And many of the Jews came to Martha and Mary, to comfort them concerning their brother.

11:20 Then Martha, as soon as she heard that Jesus was coming, went and met him: but Mary sat still in the house.

11:21 Then said Martha unto Jesus, Lord, if thou hadst been here, my brother had not died.

11:22 But I know, that even now, whatsoever thou wilt ask of God,

God will give it thee.

11:23 Jesus saith unto her, Thy brother shall rise again.

11:24 Martha saith unto him, I know that he shall rise again in the resurrection at the last day.

11:25 Jesus said unto her, I am the resurrection, and the life: he that believeth in me, though he were dead, yet shall he live:

11:26 And whosoever liveth and believeth in me shall never die. Believest thou this?

11:27 She saith unto him, Yea, Lord: I believe that thou art the Christ, the Son of God, which should come into the world.

11:28 And when she had so said, she went her way, and called Mary her sister secretly, saying, The Master is come, and calleth for thee.

11:29 As soon as ~~she~~ *Mary* heard that *Jesus was come*, she arose quickly, and came unto him.

11:30 Now Jesus was not yet come into the town, but was in that place where Martha met him.

11:31 The Jews then which were with her in the house, and comforted her, when they saw Mary, that she rose up hastily and went out, followed her, saying, She goeth unto the grave to weep there.

11:32 Then when Mary was come where Jesus was, and saw him, she fell down at his feet, saying unto him, Lord, if thou hadst been here, my brother had not died.

11:33 When Jesus therefore saw her weeping, and the Jews also weeping which came with her, he groaned in the spirit, and was troubled,

11:34 And said, Where have ye laid him? They said unto him, Lord, come and see.

11:35 Jesus wept.

11:36 Then said the Jews, Behold how he loved him!

11:37 And some of them said, Could not this man, which opened the eyes of the blind, have caused that even this man should not have died?

11:38 Jesus therefore again groaning in himself cometh to the grave. It was a cave, and a stone lay upon it.

11:39 Jesus said, Take ye away the stone. Martha, the sister of him that was dead, saith unto him, Lord, by this time he stinketh: for he hath been dead four days.

11:40 Jesus saith unto her, Said I not unto thee, that, if thou wouldest believe, thou shouldest see the glory of God?

11:41 Then they took away the stone from the place where the

MATTHEW	MARK	LUKE	JOHN

dead was laid. And Jesus lifted up his eyes, and said, Father, I thank thee that thou hast heard me.

11:42 And I knew that thou hearest me always: but because of the people which stand by I said it, that they may believe that thou hast sent me.

11:43 And when he thus had spoken, he cried with a loud voice, Lazarus, come forth.

11:44 And he that was dead came forth, bound hand and foot with graveclothes: and his face was bound about with a napkin. Jesus saith unto them, Loose him, and let him go.

11:45 Then many of the Jews which came to Mary, and had seen the things which Jesus did, believed on him.

11:46 But some of them went their ways to the Pharisees, and told them what things Jesus had done.

G-16. CHIEF PRIESTS AND PHARISEES PLOT AGAINST JESUS

11:47 Then gathered the chief priests and the Pharisees a council, and said, What ~~do we~~ *shall we do*? for this man doeth many miracles.

11:48 If we let him thus alone, all men will believe on him: and the Romans shall come and take away both our place and nation.

11:49 And one of them, named Caiaphas, being the high priest that same year, said unto them, Ye know nothing at all,

11:50 Nor consider that it is expedient for us, that one man should die for the people, and that the whole nation perish not.

11:51 And this spake he not of himself: but being high priest that year, he prophesied that Jesus should die for that nation;

11:52 And not for that nation only, but that also he should gather together in one the children of God that were scattered abroad.

11:53 Then from that day forth they took counsel together for to put him to death.

MATTHEW	MARK	LUKE	JOHN

G-17. JESUS GOES TO EPHRAIM

11:54 Jesus therefore walked no more openly among the Jews; but went thence unto a country near to the wilderness, into a city called Ephraim, and there continued with his disciples.

G-18. THE BEGINNING OF THE FINAL JOURNEY TO JERUSALEM

17:11 ~~And~~ it came to pass, as he went to Jerusalem, that he passed through the midst of ~~Samaria and~~ Galilee *and Samaria*.

G-19. THE HEALING OF THE TEN LEPERS

17:12 And as he entered into a certain village, there met him ten men ~~that~~ *who* were lepers, ~~which~~ *who* stood afar off:

17:13 And they lifted up their voices, and said, Jesus, Master, have mercy on us.

17:14 And ~~when he saw them,~~ he said unto them, Go ~~shew~~ *show* yourselves unto the priests. And it came to pass, ~~that,~~ as they went, they were cleansed.

17:15 ~~And~~ one of them, when he saw ~~that~~ he was healed, turned back, and with a loud voice glorified God,

17:16 And fell down on his face at ~~his~~ *Jesus'* feet, giving him thanks: and he was a Samaritan.

17:17 And Jesus answering said, Were there not ten cleansed? but where are the nine?

17:18 There are not found that returned to give glory to God, save this stranger.

17:19 And he said unto him, Arise, go thy way: thy faith hath made thee whole.

G-20. SIGNS, TIMES AND COMING OF THE KINGDOM OF GOD

17:20 And when he was demanded of the Pharisees, when the kingdom of God should come, he answered them and said, The kingdom of God cometh not with observation:

17:21 Neither shall they say, Lo here! or, lo there! for, behold, the kingdom of God ~~is within~~ *has already come unto* you.

17:22 And he said unto ~~the~~ *his* disciples, The days will come, when ~~ye shall~~ *they will* desire to see one of the days of the Son of ~~m~~*M*an, and ~~ye~~ *they* shall not see it.

17:23 And *if* they shall say to you, See here; or, see there: go not after them, nor follow them.

MATTHEW	MARK	LUKE	JOHN

17:24 For as the ~~lightning~~ *light of the morning*, that ~~lighteneth~~ *shineth* out of the one part under heaven, ~~shineth~~ *and lighteneth* ~~un~~to the other part under heaven; so shall also the Son of ~~m~~*M*an be in his day.

17:25 But first must he suffer many things, and be rejected of this generation.

17:26 And as it was in the days of Noe, so shall it be also in the days of the Son of man.

17:27 They did eat, they drank, they married wives, they were given in marriage, until the day that Noe entered into the ark, and the flood came, and destroyed them all.

17:28 Likewise also as it was in the days of Lot; they did eat, they drank, they bought, they sold, they planted, they builded;

17:29 But the same day that Lot went out of Sodom it rained fire and brimstone from heaven, and destroyed them all.

17:30 Even thus shall it be in the day when the Son of man is revealed.

17:31 In that day, ~~he which~~ *the disciple who* shall be ~~up~~on the housetop, and his stuff in the house, let him not come down to take it away: and he ~~that~~ *who* is in the field, let him likewise not return back.

17:32 Remember Lot's wife.

17:33 Whosoever shall seek to save his life shall lose it; and whosoever shall lose his life shall preserve it.

17:34 I tell you, in that night there shall be two ~~men~~ in one bed; the one shall be taken, and the other shall be left.

17:35 Two ~~women~~ shall be grinding together; the one shall be taken, and the other left.

17:36 Two ~~men~~ shall be in the field; the one shall be taken, and the other left.

17:37 And they answered and said unto him, Where, Lord, *shall they be taken*? And he said unto them, Wheresoever the body is *gathered; or in other words, whithersoever the saints are gathered,* thither will the eagles be gathered together*; or, thither will the remainder be gathered together. This he spake, signifying the gathering of his saints; and of angels descending and gathering the remainder unto them; the one from the bed, the other from the grinding, and the other from the field, whithersoever he listeth. For verily there shall be new heavens, and a new earth, wherein dwelleth righteousness. And there shall be no unclean* *thing; for the earth becoming old, even as a garment, having waxed in corruption, wherefore it vanisheth away, and the footstool remaineth sanctified, cleansed from all sin.*

G-21. PARABLE OF THE IMPORTUNATE WIDOW

18:1 And he spake a parable unto them ~~to this end~~ , *saying*, that men ought always to pray, and not ~~to~~ faint;

18:2 Saying, There was in a city a judge, ~~which~~ *who* feared not God, ~~neither~~ *nor* regarded man:

18:3 And there was a widow in that city; and she came unto him, saying, Avenge me of mine adversary.

18:4 And he would not for a while: but afterward he said within himself, Though I fear not God, nor regard man;

18:5 Yet because this widow troubleth me, I will avenge her, lest by her continual coming she weary me.

18:6 And the Lord said, Hear what the unjust judge saith.

18:7 And shall not God avenge his own elect, ~~which~~ *who* cry day and night unto him, though he bear long with ~~them~~ *men*?

18:8 I tell you that he will *come, and when he does come, he will* avenge ~~them~~ *his saints* speedily. Nevertheless when the Son of ~~m~~*M*an cometh, shall he find faith on the earth?

G-22. PARABLE OF THE PHARASEE AND THE PUBLICAN

18:9 ~~And~~ he spake this parable unto certain *men,* ~~which~~ *who* trusted in themselves that they were righteous, and despised others:

18:10 Two men went up into the temple to pray; the one a Pharisee, and the other a publican.

18:11 The Pharisee stood and prayed thus with himself, God, I thank thee, that I am not as other men ~~are~~, extortioners, unjust, adulterers, or even as this publican.

18:12 I fast twice in the week, I give tithes of all that I possess.

18:13 ~~And~~ *But* the publican, standing afar off, would not lift up so much as his eyes unto heaven, but smote upon his breast, saying, God be merciful to me a sinner.

18:14 I tell you, this man went down to his house justified rather than the other: for every one ~~that~~ *who* exalteth himself shall be abased; and he ~~that~~ *who* humbleth himself shall be exalted.

MATTHEW	MARK	LUKE	JOHN

G-23. JESUS CROSSES JORDAN, GOING TOWARDS JERUSALEM

19:1 And it came to pass, ~~that~~ when Jesus had finished these sayings, he departed from Galilee, and came into the coasts of ~~Judaea~~ *Judea* beyond Jordan;
19:2 And great multitudes followed him;

and many believed on him, and he healed them there.

10:1 And he arose from thence, and cometh into the coasts of ~~Judaea~~ *Judea* by the farther side of Jordan:
and the people resort unto him again;
and, as he was ~~wont~~ *accustomed to teach*, he *also* taught them again.

G-24. THE PHARISEES TEMPT JESUS ABOUT MARRIAGE AND DIVORCE

19:3 The Pharisees ~~also~~ came *also* unto him, tempting him, and saying unto him, Is it lawful for a man to put away his wife for every cause?

10:2 And the Pharisees came to him, and asked him,
Is it lawful for a man to put away his wife?
~~tempting~~ *This they said, thinking to tempt* him.
10:3 And he answered and said unto them, What did Moses command you?
10:4 And they said, Moses suffered to write a bill of divorcement, and to put her away.

19:4 And he answered and said unto them, Have ye not read, that he ~~which~~ *who* made ~~them~~ *man* at the beginning made ~~them~~ *him,* male and female,
19:5 And said, For this cause shall a man leave father and mother, and shall cleave to his wife: and they twain shall be one flesh?
19:6 Wherefore they are no more twain, but one flesh.
What therefore God hath joined together, let not man put asunder.

10:6 But from the beginning of the creation God made them male and female.
10:7 For this cause shall a man leave his father and mother, and cleave to his wife;
10:8 And they twain shall be one flesh:
so then they are no more twain, but one flesh.
10:9 What therefore God hath joined together, let not man put asunder.

19:7 They say unto him, Why did Moses then command to give a writing of divorcement, and to put her away?
19:8 He sai~~th~~*d* unto them, Moses because of the hardness of your hearts suffered you to put away your wives: but from the beginning it was not so.

10:5 ~~And~~ Jesus answered and said unto them, For the hardness of your heart*s* he wrote you this precept.

10:10 And in the house his disciples asked him again of the same matter.

19:9 And I say unto you, Whosoever shall put away his wife, except ~~it be~~ for fornication, and shall marry another, committeth adultery:
and whoso marrieth her ~~which~~ *that* is put away doth commit adultery.

10:11 And he sai~~th~~*d* unto them, Whosoever shall put away his wife, and marry another,
committeth adultery against her.

10:12 And if a woman shall put away her husband, and be married to another, she committeth adultery.

MATTHEW	MARK	LUKE	JOHN

19:10 His disciples say unto him, If the case of the man be so with ~~his~~ *a* wife, it is not good to marry.
19:11 But he said unto them, All ~~men~~ cannot receive this saying, *it is not for them,* save ~~they~~ to whom it is given.
19:12 For there are some eunuchs, which were so born from their mother's womb: and there are some eunuchs, which were made eunuchs of men: and there be eunuchs, which have made themselves eunuchs for the kingdom of heaven's sake. He that is able to receive ~~it~~, let him receive ~~it~~ *my sayings*.

G-25. JESUS BLESSES THE LITTLE CHILDREN

19:13 Then were there brought unto him little children, that he should put his hands on them, and pray: and the disciples rebuked them, *saying, There is no need, for Jesus hath said, Such shall be saved.*

19:14 But Jesus said,

Suffer little children *to come unto me*, and forbid them not, ~~to come unto me:~~ for of such is the kingdom of heaven.

19:15 And he laid ~~his~~ hands on them,

and departed thence.

10:13 And they brought young children to him, that he should touch them:
and ~~his~~ *the* disciples rebuked those that brought them.

10:14 But when Jesus saw ~~it~~ *and heard them*, he was much displeased,
and said unto them,

Suffer the little children to come unto me, and forbid them not: for of such is the kingdom of God.

10:15 Verily I say unto you, Whosoever shall not receive the kingdom of God as a little child, he shall not enter therein.
10:16 And he took them up in his arms, put his hands upon them, and blessed them.

18:15 And they brought unto him also infants, that he ~~would~~ *might* touch them:
but when his disciples saw it, they rebuked them.

18:16 But Jesus called them ~~unto him~~, and said,
Suffer little children to come unto me, and forbid them not: for of such is the kingdom of God.

18:17 Verily I say unto you, Whosoever ~~shall~~ *will* not receive the kingdom of God as a little child shall in no wise enter therein.

G-26. JESUS TEACHES A RICH YOUNG RULER

19:16 And, behold, one came and said ~~unto him~~,
Good Master, what good thing shall I do, that I may have eternal life?

19:17 And he said unto him, Why callest thou me good? there is none good but one, that is, God: but if thou wilt enter into life, keep the commandments.

19:18 He sai~~th~~*d* unto him, Which? Jesus said,
Thou shalt ~~do no murder~~ *not kill*, Thou shalt not commit adultery, Thou shalt not steal, Thou shalt not bear false witness,

19:19 ~~Honour~~ *Honor* thy father and ~~thy~~ mother: and,

10:17 And when he was gone forth into the way, there came one running, and kneeled to him, and asked him, Good Master, what shall I do that I may inherit eternal life?
10:18 And Jesus said unto him, Why callest thou me good? ~~there is~~ none *is* good but one, that is, God.

10:19 Thou knowest the commandments,

Do not commit adultery,
Do not kill,
Do not steal,
Do not bear false witness,
Defraud not,
Honour thy father and mother.

18:18 And a certain ruler asked him, saying,
Good Master, what shall I do to inherit eternal life?

18:19 And Jesus said unto him, Why callest thou me good? none is good, save one, that is, God.

18:20 Thou knowest the commandments,

Do not commit adultery,
Do not kill,
Do not steal,
Do not bear false witness,

Honour thy father and thy mother.

MATTHEW	MARK	LUKE	JOHN

Thou shalt love thy neighbour as thyself.

19:20 The young man saith unto him, All these things have I kept from my youth up: what lack I yet?

19:21 Jesus said unto him,

If thou wilt be perfect,
go ~~and~~ sell that thou hast, and give to the poor, and thou shalt have treasure in heaven:
and come and follow me.

19:22 But when the young man heard that saying, he went away sorrowful: for he had great possessions.

19:23 Then said Jesus unto his disciples,
Verily I say unto you, That a rich man shall hardly enter into the kingdom of heaven.

19:24 And again I say unto you,

It is easier for a camel to go through the eye of a needle, than for a rich man to enter ~~into~~ the kingdom of God.

19:25 When his disciples heard ~~it~~, *this* they were exceedingly amazed, saying,
Who then can be saved?

19:26 But Jesus beheld ~~them~~ *their thoughts*, and said unto them, With men this is impossible; but *if they will forsake all things for my sake,*

with God ~~all~~ *whatsoever* things *I speak* are possible .

10:20 And ~~he~~ *the man* answered and said unto him, Master, all these have I observed from my youth.

10:21 Then Jesus beholding him loved him, and said unto him, One thing thou lackest:

go thy way, sell whatsoever thou hast, and give to the poor, and thou shalt have treasure in heaven: and come, take up the cross, and follow me.

10:22 And ~~he~~ *the man* was sad at that saying, and went away grieved: for he had great possessions.

10:23 And Jesus looked round about, and saith~~d~~ unto his disciples, How hardly shall they that have riches enter into the kingdom of ~~God~~ *my Father*!

10:24 And the disciples were astonished at his words. But Jesus ~~answereth~~ *spake* again, and saith~~d~~ unto them,
Children, how hard is it for them ~~that~~ *who* trust in riches to enter into the kingdom of God!

10:25 It is easier for a camel to go through the eye of a needle, than for a rich man to enter into the kingdom of God.

10:26 And they were astonished out of measure, saying among themselves,
Who then can be saved?

10:27 And Jesus looking upon them saith~~d~~,
With men *that trust in riches* it is impossible, but not ~~with God: for with God~~ impossible

with men who trust in God and leave all for my sake, for with such all *these* things are possible.

18:21 And he said, All these have I kept from my youth up.

18:22 Now when Jesus heard these things, he said unto him, Yet ~~lackest~~ thou *lackest* one thing:

sell all that thou hast, and distribute unto the poor, and thou shalt have treasure in heaven: and come, follow me.

18:23 And when he heard this, he was very sorrowful: for he was very rich.

18:24 And when Jesus saw that he was very sorrowful, he said, How hardly shall they ~~that~~ *who* have riches enter into the kingdom of God!

18:25 For it is easier for a camel to go through a needle's eye, than for a rich man to enter into the kingdom of God.

18:26 And they ~~that~~ *who* heard it said,

Who then can be saved?

18:27 And he said ~~, The things which are impossible with men are possible with God.~~ *unto them, it is impossible for them who trust in riches, to enter into the kingdom of God;*
but he who forsaketh the things which are of this world, it is possible with God that he should enter in.

G-27. FOLLOWING JESUS BRINGS EVERLASTING LIFE

19:27 Then answered Peter and said unto him, Behold, we have forsaken all, and followed thee; what shall we have therefore?

19:28 And Jesus said unto them, Verily I say unto you, That ye ~~which~~ *who* have followed me, *shall,* in the ~~regeneration~~ *resurrection,* when the Son of ~~m~~*M*an shall ~~sit in~~ *come sitting on* the throne of his glory, ye ~~also~~ shall *also* sit upon twelve thrones, judging the twelve tribes of Israel.

19:29 And every one that ha~~ths~~ forsaken houses, or brethren, or sisters, or father, or mother, or wife, or children, or lands, for my name's sake,
shall receive an hundredfold, and

10:28 Then Peter began to say unto him, Lo, we have left all, and have followed thee.

10:29 And Jesus answered and said, Verily I say unto you,

There is no man that hath left house, or brethren, or sisters, or father, or mother, or wife, or children, or lands, for my sake, and the gospel's,

10:30 But he shall receive an hundredfold now in this time,

18:28 Then Peter said, Lo, we have left all, and followed thee.

18:29 And he said unto them, Verily I say unto you,

There is no man ~~that hath~~ *who has* left house, or parents, or brethren, or wife, or children, for the kingdom of God's sake,

18:30 Who shall not receive manifold more in this present time,

MATTHEW	MARK	LUKE	JOHN

shall inherit everlasting life.

19:30 But many ~~that are~~ *of the* first shall be last; and the last ~~shall be~~ first.

houses, and brethren, and sisters, and mothers, and children, and lands, with persecutions; and in the world to come eternal life.

10:31 But ~~many that are first~~ *there are many who make themselves first, that* shall be last; and the last first.

10:32(a) *This he said, rebuking Peter;*

and in the world to come life everlasting.

G-28. PARABLE OF THE VINEYARD

20:1 For the kingdom of heaven is like unto a man ~~that is~~ *,* an householder, ~~which~~ *who* went out early in the morning to hire ~~labourers~~ *laborers* into his vineyard.

20:2 And when he had agreed with the labourers for a penny a day, he sent them into his vineyard.

20:3 And he went out about the third hour, and ~~saw~~ *found* others standing idle in the marketplace,

20:4 And said unto them; Go ye also into the vineyard, and whatsoever is right I will give you. And they went their way.

20:5 Again he went out about the sixth and ninth hour, and did likewise.

20:6 And about the eleventh hour he went out, and found others standing idle, and saith unto them, Why stand ye here all the day idle?

20:7 They ~~say~~ *said* unto him, Because no man hath hired us. He saith*d* unto them, Go ye also into the vineyard; and whatsoever is right, ~~that~~ shall ye receive.

20:8 So when even was come, the lord of the vineyard saith*d* unto his steward, Call the ~~labourers~~ *laborers*, and give them their hire, beginning from the last unto the first.

20:9 And when they came that ~~were hired~~ *began* about the eleventh hour, they received every man a penny.

20:10 But when the first came, they supposed that they should have received more; and they likewise received every man a penny.

20:11 And when they had received ~~it~~ *a penny*, they murmured against the goodman of the house,

20:12 Saying, These last have wrought ~~but~~ one hour *only*, and thou hast made them equal unto us, ~~which~~ *who* have borne the burden and heat of the day.

20:13 But he answered one of them, and said, Friend, I do thee no wrong: didst not thou agree with me for a penny?

20:14 Take ~~that~~ thine ~~is~~, and go

MATTHEW	MARK	LUKE	JOHN

thy way: I will give unto this last, even as unto thee.
20:15 Is it not lawful for me to do what I will with mine own? Is thine eye evil, because I am good?
20:16 So the last shall be first, and the first last: for many ~~be~~ *are* called, but few chosen.

G-29. JESUS FORETELLS HIS DEATH AND RESURRECTION

20:17 And Jesus going up to Jerusalem

took the twelve disciples apart in the way, and said unto them,

20:18 Behold, we go up to Jerusalem;

and the Son of ~~m~~*M*an shall be betrayed unto the chief priests and unto the scribes, and they shall condemn him to death,
20:19 And shall deliver him to the Gentiles
to mock, and to scourge, and to crucify ~~him~~:

and the third day he shall rise again.

10:32(b) And they were in the way going up to Jerusalem; and Jesus went before ~~them~~: and they were amazed; and as they followed, they were afraid.
And he took again the twelve, and began to tell them what things should happen unto him,
10:33 ~~Saying~~ *And Jesus said*, Behold, we go up to Jerusalem;

and the Son of ~~m~~*M*an shall be delivered unto the chief priests, and unto the scribes; and they shall condemn him to death,
and shall deliver him to the Gentiles:
10:34 And they shall mock him, and shall scourge him, and shall spit upon him, and shall kill him: and the third day he shall rise again.

18:31 Then he took ~~unto him~~ the twelve, and said unto them,

Behold, we go up to Jerusalem, and all things ~~that~~ *which* are written by the prophets concerning the Son of ~~m~~*M*an shall be accomplished.

18:32 For he shall be delivered unto the Gentiles, and shall be mocked, and spitefully entreated, and spitted on:
18:33 And they shall scourge ~~him,~~ and put him to death: and the third day he shall rise again.
18:34 And they understood none of these things: and this saying was hid from them, neither ~~knew~~ *remembered* they the things which were spoken.

G-30. THE AMBITION OF JAMES AND JOHN

20:20 Then came to him the mother of Zebedee's children with her sons, worshipping ~~him~~ *Jesus*, and desiring a certain thing of him.

20:21 And he said unto her, What wilt thou *that I should do*?

And She saith~~d~~ unto him, Grant that these my two sons may sit, the one on thy right hand, and the other on ~~the~~ *thy* left, in thy kingdom.
20:22 But Jesus answered and said, Ye know not what ye ask. Are ye able to drink of the cup that I shall drink of, and to be baptized with the baptism that I am baptized with?
They say unto him, We are able.

20:23 And he saith~~d~~ unto them, Ye shall drink indeed of my cup, and be baptized with the baptism

10:35 And James and John, the sons of Zebedee, ~~come~~ *came* unto him, saying, Master, we would that thou shouldest do for us whatsoever we shall desire.
10:36 And he said unto them, What ~~would~~ *will* ye that I should do ~~for~~ *unto* you?
10:37 They said unto him, Grant unto us that we may sit, one on thy right hand, and the other on thy left hand, in thy glory.
10:38 But Jesus said unto them, Ye know not what ye ask: can ye drink of the cup that I drink of? and be baptized with the baptism that I am baptized with?
10:39 And they said unto him, We can.
And Jesus said unto them, Ye shall indeed drink of the cup that I drink of; and *be baptized* with the

MATTHEW	MARK	LUKE	JOHN

MATTHEW

that I am baptized with:

but to sit on my right hand, and on my left, is ~~not mine to give, but it shall be given to them~~ for whom it is prepared of my Father, *but not mine to give*.
20:24 And when the ten heard ~~it~~ *this*, they were moved with indignation against the two brethren.
20:25 But Jesus called them ~~unto him~~, and said, Ye know that the princes of the Gentiles exercise dominion over them,

and they that are great exercise authority upon them.
20:26 But it shall not be so among you: but whosoever will be great among you, let him be your minister;
20:27 And whosoever will be chief among you, let him be your servant:
20:28 Even as the Son of man came not to be ministered unto, but to minister, and to give his life a ransom for many.

MARK

baptism that I am baptized with~~al shall ye be baptized~~:
10:40 But to sit on my right hand and on my left hand is not mine to give; but ~~it shall be given to them~~ *they shall receive it* for whom it is prepared.
10:41 And when the ten heard ~~it~~, they began to be much displeased with James and John.

10:42 But Jesus called them ~~to him~~, and sai~~th~~*d* unto them, Ye know that they ~~which~~ *who* are ~~accounted~~ *appointed* to rule over the Gentiles exercise lordship over them; and their great ones exercise authority upon them.
10:43 But ~~so shall it not be~~ *it shall not be so* among you: but whosoever will be great among you, shall be your minister:
10:44 And whosoever of you will be the chiefest, shall be servant of all.
10:45 For even the Son of man came not to be ministered unto, but to minister, and to give his life a ransom for many.

G-31. BARTIMAEUS HEALED OF BLINDNESS NEAR JERICHO

MATTHEW

20:29 And as they departed from Jericho, a great multitude followed him.
20:30 And, behold, two blind men sitting by the way side,

when they heard that Jesus passed by,
cried out, saying,
Have mercy on us, O Lord, ~~thou~~ Son of David.
20:31 And the multitude rebuked them, ~~because~~ *saying* they should hold their peace: but they cried the more, saying, Have mercy on us, O Lord, ~~thou~~ Son of David.

20:32 And Jesus stood still, and called them,

and said, What will ye that I shall do unto you?

20:33 They say unto him, Lord, that our eyes may be opened.

MARK

10:46 And they came to Jericho: and as he went out of Jericho with his disciples and a great number of people,
blind Bartimaeus, the son of Timaeus, sat by the highway side begging.

10:47 And when he heard that it was Jesus of Nazareth,
he began to cry out, and say, Jesus, ~~thou~~ Son of David, have mercy on me.
10:48 And many charged him that he should hold his peace: but he cried the more ~~a great deal~~ *exceedingly, saying*, ~~Thou~~ Son of David, have mercy on me.

10:49 And Jesus stood still, and commanded him to be called.

And they call*ed* the blind man, saying unto him, Be of good comfort, rise; he calleth thee.
10:50 And he, casting away his garment, *a*rose, and came to Jesus.
10:51 And Jesus ~~answered and~~ said unto him, What wilt thou that I should do unto thee?

And The blind man said unto him, Lord, that I might receive my sight.

LUKE

18:35 And it came to pass, ~~that~~ as he was come nigh unto Jericho,

a certain blind man sat by the way side begging:

18:36 And hearing the multitude pass by, he asked what it meant.
18:37 And they told him, that Jesus of Nazareth passe~~th~~*d* by.
18:38 And he cried, saying, Jesus, ~~thou~~ *S*son of David, have mercy on me.
18:39 And they ~~which~~ *who* went before rebuked him, *telling him* that he should hold his peace: but he cried so much the more, *saying*, Thou Son of David, have mercy on me.
18:40 And Jesus stood, and commanded him to be brought unto him:

and when he was come near,

he asked him,
18:41 Saying, What wilt thou that I shall do unto thee?
And he said, Lord, that I may receive my sight.

MATTHEW	MARK	LUKE	JOHN

20:34 So Jesus had compassion ~~on them~~, and touched their eyes:

and immediately their eyes received sight, and they followed him.

10:52 And Jesus said unto him, Go thy way; thy faith hath made thee whole.
And immediately he received his sight, and followed Jesus in the way.

18:42 And Jesus said unto him, Receive thy sight: thy faith hath saved thee.
18:43 And immediately he received his sight, and *he* followed him, glorifying God: and all the ~~people,~~ *disciples* when they saw ~~it~~ *this*, gave praise unto God.

G-32. ZACCHAEUS THE PUBLICAN IS SAVED

19:1 And Jesus entered and passed through Jericho.
19:2 And, behold, there was a man named ~~Zacchaeus, which~~ *Zaccheus, who* was the chief among the publicans, and he was rich.
19:3 And he sought to see Jesus who he was; and could not for the press, because he was little of stature.
19:4 And he ran before, and climbed up into a sycomore tree to see him: for he was to pass that way.
19:5 And when Jesus came to the place, he looked up, and saw him, and said unto him, *Zaccheus* ~~Zacchaeus~~, make haste, and come down; for to day I must abide at thy house.
19:6 And he made haste, and came down, and received him joyfully.
19:7 And when ~~they~~ *the disciples* saw it, they all murmured, saying, That he was gone to be guest with a man ~~that~~ *who* is a sinner.
19:8 And *Zaccheus* ~~Zacchaeus~~ stood, and said unto the Lord; Behold, Lord, the half of my goods I give to the poor; and if I have taken any thing from any man by ~~false accusation~~ *unjust means*, I restore him fourfold.
19:9 And Jesus said unto him, This day is salvation come to this house, ~~forsomuch~~ *forasmuch* as he also is a son of Abraham.
19:10 For the Son of man is come to seek and to save that which was lost.

G-33. PARABLE OF THE TEN POUNDS

19:11 And as they heard these things, he added and spake a parable, because he was nigh to Jerusalem, and because ~~they thought~~ *the Jews taught* that the kingdom of God should immediately appear.
19:12 He said therefore, A certain nobleman went into a far country to receive for himself a kingdom, and to return.

MATTHEW	MARK	LUKE	JOHN

19:13 And he called his ten servants, and delivered them ten pounds, and said unto them, Occupy till I come.

19:14 But his citizens hated him, and sent a ~~message~~ *messenger* after him, saying, We will not have this man to reign over us.

19:15 And it came to pass, that when he was returned, having received the kingdom, then he commanded these servants to be called unto him, to whom he had given the money, that he might know how much every man had gained by trading.

19:16 Then came the first, saying, Lord, thy pound hath gained ten pounds.

19:17 And he said unto him, Well *done*, thou good servant: because thou hast been faithful in a very little, have thou authority over ten cities.

19:18 And the second came, saying, Lord, thy pound hath gained five pounds.

19:19 And he said likewise to him, Be thou also over five cities.

19:20 And another came, saying, Lord, behold, ~~here is~~ thy pound, which I have kept laid up in a napkin:

19:21 For I feared thee, because thou art an austere man: thou takest up that thou layedst not down, and reapest that *which* thou didst not sow.

19:22 And he sai~~th~~*d* unto him, Out of thine own mouth will I judge thee, ~~thou~~ *O* wicked servant. Thou knewest that I was an austere man, taking up that I laid not down, and reaping that I did not sow:

19:23 Wherefore then gavest not thou my money into the bank, that at my coming I might have ~~required~~ *received* mine own with usury?

19:24 And he said unto them ~~that~~ *who* stood by, Take from him the pound, and give it to him ~~that~~ *who* hath ten pounds.

19:25 ~~(And they said unto him, Lord, he hath ten pounds.)~~

19:26 For I say unto you, That unto every one ~~which hath~~ *who occupieth* shall be given; and from him ~~that hath~~ *who occupieth* not, even that he hath *received* shall be taken away from him.

19:27 But those mine enemies, ~~which~~ *who* would not that I should reign over them, bring *them* hither, and slay them before me.

MATTHEW	MARK	LUKE	JOHN

G-34. JESUS APPROACHES JERUSALEM

| | | 19:28 And when he had thus spoken, he went before, ascending up to Jerusalem. | |

G-35. MANY SEEK JESUS AT PASSOVER

| | | | 11:55 And the Jews' passover was nigh at hand: and many went out of the country up to Jerusalem before the passover, to purify themselves. 11:56 Then sought they for Jesus, and spake among themselves, as they stood in the temple, What think ye *of Jesus*, ~~that he~~ will *he* not come to the feast? 11:57 Now both the chief priests and the Pharisees had given a commandment, that, if any man knew where he ~~were~~ *was*, he should ~~shew it~~ *show them*, that they might take him. |

G-36. MARY ANNOINTS JESUS

MATTHEW	MARK	LUKE	JOHN
26:6 Now when *Jesus* was in Bethany, in the house of Simon the leper,	14:3 And *Jesus* being in Bethany in the house of Simon the leper,		12:1 Then Jesus six days before the passover came to Bethany, where Lazarus was which had been dead, whom he raised from the dead.
26:7(b) as he sat ~~at meat~~ *in the house*.	as he sat at meat,		12:2 There they made him a supper; and Martha served: but Lazarus was one of them that sat at the table with him.
26:7(a) There came unto him a woman having an alabaster box of very precious ointment,	there came a woman having an alabaster box of ointment of spikenard very precious; and she brake the box,		12:3 Then took Mary a pound of ointment of spikenard, very costly,
and poured it on his head,	and poured ~~it~~ *the ointment* on his head.		and anointed the feet of Jesus, and wiped his feet with her hair: and the house was filled with the odour of the ointment.
26:8 But when ~~his disciples~~ *some* saw ~~it~~ *this*, they had indignation, saying, *un*To what purpose is this waste?	14:4 ~~And~~ there were some ~~that~~ *among the disciples who* had indignation within themselves, and said, Why was this waste of the ointment made?		12:4 Then saith one of his disciples, Judas Iscariot, Simon's son, which should betray him,
26:9 For this ointment might have been sold for much, and given to the poor.	14:5 For it might have been sold for more than three hundred pence, and have been given to the poor. And they murmured against her.		12:5 Why was not this ointment sold for three hundred pence, and given to the poor?
			12:6 This he said, not that he cared for the poor; but because he was a thief, and had the bag, and bare what was put therein. 12:7 Then said Jesus,
26:10 When ~~Jesus understood it,~~ *they had said thus, Jesus understood them, and* he said unto them, Why trouble ye the woman? for she hath wrought a good work upon me.	14:6 And Jesus said *unto them*, Let her alone; why trouble ye her? *for* she hath wrought a good work on me.		Let her alone: ~~against the day of my burying hath she kept this~~ *for she hath preserved this ointment until now, that she might anoint me in token of my burial*.

MATTHEW	MARK	LUKE	JOHN
26:11 For ye have the poor always with you; but me ye have not always.	14:7 ~~For~~ ye have the poor with you always, and whensoever ye will ye may do them good: but me ye have not always.		12:8 For the poor always ye have with you; but me ye have not always.
26:12 For ~~in that~~ she hath poured this ointment on my body, ~~she did it~~ for my burial. 26:13 *And in this thing that she hath done, she shall be blessed;*	14:8(b) *for verily* she ~~is~~ *has* come ~~aforehand~~ *beforehand* to anoint my body to the burying.		
	14:8(a) She ~~hath~~ *has* done what she could: *and this which she has done unto me, shall be had in remembrance in generations to come, wheresoever my gospel shall be preached;*		
for Verily I say unto you, Wheresoever this gospel shall be preached in the whole world, ~~there shall also this,~~ *this thing* that this woman hath done, *shall also* be told for a memorial of her.	14:9 Verily I say unto you, Wheresoever this gospel shall be preached throughout the whole world, ~~this also that~~ *what* she hath done shall be spoken of *also* for a memorial of her.		

G-37. SEEING LAZARUS, MANY BELIEVE

12:9 Much people of the Jews therefore knew that he was there: and they came not for Jesus' sake only, but that they might see Lazarus also, whom he had raised from the dead.
12:10 But the chief priests consulted that they might put Lazarus also to death;
12:11 Because that by reason of him many of the Jews went away, and believed on Jesus.

MATTHEW	MARK	LUKE	JOHN

Sunday--The First Day of the Week

H-1. THE TRIUMPHAL ENTRY INTO JERUSALEM

MATTHEW

21:1 And when ~~they~~ *Jesus* drew nigh unto Jerusalem, and *they* were come to Bethphage, unto the mount of Olives, then sent Jesus two disciples,
21:2 Saying unto them, Go into the village over against you,

and straightway ye shall find ~~an ass tied, and a colt with her: loose them, and bring them unto me~~ *a colt tied; loose it, and bring it unto me*.

21:3 And if any ~~man~~ *shall* say ought unto you, ye shall say, The Lord hath need of ~~them~~ *it*; and straightway he will send ~~them~~ *it*.
21:6 And the disciples went, and did as Jesus commanded them,

21:7 And brought ~~the ass, and~~ the colt, and put on ~~them~~ *it* their clothes,
and ~~they set him thereon~~ *Jesus took the colt and sat thereon; and they followed him*.
21:4 All this was done, that it might be fulfilled which was spoken by the prophet, saying,
21:5 Tell ye the daughter of ~~S~~*Z*ion, Behold, thy King cometh unto thee, *and he is* meek, and sitting upon an ass, and a colt the foal of an ass.

21:8 And a very great multitude

spread their garments in the way; others cut down branches from the trees, and ~~strawed them~~ *strewed* in the way.

MARK

11:1 And when they came nigh to Jerusalem, unto Bethphage and Bethany, at the mount of Olives, he sendeth forth two of his disciples,
11:2 And sai~~th~~*d* unto them, Go your way into the village over against you:
and as soon as ye ~~be~~ *have* entered into it, ye shall find

a colt tied, whereon ~~never~~ *no* man *ever* sat; loose him, and bring him *to me*.
11:3 And if any man say unto you, Why do ye this? say ye that the Lord hath need of him; and straightway he will send him hither.
11:4 And they went their way, and found the colt tied by the door without in a place where two ways met; and they loose*d* him.
11:5 And certain of them ~~that~~ *who* stood there said unto ~~them~~ *the disciples*, ~~What do ye, loosing~~ *why loose ye* the colt?
11:6 And they said unto them even as Jesus had commanded: and they let them go.
11:7 And they brought the colt to Jesus, and cast their garments on him *it*;
and ~~he~~ *Jesus* sat upon ~~him~~ *it*.

1:8 And many spread their garments in the way:
and others cut down branches ~~off the~~ *of* trees, and strawed *strewed* them in the way.

LUKE

19:29 And it came to pass, when he was come nigh to Bethphage and Bethany, at the mount called the mount of Olives, he sent two of his disciples,
19:30 Saying, Go ye into the village over against you;

in the which at your entering ye shall find

a colt tied, whereon yet never man sat: loose him, and bring him ~~hither~~ *to me*.
19:31 And if any man ask you, Why do ye loose ~~him~~ *the colt*? thus shall ye say unto him, Because the Lord hath need of him.
19:32 And they ~~that~~ *who* were sent went their way, and found even as he had said unto them.

19:33 And as they were loosing the colt, the owners thereof said unto them, Why loose ye the colt?

19:34 And they said, The Lord hath need of him.

19:35 And they brought him to Jesus: and they cast their garments upon the colt,
and they set Jesus thereon.

19:36 And as he went, they spread their clothes in the way.

JOHN

12:14 And Jesus, when he had ~~found~~ *sent two of his disciples and got* a young ass, sat thereon;

as it is written,
12:15 Fear not, daughter of Sion: behold, thy King cometh,

sitting on an ass's colt.

12:16 These things understood not his disciples at the first: but when Jesus was glorified, then remembered they that these things were written of him, and that they had done these things unto him.
12:17 The people therefore that was with him when he called Lazarus out of his grave, and raised him from the dead, bare record.
12:18 For this cause the people also met him, for that they heard that he had done this miracle.
12:12 On the next day much people that were come to the feast, when they heard that Jesus was coming to Jerusalem,
12:13(a) Took branches of palm trees, and went forth to meet him,

MATTHEW	MARK	LUKE	JOHN
21:9 And the multitudes that went before, and *also* that followed *after*,	11:9 And they that went before *him*, and they that followed *after*,	19:37 And when he was come nigh, even now at the descent of the mount of Olives, the whole multitude of the disciples began to rejoice and praise God with a loud voice for all the mighty works that they had seen;	
cried, saying, Hosanna to the Son of David: Blessed is he that cometh in the name of the Lord; Hosanna in the highest.	cried, saying, Hosanna; Blessed is he that cometh in the name of the Lord:	19:38 Saying, Blessed ~~be~~ *is* the King ~~that~~ *who* cometh in the name of the Lord: peace in heaven, and glory in the highest.	12:13(b) and cried, Hosanna: Blessed is the King of Israel that cometh in the name of the Lord.
	11:10 ~~Blessed be~~ *That bringeth* the kingdom of our father David, *Blessed is he* that cometh in the name of the Lord: Hosanna in the highest.		
		19:39 And some of the Pharisees from among the multitude said unto him, Master, rebuke thy disciples. 19:40 And he answered and said unto them, ~~I tell you that,~~ if these should hold their peace, the stones would immediately cry out.	
			12:19 The Pharisees therefore said among themselves, Perceive ye how ye prevail nothing? behold, the world is gone after him.
		19:41 And when he was come near, he beheld the city, and wept over it, 19:42 Saying, If thou hadst known, even thou, at least in this thy day, the things which belong unto thy peace! but now they are hid from thine eyes. 19:43 For the days shall come upon thee, that thine enemies shall cast a trench about thee, and compass thee round, and keep thee in on every side, 19:44 And shall lay thee even with the ground, and thy children within thee; and they shall not leave in thee one stone upon another; because thou knewest not the time of thy visitation.	
21:10 And when he was come into Jerusalem, all the city was moved, saying, Who is this? 21:11 And the multitude said, This is Jesus ~~the prophet~~ of Nazareth, *the prophet* of Galilee.	11:11 And Jesus entered into Jerusalem,		
	and into the temple: and when he had looked round about upon all things, and ~~now~~ *blessed the disciples,* the eventide was come, *and* he went out unto Bethany with the twelve.		

MATTHEW	MARK	LUKE	JOHN

Monday--The Second Day of the Week

H-2. THE BARREN FIG TREE

21:18 Now in the morning as he returned into the city, he hungered.

21:19 And when he saw a fig tree in the way,

he came to it, and ~~found nothing thereon~~ *there was not any fruit on it*, but leaves only,

and *he* said unto it, Let no fruit grow on thee henceforward for ever. And presently the fig tree withered away.

11:12 And on the morrow, when they ~~were come~~ *came* from Bethany, he was hungry:
11:13 And seeing a fig tree afar off having leaves, he came *to it with his disciples; and as they supposed, he came to it to see* if ~~haply~~ he might find any thing thereon:
and when he came to it, ~~he found~~ *there was* nothing but leaves; for ~~the time of figs was not yet~~ *; for as yet the figs were not ripe*.
11:14 And Jesus ~~answered~~ *spake* and said unto it, No man eat fruit of thee hereafter for ever.

And ~~his~~ *the* disciples heard ~~it~~ *him*.

H-3. SECOND CLEANSING OF THE TEMPLE

21:12 And Jesus went into the temple of God, and cast out all them that sold and bought in the temple,
and overthrew the tables of the moneychangers, and the seats of them that sold doves,

21:13 And said unto them,
It is written, My house shall be called the house of prayer;

but ye have made it a den of thieves.
21:14 And the blind and the lame came to him in the temple; and he healed them.
21:15 And when the chief priests and scribes saw the wonderful things that he did, and the children *of the kingdom* crying in the temple, and saying, Hosanna to the Son of David; they were sore displeased,
21:16 And said unto him, Hearest thou what these say? And Jesus sai~~th~~*d* unto them, Yea; have ye never read *the scriptures which saith*, Out of the mouth*s* of babes and sucklings, *O Lord,* thou hast perfected praise?

11:15 And they ~~come~~ *came* to Jerusalem: and Jesus went into the temple, and began to cast out them that sold and bought in the temple, and overthrew the tables of the moneychangers, and the seats of them ~~that~~ *who* sold doves;
11:16 And would not suffer that any man should carry ~~any~~ *a* vessel through the temple.
11:17 And he taught, saying unto them, Is it not written, My house shall be called of all nations the house of prayer?
but ye have made it a den of thieves.

19:45 And he went into the temple, and began to cast out them ~~that~~ *who* sold therein, and them ~~that~~ *who* bought;

19:46 Saying unto them, It is written, My house is ~~the~~ *a* house of prayer:

but ye have made it a den of thieves.

11:18 And the scribes and chief priests heard ~~it~~ *him*, and sought how they might destroy him: for they feared him,

because all the people ~~was~~ *were* astonished at his doctrine.

19:47 And he taught daily in the temple.
But the chief priests and the scribes and the chief of the people sought to destroy him,

19:48 And could not find what they might do: for all the people were very attentive to hear him.

MATTHEW	MARK	LUKE	JOHN

H-4. RETURN TO BETHANY

		21:37 And in the day time he was teaching in the temple; and at night he went out, and abode in the mount that is called ~~the mount of~~ Olives.	
21:17 And he left them, and went out of the city *iu*nto Bethany; and he lodged there.	11:19 And when even was come, he went out of the city.		

Tuesday--The Third Day of the Week

H-5. DISCOURSE ON FAITH, PRAYER AND FORGIVENESS

MATTHEW	MARK
	11:20 And in the morning, as they passed by, they saw the fig tree dried up from the roots.
21:20 And when the disciples saw ~~it~~ *this*, they marvelled, ~~saying~~ *and said*, How soon is the fig tree withered away!	
	11:21 And Peter calling to remembrance sait~~h~~*d* unto him, Master, behold, the fig tree which thou cursedst is withered away.
21:21 Jesus answered and said unto them,	11:22 And Jesus ~~answering saith unto them~~ *spake and said unto him*, Have faith in God.
Verily I say unto you, If ye have faith, and doubt not, ye shall not only do this ~~which is done~~ to the fig tree, but also if ye shall say unto this mountain, Be thou removed, and be thou cast into the sea; it shall be done.	11:23 For verily I say unto you, That whosoever shall say unto this mountain, Be thou removed, and be thou cast into the sea; and shall not doubt in his heart, but shall believe that those things which he saith shall come to pass; he shall have whatsoever he saith *fulfilled*.
	11:24 Therefore I say unto you, What*soever* things ~~soever~~ ye desire, when ye pray, believe that ye receive ~~them~~, and ye shall have ~~them~~ *whatsoever ye ask*.
21:22 And all things, whatsoever ye shall ask in prayer, *in faith* believing, ye shall receive.	11:25 And when ye stand praying, forgive, if ye have ~~ought~~ *aught* against any: that your Father also ~~which~~ *who* is in heaven may forgive you your trespasses.
	11:26 But if ~~ye~~ *you* do not forgive, neither will your Father ~~which~~ *who* is in heaven forgive your trespasses.

MATTHEW	MARK	LUKE	JOHN

H-6. JESUS' AUTHORITY IS CHALLENGED

21:23 And when he was come into the temple, the chief priests and the elders of the people came unto him as he was teaching, and said,
By what authority doest thou these things? and who gave thee this authority?

21:24 And Jesus answered and said unto them, I also will ask you one thing, which if ye tell me, I in like wise will tell you by what authority I do these things.
21:25 The baptism of John, whence was it? from heaven, or of men?
And they reasoned with themselves, saying, If we shall say, From heaven; he will say unto us, Why did ye not then believe him?
21:26 But if we shall say, Of men; we fear the people;

for all hold *people held* John as a prophet.

21:27 And they answered Jesus, and said, We cannot tell.
And he said unto them,
Neither tell I you by what authority I do these things.

11:27 And they come *came* again to Jerusalem: and as he was walking in the temple, there come *came* to him the chief priests, and the scribes, and the elders,

11:28 And say *said* unto him, By what authority doest thou these things? and who gave thee this authority to do these things?
11:29 And Jesus answered and said unto them, I will also ask of you one question, and answer me, and *then* I will tell you by what authority I do these things.
11:30 *Was* The baptism of John, was it from heaven, or of men *man*? answer me.
11:31 And they reasoned with themselves, saying, If we shall say, From heaven; he will say, Why then did ye not believe him?
11:32 But if we shall say, Of men; *we shall offend the people. Therefore* they feared the people: for all men counted *people believed* John, that he was a prophet indeed.
11:33 And they answered and said unto Jesus, We cannot tell. And Jesus answering saithd unto them, Neither do I tell you by what authority I do these things.

21:38 And all the people came early in the morning to him in the temple, for to hear him.
20:1 And it came to pass, that on one of those days, as he taught the people in the temple, and preached the gospel, the chief priests and the scribes came upon him with the elders,
20:2 And spake unto him, saying, Tell us, by what authority doest thou these things? or who is he that *who* gave thee this authority?
20:3 And he answered and said unto them, I will also ask you one thing; and answer me:

20:4 The baptism of John, was it from heaven, or of men?

20:5 And they reasoned with themselves, saying, If we shall say, From heaven; he will say, Why then believed ye him not?
20:6 But and if we say, Of men; all the people will stone us:

for they be *are* persuaded that John was a prophet.

20:7 And they answered, that they could not tell whence it was.
20:8 And Jesus said unto them, Neither tell I you by what authority I do these things.

H-7. PARABLE OF THE TWO SONS

21:28 But what think ye? A certain man had two sons; and he came to the first, and said *saying*, Son, go work to day in my vineyard.
21:29 He answered and said, I will not: but afterward he repented, and went.
21:30 And he came to the second, and said likewise. And he answered and said, I go, sir *will serve*: and went not.
21:31 Whether of them *these* twain did the will of his father? They say unto him, The first. Jesus saithd unto them, Verily I say unto you, That the publicans and the harlots *shall* go into the kingdom of God before you.
21:32 For John came unto you in the way of righteousness, *and bore record of me.* and ye believed him not: but the publicans and the harlots believed him: and ye, *afterward,* when ye had seen it *me*, repented not afterward, that ye might believe him.

MATTHEW	MARK	LUKE	JOHN

H-8. PARABLE OF THE WICKED HUSBANDMEN

MATTHEW

21:33 ~~Hear another parable:~~ *For he that believed not John concerning me, cannot believe me, except he first repent. And except ye repent, the preaching of John shall condemn you in the day of judgement. And, again, hear another parable; for unto you that believe not, I speak in parables; that your unrighteousness may be rewarded unto you.*

Behold, There was a certain householder, ~~which~~ *who* planted a vineyard, and hedged it round about, and digged a winepress in it, and built a tower, and let it out to husbandmen, and went into a far country:

21:34 And when the time of the fruit drew near, he sent his servants to the husbandmen, that they might receive the fruits of it.

21:35 And the husbandmen took his servants, and beat one, and killed another, and stoned another.

21:36 Again, he sent other servants more than the first: and they did unto them likewise.

21:37 But last of all he sent unto them his son, saying,

They will reverence my son.

21:38 But when the husbandmen saw the son, they said among themselves, This is the heir; come, let us kill him, and let us seize on his inheritance.

21:39 And they caught him, and cast him out of the vineyard, and slew him.

21:40 *And Jesus said unto them,* When the ~~l~~Lord therefore of the vineyard cometh, what will he do unto those husbandmen?

21:41 They say unto him,

He will ~~miserably~~ destroy those *miserable,* wicked men,

and will let out ~~his~~ *the* vineyard unto other husbandmen, ~~which~~ *who* shall render him the fruits in their seasons.

MARK

12:1 And ~~he~~ *Jesus* began to speak unto them by parables.

saying, A ~~certain~~ man planted a vineyard, and set ~~an~~ hedge about it, and digged ~~a place for the winefat~~ *the wine vat*, and built a tower, and let it out to husbandmen, and went into a far country.

12:2 And at the season he sent to the husbandmen a servant, that he might receive from the husbandmen of the fruit of the vineyard.

12:3 And they caught ~~him,~~ *the servant* and beat him, and sent him away empty.

12:4 And again he sent unto them another servant; and at him they cast stones, and wounded him in the head, and sent him away shamefully handled.

12:5 And again he sent another; and him they killed, and many others; beating some, and killing some.

12:6 Having yet therefore one son, his wellbeloved, he sent him also last unto them, saying, They will reverence my son.

12:7 But those husbandmen said among themselves, This is the heir; come, let us kill him, and the inheritance shall be ours.

12:8 And they took him, ~~and killed him,~~ and cast him out of the vineyard *and killed him*.

12:9 What shall therefore the lord of the vineyard do?

Lo, he will come and destroy the husbandmen, and will give the vineyard unto others.

LUKE

20:9 Then began he to speak to the people this parable;

A certain man planted a vineyard,

and let it ~~forth~~ *out* to husbandmen, and went into a far country for a long time.

20:10 And at the season *of the harvest* he sent ~~a~~ *his* servant to the husbandmen, that they should give him of the fruit of the vineyard: but the husbandmen beat him, and sent him away empty.

20:11 And again he sent another servant: and they beat him also, and entreated him shamefully, and sent him away empty.

20:12 And again he sent a third: and they wounded him also, and cast him out.

20:13 Then said the lord of the vineyard, What shall I do? I will send my beloved son:

it may be they will reverence him when they see him.

20:14 But when the husbandmen saw him, they reasoned among themselves, saying, This is the heir: come, let us kill him, that the inheritance may be ours.

20:15 So they cast him out of the vineyard, and killed him.

What therefore shall the lord of the vineyard do unto them?

20:16 He shall come and destroy these husbandmen, and shall give the vineyard to others.

And when they heard ~~it~~ *this*, they said, God forbid.

20:17 And he beheld them, and said,

MATTHEW	MARK	LUKE	JOHN

21:42 Jesus saithd unto them, Did ye never read in the scriptures,

12:10 And *Again,* have ye not read this sScripture;

What is this then that *which* is written,
The stone which the builders rejected, the same is become the head of the corner?

The stone which the builders rejected, the same is become the head of the corner: this is the Lord's doing, and it is marvellous in our eyes?

The stone which the builders rejected is become the head of the corner:
12:11 This was the Lord's doing, and it is marvellous in our eyes?

21:43 Therefore say I unto you, The kingdom of God shall be taken from you, and given to a nation bringing forth the fruits thereof.

21:44 And *For* whosoever shall fall on this stone shall be broken: but on whomsoever it shall fall, it will grind him to powder.

20:18 Whosoever shall fall upon that stone shall be broken; but on whomsoever it shall fall, it will *shall* grind him to powder.

21:45 And when the chief priests and Pharisees had heard his parables, they perceived that he spake of them. *And they said among themselves, Shall this man think that he alone can spoil this great kingdom?*
And they were angry with him.

12:12 *And now they were angry when they heard these words;*

20:19 And the chief priests and the scribes the same hour sought to lay hands on him; and *but* they feared the people:

21:46 But when they sought to lay hands on him, they feared the multitude,
because they *learned that the multitude* took him for a prophet.

And they sought to lay hold on him, but feared the people:

for they knew that he had spoken the parable against them: and they left him, and went their way.

for they perceived that he had spoken this parable against them.

And now his disciples came to him, and Jesus said unto them, Marvel ye at the words of the parable which I spake unto them? Verily, I say unto you, I am the stone, and those wicked ones reject me. I am the head of the corner. These Jews shall fall upon me, and shall be broken. And the kingdom of God shall be taken from them, and shall be given to a nation bringing forth the fruits thereof; (meaning the Gentiles.) Wherefore, on whomsoever this stone shall fall, it shall grind him to powder. And when the Lord therefore of the vineyard cometh, he will destroy those miserable, wicked men, and will let again his vineyard unto other husbandmen, even in the last days, who shall render him the fruits in their seasons. And then understood they the parable which he spake unto them, that the Gentiles should be destroyed also, when the Lord should descend out of heaven to reign in his vineyard, which is the earth and the inhabitants thereof.

H-9. PARABLE OF THE MARRIAGE OF THE KING'S SON

22:1 And Jesus answered *the people again* and spake unto them ~~again by~~ *in* parables, and said,

22:2 The kingdom of heaven is like unto a certain king, ~~which~~ *who* made a marriage for his son,

22:3 And *when the marriage was ready, he* sent forth his servants to call them that were bidden to the wedding: and they would not come.

22:4 Again, he sent forth other servants, saying, Tell them ~~which~~ *that* are bidden, Behold, I have prepared my ~~dinner: my~~ oxen and my fatlings ~~are~~ *have been* killed, *and my dinner is ready,* and all things are ~~ready~~ *prepared*: come unto the marriage.

22:5 But they made light of ~~it~~ *the servants*, and went their ways, one to his farm, another to his merchandise:

22:6 And the remnant took his servants, and entreated them spitefully, and slew them.

22:7 But when the king heard ~~thereof~~ *that his servants were dead*, he was wroth: and he sent forth his armies, and destroyed those murderers, and burned up their city.

22:8 Then sai~~th~~*d* he to his servants, The wedding is ready, but they ~~which~~ *who* were bidden were not worthy.

22:9 Go ye therefore into the highways, and as many as ye shall find, bid to the marriage.

22:10 So those servants went out into the highways, and gathered together all as many as they found, both bad and good: and the wedding was furnished with guests.

22:11 ~~And~~ *But* when the king came in to see the guests, he saw there a man ~~which~~ *who* had not ~~on~~ a wedding garment:

22:12 And he sai~~th~~*d* unto him, Friend, how camest thou in hither not having a wedding garment? And he was speechless.

22:13 Then said the king *un*to the servants, Bind him hand and foot, and take ~~him away,~~ and cast him *away* into outer darkness; there shall be weeping and gnashing of teeth.

22:14 For many are called, but few ~~are~~ chosen. *Wherefore all do not have on the wedding garment.*

MATTHEW	MARK	LUKE	JOHN

H-10. PAYING TRIBUTE TO CAESAR

MATTHEW

22:15   Then went the Pharisees, and took counsel how they might entangle him in his talk.
22:16   And they sent out unto him their disciples with the Herodians,

saying, Master, we know that thou art true, and teachest the way of God in truth, neither carest thou for any ~~man~~:
for thou regardest not the person of men.

22:17   Tell us therefore, What thinkest thou?
Is it lawful to give tribute unto Caesar, or not?

22:18   But Jesus perceived their wickedness, and said, *Ye hypocrites!* Why tempt ye me, ~~ye hypocrites~~ ?
22:19   ~~Shew~~ *Show* me the tribute money.
And they brought unto him a penny.
22:20   And he sai~~th~~*d* unto them, Whose *image* is this ~~image~~ and superscription?
22:21   They say unto him, Caesar's.   Then sai~~th~~*d* he unto them, Render therefore unto Caesar the things which are Caesar's; and unto God the things ~~that~~ *which* are God's.

22:22   *And* When they had heard *him say* these words,
they marvelled, and left him, and went their way.

MARK

12:13   And they ~~send~~ *sent* unto him certain of the Pharisees and of the Herodians, to catch him in his words.

12:14   And when they were come, they say unto him, Master, we know that thou art true, and carest for no man:
for thou regardest not the person of men, but teachest the way of God in truth:

Is it lawful to give tribute to Caesar, or not?
12:15   Shall we give, or shall we not give?
But he, knowing their hypocrisy, said unto them,
Why tempt ye me?

bring me a penny, that I may see it.

12:16   And they brought ~~it~~ *the penny*.
And he sai~~th~~*d* unto them, Whose ~~is this~~ image and superscription *is this*?
And they said unto him, Caesar's.
12:17   And Jesus answering said unto them, Render to Caesar the things ~~that~~ *which* are Caesar's, and to God the things that are God's.

And they marvelled at ~~him~~ *it*.

LUKE

20:20   And they watched him,

and sent forth spies, ~~which~~ *who* should feign themselves just men, that they might take hold of his words, that so *doing,* they might deliver him unto the power and authority of the governor.
20:21   And they asked him, saying, Master, we know that thou sayest and teachest rightly,

neither ~~acceptest~~ *regardest* thou the person of any,
but teachest the way of God truly:

20:22   Is it lawful for us to give tribute unto Caesar, or no?

20:23   But he perceived their craftiness, and said unto them, Why tempt ye me?

20:24   Shew me a penny.

Whose image and superscription hath it?

They answered and said, Caesar's.
20:25   And he said unto them, Render therefore unto Caesar the things which be Caesar's, and unto God the things which be God's.

20:26   And they could not take hold of his words before the people:

and they marvelled at his answer, and held their peace.

H-11. MARRIAGE AFTER THE RESURRECTION

MATTHEW

22:23   The same day came ~~to him~~ the Sadducees *to him*, ~~which~~ *who* say that there is no resurrection, and asked him,
22:24   Saying, Master, Moses said, If a man die,

having no children,
his brother shall marry his wife, and raise up seed unto his brother.
22:25   Now there were with us seven brethren: and the first, when he had married a wife, deceased, and, having no issue, left his wife unto his brother:
22:26   Likewise the second also, and the third,

MARK

12:18   Then ~~come~~ *came* unto him the Sadducees, ~~which~~ *who* say there is no resurrection; and they asked him, saying,
12:19   Master, Moses wrote unto us *in his law*, If a man's brother die, and leave ~~his wife behind him~~ *a wife*, and leave no children, that his brother should take his wife, and raise up seed unto his brother.
12:20   Now there were seven brethren: ~~and~~ the first took a wife, and dying left no seed.

12:21   And the second took her, and died, neither left he any seed:

LUKE

20:27   Then came to him certain of the Sadducees, ~~which~~ *who* deny ~~that~~ there is any resurrection; and they asked him,
20:28   Saying, Master, Moses wrote unto us, *saying,* If any man's brother die, having a wife, and he die without children, that his brother should take his wife, and raise up seed unto his brother.
20:29   There were therefore seven brethren: ~~and~~ the first took a wife, and died without children.

20:30   And the second took her to wife, and he died childless.

MATTHEW	MARK	LUKE	JOHN

and the third likewise.

20:31 And the third took her *in like manner*; and ~~in like manner~~ the seven also: and they left no children, and died.

unto the seventh.

12:22 And the seven had her, and left no seed:
last of all the woman died also.

20:32 *And* Last of all the woman died also.

22:27 And last of all the woman died also.
22:28 Therefore in the resurrection whose wife shall she be of the seven?
for they all had her.
22:29 Jesus answered and said unto them, Ye do err, not knowing the scriptures, nor the power of God.

12:23 In the resurrection therefore, when they shall rise, whose wife shall she be of them? for the seven had her to wife.
12:24 And Jesus answering said unto them, ~~Do ye not therefore err~~ *ye do err therefore*, because ye know not*, and understand not* the ~~s~~Scriptures, neither the power of God?

20:33 Therefore in the resurrection whose wife of them is she?

for seven had her to wife.

20:34 And Jesus answering said unto them, The children of this world marry, and are given in marriage:
20:35 But they ~~which~~ *who* shall be accounted worthy to obtain that world, ~~and the~~ *through* resurrection from the dead, neither marry, nor are given in marriage:
20:36 Neither can they die any more: for they are equal unto the angels; and are the children of God, being the children of the resurrection.

22:30 For in the resurrection they neither marry, nor are given in marriage,

but are as the angels of God in heaven.

12:25 For when they shall rise from the dead, they neither marry, nor are given in marriage;

but are as the angels ~~which~~ *of God who* are in heaven.

22:31 But as touching the resurrection of the dead, have ye not read that which was spoken unto you ~~by~~ *of* God, saying,
22:32 I am the God of Abraham, and the God of Isaac, and the God of Jacob?
God is not the God of the dead, but of the living.

12:26 And as touching the dead, that they rise: have ye not read in the book of Moses, how in the bush God spake unto him, saying,
I am the God of Abraham, and the God of Isaac, and the God of Jacob?
12:27 He is not *therefore* the God of the dead, but the God of the living:
for he raiseth them up out of their graves. ye therefore do greatly err.

20:37 Now that the dead are raised, even Moses shewed at the bush, when he calleth the Lord

the God of Abraham, and the God of Isaac, and the God of Jacob.

20:38 For he is not a God of the dead, but of the living: for all live unto him.

22:33 And when the multitude heard ~~this~~ *him*, they were astonished at his doctrine.

20:39 Then certain of the scribes answering said, Master, thou hast well said.

H-12. LAWYER ASKS ABOUT THE GREAT COMMANDMENT

22:34 But when the Pharisees had heard that he had put the Sadducees to silence, they were gathered together.

12:28 And one of the scribes came, and having heard them reasoning together, and perceiving that he had answered them well,

22:35 Then one of them, ~~which was~~ a lawyer, ~~asked him a question,~~ tempting him, *asked, and* saying,
22:36 Master, which is the great commandment in the law?
22:37 Jesus said unto him,

asked him, Which is the first commandment of all?
12:29 And Jesus answered him, The first of all the commandments is, *Hearken, and* Hear, O Israel; The Lord our God is one Lord:

MATTHEW	MARK	LUKE	JOHN

Thou shalt love the Lord thy God with all thy heart, and with all thy soul, and with all thy mind.

12:30 And thou shalt love the Lord thy God with all thy heart, and with all thy soul, and with all thy mind, and with all thy strength: this is the first commandment.

22:38 This is the first and great commandment.

22:39 And the second is like unto it, Thou shalt love thy neighbour as thyself.

12:31 And the second is like, namely this, Thou shalt love thy neighbour *neighbor* as thyself. There is none other comman-dment greater than these.

22:40 On these two command-ments hang all the law and the prophets.

12:32 And the scribe said unto him, Well, Master, thou hast said the truth: for there is one God; and there is none other but he *him*:

12:33 And to love him with all the heart, and with all the understanding, and with all the soul, and with all the strength, and to love his neighbour as himself, is more than all whole burnt offerings and sacrifices.

12:34(a) And when Jesus saw that he answered discreetly, he said unto him, Thou art not far from the kingdom of God.

H-13. WHAT THINK YE OF CHRIST?

22:41 While the Pharisees were gathered together, Jesus asked them,

12:35 And Jesus answered *spake* and said, while he taught in the temple,

22:42 Saying, What think ye of Christ? whose son is he? They say unto him, The Son of David.

How say the scribes that Christ is the Son of David?

20:41 And he said unto them, How say they that Christ is David's son?

22:43 He saith*d* unto them, How then doth David in spirit call him Lord, saying,

22:44 The LORD said unto my Lord, Sit thou on my right hand, till I make thine enemies thy footstool?

22:45 If David then call him Lord, how is he his son?

12:36 For David himself said by the Holy Ghost, The Lord said to my Lord, Sit thou on my right hand, till *until* I make thine enemies thy footstool.

12:37 David therefore himself calleth him Lord; and whence is he then his son? And the common people heard him gladly*; but the high priest and the elders were offended at him.*

20:42 And David himself saith*d* in the book of Psalms, The LORD said unto my Lord, Sit thou on my right hand,

20:43 Till I make thine enemies thy footstool.

20:44 David therefore calleth him Lord, how is he then his son?

22:46 And no man was able to answer him a word, neither durst any man from that day forth ask him any more questions.

12:34(b) And no man after that durst ask him any question , *saying, Who art thou?*

20:40 And after that they durst not ask him any question at all.

MATTHEW	MARK	LUKE	JOHN

H-14. JESUS WARNS AGAINST THE SCRIBES AND PHARISEES

23:1 Then spake Jesus to the multitude, and to his disciples, 23:2 Saying,

The scribes and the Pharisees sit in Moses' seat:
23:3 All therefore whatsoever they bid you observe, that observe and do *they will make you observe and do; for they are ministers of the law, and they make themselves your judges*; but do not ye after their works: for they say, and do not.
23:4 For they bind heavy burdens and grievous to be borne, and lay them on men's shoulders, *and they are grievous to be borne*; but they themselves will not move them with one of their fingers.
23:5 But *And* all their works they do for to be seen of men: they make broad their phylacteries, and enlarge the borders of their garments,
23:6 And love the uppermost rooms at feasts,
and the chief seats in the synagogues,
23:7 And greetings in the markets,
and to be called of men, Rabbi, Rabbi, *(which is master)*.
23:8 But be not ye called Rabbi: for one is your Master, even *which is* Christ; and all ye are brethren.
23:9 And call no man *one* your father *creator* upon the earth, *or your heavenly Father*: for one is your *creator and heavenly* Father, which *even he who* is in heaven.
23:10 Neither be ye called masters: for one is your Master, even *he whom your heavenly Father sent, which is* Christ; *For he hath sent him among you that ye might have life.*
23:11 But he that is greatest among you shall be your servant.
23:12 And whosoever shall exalt himself shall be abased *of him*; and he that shall humble himself shall be exalted *of him*.
23:13 But woe unto you, scribes and Pharisees, hypocrites! for ye shut up the kingdom of heaven against men: for ye neither go in yourselves, neither suffer ye them that are entering to go in.
23:14 Woe unto you, scribes and Pharisees, *for ye are* hypocrites! for ye devour widows' houses, and for a pretence make long prayers: therefore ye shall receive the greater damnation *punishment*.
23:15 Woe unto you, scribes and Pharisees, hypocrites! for ye compass sea and land to make one proselyte, and when he is made, ye

12:38(a) And he said unto them in his doctrine,

Beware of the scribes,

which love to go in long clothing,

12:39(b) and the uppermost rooms at feasts:
12:39(a) And the chief seats in the synagogues,
12:38(b) and love *have* salutations in the marketplaces,

12:40 Which *Who* devour widows' houses, and for a pretence make long prayers: these shall receive greater damnation.

20:45 Then in the audience of all the people he said unto his disciples,
20:46(a) Beware of the scribes,

which *who* desire to walk in long robes,

20:46(d) and the chief rooms at feasts;
20:46(c) and the highest seats in the synagogues,
20:46(b) and love greetings in the markets,

20:47 Which *Who* devour widows' houses, and for a shew *show* make long prayers: the same shall receive greater damnation.

MATTHEW	MARK	LUKE	JOHN

make him twofold more the child of hell than *he was before, like unto* yourselves.

23:16 Woe unto you, ~~ye~~ blind guides, ~~which~~ *who* say, Whosoever shall swear by the temple, it is nothing; but whosoever shall swear by the gold of the temple, he *committeth sin, and* is a debtor!

23:17 ~~Ye~~ *You are* fools and blind: for ~~whether~~ *which* is *the* greater, the gold, or the temple that sanctifieth the gold?

23:18 And *ye say*, Whosoever ~~shall~~ swear*eth* by the altar, it is nothing; but whosoever sweareth by the gift that is upon it, he is guilty.

23:19 ~~Ye~~ *O* fools and blind: for ~~whether~~ *which* is *the* greater, the gift, or the altar that sanctifieth the gift?

23:20 *Verily I say unto you,* Whoso therefore ~~shall swear by the altar~~, sweareth by it, *sweareth by the altar,* and by all things thereon.

23:21 And whoso shall swear by the temple, sweareth by it, and by him ~~that~~ *who* dwelleth therein.

23:22 And he that shall swear by heaven, sweareth by the throne of God, and by him ~~that~~ *who* sitteth thereon.

23:23 Woe unto you, scribes and Pharisees, hypocrites! for ye pay tithe of mint and anise and cummin, and have omitted the weightier ~~matters~~ *things* of the law, judgment, mercy, and faith: these ought ye to have done, and not to leave the other undone.

23:24 Ye blind guides, ~~which~~ *who* strain at a gnat, and swallow a camel*; who make yourselves appear unto men that ye would not commit the least sin, and yet ye yourselves, transgress the whole law*.

23:25 Woe unto you, scribes and Pharisees, hypocrites! for ye make clean the outside of the cup and of the platter, but within they are full of extortion and excess.

23:26 ~~Thou~~ *Ye* blind Pharisee*s*, cleanse first ~~that which is within~~ the cup and platter *within*, that the outside of them may be clean also.

23:27 Woe unto you, scribes and Pharisees, hypocrites! for ye are like unto whited sepulchres, which indeed appear beautiful outward*ly*, but are within full of *the bones of the* dead ~~men's bones~~, and of all uncleanness.

23:28 Even so ye also outwardly appear righteous unto men, but within ye are full of hypocrisy and iniquity.

23:29 Woe unto you, scribes and Pharisees, hypocrites! because ye build the tombs of the prophets, and garnish the sepulchres of the righteous,

23:30 And say, If we had been in the days of our fathers, we would not have been partakers with them in the blood of the prophets.

23:31 Wherefore ye ~~be~~ *are* witnesses unto yourselves *of your own wickedness*, ~~that~~ *and* ye are the children of them ~~which~~ *who* killed the prophets.

23:32 ~~Fill ye~~ *And will fill* up ~~then~~ the measure *then* of your fathers *for ye, yourselves, kill the prophets like unto your fathers*.

23:33 Ye serpents, ~~ye~~ *and* generation of vipers, how can ye escape the damnation of hell?

23:34 Wherefore, behold, I send unto you prophets, and wise men, and scribes: and ~~some~~ of them ye shall kill and crucify; and ~~some~~ of them shall ye scourge in your synagogues, and persecute ~~them~~ from city to city:

23:35 That upon you may come all the righteous blood shed upon the earth, from the blood of righteous Abel unto the blood of Zacharias son of Barachias, whom ye slew between the temple and the altar.

23:36 Verily I say unto you, All these things shall come upon this generation.

H-15. JESUS' LAMENTATION OVER JERUSALEM

23:37 *Ye bear testimony against your fathers, when ye, yourselves, are partakers of the same wickedness. Behold your fathers did it through ignorance, but ye do not; wherefore, their sins shall be upon your heads. Then Jesus began to weep over Jerusalem, saying,* O Jerusalem, Jerusalem, ~~thou that killest~~ *ye who will kill* the prophets, and ~~stonest~~ *will stone* them ~~which~~ *who* are sent unto ~~thee~~ *you*, how often would I have gathered ~~thy~~ *your* children together, even as a hen ~~gathereth~~ *gathers* her chickens under her wings, and ye would not!

23:38 Behold, your house is left unto you desolate.

23:39 For I say unto you, *that* Ye shall not see me henceforth, *and know that I am he of whom it is written by the prophets,* ~~till~~ *until* ye shall say, Blessed is he ~~that~~ *who* cometh in the name of the Lord, *in the clouds of heaven, and all the holy angels with him. Then understood his disciples that he should come again on the earth, after that he was glorified and crowned on the right hand of God.*

MATTHEW	MARK	LUKE	JOHN

H-16. THE WIDOW'S MITE

	MARK	**LUKE**	

MARK

12:41 And *after this,* Jesus sat over against the treasury, and beheld how the people cast money into the treasury: and many that were rich cast in much.

12:42 And there came a certain poor widow, and she ~~threw~~ *cast* in two mites, which make a farthing.

12:43 And ~~he~~ *Jesus* called ~~unto him~~ his disciples, and sai~~th~~*d* unto them, Verily I say unto you, That this poor widow hath cast more in, than all they ~~which~~ *who* have cast into the treasury:

12:44 For all ~~they~~ *the rich* did cast in of their abundance; but she ~~of~~ *, notwithstanding* her want did cast in all that she had, *yea,* even all her living.

LUKE

21:1 And he looked up, and saw the rich men casting their gifts into the treasury.

21:2 And ~~he~~ saw also a certain poor widow casting in thither two mites.

21:3 And he said, Of a truth I say unto you, that this poor widow hath cast in more than they all:

21:4 For all these have of their abundance cast in unto the offerings of God: but she of her penury hath cast in all the living that she had.

H-17. JESUS TESTIFIES OF HIS DEATH

JOHN

12:20 And there were certain Greeks among them that came up to worship at the feast:

12:21 The same came therefore to Philip, which was of Bethsaida of Galilee, and desired him, saying, Sir, we would see Jesus.

12:22 Philip cometh and telleth Andrew: and again Andrew and Philip tell Jesus.

12:23 And Jesus answered them, saying, The hour is come, that the Son of man should be glorified.

12:24 Verily, verily, I say unto you, Except a corn of wheat fall into the ground and die, it abideth alone: but if it die, it bringeth forth much fruit.

12:25 He that loveth his life shall lose it; and he that hateth his life in this world shall keep it unto life eternal.

12:26 If any man serve me, let him follow me; and where I am, there shall also my servant be: if any man serve me, him will my Father honour.

12:27 Now is my soul troubled; and what shall I say? Father, save me from this hour: but for this cause came I unto this hour.

12:28 Father, glorify thy name. Then came there a voice from heaven, saying, I have both glorified it, and will glorify it again.

12:29 The people therefore, that stood by, and heard it, said that it thundered: others said, An angel spake to him.

12:30 Jesus answered and said, This voice came not because of me, but for your sakes.

12:31 Now is the judgment of this

MATTHEW	MARK	LUKE	JOHN

world: now shall the prince of this world be cast out.

12:32 And I, if I be lifted up from the earth, will draw all men unto me.

12:33 This he said, signifying what death he should die.

12:34 The people answered him, We have heard out of the law that Christ abideth for ever: and how sayest thou, The Son of man must be lifted up? who is this Son of man?

12:35 Then Jesus said unto them, Yet a little while is the light with you. Walk while ye have the light, lest darkness come upon you: for he that walketh in darkness knoweth not whither he goeth.

12:36(a) While ye have light, believe in the light, that ye may be the children of light.

H-18. JESUS AND HIS FATHER

12:44 Jesus cried and said, He that believeth on me, believeth not on me, but on him that sent me.

12:45 And he that seeth me seeth him that sent me.

12:46 I am come a light into the world, that whosoever believeth on me should not abide in darkness.

12:47 And if any man hear my words, and believe not, I judge him not: for I came not to judge the world, but to save the world.

12:48 He that rejecteth me, and receiveth not my words, hath one that judgeth him: the word that I have spoken, the same shall judge him in the last day.

12:49 For I have not spoken of myself; but the Father which sent me, he gave me a commandment, what I should say, and what I should speak.

12:50 And I know that his commandment is life everlasting: whatsoever I speak therefore, even as the Father said unto me, so I speak.

H-19. JESUS LEAVES THE TEMPLE

12:36(b) These things spake Jesus, and departed, and did hide himself from them.

MATTHEW	MARK	LUKE	JOHN

H-20. PEOPLE'S REACTION TO THE TEACHINGS OF JESUS

| | | | 12:37 But though he had done so many miracles before them, yet they believed not on him: |

12:37 But though he had done so many miracles before them, yet they believed not on him:

12:38 That the saying of Esaias the prophet might be fulfilled, which he spake, Lord, who hath believed our report? and to whom hath the arm of the Lord been revealed?

12:39 Therefore they could not believe, because that Esaias said again,

12:40 He hath blinded their eyes, and hardened their heart; that they should not see with their eyes, nor understand with their heart, and be converted, and I should heal them.

12:41 These things said Esaias, when he saw his glory, and spake of him.

12:42 Nevertheless among the chief rulers also many believed on him; but because of the Pharisees they did not confess him, lest they should be put out of the synagogue:

12:43 For they loved the praise of men more than the praise of God.

H-21. THE OLIVET DISCOURSE

MATTHEW

24:1 And Jesus went out, and departed from the temple: and his disciples came to him for to ~~shew him~~ *hear him, saying, Master,*

show us concerning the buildings of the temple, *as thou hast said; They shall be thrown down and left unto you desolate*.

24:2 And Jesus said unto them,

See ye not all these things? *And do ye not understand them?* verily I say unto you,

There shall not be left here , *upon this temple,* one stone upon another, that shall not be thrown down.

24:3 *And Jesus left them and went upon the mount of Olives.* And as he sat upon the mount of Olives,

the disciples came unto him

MARK

13:1 And as ~~he~~ *Jesus* went out of the temple, ~~one of~~ his disciples ~~saith unto~~ *came to* him *saying,* Master, ~~see what manner of stones and what buildings are here!~~ *show us concerning the buildings of the Temple.*

13:2 And ~~Jesus answering~~ *he* said unto him, ~~Seest thou these great buildings?~~ *Behold ye these stones of the temple, and all this great work, and buidings of the temple? Verily I say unto you, they shall be thrown down and left unto the Jews desolate. And Jesus said unto them, See ye not all these things, and do ye not understand them? Verily I say unto you,*

there shall not be left *here upon this temple,* one stone upon another, that shall not be thrown down.

And Jesus left them and went upon the mount of Olives. 13:3 And as he sat upon the mount of Olives ~~over against the temple~~, ~~Peter and James and John and Andrew asked~~ *the disciples came*

LUKE

21:5 And as some spake of the temple, how it was adorned with goodly stones and gifts, he said,

21:6 ~~As for~~ these things which ye behold, the days will come, in the which there shall not be left one stone upon another, ~~that~~ *which* shall not be thrown down.

21:7 And ~~they~~ *the disciples* asked

MATTHEW	MARK	LUKE	JOHN

MATTHEW

privately, saying,
Tell us, when shall these things be *which thou hast said concerning the destruction of the temple, and the Jews?*
and what ~~shall be~~ *is* the sign of thy coming, and of the end of the world? *(or the destruction of the wicked, which is the end of the world.)*

24:4 And Jesus answered and said unto them,

Take heed that no man deceive you.
24:5 For many shall come in my name, saying, I am Christ; and shall deceive many.

24:9 Then shall they deliver you up to be afflicted, and shall kill you: and ye shall be hated of all nations for my name's sake.

24:10 And then shall many be offended, and shall betray one another, and shall hate one another.
24:11 And many false prophets shall rise, and shall deceive many.
24:12 And because iniquity shall abound, the love of many shall wax cold.
24:13 But he that ~~shall endure unto the end~~ *remaineth steadfast, and is not overcome*, the same shall be saved.
24:15 When ye therefore shall see the abomination of desolation, spoken of by Daniel the prophet,

MARK

unto him privately, *saying,*
13:4 Tell us, when shall these things be *which thou has said, concerning the destruction of the temple, and the Jews?*
and what ~~shall be~~ *is* the sign ~~when all these things shall be fulfilled?~~ *of thy coming, and of the end of the world, (or destruction of the wicked, which is the end of the world?)*
13:5 And Jesus ~~answering them began to say~~ *answered and said unto them,*

Take heed ~~lest any~~ *that no* man deceive you:
13:6 For many shall come in my name, saying, I am Christ; and shall deceive many.

13:9 ~~But take heed to yourselves:~~

~~for they shall deliver you up to councils; and in the synagogues ye shall be beaten:~~
~~and ye shall be brought before rulers and kings for my sake, for a testimony against them.~~

~~13:11 But when they shall lead you, and deliver you up,~~

~~take no thought beforehand what ye shall speak, neither do ye premeditate: but whatsoever shall be given you in that hour, that speak ye: for it is not ye that speak, but the Holy Ghost.~~

13:13(a) *Then shall they deliver you up to be afflicted, and shall kill you,* And ye shall be hated of all men for my name's sake:
13:12 ~~Now the brother shall betray the brother to death, and the father the son; and children shall rise up against their parents, and shall cause them to be put to death.~~ *And then shall many be offended, and shall betray one another;*

and many false prophets shall arise, and shall deceive many;
13:13(b) *And because iniquity shall abound, the love of many shall wax cold;*
but he that shall endure unto the end, the same shall be saved.

13:14 ~~But~~ when ye *therefore* shall see the abomination of desolation, spoken of by Daniel the prophet,

LUKE

him, saying,
Master, ~~but~~ when shall these things be?

and what sign ~~will there be~~ *wilt thou show,* when these things shall come to pass?

21:8 And he said,

the time draweth near, and therefore
Take heed that ye be not deceived:

for many shall come in my name, saying, I am Christ;

and the time draweth near: go ye not therefore after them.

21:12 But before all these *things shall come*, they shall lay their hands on you, and persecute you, delivering you up to the synagogues, and into prisons, being brought before kings and rulers for my name's sake.
21:13 And it shall turn to you for a testimony.

21:14 Settle ~~it~~ *this* therefore in your hearts, not to meditate before what ye shall answer:

21:15 For I will give you a mouth and wisdom, which all your adversaries shall not be able to gainsay nor resist.

21:17 And ye shall be hated of all ~~men~~ *the world* for my name's sake.
21:16 And ye shall be betrayed both by parents, and brethren, and kinsfolks, and friends;
and some of you shall they cause to be put to death.

MATTHEW	MARK	LUKE	JOHN

concerning the destruction of Jerusalem,
then ye shall stand in the holy place, (whoso readeth, let him understand:)

concerning the destruction of Jerusalem, ~~standing where it ought not,~~ then ye shall stand in the holy place. (~~let him that~~ *Whoso* readeth understand,)

21:18 But there shall not ~~an~~ hair of your head perish.
21:19 In your patience possess ye your souls.
21:20 And when ye shall see Jerusalem compassed with armies, then know that the desolation thereof is nigh.

24:16 Then let them ~~which be~~ *who are* in ~~Judaea~~ *Judea* flee into the mountains:
24:17 Let him ~~which~~ *who* is on the housetop ~~not come down~~ *flee, and not return* to take any thing out of his house:

then let them that be in ~~Judaea~~ *Judea* flee *in*to the mountains:

13:15 And let him ~~that~~ *who* is on the housetop ~~not go down into the house, neither enter therein,~~ *flee, and not return* to take any thing out of his house:

21:21 Then let them ~~which~~ *who* are in ~~Judaea~~ *Judea* flee to the mountains;

and let them ~~which~~ *who* are in the midst of it depart out;
and let not them ~~that~~ *who* are in the countries *return to* enter ~~thereinto~~ *into the city*.

24:18 Neither let him ~~which~~ *who* is in the field return back to take his clothes.

13:16 And let him that is in the field ~~not~~ *re*turn back ~~again for~~ to take ~~up~~ his ~~garment~~ *clothes*.

21:22 For these be the days of vengeance, that all things which are written may be fulfilled.
21:23 But woe unto them ~~that~~ *who* are with child, and to them ~~that~~ *who* give suck, in those days! for there shall be great distress in the land, and wrath upon this people.

24:19 And woe unto them that are with child, and *un*to them that give suck in those days!

13:17 ~~But~~ *And* woe un*to* them that are with child, and to them that give suck in those days!

24:20 ~~But~~ *Therefore,* pray ye *the Lord* that your flight be not in the winter, neither on the ~~s~~Sabbath day:
24:21 For then, *in those days,* shall be great tribulation*s on the Jews, and upon the inhabitants of Jerusalem,* such as was not *before sent upon Israel, of God,* since the beginning of ~~the world to~~ *their kingdom*

13:18 ~~And~~ *Therefore* pray ye *the Lord,* that your flight be not in the winter, *neither on the Sabbath day.*
13:19 For in those days shall be ~~affliction~~ *great tribulation on the Jews, and upon th inhabitants of Jerusalem;* such as was not *before sent upon Israel, of God,* ~~from~~ *since* the beginning of ~~the creation which God created unto this time, neither shall be~~ *their kingdom, (for it is written their enemies shall scatter them,)*

until this time, no, nor ever shall be *sent again upon Israel.*
24:8 All ~~these~~ *things which have befallen them,* are *only* the beginning of sorrows *which shall come upon them;*
24:22 And except those days should be shortened, there should no*ne of their* flesh be saved:

until this time; no, nor ever shall be sent again upon Israel
13:8(b) *All* these *things* are the beginnings of sorrows.

but for the elect's sake, *according to the covenant,* those days shall be shortened.

13:20 And except ~~that the Lord had shortened~~ those days *should be shortened, there should* no flesh should be saved:
but for the elect's sake, ~~whom he hath chosen, he hath shortened the days~~ *according to the covenant, those days shall be shortened.*

Behold these things I have spoken unto you concerning the Jews.

Behold these things I have spoken unto you concerning the Jews.

21:24 And they shall fall by the edge of the sword, and shall be led away captive into all nations: and

MATTHEW	MARK	LUKE	JOHN

Jerusalem shall be trodden down of the Gentiles, until the times of the Gentiles be fulfilled.

24:23 ~~Then~~ *And again, after the tribulation of those days which shall come upon Jerusalem,* if any man shall say unto you, Lo, here is Christ, or there; believe ~~it~~ *him* not.

24:24 For *in those days,* there shall *also* arise false Christs, and false prophets, and shall ~~shew~~ *show* great signs and wonders; insomuch that, if ~~it were~~ possible,
they shall deceive the very elect, *who are the elect according to the covenant.*

Behold, I speak these things unto you for the elect's sake.

13:21 And then *immediately after the tribulation of those days which shall come upon Jerusalem,* if any man shall say to you, Lo, here is Christ; or ~~, lo, he is~~ there; believe him not:

13:22 For *in those days there shall also arise* false Christs and false prophets ~~shall rise~~, and shall ~~shew~~ *show great* signs and wonders, ~~to seduce, if it were possible, even the elect~~ *insomuch, that if possible, they shall deceive the very elect, who are the elect according to the covenant.*
13:23 ~~But take ye heed: behold, I have foretold you all things~~ *Behold, I speak these things unto you, for the elect's sake.*

Now these things he spake unto them, concerning the destruction of Jerusalem.   And then his disciples asked him, saying, Master, tell us concerning thy coming?
21:9 ~~But~~ *And* when ye shall hear of wars and commotions, be not terrified:

24:6 And ye *also* shall hear of wars, and ~~rumours~~ *rumors* of wars: see that ye be not troubled:

for all ~~these things~~ *I have told you* must come to pass, but the end is not yet.
24:25 Behold, I have told you before.
24:26 Wherefore if they shall say unto you, Behold, he is in the desert; go not forth: behold, he is in the secret chambers; believe it not.
24:27 For as the ~~lightning~~ *light of the morning* cometh out of the east, and shineth even unto the west*, and covereth the whole earth*; so shall also the coming of the Son of ~~m~~*M*an be.
24:28 ~~For~~ *And now I show unto you a parable. Behold,* wheresoever the ~~carcase~~ *carcass* is, there will the eagles be gathered together*;
so likewise shall mine elect be gathered from the four quarters of the earth.
 For they shall hear of wars, and rumors of wars. Behold, I speak unto you for mine elect's sake.*
24:7 For nation shall rise against nation, and kingdom against kingdom:
~~and~~ there shall be famines, and pestilences, and earthquakes, in divers places. *(verse order changed by JST)*

13:7 And ~~when~~ ye *also* shall hear of wars and ~~rumours~~ *rumors* of wars, ~~be~~ *see that* ye *be* not troubled:
for ~~such things must needs be~~ *all I have told you must come to pass*; but the end ~~shall~~ *is* not ~~be~~ yet.
Behold, I have told you before,

*wherefore if they shall say unto you, Behold, he is in the desert; go not forth; Behold, he is in the secret chambers; believe it not.
For as the light of the morning cometh out of the east, and shineth even unto the west, and covereth the whole earth, so shall also the coming of the Son of Man be.
And now I show unto you a parable. Behold, wheresoever the carcass is, there will the eagles be gathered together;*

*So likewise, shall mine elect be gathered from the four quarters of the earth.
And they shall hear of wars and rumors of wars. Behold, I speak unto you for mine elect's sake.*
13:8(a) For nation shall rise against nation, and kingdom against kingdom:
and there shall be *famines and pestilences, and* earthquakes in divers places. ~~, and there shall be famines and troubles:~~

for these things must first come to pass; but ~~the end is not by and by~~ *this is not the end*.

21:10 Then said he unto them, Nation shall rise against nation, and kingdom against kingdom:
21:11 And great earthquakes shall be in divers places, and famines, and pestilences;

and fearful sights and great signs shall there be from heaven.

And again, because iniquity shall abound, the love of men shall wax cold; but he that shall not be overcome, the same shall be saved.

And again, because iniquity shall abound, the love of men shall wax cold; but he who shall not be overcome, the same shall be saved.

MATTHEW	MARK	LUKE	JOHN

MATTHEW

24:14 And *again* this gospel of the kingdom shall be preached in all the world for a witness unto all nations; and then shall the end come, *or the destruction of the wicked.*

And again shall the abomination of desolation, spoken of by Daniel the prophet, be fulfilled. (verse order changed by JST)

24:29 *And* Immediately after the tribulation of those days ~~shall~~ the sun *shall* be darkened, and the moon shall not give her light,

and the stars shall fall from heaven,

and the powers of ~~the~~ heavens shall be shaken:
24:34 Verily I say unto you, This generation, *in which these things shall be shown forth,* shall not pass *away,* ~~till all these things be~~ *until all I have told you shall be* fulfilled.
24:35 *Although the days will come that* heaven and earth shall pass away, but my words shall not pass away; *but all shall be fulfilled.*

24:30 *And as I said before, after the tribulation of those days, and the powers of the heavens shall be shaken,* then shall appear the sign of the Son of ~~m~~*M*an in heaven: and then shall all the tribes of the earth mourn,
and they shall see the Son of man coming in the clouds of heaven with power and great glory.

And whoso treasureth up my words, shall not be deceived.
24:31 *For the Son of Man shall come,* And he shall send his angels *before him* with ~~a~~ *the* great sound of a trumpet,
and they shall gather together *the remainder of* his elect from the four winds, from one end of heaven to the other.

MARK

13:10 And ~~the~~ *again this* gospel *of the kingdom* ~~must first be published among all~~ *shall be preached in all the world, for a witness unto all* nations, *and then shall the end come, or the destructon of the wicked.*
And again shall the abomination of desolation, spoken of by Daniel the prophet, be fulfilled. (verse order changed by JST)

13:24 ~~But in~~ *And immediately after the tribulation of* those days, ~~after that tribulation,~~ the sun shall be darkened, and the moon shall not give her light,
13:25 And the stars of heaven shall fall,

and the powers ~~that are in~~ *of* heaven shall be shaken.
13:30 Verily I say unto you, that this generation, *in which these things shall be shown forth,* shall not pass *away,* till all ~~these things be done~~ *I have told you shall be fulfilled.*
13:31 *Although the days will come that* Heaven and earth shall pass away: ~~but~~ *yet* my words shall not pass away *but all shall be fulfilled.*

And as I said before, after the tribulation of those days, and the powers of the heavens shall be shaken, then shall appear the sign of the Son of Man in heaven: and then shall all the tribes of the earth mourn;
13:26 And ~~then shall~~ they *shall* see the Son of ~~m~~*M*an coming in the clouds *of heaven,* with ~~great~~ power and *great* glory.
And whoso treasureth up my word, shall not be deceived.
13:27 *For the Son of Man shall come;* And ~~then shall~~ he *shall send* send his angels *before him with the great sound of a trumpet,*
and *they* shall gather together his elect from the four winds, from ~~the uttermost part of the earth to the uttermost part~~ *one end* of heaven *to*

LUKE

21:25 And *he answered them, and said, In the generation in which the times of the Gentiles shall be fulfilled,*

there shall be signs in the sun,
and in the moon,

and in the stars;

and upon the earth distress of nations, with perplexity; *like* the sea and the waves roaring; *The earth shall also be troubled, and the waters of the great deep;*
21:26 Men's hearts failing them for fear, and for looking after those things which are coming on the earth: for the powers of heaven shall be shaken.
21:32 Verily I say unto you, This generation, *the generation when the times of the Gentiles be fulfilled,*
shall not pass away, till all be fulfilled.

21:33 Heaven and earth shall pass away: but my words shall not pass away.

21:28 And when these things begin to come to pass, then look up, and lift up your heads; for *the day of* your redemption draweth nigh. *(verse order of 21:27 & 21:28 changed order by JST)*

21:27 And then shall they see the Son of ~~m~~*M*an coming in a cloud with power and great glory.

MATTHEW	MARK	LUKE	JOHN

MATTHEW

24:32 Now learn a parable of the fig tree; When his branch*es* ~~is~~ *are* yet tender,

and ~~putteth~~ *it begins to put* forth leaves, ye know that summer is nigh *at hand*:

24:33 So likewise ~~ye~~ *mine elect*, when ~~ye~~ *they* shall see all these things,

they shall know that ~~it~~ *he* is near, even at the doors.

24:36 But of that day and hour ~~knoweth~~ ~~no man~~ *no one knoweth;* no, not the angels of *God in* heaven, but my Father only.

24:37 But as ~~the days of Noe were~~ *it was in the days of Noah,* so ~~shall also~~ *it shall be also at* the coming of the Son of ~~m~~*M*an ~~be~~.

24:38 For ~~as~~ *it shall be with them as it was* in the days ~~that~~ *which* were before the flood*;*

for until the day that Noah entered the ark, they were eating and drinking, marrying and giving in marriage, ~~until the day that Noe entered into the ark,~~

24:39 And knew not until the flood came, and took them all away; so shall also the coming of the Son of ~~m~~*M*an be.

24:40 *Then shall be fulfilled that which is written, that, In the last days,*

~~Then shall~~ two *shall* be in the field; the one shall be taken, and the other left.

24:41 Two ~~women~~ shall be grinding at the mill; the one ~~shall be~~ taken, and the other left.

24:42 *And what I say unto one, I say unto all men;* Watch therefore:

for ye know not *at* what hour your Lord doth come.

MARK

the other.

13:28 Now learn a parable of the fig tree; When ~~her~~ *his* branch*es* ~~is~~ *are* yet tender,

and putteth forth leaves, ye know that summer is ~~near:~~ *nigh at hand.*

13:29 So ~~ye in like manner~~ *likewise, mine elect,* when ~~ye~~ *they* shall see *all* these things ~~come to pass~~, *they* shall know that ~~it is nigh~~ *he is near*, even at the doors.

13:32 But of that day and ~~that~~ hour *no one* knoweth ~~no man,~~ *;* no, not the angels ~~which are~~ *of God* in heaven, ~~neither the Son,~~ but ~~the~~ *my* Father *only*.

But as it was in the days of Noah, so it shall be also at the coming of the Son of Man;

for it shall be with them as it was in the days which were before the flood.

Until the day that Noah entered into the ark, they were eating and drinking, marrying and giving in marriage,

and knew not until the flood came and took them all away; so shall also the coming of the Son of Man be.

Then shall be fulfilled that which is written, That in the last days,

two shall be in the field, one shall be taken and the other left.

Two shall be grinding at the mill; the one taken, and the other left.

13:33 ~~Take ye heed,~~

~~watch and pray: for ye know not when the time is.~~

13:37 And what I say unto you I say unto all *men*,. Watch *therefore,*

for ye know not at what hour your Lord doth come.

LUKE

21:29 And he spake to them a parable; *saying,* Behold the fig tree, and all the trees;

21:30 When they now shoot forth, ye see and know of your own selves that summer is now nigh at hand.

21:31 So likewise ye, when ye see these things come to pass,

know ye that the kingdom of God is nigh at hand.

21:34 ~~And~~ *let my disciples therefore* take heed to ~~yourselves~~ *themselves*, lest at any time ~~your~~ *their* hearts be overcharged with surfeiting, and drunkenness, and cares of this life, and ~~so~~ *that* day come upon ~~you~~ *them* unawares.

21:35 For as a snare shall it come on all them ~~that~~ *who* dwell on the face of the whole earth.

21:36 *And what I say unto one, I say unto all,* Watch ye therefore, and pray always, *and keep my commandments,*

that ye may be ~~accounted~~ worthy to escape all these things ~~that~~ *which* shall come to pass, and to stand before the Son of ~~m~~*M*an *when he shall come clothed in the glory of his Father*.

H-22. PARABLE OF THE SERVANTS

13:34 ~~For the Son of man is as a man taking a far journey, who left his house, and gave authority to his servants, and to every man his work, and commanded the porter to watch.~~

13:35 ~~Watch ye therefore: for ye know not when the master of the house cometh, at even, or at midnight, or at the cockcrowing, or in the morning:~~

13:36 ~~Lest coming suddenly he find you sleeping.~~

24:43 But know this, ~~that~~ if the goodman of the house had known in what watch the thief would come, he would have watched, and would not have suffered his house to be broken up*; but would have been ready*.

But know this, if the goodman of the house had known in what watch the thief would come, he would have watched, and would not have suffered his house to be broken up; but would have been ready.

24:44 Therefore be ye also ready: for in such an hour as ye think not the Son of ~~m~~Man cometh.

Therefore, be ye also ready, for in such an hour as ye think not, the Son of Man cometh.

24:45 Who then is a faithful and wise servant, whom his lord hath made ruler over his household, to give them meat in due season?

Who then is a faithful and wise servant, whom his lord hath made ruler over his household, to give them meat in due season?

24:46 Blessed is that servant, whom his lord when he cometh shall find so doing.

Blessed is that servant, whom his lord, when he cometh, shall find so doing.

24:47 *And,* Verily I say unto you, ~~That~~ he shall make him ruler over all his goods.

And verily I say unto you, he shall make him ruler over all his goods.

24:48 But ~~and~~ if that evil servant shall say in his heart, My lord delayeth his coming;

But if that evil servant shall say in his heart, My lord delayeth his coming;

24:49 And shall begin to smite his fellow-servants, and to eat and drink with the drunken;

And shall begin to smite his fellow servants, and to eat and drink with the drunken;

24:50 The lord of that servant shall come in a day when he looketh not for him, and in an hour that he is not aware of,

The lord of that servant shall come in a day when he looketh not for him, and in an hour that he is not aware of,

24:51 And shall cut him asunder, and appoint him his portion with the hypocrites:

And shall cut him asunder, and appoint him his portion with the hypocrites:

there shall be weeping and gnashing of teeth.

there shall be weeping and gnashing of teeth.

And thus cometh the end of the wicked according to the prophecy of Moses, saying, They should be cut off from among the people. But the end of the earth is not yet; but bye and bye.

And thus cometh the end.

MATTHEW	MARK	LUKE	JOHN

H-23. PARABLE OF THE TEN VIRGINS

25:1 *And* Then*, at that day, before the Son of Man comes,* ~~shall~~ the kingdom of heaven *shall* be likened unto ten virgins, ~~which~~ *who* took their lamps, and went forth to meet the bridegroom.

25:2 And five of them were wise, and five *of them* were foolish.

25:3 They that were foolish took their lamps, and took no oil with them:

25:4 But the wise took oil in their vessels with their lamps.

25:5 While the bridegroom tarried, they all slumbered and slept.

25:6 And at midnight there was a cry made, Behold, the bridegroom cometh; go ye out to meet him.

25:7 Then all those virgins arose, and trimmed their lamps.

25:8 And the foolish said unto the wise, Give us of your oil; for our lamps are gone out.

25:9 But the wise answered, saying, ~~Not so;~~ lest there be not enough for us and you: ~~but~~ go ye rather to them that sell, and buy for yourselves.

25:10 And while they went to buy, the bridegroom came; and they that were ready went in with him to the marriage: and the door was shut.

25:11 Afterward came also the other virgins, saying, Lord, Lord, open *un*to us.

25:12 But he answered and said, Verily I say unto you, ~~I know you not~~ *Ye know me not*.

25:13 Watch therefore, for ye know neither the day nor the hour wherein the Son of ~~m~~*M*an cometh.

H-24. PARABLE OF THE TALENTS

25:14 *Now I will liken these things unto a parable.* For ~~the kingdom of heaven is~~ *it is like* as a man travelling into a far country, who called his own servants, and delivered unto them his goods.

25:15 And unto one he gave five talents, to another two, and to another one; to every man according to his several ability; and straightway ~~took~~ *went on* his journey.

25:16 Then he that had received the five talents went and traded with the same, and ~~made them~~ *gained* other five talents.

25:17 And likewise he ~~that had~~ *who* received two *talents*, he also gained other two.

25:18 But he ~~that~~ *who* had

MATTHEW	MARK	LUKE	JOHN

received one went and digged in the earth, and hid his lord's money.

25:19 After a long time the lord of those servants cometh, and reckoneth with them.

25:20 And so he that had received *the* five talents came and brought other five talents, saying, Lord, thou deliveredst unto me five talents: behold, I have gained beside*s* them five talents more.

25:21 His lord said unto him, Well done, ~~thou~~ good and faithful servant: thou hast been faithful over a few things, I will make thee ruler over many things: enter thou into the joy of thy lord.

25:22 He also that had received two talents came and said, Lord, thou deliveredst unto me two talents: behold, I have gained two ~~other~~ talents beside*s* them.

25:23 His lord said unto him, Well done, good and faithful servant; thou hast been faithful over a few things, I will make thee ruler over many things: enter thou into the joy of thy lord.

25:24 Then he ~~which~~ *who* had received the one talent came and said, Lord, I knew thee that thou art ~~an~~ hard man, reaping where thou hast not sown, and gathering where thou hast not ~~strawed~~ *scattered*:

25:25 And I was afraid, and went and hid thy talent in the earth: *and* lo, ~~there thou hast that is thine~~ *here is thy talent; take it from me as thou hast from thine other servants, for it is thine*.

25:26 His lord answered and said unto him, ~~Thou~~ *O* wicked and slothful servant, thou knewest that I reap where I sowed not, and gather where I have not ~~strawed~~ *scattered*:

25:27 *Having known this, therefore,* Thou oughtest ~~therefore~~ to have put my money to the exchangers, and ~~then~~ at my coming I should have received mine own with usury.

25:28 *I will* Take therefore the talent from ~~him~~ *you*, and give it unto him ~~which~~ *who* hath ten talents.

25:29 For unto every one ~~that~~ *who* hath *obtained other talents,* shall be given, and he shall have *in* abundance: but from him that hath not *obtained other talents,* shall be taken away even that which he hath *received*.

25:30 And *his lord shall say unto his servants,* cast ye the unprofitable servant into outer darkness: there shall be weeping and gnashing of teeth.

H-25. JESUS WILL JUDGE THE WORLD

25:31 When the Son of mMan shall come in his glory, and all the holy angels with him, then ~~shall~~ he *shall* sit upon the throne of his glory:

25:32 And before him shall be gathered all nations: and he shall separate them one from another, as a shepherd divideth ~~his~~ sheep from the goats:

25:33 ~~And he shall set~~ the sheep on his right hand, but the goats on ~~the~~ *his* left.

25:34 *And he shall sit upon his throne, and the twelve apostles with him.* Then shall the King say unto them on his right hand, Come, ye blessed of my Father, inherit the kingdom prepared for you from the foundation of the world:

25:35 For I was an ~~hungred~~ *hungered*, and ye gave me meat: I was thirsty, and ye gave me drink: I was a stranger, and ye took me in:

25:36 Naked, and ye clothed me: I was sick, and ye visited me: I was in prison, and ye came unto me.

25:37 Then shall the righteous answer him, saying, Lord, when saw we thee an hungred, and fed thee? or thirsty, and gave thee drink?

25:38 When saw we thee a stranger, and took thee in? or naked, and clothed thee?

25:39 Or when saw we thee sick, or in prison, and came unto thee?

25:40 And the King shall answer and say unto them, Verily I say unto you, Inasmuch as ye have done it unto one of the least of these my brethren, ye have done it unto me.

25:41 Then shall he say also unto them on the left hand, Depart from me, ye cursed, into everlasting fire, prepared for the devil and his angels:

25:42 For I was an hungred, and ye gave me no meat: I was thirsty, and ye gave me no drink:

25:43 I was a stranger, and ye took me not in: naked, and ye clothed me not: sick, and in prison, and ye visited me not.

25:44 Then shall they also answer him, saying, Lord, when saw we thee an hungred, or athirst, or a stranger, or naked, or sick, or in prison, and did not minister unto thee?

MATTHEW	MARK	LUKE	JOHN

25:45 Then shall he answer them, saying, Verily I say unto you, Inasmuch as ye did it not to one of the least of these *my brethren*, ye did it not to me.
25:46 And these shall go away into everlasting punishment: but the righteous into life eternal.

H-26. JESUS FORETELLS HIS BETRAYAL AND CRUCIFIXION

MATTHEW	MARK	LUKE
	14:1(a) After two days was ~~the feast of~~ the passover, and *the feast* of unleavened bread:	22:1 Now the feast of unleavened bread drew nigh, which is called the Passover.
26:1 And it came to pass, when Jesus had finished all these sayings, he said unto his disciples, 26:2 Ye know that after two days is the ~~feast of the~~ passover, and *then* the Son of man is betrayed to be crucified.		

H-27. THE PLOT TO KILL JESUS

MATTHEW	MARK	LUKE
26:3 Then assembled together the chief priests, and the scribes, and the elders of the people, unto the palace of the high priest, who was called Caiaphas, 26:4 And consulted that they might take Jesus by subtilty, and kill him.	14:1(b) and the chief priests and the scribes sought how they might take ~~him~~ *Jesus* by craft, and put him to death.	22:2 And the chief priests and *the* scribes sought how they might kill him;
		~~for~~ *but* they feared the people.
26:5 But they said,	14:2 But they said *among themselves*, ~~Not~~ *let us not take him* on the feast day, lest there be an uproar of the people.	
Not on the feast day, lest there be an uproar among the people.		

H-28. JUDAS ISCARIOT ARRANGES BETRAYAL

MATTHEW	MARK	LUKE
26:14 Then one of the twelve, called Judas Iscariot,	14:10 ~~And~~ *Nevertheless,* Judas Iscariot, *even* one of the twelve,	22:3 Then entered Satan into Judas surnamed Iscariot, being of the number of the twelve.
went unto the chief priests,	went unto the chief priests, to betray ~~him~~ *Jesus* unto them,	22:4 And he went his way, and communed with the chief priests and captains, how he might betray him unto them.
	for he turned away from him, and was offended because of his words.	
26:15 And said ~~unto them~~, What will ye give me, and I will deliver him unto you?		
		22:5 And they were glad, and
	14:11 And when ~~they~~ *the chief priests* heard ~~it~~ *of him*, they were glad,	
And they covenanted with him for thirty pieces of silver.	and promised to give him money.	covenanted to give him money.
26:16 And from that time he sought opportunity to betray ~~him~~ *Jesus*.	And he sought how he might conveniently betray ~~him~~ *Jesus*.	22:6 And he promised *them*, and sought opportunity to betray him unto them in the absence of the multitude.

MATTHEW	MARK	LUKE	JOHN

Wednesday--The Fourth Day of the Week--No Record

Thursday--The Fifth Day of the Week

H-29. DISCIPLES ARRANGE FOR PASSOVER MEAL

26:17 Now *on* the first day of the feast of unleavened bread

14:12 And *now* the first day of unleavened bread, when they killed the passover,

22:7 Then came the day of unleavened bread, when the passover must be killed.
22:8 And he sent Peter and John, saying, Go and prepare us the passover, that we may eat.
22:9 And they said unto him, Where wilt thou that we prepare?

the disciples came to Jesus, saying unto him, Where wilt thou that we prepare for thee to eat the passover?

his disciples said unto him, Where wilt thou that we go and prepare that thou mayest eat the passover?

26:18 And he said, Go into the city to such a man,

14:13 And he sendeth forth two of his disciples, and saith̶d̶ unto them, Go ye into the city, and there shall meet you a man bearing a pitcher of water: follow him.
14:14 And wheresoever he shall go in,

22:10 And he said unto them, Behold, when ye a̶r̶e̶ *have* entered into the city, there shall a man meet you, bearing a pitcher of water; follow him into the house where he entereth in.

and say unto him, The Master saith,

say ye to the goodman of the house, The Master saith,
Where is the guestchamber, where I shall eat the passover with my disciples?

22:11 And ye shall say unto the goodman of the house, The Master saith unto t̶h̶e̶e̶ *you*,
Where is the guestchamber, where I shall eat the passover with my disciples?

My time is at hand; I will keep the passover at thy house with my disciples.

14:15 And he will s̶h̶e̶w̶ *show* you a large upper room furnished and prepared: there make ready for us.
14:16 And his disciples went forth, and came into the city, and found as he had said unto them: and they made ready the passover.

22:12 And he shall shew you a large upper room furnished: there make ready.
22:13 And they went,

and found as he had said unto them: and they made ready the passover.

26:19 And the disciples did as Jesus h̶a̶d̶ appointed them;

and they made ready the passover.

H-30. THE LAST SUPPER

26:20 Now when the eve*ning* was come, he sat down with the twelve.

14:17 And in the evening he cometh with the twelve.

22:14 And when the hour was come, he sat down, and the twelve apostles with him.
22:15 And he said unto them, With desire I have desired to eat this passover with you before I suffer:
22:16 For I say unto you, I will not any more eat thereof, until it be fulfilled *which is written in the prophets concerning me. Then I will partake with you,* in the kingdom of God.
22:17 And he took the cup, and gave thanks, and said, Take this, and divide i̶t̶ among yourselves:
22:18 For I say unto you, *that* I will not drink of the fruit of the vine, until the kingdom of God shall come.

MATTHEW	MARK	LUKE	JOHN

H-31. STRIFE AMONG THE APOSTLES OVER PRECEDENCE

		22:24 ~~And~~ there was also a strife among them, ~~which~~ *who* of them should be accounted the greatest. 22:25 And he said unto them, The kings of the Gentiles exercise lordship over them; and they ~~that~~ *who* exercise authority upon them are called benefactors. 22:26 But ~~ye shall not be so~~ *it ought not to be so with you*: but he ~~that~~ *who* is greatest among you, let him be as the younger; and he ~~that~~ *who* is chief, as he ~~that~~ *who* doth serve. 22:27 For whether is *he* greater, ~~he that~~ *who* sitteth at meat, or he ~~that~~ *who* serveth? ~~is not he that~~ *I am not as he who* sitteth at meat ~~?~~ but I am among you as he ~~that~~ *who* serveth. 22:28 Ye are they ~~which~~ *who* have continued with me in my temptations. 22:29 And I appoint unto you a kingdom, as my Father hath appointed unto me; 22:30 That ye may eat and drink at my table in my kingdom, and sit on *twelve* thrones judging the twelve tribes of Israel.	

H-32. JESUS WASHES THE APOSTLES' FEET

			13:1 Now before the feast of the passover, when Jesus knew that his hour was come that he should depart out of this world unto the Father, having loved his own which were in the world, he loved them unto the end. 13:2 And supper being ended, the devil having now put into the heart of Judas Iscariot, Simon's son, to betray him; 13:3 Jesus knowing that the Father had given all things into his hands, and that he was come from God, and went to God; 13:4 He riseth from supper, and laid aside his garments; and took a towel, and girded himself. 13:5 After that he poureth water into a ~~bason~~ *basin*, and *he* began to wash the disciples' feet, and to wipe them with the towel wherewith he was girded. 13:6 Then cometh he to Simon Peter: and Peter saith unto him, Lord, dost thou wash my feet? 13:7 Jesus answered and said unto him, What I do thou knowest not now; but thou shalt know hereafter. 13:8 Peter sai~~th~~d unto him, Thou ~~shalt never~~ *needest not to* wash my feet. Jesus answered him, If I wash thee not, thou hast no part

MATTHEW	MARK	LUKE	JOHN

with me.

13:9 Simon Peter saith unto him, Lord, not my feet only, but also my hands and my head.

13:10 Jesus saith to him, He that ~~is washed~~ *has washed his hands and his head,* needeth not save to wash his feet, but is clean every whit: and ye are clean, but not all. *Now this was the custom of the Jews under their law; wherefore, Jesus did this that the law might be fulfilled.*

13:11 For he knew who should betray him; therefore said he, Ye are not all clean.

13:12 So after he had washed their feet, and had taken his garments, and was set down again, he said unto them, Know ye what I have done to you?

13:13 Ye call me Master and Lord: and ye say well; for so I am.

13:14 If I then, your Lord and Master, have washed your feet; ye also ought to wash one another's feet.

13:15 For I have given you an example, that ye should do as I have done to you.

13:16 Verily, verily, I say unto you, The servant is not greater than his lord; neither he that is sent greater than he that sent him.

13:17 If ye know these things, happy are ye if ye do them.

13:20 Verily, verily, I say unto you, He that receiveth whomsoever I send receiveth me; and he that receiveth me receiveth him that sent me.

H-33. JESUS ANNOUNCES HIS BETRAYAL

26:21 And as they did eat, he said,
Verily I say unto you, that one of you shall betray me.

14:18 And as they sat and did eat, Jesus said,
Verily I say unto you, One of you ~~which~~ *who* eateth with me shall betray me.

13:21 When Jesus had thus said, he was troubled in spirit, and testified, and said, Verily, verily, I say unto you, that one of you shall betray me.

13:22 Then the disciples looked one on another, doubting of whom he spake.

13:18 I speak not of you all: I know whom I have chosen: but that the scripture may be fulfilled, He that eateth bread with me hath lifted up his heel against me.

26:22 And they were exceeding sorrowful, and began every one of them to say unto him, Lord, is it I?

14:19 And they *all* began to be *very* sorrowful, and *began* to say unto him one by one, Is it I? and another said, Is it I?

22:23 And they began to inquire among themselves, ~~which~~ *who* of them it was ~~that~~ *who* should do this thing.

26:23 And he answered and said, He that dippeth his hand with me in the dish, the same shall betray me.

14:20 And he answered and said unto them, It is one of the twelve, ~~that~~ *who* dippeth with me in the dish.

22:21 But, behold, the hand of him ~~that~~ *who* betrayeth me is with me on the table.

26:24 *But* The Son of ~~m~~*M*an goeth as it is written of him: but woe unto that man by whom the Son of man is betrayed! it had

14:21 The Son of ~~m~~*M*an indeed goeth, as it is written of him: but woe to that man by whom the Son of ~~m~~*M*an is betrayed! good were it

22:22 And truly the Son of man goeth, as it was determined: but woe unto that man by whom he is betrayed!

MATTHEW	MARK	LUKE	JOHN

MATTHEW	MARK	LUKE	JOHN
been good for that man if he had not been born.	for that man if he had never been born.		
			13:19 Now I tell you before it come, that, when it is come to pass, ye may believe that I am ~~he~~ *the Christ.*
26:25 Then Judas, ~~which~~ *who* betrayed him, answered and said, Master, is it I? He said unto him, Thou hast said.			

H-34. JUDAS LEAVES THE UPPER ROOM

MATTHEW	MARK	LUKE	JOHN
			13:23 Now there was leaning on Jesus' bosom one of his disciples, whom Jesus loved.
			13:24 Simon Peter therefore beckoned to him, that he should ask who it should be of whom he spake.
			13:25 He then lying on Jesus' breast saith unto him, Lord, who is it?
			13:26 Jesus answered, He it is, to whom I shall give a sop, when I have dipped it. And when he had dipped the sop, he gave it to Judas Iscariot, the son of Simon.
			13:27 And after the sop Satan entered into him.
	14:28(b) *And he said unto Judas Iscariot, What thou doest, do quickly; but beware of innocent blood.*		Then said Jesus unto him, That thou doest, do quickly.
			13:28 Now no man at the table knew for what intent he spake this unto him.
			13:29 For some of them thought, because Judas had the bag, that Jesus had said unto him, Buy those things that we have need of against the feast; or, that he should give something to the poor.
			13:30 He then having received the sop went immediately out: and it was night.

H-35. THE NEW COMMANDMENT: TO LOVE ONE ANOTHER

MATTHEW	MARK	LUKE	JOHN
			13:31 Therefore, when he was gone out, Jesus said, Now is the Son of man glorified, and God is glorified in him.
			13:32 If God be glorified in him, God shall also glorify him in himself, and shall straightway glorify him.
			13:33 Little children, yet a little while I am with you. Ye shall seek me: and as I said unto the Jews, Whither I go, ye cannot come; so now I say to you.

MATTHEW	MARK	LUKE	JOHN

| | | | 13:34 A new commandment I give unto you, That ye love one another; as I have loved you, that ye also love one another.
 13:35 By this shall all men know that ye are my disciples, if ye have love one to another. |

H-36. THE SACRAMENT

MATTHEW	MARK	LUKE	JOHN
26:26 And as they were eating, Jesus took bread *and brake it*, and blessed it, ~~and brake it,~~ and gave it to ~~the~~ *his* disciples, and said, Take, eat; this is *in remembrance of* my body *which I give a ransom for you*.	14:22 And as they did eat, Jesus took bread, and blessed *it*, and brake ~~it~~, and gave to them, and said, Take *it, and* eat: ~~this is my body~~ *Behold, this is for you to do in remembrance of my body; for as oft as ye do this ye will remember this hour that I was with you.*	22:19 And he took bread, and gave thanks, and brake ~~it~~, and gave unto them, saying, This is my body which is given for you: this do in remembrance of me.	
26:27 And he took the cup, and gave thanks, and gave it to them, saying, Drink ye all of it;	14:23 And he took the cup, and when he had given thanks, he gave it to them: and they all drank of it. 14:24 And he said unto them, ~~This is my blood of the new testament, which is shed for many~~ *This is in remembrance of my blood which is shed for many, and the new testament which I give unto you;*	22:20 Likewise also the cup after supper, saying,	
26:28 For this is *in remembrance of* my blood of the new testament, which is shed for *as* many *as shall believe on my name,* for the remission of sins. 26:29 *And I give unto you a commandment, that ye shall observe to do the things which ye have seen me do, and bear record of me even unto the end.*	*for of me ye shall bear record unto all the world.* *And as oft as ye do this ordinance, ye will remember me in this hour that I was with you and drank with you of this cup, even the last time in my ministry.*	This cup is the new testament in my blood, which is shed for you.	
But I say unto you, I will not drink henceforth of this fruit of the vine, until that day when I *shall come and* drink it new with you in my Father's kingdom.	14:25 Verily I say unto you, *Of this ye shall bear record; for* I will ~~drink~~ no more *drink* of the fruit of the vine *with you*, until that day that I drink it new in the kingdom of God. *And now they were grieved, and wept over him.*		

H-37. JESUS FORETELLS PETER'S DENIAL

MATTHEW	MARK	LUKE	JOHN
26:31 Then sai~~th~~*d* Jesus unto them, All ye shall be offended because of me this night: for it is written, I will smite the shepherd, and the sheep of the flock shall be scattered abroad. 26:32 But after I am risen again, I will go before you into Galilee. 26:33 Peter answered and said unto him, Though all men shall be offended because of thee, ~~yet will I~~ *will* never be offended.	14:27 And Jesus sai~~th~~*d* unto them, All ye shall be offended because of me this night: for it is written, I will smite the shepherd, and the sheep shall be scattered. 14:28(a) But after that I am risen, I will go before you into Galilee. 14:29 But Peter said unto ~~him~~ *Jesus*, Although all *men* shall be offended *with thee*, yet ~~will not I~~ *I will never be offended*.		
		22:31 And the Lord said, Simon, Simon, behold, Satan hath desired ~~to have~~ you, that he may sift ~~you~~ *the children of the kingdom* as wheat:	

MATTHEW	MARK	LUKE	JOHN
		22:32 But I have prayed for ~~thee~~ *you*, that ~~thy~~ *your* faith fail not: and when ~~thou art~~ *you are* converted, strengthen ~~thy~~ *your* brethren.	
			13:36 Simon Peter said unto him, Lord, whither goest thou? Jesus answered him, Whither I go, thou canst not follow me now; but thou shalt follow me afterwards.
		22:33 And he said unto him, *being aggrieved,* Lord, I am ready to go with ~~thee~~ *you*, both into prison, and *un*to death.	13:37 Peter said unto him,
26:34 Jesus said unto him,	14:30 And Jesus sait~~h~~*d* unto him,	22:34 And ~~he~~ *the Lord* said,	Lord, why cannot I follow thee now? I will lay down my life for thy sake. 13:38 Jesus answered him, Wilt thou lay down thy life for my sake? Verily, verily, I say unto thee, The cock shall not crow,
Verily I say unto thee, That this night, before the cock crow, thou shalt deny me thrice.	Verily I say unto thee, That this day, even in this night, before the cock crow twice, thou shalt deny me thrice.	I tell ~~thee~~ *you*, Peter, *that* the cock shall not crow this day, before that ~~thou shalt~~ *you will* thrice deny that ~~thou~~ *you* know~~est~~ me.	till thou hast denied me thrice.
26:35 Peter said unto him, Though I should die with thee, yet will I not deny thee.	14:31 But he spake the more vehemently, If I should die with thee, ~~I will~~ *yet will I* not deny thee in any wise.		
Likewise also said all the disciples.	Likewise also said they all.		
		22:35 And he said unto them, When I sent you without purse, and scrip, and shoes, lacked ye any thing? And they said, Nothing. 22:36 Then said he unto them, ~~But now~~ *I say unto you again*, he ~~that~~ *who* hath a purse, let him take it, and likewise his scrip: and he ~~that~~ *who* hath no sword, let him sell his garment, and buy one. 22:37 For I say unto you, ~~that~~ this *that* is written must yet be accomplished in me, And he was reckoned among the transgressors: for the things concerning me have an end. 22:38 And they said, Lord, behold, here are two swords. And he said unto them, It is enough.	

H-38. DISCOURSE ON THE COMFORTER

MATTHEW	MARK	LUKE	JOHN
			14:1 Let not your heart be troubled: ye believe in God, believe also in me. 14:2 In my Father's house are many mansions: if it were not so, I would have told you. I go to prepare a place for you. 14:3 And ~~if~~ *when* I go ~~and~~ *I will* prepare a place for you, ~~I will~~ *and* come again, and receive you unto myself; that where I am, ~~there~~ ye may be also. 14:4 And whither I go ye know, and the way ye know. 14:5 Thomas saith unto him, Lord, we know not whither thou goest; and how can we know the way? 14:6 Jesus saith unto him, I am

MATTHEW	MARK	LUKE	JOHN

the way, the truth, and the life: no man cometh unto the Father, but by me.

14:7 If ye had known me, ye should have known my Father also: and from henceforth ye know him, and have seen him.

14:8 Philip saith unto him, Lord, shew us the Father, and it sufficeth us.

14:9 Jesus saith unto him, Have I been so long time with you, and yet hast thou not known me, Philip? he that hath seen me hath seen the Father; and how sayest thou then, Shew us the Father?

14:10 Believest thou not that I am in the Father, and the Father in me? the words that I speak unto you I speak not of myself: but the Father that dwelleth in me, he doeth the works.

14:11 Believe me that I am in the Father, and the Father in me: or else believe me for the very works' sake.

14:12 Verily, verily, I say unto you, He that believeth on me, the works that I do shall he do also; and greater works than these shall he do; because I go unto my Father.

14:13 And whatsoever ye shall ask in my name, that will I do, that the Father may be glorified in the Son.

14:14 If ye shall ask any thing in my name, I will do it.

14:15 If ye love me, keep my commandments.

14:16 And I will pray the Father, and he shall give you another Comforter, that he may abide with you for ever;

14:17 Even the Spirit of truth; whom the world cannot receive, because it seeth him not, neither knoweth him: but ye know him; for he dwelleth with you, and shall be in you.

14:18 I will not leave you comfortless: I will come to you.

14:19 Yet a little while, and the world seeth me no more; but ye see me: because I live, ye shall live also.

14:20 At that day ye shall know that I am in my Father, and ye in me, and I in you.

14:21 He that hath my commandments, and keepeth them, he it is that loveth me: and he that loveth me shall be loved of my Father, and I will love him, and will manifest myself to him.

14:22 Judas saith unto him, not Iscariot, Lord, how is it that thou wilt manifest thyself unto us, and not unto the world?

14:23 Jesus answered and said

MATTHEW	MARK	LUKE	JOHN

unto him, If a man love me, he will keep my words: and my Father will love him, and we will come unto him, and make our abode with him.

14:24 He that loveth me not keepeth not my sayings: and the word which ye hear is not mine, but the Father's which sent me.

14:25 These things have I spoken unto you, being yet present with you.

14:26 But the Comforter, which is the Holy Ghost, whom the Father will send in my name, he shall teach you all things, and bring all things to your remembrance, whatsoever I have said unto you.

14:27 Peace I leave with you, my peace I give unto you: not as the world giveth, give I unto you. Let not your heart be troubled, neither let it be afraid.

14:28 Ye have heard how I said unto you, I go away, and come again unto you. If ye loved me, ye would rejoice, because I said, I go unto the Father: for my Father is greater than I.

14:29 And now I have told you before it come to pass, that, when it is come to pass, ye might believe.

14:30 Hereafter I will not talk much with you: for the prince of ***darkness, who is of*** this world cometh, ~~and hath nothing in me~~ *but hath no power over me, but he hath power over you*.

14:31 ~~But that the world~~ *And I tell you these things, that ye* may know that I love the Father; and as the Father gave me commandment, even so I do. Arise, let us go hence.

H-39. JESUS DEPARTS TO MOUNT OF OLIVES

26:30 And when they had sung ~~an~~ hymn,
they went out into the mount of Olives.

14:26 And when they had sung an hymn,
they went out into the mount of Olives.

22:39 And he came out, and went, as he was ~~wont~~ *accustomed*, to the mount of Olives; and his disciples ~~also~~ followed him.

H-40. THE TRUE VINE

15:1 I am the true vine, and my Father is the husbandman.

15:2 Every branch in me that beareth not fruit he taketh away: and every branch that beareth fruit, he purgeth it, that it may bring forth more fruit.

15:3 Now ye are clean through the word which I have spoken unto you.

15:4 Abide in me, and I in you. As the branch cannot bear fruit of itself, except it abide in the vine; no more can ye, except ye abide in me.

15:5 I am the vine, ye are the branches: He that abideth in me, and I in him, the same bringeth forth much fruit: for without me ye can do nothing.

15:6 If a man abide not in me, he is cast forth as a branch, and is withered; and men gather them, and cast them into the fire, and they are burned.

15:7 If ye abide in me, and my words abide in you, ye shall ask what ye will, and it shall be done unto you.

15:8 Herein is my Father glorified, that ye bear much fruit; so shall ye be my disciples.

15:9 As the Father hath loved me, so have I loved you: continue ye in my love.

15:10 If ye keep my commandments, ye shall abide in my love; even as I have kept my Father's commandments, and abide in his love.

15:11 These things have I spoken unto you, that my joy might remain in you, and that your joy might be full.

H-41. APOSTLES AGAIN COMMANDED TO LOVE ONE ANOTHER

15:12 This is my commandment, That ye love one another, as I have loved you.

15:13 Greater love hath no man than this, that a man lay down his life for his friends.

15:14 Ye are my friends, if ye do whatsoever I command you.

15:15 Henceforth I call you not servants; for the servant knoweth not what his lord doeth: but I have called you friends; for all things that I have heard of my Father I have made known unto you.

15:16 Ye have not chosen me, but I have chosen you, and ordained you, that ye should go and bring forth fruit, and that your fruit should remain: that whatsoever ye

MATTHEW	MARK	LUKE	JOHN

shall ask of the Father in my name, he may give it you.

15:17 These things I command you, that ye love one another.

H-42. THE WORLD WILL HATE THE APOSTLES

15:18 If the world hate you, ye know that it hated me before it hated you.

15:19 If ye were of the world, the world would love his own: but because ye are not of the world, but I have chosen you out of the world, therefore the world hateth you.

15:20 Remember the word that I said unto you, The servant is not greater than his lord. If they have persecuted me, they will also persecute you; if they have kept my saying, they will keep yours also.

15:21 But all these things will they do unto you for my name's sake, because they know not him that sent me.

15:22 If I had not come and spoken unto them, they had not had sin: but now they have no cloke for their sin.

15:23 He that hateth me hateth my Father also.

15:24 If I had not done among them the works which none other man did, they had not had sin: but now have they both seen and hated both me and my Father.

15:25 But this cometh to pass, that the word might be fulfilled that is written in their law, They hated me without a cause.

15:26 But when the Comforter is come, whom I will send unto you from the Father, even the Spirit of truth, which proceedeth from the Father, he shall testify of me:

15:27 And ye also shall bear witness, because ye have been with me from the beginning.

16:1 These things have I spoken unto you, that ye should not be offended.

16:2 They shall put you out of the synagogues: yea, the time cometh, that whosoever killeth you will think that he doeth God service.

16:3 And these things will they do unto you, because they have not known the Father, nor me.

H-43. JESUS AGAIN EXPLAINS HIS DEATH

16:4 But these things have I told you, that when the time shall come, ye may remember that I told you of them. And these things I said not unto you at the beginning, because I was with you.

MATTHEW	MARK	LUKE	JOHN

16:5 But now I go my way to him that sent me; and none of you asketh me, Whither goest thou?

16:6 But because I have said these things unto you, sorrow hath filled your heart.

16:7 Nevertheless I tell you the truth; It is expedient for you that I go away: for if I go not away, the Comforter will not come unto you; but if I depart, I will send him unto you.

16:8 And when he is come, he will reprove the world of sin, and of righteousness, and of judgment:

16:9 Of sin, because they believe not on me;

16:10 Of righteousness, because I go to my Father, and ~~ye~~ *they* see me no more;

16:11 Of judgment, because the prince of this world is judged.

16:12 I have yet many things to say unto you, but ye cannot bear them now.

16:13 Howbeit when he, the Spirit of truth, is come, he will guide you into all truth: for he shall not speak of himself; but whatsoever he shall hear, that shall he speak: and he will shew you things to come.

16:14 He shall glorify me: for he shall receive of mine, and shall shew it unto you.

16:15 All things that the Father hath are mine: therefore said I, that he shall take of mine, and shall shew it unto you.

16:16 A little while, and ye shall not see me: and again, a little while, and ye shall see me, because I go to the Father.

16:17 Then said some of his disciples among themselves, What is this that he saith unto us, A little while, and ye shall not see me: and again, a little while, and ye shall see me: and, Because I go to the Father?

16:18 They said therefore, What is this that he saith, A little while? we cannot tell what he saith.

16:19 Now Jesus knew that they were desirous to ask him, and said unto them, Do ye inquire among yourselves of that I said, A little while, and ye shall not see me: and again, a little while, and ye shall see me?

16:20 Verily, verily, I say unto you, That ye shall weep and lament, but the world shall rejoice: and ye shall be sorrowful, but your sorrow shall be turned into joy.

16:21 A woman when she is in travail hath sorrow, because her hour is come: but as soon as she is delivered of the child, she remembereth no more the anguish, for joy that a man is born into the

MATTHEW	MARK	LUKE	JOHN

world.

16:22 And ye now therefore have sorrow: but I will see you again, and your heart shall rejoice, and your joy no man taketh from you.

16:23 And in that day ye shall ask me nothing *but it shall be done unto you*. Verily, verily, I say unto you, Whatsoever ye shall ask the Father in my name, he will give it you.

16:24 Hitherto have ye asked nothing in my name: ask, and ye shall receive, that your joy may be full.

16:25 These things have I spoken unto you in proverbs: but the time cometh, when I shall no more speak unto you in proverbs, but I shall shew you plainly of the Father.

16:26 At that day ye shall ask in my name: and I say not unto you, that I will pray the Father for you:

16:27 For the Father himself loveth you, because ye have loved me, and have believed that I came out from God.

16:28 I came forth from the Father, and am come into the world: again, I leave the world, and go to the Father.

16:29 His disciples said unto him, Lo, now speakest thou plainly, and speakest no proverb.

16:30 Now are we sure that thou knowest all things, and needest not that any man should ask thee: by this we believe that thou camest forth from God.

16:31 Jesus answered them, Do ye now believe?

16:32 Behold, the hour cometh, yea, is now come, that ye shall be scattered, every man to his own, and shall leave me alone: and yet I am not alone, because the Father is with me.

16:33 These things I have spoken unto you, that in me ye might have peace. In the world ye shall have tribulation: but be of good cheer; I have overcome the world.

H-44. THE INTERCESSORY PRAYER

17:1 These words spake Jesus, and lifted up his eyes to heaven, and said, Father, the hour is come; glorify thy Son, that thy Son also may glorify thee:

17:2 As thou hast given him power over all flesh, that he should give eternal life to as many as thou hast given him.

17:3 And this is life eternal, that they might know thee the only true God, and Jesus Christ, whom thou hast sent.

MATTHEW	MARK	LUKE	JOHN

17:4 I have glorified thee on the earth: I have finished the work which thou gavest me to do.

17:5 And now, O Father, glorify thou me with thine own self with the glory which I had with thee before the world was.

17:6 I have manifested thy name unto the men which thou gavest me out of the world: thine they were, and thou gavest them me; and they have kept thy word.

17:7 Now they have known that all things whatsoever thou hast given me are of thee.

17:8 For I have given unto them the words which thou gavest me; and they have received them, and have known surely that I came out from thee, and they have believed that thou didst send me.

17:9 I pray for them: I pray not for the world, but for them which thou hast given me; for they are thine.

17:10 And all mine are thine, and thine are mine; and I am glorified in them.

17:11 And now I am no more in the world, but these are in the world, and I come to thee. Holy Father, keep through thine own name those whom thou hast given me, that they may be one, as we are.

17:12 While I was with them in the world, I kept them in thy name: those that thou gavest me I have kept, and none of them is lost, but the son of perdition; that the scripture might be fulfilled.

17:13 And now come I to thee; and these things I speak in the world, that they might have my joy fulfilled in themselves.

17:14 I have given them thy word; and the world hath hated them, because they are not of the world, even as I am not of the world.

17:15 I pray not that thou shouldest take them out of the world, but that thou shouldest keep them from the evil.

17:16 They are not of the world, even as I am not of the world.

17:17 Sanctify them through thy truth: thy word is truth.

17:18 As thou hast sent me into the world, even so have I also sent them into the world.

17:19 And for their sakes I sanctify myself, that they also might be sanctified through the truth.

17:20 Neither pray I for these alone, but for them also which shall believe on me through their word;

17:21 That they all may be one; as thou, Father, art in me, and I in

MATTHEW	MARK	LUKE	JOHN

thee, that they also may be one in us: that the world may believe that thou hast sent me.

17:22 And the glory which thou gavest me I have given them; that they may be one, even as we are one:

17:23 I in them, and thou in me, that they may be made perfect in one; and that the world may know that thou hast sent me, and hast loved them, as thou hast loved me.

17:24 Father, I will that they also, whom thou hast given me, be with me where I am; that they may behold my glory, which thou hast given me: for thou lovedst me before the foundation of the world.

17:25 O righteous Father, the world hath not known thee: but I have known thee, and these have known that thou hast sent me.

17:26 And I have declared unto them thy name, and will declare it: that the love wherewith thou hast loved me may be in them, and I in them.

H-45. GETHSEMANE

18:1 When Jesus had spoken these words, he went forth with his disciples over the brook Cedron, where was a garden, into the which he entered, and his disciples.

26:36 Then cometh Jesus with them unto a place called Gethsemane,

14:32 And they came to a place which was named Gethsemane: ~~and he saith~~ *which was a garden; and the disciples began to be sore amazed, and to be very heavy, and to complain in their hearts, wondering if this be the Messiah. And Jesus knowing their hearts, said* to his disciples,

22:40 And when he was at the place,

and sai~~th~~*d* unto the disciples,
Sit ye here, while I go *yonder* and pray ~~yonder~~.

Sit ye here, while I shall pray.

he said unto them,

Pray that ye enter not into temptation.

26:37 And he took with him Peter and the two sons of Zebedee, and began to be sorrowful and very heavy.

14:33 And he taketh with him Peter and James and John, and ~~began to be sore amazed, and to be very heavy;~~ *rebuked them,*

26:38 Then sai~~th~~*d* he unto them, My soul is exceeding sorrowful, even unto death: tarry ye here, and watch with me.

14:34 And sai~~th~~*d* unto them, My soul is exceeding sorrowful*, even* unto death: tarry ye here, and watch.

26:39 And he went a little further, and fell on his face, and prayed,

14:35 And he went forward a little, and fell on the ground, and prayed

22:41 And he was withdrawn from them about a stone's cast, and kneeled down, and prayed,

saying, O my Father, if it be possible, let this cup pass from me:

that, if it were possible, the hour might pass from him.

2:42 Saying, Father, if thou be willing, remove this cup from me:

14:36 And he said, Abba, Father, all things are possible unto thee; take away this cup from me:

nevertheless not as I will, but as thou wilt.

nevertheless not ~~what I will, but what thou wilt~~ *my will, but thine be done*.

nevertheless not my will, but thine, be done.

MATTHEW	MARK	LUKE	JOHN

LUKE

22:43   And there appeared an angel unto him from heaven, strengthening him.
22:44   And being in an agony he prayed more earnestly: and ~~his~~ *he* sweat ~~was~~ as it were great drops of blood falling down to the ground.
22:45   And when he rose up from prayer,

MATTHEW

26:40   And he cometh unto the disciples, and findeth them asleep,

and saith unto Peter, What, could ye not watch with me one hour?

26:41   Watch and pray, that ye enter not into temptation:
the spirit indeed is willing, but the flesh is weak.

26:42   He went away again the second time, and prayed,

saying, O my Father, if this cup may not pass away from me, except I drink it, thy will be done.
26:43   And he came and found them asleep again: for their eyes were heavy.

26:44   And he left them, and went away again, and prayed the third time, saying the same words.
26:45   Then cometh he to his disciples, and saith unto them, Sleep on now, and take ~~your~~ rest: behold, the hour is at hand, and the Son of man is betrayed into the hands of sinners.
26:46   *And after they had slept, he said unto them, A*rise, *and* let us be going: behold, he is at hand that doth betray me.

MARK

14:37   And he cometh, and findeth them sleeping,

and sai~~th~~*d* unto Peter, Simon, sleepest thou? couldest not thou watch one hour?
14:38   Watch ye and pray, lest ye enter into temptation.
And they said unto him, The spirit truly is ready, but the flesh is weak.
14:39   And again he went away, and prayed,
and spake the same words.

14:40   And when he returned, he found them asleep again, (for their eyes were heavy,) neither ~~wist~~ *knew* they what to answer him.

14:41   And he cometh *to them* the third time, and sai~~th~~*d* unto them, Sleep on now, and take ~~your~~ rest: it is enough, the hour is come; behold, the Son of man is betrayed into the hands of sinners.
14:42   *And after they had finished their sleep, he said,* Rise up, let us go; lo, he ~~that~~ *who* betrayeth me is at hand.

LUKE (cont.)

and was come to his disciples, he found them sleeping ~~for sorrow~~, *for they were filled with sorrow;*
22:46   And *he* said unto them, Why sleep ye?

rise and pray, lest ye enter into temptation.

MATTHEW	MARK	LUKE	JOHN

Friday--The Sixth Day of the Week

H-46. THE BETRAYAL

MATTHEW	MARK	LUKE	JOHN
			18:2 And Judas also, which betrayed him, knew the place: for Jesus ofttimes resorted thither with his disciples. 18:3 Judas then, having received a band of men and officers from the chief priests and Pharisees, cometh thither with lanterns and torches and weapons.
26:47 And while he yet spake, lo, Judas, one of the twelve, came, and with him a great multitude with swords and staves, from the chief priests and elders of the people. 26:48 Now he that betrayed him gave them a sign, saying, Whomsoever I shall kiss, that same is he: hold him fast. 26:49 And forthwith he came to Jesus, and said, Hail, master; and kissed him. 26:50(a) And Jesus said unto him, Friend *Judas*, wherefore art thou come *to betray me with a kiss*?	14:43 And immediately, while he yet spake, cometh Judas, one of the twelve, and with him a great multitude with swords and staves, from the chief priests and the scribes and the elders. 14:44 And he that *who* betrayed him had given them a token, saying, Whomsoever I shall kiss, that same is he; take him, and lead him away safely. 14:45 And as soon as he was come, he goeth straightway to him, and saithd, Master, master; and kissed him.	22:47 And while he yet spake, behold a multitude, and he that *who* was called Judas, one of the twelve, went before them, and drew near unto Jesus to kiss him. 22:48 But Jesus said unto him, Judas, betrayest thou the Son of man with a kiss?	
			18:4 Jesus therefore, knowing all things that should come upon him, went forth, and said unto them, Whom seek ye? 18:5 They answered him, Jesus of Nazareth. Jesus saith unto them, I am he. And Judas also, which betrayed him, stood with them. 18:6 As soon then as he had said unto them, I am he, they went backward, and fell to the ground. 18:7 Then asked he them again, Whom seek ye? And they said, Jesus of Nazareth. 18:8 Jesus answered, I have told you that I am he: if therefore ye seek me, let these go their way: 18:9 That the saying might be fulfilled, which he spake, Of them which thou gavest me have I lost none.

H-47. PETER TRIES TO STOP THE ARREST

MATTHEW	MARK	LUKE	JOHN
		22:49 When they which *who* were about him saw what would follow, they said unto him, Lord, shall we smite with the *a* sword?	
26:51 And, behold, one of them which were with Jesus stretched out his hand, and drew his sword, and struck a servant of the high priest's, and smote off his ear. 26:52 Then said Jesus unto him, Put up again thy sword into his *its*	14:47 And one of them that *who* stood by drew a *his* sword, and smote a servant of the high priest, and cut off his ear. *But Jesus commanded him to return his sword,*	22:50 And one of them smote the servant of the high priest, and cut off his right ear. 22:51 And Jesus answered and said,	18:10 Then Simon Peter having a sword drew it, and smote the high priest's servant, and cut off his right ear. The servant's name was Malchus. 18:11 Then said Jesus unto Peter, Put up thy sword into the sheath:

MATTHEW	MARK	LUKE	JOHN
place: for all they that take the sword shall perish with the sword.	*saying, He who taketh the sword shall perish with the sword.* *And he put forth his finger and healed the servant of the high priest.*	Suffer ye thus far. And he touched his ear, and healed him.	
26:53 Thinkest thou that I cannot now pray to my Father, and he shall presently give me more than twelve legions of angels? 26:55 In that same hour said Jesus *un*to the multitudes,	14:48 And Jesus answered and said unto them,	22:52 Then Jesus said unto the chief priests, and captains of the temple, and the elders, ~~which~~ *who* were come to him,	
Are ye come out as against a thief with swords and staves for to take me? I sat daily with you ~~teaching~~ in the temple, *teaching,* and ye laid no hold on me.	Are ye come out, as against a thief, with swords and ~~with~~ staves to take me? 14:49 I was daily with you in the temple teaching, and ye took me not:	~~Be~~ *Are* ye come out, as against a thief, with swords and staves? 22:53 When I was daily with you in the temple, ye stretched forth no hands against me: but this is your hour, and the power of darkness.	
			the cup which my Father hath given me, shall I not drink it?
26:54 But how then shall the scriptures be fulfilled, that thus it must be?	but the ~~s~~Scriptures must be fulfilled.		

H-48. THE ARREST

MATTHEW	MARK	LUKE	JOHN
26:50(b) Then came they, and laid hands on Jesus, and took him. 26:56 But all this was done, that the scriptures of the prophets might be fulfilled. Then all the disciples forsook him, and fled.	14:46 And they laid their hands on him, and took him. 14:50 And ~~they~~ *the disciples, when they heard this saying,* all forsook him, and fled. 14:51 And there followed him a certain young man, *a disciple,* having a linen cloth cast about his naked body; and the young ~~men~~ *man* laid hold on him: 14:52 And he left the linen cloth, and fled from them naked, *and saved himself out of their hands.*		18:12 Then the band and the captain and officers of the Jews took Jesus, and bound him,

H-49. JESUS TAKEN TO THE PALACE OF ANNAS AND CAIAPHAS

MATTHEW	MARK	LUKE	JOHN
26:57 And they that had laid hold on Jesus led him away to Caiaphas the high priest, where the scribes and the elders were assembled.	14:53 And they led Jesus away to the high priest: and with him were assembled all the chief priests and the elders and the scribes.	22:54 Then took they him, and led him, and brought him into the high priest's house.	18:13 And led him away to Annas first; for he was father in law to Caiaphas, which was the high priest that same year. 18:14 Now Caiaphas was he, which gave counsel to the Jews, that it was expedient that one man should die for the people.
26:58 But Peter followed him afar off unto the high priest's palace,	14:54 And Peter followed him afar off, even into the palace of the high priest:	And Peter followed afar off.	18:15 And Simon Peter followed Jesus, and so did another disciple: that disciple was known unto the high priest, and went in with Jesus into the palace of the high priest. 18:16 But Peter stood at the door without. Then went out that other disciple, which was known unto the high priest, and spake unto her that kept the door, and brought in Peter.

MATTHEW	MARK	LUKE	JOHN
			18:18 And the servants and officers stood there, who had made a fire of coals; for it was cold: and they warmed themselves:
		22:55 And when they had kindled a fire in the midst of the hall, and were set down together, Peter sat down among them.	
and went in, and sat with the servants, to see the end.	and he sat with the servants, and warmed himself at the fire.		and Peter stood with them, and warmed himself.

H-50. JESUS BEFORE ANNAS

18:19 The high priest then asked Jesus of his disciples, and of his doctrine.
18:20 Jesus answered him, I spake openly to the world; I ever taught in the synagogue, and in the temple, whither the Jews always resort; and in secret have I said nothing.
18:21 Why askest thou me? ask them which heard me, what I have said unto them: behold, they know what I said.
18:22 And when he had thus spoken, one of the officers which stood by struck Jesus with the palm of his hand, saying, Answerest thou the high priest so?
18:23 Jesus answered him, If I have spoken evil, bear witness of the evil: but if well, why smitest thou me?
18:24 Now Annas had sent him bound unto Caiaphas the high priest.

H-51. JESUS BEFORE CAIAPHAS AND THE COUNCIL

MATTHEW

26:59 Now the chief priests, and elders, and all the council, sought false witness against Jesus, to put him to death;
26:60 ~~But found none:~~ yea, though many false witnesses came, ~~yet found they none~~ *they found none that could accuse him*.
At the last came two false witnesses,

26:61 And said, This ~~fellow~~ *man* said, I am able to destroy the temple of God, and to build it in three days.

26:62 And the high priest arose, and said unto him,
Answerest thou nothing?
~~what is it which~~ *Knowest thou what* these witness against thee?
26:63 But Jesus held his peace.
And the high priest answered and said unto him,

I adjure thee by the living God, that thou tell us whether thou be the

MARK

14:55 And the chief priests and all the council sought for witness against Jesus to put him to death;

~~and~~ *but* found none.
14:56 ~~For~~ *Though* many bare false witness against him, ~~but~~ *yet* their witness agreed not together.
14:57 And there arose certain *men*, and bare false witness against him, saying,
14:58 We heard him say, I will destroy this temple that is made with hands, and within three days I will build another made without hands.
14:59 But neither ~~so~~ did their witness agree together.
14:60 And the high priest stood up in the midst, and asked Jesus, saying, Answerest thou nothing?
~~what is it which~~ *knowest thou not what* these witness against thee?
14:61 But he held his peace, and answered nothing. Again the high priest asked him, and said unto him,
Art thou the Christ, the Son of the Blessed?

MATTHEW	MARK	LUKE	JOHN

Christ, the Son of God.

26:64 Jesus saithd unto him, Thou hast said: nevertheless I say unto you,
Hereafter shall ye see the Son of man sitting on the right hand of power, and coming in the clouds of heaven.
26:65 Then the high priest rent his clothes, saying, He hath spoken blasphemy; what further need have we of witnesses?
 behold, now ye have heard his blasphemy.
26:66 What think ye? They answered and said, He is guilty, *and worthy* of death.

14:62 And Jesus said, I am:

and ye shall see the Son of mMan sitting on the right hand of power, and coming in the clouds of heaven.
14:63 Then the high priest rent his clothes, and saith *said*, What need we any further witnesses?

14:64 Ye have heard the blasphemy:
what think ye? And they all condemned him to be guilty of death.

H-52. JESUS IS MOCKED

26:67 Then did they spit in his face, and buffeted him;

and others smote him with the palms of their hands,

26:68 Saying, Prophesy unto us, thou Christ, Who is he *it* that smote thee?

14:65 And some began to spit on him, and to cover his face, and to buffet him,
and to say unto him, Prophesy: and the servants did strike him with the palms of their hands.

22:63 And the men that *who* held Jesus mocked him, and smote him.

22:64 And when they had blindfolded him, they struck him on the face,
and asked him, saying, Prophesy, who is it that *who* smote thee?

22:65 And many other things blasphemously spake they against him.

H-53. PETER DENIES JESUS

26:69 Now Peter sat without in the palace: and a damsel came unto him,

saying,
Thou also wast with Jesus of Galilee.
26:70 But he denied before them all, saying, I know not what thou sayest.
26:71 And when he was gone out into the porch,
another maid saw him, and said unto them that were there,

This fellow *man* was also with Jesus of Nazareth.
26:72 And again he denied with an oath, I do not know the man.
26:73 And after a while came unto him they that stood by, and said to Peter, Surely thou also art one of them; for thy speech bewrayeth *betrayeth* thee.
26:74 Then began he to curse and to swear, saying, I know not the man.
And immediately the cock crew.

14:66 And as Peter was beneath in the palace, there cometh one of the maids of the high priest:
14:67 And when she saw Peter warming himself, she looked upon him, and said,
And thou also wast with Jesus of Nazareth.
14:68 But he denied, saying, I know not, neither understand I what thou sayest.
And he went out into the porch; and the cock crew.
14:69 And a maid saw him again, and began to say to them that *who* stood by,
This is one of them.

14:70 And he denied it again.

And a little after, they that *who* stood by said again to Peter, Surely thou art one of them: for thou art a Galilaean, and thy speech agreeth thereto.
14:71 But he began to curse and to swear, saying, I know not this man of whom ye speak.
14:72 And the second time the cock crew.

22:56 But a certain maid beheld him as he sat by the fire,

and earnestly looked upon him, and said,
This man was also with him.

22:57 And he denied him, saying, Woman, I know him not.

22:58 And after a little while another saw him, and said,
Thou art also of them.

And Peter said, Man, I am not.

22:59 And about the space of one hour after another confidently affirmed, saying, Of a truth this fellow also was *man was also* with him: for he is a Galilaean *Galilean*.
22:60 And Peter said, Man, I know not what thou sayest.

And immediately, while he yet spake, the cock crew.
22:61 And the Lord turned, and looked upon Peter.

18:17 Then saith the damsel that kept the door unto Peter,

Art not thou also one of this man's disciples?
He saith, I am not.

18:25 And Simon Peter stood and warmed himself.

They said therefore unto him, Art not thou also one of his disciples? He denied it, and said, I am not.

18:26 One of the servants of the high priest, being his kinsman whose ear Peter cut off, saith, Did not I *not* see thee in the garden with him?
18:27 Peter then denied again:

and immediately the cock crew.

MATTHEW	MARK	LUKE	JOHN

26:75 And Peter remembered the words of Jesus, which *he* said unto him, Before the cock crow, thou shalt deny me thrice.
And he went out, and wept bitterly.

And Peter called to mind the word*s* ~~that~~ *which* Jesus said unto him, Before the cock crow twice, thou shalt deny me thrice.
~~And when he thought thereon, he wept~~ *And he went out, and fell upon his face, and wept bitterly.*

And Peter remembered the word of the Lord, how he had said unto him, Before the cock crow, thou shalt deny me thrice.
22:62 And Peter went out, and wept bitterly.

H-54. THE TRIAL AND CONDEMNATION

27:1   When the morning was come, all the chief priests and elders of the people took counsel against Jesus
to put him to death:

15:1(a) And straightway in the morning the chief priests held a consultation with the elders and scribes

22:66 And as soon as it was day, the elders of the people and the chief priests and the scribes came together,

and led him into their council, saying,
22:67 Art thou the Christ? tell us. And he said unto them, If I tell you, ye will not believe:
22:68 And if I also ask you, ye will not answer me, nor let me go.
22:69 Hereafter shall the Son of man sit on the right hand of the power of God.
22:70 Then said they all, Art thou then the Son of God? And he said unto them, Ye say that I am.
22:71 And they said, What need we *of* any further witness? for we ourselves have heard of his own mouth.

and the whole council *condemned him,*

H-55. JUDAS COMMITS SUICIDE

27:3 Then Judas, ~~which~~ *who* had betrayed him, when he saw that he was condemned, repented himself, and brought again the thirty pieces of silver to the chief priests and elders,
27:4 Saying, I have sinned in that I have betrayed the innocent blood. And they said *unto him,* What is that to us? see thou to ~~that~~ *it; thy sins be upon thee.*
27:5 And he cast down the pieces of silver in the temple, and departed, and went and hanged himself *on a tree. And straightway he fell down, and his bowels gushed out, and he died.*
27:6 And the chief priests took the silver pieces, and said, It is not lawful for to put them into the treasury, because it is the price of blood.
27:7 And they took counsel, and bought with them the potter's field, to bury strangers in.
27:8 Wherefore that field was called, The field of blood, unto this day.
27:9 Then was fulfilled that which was spoken by Jeremy the prophet,

MATTHEW	MARK	LUKE	JOHN

saying, And they took the thirty pieces of silver, the price of him that was valued, whom they of the children of Israel did value;

27:10 *And therefore they took the pieces of silver,* And gave them for the potter's field, as the Lord appointed ~~me~~ *by the mouth of Jeremy.*

H-56. JESUS BEFORE PILATE

MATTHEW	MARK	LUKE	JOHN
27:2 And when they had bound him, they led him away, and delivered him to Pontius Pilate the governor.	15:1(b) and bound ~~Jesus~~ *him,* and carried him away, and delivered him to Pilate.	23:1 And the whole multitude of them arose, and led him unto Pilate.	18:28 Then led they Jesus from Caiaphas unto the hall of judgment:

and it was early; and they themselves went not into the judgment hall, lest they should be defiled; but that they might eat the passover.

18:29 Pilate then went out unto them, and said, What accusation bring ye against this man?

18:30 They answered and said unto him, If he were not a malefactor, we would not have delivered him up unto thee.

23:2 And they began to accuse him, saying, We found this ~~fellow~~ *man* perverting the nation, and forbidding to give tribute to Caesar, saying that he himself is Christ a King.

18:31 Then said Pilate unto them, Take ye him, and judge him according to your law. The Jews therefore said unto him, It is not lawful for us to put any man to death:

18:32 That the saying of Jesus might be fulfilled, which he spake, signifying what death he should die.

18:33 Then Pilate entered into the judgment hall again, and called Jesus, and said unto him, Art thou the King of the Jews?

| 27:11 And Jesus stood before the governor: and the governor asked him, saying, Art thou the King of the Jews? | 15:2 And Pilate asked him, Art thou the King of the Jews? | 23:3 And Pilate asked him, saying, Art thou the King of the Jews? | |

18:34 Jesus answered him, Sayest thou this thing of thyself, or did others tell it thee of me?

18:35 Pilate answered, Am I a Jew? Thine own nation and the chief priests have delivered thee unto me: what hast thou done?

18:36 Jesus answered, My kingdom is not of this world: if my kingdom were of this world, then would my servants fight, that I should not be delivered to the Jews: but now is my kingdom not from hence.

18:37 Pilate therefore said unto him, Art thou a king then?

| And Jesus said unto him, Thou sayest *truely; for thus it is written of me.* | And ~~he~~ *Jesus* answering said unto him, ~~Thou sayest it~~ *I am, even as thou sayest.* | And he answered him and said, *Yea,* Thou sayest it. | Jesus answered, Thou sayest that I am a king. To this end was I born, and for this cause came I into the |

MATTHEW	MARK	LUKE	JOHN
			world, that I should bear witness unto the truth. Every one that is of the truth heareth my voice.
			18:38 Pilate saith unto him, What is truth? And when he had said this, he went out again unto the Jews, and saith unto them, I find in him no fault at all.
		23:4 Then said Pilate to the chief priests and to the people, I find no fault in this man.	
27:12 And when he was accused of the chief priests and elders, he answered nothing.	15:3 And the chief priests accused him of many things: but he answered nothing.		
27:13 Then said Pilate unto him, Hearest thou not how many things they witness against thee?	15:4 And Pilate asked him again, saying, Answerest thou nothing? behold how many things they witness against thee.		
27:14 And he answered him to *not to his questions; yea* never a word; insomuch that the governor marvelled greatly.	15:5 But Jesus yet answered nothing; so that Pilate marvelled.		
		23:5 And they were the more fierce, saying, He stirreth up the people, teaching throughout all Jewry, beginning from Galilee to this place.	
		23:6 When Pilate heard of Galilee, he asked whether the man were a Galilaean.	
		23:7 And as soon as he knew that he belonged unto Herod's jurisdiction, he sent him to Herod, who himself also was at Jerusalem at that time.	

H-57. JESUS BEFORE HEROD

MATTHEW	MARK	LUKE	JOHN
		23:8 And when Herod saw Jesus, he was exceeding glad: for he was desirous to see him of a long season *time*, because he had heard many things of him; and he hoped to have seen some miracle done by him.	
		23:9 Then he questioned with him in many words; but he answered him nothing.	
		23:10 And the chief priests and scribes stood and vehemently accused him.	
		23:11 And Herod with his men of war set him at nought, and mocked him, and arrayed him in a gorgeous robe, and sent him again to Pilate.	
		23:12 And the same day Pilate and Herod were made friends together: for before *this* they were at enmity between themselves.	

MATTHEW	MARK	LUKE	JOHN

H-58. SECOND APPEARANCE BEFORE PILATE

		23:13 And Pilate, when he had called together the chief priests and the rulers and the people,	
		23:14 Said unto them, ~~Ye~~ *You* have brought this man unto me, as one ~~that~~ *who* perverteth the people: and, behold, I, having examined him before you, have found no fault in this man touching those things whereof ye accuse him:	
		23:15 No, nor yet Herod: for I sent you to him; and, lo, nothing worthy of death is done unto him.	
		23:16 I will therefore chastise him, and release him.	
27:15 Now at that feast the governor was wont to release unto the people a prisoner, whom they would.	15:6 Now *it was common* at that feast ~~he released~~ *for Pilate to release* unto them one prisoner, whomsoever they desired.	23:17 (For of necessity he must release one unto them at the feast.)	18:39(a) But ye have a custom, that I should release unto you one at the passover:
27:16 And they had then a notable prisoner, called Barabbas.	15:7 And there was ~~one~~ *a man* named Barabbas, ~~which lay~~ bound with them ~~that~~ *who* had made insurrection with him, who had committed murder in the insurrection.		
	15:8 And the multitude crying aloud began to desire him to ~~do as he had ever done~~ *deliver Jesus* unto them.		
27:17 Therefore when they were gathered together, Pilate said unto them, Whom will ye that I release unto you? Barabbas, or Jesus which is called Christ?	15:9 But Pilate answered *unto* them, saying, Will ye that I release unto you the King of the Jews?		18:39(b) will ye therefore that I release unto you the King of the Jews?
27:18 For he knew that for envy they had delivered him.	15:10 For he knew that the chief priests had delivered him for envy.		
27:19 When he was set down on the judgment seat, his wife sent unto him, saying, Have thou nothing to do with that just man: for I have suffered many things this day in a ~~dream~~ *vision* because of him.			
27:20 But the chief priests and elders persuaded the multitude that they should ask Barabbas, and destroy Jesus.	15:11 But the chief priests moved the people, that he should rather release Barabbas unto them, *as he had before done unto them.*	23:18 ~~And~~ *But* they cried out all at once, saying, Away with this man, and release unto us Barabbas:	
		23:19 (Who for a certain sedition made in the city, and for murder, was cast into prison.)	
		23:20 Pilate therefore, willing to release Jesus, spake again to them.	
27:21 *And* The governor ~~answered and~~ said unto them, Whether of the twain will ye that I release unto you? They said, Barabbas.			
27:22 Pilate sai~~th~~d unto them,	15:12 And Pilate ~~answered and said~~ *spake* again *and said* unto them,		
What shall I do ~~then~~ with Jesus which is called Christ?	What will ye then that I shall do unto him whom ye call the King of the Jews?		
~~They all say~~ *And all said* unto him, Let him be crucified.	15:13 And they cried out again, *Deliver him unto us to be crucified. Away with him.* Crucify him.	23:21 But they cried, saying, crucify him, crucify him.	
27:23(a) And the governor said,		23:22 And he said unto them the	

MATTHEW	MARK	LUKE	JOHN
Why, what evil hath he done?	15:14(a) Then Pilate said unto them, Why, what evil hath he done?	third time, Why, what evil hath he done? I have found no cause of death in him: I will therefore chastise him, and let him go.	
			18:40 Then cried they all again, saying, Not this man, but Barabbas. Now Barabbas was a robber.

H-59. SOLDIERS SCOURGE AND MOCK OF JESUS

MATTHEW	MARK	LUKE	JOHN
			19:1 Then Pilate therefore took Jesus, and scourged him.
27:27 Then the soldiers of the governor took Jesus into the common hall, and gathered unto him the whole band ~~of soldiers~~. 27:28 And they stripped him, and put on him a ~~scarlet~~ *purple* robe. 27:29 And when they had platted a crown of thorns, they put it upon his head, and a reed in his right hand: and they bowed the knee before him, and mocked him, saying, Hail, King of the Jews! 27:30 And they spit upon him, and took the reed, and smote him on the head.	15:16 And the soldiers led him away into the hall, called Praetorium; and they call together the whole band. 15:17 And they clothed him with purple, and platted a crown of thorns, and put it ~~about~~ *upon* his head, 15:18 And began to salute him, *saying,* Hail, King of the Jews! 15:19 And they smote him on the head with a reed, and did spit upon him, and bowing their knees worshipped him.		19:2 And the soldiers platted a crown of thorns, and put it on his head, and they put on him a purple robe, 19:3 And said, Hail, King of the Jews! and they smote him with their hands.

H-60. PILATE PLEADS FOR JESUS, THEN DELIVERS HIM

MATTHEW	MARK	LUKE	JOHN
			19:4 Pilate therefore went forth again, and saith unto them, Behold, I bring him forth to you, that ye may know that I find no fault in him. 19:5 Then came Jesus forth, wearing the crown of thorns, and the purple robe. And Pilate saith unto them, Behold the man! 19:6 When the chief priests therefore and officers saw him, they cried out, saying, Crucify him, crucify him. Pilate saith unto them, Take ye him, and crucify him: for I find no fault in him. 19:7 The Jews answered him, We have a law, and by our law he ought to die, because he made himself the Son of God. 19:8 When Pilate therefore heard that saying, he was the more afraid; 19:9 And went again into the judgment hall, and saith unto Jesus, Whence art thou? But Jesus gave him no answer. 19:10 Then saith Pilate unto him, Speakest thou not unto me? knowest thou not that I have power to crucify thee, and have power to release thee? 19:11 Jesus answered, Thou couldest have no power ~~at all~~

MATTHEW	MARK	LUKE	JOHN
			against me, except it were given thee from above: therefore he that delivered me unto thee hath the greater sin. 19:12 And from thenceforth Pilate sought to release him: but the Jews cried out, saying, If thou let this man go, thou art not Caesar's friend: whosoever maketh himself a king speaketh against Caesar. 19:13 When Pilate therefore heard that saying, he brought Jesus forth, and sat down in the judgment seat in a place that is called the Pavement, but in the Hebrew, Gabbatha. 19:14 And it was the preparation of the passover, and about the sixth hour: and he saith unto the Jews, Behold your King!
27:23(b) But they cried out the more, saying, Let him be crucified.	15:14(b) ~~And~~ *But* they cried out the more exceedingly, Crucify him.	23:23 And they were instant ~~with~~ *in* loud voices, requiring that he might be crucified.	19:15 But they cried out, Away with him, away with him, crucify him. Pilate saith unto them, Shall I crucify your King? The chief priest answered, We have no king but Caesar.
		And the voices of them and of the chief priests prevailed.	
27:24 When Pilate saw that he could prevail nothing, but ~~that~~ rather *that* a tumult was made, he took water, and washed his hands before the multitude, saying, I am innocent of the blood of this just person: see ~~ye to it~~ *that ye do nothing unto him*. 27:25 Then answered all the people, and said, His blood ~~be on~~ *come upon* us, and ~~on~~ our children.	15:15 And ~~so~~ *now* Pilate, willing to content the people,		
		23:24 And Pilate gave sentence that it should be as they required. 23:25 And he released unto them him ~~that~~ *who* for sedition and murder was cast into prison, whom they had desired; ~~but he~~ *and* delivered Jesus to their will.	
27:26 Then released he Barabbas unto them: and when he had scourged Jesus,	released Barabbas unto them, and		
he delivered him to be crucified.	delivered Jesus, when he had scourged him, to be crucified.		19:16(a) Then delivered he him therefore unto them to be crucified.

H-61. JESUS IS MOCKED AND CRUCIFIED

MATTHEW	MARK	LUKE	JOHN
27:31 And after that they had mocked him, they took the robe off from him, and put his own raiment on him, and led him away to crucify him. 27:32 And as they came out, they found a man of Cyrene, Simon by name: him they compelled to bear his cross.	15:20 And when they had mocked him, they took off the purple from him, and put his own clothes on him, and led him out to crucify him. 15:21 And they compel*led* one Simon a Cyrenian, who passed by, coming out of the country, the father of Alexander and Rufus, to bear his cross.	23:26 And as they led him away, they laid hold upon one Simon, a Cyrenian, coming out of the country, and on him they laid the cross, that he might bear it after Jesus. 23:27 And there followed him a great company of people, and of women, ~~which~~ *who* also bewailed and lamented him. 23:28 But Jesus ~~turned~~ *turned*	19:16(b) And they took Jesus, and led him away.

MATTHEW	MARK	LUKE	JOHN
		unto them said, Daughters of Jerusalem, weep not for me, but weep for yourselves, and for your children.	

23:29 For, behold, the days are coming, in the which they shall say, Blessed are the barren, and the wombs ~~that~~ *which* never bare, and the paps which never gave suck.

23:30 Then shall they begin to say to the mountains, Fall on us; and to the hills, Cover us.

23:31 For if ~~they do~~ these things *are done* in ~~a~~ *the* green tree, what shall be done in the dry *tree? This he spake, signifying the scattering of Israel, and the desolation of the heathen, or in other words, the Gentiles.*

23:32 And there were also two other*s*, malefactors, led with him to be put to death.

MATTHEW	MARK	LUKE	JOHN
27:33 And when they were come unto a place called Golgotha, that is to say, a place of ~~a skull~~ *burial*,	15:22 And they bring him unto the place Golgotha, which is, being interpreted, The place of a ~~skull~~ *burial*.		19:17 And he bearing his cross went forth into a place called the place of a ~~skull~~ *burial*, which is called in the Hebrew Golgotha:
		23:33 And when they were come to the place, which is called Calvary,	
27:34 They gave him vinegar to drink mingled with gall: and when he had tasted ~~thereof~~ *the vinegar*, he would not drink.	15:23 And they gave him to drink ~~wine mingled with myrrh: but he received it not~~ *vinegar mingled with gall; and when he had tasted the vinegar, he would not drink*. 15:25 And it was the third hour, ~~and~~ *when* they crucified him.		
27:38 Then were there two thieves crucified with him, one on the right hand, and another on the left.	15:27 And with him they crucif~~y~~*ied* two thieves; the one on his right hand, ~~and~~ the other on his left. 15:28 And the scripture was fulfilled, which sait~~h~~*d*, And he was numbered with the transgressors.	there they crucified him, and the malefactors, one on the right hand, and the other on the left.	19:18 Where they crucified him, and two other with him, on either side one, and Jesus in the midst.

H-62. "THIS IS JESUS THE KING OF THE JEWS"

MATTHEW	MARK	LUKE	JOHN
27:37 ~~And set up over his head his accusation written, THIS IS JESUS THE KING OF THE JEWS.~~ *And Pilate wrote a title, and put it on the cross, and the writing was,*	15:26 ~~And the superscription of his accusation was written over~~ *And Pilate wrote his accusation and put it upon the cross,*	23:38 And a superscription also was written over him	19:19 And Pilate wrote a title, and put it on the cross.
JESUS OF NAZARETH, THE KING OF THE JEWS, in letters of Greek, and Latin, and Hebrew.	THE KING OF THE JEWS.	in letters of Greek, and Latin, and Hebrew, THIS IS THE KING OF THE JEWS.	And the writing was, JESUS OF NAZARETH THE KING OF THE JEWS. 19:20 This title then read many of the Jews: for the place where Jesus was crucified was nigh to the city: and it was written in Hebrew, and Greek, and Latin. 19:21 Then said the chief priests of the Jews to Pilate, Write not, The King of the Jews; but that he said, I am King of the Jews.
And the chief priests said unto Pilate, It should be written and set up over his head, his accusation, This is he that said he was Jesus, the King of the Jews. *But Pilate answered and said, What I have written, I have written; let it alone.*	*There were certain of the chief priests who stood by, that said unto Pilate, write, that he said, I am King of the Jews.* *But Pilate said unto them, What I have written, I have written.*		19:22 Pilate answered, What I have written I have written.

MATTHEW	MARK	LUKE	JOHN

H-63. FIRST WORDS FROM THE CROSS: "FATHER, FORGIVE THEM"

| | | 23:34 Then said Jesus, Father, forgive them; for they know not what they do. *(Meaning the soldiers who crucified him,)* | |

H-64. SOLDIERS CAST LOTS FOR JESUS' GARMENTS

27:35 And they crucified him, and parted his garments,	15:24 And when they had crucified him, they parted his garments,	And they parted his raiment,	19:23 Then the soldiers, when they had crucified Jesus, took his garments, and made four parts, to every soldier a part; and also his coat: now the coat was without seam, woven from the top throughout. 19:24 They said therefore among themselves, Let us not rend it, but cast lots for it, whose it shall be:
casting lots:	casting lots upon them, what every man should take.	and cast lots.	
that it might be fulfilled which was spoken by the prophet, They parted my garments among them, and ~~upon~~ *for* my vesture ~~did~~ they *did* cast lots. 27:36 And sitting down they watched him there;			that the scripture might be fulfilled, which saith, They parted my raiment among them, and for my vesture they did cast lots. These things therefore the soldiers did.

H-65. FURTHER MOCKING BY THE RULERS AND THE PEOPLE

27:39 And they that passed by reviled him, wagging their heads, 27:40 And saying, Thou that destroyest the temple, and buildest it *again* in three days, save thyself.	15:29 And they ~~that~~ *who* passed by railed on him, wagging their heads, and saying, Ah, thou ~~that~~ *who* destroyest the temple, and buildest it in three days, 15:30 Save thyself, and come down from the cross.	23:35 And the people stood beholding.	
If thou be the Son of God, come down from the cross. 27:41 Likewise also the chief priests mocking ~~him,~~ with the scribes and elders, said, 27:42 He saved others; himself he cannot save.	15:31 Likewise also the chief priests mocking said among themselves with the scribes, He saved others; himself he cannot save.	And the rulers also with them derided ~~him~~, saying, He saved others; let him save himself, if he be *the* Christ, the chosen of God.	
If he be the King of Israel, let him now come down from the cross, and we will believe him. 27:43 He trusted in God; let him deliver him now, if he will ~~have~~ *save* him: for he said, I am the Son of God.	15:32(a) Let Christ the King of Israel descend now from the cross, that we may see and believe.		
		23:36 And the soldiers also mocked him, coming to him, and offering him vinegar, 23:37 And saying, If thou be the king of the Jews, save thyself.	

MATTHEW	MARK	LUKE	JOHN

H-66. SECOND WORDS FROM THE CROSS: TO THE THIEF

27:44 *One of* The thieves also, which were crucified with him, cast the same in his teeth.

But the other rebuked him, saying, Dost thou not fear God, seeing thou art under the same condemnation;

and this man is just, and hath not sinned;
and he cried unto the Lord that he would save him.

And the Lord said unto him, This day thou shalt be with me in paradise.

15:32(b) And ~~they that were crucified with him reviled him~~ *one of them who was crucified with him, reviled him also, saying, If thou are the Christ, save thyself and us.*

23:39 And one of the malefactors ~~which were hanged~~ *who was crucified with him,* railed on him, saying, If thou be *the* Christ, save thyself and us.
23:40 But the other answering rebuked him, saying, Dost ~~not thou~~ *thou not* fear God, seeing thou art in the same condemnation?
23:41 And we indeed justly; for we receive the due reward of our deeds: but this man hath done nothing amiss.
23:42 And he said ~~un~~to Jesus, Lord, remember me when thou comest into thy kingdom.
23:43 And Jesus said unto him, Verily I say unto thee, To day shalt thou be with me in paradise.

H-67. THIRD WORDS FROM THE CROSS: TO HIS MOTHER

19:25 Now there stood by the cross of Jesus his mother, and his mother's sister, Mary the wife of Cleophas, and Mary Magdalene.
19:26 When Jesus therefore saw his mother, and the disciple standing by, whom he loved, he saith unto his mother, Woman, behold thy son!
19:27 Then saith he to the disciple, Behold thy mother! And from that hour that disciple took her unto his own home.

H-68. DARKNESS FROM THE SIXTH TO THE NINTH HOUR

27:45 Now from the sixth hour there was darkness over all the land unto the ninth hour.

15:33 And when the sixth hour was come, there was darkness over the whole land until the ninth hour.

23:44 And it was about the sixth hour, and there was ~~a~~ darkness over all the earth until the ninth hour.
23:45(a) And the sun was darkened,

H-69. FINAL WORDS FROM THE CROSS

27:46 And about the ninth hour Jesus cried with a loud voice, saying, Eli, Eli, lama sabachthani? that is to say, My God, my God, why hast thou forsaken me?

27:47 Some of them that stood there, when they heard ~~that~~ *him*, said, This man calleth for Elias.

15:34 And at the ninth hour Jesus cried with a loud voice, saying, Eloi, Eloi, lama sabachthani? which is, being interpreted, My God, my God, why hast thou forsaken me?

15:35 And some of them ~~that~~ *who* stood by, when they heard ~~it~~ *him*, said, Behold, he calleth Elias.

19:28 After this, Jesus knowing that all things were now accomplished, that the scripture might be fulfilled, saith, I thirst.
19:29 Now there was ~~set~~ a vessel full of vinegar, *mingled with gall*:

MATTHEW	MARK	LUKE	JOHN
27:48 And straightway one of them ran, and took a spunge, and filled it with vinegar, and put it on a reed, and gave him to drink.	15:36 And one ran and filled a spunge full of vinegar, and put it on a reed, and gave him to drink;		and they filled a ~~spunge~~ *sponge* with ~~vinegar~~ *it*, and put ~~it~~ upon hyssop, and put ~~it~~ to his mouth.
			19:30 When Jesus therefore had received the vinegar,
27:49 The rest said, Let *him* be, let us see whether Elias will come to save him.	*others spake,,* saying, Let *him* alone; let us see whether Elias will come to take him down.		
27:50 Jesus, when he had cried again with a loud voice, *saying, Father it is finished, thy will is done,*	15:37 And Jesus cried with a loud voice,	23:46 And when Jesus had cried with a loud voice, he said, Father,	he said, It is finished:
		into thy hands I commend my spirit:	
yielded up the ghost.	and gave up the ghost.	and having said thus, he gave up the ghost.	and he bowed his head, and gave up the ghost.

H-70. VEIL OF TEMPLE RENT

MATTHEW	MARK	LUKE	JOHN
27:51 And, behold, the veil of the temple was rent in twain from the top to the bottom; and the earth did quake, and the rocks rent;	15:38 And the veil of the temple was rent in twain from the top to the bottom.	23:45(b) and the veil of the temple was rent in the midst.	

H-71. TESTIMONY OF THE CENTURION AND OTHER WITNESSES

MATTHEW	MARK	LUKE	JOHN
27:54 Now when the centurion, and they that were with him, watching Jesus, ~~saw~~ *heard* the earthquake, and *saw* those things ~~that~~ *which* were done,	15:39 And when the centurion, ~~which~~ *who* stood over against him,	23:47 Now when the centurion saw what was done,	
	saw that he so cried out, and gave up the ghost, he said,		
they feared greatly, saying, Truly this was the Son of God.	Truly this man ~~was~~ *is* the Son of God.	he glorified God, saying, Certainly this was a righteous man.	
		23:48 And all the people ~~that~~ *who* came together to that sight, beholding the things which were done, smote their breasts, and returned.	
27:55 And many women were there beholding afar off, which followed Jesus from Galilee, ministering unto him *for his burial*:	15:40 There were also women looking on afar off:	23:49 And all his acquaintance, and ~~the~~ women ~~that~~ *who* followed him from Galilee, stood afar off, beholding these things.	
27:56 Among ~~which~~ *whom* was Mary Magdalene, and Mary the mother of James and Joses, and the mother of Zebedee's children.	among whom was Mary Magdalene, and Mary the mother of James the ~~less~~ *younger* and of Joses, and Salome;		
	15:41 (Who also, when he was in Galilee, followed him, and ministered unto him;) and many other women ~~which~~ *who* came ~~up~~ with him unto Jerusalem.		

H-72. SOLDIERS PIERCE HIS SIDE

MATTHEW	MARK	LUKE	JOHN
			19:31 The Jews therefore, because it was the preparation, that the bodies should not remain upon the cross on the sabbath day, (for that sabbath day was an high day,) besought Pilate that their legs might be broken, and that they might be taken away.

MATTHEW	MARK	LUKE	JOHN
			19:32 Then came the soldiers, and brake the legs of the first, and of the other which was crucified with him. 19:33 But when they came to Jesus, and saw that he was dead already, they brake not his legs: 19:34 But one of the soldiers with a spear pierced his side, and forthwith came there out blood and water. 19:35 And he that saw it bare record, and his record is true: and he knoweth that he saith true, that ye might believe. 19:36 For these things were done, that the scripture should be fulfilled, A bone of him shall not be broken. 19:37 And again another scripture saith, They shall look on him whom they pierced.

H-73. THE BURIAL OF JESUS

MATTHEW	MARK	LUKE	JOHN
27:57 When the even*ing* was come,	15:42 And now when the even was come, because it was the preparation *day*, that is, the day before the sSabbath,		
there came a rich man of Arimathaea, named Joseph,	15:43 Joseph of Arimathaea, and honourable *honorable* counsellor,	23:50 And, behold, there was a man named Joseph, a counsellor; and he was a good man, and a just *one*: 23:51 (The same *day* had not consented to the counsel and deed of them;) he was *a man* of Arimathaea, a city of the Jews:	19:38 And after this Joseph of Arimathaea,
who also himself was Jesus' disciple:	which *who* also waited for the kingdom of God, came,	who also himself waited for the kingdom of God.	being a disciple of Jesus,
			but secretly for fear of the Jews, besought Pilate that he might take away the body of Jesus:
27:58 He went to Pilate, and begged the body of Jesus.	and went in boldly unto Pilate, and craved the body of Jesus.	23:52 This man *He* went unto Pilate, and begged the body of Jesus.	
	15:44 And Pilate marvelled, *and asked him* if he were already dead: and calling unto him the centurion, he asked him whether *if* he had been any while dead.		
Then Pilate commanded the body to be delivered.	15:45 And when he knew it of the centurion, he gave the body to Joseph.		and Pilate gave him leave.
			He came therefore, and took the body of Jesus. 19:39 And there came also Nicodemus, which at the first came to Jesus by night, and brought a mixture of myrrh and aloes, about an hundred pound weight.
27:59 And when Joseph had taken the body, he wrapped it in a clean linen cloth,	15:46 And he *Joseph* bought fine linen, and took him down, and wrapped him in the linen,	23:53 And he took it down, and wrapped it in linen,	19:40 Then took they the body of Jesus, and wound it in linen clothes with the spices, as the manner of the Jews is to bury. 19:41 Now in the place where he was crucified there was a garden; and in the garden a new sepulchre, wherein was never man yet laid.
27:60 And laid it in his own new tomb, which he had hewn out in the rock:	and laid him in a sepulchre which was hewn out of a rock,	and laid it in a sepulchre that *which* was hewn *hewed* in *a* stone, wherein never man before was laid.	19:42 There laid they Jesus

MATTHEW	MARK	LUKE	JOHN
and he rolled a great stone to the door of the sepulchre, and departed.	and rolled a stone unto the door of the ~~sepulchre~~ *sepulcher*.		therefore because of the Jews' preparation day;
		23:54 And that day was the preparation, and the sSabbath drew on.	for the sepulchre was nigh at hand.
27:61 And there was Mary Magdalene, and the other Mary, sitting over against the sepulchre.	15:47 And Mary Magdalene and Mary the mother of Joses beheld where he was laid.	23:55 And the women also, ~~which~~ *who* came with him from Galilee, followed after, and beheld the sepulchre, and how his body was laid.	
		23:56 And they returned, and prepared spices and ointments; and rested the sSabbath day according to the commandment.	

Saturday--The Seventh Day of the Week

H-74. GUARDS AT THE TOMB

27:62 Now the next day, that followed the day of the preparation, the chief priests and Pharisees came together unto Pilate,

27:63 Saying, Sir, we remember that that deceiver said, while he was yet alive, After three days I will rise again.

27:64 Command therefore that the sepulchre be made sure until the third day, lest his disciples come by night, and steal him away, and say unto the people, He is risen from the dead: so the last ~~error shall~~ *imposture will* be worse than the first.

27:65 Pilate said unto them, Ye have a watch: go your way, make it as sure as ye can.

27:66 So they went, and made the sepulchre sure, sealing the stone, and setting a watch.

MATTHEW	MARK	LUKE	JOHN

I-1. THE STONE IS ROLLED AWAY

28:2 And, behold, there ~~was~~ *had been* a great earthquake: for ~~the~~ *two* angel*s* of the Lord descended from heaven, and came and rolled back the stone from the door, and sat upon it.
28:3 ~~His~~ *And their* countenance was like lightning, and ~~his~~ *their* raiment white as snow:
28:4 And for fear of ~~him~~ *them* the keepers did shake, and became as ~~dead men~~ *though they were dead*.

I-2. WOMEN COME TO THE TOMB

	16:1 And when the ~~s~~*S*abbath was ~~past~~ *passed*, Mary Magdalene, and Mary the mother of James, and Salome, ~~had~~ bought sweet spices, that they might come and anoint him.		
28:1 In the end of the sabbath *day*, as it began to dawn towards the first day of the week, *early in the morning,* came Mary Magdalene and the other Mary to see the sepulchre.	16:2 And very early in the morning the first day of the week, they came unto the ~~sepulchre~~ *sepulcher* at the rising of the sun.	24:1 Now upon the first day of the week, very early in the morning, ~~they~~ *the women* came unto the sepulchre, bringing the spices which they had prepared, and certain others with them.	20:1(a) The first day of the week cometh Mary Magdalene early, when it was yet dark, unto the sepulchre,
	16:3 And they said among themselves, Who shall roll us away the stone from the door of the ~~sepulchre~~ *sepulcher*?		

I-3. WOMEN FIND STONE ROLLED AWAY

	16:4(a) ~~And~~ *But* when they looked, they saw that the stone was rolled away: for it was very great, *and two angels sitting thereon, clothed in long white garments;*	24:2 And they found the stone rolled away from the sepulchre, *and two angels standing by it in shining garments.*	20:1(b) and seeth the stone taken away from the sepulchre, *and two angels sitting thereon.*
		24:4 ~~And it came to pass, as~~ they were much perplexed thereabout, ~~behold, two men stood by them in shining garments:~~ 24:5 And ~~as~~ *they* were ~~afraid~~ *affrighted*, and bowed down their faces to the earth, ~~they~~	
	and they were affrighted.		
	16:5 ~~And entering into the sepulchre, they saw a young man sitting on the right side, clothed in a long white garment; and they were affrighted.~~		
28:5 And the angel*s* answered and said unto the women, Fear not ye: for ~~I~~ *we* know that ye seek Jesus, which was crucified.	16:6 ~~And he saith~~ *But the angels said* unto them, Be not affrighted: Ye seek Jesus of Nazareth, ~~which~~ *who* was crucified:	*But behold the angels* said unto them, Why seek ye the living among the dead?	
28:6 He is not here: for he is risen, as he said.	he is risen; he is not here:	24:6 He is not here, but is risen: remember how he spake unto you when he was yet in Galilee, 24:7 Saying, The Son of ~~m~~*M*an must be delivered into the hands of sinful men, and be crucified, and the third day rise again.	

MATTHEW	MARK	LUKE	JOHN
		24:8 And they remembered his words,	
Come, see the place where the Lord lay.	behold the place where they laid him. 16:8(a) *And they, entering into the sepulcher, saw the place where they laid Jesus.*	24:3 And they entered *to the sepulcher,* and ~~found not~~ *not finding* the body of the Lord Jesus,	
28:7 And go quickly, and tell his disciples that he is risen from the dead; and, behold, he goeth before you into Galilee; there shall ye see him: lo, I have told you.	16:7 ~~But~~ *And* go your way, tell his disciples and Peter that he goeth before you into Galilee: there shall ye see him, as he said unto you.		

I-4. WOMEN LEAVE TOMB TO TELL DISCIPLES

MATTHEW	MARK	LUKE	JOHN
28:8 And they departed quickly from the sepulchre with fear and great joy;	16:8(b) And they went out quickly, and fled from the ~~sepulchre~~ *sepulcher;* for they trembled and were amazed: neither said they any thing to any man; for they were afraid.	24:9 And returned from the sepulchre,	
and did run to bring his disciples word.		and told all these things unto the eleven, and to all the rest.	20:2 Then she runneth, and cometh to Simon Peter, and to the other disciple, whom Jesus loved, and saith unto them, They have taken away the Lord out of the sepulchre, and we know not where they have laid him.

I-5. PETER AND JOHN VISIT TOMB

MATTHEW	MARK	LUKE	JOHN
		24:12 Then arose Peter, and ran unto the sepulchre;	20:3 Peter therefore went forth, and that other disciple, and came to the sepulchre. 20:4 So they ran both together: and the other disciple did outrun Peter, and came first to the sepulchre. 20:5 And he stooping down, and looking in, saw the linen clothes lying; yet went he not in. 20:6 Then cometh Simon Peter following him, and went into the sepulchre, and seeth the linen clothes lie, 20:7 And the napkin, that was about his head, not lying with the linen clothes, but wrapped together in a place by itself. 20:8 Then went in also that other disciple, which came first to the sepulchre, and he saw, and believed. 20:9 For as yet they knew not the scripture, that he must rise again from the dead.
		and ~~stooping down,~~ *went in, and* he beheld the linen clothes laid by themselves,	
		and *he* departed, wondering in himself at that which was come to pass.	20:10 Then the disciples went away again unto their own homes.

MATTHEW	MARK	LUKE	JOHN

I-6. JESUS APPEARS TO MARY

MARK

16:9 Now when Jesus was risen early *on* the first day of the week, he appeared first to Mary Magdalene, out of whom he had cast seven devils.

JOHN

20:11 But Mary stood without at the sepulchre weeping: and as she wept, she stooped down, and looked into the sepulchre,

20:12 And seeth two angels in white sitting, the one at the head, and the other at the feet, where the body of Jesus had lain.

20:13 And they say unto her, Woman, why weepest thou? She saith unto them, Because they have taken away my Lord, and I know not where they have laid him.

20:14 And when she had thus said, she turned herself back, and saw Jesus standing, and knew not that it was Jesus.

20:15 Jesus saith unto her, Woman, why weepest thou? whom seekest thou? She, supposing him to be the gardener, saith unto him, Sir, if thou have borne him hence, tell me where thou hast laid him, and I will take him away.

20:16 Jesus saith unto her, Mary. She turned herself, and saith unto him, Rabboni; which is to say, Master.

20:17 Jesus saith unto her, ~~Touch~~ *Hold* me not; for I am not yet ascended to my Father: but go to my brethren, and say unto them, I ascend unto my Father, and your Father; and to my God, and your God.

I-7. JESUS APPEARS TO THE OTHER WOMEN

MATTHEW

28:9 And as they went to tell his disciples, behold, Jesus met them, saying, All hail. And they came and held him by the feet, and worshipped him.

28:10 Then said Jesus unto them, Be not afraid: go tell my brethren that they go into Galilee, and there shall they see me.

MATTHEW	MARK	LUKE	JOHN

I-8. TESTIMONY OF MARY AND OTHER WOMEN

MATTHEW	MARK	LUKE	JOHN
	16:10 And she went and told them ~~that~~ *who* had been with him, as they mourned and wept.		20:18 Mary Magdalene came and told the disciples that she had seen the Lord, and that he had spoken these things unto her.
		24:10 It was Mary Magdalene, and Joanna, and Mary the mother of James, and other women ~~that~~ *who* were with them, ~~which~~ *who* told these things unto the apostles.	
	16:11 And they, when they had heard that he was alive, and had been seen of her, believed not.	24:11 And their words seemed to them as idle tales, and they believed them not.	

I-9. OTHERS RESURRECTED AFTER JESUS

27:52 And the graves were opened; and ~~many~~ *the* bodies of the saints which slept arose, *who were many,*
27:53 And came out of the graves after his resurrection, ~~and~~ went into the holy city, and appeared unto many.

I-10. CHIEF PRIESTS TOLD OF RESURRECTION

28:11 Now when they were going, behold, some of the watch came into the city, and ~~shewed~~ *showed* unto the chief priests all the things that were done.
28:12 And when they were assembled with the elders, and had taken counsel, they gave large money unto the soldiers,
28:13 Saying, Say ye, His disciples came by night, and stole him ~~away~~ while we slept.
28:14 And if this come to the governor's ears, we will persuade him, and secure you.
28:15 So they took the money, and did as they were taught: and this saying is commonly reported among the Jews until this day.

I-11. JESUS APPEARS ON THE ROAD TO EMMAUS

MATTHEW	MARK	LUKE	JOHN
		24:13 And, behold, two of them went that same day to a village called Emmaus, which was from Jerusalem ~~about~~ threescore furlongs.	
		24:14 And they talked together of all these things which had happened.	
		24:15 And it came to pass, that, while they communed together and reasoned,	
	16:12 After that he appeared in another form unto two of them, as they walked, and went into the country.	Jesus himself drew near, and went with them.	

MATTHEW	MARK	LUKE	JOHN

LUKE

24:16 But their eyes were holden, *or covered,* that they ~~should~~ *could* not know him.

24:17 And he said unto them, What manner of communications are these ~~that~~ *which* ye have one ~~to~~ *with* another, as ye walk, and are sad?

24:18 And ~~the~~ one of them, whose name was Cleopas, answering said unto him, Art thou ~~only~~ a stranger in Jerusalem, and hast not known the things which are come to pass there in these days?

24:19 And he said unto them, What things? And they said unto him, Concerning Jesus of Nazareth, ~~which~~ *who* was a prophet mighty in deed and word before God and all the people:

24:20 And how the chief priests and our rulers delivered him to be condemned to death, and have crucified him.

24:21 But we trusted that it had been he ~~which~~ *who* should have redeemed Israel: and besides all this, to day is the third day since these things were done.

24:22 Yea, and certain women also of our company made us astonished, ~~which~~ *who* were early at the sepulchre;

24:23 And when they found not his body, they came, saying, that they had also seen a vision of angels, ~~which~~ *who* said that he was alive.

24:24 And certain of them ~~which~~ *who* were with us went to the sepulchre, and found it even so as the women had said: but him they saw not.

24:25 Then he said unto them, O fools, and slow of heart to believe all that the prophets have spoken:

24:26 Ought not Christ to have suffered these things, and to enter into his glory?

24:27 And beginning at Moses and all the prophets, he expounded unto them in all the scriptures the things concerning himself.

24:28 And they drew nigh unto the village, whither they went: and he made as though he would have gone ~~further~~ *farther*.

24:29 But they constrained him, saying, Abide with us: for it is toward evening, and the day is far spent. And he went in to tarry with them.

24:30 And it came to pass, as he sat at meat with them, he took bread, and blessed ~~it~~, and brake, and gave to them.

24:31 And their eyes were opened, and they knew him; and he ~~vanished~~ *was taken up* out of their

MATTHEW	MARK	LUKE	JOHN

sight.
24:32　And they said one to another, Did not our heart*s* burn within us, while he talked with us by the way, and while he opened to us the scriptures?

I-12. TWO DISCIPLES TELL APOSTLES OF CHRIST'S APPEARANCE

16:13　And they went

and told it unto the residue:

neither believed they them.

24:33　And they rose up the same hour, and returned to Jerusalem, and found the eleven gathered together, and ~~them that~~ *those who* were with them,
24:34　Saying, The Lord is risen indeed, and hath appeared to Simon.
24:35　And they told what things ~~were done~~ *they saw and heard* in the way, and how he was known ~~of~~ *to* them in breaking of bread.

I-13. JESUS APPEARS TO TEN APOSTLES

16:14　Afterward he appeared unto the eleven as they sat at meat,

and upbraided them with their unbelief and hardness of heart, because they believed not them ~~which~~ *who* had seen him after he was risen.

24:36　And as they thus spake, Jesus himself stood in the midst of them,
and saith*d* unto them, Peace be unto you.
24:37　But they were terrified and affrighted, and supposed that they had seen a spirit.
24:38　And he said unto them, Why are ~~ye~~ *you* troubled? and why do thoughts arise in your hearts?

24:39　Behold my hands and my feet, that it is I myself: handle me, and see; for a spirit hath not flesh and bones, as ~~ye~~ *you* see me have.
24:40　~~And~~ when he had thus spoken, he ~~shewed~~ *showed* them his hands and his feet.

24:41　And while they yet *wondered and* believed not for joy, ~~and wondered,~~ he said unto them, Have ye here any meat?
24:42　And they gave him a piece of a broiled fish, and ~~of an~~ *a* honeycomb.
24:43　And he took it, and did eat before them.
24:44　And he said unto them, These are the words which I spake

20:19　Then the same day at evening, being the first day of the week, when the doors were shut where the disciples were assembled for fear of the Jews,

came Jesus and stood in the midst,

and saith unto them, Peace be unto you.

20:20　And when he had so said, he shewed unto them his hands and his side.
Then were the disciples glad, when they saw the Lord.

MATTHEW	MARK	LUKE	JOHN

unto you, while I was yet with you, that all things must be fulfilled, which were written in the law of Moses, and in the prophets, and in the ᵽPsalms, concerning me.

24:45 Then opened he their understanding, that they might understand the scriptures,

24:46 And said unto them, Thus it is written, and thus it behoved Christ to suffer, and to rise from the dead the third day:

24:47 And that repentance and remission of sins should be preached in his name among all nations, beginning at Jerusalem.

24:48 And ye are witnesses of these things.

20:21 Then said Jesus to them again, Peace be unto you: as my Father hath sent me, even so send I you.

20:22 And when he had said this, he breathed on them, and saith unto them, Receive ye the Holy Ghost:

20:23 Whose soever sins ye remit, they are remitted unto them; and whose soever sins ye retain, they are retained.

I-14. JESUS APPEARS TO THOMAS AND THE OTHER APOSTLES

20:24 But Thomas, one of the twelve, called Didymus, was not with them when Jesus came.

20:25 The other disciples therefore said unto him, We have seen the Lord. But he said unto them, Except I shall see in his hands the print of the nails, and put my finger into the print of the nails, and thrust my hand into his side, I will not believe.

20:26 And after eight days again his disciples were within, and Thomas with them: then came Jesus, the doors being shut, and stood in the midst, and said, Peace be unto you.

20:27 Then saith he to Thomas, reach hither thy finger, and behold my hands; and reach hither thy hand, and thrust it into my side: and be not faithless, but believing.

20:28 And Thomas answered and said unto him, My Lord and my God.

20:29 Jesus saith unto him, Thomas, because thou hast seen me, thou hast believed: blessed are they that have not seen, and yet have believed.

I-15. JESUS VISITS HIS DISCIPLES AT THE SEA OF TIBERIAS

21:1 After these things Jesus shewed himself again to the disciples at the sea of Tiberias; and on this wise shewed he himself.

21:2 There were together Simon Peter, and Thomas called Didymus, and Nathanael of Cana in Galilee, and the sons of Zebedee, and two other of his disciples.

21:3 Simon Peter saith unto them, I go a fishing. They say unto him, We also go with thee. They went forth, and entered into a ship immediately; and that night they caught nothing.

21:4 But when the morning was now come, Jesus stood on the shore: but the disciples knew not that it was Jesus.

21:5 Then Jesus saith unto them, Children, have ye any meat? They answered him, No.

21:6 And he said unto them, Cast the net on the right side of the ship, and ye shall find. They cast therefore, and now they were not able to draw it for the multitude of fishes.

21:7 Therefore that disciple whom Jesus loved saith unto Peter, It is the Lord. Now when Simon Peter heard that it was the Lord, he girt his fisher's coat unto him, (for he was naked,) and did cast himself into the sea.

21:8 And the other disciples came in a little ship; (for they were not far from land, but as it were two hundred cubits,) dragging the net with fishes.

21:9 As soon then as they were come to land, they saw a fire of coals there, and fish laid thereon, and bread.

21:10 Jesus saith unto them, Bring of the fish which ye have now caught.

21:11 Simon Peter went up, and drew the net to land full of great fishes, and hundred and fifty and three: and for all there were so many, yet was not the net broken.

21:12 Jesus saith unto them, Come and dine. And none of the disciples durst ask him, Who art thou? knowing that it was the Lord.

21:13 Jesus then cometh, and taketh bread, and giveth them, and fish likewise.

21:14 This is now the third time that Jesus shewed himself to his disciples, after that he was risen from the dead.

MATTHEW	MARK	LUKE	JOHN

I-16. FEED MY SHEEP

21:15 So when they had dined, Jesus saith to Simon Peter, Simon, son of Jonas, lovest thou me more than these? He saith unto him, Yea, Lord; thou knowest that I love thee. He saith unto him, Feed my lambs.

21:16 He saith to him again the second time, Simon, son of Jonas, lovest thou me? He saith unto him, Yea, Lord; thou knowest that I love thee. He saith unto him, Feed my sheep.

21:17 He saith unto him the third time, Simon, son of Jonas, lovest thou me? Peter was grieved because he said unto him the third time, Lovest thou me? And he said unto him, Lord, thou knowest all things; thou knowest that I love thee. Jesus saith unto him, Feed my sheep.

21:18 Verily, verily, I say unto thee, When thou wast young, thou girdedst thyself, and walkedst whither thou wouldest: but when thou shalt be old, thou shalt stretch forth thy hands, and another shall gird thee, and carry thee whither thou wouldest not.

21:19 This spake he, signifying by what death he should glorify God. And when he had spoken this, he saith unto him, Follow me.

I-17. PETER ASKS JESUS ABOUT JOHN'S FUTURE

21:20 Then Peter, turning about, seeth the disciple whom Jesus loved following; which also leaned on his breast at supper, and said, Lord, which is he that betrayeth thee?

21:21 Peter seeing him saith to Jesus, Lord, and what shall this man do?

21:22 Jesus saith unto him, If I will that he tarry till I come, what is that to thee? follow thou me.

21:23 Then went this saying abroad among the brethren, that that disciple should not die: yet Jesus said not unto him, He shall not die; but, If I will that he tarry till I come, what is that to thee?

I-18. JESUS APPEARS IN GALILEE

28:16 Then the eleven disciples went away into Galilee, into a mountain where Jesus had appointed them.

28:17 And when they saw him, they worshipped him: but some doubted.

28:18 And Jesus came and spake

MATTHEW	MARK	LUKE	JOHN

unto them, saying, All power is given unto me in heaven and in earth.

28:19 Go ye therefore, and teach all nations,
baptizing them in the name of the Father, and of the Son, and of the Holy Ghost:

16:15 And he said unto them, Go ye into all the world, and preach the gospel to every creature.

16:16 He that believeth and is baptized shall be saved;
but he that believeth not shall be damned.
16:17 And these signs shall follow them that believe; In my name shall they cast out devils; they shall speak with new tongues;
16:18 They shall take up serpents; and if they drink any deadly thing, it shall not hurt them; they shall lay hands on the sick, and they shall recover.

28:20 Teaching them to observe all things whatsoever I have commanded you: and, lo, I am with you always, ~~even~~ unto the end of the world. Amen.

I-19. THE ASCENSION

24:49 And, behold, I send the promise of my Father upon you: but tarry ye in the city of Jerusalem, until ye be endued with power from on high.
24:50 And he led them out as far as to Bethany, and he lifted up his hands, and blessed them.

16:19 So then after the Lord had spoken unto them, he was received up into heaven, and sat on the right hand of God.

24:51 And it came to pass, while he blessed them, he was ~~parted~~ *taken* from them, and carried up into heaven.
24:52 And they worshipped him, and returned to Jerusalem with great joy:
24:53 And were continually in the temple, praising and blessing God. Amen.

16:20 And they went forth, and preached everywhere, the Lord working with them, and confirming the word with signs following. Amen.

MATTHEW	MARK	LUKE	JOHN

I-20. JOHN'S FINAL TESTIMONY

20:30 And many other signs truly did Jesus in the presence of his disciples, which are not written in this book:

20:31 But these are written, that ye might believe that Jesus is the Christ, the Son of God; and that believing ye might have life through his name.

21:24 This is the disciple which testifieth of these things, and wrote these things: and we know that his testimony is true.

21:25 And there are also many other things which Jesus did, the which, if they should be written every one, I suppose that even the world itself could not contain the books that should be written. Amen.

The
New Testament

---

with the
Joseph Smith Translation

Section II

The Acts
to
Revelation

followed by a suggested
Chronology of Events

Chapter 1

1 The former treatise have I made, O Theophilus, of all that Jesus began both to do and teach,

2 Until the day in which he was taken up, after that he through the Holy Ghost had given commandments unto the apostles whom he had chosen:

3 To whom also he shewed *showed* himself alive after his passion *sufferings* by many infallible proofs, being seen of them forty days, and speaking of the things pertaining to the kingdom of God:

4 And, being assembled together with them *when they were assembled together*, commanded them that they should not depart from Jerusalem, but wait for the promise of the Father, which, saith he, ye have heard of me.

5 For John truly baptized with water; but ye shall be baptized with the Holy Ghost not many days hence.

6 When they therefore were come together, they asked of him, saying, Lord, wilt thou at this time restore again the kingdom to Israel?

7 And he said unto them, It is not for you to know the times or the seasons, which the Father hath put in his own power.

8 But ye shall receive power, after that the Holy Ghost is come upon you: and ye shall be witnesses unto me both in Jerusalem, and in all Judaea, and in Samaria, and unto the uttermost part of the earth.

9 And when he had spoken these things, while they beheld, he was taken up; and a cloud received him out of their sight.

10 And while they looked stedfastly toward heaven as he went up, behold, two men stood by them in white apparel;

11 Which also said, Ye men of Galilee, why stand ye gazing up into heaven? this same Jesus, which is taken up from you into heaven, shall so come in like manner as ye have seen him go into heaven.

12 Then returned they unto Jerusalem from the mount called Olivet, which is from Jerusalem a sabbath day's journey.

13 And when they were come in, they went up into an upper room, where abode both Peter, and James, and John, and Andrew, Philip, and Thomas, Bartholomew, and Matthew, James the son of Alphaeus, and Simon Zelotes, and Judas the brother of James.

14 These all continued with one accord in prayer and supplication, with the women, and Mary the mother of Jesus, and with his brethren.

15 And in those days Peter stood up in the midst of the disciples, and said, (the number of names together were about an hundred and twenty,)

16 Men and brethren, this scripture must needs have been fulfilled, which the Holy Ghost by the mouth of David spake before concerning Judas, which was guide to them that took Jesus.

17 For he was numbered with us, and had obtained part of this ministry.

18 Now this man purchased a field with the reward of iniquity; and falling headlong, he burst asunder in the midst, and all his bowels gushed out.

19 And it was known unto all the dwellers at Jerusalem; insomuch as that field is called in their proper tongue, Aceldama, that is to say, The field of blood.

20 For it is written in the book of Psalms, Let his habitation be desolate, and let no man dwell therein: and his bishopric let another take.

21 Wherefore of these men which have companied with us all the time that the Lord Jesus went in and out among us,

22 Beginning from the baptism of John, unto that same day that he was taken up from us, must one be ordained to be a witness with us of his resurrection.

23 And they appointed two, Joseph called Barsabas, who was surnamed Justus, and Matthias.

24 And they prayed, and said, Thou, Lord, which knowest the hearts of all men, show whether of these two thou hast chosen,

25 That he may take part of this ministry and apostleship, from which Judas by transgression fell, that he might go to his own place.

26 And they gave forth their lots; and the lot fell upon Matthias; and he was numbered with the eleven apostles.

Chapter 2

1 And when the day of Pentecost was fully come, they were all with one accord in one place.

2 And suddenly there came a sound from heaven as of a rushing mighty wind, and it filled all the house where they were sitting.

3 And there appeared unto them cloven tongues like as of fire, and it sat *rested* upon each of them.

4 And they were all filled with the Holy Ghost, and began to speak with other tongues, as the Spirit gave them utterance.

5 And there were dwelling at Jerusalem Jews, devout men, out of every nation under heaven.

6 Now when this was noised abroad, the multitude came together, and were confounded, because that every man heard them speak in his own language.

7 And they were all amazed and marvelled, saying one to another, Behold, are not all these which speak Galilaeans?

8 And how hear we every man in our own tongue, wherein we were born?

9 Parthians, and Medes, and Elamites, and the dwellers in Mesopotamia, and in Judaea, and Cappadocia, in Pontus, and Asia,

10 Phrygia, and Pamphylia, in Egypt, and in the parts of Libya about Cyrene, and strangers of Rome, Jews and proselytes,

11 Cretes and Arabians, we do hear them speak in our tongues the wonderful works of God.

12 And they were all amazed, and were in doubt, saying one to another, What meaneth this?

13 Others mocking said, These men are full of new wine.

14 But Peter, standing up with the eleven, lifted up his voice, and said unto them, Ye men of Judaea, and all ye that dwell at Jerusalem, be this known unto you, and hearken to my words:

15 For these are not drunken, as ye suppose, seeing it is but the third hour of the day.

16 But this is that which was spoken by the prophet Joel;

17 And it shall come to pass in the last days, saith God, I will pour out of my Spirit upon all flesh: and your sons and your daughters shall prophesy, and your young men shall see visions, and your old men shall dream dreams:

18 And on my servants and on my handmaidens I will pour out in those days of my Spirit; and they shall prophesy:

19 And I will show wonders in heaven above, and signs in the earth beneath; blood, and fire, and vapour of smoke:

20 The sun shall be turned into darkness, and the moon into blood, before that great and notable day of the Lord come:

21 And it shall come to pass, that whosoever shall call on the name of the Lord shall be saved.

22 Ye men of Israel, hear these words; Jesus of Nazareth, a man approved of God among you by miracles and wonders and signs, which God did by him in the midst of you, as ye yourselves also know:

23 Him, being delivered by the determinate counsel and foreknowledge of God, ye have taken, and by wicked hands have crucified and slain:

24 Whom God hath raised up, having loosed the pains of death: because it was not possible that he should be holden of it.

25 For David speaketh concerning him, I foresaw the Lord always before my face, for he is on my right hand, that I should not be moved:

26 Therefore did my heart rejoice, and my tongue was glad; moreover also my flesh shall rest in hope:

27 Because thou wilt not leave my soul in ~~hell~~ *prison*, neither wilt thou suffer thine Holy One to see corruption.

28 Thou hast made known to me the ways of life; thou shalt make me full of joy with thy countenance.

29 Men and brethren, let me freely speak unto you of the patriarch David, that he is both dead and buried, and his sepulchre is with us unto this day.

30 Therefore being a prophet, and knowing that God had sworn with an oath to him, that of the fruit of his loins, according to the flesh, he would raise up Christ to sit on his throne;

31 He seeing this before spake of the resurrection of Christ, that his soul was not left in hell, neither his flesh did see corruption.

32 This Jesus hath God raised up, whereof we all are witnesses.

33 Therefore being by the right hand of God exalted, and having received of the Father the promise of the Holy Ghost, he hath shed forth this, which ye now see and hear.

34 For David is not ascended into the heavens: but he saith himself, The Lord said unto my Lord, Sit thou on my right hand,

35 Until I make thy foes thy footstool.

36 Therefore let all the house of Israel know assuredly, that God hath made that same Jesus, whom ye have crucified, both Lord and Christ.

37 Now when they heard this, they were pricked in their heart, and said unto Peter and to the rest of the apostles, Men and brethren, what shall we do?

38 Then Peter said unto them, Repent, and be baptized every one of you in the name of Jesus Christ for the remission of sins, and ye shall receive the gift of the Holy Ghost.

39 For the promise is unto you, and to your children, and to all that are afar off, even as many as the Lord our God shall call.

40 And with many other words did he testify and exhort, saying, Save yourselves from this untoward generation.

41 Then they that gladly received his word were baptized: and the same day there were added unto them about three thousand souls.

42 And they continued stedfastly in the apostles' doctrine and fellowship, and in breaking of bread, and in prayers.

43 And fear came upon every soul: and many wonders and signs were done by the apostles.

44 And all that believed were together, and had all things common;

45 And sold their possessions and goods, and parted them to all men, as every man had need.

46 And they, continuing daily with one accord in the temple, and breaking bread from house to house, did eat their meat with gladness and singleness of heart,

47 Praising God, and having favour with all the people. And the Lord added to the church daily such as should be saved.

Chapter 3

1 Now Peter and John went up together into the temple ~~at the hour of prayer, being the ninth hour~~ *at the ninth hour, for prayer*.

2 And a certain man lame from his mother's womb was carried, whom they laid daily at the gate of the temple which is called Beautiful, to ask alms of them that entered into the temple;

3 Who seeing Peter and John about to go into the temple asked an alms.

4 And Peter *and John*, fastening ~~his~~ *their* eyes upon him ~~with John~~, said, Look on us.

5 And he gave heed unto them, expecting to receive something of them.

6 Then Peter said, Silver and gold have I none; but such as I have give I thee: In the name of Jesus Christ of Nazareth rise up and walk.

7 And he took him by the right hand, and lifted him up: and immediately his feet and ankle bones received strength.

8 And he leaping up stood, and walked, and entered with them into the temple, walking, and leaping, and praising God.

9 And all the people saw him walking and praising God:

10 And they knew that it was he which sat for alms at the Beautiful gate of the temple: and they were filled with wonder and amazement at that which had happened unto him.

11 And as the lame man which was healed held Peter and John, all the people ran together unto them in the porch that is called Solomon's, greatly wondering.

12 And when Peter saw ~~it~~ *this*, he answered *and said* unto the people, Ye men of Israel, why marvel ye at this? or why look ye so earnestly on us, as though by our own power or holiness we had made this man to walk?

13 The God of Abraham, and of Isaac, and of Jacob, the God of our fathers, hath glorified his Son Jesus; whom ye delivered up, and denied him in the presence of Pilate, when he was determined to let him go.

14 But ye denied the Holy One and the Just, and desired a murderer to be granted unto you;

15 And killed the Prince of life, whom God hath raised from the dead; whereof we are witnesses.

16 And ~~his name~~ *this man,* through faith in his name, hath *been* made ~~this man~~ strong, whom ye see and know: yea, the faith which is ~~by~~ *in* him hath given him this perfect soundness in the presence of you all.

17 And now, brethren, I ~~wot~~ *know* that through ignorance ye ~~did it~~ *have done this*, as ~~did~~ also your rulers.

18 But those things, which God before had showed by the mouth of all his prophets, that Christ should suffer, he hath so fulfilled.

19 Repent ye therefore, and be converted, that your sins may be blotted out, when the times of refreshing shall come from the presence of the Lord;

20 And he shall send Jesus Christ, which before was preached unto you*, whom ye have crucified*:

21 Whom the heaven must receive until the times of restitution of all things, which God hath spoken by the mouth of all his holy prophets since the world began.

22 For Moses truly said unto the fathers, A prophet shall the Lord your God raise up unto you of your brethren, like unto me; him shall ye hear in all things whatsoever he shall say unto you.

23 And it shall come to pass, that every soul, which will not hear that prophet, shall be destroyed from among the people.

24 Yea, and all the prophets from Samuel and those that follow after, as many as have spoken, have likewise foretold of these days.

25 Ye are the children of the prophets, and of the covenant which God made with our fathers, saying unto Abraham, And in thy seed shall all the kindreds of the earth be blessed.

26 Unto you first God, having raised up his Son Jesus, sent him to bless you, in turning away every one of you from his iniquities.

Chapter 4

1 And as they spake unto the people, the priests, and the captain of the temple, and the Sadducees, came upon them,

2 Being grieved that they taught the people, and preached through Jesus the resurrection from the dead.

3 And they laid hands on them, and put them in hold unto the next day: for it was now eventide.

4 Howbeit many of them which heard the word believed; and the number of the men was about five thousand.

5 And it came to pass on the morrow, that their rulers, and elders, and scribes,

6 And Annas the high priest, and Caiaphas, and John, and Alexander, and as many as were of the kindred of the high priest, were gathered together at Jerusalem.

7 And when they had set them in the midst, they asked, By what power, or by what name, have ye done this?

8 Then Peter, filled with the Holy Ghost, said unto them, Ye rulers of the people, and elders of Israel,

9 If we this day be examined of the good deed done to the impotent man, by what means he is made whole;

10 Be it known unto you all, and to all the people of Israel, that by the name of Jesus Christ of Nazareth, whom ye crucified, whom God

raised from the dead, even by him doth this man stand here before you whole.

11 This is the stone which was set at nought of you builders, which is become the head of the corner.

12 Neither is there salvation in any other: for there is none other name under heaven given among men, whereby we must be saved.

13 Now when they saw the boldness of Peter and John, and perceived that they were unlearned and ignorant men, they marvelled; and they took knowledge of them, that they had been with Jesus.

14 And beholding the man which was healed standing with them, they could say nothing against it.

15 But when they had commanded them to go aside out of the council, they conferred among themselves,

16 Saying, What shall we do to these men? for that indeed a notable miracle hath been done by them is manifest to all them that dwell in Jerusalem; and we cannot deny it.

17 But that it spread no further among the people, let us straitly threaten them, that they speak henceforth to no man in this name.

18 And they called them, and commanded them not to speak at all nor teach in the name of Jesus.

19 But Peter and John answered and said unto them, Whether it be right in the sight of God to hearken unto you more than unto God, judge ye.

20 For we cannot but speak the things which we have seen and heard.

21 So when they had further threatened them, they let them go, finding nothing how they might punish them, because of the people: for ~~all men~~ *many* glorified God for that which was done.

22 For the man was above forty years old, on whom this miracle of healing was showed.

23 And being let go, they went to their own company, and reported all that the chief priests and elders had said unto them.

24 And when they heard that, they lifted up their voice to God with one accord, and said, Lord, thou art God, which hast made heaven, and earth, and the sea, and all that in them is:

25 Who by the mouth of thy servant David hast said, Why did the heathen rage, and the people imagine vain things?

26 The kings of the earth stood up, and the rulers were gathered together against the Lord, and against his Christ.

27 For of a truth against thy holy child Jesus, whom thou hast anointed, both Herod, and Pontius Pilate, with the Gentiles, and the people of Israel, were gathered together,

28 For to do whatsoever thy hand and thy counsel determined before to be done.

29 And now, Lord, behold their threatenings: and grant unto thy servants, that with all boldness they may speak thy word,

30 By stretching forth thine hand to heal; and that signs and wonders may be done by the name of thy holy child Jesus.

31 And when they had prayed, the place was shaken where they were assembled together; and they were all filled with the Holy Ghost, and they spake the word of God with boldness.

32 And the multitude of them that believed were of one heart and of one soul: neither said any of them that ought of the things which he possessed was his own; but they had all things common.

33 And with great power gave the apostles witness of the resurrection of the Lord Jesus: and great grace was upon them all.

34 Neither was there any among them that lacked: for as many as were possessors of lands or houses sold them, and brought the prices of the things that were sold,

35 And laid them down at the apostles' feet: and distribution was made unto every man according as he had need.

36 And Joses, who by the apostles was surnamed Barnabas, (which is, being interpreted, The son of consolation,) a Levite, and of the country of Cyprus,

37 Having land, sold it, and brought the money, and laid it at the apostles' feet.

Chapter 5

1 But a certain man named Ananias, with Sapphira his wife, sold a possession,

2 And kept back part of the price, his wife also being privy to it, and brought a certain part, and laid it, at the apostles' feet.

3 But Peter said, Ananias, why hath Satan filled thine heart to lie to the Holy Ghost, and to keep back part of the price of the land?

4 Whiles it remained, was it not thine own? and after it was sold, was it not in thine own power? why hast thou conceived this thing in thine heart? thou hast not lied unto men, but unto God.

5 And Ananias hearing these words fell down, and gave up the ghost: and great fear came on all them that heard these things.

6 And the young men arose, wound him up, and carried him out, and buried him.

7 And it was about the space of three hours after, when his wife, not knowing what was done, came in.

8 And Peter answered unto her, Tell me whether ye sold the land for so much? And she said, Yea, for so much.

9 Then Peter said unto her, How is it that ye have agreed together to tempt the Spirit of the Lord? behold, the feet of them which have buried

thy husband are at the door, and shall carry thee out.

10 Then fell she down straightway at his feet, and yielded up the ghost: and the young men came in, and found her dead, and, carrying her forth, buried her by her husband.

11 And great fear came upon all the church, and upon as many as heard these things.

12 And by the hands of the apostles were many signs and wonders wrought among the people; (and they were all with one accord in Solomon's porch.

13 And of the ~~rest~~ *rulers* durst no man join himself to them: but the people magnified them.

14 And believers were the more added to the Lord, multitudes both of men and women.)

15 Insomuch that they brought forth the sick into the streets, and laid them on beds and couches, that at the least the shadow of Peter passing by might overshadow some of them.

16 There came also a multitude out of the cities round about unto Jerusalem, bringing sick folks, and them which were vexed with unclean spirits: and they were healed every one.

17 Then the high priest rose up, and all they that were with him, (which is the sect of the Sadducees,) and were filled with indignation,

18 And laid their hands on the apostles, and put them in the common prison.

19 But the angel of the Lord by night opened the prison doors, and brought them forth, and said,

20 Go, stand and speak in the temple to the people all the words of this life.

21 And when they heard that, they entered into the temple early in the morning, and taught. But the high priest came, and they that were with him, and called the council together, and all the senate of the children of Israel, and sent to the prison to have them brought.

22 But when the officers came, and found them not in the prison, they returned, and told,

23 Saying, The prison truly found we shut with all safety, and the keepers standing without before the doors: but when we had opened, we found no man within.

24 Now when the high priest and the captain of the temple and the chief priests heard these things, they doubted of them whereunto this would grow.

25 Then came one and told them, saying, Behold, the men whom ye put in prison are standing in the temple, and teaching the people.

26 Then went the captain with the officers, and brought them without violence: for they feared the people, lest they should have been stoned.

27 And when they had brought them, they set them before the council: and the high priest asked them,

28 Saying, Did not we straitly command you that ye should not teach in this name? and, behold, ye have filled Jerusalem with your doctrine, and intend to bring this man's blood upon us.

29 Then Peter and the other apostles answered and said, We ought to obey God rather than men.

30 The God of our fathers raised up Jesus, whom ye slew and hanged on a tree.

31 Him hath God exalted with his right hand to be a Prince and a Saviour, for to give repentance to Israel, and forgiveness of sins.

32 And we are his witnesses of these things; and so is also the Holy Ghost, whom God hath given to them that obey him.

33 When they heard that, they were cut to the heart, and took counsel to slay them.

34 Then stood there up one in the council, a Pharisee, named Gamaliel, a doctor of the law, had in reputation among all the people, and commanded to put the apostles forth a little space;

35 And said unto them, Ye men of Israel, take heed to yourselves what ye intend to do as touching these men.

36 For before these days rose up Theudas, boasting himself to be somebody; to whom a number of men, about four hundred, joined themselves: who was slain; and all, as many as obeyed him, were scattered, and brought to nought.

37 After this man rose up Judas of Galilee in the days of the taxing, and drew away much people after him: he also perished; and all, even as many as obeyed him, were dispersed.

38 And now I say unto you, Refrain from these men, and let them alone: for if this counsel or this work be of men, it will come to nought:

39 But if it be of God, ye cannot overthrow it; *be careful, therefore,* lest ~~haply~~ ye be found even to fight against God.

40 And to him they agreed: and when they had called the apostles, and beaten them, they commanded that they should not speak in the name of Jesus, and let them go.

41 And they departed from the presence of the council, rejoicing that they were counted worthy to suffer shame for his name.

42 And daily in the temple, and in every house, they ceased not to teach and preach Jesus Christ.

Chapter 6

1 And in those days, when the number of the disciples was multiplied, there arose a murmuring of the Grecians against the Hebrews, because their widows were neglected in the daily ministration.

2 Then the twelve called the multitude of the disciples unto them, and said, It is not reason

that we should leave the word of God, and serve tables.

3 Wherefore, brethren, look ye out among you seven men of honest report, full of the Holy Ghost and wisdom, whom we may appoint over this business.

4 But we will give ourselves continually to prayer, and to the ministry of the word.

5 And the saying pleased the whole multitude: and they chose Stephen, a man full of faith and of the Holy Ghost, and Philip, and Prochorus, and Nicanor, and Timon, and Parmenas, and Nicolas a proselyte of Antioch:

6 Whom they set before the apostles: and when they had prayed, they laid their hands on them.

7 And the word of God increased; and the number of the disciples multiplied in Jerusalem greatly; and a great company of the priests were obedient to the faith.

8 And Stephen, full of faith and power, did great wonders and miracles among the people.

9 ~~Then~~ *And* there arose certain of the synagogue, ~~which is called the synagogue of the~~ *who are called* Libertines, and *also* Cyrenians, and Alexandrians, and of them of Cilicia and of Asia, disputing with Stephen.

10 And they were not able to resist the wisdom and the spirit by which he spake.

11 Then they suborned men, which said, We have heard him speak blasphemous words against Moses, and against God.

12 And they stirred up the people, and the elders, and the scribes, and came upon him, and caught him, and brought him to the council,

13 And set up false witnesses, which said, This man ceaseth not to speak blasphemous words against this holy place, and the law:

14 For we have heard him say, that this Jesus of Nazareth shall destroy this place, and shall change the customs which Moses delivered us.

15 And all that sat in the council, looking stedfastly on him, saw his face as it had been the face of an angel.

Chapter 7

1 Then said the high priest, Are these things so?

2 And he said, Men, brethren, and fathers, hearken; The God of glory appeared unto our father Abraham, when he was in Mesopotamia, before he dwelt in Charran,

3 And said unto him, Get thee out of thy country, and from thy kindred, and come into the land which I shall show thee.

4 Then came he out of the land of the Chaldaeans, and dwelt in Charran: and from thence, when his father was dead, he removed him into this land, wherein ye now dwell.

5 And he gave him none inheritance in it, no, not so much as to set his foot on: yet he promised that he would give it to him for a possession, and to his seed after him, when as yet he had no child.

6 And God spake on this wise, That his seed should sojourn in a strange land; and that they should bring them into bondage, and entreat them evil four hundred years.

7 And the nation to whom they shall be in bondage will I judge, said God: and after that shall they come forth, and serve me in this place.

8 And he gave him the covenant of circumcision: and so Abraham begat Isaac, and circumcised him the eighth day; and Isaac begat Jacob; and Jacob begat the twelve patriarchs.

9 And the patriarchs, moved with envy, sold Joseph into Egypt: but God was with him,

10 And delivered him out of all his afflictions, and gave him favour and wisdom in the sight of Pharaoh king of Egypt; and he made him governor over Egypt and all his house.

11 Now there came a dearth over all the land of Egypt and Chanaan, and great affliction: and our fathers found no sustenance.

12 But when Jacob heard that there was corn in Egypt, he sent out our fathers first.

13 And at the second time Joseph was made known to his brethren; and Joseph's kindred was made known unto Pharaoh.

14 Then sent Joseph, and called his father Jacob to him, and all his kindred, threescore and fifteen souls.

15 So Jacob went down into Egypt, and died, he, and our fathers,

16 And were carried over into Sychem, and laid in the sepulchre that Abraham bought for a sum of money of the sons of Emmor the father of Sychem.

17 But when the time of the promise drew nigh, which God had sworn to Abraham, the people grew and multiplied in Egypt,

18 Till another king arose, which knew not Joseph.

19 The same dealt subtly with our kindred, and evil entreated our fathers, so that they cast out their young children, to the end they might not live.

20 In which time Moses was born, and was exceeding fair, and nourished up in his father's house three months:

21 And when he was cast out, Pharaoh's daughter took him up, and nourished him for her own son.

22 And Moses was learned in all the wisdom of the Egyptians, and was mighty in words and in deeds.

23 And when he was full forty years old, it came into his heart to visit his brethren the children of Israel.

24 And seeing one of them suffer wrong, he

defended him, and avenged him that was oppressed, and smote the Egyptian:

25 For he supposed his brethren would have understood how that God by his hand would deliver them: but they understood not.

26 And the next day he showed himself unto them as they strove, and would have set them at one again, saying, Sirs, ye are brethren; why do ye wrong one to another?

27 But he that did his neighbour wrong thrust him away, saying, Who made thee a ruler and a judge over us?

28 Wilt thou kill me, as thou diddest the Egyptian yesterday?

29 Then fled Moses at this saying, and was a stranger in the land of Madian, where he begat two sons.

30 And when forty years were expired, there appeared to him in the wilderness of mount Sina an angel of the Lord in a flame of fire in a bush.

31 When Moses saw it, he wondered at the sight: and as he drew near to behold it, the voice of the Lord came unto him,

32 Saying, I am the God of thy fathers, the God of Abraham, and the God of Isaac, and the God of Jacob. Then Moses trembled, and durst not behold.

33 Then said the Lord to him, Put off thy shoes from thy feet: for the place where thou standest is holy ground.

34 I have seen, I have seen the affliction of my people which is in Egypt, and I have heard their groaning, and am come down to deliver them. And now come, I will send thee into Egypt.

35 This Moses whom they refused, saying, Who made thee a ruler and a judge? thåsame did God send to be a ruler and a deliverer by the hand of the angel which appeared to him in the bush.

36 He brought them out, after that he had showed wonders and signs in the land of Egypt, and in the Red sea, and in the wilderness forty years.

37 This is that Moses, which said unto the children of Israel, A prophet shall the Lord your God raise up unto you of your brethren, like unto me; him shall ye hear.

38 This is he, that was in the church in the wilderness with the angel which spake to him in the mount Sina, and with our fathers: who received the lively oracles to give unto us:

39 To w*Wh*om our fathers would not obey, but thrust him from them, and in their hearts turned back again into Egypt,

40 Saying unto Aaron, Make us gods to go before us: for as for this Moses, which brought us out of the land of Egypt, we wot *know* not what is become of him.

41 And they made a calf in those days, and offered sacrifice unto the idol, and rejoiced in the works of their own hands.

42 Then God turned, and gave them up to worship the host of heaven; as it is written in the book of the prophets, O ye house of Israel, have ye offered to me slain beasts and sacrifices by the space of forty years in the wilderness?

43 Yea, ye took up the tabernacle of Moloch, and the star of your god Remphan, figures which ye made to worship them: and I will carry you away beyond Babylon.

44 Our fathers had the tabernacle of witness in the wilderness, as he had appointed, speaking unto Moses, that he should make it according to the fashion *pattern* that he had seen.

45 Which also our fathers that came after brought in with Jesus into the possession of the Gentiles, whom God drave out before the face of our fathers, unto the days of David;

46 Who found favour before God, and desired to find a tabernacle for the God of Jacob.

47 But Solomon built him an house.

48 Howbeit the most High dwelleth not in temples made with hands; as saith the prophet,

49 Heaven is my throne, and earth is my footstool: what house will ye build me? saith the Lord: or what is the place of my rest?

50 Hath not my hand made all these things?

51 Ye stiffnecked and uncircumcised in heart and ears, ye do always resist the Holy Ghost: as your fathers did, so do ye.

52 Which of the prophets have not your fathers persecuted? and they have slain them which showed before of the coming of the Just One; of whom ye have been now the betrayers and murderers:

53 Who have received the law by the disposition of angels, and have not kept it.

54 When they heard these things, they were cut to the heart, and they gnashed on him with their teeth.

55 But he, being full of the Holy Ghost, looked up stedfastly into heaven, and saw the glory of God, and Jesus standing on the right hand of God,

56 And said, Behold, I see the heavens opened, and the Son of man standing on the right hand of God.

57 Then they cried out with a loud voice, and stopped their ears, and ran upon him with one accord,

58 And cast him out of the city, and stoned him: and the witnesses laid down their clothes at a young man's feet, whose name was Saul.

59 And they stoned Stephen*; and he*, calling upon God, and saying *said*, Lord Jesus, receive my spirit.

60 And he kneeled down, and cried with a loud voice, Lord, lay not this sin to their charge. And when he had said this, he fell asleep.

Chapter 8

1 And Saul was consenting unto his death. And at that time there was a great persecution against the church which was at Jerusalem; and they were all scattered abroad throughout the regions of Judaea and Samaria, except the apostles.

2 And devout men carried Stephen to his burial, and made great lamentation over him.

3 As for Saul, he made havock of the church, entering into every house, and haling men and women committed them to prison.

4 Therefore they that were scattered abroad went every where preaching the word.

5 Then Philip went down to the city of Samaria, and preached Christ unto them.

6 And the people with one accord gave heed unto those things which Philip spake, hearing and seeing the miracles which he did.

7 For unclean spirits, crying with loud voice, came out of many that were possessed with them: and many taken with palsies, and that were lame, were healed.

8 And there was great joy in that city.

9 But there was a certain man, called Simon, which beforetime in the same city used sorcery, and bewitched the people of Samaria, giving out that himself was some great one:

10 To whom they all gave heed, from the least to the greatest, saying, This man is the great power of God.

11 And to him they had regard, because that of long time he had bewitched them with sorceries.

12 But when they believed Philip preaching the things concerning the kingdom of God, and the name of Jesus Christ, they were baptized, both men and women.

13 Then Simon himself believed also: and when he was baptized, he continued with Philip, and wondered, beholding the miracles and signs which were done.

14 Now when the apostles which were at Jerusalem heard that Samaria had received the word of God, they sent unto them Peter and John:

15 Who, when they were come down, prayed for them, that they might receive the Holy Ghost:

16 (For as yet he was fallen upon none of them: only they were baptized in the name of the Lord Jesus.)

17 Then laid they their hands on them, and they received the Holy Ghost.

18 And when Simon saw that through laying on of the apostles' hands the Holy Ghost was given, he offered them money,

19 Saying, Give me also this power, that on whomsoever I lay hands, he may receive the Holy Ghost.

20 But Peter said unto him, Thy money perish with thee, because thou hast thought that the gift of God may be purchased with money.

21 Thou hast neither part nor lot in this matter: for thy heart is not right in the sight of God.

22 Repent therefore of this thy wickedness, and pray God, if perhaps the thought of thine heart may be forgiven thee.

23 For I perceive that thou art in the gall of bitterness, and in the bond of iniquity.

24 Then answered Simon, and said, Pray ye to the Lord for me, that none of these things which ye have spoken come upon me.

25 And they, when they had testified and preached the word of the Lord, returned to Jerusalem, and preached the gospel in many villages of the Samaritans.

26 And the angel of the Lord spake unto Philip, saying, Arise, and go toward the south unto the way that goeth down from Jerusalem unto Gaza, which is desert.

27 And he arose and went: and, behold, a man of Ethiopia, an eunuch of great authority under Candace queen of the Ethiopians, who had the charge of all her treasure, and had come to Jerusalem for to worship,

28 Was returning, and sitting in his chariot read Esaias the prophet.

29 Then the Spirit said unto Philip, Go near, and join thyself to this chariot.

30 And Philip ran thither to him, and heard him read the prophet Esaias, and said, Understandest thou what thou readest?

31 And he said, How can I, except some man should guide me? And he desired Philip that he would come up and sit with him.

32 The place of the scripture which he read was this, He was led as a sheep to the slaughter; and like a lamb dumb before his shearer, so opened he not his mouth:

33 In his humiliation his judgment was taken away: and who shall declare his generation? for his life is taken from the earth.

34 And the eunuch answered Philip, and said, I pray thee, of whom speaketh the prophet this? of himself, or of some other man?

35 Then Philip opened his mouth, and began at the same scripture, and preached unto him Jesus.

36 And as they went on their way, they came unto a certain water: and the eunuch said, See, here is water; what doth hinder me to be baptized?

37 And Philip said, If thou believest with all thine heart, thou mayest. And he answered and said, I believe that Jesus Christ is the Son of God.

38 And he commanded the chariot to stand still: and they went down both into the water, both Philip and the eunuch; and he baptized him.

39 And when they were come up out of the water, the Spirit of the Lord caught away Philip, that the eunuch saw him no more: and he went

on his way rejoicing.

40 But Philip was found at Azotus: and passing through he preached in all the cities, till he came to Caesarea.

Chapter 9

1 And Saul, yet breathing out threatenings and slaughter against the disciples of the Lord, went unto the high priest,

2 And desired of him letters to Damascus to the synagogues, that if he found any of this way, whether they were men or women, he might bring them bound unto Jerusalem.

3 And as he journeyed, he came near Damascus: and suddenly there shined round about him a light from heaven:

4 And he fell to the earth, and heard a voice saying unto him, Saul, Saul, why persecutest thou me?

5 And he said, Who art thou, Lord? And the Lord said, I am Jesus whom thou persecutest: it is hard for thee to kick against the pricks.

6 And he trembling and astonished said, Lord, what wilt thou have me to do? And the Lord said unto him, Arise, and go into the city, and it shall be told thee what thou must do.

7 And ~~the men which journeyed with him stood speechless, hearing a voice, but seeing no man~~ *they who were journeying with him saw indeed the light, and were afraid; but they heard not the voice of him who spake to him.*

8 And Saul arose from the earth; and when his eyes were opened, he saw no man: but they led him by the hand, and brought him into Damascus.

9 And he was three days without sight, and neither did eat nor drink.

10 And there was a certain disciple at Damascus, named Ananias; and to him said the Lord in a vision, Ananias. And he said, Behold, I am here, Lord.

11 And the Lord said unto him, Arise, and go into the street which is called Straight, and inquire in the house of Judas for one called Saul, of Tarsus: for, behold, he prayeth,

12 And hath seen in a vision a man named Ananias coming in, and putting his hand on him, that he might receive his sight.

13 Then Ananias answered, Lord, I have heard by many of this man, how much evil he hath done to thy saints at Jerusalem:

14 And here he hath authority from the chief priests to bind all that call on thy name.

15 But the Lord said unto him, Go thy way: for he is a chosen vessel unto me, to bear my name before the Gentiles, and kings, and the children of Israel:

16 For I will show him how great things he must suffer for my name's sake.

17 And Ananias went his way, and entered into the house; and putting his hands on him said, Brother Saul, the Lord, even Jesus, that appeared unto thee in the way as thou camest, hath sent me, that thou mightest receive thy sight, and be filled with the Holy Ghost.

18 And immediately there fell from his eyes as it had been scales: and he received sight forthwith, and arose, and was baptized.

19 And when he had received meat, he was strengthened. Then was Saul certain days with the disciples which were at Damascus.

20 And straightway he preached Christ in the synagogues, that he is the Son of God.

21 But all that heard him were amazed, and said; Is not this he that destroyed them which called on this name in Jerusalem, and came hither for that intent, that he might bring them bound unto the chief priests?

22 But Saul increased the more in strength, and confounded the Jews which dwelt at Damascus, proving that this is very Christ.

23 And after that many days were fulfilled, the Jews took counsel to kill him:

24 But their ~~laying await~~ *lying in wait* was known of Saul. And they watched the gates day and night to kill him.

25 Then the disciples took him by night, and let him down by the wall in a basket.

26 And when Saul was come to Jerusalem, he assayed to join himself to the disciples: but they were all afraid of him, and believed not that he was a disciple.

27 But Barnabas took him, and brought him to the apostles, and declared unto them how he had seen the Lord in the way, and that he had spoken to him, and how he had preached boldly at Damascus in the name of Jesus.

28 And he was with them coming in and going out at Jerusalem.

29 And he spake boldly in the name of the Lord Jesus, and disputed against the Grecians: but they went about to slay him.

30 ~~Which w~~*W*hen the brethren knew *this*, they brought him down to Caesarea, and sent him forth to Tarsus.

31 Then had the churches rest throughout all Judaea and Galilee and Samaria, and were edified; and walking in the fear of the Lord, and in the comfort of the Holy Ghost, were multiplied.

32 And it came to pass, as Peter passed throughout all ~~quarters~~ *these regions*, he came down also to the saints which dwelt at Lydda.

33 And there he found a certain man named Æneas, which had kept his bed eight years, and was sick of the palsy.

34 And Peter said unto him, Æneas, Jesus Christ maketh thee whole: arise, and make thy

bed. And he arose immediately.

35 And all that dwelt at Lydda and Saron saw him, and turned to the Lord.

36 Now there was at Joppa a certain disciple named Tabitha, which by interpretation is called Dorcas: this woman was full of good works and almsdeeds which she did.

37 And it came to pass in those days, that she was sick, and died: whom when they had washed, they laid her in an upper chamber.

38 And forasmuch as Lydda was nigh to Joppa, and the disciples had heard that Peter was there, they sent unto him two men, desiring him that he would not delay to come to them.

39 Then Peter arose and went with them. When he was come, they brought him into the upper chamber: and all the widows stood by him weeping, and showing the coats and garments which Dorcas made, while she was with them.

40 But Peter put them all forth, and kneeled down, and prayed; and turning him to the body said, Tabitha, arise. And she opened her eyes: and when she saw Peter, she sat up.

41 And he gave her his hand, and lifted her up, and when he had called the saints and widows, *he* presented her alive.

42 And it was known throughout all Joppa; and many believed in the Lord.

43 And it came to pass, that he tarried many days in Joppa with one Simon a tanner.

Chapter 10

1 There was a certain man in Caesarea called Cornelius, a centurion of the band called the Italian band,

2 A devout man, and one that feared God with all his house, which gave much alms to the people, and prayed to God alway.

3 He saw in a vision evidently about the ninth hour of the day an angel of God coming in to him, and saying unto him, Cornelius.

4 And when he looked on him, he was afraid, and said, What is it, Lord? And he said unto him, Thy prayers and thine alms are come up for a memorial before God.

5 And now send men to Joppa, and call for one Simon, whose surname is Peter:

6 He lodgeth with one Simon a tanner, whose house is by the sea side: he shall tell thee what thou oughtest to do.

7 And when the angel which spake unto Cornelius was departed, he called two of his household servants, and a devout soldier of them that waited on him continually;

8 And when he had declared all these things unto them, he sent them to Joppa.

9 On the morrow, as they went on their journey, and drew nigh unto the city, Peter went up upon the housetop to pray about the sixth hour:

10 And he became very hungry, and would have eaten: but while they made ready, he fell into a trance,

11 And saw heaven opened, and a certain vessel descending unto him, as it had been a great sheet knit at the four corners, and let down to the earth:

12 Wherein were all manner of fourfooted beasts of the earth, and wild beasts, and creeping things, and fowls of the air.

13 And there came a voice to him, Rise, Peter; kill, and eat.

14 But Peter said, Not so, Lord; for I have never eaten any thing that is common or unclean.

15 And the voice spake unto him again the second time, What God hath cleansed, that call not thou common.

16 This was done thrice: and the vessel was received up again into heaven.

17 Now while Peter doubted in himself what this vision which he had seen should mean, behold, the men which were sent from Cornelius had made inquiry for Simon's house, and stood before the gate,

18 And called, and asked whether Simon, which was surnamed Peter, were lodged there.

19 While Peter thought on the vision, the Spirit said unto him, Behold, three men seek thee.

20 Arise therefore, and get thee down, and go with them, doubting nothing: for I have sent them.

21 Then Peter went down to the men which were sent unto him from Cornelius; and said, Behold, I am he whom ye seek: what is the cause wherefore ye are come?

22 And they said, Cornelius the centurion, a just man, and one that feareth God, and of good report among all the nation of the Jews, was warned from God by an holy angel to send for thee into his house, and to hear words of thee.

23 Then called he them in, and lodged them. And on the morrow Peter went away with them, and certain brethren from Joppa accompanied him.

24 And the morrow after they entered into Caesarea. And Cornelius waited for them, and had called together his kinsmen and near friends.

25 And as Peter was coming in, Cornelius met him, and fell down at his feet, and worshipped him.

26 But Peter took him up, saying, Stand up; I myself also am a man.

27 And as he talked with him, he went in, and found many that were come together.

28 And he said unto them, Ye know how that it is an unlawful thing for a man that is a Jew to keep company, or come unto one of another nation; but God hath showed me that I should not call any man common or unclean.

29 Therefore came I unto you without gainsaying, as soon as I was sent for: I ask therefore for what intent ye have sent for me?

30 And Cornelius said, Four days ago I was fasting until this hour; and at the ninth hour I prayed in my house, and, behold, a man stood before me in bright clothing,

31 And said, Cornelius, thy prayer is heard, and thine alms are had in remembrance in the sight of God.

32 Send therefore to Joppa, and call hither Simon, whose surname is Peter; he is lodged in the house of one Simon a tanner by the sea side: who, when he cometh, shall speak unto thee.

33 Immediately therefore I sent to thee; and thou hast well done that thou art come. Now therefore are we all here present before God, to hear all things that are commanded thee of God.

34 Then Peter opened his mouth, and said, Of a truth I perceive that God is no respecter of persons:

35 But in every nation he that feareth him, and worketh righteousness, is accepted with him.

36 The word which God sent unto the children of Israel, preaching peace by Jesus Christ: (he is Lord of all:)

37 That word, I say, ye know, which was published throughout all Judaea, and began from Galilee, after the baptism which John preached;

38 How God anointed Jesus of Nazareth with the Holy Ghost and with power: who went about doing good, and healing all that were oppressed of the devil; for God was with him.

39 And we are witnesses of all things which he did both in the land of the Jews, and in Jerusalem; whom they slew and hanged on a tree:

40 Him God raised up the third day, and showed him openly;

41 Not to all the people, but unto witnesses chosen before of God, even to us, who did eat and drink with him after he rose from the dead.

42 And he commanded us to preach unto the people, and to testify that it is he which was ordained of God to be the Judge of quick and dead.

43 To him give all the prophets witness, that through his name whosoever believeth in him shall receive remission of sins.

44 While Peter yet spake these words, the Holy Ghost fell on all them which heard the word.

45 And they of the circumcision which believed were astonished, as many as came with Peter, because that on the Gentiles also was poured out the gift of the Holy Ghost.

46 For they heard them speak with tongues, and magnify God. Then answered Peter,

47 Can any man forbid water, that these should not be baptized, which have received the Holy Ghost as well as we?

48 And he commanded them to be baptized in the name of the Lord. Then prayed they him to tarry certain days.

Chapter 11

1 And the apostles and brethren that were in Judaea heard that the Gentiles had also received the word of God.

2 And when Peter was come up to Jerusalem, they that were of the circumcision contended with him,

3 Saying, Thou wentest in to men uncircumcised, and didst eat with them.

4 But Peter rehearsed the matter from the beginning, and expounded it by order unto them, saying,

5 I was in the city of Joppa praying: and in a trance I saw a vision, A certain vessel descend, as it had been a great sheet, let down from heaven by four corners; and it came even to me:

6 Upon the which when I had fastened mine eyes, I considered, and saw fourfooted beasts of the earth, and wild beasts, and creeping things, and fowls of the air.

7 And I heard a voice saying unto me, Arise, Peter; slay and eat.

8 But I said, Not so, Lord: for nothing common or unclean hath at any time entered into my mouth.

9 But the voice answered me again from heaven, What God hath cleansed, that call not thou common.

10 And this was done three times: and all were drawn up again into heaven.

11 And, behold, immediately there were three men already come unto the house where I was, sent from Caesarea unto me.

12 And the Spirit bade me go with them, nothing doubting. Moreover these six brethren accompanied me, and we entered into the man's house:

13 And he showed us how he had seen an angel in his house, which stood and said unto him, Send men to Joppa, and call for Simon, whose surname is Peter;

14 Who shall tell thee words, whereby thou and all thy house shall be saved.

15 And as I began to speak, the Holy Ghost fell on them, as on us at the beginning.

16 Then remembered I the word of the Lord, how that he said, John indeed baptized with water; but ye shall be baptized with the Holy Ghost.

17 Forasmuch then as God gave them the like gift as he did unto us, who believed on the Lord Jesus Christ; what was I, that I could withstand God?

18 When they heard these things, they held their peace, and glorified God, saying, Then hath God also to the Gentiles granted repentance unto life.

19 Now they which were scattered abroad upon

the persecution that arose about Stephen travelled as far as Phenice, and Cyprus, and Antioch, preaching the word to none but unto the Jews only.

20 And some of them were men of Cyprus and Cyrene, which, when they were come to Antioch, spake unto the Grecians, preaching the Lord Jesus.

21 And the hand of the Lord was with them: and a great number believed, and turned unto the Lord.

22 Then tidings of these things came unto the ears of the church which was in Jerusalem: and they sent forth Barnabas, that he should go as far as Antioch.

23 Who, when he came, and had seen the grace of God, was glad, and exhorted them all, that with purpose of heart they would cleave unto the Lord.

24 For he was a good man, and full of the Holy Ghost and of faith: and much people was added unto the Lord.

25 Then departed Barnabas to Tarsus, for to seek Saul:

26 And when he had found him, he brought him unto Antioch. And it came to pass, that a whole year they assembled themselves with the church, and taught much people. And the disciples were called Christians first in Antioch.

27 And in these days came prophets from Jerusalem unto Antioch.

28 And there stood up one of them named Agabus, and signified by the Spirit that there should be great dearth throughout all the world: which came to pass in the days of Claudius Caesar.

29 Then the disciples, every man according to his ability, determined to send relief unto the brethren which dwelt in Judaea:

30 Which also they did, and sent it to the elders by the hands of Barnabas and Saul.

Chapter 12

1 Now about that time Herod the king stretched forth his hands to vex certain of the church.

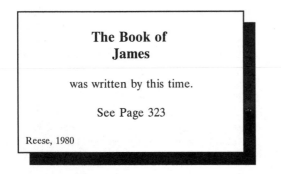

**The Book of
James**

was written by this time.

See Page 323

Reese, 1980

2 And he killed James the brother of John with the sword.

3 And because he saw it pleased the Jews, he proceeded further to take Peter also. (Then were the days of unleavened bread.)

4 And when he had apprehended him, he put him in prison, and delivered him to four quaternions of soldiers to keep him; intending after Easter to bring him forth to the people.

5 Peter therefore was kept in prison: but prayer was made without ceasing of the church unto God for him.

6 And when Herod would have brought him forth, the same night Peter was sleeping between two soldiers, bound with two chains: and the keepers before the door kept the prison.

7 And, behold, the angel of the Lord came ~~upon~~ *unto* him, and a light shined in the prison: and he smote Peter on the side, and raised him up, saying, Arise up quickly. And his chains fell off from his hands.

8 And the angel said unto him, Gird thyself, and bind on thy sandals. And so he did. And he saith unto him, Cast thy garment about thee, and follow me.

9 And he went out, and followed him; and wist not that it was true which was done by the angel; but thought he saw a vision.

10 When they were past the first and the second ward, they came unto the iron gate that leadeth unto the city; which opened to them of his own accord: and they went out, and passed on through one street; and forthwith the angel departed from him.

11 And when Peter was come to himself, he said, Now I know of a surety, that the Lord hath sent his angel, and hath delivered me out of the hand of Herod, and from all the expectation of the people of the Jews.

12 And when he had considered the thing, he came to the house of Mary the mother of John, whose surname was Mark; where many were gathered together praying.

13 And as Peter knocked at the door of the gate, a damsel came to hearken, named Rhoda.

14 And when she knew Peter's voice, she opened not the gate for gladness, but ran in, and told how Peter stood before the gate.

15 And they said unto her, Thou art mad. But she constantly affirmed that it was even so. Then said they, It is his angel.

16 But Peter continued knocking: and when they had opened the door, and saw him, they were astonished.

17 But he, beckoning unto them with the hand to hold their peace, declared unto them how the Lord had brought him out of the prison. And he said, Go show these things unto James, and to the brethren. And he departed, and went into another place.

18 Now as soon as it was day, there was no small stir among the soldiers, what was become of Peter.

19 And when Herod had sought for him, and found him not, he examined the keepers, and commanded that they should be put to death. And he went down from Judaea to Caesarea, and there abode.

20 And Herod was highly displeased with them of Tyre and Sidon: but they came with one accord to him, and, having made Blastus the king's chamberlain their friend, desired peace; because their country was nourished by the king's country.

21 And upon a set day Herod, arrayed in royal apparel, sat upon his throne, and made an oration unto them.

22 And the people gave a shout, saying, It is the voice of a god, and not of a man.

23 And immediately the angel of the Lord smote him, because he gave not God the glory: and he was eaten of worms, and gave up the ghost.

24 But the word of God grew and multiplied.

25 And Barnabas and Saul returned from Jerusalem, when they had fulfilled their ministry, and took with them John, whose surname was Mark.

Chapter 13

1 Now there were in the church that was at Antioch certain prophets and teachers; as Barnabas, and Simeon that was called Niger, and Lucius of Cyrene, and Manaen, which had been brought up with Herod the tetrarch, and Saul.

2 As they ministered to the Lord, and fasted, the Holy Ghost said, Separate me Barnabas and Saul for the work whereunto I have called them.

3 And when they had fasted and prayed, and laid their hands on them, they sent them away.

4 So they, being sent forth by the Holy Ghost, departed unto Seleucia; and from thence they sailed to Cyprus.

5 And when they were at Salamis, they preached the word of God in the synagogues of the Jews: and they had also John to their minister.

6 And when they had gone through the isle unto Paphos, they found a certain sorcerer, a false prophet, a Jew, whose name was Barjesus:

7 Which was with the deputy of the country, Sergius Paulus, a prudent man; who called for Barnabas and Saul, and desired to hear the word of God.

8 But Elymas the sorcerer (for so is his name by interpretation) withstood them, seeking to turn away the deputy from the faith.

9 Then Saul, (who also is called Paul,) filled with the Holy Ghost, set his eyes on him,

10 And said, O full of all subtlety and all mischief, thou child of the devil, thou enemy of all righteousness, wilt thou not cease to pervert the right ways of the Lord?

11 And now, behold, the hand of the Lord is upon thee, and thou shalt be blind, not seeing the sun for a season. And immediately there fell on him a mist and a darkness; and he went about seeking some to lead him by the hand.

12 Then the deputy, when he saw what was done, believed, being astonished at the doctrine of the Lord.

13 Now when Paul and his company loosed from Paphos, they came to Perga in Pamphylia: and John departing from them returned to Jerusalem.

14 But when they departed from Perga, they came to Antioch in Pisidia, and went into the synagogue on the sabbath day, and sat down.

15 And after the reading of the law and the prophets the rulers of the synagogue sent unto them, saying, Ye men and brethren, if ye have any word of exhortation for the people, say on.

16 Then Paul stood up, and beckoning with his hand said, Men of Israel, and ye that fear God, give audience.

17 The God of this people of Israel chose our fathers, and exalted the people when they dwelt as strangers in the land of Egypt, and with an high arm brought he them out of it.

18 And about the time ~~of~~ *for* forty years suffered he their manners in the wilderness.

19 And when he had destroyed seven nations in the land of Chanaan, he divided their land to them by lot.

20 And after that he gave unto them judges about the space of four hundred and fifty years, until Samuel the prophet.

21 And afterward they desired a king: and God gave unto them Saul the son of Cis, a man of the tribe of Benjamin, by the space of forty years.

22 And when he had removed him, he raised up unto them David to be their king; to whom also he gave testimony, and said, I have found David the son of Jesse, a man after mine own heart, which shall fulfil all my will.

23 Of this man's seed hath God according to his promise raised unto Israel a Saviour, Jesus:

24 When John had first preached before his coming the baptism of repentance to all the people of Israel.

25 And as John fulfilled his course, he said, Whom think ye that I am? I am not he. But, behold, there cometh one after me, whose shoes of his feet I am not worthy to loose.

26 Men and brethren, children of the stock of Abraham, and whosoever among you feareth God, to you is the word of this salvation sent.

27 For they that dwell at Jerusalem, and their rulers, because they knew him not, nor yet the voices of the prophets which are read every

sabbath day, they have fulfilled them in condemning him.

28 And though they found no cause of death in him, yet desired they Pilate that he should be slain.

29 And when they had fulfilled all that was written of him, they took him down from the tree, and laid him in a sepulchre.

30 But God raised him from the dead:

31 And he was seen many days of them which came up with him from Galilee to Jerusalem, who are his witnesses unto the people.

32 And we declare unto you glad tidings, how that the promise which was made unto the fathers,

33 God hath fulfilled the same unto us their children, in that he hath raised up Jesus again; as it is also written in the second psalm, Thou art my Son, this day have I begotten thee.

34 And as concerning that he raised him up from the dead, now no more to return to corruption, he said on this wise, I will give you the sure mercies of David.

35 Wherefore he saith also in another psalm, Thou shalt not suffer thine Holy One to see corruption.

36 For David, after he had served his own generation by the will of God, fell on sleep, and was laid unto his fathers, and saw corruption:

37 But he, whom God raised again, saw no corruption.

38 Be it known unto you therefore, men and brethren, that through this man is preached unto you the forgiveness of sins:

39 And by him all that believe are justified from all things, from which ye could not be justified by the law of Moses.

40 Beware therefore, lest that come upon you, which is spoken of in the prophets;

41 Behold, ye despisers, and wonder, and perish: for I work a work in your days, a work which ye shall in no wise believe, though a man declare it unto you.

42 And when the Jews were gone out of the synagogue, the Gentiles besought that these words might be preached to them the next sabbath.

43 Now when the congregation was broken up, many of the Jews and religious proselytes followed Paul and Barnabas: who, speaking to them, persuaded them to continue in the grace of God.

44 And the next sabbath day came almost the whole city together to hear the word of God.

45 But when the Jews saw the multitudes, they were filled with envy, and spake against those things which were spoken by Paul, contradicting and blaspheming.

46 Then Paul and Barnabas waxed bold, and said, It was necessary that the word of God should first have been spoken to you: but seeing ye put it from you, and judge yourselves unworthy of everlasting life, lo, we turn to the Gentiles.

47 For so hath the Lord commanded us, saying, I have set thee to be a light of the Gentiles, that thou shouldest be for salvation unto the ends of the earth.

48 And when the Gentiles heard this, they were glad, and glorified the word of the Lord: and as many as *believed* were ordained to eternal life believed.

49 And the word of the Lord was published throughout all the region.

50 But the Jews stirred up the devout and honourable women, and the chief men of the city, and raised persecution against Paul and Barnabas, and expelled them out of their coasts.

51 But they shook off the dust of their feet against them, and came unto Iconium.

52 And the disciples were filled with joy, and with the Holy Ghost.

Chapter 14

1 And it came to pass in Iconium, that they went both together into the synagogue of the Jews, and so spake, that a great multitude both of the Jews and also of the Greeks believed.

2 But the unbelieving Jews stirred up the Gentiles, and made their minds evil affected against the brethren.

3 Long time therefore abode they speaking boldly in the Lord, which gave testimony unto the word of his grace, and granted signs and wonders to be done by their hands.

4 But the multitude of the city was divided: and part held with the Jews, and part with the apostles.

5 And when there was an assault made both of the Gentiles, and also of the Jews with their rulers, to use them despitefully, and to stone them,

6 They were ware of it, and fled unto Lystra and Derbe, cities of Lycaonia, and unto the region that lieth round about:

7 And there they preached the gospel.

8 And there sat a certain man at Lystra, impotent in his feet, being a cripple from his mother's womb, who never had walked:

9 The same heard Paul speak: who stedfastly beholding him, and perceiving that he had faith to be healed,

10 Said with a loud voice, Stand upright on thy feet. And he leaped and walked.

11 And when the people saw what Paul had done, they lifted up their voices, saying in the speech of Lycaonia, The gods are come down to us in the likeness of men.

12 And they called Barnabas, Jupiter; and Paul, Mercurius, because he was the chief speaker.

13 Then the priest of Jupiter, which was before their city, brought oxen and garlands unto the gates, and would have done sacrifice with the people.

14 ~~Which w~~When the apostles, Barnabas and Paul, heard ~~of~~ *this*, they rent their clothes, and ran in among the people, crying out,

15 And saying, Sirs, why do ye these things? We also are men of like passions with you, and preach unto you that ye should turn from these vanities unto the living God, which made heaven, and earth, and the sea, and all things that are therein:

16 Who in times past suffered all nations to walk in their own ways.

17 Nevertheless he left not himself without witness, in that he did good, and gave us rain from heaven, and fruitful seasons, filling our hearts with food and gladness.

18 And with these sayings scarce restrained they the people, that they had not done sacrifice unto them.

19 And there came thither certain Jews from Antioch and Iconium, who persuaded the people, and, having stoned Paul, drew him out of the city, supposing he had been dead.

20 Howbeit, as the disciples stood round about him, he rose up, and came into the city: and the next day he departed with Barnabas to Derbe.

21 And when they had preached the gospel to that city, and had taught many, they returned again to Lystra, and to Iconium, and Antioch,

22 Confirming the souls of the disciples, and exhorting them to continue in the faith, and that we must through much tribulation enter into the kingdom of God.

23 And when they had ordained them elders in every church, and had prayed with fasting, they commended them to the Lord, on whom they believed.

24 And after they had passed throughout Pisidia, they came to Pamphylia.

25 And when they had preached the word in Perga, they went down into Attalia:

26 And thence sailed to Antioch, from whence they had been recommended to the grace of God for the work which they fulfilled.

27 And when they were come, and had gathered the church together, they rehearsed all that God had done with them, and how he had opened the door of faith unto the Gentiles.

28 And there they abode long time with the disciples.

Chapter 15

1 And certain men which came down from Judaea taught the brethren, and said, Except ye be circumcised after the manner of Moses, ye cannot be saved.

2 When therefore Paul and Barnabas had no small dissension and disputation with them, they determined that Paul and Barnabas, and certain other of them, should go up to Jerusalem unto the apostles and elders about this question.

3 And being brought on their way by the church, they passed through Phenice and Samaria, declaring the conversion of the Gentiles: and they caused great joy unto all the brethren.

4 And when they were come to Jerusalem, they were received of the church, and of the apostles and elders, and they declared all things that God had done with them.

5 But there rose up certain of the sect of the Pharisees which believed, saying, That it was needful to circumcise them, and to command them to keep the law of Moses.

6 And the apostles and elders came together for to consider of this matter.

7 And when there had been much disputing, Peter rose up, and said unto them, Men and brethren, ye know how that a good while ago God made choice among us, that the Gentiles by my mouth should hear the word of the gospel, and believe.

8 And God, which knoweth the hearts, bare them witness, giving them the Holy Ghost, even as he did unto us;

9 And put no difference between us and them, purifying their hearts by faith.

10 Now therefore why tempt ye God, to put a yoke upon the neck of the disciples, which neither our fathers nor we were able to bear?

11 But we believe that through the grace of the Lord Jesus Christ we shall be saved, even as they.

12 Then all the multitude kept silence, and gave audience to Barnabas and Paul, declaring what miracles and wonders God had wrought among the Gentiles by them.

13 And after they had held their peace, James answered, saying, Men and brethren, hearken unto me:

14 Simeon hath declared how God at the first did visit the Gentiles, to take out of them a people for his name.

15 And to this agree the words of the prophets; as it is written,

16 After this I will return, and will build again the tabernacle of David, which is fallen down; and I will build again the ruins thereof, and I will set it up:

17 That the residue of men might seek after the Lord, and all the Gentiles, upon whom my name is called, saith the Lord, who doeth all these things.

18 Known unto God are all his works from the beginning of the world.

19 Wherefore my sentence is, that we trouble

not them, which from among the Gentiles are turned to God:

20 But that we write unto them, that they abstain from pollutions of idols, and from fornication, and from things strangled, and from blood.

21 For Moses of old time hath in every city them that preach him, being read in the synagogues every sabbath day.

22 Then pleased it the apostles and elders, with the whole church, to send chosen men of their own company to Antioch with Paul and Barnabas; namely, Judas surnamed Barsabas, and Silas, chief men among the brethren:

23 And they wrote letters by them after this manner; The apostles and elders and brethren send greeting unto the brethren which are of the Gentiles in Antioch and Syria and Cilicia:

24 Forasmuch as we have heard, that certain *men* which went out from us have troubled you with words, subverting your souls, saying, Ye must be circumcised, and keep the law: to whom we gave no such commandment:

25 It seemed good unto us, being assembled with one accord, to send chosen men unto you with our beloved Barnabas and Paul,

26 Men that have hazarded their lives for the name of our Lord Jesus Christ.

27 We have sent therefore Judas and Silas, who shall also tell you the same things by mouth.

28 For it seemed good to the Holy Ghost, and to us, to lay upon you no greater burden than these necessary things;

29 That ye abstain from meats offered to idols, and from blood, and from things strangled, and from fornication: from which if ye keep yourselves, ye shall do well. Fare ye well.

30 So when they were dismissed, they came to Antioch: and when they had gathered the multitude together, they delivered the epistle:

31 Which when they had read, they rejoiced for the consolation.

32 And Judas and Silas, being prophets also themselves, exhorted the brethren with many words, and confirmed them.

33 And after they had tarried there a space, they were let go in peace from the brethren unto the apostles.

34 Notwithstanding it pleased Silas to abide there still.

35 Paul also and Barnabas continued in Antioch, teaching and preaching the word of the Lord, with many others also.

36 And some days after Paul said unto Barnabas, Let us go again and visit our brethren in every city where we have preached the word of the Lord, and see how they do.

37 And Barnabas determined to take with them John, whose surname was Mark.

38 But Paul thought not good to take him with

them, who departed from them from Pamphylia, and went not with them to the work.

39 And the contention was so sharp between them, that they departed asunder one from the other: and so Barnabas took Mark, and sailed unto Cyprus;

40 And Paul chose Silas, and departed, being recommended by the brethren unto the grace of God.

41 And he went through Syria and Cilicia, confirming the churches.

Chapter 16

1 Then came he to Derbe and Lystra: and, behold, a certain disciple was there, named Timotheus, the son of a certain woman, which was a Jewess, and believed; but his father was a Greek:

2 Which was well reported of by the brethren that were at Lystra and Iconium.

3 Him would Paul have to go forth with him; and took and circumcised him because of the Jews which were in those quarters: for they knew all that his father was a Greek.

4 And as they went through the cities, they delivered them the decrees for to keep, that were ordained of the apostles and elders which were at Jerusalem.

5 And so were the churches established in the faith, and increased in number daily.

6 Now when they had gone throughout Phrygia and the region of Galatia, and were forbidden of the Holy Ghost to preach the word in Asia,

7 After they were come to Mysia, they assayed to go into Bithynia: but the Spirit suffered them not.

8 And they passing by Mysia came down to Troas.

9 And a vision appeared to Paul in the night; There stood a man of Macedonia, and prayed him, saying, Come over into Macedonia, and help us.

10 And after he had seen the vision, immediately we endeavoured to go into Macedonia, assuredly gathering that the Lord had called us for to preach the gospel unto them.

11 Therefore loosing from Troas, we came with a straight course to Samothracia, and the next day to Neapolis;

12 And from thence to Philippi, which is the chief city of that part of Macedonia, and a colony: and we were in that city abiding certain days.

13 And on the sSabbath we went out of the city by a river side, where *the people resorted for* prayer was wont to be made; and we sat down, and spake unto the women which resorted thither.

14 And a certain woman named Lydia, a seller

of purple, of the city of Thyatira, which worshipped God, heard us: whose heart the Lord opened, that she attended unto the things which were spoken of Paul.

15 And when she was baptized, and her household, she besought us, saying, If ye have judged me to be faithful to the Lord, come into my house, and abide there. And she constrained us.

16 And it came to pass, as we went to prayer, a certain damsel possessed with a spirit of divination met us, which brought her masters much gain by soothsaying:

17 The same followed Paul and us, and cried, saying, These men are the servants of the most high God, which show unto us the way of salvation.

18 And this did she many days. But Paul, being grieved, turned and said to the spirit, I command thee in the name of Jesus Christ to come out of her. And he came out the same hour.

19 And when her masters saw that the hope of their gains was gone, they caught Paul and Silas, and drew them into the marketplace unto the rulers,

20 And brought them to the magistrates, saying, These men, being Jews, do exceedingly trouble our city,

21 And teach customs, which are not lawful for us to receive, neither to observe, being Romans.

22 And the multitude rose up together against them: and the magistrates rent off their clothes, and commanded to beat them.

23 And when they had laid many stripes upon them, they cast them into prison, charging the jailor to keep them safely:

24 Who, having received such a charge, thrust them into the inner prison, and made their feet fast in the stocks.

25 And at midnight Paul and Silas prayed, and sang praises unto God: and the prisoners heard them.

26 And suddenly there was a great earthquake, so that the foundations of the prison were shaken: and immediately all the doors were opened, and every one's bands were loosed.

27 And the keeper of the prison awaking out of his sleep, and seeing the prison doors open, he drew out his sword, and would have killed himself, supposing that the prisoners had been fled.

28 But Paul cried with a loud voice, saying, Do thyself no harm: for we are all here.

29 Then he called for a light, and sprang in, and came trembling, and fell down before Paul and Silas,

30 And brought them out, and said, Sirs, what must I do to be saved?

31 And they said, Believe on the Lord Jesus Christ, and thou shalt be saved, and thy house.

32 And they spake unto him the word of the Lord, and to all that were in his house.

33 And he took them the same hour of the night, and washed their stripes; and was baptized, he and all his, straightway.

34 And when he had brought them into his house, he set meat before them, and rejoiced, believing in God with all his house.

35 And when it was day, the magistrates sent the serjeants, saying, Let those men go.

36 And the keeper of the prison told this saying to Paul, The magistrates have sent to let you go: now therefore depart, and go in peace.

37 But Paul said unto them, They have beaten us openly uncondemned, being Romans, and have cast us into prison; and now do they thrust us out privily? nay verily; but let them come themselves and fetch us out.

38 And the serjeants told these words unto the magistrates: and they feared, when they heard that they were Romans.

39 And they came and besought them, and brought them out, and desired them to depart out of the city.

40 And they went out of the prison, and entered into the house of Lydia: and when they had seen the brethren, they comforted them, and departed.

Chapter 17

1 Now when they had passed through Amphipolis and Apollonia, they came to Thessalonica, where was a synagogue of the Jews:

2 And Paul, as his manner was, went in unto them, and three sabbath days reasoned with them out of the scriptures,

3 Opening and alleging, that Christ must needs have suffered, and risen again from the dead; and that this Jesus, whom I preach unto you, is Christ.

4 And some of them believed, and consorted with Paul and Silas; and of the devout Greeks a great multitude, and of the chief women not a few.

5 But the Jews which believed not, moved with envy, took unto them certain lewd fellows of the baser sort, and gathered a company, and set all the city on an uproar, and assaulted the house of Jason, and sought to bring them out to the people.

6 And when they found them not, they drew Jason and certain brethren unto the rulers of the city, crying, These that have turned the world upside down are come hither also;

7 Whom Jason hath received: and these all do contrary to the decrees of Caesar, saying that there is another king, one Jesus.

8 And they troubled the people and the rulers of the city, when they heard these things.

9 And when they had taken security of Jason, and of the other, they let them go.

10 And the brethren immediately sent away Paul and Silas by night unto Berea: who coming thither went into the synagogue of the Jews.

11 These were more noble than those in Thessalonica, in that they received the word with all readiness of mind, and searched the scriptures daily, whether those things were so.

12 Therefore many of them believed; also of honourable women which were Greeks, and of men, not a few.

13 But when the Jews of Thessalonica had knowledge that the word of God was preached of Paul at Berea, they came thither also, and stirred up the people.

14 And then immediately the brethren sent away Paul to go as it were to the sea: but Silas and Timotheus abode there still.

15 And they that conducted Paul brought him unto Athens: and receiving a commandment unto Silas and Timotheus for to come to him with all speed, they departed.

16 Now while Paul waited for them at Athens, his spirit was stirred in him, when he saw the city wholly given to idolatry.

17 Therefore disputed he in the synagogue with the Jews, and with the devout persons, and in the market daily with them that met with him.

18 Then certain philosophers of the Epicureans, and of the Stoicks, encountered him. And some said, What will this babbler say? other some, He seemeth to be a setter forth of strange gods: because he preached unto them Jesus, and the resurrection.

19 And they took him, and brought him unto *the* Areopagus, saying, May we know what this new doctrine *is*, whereof thou speakest, ~~is~~?

20 For thou bringest certain strange things to our ears: we would know therefore what these things mean.

21 (For all the Athenians and strangers which were there spent their time in nothing else, but either to tell, or to hear some new thing.)

22 Then Paul stood in the midst of Mars' hill, and said, Ye men of Athens, I perceive that in all things ye are too superstitious.

23 For as I passed by, and beheld your devotions, I found an altar with this inscription, TO THE UNKNOWN GOD. Whom therefore ye ignorantly worship, him declare I unto you.

24 God that made the world and all things therein, seeing that he is Lord of heaven and earth, dwelleth not in temples made with hands;

25 Neither is worshipped with men's hands, as though he needed any thing, seeing he giveth to all life, and breath, and all things;

26 And hath made of one blood all nations of men for to dwell on all the face of the earth, and hath determined the times before appointed, and the bounds of their habitation;

27 That they should seek the Lord, if ~~haply they~~ ~~might feel after him, and~~ *they are willing to* find him, ~~though he be~~ *for he is* not far from every one of us:

28 For in him we live, and move, and have our being; as certain also of your own poets have said, For we are also his offspring.

29 Forasmuch then as we are the offspring of God, we ought not to think that the Godhead is like unto gold, or silver, or stone, graven by art and man's device.

30 And the times of this ignorance God winked at; but now commandeth all men every where to repent:

31 Because he hath appointed a day, in the which he will judge the world in righteousness by ~~that man~~ *him* whom he hath ordained; ~~whereof~~ *and* he hath given assurance *of this* unto all men, in that he hath raised him from the dead.

32 And when they heard of the resurrection of the dead, some mocked: and others said, We will hear thee again of this matter.

33 So Paul departed from among them.

34 Howbeit certain men clave unto him, and believed: among the which was Dionysius the Areopagite, and a woman named Damaris, and others with them.

Chapter 18

1 After these things Paul departed from Athens, and came to Corinth;

2 And found a certain Jew named Aquila, born in Pontus, lately come from Italy, with his wife Priscilla; (because that Claudius had commanded all Jews to depart from Rome:) and came unto them.

3 And because he was of the same craft, he abode with them, and wrought: for by their occupation they were tentmakers.

4 And he reasoned in the synagogue every sabbath, and persuaded the Jews and the Greeks.

5 And when Silas and Timotheus were come from Macedonia,

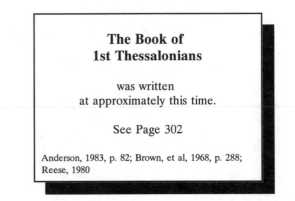

**The Book of
1st Thessalonians**

was written
at approximately this time.

See Page 302

Anderson, 1983, p. 82; Brown, et al, 1968, p. 288; Reese, 1980

Paul was pressed in the spirit, and testified to the Jews that Jesus was Christ.

6 And when they opposed themselves, and blasphemed, he shook his raiment, and said unto them, Your blood be upon your own heads; I am clean: from henceforth I will go unto the Gentiles.

7 And he departed thence, and entered into a certain man's house, named Justus, one that worshipped God, whose house joined hard to the synagogue.

8 And Crispus, the chief ruler of the synagogue, believed on the Lord with all his house; and many of the Corinthians hearing believed, and were baptized.

9 Then spake the Lord to Paul in the night by a vision, Be not afraid, but speak, and hold not thy peace:

10 For I am with thee, and no man shall set on thee to hurt thee: for I have much people in this city.

11 And he continued there a year and six months, teaching the word of God among them.

12 And when Gallio was the deputy of Achaia, the Jews made insurrection with one accord against Paul, and brought him to the judgment seat,

13 Saying, This fellow persuadeth men to worship God contrary to the law.

14 And when Paul was now about to open his mouth, Gallio said unto the Jews, If it were a matter of wrong or wicked lewdness, O ye Jews, reason would that I should bear with you:

15 But if it be a question of words and names, and of your law, look ye to it; for I will be no judge of such matters.

16 And he drave them from the judgment seat.

17 Then all the Greeks took Sosthenes, the chief ruler of the synagogue, and beat him before the judgment seat. And Gallio cared for none of those things.

The Book of
2nd Thessalonians

was written
at approximately this time.

See Page 305

Anderson, 1983, p. 82; Reese, 1980

---

18 And Paul after this tarried there yet a good while, and then took his leave of the brethren, and sailed thence into Syria, and with him

Priscilla and Aquila; having shorn his head in Cenchrea: for he had a vow.

19 And he came to Ephesus, and left them there: but he himself entered into the synagogue, and reasoned with the Jews.

20 When they desired him to tarry longer time with them, he consented not;

21 But bade them farewell, saying, I must by all means keep this feast that cometh in Jerusalem: but I will return again unto you, if God will. And he sailed from Ephesus.

22 And when he had landed at Caesarea, and gone up, and saluted the church, he went down to Antioch.

23 And after he had spent some time there, he departed, and went over all the country of Galatia and Phrygia in order, strengthening all the disciples.

24 And a certain Jew named Apollos, born at Alexandria, an eloquent man, and mighty in the scriptures, came to Ephesus.

25 This man was instructed in the way of the Lord; and being fervent in the spirit, he spake and taught diligently the things of the Lord, knowing only the baptism of John.

26 And he began to speak boldly in the synagogue: whom when Aquila and Priscilla had heard, they took him unto them, and expounded unto him the way of God more perfectly.

27 And when he was disposed to pass into Achaia, the brethren wrote, exhorting the disciples to receive him: who, when he was come, helped them much which had believed through grace:

28 For he mightily convinced the Jews, and that publicly, showing by the scriptures that Jesus was Christ.

Chapter 19

1 And it came to pass, that, while Apollos was at Corinth, Paul having passed through the upper coasts came to Ephesus: and finding certain disciples,

2 He said unto them, Have ye received the Holy Ghost since ye believed? And they said unto him, We have not so much as heard whether there be any Holy Ghost.

3 And he said unto them, Unto what then were ye baptized? And they said, Unto John's baptism.

4 Then said Paul, John verily baptized with the baptism of repentance, saying unto the people, that they should believe on him which should come after him, that is, on Christ Jesus.

5 When they heard this, they were baptized in the name of the Lord Jesus.

6 And when Paul had laid his hands upon them, the Holy Ghost came on them; and they spake

with tongues, and prophesied.

7 And all the men were about twelve.

8 And he went into the synagogue, and spake boldly for the space of three months, disputing and persuading the things concerning the kingdom of God.

9 But when divers were hardened, and believed not, but spake evil of that way before the multitude, he departed from them, and separated the disciples, disputing daily in the school of one Tyrannus.

10 And this continued by the space of two years; so that all they which dwelt in Asia heard the word of the Lord Jesus, both Jews and Greeks.

11 And God wrought special miracles by the hands of Paul:

12 So that from his body were brought unto the sick handkerchiefs or aprons, and the diseases departed from them, and the evil spirits went out of them.

13 Then certain of the vagabond Jews, exorcists, took upon them to call over them which had evil spirits the name of the Lord Jesus, saying, We adjure you by Jesus whom Paul preacheth.

14 And there were seven sons of one Sceva, a Jew, and chief of the priests, which did so.

15 And the evil spirit answered and said, Jesus I know, and Paul I know; but who are ye?

16 And the man in whom the evil spirit was leaped on them, and overcame them, and prevailed against them, so that they fled out of that house naked and wounded.

17 And this was known to all the Jews and Greeks also dwelling at Ephesus; and fear fell on them all, and the name of the Lord Jesus was magnified.

18 And many that believed came, and confessed, and showed their deeds.

19 Many of them also which used curious arts brought their books together, and burned them before all men: and they counted the price of them, and found it fifty thousand pieces of silver.

20 So mightily grew the word of God and prevailed.

21 After these things were ended, Paul purposed in the spirit, when he had passed through Macedonia and Achaia, to go to Jerusalem, saying, After I have been there, I must also see Rome.

22 So he sent into Macedonia two of them that ministered unto him, Timotheus and Erastus; but he himself stayed in Asia for a season.

23 And the same time there arose no small stir about that way.

24 For a certain man named Demetrius, a silversmith, which made silver shrines for Diana, brought no small gain unto the craftsmen;

25 Whom he called together with the workmen of like occupation, and said, Sirs, ye know that by this craft we have our wealth.

26 Moreover ye see and hear, that not alone at Ephesus, but almost throughout all Asia, this Paul hath persuaded and turned away much people, saying that they be no gods, which are made with hands:

27 So that not only this our craft is in danger to be set at nought; but also that the temple of the great goddess Diana should be despised, and her magnificence should be destroyed, whom all Asia and the world worshippeth.

28 And when they heard these sayings, they were full of wrath, and cried out, saying, Great is Diana of the Ephesians.

29 And the whole city was filled with confusion: and having caught Gaius and Aristarchus, men of Macedonia, Paul's companions in travel, they rushed with one accord into the theatre.

30 And when Paul would have entered in unto the people, the disciples suffered him not.

31 And certain of the chief of Asia, which were his friends, sent unto him, desiring him that he would not adventure himself into the theatre.

32 Some therefore cried one thing, and some another: for the assembly was confused; and the more part knew not wherefore they were come together.

33 And they drew Alexander out of the multitude, the Jews putting him forward. And Alexander beckoned with the hand, and would have made his defence unto the people.

34 But when they knew that he was a Jew, all with one voice about the space of two hours cried out, Great is Diana of the Ephesians.

35 And when the townclerk had appeased the people, he said, Ye men of Ephesus, what man is there that knoweth not how that the city of the Ephesians is a worshipper of the great goddess Diana, and of the image which fell down from Jupiter?

36 Seeing then that these things cannot be spoken against, ye ought to be quiet, and to do nothing rashly.

37 For ye have brought hither these men, which are neither robbers of churches, nor yet blasphemers of your goddess.

38 Wherefore if Demetrius, and the craftsmen which are with him, have a matter against any man, the law is open, and there are deputies: let them implead one another.

39 But if ye inquire any thing concerning other matters, it shall be determined in a lawful assembly.

40 For we are in danger to be called in question for this day's uproar, there being no cause whereby we may give an account of this concourse.

41 And when he had thus spoken, he dismissed the assembly.

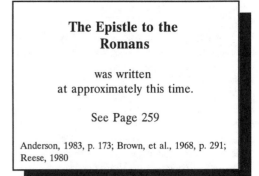

**The Book of
1st Corinthians**

was written
at approximately this time. .

See Page 271

Anderson, 1983, p. 95,130;
Brown, et al, 1968, p. 255; Reese, 1980

**The Epistle to the
Romans**

was written
at approximately this time.

See Page 259

Anderson, 1983, p. 173; Brown, et al., 1968, p. 291;
Reese, 1980

Chapter 20

1 And after the uproar was ceased, Paul called unto him the disciples, and embraced them, and departed for to go into Macedonia.

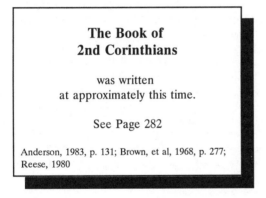

**The Book of
2nd Corinthians**

was written
at approximately this time.

See Page 282

Anderson, 1983, p. 131; Brown, et al, 1968, p. 277;
Reese, 1980

2 And when he had gone over those parts, and had given them much exhortation, he came into Greece,

3 And there abode three months. And when the Jews laid wait for him, as he was about to sail into Syria, he purposed to return through Macedonia.

**The Book of
Galatians**

Exact date of writing unknown

See Page 289

Anderson, 1983, p. 130; Brown, et al, 1968, p. 150;
Reese, 1980

4 And there accompanied him into Asia Sopater of Berea; and of the Thessalonians, Aristarchus and Secundus; and Gaius of Derbe, and Timotheus; and of Asia, Tychicus and Trophimus.

5 These going before tarried for us at Troas.

6 And we sailed away from Philippi after the days of unleavened bread, and came unto them to Troas in five days; where we abode seven days.

7 And upon the first day of the week, when the disciples came together to break bread, Paul preached unto them, ready to depart on the morrow; and continued his speech until midnight.

8 And there were many lights in the upper chamber, where they were gathered together.

9 And there sat in a window a certain young man named Eutychus, being fallen into a deep sleep: and as Paul was long preaching, he sunk down with sleep, and fell down from the third loft, and was taken up dead.

10 And Paul went down, and fell on him, and embracing him said, Trouble not yourselves; for his life is in him.

11 When he therefore was come up again, and had broken bread, and eaten, and talked a long while, even till break of day, so he departed.

12 And they brought the young man alive, and were not a little comforted.

13 And ~~we~~ *he* went before to ship, and sailed unto Assos, there intending to take in Paul: for so had he appointed, minding himself to go afoot.

14 And when he met with us at Assos, we took him in, and came to Mitylene.

15 And we sailed thence, and came the next day over against Chios; and the next day we arrived at Samos, and tarried at Trogyllium; and the next day we came to Miletus.

16 For Paul had determined to sail by Ephesus, because he would not spend the time in Asia: for he hasted, if it were possible for him, to be at Jerusalem the day of Pentecost.

17 And from Miletus he sent to Ephesus, and called the elders of the church.

18 And when they were come to him, he said unto them, Ye know, from the first day that I

came into Asia, after what manner I have been with you at all seasons,

19 Serving the Lord with all humility of mind, and with many tears, and temptations, which befell me by the lying in wait of the Jews:

20 And how I kept back nothing that was profitable unto you, but have showed you, and have taught you publicly, and from house to house,

21 Testifying both to the Jews, and also to the Greeks, repentance toward God, and faith ~~toward~~ *on the name of* our Lord Jesus Christ.

22 And now, behold, I go bound in the spirit unto Jerusalem, not knowing the things that shall befall me there:

23 Save that the Holy Ghost witnesseth in every city, saying that bonds and afflictions abide me.

24 But none of these things move me, neither count I my life dear unto myself, so that I might finish my course with joy, and the ministry, which I have received of the Lord Jesus, to testify the gospel of the grace of God.

25 And now, behold, I know that ye all, among whom I have gone preaching the kingdom of God, shall see my face no more.

26 Wherefore I take you to record this day, that I am pure from the blood of all men.

27 For I have not shunned to declare unto you all the counsel of God.

28 Take heed therefore unto yourselves, and to all the flock, over the which the Holy Ghost hath made you overseers, to feed the church of God, which he hath purchased with his own blood.

29 For I know this, that after my departing shall grievous wolves enter in among you, not sparing the flock.

30 Also of your own selves shall men arise, speaking perverse things, to draw away disciples after them.

31 Therefore watch, and remember, that by the space of three years I ceased not to warn every one night and day with tears.

32 And now, brethren, I commend you to God, and to the word of his grace, which is able to build you up, and to give you an inheritance among all them which are sanctified.

33 I have coveted no man's silver, or gold, or apparel.

34 Yea, ye yourselves know, that these hands have ministered unto my necessities, and to them that were with me.

35 I have showed you all things, how that so labouring ye ought to support the weak, and to remember the words of the Lord Jesus, how he said, It is more blessed to give than to receive.

36 And when he had thus spoken, he kneeled down, and prayed with them all.

37 And they all wept sore, and fell on Paul's neck, and kissed him,

38 Sorrowing most of all for the words

which he spake, that they should see his face no more. And they accompanied him unto the ship.

Chapter 21

1 And it came to pass, that after we were gotten from them, and had launched, we came with a straight course unto Coos, and the day following unto Rhodes, and from thence unto Patara:

2 And finding a ship sailing over unto Phenicia, we went aboard, and set forth.

3 Now when we had discovered Cyprus, we left it on the left hand, and sailed into Syria, and landed at Tyre: for there the ship was to unlade her burden.

4 And finding disciples, we tarried there seven days: who said to Paul through the Spirit, that he should not go up to Jerusalem.

5 And when we had accomplished those days, we departed and went our way; and they all brought us on our way, with wives and children, till we were out of the city: and we kneeled down on the shore, and prayed.

6 And when we had taken our leave one of another, we took ship; and they returned home again.

7 And when we had finished our course from Tyre, we came to Ptolemais, and saluted the brethren, and abode with them one day.

8 And the next day we that were of Paul's company departed, and came unto Caesarea: and we entered into the house of Philip the evangelist, which was one of the seven; and abode with him.

9 And the same man had four daughters, virgins, which did prophesy.

10 And as we tarried there many days, there came down from Judaea a certain prophet, named Agabus.

11 And when he was come unto us, he took Paul's girdle, and bound his own hands and feet, and said, Thus saith the Holy Ghost, So shall the Jews at Jerusalem bind the man that owneth this girdle, and shall deliver him into the hands of the Gentiles.

12 And when we heard these things, both we, and they of that place, besought him not to go up to Jerusalem.

13 Then Paul answered, What mean ye to weep and to break mine heart? for I am ready not to be bound only, but also to die at Jerusalem for the name of the Lord Jesus.

14 And when he would not be persuaded, we ceased, saying, The will of the Lord be done.

15 And after those days we took up our carriages, and went up to Jerusalem.

16 There went with us also certain of the disciples of Caesarea, and brought with them one

Mnason of Cyprus, an old disciple, with whom we should lodge.

17 And when we were come to Jerusalem, the brethren received us gladly.

18 And the day following Paul went in with us unto James; and all the elders were present.

19 And when he had saluted them, he declared particularly what things God had wrought among the Gentiles by his ministry.

20 And when they heard it, they glorified the Lord, and said unto him, Thou seest, brother, how many thousands of Jews there are which believe; and they are all zealous of the law:

21 And they are informed of thee, that thou teachest all the Jews which are among the Gentiles to forsake Moses, saying that they ought not to circumcise their children, neither to walk after the customs.

22 What is it therefore? the multitude must needs come together: for they will hear that thou art come.

23 Do therefore this that we say to thee: We have four men which have a vow on them;

24 Them take, and purify thyself with them, and be at charges with them, that they may shave their heads: and all may know that those things, whereof they were informed concerning thee, are nothing; but that thou thyself also walkest orderly, and keepest the law.

25 As touching the Gentiles which believe, we have written and concluded that they observe no such thing, save only that they keep themselves from things offered to idols, and from blood, and from *things* strangled, and from fornication.

26 Then Paul took the men, and the next day purifying himself with them entered into the temple, to signify the accomplishment of the days of purification, until that an offering should be offered for every one of them.

27 And when the seven days were almost ended, the Jews which were of Asia, when they saw him in the temple, stirred up all the people, and laid hands on him,

28 Crying out, Men of Israel, help: This is the man, that teacheth all men every where against the people, and the law, and this place: and further brought Greeks also into the temple, and hath polluted this holy place.

29 (For they had seen before with him in the city Trophimus an Ephesian, whom they supposed that Paul had brought into the temple.)

30 And all the city was moved, and the people ran together: and they took ~~Paul~~, and drew him out of the temple: and forthwith the doors were shut.

31 And as they went about to kill him, tidings came unto the chief captain of the band, that all Jerusalem was in an uproar.

32 Who immediately took soldiers and centurions, and ran down unto them: and when they saw the chief captain and the soldiers, they left beating of Paul.

33 Then the chief captain came near, and took him, and commanded him to be bound with two chains; and demanded who he was, and what he had done.

34 And some cried one thing, some another, among the multitude: and when he could not know the certainty for the tumult, he commanded him to be carried into the castle.

35 And when he came upon the stairs, so it was, that he was borne of the soldiers for the violence of the people.

36 For the multitude of the people followed after, crying, Away with him.

37 And as Paul was to be led into the castle, he said unto the chief captain, May I speak unto thee? Who said, Canst thou speak Greek?

38 Art not thou that Egyptian, which before these days madest an uproar, and leddest out into the wilderness four thousand men that were murderers?

39 But Paul said, I am a man which am a Jew of Tarsus, a city in Cilicia, a citizen of no mean city: and, I beseech thee, suffer me to speak unto the people.

40 And when he had given him licence, Paul stood on the stairs, and beckoned with the hand unto the people. And when there was made a great silence, he spake unto them in the Hebrew tongue, saying,

Chapter 22

1 Men, brethren, and fathers, hear ye my defence which I make now unto you.

2 (And when they heard that he spake in the Hebrew tongue to them, they kept the more silence: and he saith,)

3 I am verily a man which am a Jew, born in Tarsus, a city in Cilicia, yet brought up in this city at the feet of Gamaliel, and taught according to the perfect manner of the law of the fathers, and was zealous toward God, as ye all are this day.

4 And I persecuted this way unto the death, binding and delivering into prisons both men and women.

5 As also the high priest doth bear me witness, and all the estate of the elders: from whom also I received letters unto the brethren, and went to Damascus, to bring them which were there bound unto Jerusalem, for to be punished.

6 And it came to pass, that, as I made my journey, and was come nigh unto Damascus about noon, suddenly there shone from heaven a great light round about me.

7 And I fell unto the ground, and heard a voice saying unto me, Saul, Saul, why persecutest thou

me?

8 And I answered, Who art thou, Lord? And he said unto me, I am Jesus of Nazareth, whom thou persecutest.

9 And they that were with me saw indeed the light, and were afraid; but they heard not the voice of him that spake to me.

10 And I said, What shall I do, Lord? And the Lord said unto me, Arise, and go into Damascus; and there it shall be told thee of all things which are appointed ~~for~~ *of* thee to do.

11 And when I could not see for the glory of that light, being led by the hand of them that were with me, I came into Damascus.

12 And one Ananias, a devout man according to the law, having a good report of all the Jews which dwelt there,

13 Came unto me, and stood, and said unto me, Brother Saul, receive thy sight. And the same hour I looked up upon him.

14 And he said, The God of our fathers hath chosen thee, that thou shouldest know his will, and see that Just One, and shouldest hear the voice of his mouth.

15 For thou shalt be his witness unto all men of what thou hast seen and heard.

16 And now why tarriest thou? arise, and be baptized, and wash away thy sins, calling on the name of the Lord.

17 And it came to pass, that, when I was come again to Jerusalem, even while I prayed in the temple, I was in a trance;

18 And saw him saying unto me, Make haste, and get thee quickly out of Jerusalem: for they will not receive thy testimony concerning me.

19 And I said, Lord, they know that I imprisoned and beat in every synagogue them that believed on thee:

20 And when the blood of thy martyr Stephen was shed, I also was standing by, and consenting unto his death, and kept the raiment of them that slew him.

21 And he said unto me, Depart: for I will send thee far hence unto the Gentiles.

22 And they gave him audience unto this word, and then lifted up their voices, and said, Away with such a fellow from the earth: for it is not fit that he should live.

23 And as they cried out, and cast off their clothes, and threw dust into the air,

24 The chief captain commanded him to be brought into the castle, and bade that he should be examined by scourging; that he might know wherefore they cried so against him.

25 And as they bound him with thongs, Paul said unto the centurion that stood by, Is it lawful for you to scourge a man that is a Roman, and uncondemned?

26 When the centurion heard that, he went and told the chief captain, saying, Take heed what

thou doest: for this man is a Roman.

27 Then the chief captain came, and said unto him, Tell me, art thou a Roman? He said, Yea.

28 And the chief captain answered, With a great sum obtained I this freedom. And Paul said, But I was free born.

29 Then straightway they departed from him which should have examined him: and the chief captain also was afraid, after he knew that he was a Roman, ~~and~~ because he had bound him, *and he loosed him from his bands*.

30 On the morrow, because he would have known the certainty wherefore he was accused of the Jews, he ~~loosed him from his bands, and~~ commanded the chief priests and all their council to appear, and brought Paul down, and set him before them.

Chapter 23

1 And Paul, earnestly beholding the council, said, Men and brethren, I have lived in all good conscience before God until this day.

2 And the high priest Ananias commanded them that stood by him to smite him on the mouth.

3 Then said Paul unto him, God shall smite thee, thou whited wall: for sittest thou to judge me after the law, and commandest me to be smitten contrary to the law?

4 And they that stood by said, Revilest thou God's high priest?

5 Then said Paul, I ~~wist not~~ *did not know*, brethren, that he was the high priest: for it is written, Thou shalt not speak evil of the ruler of thy people.

6 But when Paul perceived that the one part were Sadducees, and the other Pharisees, he cried out in the council, Men and brethren, I am a Pharisee, the son of a Pharisee: of the hope and resurrection of the dead I am called in question.

7 And when he had so said, there arose a dissension between the Pharisees and the Sadducees: and the multitude was divided.

8 For the Sadducees say that there is no resurrection, neither angel, nor spirit: but the Pharisees confess both.

9 And there arose a great cry: and the scribes that were of the Pharisees' part arose, and strove, saying, We find no evil in this man: but if a spirit or an angel hath spoken to him, let us not fight against God.

10 And when there arose a great dissension, the chief captain, fearing lest Paul should have been pulled in pieces of them, commanded the soldiers to go down, and to take him by force from among them, and to bring him into the castle.

11 And the night following the Lord stood by

him, and said, Be of good cheer, Paul: for as thou hast testified of me in Jerusalem, so must thou bear witness also at Rome.

12 And when it was day, certain of the Jews banded together, and bound themselves under a curse, saying that they would neither eat nor drink till they had killed Paul.

13 And they were more than forty which had made this conspiracy.

14 And they came to the chief priests and elders, and said, We have bound ourselves under a great curse, that we will eat nothing until we have slain Paul.

15 Now therefore ye with the council signify to the chief captain that he bring him down unto you to morrow, as though ye would ~~inquire~~ *enquire* something more perfectly concerning him: and we, ~~or ever~~ *before* he come near, are ready to kill him.

16 And when Paul's sister's son heard of their lying in wait, he went and entered into the castle, and told Paul.

17 Then Paul called one of the centurions unto him, and said, Bring this young man unto the chief captain: for he hath a certain thing to tell him.

18 So he took him, and brought him to the chief captain, and said, Paul the prisoner called me unto him, and prayed me to bring this young man unto thee, who hath something to say unto thee.

19 Then the chief captain took him by the hand, and went with him aside privately, and asked him, What is that thou hast to tell me?

20 And he said, The Jews have agreed to desire thee that thou wouldest bring down Paul to morrow into the council, as though they would inquire somewhat of him more perfectly.

21 But do not thou yield unto them: for there lie in wait for him of them more than forty men, which have bound themselves with an oath, that they will neither eat nor drink till they have killed him: and now are they ready, looking for a promise from thee.

22 So the chief captain then let the young man depart, and charged him, See thou tell no man that thou hast showed these things to me.

23 And he called unto him two centurions, saying, Make ready two hundred soldiers to go to Caesarea, and horsemen threescore and ten, and spearmen two hundred, at the third hour of the night;

24 And provide them beasts, that they may set Paul on, and bring him safe unto Felix the governor.

25 And he wrote a letter after this manner:

26 Claudius Lysias unto the most excellent governor Felix sendeth greeting.

27 This man was taken of the Jews, and ~~should~~ *would* have been killed of them: then came I with an army, and rescued him, having understood that he was a Roman.

28 And when I would have known the cause wherefore they accused him, I brought him forth into their council:

29 Whom I perceived to be accused of questions of their law, but to have nothing laid to his charge worthy of death or of bonds.

30 And when it was told me how that the Jews laid wait for the man, I sent straightway to thee, and gave commandment to his accusers also to say before thee what they had against him. Farewell.

31 Then the soldiers, as it was commanded them, took Paul, and brought him by night to Antipatris.

32 On the morrow they left the horsemen to go with him, and returned to the castle:

33 Who, when they came to Caesarea, and delivered the epistle to the governor, presented Paul also before him.

34 And when the governor had read the letter, he asked of what province he was. And when he understood that he was of Cilicia;

35 I will hear thee, said he, when thine accusers are also come. And he commanded him to be kept in Herod's judgment hall.

Chapter 24

1 And after five days Ananias the high priest descended with the elders, and with a certain orator named Tertullus, who informed the governor against Paul.

2 And when he was called forth, Tertullus began to accuse him, saying, Seeing that by thee we enjoy great quietness, and that very worthy deeds are done unto this nation by thy providence,

3 We accept it always, and in all places, most noble Felix, with all thankfulness.

4 Notwithstanding, that I be not further tedious unto thee, I pray thee that thou wouldest hear us of thy clemency a few words.

5 For we have found this man a pestilent fellow, and a mover of sedition among all the Jews throughout the world, and a ringleader of the sect of the Nazarenes:

6 Who also hath gone about to profane the temple: whom we took, and would have judged according to our law.

7 But the chief captain Lysias came upon us, and with great violence took him away out of our hands,

8 Commanding his accusers to come unto thee: by examining of whom thyself mayest take knowledge of all these things, whereof we accuse him.

9 And the Jews also assented, saying that these things were so.

10 Then Paul, after that the governor had

beckoned unto him to speak, answered, Forasmuch as I know that thou hast been of many years a judge unto this nation, I do the more cheerfully answer for myself:

11 Because that thou mayest understand, that there are yet but twelve days since I went up to Jerusalem for to worship.

12 And they neither found me in the temple disputing with any man, neither raising up the people, neither in the synagogues, nor in the city:

13 Neither can they prove the things whereof they now accuse me.

14 But this I confess unto thee, that after the way which they call heresy, so worship I the God of my fathers, believing all things which are written in the law and in the prophets:

15 And have hope toward God, which they themselves also allow, that there shall be a resurrection of the dead, both of the just and unjust.

16 And herein do I exercise myself, to have always a conscience void of offence toward God, and toward men.

17 Now after many years I came to bring alms to my nation, and offerings.

18 Whereupon certain Jews from Asia found me purified in the temple, neither with multitude, nor with tumult.

19 Who ought to have been here before thee, and object, if they had ought against me.

20 Or else let these same here say, if they have found any evil doing in me, while I stood before the council,

21 Except it be for this one voice, that I cried standing among them, Touching the resurrection of the dead I am called in question by you this day.

22 And when Felix heard these things, having more perfect knowledge of that way, he deferred them, and said, When Lysias the chief captain shall come down, I will know the uttermost of your matter.

23 And he commanded a centurion to keep Paul, and to let him have liberty, and that he should forbid none of his acquaintance to minister or come unto him.

24 And after certain days, when Felix came with his wife Drusilla, which was a Jewess, he sent for Paul, and heard him concerning the faith in Christ.

25 And as he reasoned of righteousness, temperance, and judgment to come, Felix trembled, and answered, Go thy way for this time; when I have a convenient season, I will call for thee.

26 He hoped also that money should have been given him of Paul, that he might loose him: wherefore he sent for him the oftener, and communed with him.

27 But after two years Porcius Festus came into

Felix' room: and Felix, willing to show the Jews a pleasure, left Paul bound.

Chapter 25

1 Now when Festus was come into the province, after three days he ascended from Caesarea to Jerusalem.

2 Then the high priest and the chief of the Jews informed him against Paul, and besought him,

3 And desired favour against him, that he would send for him to Jerusalem, laying wait in the way to kill him.

4 But Festus answered, that Paul should be kept at Caesarea, and that he himself would depart shortly thither.

5 Let them therefore, said he, which among you are able, go down with me, and accuse this man, if there be any wickedness in him.

6 And when he had tarried among them more than ten days, he went down unto Caesarea; and the next day sitting on the judgment seat commanded Paul to be brought.

7 And when he was come, the Jews which came down from Jerusalem stood round about, and laid many and grievous complaints against Paul, which they could not prove.

8 While he answered for himself, Neither against the law of the Jews, neither against the temple, nor yet against Caesar, have I offended any thing at all.

9 But Festus, willing to do the Jews a pleasure, answered Paul, and said, Wilt thou go up to Jerusalem, and there be judged of these things before me?

10 Then said Paul, I stand at Caesar's judgment seat, where I ought to be judged: to the Jews have I done no wrong, as thou very well knowest.

11 For if I be an offender, or have committed any thing worthy of death, I refuse not to die: but if there be none of these things whereof these accuse me, no man may deliver me unto them. I appeal unto Caesar.

12 Then Festus, when he had conferred with the council, answered, Hast thou appealed unto Caesar? unto Caesar shalt thou go.

13 And after certain days king Agrippa and Bernice came unto Caesarea to salute Festus.

14 And when they had been there many days, Festus declared Paul's cause unto the king, saying, There is a certain man left in bonds by Felix:

15 About whom, when I was at Jerusalem, the chief priests and the elders of the Jews informed me, desiring to have judgment against him.

16 To whom I answered, It is not the manner of the Romans to deliver any man to die, before that he which is accused have the accusers face to

face, and have licence to answer for himself concerning the crime laid against him.

17 Therefore, when they were come hither, without any delay on the ~~morrow~~ *day following* I sat on the judgment seat, and commanded the man to be brought forth.

18 Against whom when the accusers stood up, they brought none accusation of such things as I supposed:

19 But had certain questions against him of their own superstition, and of one Jesus, which was dead, whom Paul affirmed to be alive.

20 And because I doubted of such manner of questions, I asked him whether he would go to Jerusalem, and there be judged of these matters.

21 But when Paul had appealed to be reserved unto the hearing of Augustus, I commanded him to be kept till I might send him to Caesar.

22 Then Agrippa said unto Festus, I would also hear the man myself. To morrow, said he, thou shalt hear him.

23 And on the morrow, when Agrippa was come, and Bernice, with great pomp, and was entered into the place of hearing, with the chief captains, and principal men of the city, at Festus' commandment Paul was brought forth.

24 And Festus said, King Agrippa, and all men which are here present with us, ye see this man, about whom all the multitude of the Jews have dealt with me, both at Jerusalem, and also here, crying that he ought not to live any longer.

25 But when I found that he had committed nothing worthy of death, and that he himself hath appealed to Augustus, I have determined to send him.

26 Of whom I have no certain thing to write unto my lord. Wherefore I have brought him forth before you, and specially before thee, O king Agrippa, that, after examination had, I might have somewhat to write.

27 For it seemeth to me unreasonable to send a prisoner, and not withal to signify the crimes laid against him.

Chapter 26

1 Then Agrippa said unto Paul, Thou art permitted to speak for thyself. Then Paul stretched forth the hand, and answered for himself:

2 I think myself happy, king Agrippa, because I shall answer for myself this day before thee touching all the things whereof I am accused of the Jews:

3 Especially because I know thee to be expert in all customs and questions which are among the Jews: wherefore I beseech thee to hear me patiently.

4 My manner of life from my youth, which was at the first among mine own nation at Jerusalem, know all the Jews;

5 Which knew me from the beginning, if they would testify, that after the most straitest sect of our religion I lived a Pharisee.

6 And now I stand and am judged for the hope of the promise made of God unto our fathers:

7 Unto which promise our twelve tribes, instantly serving God day and night, hope to come. For which hope's sake, king Agrippa, I am accused of the Jews.

8 Why should it be thought a thing incredible with you, that God should raise the dead?

9 I verily thought with myself, that I ought to do many things contrary to the name of Jesus of Nazareth.

10 Which thing I also did in Jerusalem: and many of the saints did I shut up in prison, having received authority from the chief priests; and when they were put to death, I gave my voice against them.

11 And I punished them oft in every synagogue, and compelled them to blaspheme; and being exceedingly mad against them, I persecuted them even unto strange cities.

12 Whereupon as I went to Damascus with authority and commission from the chief priests,

13 At midday, O king, I saw in the way a light from heaven, above the brightness of the sun, shining round about me and them which journeyed with me.

14 And when we were all fallen to the earth, I heard a voice speaking unto me, and saying in the Hebrew tongue, Saul, Saul, why persecutest thou me? it is hard for thee to kick against the pricks.

15 And I said, Who art thou, Lord? And he said, I am Jesus whom thou persecutest.

16 But rise, and stand upon thy feet: for I have appeared unto thee for this purpose, to make thee a minister and a witness both of these things which thou hast seen, and of those things in the which I will appear unto thee;

17 Delivering thee from the people, and from the Gentiles, unto whom now I send thee,

18 To open their eyes, and to turn them from darkness to light, and from the power of Satan unto God, that they may receive forgiveness of sins, and inheritance among them which are sanctified by faith that is in me.

19 Whereupon, O king Agrippa, I was not disobedient unto the heavenly vision:

20 But showed first unto them of Damascus, and at Jerusalem, and throughout all the coasts of Judaea, and then to the Gentiles, that they should repent and turn to God, and do works meet for repentance.

21 For these causes the Jews caught me in the temple, and went about to kill me.

22 Having therefore obtained help of God, I continue unto this day, witnessing both to small and great, saying none other things than those which the prophets and Moses did say should come:

23 That Christ should suffer, and that he should be the first that should rise from the dead, and should show light unto the people, and to the Gentiles.

24 And as he thus spake for himself, Festus said with a loud voice, Paul, thou art beside thyself; much learning doth make thee mad.

25 But he said, I am not mad, most noble Festus; but speak forth the words of truth and soberness.

26 For the king knoweth of these things, before whom also I speak freely: for I am persuaded that none of these things are hidden from him; for this thing was not done in a corner.

27 King Agrippa, believest thou the prophets? I know that thou believest.

28 Then Agrippa said unto Paul, Almost thou persuadest me to be a Christian.

29 And Paul said, I would to God, that not only thou, but also all that hear me this day, were both almost, and altogether such as I am, except these bonds.

30 And when he had thus spoken, the king rose up, and the governor, and Bernice, and they that sat with them:

31 And when they were gone aside, they talked between themselves, saying, This man doeth nothing worthy of death or of bonds.

32 Then said Agrippa unto Festus, This man might have been set at liberty, if he had not appealed unto Caesar.

Chapter 27

1 And when it was determined that we should sail into Italy, they delivered Paul and certain other prisoners unto one named Julius, a centurion of Augustus' band.

2 And entering into a ship of Adramyttium, we launched, meaning to sail by the coasts of Asia; one Aristarchus, a Macedonian of Thessalonica, being with us.

3 And the next day we touched at Sidon. And Julius courteously entreated Paul, and gave him liberty to go unto his friends to refresh himself.

4 And when we had launched from thence, we sailed under Cyprus, because the winds were contrary.

5 And when we had sailed over the sea of Cilicia and Pamphylia, we came to Myra, a city of Lycia.

6 And there the centurion found a ship of Alexandria sailing into Italy; and he put us therein.

7 And when we had sailed slowly many days, and scarce were come over against Cnidus, the wind not suffering us, we sailed under Crete, over against Salmone;

8 And, hardly passing it, came unto a place which is called The fair havens; nigh whereunto was the city of Lasea.

9 Now when much time was spent, and when sailing was now dangerous, because the fast was now already past, Paul admonished them,

10 And said unto them, Sirs, I perceive that this voyage will be with hurt and much damage, not only of the lading and ship, but also of our lives.

11 Nevertheless the centurion believed the master and the owner of the ship, more than those things which were spoken by Paul.

12 And because the haven was not commodious to winter in, the more part advised to depart thence also, if by any means they might attain to Phenice, and there to winter; which is an haven of Crete, and lieth toward the south west and north west.

13 And when the south wind blew softly, supposing that they had obtained their purpose, loosing thence, they sailed close by Crete.

14 But not long after there arose against it a tempestuous wind, called Euroclydon.

15 And when the ship was caught, and could not bear up into the wind, we let her drive.

16 And running under a certain island which is called Clauda, we had much work to come by the boat:

17 Which when they had taken up, they used helps, undergirding the ship; and, fearing lest they should fall into the quicksands, struck sail, and so were driven.

18 And we being exceedingly tossed with a tempest, the next day they lightened the ship;

19 And the third day we cast out with our own hands the tackling of the ship.

20 And when neither sun nor stars in many days appeared, and no small tempest lay on us, all hope that we should be saved was then taken away.

21 But after long abstinence Paul stood forth in the midst of them, and said, Sirs, ye should have hearkened unto me, and not have loosed from Crete, and to have gained this harm and loss.

22 And now I exhort you to be of good cheer: for there shall be no loss of any man's life among you, but of the ship.

23 For there stood by me this night the angel of God, whose I am, and whom I serve,

24 Saying, Fear not, Paul; thou must be brought before Caesar: and, lo, God hath given thee all them that sail with thee.

25 Wherefore, sirs, be of good cheer: for I believe God, that it shall be even as it was told me.

26 Howbeit we must be cast upon a certain island.

27 But when the fourteenth night was come, as we were driven up and down in Adria, about midnight the shipmen deemed that they drew near to some country;

28 And sounded, and found it twenty fathoms: and when they had gone a little further, they sounded again, and found it fifteen fathoms.

29 Then fearing lest we should have fallen upon rocks, they cast four anchors out of the stern, and wished for the day.

30 And as the shipmen were about to flee out of the ship, when they had let down the boat into the sea, under colour as though they would have cast anchors out of the foreship,

31 Paul said to the centurion and to the soldiers, Except these abide in the ship, ye cannot be saved.

32 Then the soldiers cut off the ropes of the boat, and let her fall off.

33 And while the day was coming on, Paul besought them all to take meat, saying, This day is the fourteenth day that ye have tarried and continued fasting, having taken nothing.

34 Wherefore I pray you to take some meat: for this is for your health: for there shall not an hair fall from the head of any of you.

35 And when he had thus spoken, he took bread, and gave thanks to God in presence of them all: and when he had broken it, he began to eat.

36 Then were they all of good cheer, and they also took some meat.

37 And we were in all in the ship two hundred threescore and sixteen souls.

38 And when they had eaten enough, they lightened the ship, and cast out the wheat into the sea.

39 And when it was day, they knew not the land: but they discovered a certain creek with a shore, into the which they were minded, if it were possible, to thrust in the ship.

40 And when they had taken up the anchors, they committed themselves unto the sea, and loosed the rudder bands, and hoisted up the mainsail to the wind, and made toward shore.

41 And falling into a place where two seas met, they ran the ship aground; and the forepart stuck fast, and remained unmoveable, but the hinder part was broken with the violence of the waves.

42 And the soldiers' counsel was to kill the prisoners, lest any of them should swim out, and escape.

43 But the centurion, willing to save Paul, kept them from their purpose; and commanded that they which could swim should cast themselves first into the sea, and get to land:

44 And the rest, some on boards, and some on broken pieces of the ship. And so it came to pass, that they escaped all safe to land.

Chapter 28

1 And when they were escaped, then they knew that the island was called Melita.

2 And the barbarous people showed us no little kindness: for they kindled a fire, and received us every one, because of the present rain, and because of the cold.

3 And when Paul had gathered a bundle of sticks, and laid them on the fire, there came a viper out of the heat, and fastened on his hand.

4 And when the barbarians saw the venomous beast hang on his hand, they said among themselves, No doubt this man is a murderer, whom, though he hath escaped the sea, yet vengeance suffereth not to live.

5 And he shook off the beast into the fire, and felt no harm.

6 Howbeit they looked when he should have swollen, or fallen down dead suddenly: but after they had looked a great while, and saw no harm come to him, they changed their minds, and said that he was a god.

7 In the same quarters were possessions of the chief man of the island, whose name was Publius; who received us, and lodged us three days courteously.

8 And it came to pass, that the father of Publius lay sick of a fever and of a bloody flux: to whom Paul entered in, and prayed, and laid his hands on him, and healed him.

9 So when this was done, others also, which had diseases in the island, came, and were healed:

10 Who also honoured us with many honours; and when we departed, they laded us with such things as were necessary.

11 And after three months we departed in a ship of Alexandria, which had wintered in the isle, whose sign was Castor and Pollux.

12 And landing at Syracuse, we tarried there three days.

13 And from thence we fetched a compass, and came to Rhegium: and after one day the south wind blew, and we came the next day to Puteoli:

14 Where we found brethren, and were desired to tarry with them seven days: and so we went toward Rome.

15 And from thence, when the brethren heard of us, they came to meet us as far as Appii forum, and The three taverns: whom when Paul saw, he thanked God, and took courage.

16 And when we came to Rome, the centurion delivered the prisoners to the captain of the guard: but Paul was suffered to dwell by himself with a soldier that kept him.

17 And it came to pass, that after three days Paul called the chief of the Jews together: and when they were come together, he said unto them, Men and brethren, though I have

committed nothing against the people, or customs of our fathers, yet was I delivered prisoner from Jerusalem into the hands of the Romans.

18 Who, when they had examined me, would have let me go, because there was no cause of death in me.

19 But when the Jews spake against it, I was constrained to appeal unto Caesar; not that I had ought to accuse my nation of.

20 For this cause therefore have I called for you, to see you, and to speak with you: because that for the hope of Israel I am bound with this chain.

21 And they said unto him, We neither received letters out of Judaea concerning thee, neither any of the brethren that came showed or spake any harm of thee.

22 But we desire to hear of thee what thou thinkest: for as concerning this sect, we know that every where it is spoken against.

23 And when they had appointed him a day, there came many to him into his lodging; to whom he expounded and testified the kingdom of God, persuading them concerning Jesus, both out of the law of Moses, and out of the prophets, from morning till evening.

24 And some believed the things which were spoken, and some believed not.

25 And when they agreed not among themselves, they departed, after that Paul had spoken one word, Well spake the Holy Ghost by Esaias the prophet unto our fathers,

26 Saying, Go unto this people, and say, Hearing ye shall hear, and shall not understand; and seeing ye shall see, and not perceive:

27 For the heart of this people is waxed gross, and their ears are dull of hearing, and their eyes have they closed; lest they should see with their eyes, and hear with their ears, and understand with their heart, and should be converted, and I should heal them.

28 Be it known therefore unto you, that the salvation of God is sent unto the Gentiles, and that they will hear it.

29 And when he had said these words, the Jews departed, and had great reasoning among themselves.

30 And Paul dwelt two whole years in his own hired house, and received all that came in unto him,

31 Preaching the kingdom of God, and teaching those things which concern the Lord Jesus Christ, with all confidence, no man forbidding him.

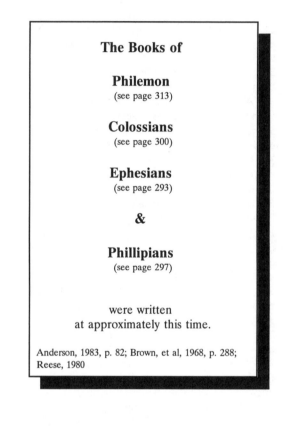

The Books of

Philemon
(see page 313)

Colossians
(see page 300)

Ephesians
(see page 293)

&

Phillipians
(see page 297)

were written
at approximately this time.

Anderson, 1983, p. 82; Brown, et al, 1968, p. 288; Reese, 1980

Chapter 1

1 Paul, *an apostle,* a servant of ~~Jesus Christ~~ *God,* called ~~to be an apostle~~ *of Jesus Christ, and* separated ~~un~~to preach the gospel ~~of God,~~

2 (Which he had promised ~~afore~~ *before* by his prophets in the holy scriptures,)

3 Concerning his Son Jesus Christ our Lord, which was made of the seed of David according to the flesh;

4 And declared ~~to be~~ the Son of God with power, *by the Spirit* according to the ~~spirit of holiness, by~~ truth through the resurrection from the dead:

5 By whom we have received grace and apostleship, ~~for~~ *through* obedience ~~to the~~ and faith *in his name, to preach the gospel* among all nations, ~~for his name~~:

6 Among whom ~~are~~ ye also ~~the~~ *are* called of Jesus Christ:

7 *Wherefore I write* To all ~~that be~~ *who are* in Rome, beloved of God, called ~~to be~~ saints: Grace to you and peace from God our Father, and the Lord Jesus Christ.

8 First, I thank my God through Jesus Christ, *that* ~~for~~ you all *are steadfast,* ~~that~~ *and* your faith is spoken of throughout the whole world.

9 For God is my witness, whom I serve, *that without ceasing I make mention of you always in my prayers, that you may be kept* ~~with my spirit~~ *through the Spirit* in the gospel of his Son, ~~that without ceasing I make mention of you always in my prayers;~~

10 Making request *of you, to remember me in your prayers, I now write unto you, that you will ask him in faith, that* if by any means ~~now~~ at length I ~~might~~ *may serve you with my labors, and may* have a prosperous journey by the will of God to come unto you.

11 For I long to see you, that I may impart unto you some spiritual gift, ~~to the end ye~~ *that it* may be established *in you to the end*;

12 That ~~is,~~ *I* may be comforted together with you by the mutual faith both of you and me.

13 Now I would not have you ignorant, brethren, that oftentimes I purposed to come unto you, (but was ~~let~~ *hindered* hitherto,) that I might have some fruit among you also, even as among other Gentiles.

14 I am debtor both to the Greeks, and to the Barbarians; both to the wise, and to the unwise.

15 ~~So~~ *And,* as much as in me is, I am ready to preach the gospel to you that are at Rome also.

16 For I am not ashamed of the gospel of Christ: for it is the power of God unto salvation to every one that believeth; to the Jew first, and also to the Greek.

17 For therein is the righteousness of God revealed ~~from faith to faith:~~ *through faith on his* name; as it is written, The just shall live by faith.

18 For the wrath of God is revealed from heaven against all ungodliness and unrighteousness of men, who ~~hold~~ *love not* the truth , *but remain* in unrighteousness;

19 ~~Because~~ *After* that which may be known of God is manifest ~~in~~ *to* them; ~~for God hath showed it unto them.~~

20 For *God hath revealed unto them* the invisible things of him from the creation of the world, *which* are clearly seen, *; things which are not seen* being understood by the things that are made, ~~even~~ *through* his eternal power and Godhead; so that they are without excuse:

21 Because that, when they knew God, they glorified him not as God, neither were they thankful; but became vain in their imaginations, and their foolish heart*s were* ~~was~~ darkened.

22 Professing themselves to be wise, they became fools,

23 And changed the glory of the uncorruptible God into an image made like to corruptible man, and to birds, and fourfooted beasts, and creeping things.

24 Wherefore God also gave them up to uncleanness through the lusts of their own hearts, to dishonour their own bodies between themselves:

25 Who changed the truth of God into a lie, and worshipped and served the creature more than the Creator, who is blessed for ever. Amen.

26 For this cause God gave them up unto vile affections: for even their women did change the natural use into that which is against nature:

27 And likewise also the men, leaving the natural use of the woman, burned in their lust one toward another; men with men working that which is unseemly, and receiving in themselves that recompense of their error which was meet.

28 And even as they did not like to retain God ~~in their~~ *according to some* knowledge, God gave them over to a reprobate mind, to do those things which are not convenient;

29 Being filled with all unrighteousness, fornication, wickedness, covetousness, maliciousness; full of envy, murder, debate, deceit, malignity; whisperers,

30 Backbiters, haters of God, despiteful, proud, boasters, inventors of evil things, disobedient to parents,

31 Without understanding, covenantbreakers, without natural affection, implacable, unmerciful:

32 ~~Who~~ *And some who,* knowing the judgment of God, that they which commit such things are worthy of death, *are inexcusable,* not only do the same, but have pleasure in them that do them.

Chapter 2

1 Therefore thou art inexcusable, O man, whosoever thou art that *thus* judgest: for wherein thou judgest another, thou condemnest thyself; for thou that judgest doest the same things.

2 But we are sure that the judgment of God is according to truth against them which commit such things.

3 And thinkest thou this, O man, that judgest them which do such things, and doest the same, that thou shalt escape the judgment of God?

4 Or despisest thou the riches of his goodness and forbearance and longsuffering; not knowing that the goodness of God leadeth thee to repentance?

5 But after thy hardness and impenitent heart treasurest up unto thyself wrath against the day of wrath and revelation of the righteous judgment of God;

6 Who will render to every man according to his deeds:

7 To them who by patient continuance in well doing seek for glory and honour and immortality, eternal life:

8 But unto them that are contentious, and do not obey the truth, but obey unrighteousness, indignation and wrath,

9 Tribulation and anguish, upon every soul of man that doeth evil, of the Jew first, and also of the Gentile;

10 But glory, honour, and peace, to every man that worketh good, to the Jew first, and also to the Gentile:

11 For there is no respect of persons with God.

12 For as many as have sinned without law shall also perish without law: and as many as have sinned in the law shall be judged by the law;

13 (For not the hearers of the law are just before God, but the doers of the law shall be justified.

14 For when the Gentiles, which have not the law, do by nature the things contained in the law, these, having not the law, are a law unto themselves:

15 Which show the work of the law written in their hearts, their conscience also bearing witness, and their thoughts the mean while accusing or else excusing one another;)

16 In the day when God shall judge the secrets of men by Jesus Christ according to ~~my~~ *the* gospel.

17 Behold, thou art called a Jew, and restest in the law, and makest thy boast of God,

18 And knowest his will, and approvest the things that are more excellent, being instructed out of the law;

19 And art confident that thou thyself art a guide of the blind, a light of them which are in darkness,

20 An instructor of the foolish, a teacher of babes, which hast the form of knowledge and of the truth in the law.

21 Thou therefore which teachest another, teachest thou not thyself? thou that preachest a man should not steal, dost thou steal?

22 Thou that sayest a man should not commit adultery, dost thou commit adultery? thou that abhorrest idols, dost thou commit sacrilege?

23 Thou that makest thy boast of the law, through breaking the law dishonourest thou God?

24 For the name of God is blasphemed among the Gentiles through you, as it is written.

25 For circumcision verily profiteth, if thou keep the law: but if thou be a breaker of the law, thy circumcision is made uncircumcision.

26 Therefore if the uncircumcision keep the righteousness of the law, shall not his uncircumcision be counted for circumcision?

27 And shall not uncircumcision which is by nature, if it fulfil the law, judge thee, who by the letter and circumcision dost transgress the law?

28 For he is not a Jew, which is one outwardly; neither is that circumcision, which is outward in the flesh:

29 But he is a Jew, which is one inwardly; and circumcision is that of the heart, in the spirit, and not in the letter; whose praise is not of men, but of God.

Chapter 3

1 What advantage then hath the Jew *over the Gentile*? or what profit ~~is there~~ of circumcision , *who is not a Jew from the heart*?

2 *But he who is a Jew from the heart, I say hath* Much every way: chiefly, because that unto them were committed the oracles of God.

3 For what if some did not believe? shall their unbelief make the faith of God without effect?

4 God forbid: yea, let God be true, but every man a liar; as it is written, That thou mightest be justified in thy sayings, and mightest overcome when thou art judged.

5 But if *we remain in* our unrighteousness *and* commend the righteousness of God, ~~what shall we say? Is~~ *how dare we say,* God *is* unrighteous who taketh vengeance? (I speak as a man *who fears God,*)

6 God forbid: for then how shall God judge the world?

7 For if the truth of God hath more abounded through my lie , *(as it is called of the Jews,)* unto his glory; why yet am I also judged as a sinner? *and not received?*

8 ~~And not rather, (as we be~~ *Because we are* slanderously reported, and ~~as~~ some affirm that we

say, *(whose damnation is just,)* Let us do evil, that good may come ~~? whose damnation is just~~ *But this is false*.

9 *If not so;* ~~Ww~~hat then~~?~~ are we better than they? No, in no wise: for we have ~~before~~ proved *before, that* ~~both~~ Jews and Gentiles~~, that they~~ are all under sin;

10 As it is written, There is none righteous, no, not one:

11 There is none that understandeth, there is none that seeketh after God.

12 They are all gone out of the way, they are together become unprofitable; there is none that doeth good, no, not one.

13 Their throat is an open sepulchre; with their tongues they have used deceit; the poison of asps is under their lips:

14 Whose mouth is full of cursing and bitterness:

15 Their feet are swift to shed blood:

16 Destruction and misery are in their ways:

17 And the way of peace have they not known:

18 There is no fear of God before their eyes.

19 Now we know that what things soever the law saith, it saith to them who are under the law: that every mouth may be stopped, and all the world may become guilty before God.

20 *For by the law is the knowledge of sin;* ~~T~~therefore by the deeds of the law ~~there~~ shall no flesh be justified in his sight~~: for by the law is the knowledge of sin~~.

21 But now the righteousness of God without the law is manifested, being witnessed by the law and the prophets;

22 Even the righteousness of God which is by faith of Jesus Christ unto all and upon all them that believe: for there is no difference:

23 For all have sinned, and come short of the glory of God;

24 *Therefore* ~~Bb~~eing justified ~~freely~~ *only* by his grace through the redemption that is in Christ Jesus:

25 Whom God hath set forth to be a propitiation through faith in his blood, to declare his righteousness for the remission of sins that are past, through the forbearance of God;

26 To declare, I say, at this time his righteousness: that he might be just, and the justifier of him which believeth in Jesus.

27 Where is boasting then? It is excluded. By what law? of works? Nay: but by the law of faith.

28 Therefore we conclude that a man is justified by faith *alone* without the deeds of the law.

29 Is he the God of the Jews only? is he not also of the Gentiles? Yes, of the Gentiles also:

30 Seeing ~~it is one~~ *that* God~~, which shall~~ *will* justify the circumcision by faith, and uncircumcision through faith.

31 Do we then make void the law through faith? God forbid: yea, we establish the law.

Chapter 4

1 What shall we say then that Abraham our father, as pertaining to the flesh, hath found?

2 For if Abraham were justified by *the law of* works, he hath ~~whereof~~ to glory *in himself*; but not ~~before~~ *of* God.

3 For what saith the scripture? Abraham believed God, and it was counted unto him for righteousness.

4 Now to him ~~that worketh~~ *who is justified by the law of works,* is the reward ~~not~~ reckoned *, not* of grace, but of debt.

5 But to him that ~~worketh not~~ *seeketh not to be justified by the law of works,* but believeth on him ~~that~~ *who* justifieth *not* the ungodly, his faith is counted for righteousness.

6 Even as David also describeth the blessedness of the man, unto whom God imputeth righteousness without *the law of* works,

7 Saying, Blessed are they *through faith* whose iniquities are forgiven, and whose sins are covered.

8 Blessed is the man to whom the Lord will not impute sin.

9 Cometh this blessedness then upon the circumcision only, or upon the uncircumcision also? for we say that faith was reckoned to Abraham for righteousness.

10 How was it then reckoned? when he was in circumcision, or in uncircumcision? Not in circumcision, but in uncircumcision.

11 And he received the sign of circumcision, a seal of the righteousness of the faith which he had yet being uncircumcised: that he might be the father of all them that believe, though they be not circumcised; that righteousness might be imputed unto them also:

12 And the father of circumcision to them who are not of the circumcision only, but who also walk in the steps of that faith of our father Abraham, which he had being yet uncircumcised.

13 For the promise, that he should be the heir of the world, was not to Abraham, or to his seed, through the law, but through the righteousness of faith.

14 For if they which are of the law be heirs, faith is made void, and the promise made of none effect:

15 Because the law worketh wrath: for where no law is, there is no transgression.

16 Therefore ~~it is~~ *ye are justified* of faith *and works,* ~~that it might be by~~ *through* grace; to the end the promise might be sure to all the seed; not to ~~that~~ *them* only ~~which is~~ *who are* of the law, but to ~~that~~ *them* also ~~which is~~ *who are* of the faith of Abraham; who is the father of us all,

17 (As it is written, I have made thee a father of many nations,) before him whom he believed,

even God, who quickeneth the dead, and calleth those things which be not as though they were.

18 Who against hope believed in hope, that he might become the father of many nations, according to that which was spoken, So shall thy seed be.

19 And being not weak in faith, he considered not his own body now dead, when he was about an hundred years old, neither yet the deadness of Sarah's womb:

20 He staggered not at the promise of God through unbelief; but was strong in faith, giving glory to God;

21 And being fully persuaded that, what he had promised, he was able also to perform.

22 And therefore it was imputed to him for righteousness.

23 Now it was not written for his sake alone, that it was imputed to him;

24 But for us also, to whom it shall be imputed, if we believe on him that raised up Jesus our Lord from the dead;

25 Who was delivered for our offences, and was raised again for our justification.

Chapter 5

1 Therefore being justified by faith, we have peace with God through our Lord Jesus Christ:

2 By whom also we have access by faith into this grace wherein we stand, and rejoice in hope of the glory of God.

3 And not only so *this*, but we glory in tribulations also: knowing that tribulation worketh patience;

4 And patience, experience; and experience, hope:

5 And hope maketh not ashamed; because the love of God is shed abroad in our hearts by the Holy Ghost which is given unto us.

6 For when we were yet without strength, in due time Christ died for the ungodly.

7 For scarcely for a righteous man will one die: yet peradventure for a good man some would even dare to die.

8 But God commendeth his love toward us, in that, while we were yet sinners, Christ died for us.

9 Much more then, being now justified by his blood, we shall be saved from wrath through him.

10 For if, when we were enemies, we were reconciled to God by the death of his Son, much more, being reconciled, we shall be saved by his life.

11 And not only so, but we also joy in God through our Lord Jesus Christ, by whom we have now received the atonement.

12 Wherefore, as by one man sin entered into the world, and death by sin; and so death passed upon all men, for that all have sinned:

13 (For until , *before* the law sin was in the world: but *yet* sin is not imputed when there is *to those who have* no law.

14 Nevertheless death reigned from Adam to Moses, even over them that had not sinned after the similitude of Adam's transgression, who is the figure of him that was to come. *For I say, that through the offence, death reigned over all.*

15 But not as the offence, so also is *not as* the free gift , *for the gift aboundeth*. For if through the offence of one many be dead, much more the grace of God, and the gift by grace, which is *hath abounded* by one man, Jesus Christ, hath abounded unto many.

16 And not as it was , by one that sinned, so is the gift: for the judgment was *is* by one to condemnation, but the free gift is of many offences unto justification.

17 For if by one man's offence death reigned by one; much more they which receive abundance of grace and of the gift of righteousness shall reign in life by one, Jesus Christ.)

18 Therefore as by the offence of one judgment came upon all men to condemnation; even so by the righteousness of one the free gift came upon all men unto justification of life.

19 For as by one man's disobedience many were made sinners, so by the obedience of one shall many be made righteous.

20 Moreover the law entered, that the offence might abound. But where sin abounded, grace did much more abound:

21 That as sin hath reigned unto death, even so might grace reign through righteousness unto eternal life by Jesus Christ our Lord.

Chapter 6

1 What shall we say then? Shall we continue in sin, that grace may abound?

2 God forbid. How shall we, that are dead to sin, live any longer therein?

3 Know ye not, that so many of us as were baptized into Jesus Christ were baptized into his death?

4 Therefore we are buried with him by baptism into death: that like as Christ was raised up from the dead by the glory of the Father, even so we also should walk in newness of life.

5 For if we have been planted together in the likeness of his death, we shall be also in the likeness of his resurrection:

6 Knowing this, that our old man is crucified with him, that the body of sin might be destroyed, that henceforth we should not serve sin.

7 For he that is dead *to sin* is freed from sin.

8 Now if we be dead with Christ, we believe that we shall also live with him:

9 Knowing that Christ being raised from the dead dieth no more; death hath no more dominion over him.

10 For in that he died, he died unto sin once: but in that he liveth, he liveth unto God.

11 Likewise reckon ye also yourselves to be dead indeed unto sin, but alive unto God through Jesus Christ our Lord.

12 Let not sin therefore reign in your mortal body, that ye should obey it in the lusts thereof.

13 Neither yield ye your members as instruments of unrighteousness unto sin: but yield yourselves unto God, as those that are alive from the dead, and your members as instruments of righteousness unto God.

14 For *in so doing* sin shall not have dominion over you: for ye are not under the law, but under grace.

15 What then? shall we sin, because we are not under the law, but under grace? God forbid.

16 Know ye not, that to whom ye yield yourselves servants to obey, his servants ye are to whom ye obey; whether of sin unto death, or of obedience unto righteousness?

17 But God be thanked, that ye ~~were~~ *are not* the servants of sin, ~~but~~ *for* ye have obeyed from the heart that form of doctrine which was delivered you.

18 Being then made free from sin, ye became the servants of righteousness.

19 I speak after the manner of men because of the infirmity of your flesh: for as ye have *in times past* yielded your members servants to uncleanness and to iniquity unto iniquity; even so now yield your members servants to righteousness unto holiness.

20 For when ye were the servants of sin, ye were free from righteousness.

21 What fruit had ye then in those things whereof ye are now ashamed? for the end of those things is death.

22 But now being made free from sin, and become servants to God, ye have your fruit unto holiness, and the end everlasting life.

23 For the wages of sin is death; but the gift of God is eternal life through Jesus Christ our Lord.

Chapter 7

1 Know ye not, brethren, (for I speak to them that know the law,) how that the law hath dominion over a man *only* as long as he liveth?

2 For the woman which hath an husband is bound by the law to her husband ~~so~~ *only as* long as he liveth; ~~but~~ *for* if the husband be dead, she is loosed from the law of her husband.

3 So then if, while her husband liveth, she be married to another man, she shall be called an adulteress: but if her husband be dead, she is free from that law; so that she is no adulteress, though she be married to another man.

4 Wherefore, my brethren, ye also are become dead to the law by the body of Christ; that ye should be married to another, even to him who is raised from the dead, that we should bring forth fruit unto God.

5 For when we were in the flesh, the motions of sins, which were ~~by~~ *not according to* the law, did work in our members to bring forth fruit unto death.

6 But now we are delivered from the law~~, that being dead~~ wherein we were held~~;~~ *, being dead to the law,* that we should serve in newness of spirit, and not in the oldness of the letter.

7 What shall we say then? is the law sin? God forbid. Nay, I had not known sin, but by the law: for I had not known lust, except the law had said, Thou shalt not covet.

8 But sin, taking occasion by the commandment, wrought in me all manner of concupiscence. For without the law sin was dead.

9 For *once* I was alive without *transgression of* the law ~~once:~~ *,* but when the commandment *of Christ* came, sin revived, and I died.

10 And *when I believed not* the commandment *of Christ which came*, which was ordained to life, I found ~~to be~~ *it condemned me* unto death.

11 For sin, taking occasion ~~by~~ *, denied* the commandment, *and* deceived me, and by it ~~slew me~~ *I was slain*.

12 ~~Wherefore~~ *Nevertheless, I found* the law ~~is~~ *to be* holy, and the commandment *to be* holy, and just, and good.

13 Was then that which is good made death unto me? God forbid. But sin, that it might appear sin~~, working death in me~~ by that which is good *working death in me*; that sin by the commandment might become exceeding sinful.

14 For we know that the ~~law~~ *commandment* is spiritual: but *when I was under the law,* I ~~am~~ *was yet* carnal, sold under sin.

15 *But now I am spiritual;* ~~F~~*f*or that which *I am commanded to do,* I do*; and that which I am commanded not to allow,* I allow not: for what I ~~would~~ *know is not right,* ~~that do I not~~ *I would not do*; ~~but what~~ *for that which is sin,* I hate~~, that do I~~.

16 If then I do *not* that which I would not *allow,* I consent unto the law that it is good*; and I am not condemned*.

17 Now then it is no more I that do ~~it~~ *sin*, but *I seek to subdue that* sin ~~that~~ *which* dwelleth in me.

18 For I know that in me ~~(~~ that is, in my flesh, ~~)~~ dwelleth no good thing: for to will is present with me; but ~~how~~ to perform that which is good

I find not, *only in Christ*.

19 For the good that I would *have done when under the law, I find not to be good; therefore,* I do *it* not: but the evil which I would not *do under the law, I find to be good*, that I do.

20 Now if I do that, *through the assistance of Christ,* I would not *do under the law, I am not under the law, and* it is no more ~~I~~ that *I seek to* do ~~it~~ *wrong,* but *to subdue* sin that dwelleth in me.

21 I find then ~~a~~ *that under the* law, that, when I would do good, evil ~~is~~ *was* present with me.

22 For I delight in the law of God after the inward man:

23 ~~But~~ *And now* I see another law, *even the commandment of Christ, and it is imprinted in my mind. But* ~~in~~ my members, *are* warring against the law of my mind, and bringing me into captivity to the law of sin which is in my members.

24 *And if I subdue not the sin which is in me, but with the flesh serve the law of sin;* O wretched man that I am! who shall deliver me from the body of this death?

25 I thank God through Jesus Christ our Lord, *then,* ~~So then~~ *that so* with the mind I myself serve the law of God; ~~but with the flesh the law of sin.~~

Chapter 8

1 There is therefore now no condemnation to them which are in Christ Jesus, who walk not after the flesh, but after the Spirit.

2 For the law of the Spirit of life in Christ Jesus hath made me free from the law of sin and death.

3 For what the law could not do, in that it was weak through the flesh, God sending his own Son in the likeness of sinful flesh, and for sin, condemned sin in the flesh:

4 That the righteousness of the law might be fulfilled in us, who walk not after the flesh, but after the Spirit.

5 For they that are after the flesh do mind the things of the flesh; but they that are after the Spirit the things of the Spirit.

6 For to be carnally minded is death; but to be spiritually minded is life and peace.

7 Because the carnal mind is enmity against God: for it is not subject to the law of God, neither indeed can be.

8 So then they that are ~~in~~ *after* the flesh cannot please God.

9 But ye are not ~~in~~ *after* the flesh, but ~~in~~ *after* the Spirit, if so be that the Spirit of God dwell in you. Now if any man have not the Spirit of Christ, he is none of his.

10 And if Christ be in you, *though* the body ~~is dead~~ *shall die* because of sin; ~~but~~ *yet* the Spirit is

life because of righteousness.

11 ~~But~~ *And* if the Spirit of him that raised up Jesus from the dead dwell in you, he that raised up Christ from the dead shall also quicken your mortal bodies by his Spirit that dwelleth in you.

12 Therefore, brethren, we are debtors, not to the flesh, to live after the flesh.

13 For if ye live after the flesh, *unto sin,* ye shall die: but if ye through the Spirit do mortify the deeds of the body, ye shall live *unto Christ*.

14 For as many as are led by the Spirit of God, they are the sons of God.

15 For ye have not received the spirit of bondage again to fear; but ye have received the Spirit of adoption, whereby we cry, Abba, Father.

16 The Spirit itself beareth witness with our spirit, that we are the children of God:

17 And if children, then heirs; heirs of God, and joint-heirs with Christ; if so be that we suffer with him, that we may be also glorified together.

18 For I reckon that the sufferings of this present time are not worthy to be ~~compared~~ *named* with the glory which shall be revealed in us.

19 For the earnest expectation of the creature waiteth for the manifestation of the sons of God.

20 For the creature was made subject to ~~vanity,~~ *tribulation* not willingly, but by reason of him who hath subjected ~~the same~~ *it* in hope,

21 Because the creature itself also shall be delivered from the bondage of corruption into the glorious liberty of the children of God.

22 For we know that the whole creation groaneth and travaileth in pain together until now.

23 And not only they, but ourselves also, which have the firstfruits of the Spirit, even we ourselves groan within ourselves, waiting for the adoption, to wit, the redemption of our body.

24 For we are saved by hope: but hope that is seen is not hope: for what a man seeth, why doth he yet hope for?

25 But if we hope for that we see not, then ~~do we~~ with patience *we do* wait for it.

26 Likewise the Spirit also helpeth our infirmities: for we know not what we should pray for as we ought: but the Spirit itself maketh intercession for us with groanings which cannot be uttered.

27 And he that searcheth the hearts knoweth what is the mind of the Spirit, because he maketh intercession for the saints according to the will of God.

28 And we know that all things work together for good to them that love God, to them who are the called according to his purpose.

29 For *him* whom he did foreknow, he also did predestinate to be conformed to ~~the~~ *his own* image ~~of his Son,~~ that he might be the firstborn

among many brethren.

30 Moreover, *him* whom he did predestinate, ~~them~~ *him* he also called: and *him* whom he called, ~~them~~ *him* he also ~~justified~~ *sanctified*: and *him* whom he ~~justified~~ *sanctified*, ~~them~~ *him* he also glorified.

31 What shall we then say to these things? If God be for us, who can ~~be~~ *prevail* against us?

32 He that spared not his own Son, but delivered him up for us all, how shall he not with him also freely give us all things?

33 Who shall lay any thing to the charge of God's elect? It is God that justifieth.

34 Who is he that condemneth? It is Christ that died, yea rather, that is risen again, who is even at the right hand of God, who also maketh intercession for us.

35 Who shall separate us from the love of Christ? shall tribulation, or distress, or persecution, or famine, or nakedness, or peril, or sword?

36 As it is written, For thy sake we are killed all the day long; we are accounted as sheep for the slaughter.

37 Nay, in all these things we are more than conquerors through him that loved us.

38 For I am persuaded, that neither death, nor life, nor angels, nor principalities, nor powers, nor things present, nor things to come,

39 Nor height, nor depth, nor any other creature, shall be able to separate us from the love of God, which is in Christ Jesus our Lord.

Chapter 9

1 I say the truth in Christ, I lie not, my conscience also bearing me witness in the Holy Ghost,

2 That I have great heaviness and continual sorrow in my heart.

3 ~~For~~ *(For once* I could ~~wish~~ *have wished* that myself were accursed from Christ,*)* for my brethren, my kinsmen according to the flesh:

4 Who are Israelites; ~~to~~ *of* whom ~~pertaineth~~ *are* the adoption, and the glory, and the covenants, and the giving of the law, and the service of God, and the promises *which are made unto the fathers*;

5 ~~Whose are the fathers,~~ and of whom as concerning the flesh , Christ ~~came~~ *was*, who is *God* over all, ~~God~~ blessed for ever. Amen.

6 Not as though the word of God hath taken none effect. For they are not all Israel, which are of Israel:

7 Neither, because they are ~~the seed~~ *all children* of Abraham, are they ~~all children~~ *the seed*: but, In Isaac shall thy seed be called.

8 That is, They which are the children of the flesh, these are not the children of God: but the children of the promise are counted for the seed.

9 For this is the word of promise, At this time will I come, and Sarah shall have a son.

10 And not only ~~this~~ *Sarah*; but when Rebecca also had conceived by one, ~~even by~~ our father Isaac;

11 (For the children being not yet born, neither having done any good or evil, that the purpose of God according to election might stand, not of works, but of him that calleth;)

12 It was said unto her, The elder shall serve the younger.

13 As it is written, Jacob have I loved, but Esau have I hated.

14 What shall we say then? Is there unrighteousness with God? God forbid.

15 For he saith to Moses, I will have mercy on whom I will have mercy, and I will have compassion on whom I will have compassion.

16 So then it is not of him that willeth, nor of him that runneth, but of God that showeth mercy.

17 For the scripture saith unto Pharaoh, Even for this same purpose have I raised thee up, that I might show my power in thee, and that my name might be declared throughout all the earth.

18 Therefore hath he mercy on whom he will have mercy, and whom he will he hardeneth.

19 Thou wilt say then unto me, Why doth he yet find fault? For who hath resisted his will?

20 Nay but, O man, who art thou that repliest against God? Shall the thing formed say to him that formed it, Why hast thou made me thus?

21 Hath not the potter power over the clay, of the same lump to make one vessel unto honour, and another unto dishonour?

22 What if God, willing to show his wrath, and to make his power known, endured with much longsuffering the vessels of wrath fitted to destruction:

23 And that he might make known the riches of his glory on the vessels of mercy, which he had afore prepared unto glory,

24 Even us, whom he hath called, not of the Jews only, but also of the Gentiles?

25 As he saith also in Osee, I will call them my people, which were not my people; and her beloved, which was not beloved.

26 And it shall come to pass, that in the place where it was said unto them, Ye are not my people; there shall they be called the children of the living God.

27 Esaias also crieth concerning Israel, Though the number of the children of Israel be as the sand of the sea, a remnant shall be saved:

28 For he will finish the work, and cut it short in righteousness: because a short work will the Lord make upon the earth.

29 And as Esaias said before, Except the Lord of Sabaoth had left us a seed, we had been as

Sodoma, and been made like unto Gomorrha.

30 What shall we say then? That the Gentiles, which followed not after righteousness, have attained to righteousness, even the righteousness which is of faith.

31 But Israel, which followed after the law of righteousness, hath not attained to the law of righteousness.

32 Wherefore? ~~Because they sought it not by faith, but as it were by the works of the law. For~~ they stumbled at that stumblingstone, *not by faith, but as it were by the works of the law*;

33 As it is written, Behold, I lay in Sion a stumblingstone and rock of offence: and whosoever believeth on him shall not be ashamed.

Chapter 10

1 Brethren, my heart's desire and prayer to God for Israel is, that they might be saved.

2 For I bear them record that they have a zeal of God, but not according to knowledge.

3 For they being ignorant of God's righteousness, and going about to establish their own righteousness, have not submitted themselves unto the righteousness of God.

4 For Christ is the end of the law for righteousness to every one that believeth.

5 For Moses describeth the righteousness which is of the law, That the man which doeth those things shall live by them.

6 But the righteousness which is of faith speaketh on this wise, Say not in thine heart, Who shall ascend into heaven? (that is, to bring Christ down from above:)

7 Or, Who shall descend into the deep? (that is, to bring up Christ again from the dead.)

8 But what saith it? The word is nigh thee, even in thy mouth, and in thy heart: that is, the word of faith, which we preach;

9 That if thou shalt confess with thy mouth the Lord Jesus, and shalt believe in thine heart that God hath raised him from the dead, thou shalt be saved.

10 For with the heart man believeth unto righteousness; and with the mouth confession is made unto salvation.

11 For the scripture saith, Whosoever believeth on him shall not be ashamed.

12 For there is no difference between the Jew and the Greek: for the same Lord over all is rich unto all that call upon him.

13 For whosoever shall call upon the name of the Lord shall be saved.

14 How then shall they call on him in whom they have not believed? and how shall they believe in him of whom they have not heard? and

how shall they hear without a preacher?

15 And how shall they preach, except they be sent? as it is written, How beautiful are the feet of them that preach the gospel of peace, and bring glad tidings of good things!

16 But they have not all obeyed the gospel. For Esaias saith, Lord, who hath believed our report?

17 So then faith cometh by hearing, and hearing by the word of God.

18 But I say, Have they not heard? Yes verily, their sound went into all the earth, and their words unto the ends of the world.

19 But I say, Did not Israel know? ~~First~~ *Now* Moses saith, I will provoke you to jealousy by them that are no people, and by a foolish nation I will anger you.

20 But Esaias is very bold, and saith, I was found of them that sought me not; I was made manifest unto them that asked not after me.

21 But to Israel he saith, All day long I have stretched forth my hands unto a disobedient and gainsaying people.

Chapter 11

1 I say then, Hath God cast away his people? God forbid. For I also am an Israelite, of the seed of Abraham, of the tribe of Benjamin.

2 God hath not cast away his people which he foreknew. ~~Wot~~ *Know* ye not what the ~~s~~*S*cripture saith of Elias? how he maketh ~~intercession~~ *complaint* to God against Israel, saying,

3 Lord, they have killed thy prophets, and digged down thine altars; and I am left alone, and they seek my life.

4 But what saith the answer of God unto him? I have reserved to myself seven thousand men, who have not bowed the knee to the image of Baal.

5 Even so then at this present time also there is a remnant according to the election of grace.

6 And if by grace, then is it no more of works: otherwise grace is no more grace. But if it be of works, then is it no more grace: otherwise work is no more work.

7 What then? Israel hath not obtained that which ~~he seeketh~~ *they seek* for; but the election hath obtained it, and the rest were blinded

8 (According as it is written, God hath given them the spirit of slumber, eyes that they should not see, and ears that they should not hear;) unto this day.

9 And David saith, Let their table be made a snare, and a trap, and a stumblingblock, and a recompense unto them:

10 Let their eyes be darkened that they may not see, and bow down their back alway.

11 I say then, Have they stumbled that they

should fall? God forbid: but rather through their fall salvation is come unto the Gentiles, for to provoke them to jealousy.

12 Now if the fall of them be the riches of the world, and the diminishing of them the riches of the Gentiles; how much more their fulness?

13 For I speak to you Gentiles, inasmuch as I am the apostle of the Gentiles, I magnify mine office:

14 If by any means I may provoke to emulation them which are my flesh, and might save some of them.

15 For if the casting away of them ~~be~~ *is* the reconciling of the world, what shall the ~~receiving~~ *restoring* of them be, but life from the dead?

16 For if the firstfruit be holy, the lump is also holy: and if the root be holy, so are the branches.

17 And if some of the branches be broken off, and thou, being a wild olive tree, wert grafted in among them, and with them partakest of the root and fatness of the olive tree;

18 Boast not against the branches. ~~But if thou boast,~~ *for* thou bearest not the root, but the root thee.

19 *For if thou boast,* Thou wilt say ~~then~~, The branches were broken off, that ~~I~~ *we* might be grafted in.

20 Well; because of unbelief they were broken off, and thou standest by faith. Be not highminded, but fear:

21 For if God spared not the natural branches, take heed lest he also spare not thee.

22 Behold therefore the goodness and severity of God: on them which fell, severity; but toward thee, goodness, if thou continue in his goodness: otherwise thou also shalt be cut off.

23 And they also, if they abide not still in unbelief, shall be grafted in: for God is able to graft them in again.

24 For if thou wert cut out of the olive tree which is wild by nature, and wert grafted contrary to nature into a good olive tree: how much more shall these, which be the natural branches, be grafted into their own olive tree?

25 For I would not, brethren, that ye should be ignorant of this mystery, lest ye should be wise in your own conceits; that blindness in part is happened to Israel, until the fulness of the Gentiles be come in.

26 And ~~so~~ *then* all Israel shall be saved: as it is written, There shall come out of Sion the Deliverer, and shall turn away ungodliness from Jacob:

27 For this is my covenant unto them, when I shall take away their sins.

28 As concerning the gospel, they are enemies for your sakes: but as touching the election, they are beloved for the fathers' sakes.

29 For the gifts and calling of God are without repentance.

30 For as ye in times past have not believed God, yet have now obtained mercy through their unbelief:

31 Even so have these also now not believed, that through your mercy they also may obtain mercy.

32 For God hath concluded them all in unbelief, that he might have mercy upon all.

33 O the depth of the riches both of the wisdom and knowledge of God! how unsearchable are his judgments, and his ways past finding out!

34 For who hath known the mind of the Lord? or who hath been his counsellor?

35 Or who hath first given to him, and it shall be recompensed unto him again?

36 For of him, and through him, and to him, are all things: to whom be glory for ever. Amen.

Chapter 12

1 I beseech you therefore, brethren, by the mercies of God, that ye present your bodies a living sacrifice, holy, acceptable unto God, which is your reasonable service.

2 And be not conformed to this world: but be ye transformed by the renewing of your mind, that ye may prove what ~~is~~ that good, and acceptable, and perfect, will of God *is*.

3 For I say, through the grace given unto me, to every man that is among you, not to think of himself more highly than he ought to think; but to think soberly, according as God hath dealt to every man the measure of faith.

4 For as we have many members in one body, and all members have not the same office:

5 So we, being many, are one body in Christ, and every one members one of another.

6 Having then gifts differing according to the grace that is given to us, whether prophecy, let us prophesy according to the proportion of faith;

7 Or ministry, let us wait on our ministering: or he that teacheth, on teaching;

8 Or he that exhorteth, on exhortation: he that giveth, let him do it with simplicity; he that ruleth, with diligence; he that showeth mercy, with cheerfulness.

9 Let love be without dissimulation. Abhor that which is ~~evil;~~ *and* cleave to that which is good.

10 Be kindly affectioned one to another with brotherly love; in honour preferring one another;

11 Not slothful in business; fervent in spirit; serving the Lord;

12 Rejoicing in hope; patient in tribulation; continuing instant in prayer;

13 Distributing to the necessity of saints; given to hospitality.

14 Bless them which persecute you: bless, and

curse not.

15 Rejoice with them that do rejoice, and weep with them that weep.

16 Be of the same mind one toward another. Mind not high things, but condescend to men of low estate. Be not wise in your own conceits.

17 Recompense to no man evil for evil. Provide things honest in the sight of all men.

18 If it be possible, as much as lieth in you, live peaceably with all men.

19 Dearly beloved, avenge not yourselves, but rather give place unto wrath: for it is written, Vengeance is mine; I will repay, saith the Lord.

20 Therefore if thine enemy hunger, feed him; if he thirst, give him drink: for in so doing thou shalt heap coals of fire on his head.

21 Be not overcome of evil, but overcome evil with good.

Chapter 13

1 Let every soul be subject unto the higher powers. For there is no power *in the church* but of God: the powers that be are ordained of God.

2 Whosoever therefore resisteth the power, resisteth the ordinance of God: and they that resist shall receive to themselves ~~damnation~~ *punishment*.

3 For rulers are not a terror to good works, but to the evil. Wilt thou then not be afraid of the power? do that which is good, and thou shalt have praise of the same:

4 For he is the minister of God to thee for good. But if thou do that which is evil, be afraid; for he beareth not the ~~sword~~ *rod* in vain: for he is the minister of God, a revenger to execute wrath upon him that doeth evil.

5 Wherefore ye must needs be subject, not only for wrath, but also for conscience sake.

6 For , for this cause pay ye ~~tribute~~ *your consecrations* also *unto them*: for they are God's ministers, attending continually upon this very thing.

7 *But first,* ~~R~~render ~~therefore~~ to all their dues~~:~~ , *according to custom,* tribute to whom tribute ~~is due~~; custom to whom custom; *that your consecrations may be done in* fear *of him* to whom fear *belongs*; *and in* ~~honour~~ *honor of him* to whom ~~honour~~ *honor belongs*.

8 *Therefore,* ~~O~~owe no man any thing, but to love one another: for he that loveth another hath fulfilled the law.

9 For this, Thou shalt not commit adultery, Thou shalt not kill, Thou shalt not steal, Thou shalt not bear false witness, Thou shalt not covet; and if there be any other commandment, it is briefly comprehended in this saying, namely, Thou shalt love thy neighbour as thyself.

10 Love worketh no ill to his neighbour: therefore love is the fulfilling of the law.

11 And that, knowing the time, that now it is high time to awake out of sleep: for now is our salvation nearer than when we believed.

12 The night is far spent, the day is at hand: let us therefore cast off the works of darkness, and let us put on the armour of light.

13 Let us walk honestly, as in the day; not in rioting and drunkenness, not in chambering and wantonness, not in strife and envying.

14 But put ye on the Lord Jesus Christ, and make not provision for the flesh, to ~~fulfil~~ *gratify* the lusts thereof.

Chapter 14

1 Him that is weak in the faith receive ye, but not to doubtful disputations.

2 For one believeth that he may eat all things: another, who is weak, eateth herbs.

3 Let not him that eateth despise him that eateth not; and let not him which eateth not judge him that eateth: for God hath received him.

4 Who art thou that judgest another man's servant? to his own master he standeth or falleth. Yea, he shall be holden up: for God is able to make him stand.

5 One man esteemeth one day above another: another esteemeth every day alike. Let every man be fully persuaded in his own mind.

6 He that regardeth the day, regardeth it unto the Lord; and he that regardeth not the day, to the Lord he doth not regard it. He that eateth, eateth to the Lord, for he giveth God thanks; and he that eateth not, to the Lord he eateth not, and giveth God thanks.

7 For none of us liveth to himself, and no man dieth to himself.

8 For whether we live, we live unto the Lord; and whether we die, we die unto the Lord: whether we live therefore, or die, we are the Lord's.

9 For to this end Christ both died, and rose, and revived, that he might be Lord both of the dead and living.

10 But why dost thou judge thy brother? or why dost thou set at nought thy brother? for we shall all stand before the judgment seat of Christ.

11 For *I live, saith the Lord, as* it is written~~, As I live, saith the Lord,~~ . *And* every knee shall bow to me, and every tongue shall ~~confess~~ *swear* to God.

12 So then every one of us shall give account of himself to God.

13 Let us not therefore judge one another any more: but judge this rather, that no man put a

stumblingblock or an occasion to fall in his brother's way.

14 I know, and am persuaded by the Lord Jesus, that there is nothing unclean of itself: but to him that esteemeth any thing to be unclean, to him it is unclean.

15 But if thy brother be grieved with thy meat, now *thou* walkest thou not charitably *if thou eatest. Therefore,* Ddestroy not him with thy meat, for whom Christ died.

16 Let not then your good be evil spoken of:

17 For the kingdom of God is not meat and drink; but righteousness, and peace, and joy in the Holy Ghost.

18 For he that in these things serveth Christ is acceptable to God, and approved of men.

19 Let us therefore follow after the things which make for peace, and things wherewith one may edify another.

20 For meat destroy not the work of God. All things indeed are pure; but it is evil for that man who eateth with offence.

21 It is good neither to eat flesh, nor to drink wine, nor any thing whereby thy brother stumbleth, or is offended, or is made weak.

22 Hast thou faith? have it to thyself before God. Happy is he that condemneth not himself in that thing which he alloweth.

23 And he that doubteth is damned *condemned* if he eat, because he eateth *it is* not of faith: for whatsoever is not of faith is sin.

Chapter 15

1 We then that are strong ought to bear the infirmities of the weak, and not to please ourselves.

2 Let every one of us please his neighbour for his good to edification.

3 For even Christ pleased not himself; but, as it is written, The reproaches of them that reproached thee fell on me.

4 For whatsoever things were written aforetime were written for our learning, that we through patience and comfort of the scriptures might have hope.

5 Now the God of patience and consolations grant you to be likeminded one toward another according to *as was* Christ Jesus:

6 That ye may with one mind and one mouth glorify God, even the Father of our Lord Jesus Christ.

7 Wherefore receive ye one another, as Christ also received us to the glory of God.

8 Now I say that Jesus Christ was a minister of the circumcision for the truth of God, to confirm the promises made unto the fathers:

9 And that the Gentiles might glorify God for his mercy; as it is written, For this cause I will confess to thee among the Gentiles, and sing unto thy name.

10 And again he saith, Rejoice, ye Gentiles, with his people.

11 And again, Praise the Lord, all ye Gentiles; and laud him, all ye people.

12 And again, Esaias saith, There shall be a root of Jesse, and he that shall rise to reign over the Gentiles; in him shall the Gentiles trust.

13 Now the God of hope fill you with all joy and peace in believing, that ye may abound in hope, through the power of the Holy Ghost.

14 And I myself also am persuaded of you, my brethren, that ye also are full of goodness, filled with all knowledge, able also to admonish one another.

15 Nevertheless, brethren, I have written the more boldly unto you in some sort, as putting you in mind, because of the grace that is given to me of God,

16 That I should be the minister of Jesus Christ to the Gentiles, ministering the gospel of God, that the offering up of the Gentiles might be acceptable, being sanctified by the Holy Ghost.

17 I have therefore whereof I may glory through Jesus Christ in those things which pertain to God.

18 For I will not dare to speak of any of those things which Christ hath not wrought by me, to make the Gentiles obedient, by word and deed,

19 Through mighty signs and wonders, by the power of the Spirit of God; so that from Jerusalem, and round about unto Illyricum, I have fully preached the gospel of Christ.

20 Yea, so have I strived to preach the gospel, not where Christ was named, lest I should build upon another man's foundation:

21 But as it is written, To whom he was not spoken of, they shall see: and they that have not heard shall understand.

22 For which cause also I have been much hindered from coming to you.

23 But now having no more place in these parts, and having a great desire these many years to come unto you;

24 Whensoever I take my journey into Spain, I will come to you: for I trust to see you in my journey, and to be brought on my way thitherward by you, if first I be somewhat filled with your company *through your prayers*.

25 But now I go unto Jerusalem to minister unto the saints.

26 For it hath pleased them of Macedonia and Achaia to make a certain contribution for the poor saints which are at Jerusalem.

27 It hath pleased them verily; and their debtors they are. For if the Gentiles have been made partakers of their spiritual things, their duty is also to minister unto them in carnal things.

28 When therefore I have performed this, and have sealed to them this fruit, I will come by you into Spain.

29 And I am sure that, when I come unto you, I shall come in the fulness of the blessing of the gospel of Christ.

30 Now I beseech you, brethren, for the Lord Jesus Christ's sake, and for the love of the Spirit, that ye strive together with me in your prayers to God for me;

31 That I may be delivered from them that do not believe in Judaea; and that my service which I have for Jerusalem may be accepted of the saints;

32 That I may come unto you with joy by the will of God, and may with you be refreshed.

33 Now the God of peace be with you all. Amen.

Chapter 16

1 I commend unto you Phebe our sister, which is a servant of the church which is at Cenchrea:

2 That ye receive her in the Lord, as becometh saints, and that ye assist her in whatsoever business she hath need of you: for she hath been a succourer of many, and of myself also.

3 Greet Priscilla and Aquila my helpers in Christ Jesus:

4 Who have for my life laid down their own necks: unto whom not only I give thanks, but also all the churches of the Gentiles.

5 Likewise greet the church that is in their house. Salute my well beloved Epaenetus, who is the firstfruits of Achaia unto Christ.

6 Greet Mary, who bestowed much labour on us.

7 Salute Andronicus and Junia, my kinsmen, and my fellow prisoners, who are of note among the apostles, who also were in Christ before me.

8 Greet Amplias my beloved in the Lord.

9 Salute Urbane, our helper in Christ, and Stachys my beloved.

10 Salute Apelles approved in Christ. Salute them which are of Aristobulus' ~~household~~ *church*.

11 Salute Herodion my kinsman. Greet them that be of the ~~household~~ *church* of Narcissus, which are in the Lord.

12 Salute Tryphena and Tryphosa, who labour in the Lord. Salute the beloved Persis, which laboured much in the Lord.

13 Salute Rufus chosen in the Lord, and his mother and mine.

14 Salute Asyncritus, Phlegon, Hermas, Patrobas, Hermes, and the brethren which are with them.

15 Salute Philologus, and Julia, Nereus, and his sister, and Olympas, and all the saints which are with them.

16 Salute one another with ~~an~~ holy ~~kiss~~ *salutation*. The churches of Christ salute you.

17 Now I beseech you, brethren, mark them which cause divisions and offences contrary to the doctrine which ye have learned; and avoid them.

18 For they that are such serve not our Lord Jesus Christ, but their own belly; and by good words and fair speeches deceive the hearts of the simple.

19 For your obedience is come abroad unto all men. I am glad therefore on your behalf: but yet I would have you wise unto that which is good, and simple concerning evil.

20 And the God of peace shall bruise Satan under your feet shortly. The grace of our Lord Jesus Christ be with you. Amen.

21 Timotheus my workfellow, and Lucius, and Jason, and Sosipater, my kinsmen, salute you.

22 I Tertius, who wrote this epistle, salute you in the Lord.

23 Gaius mine host, and of the whole church, saluteth you. Erastus the chamberlain of the city saluteth you, and Quartus a brother.

24 The grace of our Lord Jesus Christ be with you all. Amen.

25 Now to him that is of power to stablish you according to ~~my~~ *the* gospel, and the preaching of Jesus Christ, according to the revelation of the mystery, which was kept secret since the world began,

26 But now is made manifest, and by the scriptures of the prophets, according to the commandment of the everlasting God, made known to all nations for the obedience of faith:

27 To God only wise, be glory through Jesus Christ for ever. Amen.

Chapter 1

1 Paul, *an apostle,* called ~~to be an apostle~~ of Jesus Christ through the will of God, and Sosthenes our brother,

2 Unto the church of God which is at Corinth, to them that are sanctified in Christ Jesus, called to be saints, with all that in every place call upon the name of Jesus Christ our Lord, both theirs and ours:

3 Grace be unto you, and peace, from God our Father, and from the Lord Jesus Christ.

4 I thank my God always on your behalf, for the grace of God which is given you ~~by~~ *of* Jesus Christ;

5 That in every thing ye are enriched ~~by~~ *of* him, in all utterance, and in all knowledge;

6 Even as the testimony of Christ was confirmed in you:

7 So that ye come behind in no gift; waiting for the coming of our Lord Jesus Christ:

8 Who shall also confirm you unto the end, that ye may be blameless in the day of our Lord Jesus Christ.

9 God is faithful, by whom ye were called unto the fellowship of his Son Jesus Christ our Lord.

10 Now I beseech you, brethren, ~~by~~ *in* the name of our Lord Jesus Christ, that ye all speak the same thing, and that there be no divisions among you; but that ye be perfectly joined together in the same mind and in the same judgment.

11 For it hath been declared unto me of you, my brethren, by them which are of the house of Chloe, that there are contentions among you.

12 Now this I say, that ~~every one~~ *many* of you saith, I am of Paul; and I of Apollos; and I of Cephas; and I of Christ.

13 Is Christ divided? was Paul crucified for you? or were ye baptized in the name of Paul?

14 I thank God that I baptized none of you, but Crispus and Gaius;

15 Lest any should say that I had baptized in mine own name.

16 And I baptized also the household of Stephanas: besides, I know not whether I baptized any other.

17 For Christ sent me not to baptize, but to preach the gospel: not with wisdom of words, lest the cross of Christ should be made of none effect.

18 For the preaching of the cross is to them that perish foolishness; but unto us which are saved it is the power of God.

19 For it is written, I will destroy the wisdom of the wise, and will bring to nothing the understanding of the prudent.

20 Where is the wise? where is the scribe? where is the disputer of this world? hath not God made foolish the wisdom of this world?

21 For after that in the wisdom of God the world by wisdom knew not God, it pleased God by the foolishness of preaching to save them that believe.

22 For the Jews require a sign, and the Greeks seek after wisdom:

23 But we preach Christ crucified, unto the Jews a stumblingblock, and unto the Greeks foolishness;

24 But unto them ~~which are called~~ *who believe,* both Jews and Greeks, Christ the power of God, and the wisdom of God.

25 Because the foolishness of God is wiser than men; and the weakness of God is stronger than men.

26 For ye see your calling, brethren, how that not many wise men after the flesh, not many mighty, not many noble, are ~~called:~~ *chosen;*

27 ~~But~~ *For* God hath chosen the foolish things of the world to confound the wise; and God hath chosen the weak things of the world to confound the things which are mighty;

28 And base things of the world, and things which are despised, hath God chosen, yea, and things which are not, to bring to ~~nought~~ *naught* things that are *mighty*:

29 That no flesh should glory in his presence.

30 But of him are ye in Christ Jesus, who of God is made unto us wisdom, and righteousness, and sanctification, and redemption:

31 That, according as it is written, He that glorieth, let him glory in the Lord.

Chapter 2

1 And I, brethren, when I came to you, came not with excellency of speech or of wisdom, declaring unto you the testimony of God.

2 For I determined not to know any thing among you, save Jesus Christ, and him crucified.

3 And I was with you in weakness, and in fear, and in much trembling.

4 And my speech and my preaching was not with enticing words of man's wisdom, but in demonstration of the Spirit and of power:

5 That your faith should not stand in the wisdom of men, but in the power of God.

6 Howbeit we speak wisdom among them that are perfect: yet not the wisdom of this world, nor of the princes of this world, that come to nought:

7 But we speak the wisdom of God in a mystery, even the hidden wisdom, which God ordained before the world unto our glory:

8 Which none of the princes of this world knew: for had they known it, they would not have crucified the Lord of glory.

9 But as it is written, Eye hath not seen, nor ear heard, neither have entered into the heart of man, the things which God hath prepared for them that love him.

10 But God hath revealed them unto us by his Spirit: for the Spirit searcheth all things, yea, the deep things of God.

11 For what man knoweth the things of a man,

save the spirit of man which is in him? even so the things of God knoweth no man, ~~but~~ *except he has* the Spirit of God.

12 Now we have received, not the spirit of the world, but the spirit which is of God; that we might know the things that are freely given to us of God.

13 Which things also we speak, not in the words which man's wisdom teacheth, but which the Holy Ghost teacheth; comparing spiritual things with spiritual.

14 But the natural man receiveth not the things of the Spirit of God: for they are foolishness unto him: neither can he know them, because they are spiritually discerned.

15 But he that is spiritual judgeth all things, yet he himself is judged of no man.

16 For who hath known the mind of the Lord, that he may instruct him? But we have the mind of Christ.

Chapter 3

1 And I, brethren, could not speak unto you as unto spiritual, but as unto carnal, even as unto babes in Christ.

2 I have fed you with milk, and not with meat: for hitherto ye were not able to ~~bear~~ *receive* it, neither yet now are ye able.

3 For ye are yet carnal: for whereas there is among you envying, and strife, and divisions, are ye not carnal, and walk as men?

4 For while one saith, I am of Paul; and another, I am of Apollos; are ye not carnal?

5 Who then is Paul, and who is Apollos, but ministers by whom ye believed, even as the Lord gave to every man?

6 I have planted, Apollos watered; but God gave the increase.

7 So then neither is he that planteth any thing, neither he that watereth; but God that giveth the increase.

8 Now he that planteth and he that watereth are one: and every man shall receive his own reward according to his own labour.

9 For we are labourers together with God: ye are God's husbandry, ye are God's building.

10 According to the grace of God which is given unto me, as a wise masterbuilder, I have laid the foundation, and another buildeth thereon. But let every man take heed how he buildeth thereupon.

11 For other foundation can no man lay than that is laid, which is Jesus Christ.

12 Now if any man build upon this foundation gold, silver, precious stones, wood, hay, stubble;

13 Every man's work shall be made manifest: for the day shall declare it, because it shall be revealed by fire; and the fire shall try every man's work of what sort it is.

14 If any man's work abide which he hath built thereupon, he shall receive a reward.

15 If any man's work shall be burned, he shall suffer loss: but he himself ~~shall~~ *may* be saved; yet so as by fire.

16 Know ye not that ye are the temple of God, and that the Spirit of God dwelleth in you?

17 If any man defile the temple of God, him shall God destroy; for the temple of God is holy, which temple ye are.

18 Let no man deceive himself. If any man among you seemeth to be wise in this world, let him become a fool, that he may be wise.

19 For the wisdom of this world is foolishness with God. For it is written, He taketh the wise in their own craftiness.

20 And again, The Lord knoweth the thoughts of the wise, that they are vain.

21 Therefore let no man glory in men. For all things are yours;

22 Whether Paul, or Apollos, or Cephas, or the world, or life, or death, or things present, or things to come; all are yours;

23 And ye are Christ's; and Christ is God's.

Chapter 4

1 Let a man so account of us, as of the ministers of Christ, and stewards of the mysteries of God.

2 Moreover it is required ~~in~~ *of* stewards, that a man be found faithful.

3 But with me it is a very small thing that I should be judged of you, or of man's judgment: yea, I judge not mine own self.

4 For I know nothing ~~by~~ *against* myself; yet am I not hereby justified: but he ~~that~~ *who* judgeth me is the Lord.

5 Therefore *I* judge nothing before the time, until the Lord come, who both will bring to light the hidden things of darkness, and will make manifest the counsels of the hearts: and then shall every man have praise of God.

6 And these things, brethren, I have in a figure transferred to myself and to Apollos for your sakes; that ye might learn in us not to think of men above that which is written, that no one of you be puffed up for one against another.

7 For who maketh thee to differ from another? and what hast thou that thou didst not receive? now if thou didst receive it, why dost thou glory, as if thou hadst not received it?

8 Now ye are full, now ye are rich, ye have reigned as kings without us: and I would to God ye did reign, that we also might reign with you.

9 For I think that God hath set forth us the apostles last, as it were appointed to death: for we are made a spectacle unto the world, and to angels, and to men.

10 We are fools for Christ's sake, but ye are wise

in Christ; we are weak, but ye are strong; ye are honourable, but we are despised.

11 Even unto this present hour we both hunger, and thirst, and are naked, and are buffeted, and have no certain dwellingplace;

12 And labour, working with our own hands: being reviled, we bless; being persecuted, we suffer it:

13 Being defamed, we entreat: we are made as the filth of the world, and are the offscouring of all things unto this day.

14 I write not these things to shame you, but as my beloved sons I warn you.

15 For though ye have ten thousand instructors in Christ, yet have ye not many fathers: for in Christ Jesus I have begotten you through the gospel.

16 Wherefore I beseech you, be ye followers of me.

17 For this cause have I sent unto you Timotheus, who is my beloved son, and faithful in the Lord, who shall bring you into remembrance of my ways which be in Christ, as I teach every where in every church.

18 Now some are puffed up, as though I would not come to you.

19 But I will come to you shortly, if the Lord will, and will know, not the speech of them which are puffed up, but the power.

20 For the kingdom of God is not in word, but in power.

21 What will ye? shall I come unto you with a rod, or in love, and in the spirit of meekness?

Chapter 5

1 It is reported commonly that there is fornication among you, and such fornication as is not so much as named among the Gentiles, that one should have his father's wife.

2 And ye are puffed up, and have not rather mourned, that he that hath done this deed might be taken away from among you.

3 For I verily, as absent in body, but present in spirit, *I* have judged already, ~~as though I were present, concerning~~ him that hath so done this deed, *as though I were present,*

4 In the name of our Lord Jesus Christ, when ye are gathered together, and ~~my~~ *have the* ~~s~~*S*pirit, with the power of our Lord Jesus Christ,

5 To deliver such ~~an~~ one unto Satan for the destruction of the flesh, that the spirit may be saved in the day of ~~the~~ Lord Jesus.

6 Your glorying is not good. Know ye not that a little leaven leaveneth the whole lump?

7 Purge out therefore the old leaven, that ye may be a new lump, as ye are unleavened. For even Christ our passover is sacrificed for us:

8 Therefore let us keep the feast, not with old

leaven, neither with the leaven of malice and wickedness; but with the unleavened bread of sincerity and truth.

9 I wrote unto you in an epistle not to company with fornicators:

10 Yet not altogether with the fornicators of this world, or with the covetous, or extortioners, or with idolaters; for then must ye needs go out of the world.

11 But now I have written unto you not to keep company, if any man that is called a brother be a fornicator, or covetous, or an idolater, or a railer, or a drunkard, or an extortioner; with such an one no not to eat.

12 For what have I to do to judge them also that are without? do not ~~ye~~ *they* judge them that are within?

13 But them that are without God judgeth. Therefore put away from among yourselves that wicked person.

Chapter 6

1 Dare any of you, having a matter against another, go to law before the unjust, and not before the saints?

2 Do ye not know that the saints shall judge the world? and if the world shall be judged by you, are ye unworthy to judge the smallest matters?

3 Know ye not that we shall judge angels? how much more things that pertain to this life?

4 If then ye have judgments of things pertaining to this life, set them to judge who are least esteemed in the church.

5 I speak to your shame. Is it so, that there is not a wise man among you? no, not one that shall be able to judge between his brethren?

6 But brother goeth to law with brother, and that before the unbelievers.

7 Now therefore there is utterly a fault among you, because ye go to law one with another. Why do ye not rather take wrong? why do ye not rather suffer yourselves to be defrauded?

8 Nay, ye do wrong, and defraud, and that your brethren.

9 Know ye not that the unrighteous shall not inherit the kingdom of God? Be not deceived: neither fornicators, nor idolaters, nor adulterers, nor effeminate, nor abusers of themselves with mankind,

10 Nor thieves, nor covetous, nor drunkards, nor revilers, nor extortioners, shall inherit the kingdom of God.

11 And such were some of you: but ye are washed, but ye are sanctified, but ye are justified in the name of the Lord Jesus, and by the Spirit of our God.

12 All things are *not* lawful unto me, ~~but~~ *and* all things are not expedient: all things are *not* lawful

for me, ~~but~~ *therefore* I will not be brought under the power of any.

13 Meats for the belly, and the belly for meats: but God shall destroy both it and them. Now the body is not for fornication, but for the Lord; and the Lord for the body.

14 And God hath both raised up the Lord, and will also raise up us by his own power.

15 Know ye not that your bodies are the members of Christ? shall I then take the members of Christ, and make them the members of an harlot? God forbid.

16 What? know ye not that he which is joined to an harlot is one body? for two, saith he, shall be one flesh.

17 But he that is joined unto the Lord is one spirit.

18 Flee fornication. Every sin that a man ~~doeth~~ *committeth* is ~~without~~ *against* the body *of Christ*; ~~but~~ *and* he ~~that~~ *who* committeth fornication sinneth against his own body.

19 What? know ye not that your body is the temple of the Holy Ghost which is in you, which ye have of God, and ye are not your own?

20 For ye are bought with a price: therefore glorify God in your body, and in your spirit, which are God's.

Chapter 7

1 Now concerning the things whereof ye wrote unto me~~:~~ *,* *saying,* It is good for a man not to touch a woman.

2 Nevertheless, *I say,* to avoid fornication, let every man have his own wife, and let every woman have her own husband.

3 Let the husband render unto the wife due benevolence: and likewise also the wife unto the husband.

4 The wife hath not power of her own body, but the husband: and likewise also the husband hath not power of his own body, but the wife.

5 ~~Defraud~~ *Depart* ye not one *from* the other, except it be with consent for a time, that ye may give yourselves to fasting and prayer; and come together again, that Satan tempt you not for your incontinency.

6 ~~But~~ *And now what* I speak ~~this~~ *is* by permission, and not ~~of~~ *by* commandment.

7 For I would that all men were even as ~~I~~ myself. But every man hath his proper gift of God, one after this manner, and another after that.

8 I say therefore to the unmarried and widows, It is good for them if they abide even as I.

9 But if they cannot ~~contain~~ *abide*, let them marry: for it is better to marry than ~~to burn~~ *that any should commit sin*.

10 And unto the married I command, yet not I, but the Lord, Let not the wife depart from her husband:

11 But ~~and~~ if she depart, let her remain unmarried, or be reconciled to her husband: ~~and~~ *but* let not the husband put away his wife.

12 But to the rest speak I, not the Lord: If any brother hath a wife that believeth not, and she be pleased to dwell with him, let him not put her away.

13 And the woman which hath an husband that believeth not, and if he be pleased to dwell with her, let her not leave him.

14 For the unbelieving husband is sanctified by the wife, and the unbelieving wife is sanctified by the husband: else were your children unclean; but now are they holy.

15 But if the unbelieving depart, let him depart. A brother or a sister is not under bondage in such cases: but God hath called us to peace.

16 For what knowest thou, O wife, whether thou shalt save thy husband? or how knowest thou, O man, whether thou shalt save thy wife?

17 But as God hath distributed to every man, as the Lord hath called every one, so let him walk. And so ordain I in all churches.

18 Is any man called being circumcised? let him not become uncircumcised. Is any called in uncircumcision? let him not be circumcised.

19 Circumcision is nothing, and uncircumcision is nothing, but the keeping of the commandments of God.

20 Let every man abide in the same calling wherein he was called.

21 Art thou called being a servant? care not for it: but if thou mayest be made free, use it rather.

22 For he that is called in the Lord, being a servant, is the Lord's freeman: likewise also he that is called, being free, is Christ's servant.

23 Ye are bought with a price; be not ye the servants of men.

24 Brethren, let every man, wherein he is called, therein abide with God.

25 Now concerning virgins I have no commandment of the Lord: yet I give my judgment, as one that hath obtained mercy of the Lord to be faithful.

26 I suppose therefore that this is good for the present distress, ~~I say, that it is good for a man so to be~~ *for a man so to remain that he may do greater good*.

27 Art thou bound unto a wife? seek not to be loosed. Art thou loosed from a wife? seek not a wife.

28 But ~~and~~ if thou marry, thou hast not sinned; and if a virgin marry, she hath not sinned. Nevertheless such shall have trouble in the flesh~~:~~ ~~but~~ *.* *For* I spare you *not*.

29 But *I speak unto you who are called unto the ministry.* *For* this I say, brethren, the time *that remaineth* is *but* short~~: it remaineth, that both~~ *, that ye shall be sent forth unto the ministry. Even* they

that *who* have wives, *shall* be as though they had none; *for ye are called and chosen to do the Lord's work.*

30 And they that *it shall be with them who* weep, as though they wept not; and they that *them who* rejoice, as though they rejoiced not; and they that *them who* buy, as though they possessed not;

31 And they that *them who* use this world, as not abusing *using* it: for the fashion of this world passeth away.

32 But I would, *brethren, that ye magnify your calling. I would* have you without carefulness. He that *For he who* is unmarried careth for the things that belong to the Lord, how he may please the Lord: *therefore he prevaileth.*

33 But he that *who* is married careth for the things that are of the world, how he may please his wife; *therefore there is a difference, for he is hindered.*

34 There is difference also between a wife and a virgin. The unmarried woman careth for the things of the Lord, that she may be holy both in body and in spirit: but she that is married careth for the things of the world, how she may please her husband.

35 And this I speak for your own profit; not that I may cast a snare upon you, but for that which is comely, and that ye may attend upon the Lord without distraction.

36 But if any man think that he behaveth himself uncomely toward his virgin *whom he hath espoused*, if she pass the flower of her age, and need so require, let him do what he will *hath promised*, he sinneth not: let them marry.

37 Nevertheless he that standeth stedfast in his heart, having no necessity, but hath power over his own will, and hath so decreed in his heart that he will keep his virgin, doeth well.

38 So then he that giveth her *himself* in marriage doeth well; but he that giveth her *himself* not in marriage doeth better.

39 The wife is bound by the law as long as her husband liveth; but if her husband be dead, she is at liberty to be married to whom she will; only in the Lord.

40 But she is happier if she so abide, after my judgment: and I think also that I have the Spirit of God.

Chapter 8

1 Now as touching things offered unto idols, we know that we all have knowledge. Knowledge puffeth up, but charity edifieth.

2 And if any man think that he knoweth any thing, he knoweth nothing yet as he ought to know.

3 But if any man love God, the same is known of him.

4 As concerning therefore the eating of those things that *which* are *in the world* offered in sacrifice unto idols, we know that an idol is nothing in the world, and that there is none other God but one.

5 For though there be that are called gods, whether in heaven or in earth, (as there be gods many, and lords many,)

6 But to us there is but one God, the Father, of whom are all things, and we in him; and one Lord Jesus Christ, by whom are all things, and we by him.

7 Howbeit there is not in every man that knowledge: for some with conscience of the idol unto this hour eat it as a thing offered unto an idol; and their conscience being weak is defiled.

8 But meat commendeth us not to God: for neither, if we eat, are we the better; neither, if we eat not, are we the worse.

9 But take heed lest by any means this liberty of yours become a stumblingblock to them that are weak.

10 For if any man see thee which hast knowledge sit at meat in the idol's temple, shall not the conscience of him which is weak be emboldened to eat those things which are offered to idols;

11 And through thy knowledge shall the weak brother perish, for whom Christ died?

12 But when ye sin so against the brethren, and wound their weak conscience, ye sin against Christ.

13 Wherefore, if meat make my brother to offend, I will eat no flesh while the world standeth, lest I make my brother to offend.

Chapter 9

1 Am I not an apostle? am I not free? have I not seen Jesus Christ our Lord? are not ye my work in the Lord?

2 If I be not an apostle unto others, yet doubtless I am to you: for the seal of mine apostleship are ye in the Lord.

3 Mine answer to them that do examine me is this,

4 Have we not power to eat and to drink?

5 Have we not power to lead about a sister, a wife, as well as other apostles, and as the brethren of the Lord, and Cephas?

6 Or I only and Barnabas, have not we power to forbear working?

7 Who goeth a warfare any time at his own charges? who planteth a vineyard, and eateth not of the fruit thereof? or who feedeth a flock, and eateth not of the milk of the flock?

8 Say I these things as a man? or saith not the law the same also?

9 For it is written in the law of Moses, Thou shalt not muzzle the mouth of the ox that treadeth

out the corn. Doth God take care for oxen?

10 Or saith he it altogether for our sakes? For our sakes, no doubt, this is written: that he that ploweth should plow in hope; and that he that thresheth in hope should be partaker of his hope.

11 If we have sown unto you spiritual things, is it a great thing if we shall reap your carnal things?

12 If others be partakers of this power over you, are not we rather? Nevertheless we have not used this power; but suffer all things, lest we should hinder the gospel of Christ.

13 Do ye not know that they which minister about holy things live of the things of the temple? and they which wait at the altar are partakers with the altar?

14 Even so hath the Lord ordained that they which preach the gospel should live of the gospel.

15 But I have used none of these things: neither have I written these things, that it should be so done unto me: for it were better for me to die, than that any man should make my glorying void.

16 For though I preach the gospel, I have nothing to glory of: for necessity is laid upon me; yea, woe is unto me, if I preach not the gospel!

17 For if I do this thing willingly, I have a reward: but if against my will, a dispensation of the gospel is committed unto me.

18 What is my reward then? Verily that, when I preach the gospel, I may make the gospel of Christ without charge, that I abuse not my power in the gospel.

19 For though I be free from all men, yet have I made myself servant unto all, that I might gain the more.

20 And unto the Jews I became as a Jew, that I might gain the Jews; to them that are under the law, as under the law, that I might gain them that are under the law;

21 To them that are without law, as without law, (being not without law to God, but under the law to Christ,) that I might gain them that are without law.

22 To the weak became I as weak, that I might gain the weak: I am made all things to all men, that I might by all means save some.

23 And this I do for the gospel's sake, that I might be partaker thereof with you.

24 Know ye not that they which run in a race *all* run all, but *only* one receiveth the prize? So run, that ye may obtain.

25 And every man that striveth for the mastery is temperate in all things. Now they do it to obtain a corruptible crown; but we an incorruptible.

26 I therefore so run, not as uncertainly; so fight I, not as one that beateth the air:

27 But I keep under my body, and bring it into subjection: lest that by any means, when I have preached to others, I myself should be a castaway.

Chapter 10

1 Moreover, brethren, I would not that ye should be ignorant, how that all our fathers were under the cloud, and all passed through the sea;

2 And were all baptized unto Moses in the cloud and in the sea;

3 And did all eat the same spiritual meat;

4 And did all drink the same spiritual drink: for they drank of that spiritual Rock that followed them: and that Rock was Christ.

5 But with many of them God was not well pleased: for they were overthrown in the wilderness.

6 Now these things were our examples, to the intent we should not lust after evil things, as they also lusted.

7 Neither be ye idolaters, as were some of them; as it is written, The people sat down to eat and drink, and rose up to play.

8 Neither let us *to* commit fornication, as some of them committed, and fell in one day three and twenty thousand.

9 Neither let us tempt Christ, as some of them also tempted, and were destroyed of serpents.

10 Neither murmur ye, as some of them also murmured, and were destroyed of the destroyer.

11 Now all these things happened unto them for ensamples: and they are written for our admonition *also*, *and for an admonition for those* upon whom the ends *end* of the world are *shall* come.

12 Wherefore let him that thinketh he standeth take heed lest he fall.

13 There hath no temptation taken you but such as is common to man: but God is faithful, who will not suffer you to be tempted above that ye are able; but will with the temptation also make a way to escape, that ye may be able to bear it.

14 Wherefore, my dearly beloved, flee from idolatry.

15 I speak as to wise men; judge ye what I say.

16 The cup of blessing which we bless, is it not the communion of the blood of Christ? The bread which we break, is it not the communion of the body of Christ?

17 For we being many are one bread, and one body: for we are all partakers of that one bread.

18 Behold Israel after the flesh: are not they which eat of the sacrifices partakers of the altar?

19 What say I then? that the idol is any thing, or that which is offered in sacrifice to idols is any thing?

20 But I say, that the things which the Gentiles sacrifice, they sacrifice to devils, and not to God: and I would not that ye should have fellowship with devils.

21 Ye cannot drink the cup of the Lord, and the cup of devils: ye cannot be partakers of the Lord's table, and of the table of devils.

22 Do we provoke the Lord to jealousy? are we stronger than he?

23 All things are *not* lawful for me, ~~but~~ *for* all things are not expedient: all things are *not* lawful ~~for me~~, ~~but~~ *for* all things edify not.

24 Let ~~no~~ *not* man seek *therefore* his own, but every man another's ~~wealth~~ *good*.

25 Whatsoever is sold in the shambles, that eat, asking no question for conscience sake:

26 For the earth is the Lord's, and the fulness thereof.

27 If any of them that believe not bid you to a feast, and ye be disposed to ~~go~~ *eat*; whatsoever is set before you, eat, asking no question*s* for conscience' sake.

28 But if any man say unto you, This is offered in sacrifice unto idols, eat not for his sake that showed it, and for conscience sake: for the earth is the Lord's, and the fulness thereof:

29 Conscience, I say, not thine own, but of the other: for why is my liberty judged of another man's conscience?

30 For if I by grace be a partaker, why am I evil spoken of for that for which I give thanks?

31 Whether therefore ye eat, or drink, or whatsoever ye do, do all to the glory of God.

32 Give none offence, neither to the Jews, nor to the Gentiles, nor to the church of God:

33 Even as I please all men in all things, not seeking mine own profit, but ~~the profit~~ of *the* many, that they may be saved.

Chapter 11

1 Be ye followers of me, even as I also am of Christ.

2 Now I praise you, brethren, that ye remember me in all things, and keep the ordinances, as I delivered them to you.

3 But I would have you know, that the head of every man is Christ; and the head of the woman is the man; and the head of Christ is God.

4 Every man praying or prophesying, having his head covered, dishonoureth his head.

5 But every woman that prayeth or prophesieth with her head uncovered dishonoureth her head: for that is even all one as if she were shaven.

6 For if the woman be not covered, let her also be shorn: but if it be a shame for a woman to be shorn or shaven, let her be covered.

7 For a man indeed ought not to cover his head, forasmuch as he is the image and glory of God: but the woman is the glory of the man.

8 For the man is not of the woman; but the woman of the man.

9 Neither was the man created for the woman; but the woman for the man.

10 For this cause ought the woman to have ~~power~~ *a covering* on her head because of the angels.

11 Nevertheless neither is the man without the woman, neither the woman without the man, in the Lord.

12 For as the woman is of the man, even so is the man also by the woman; but all things of God.

13 Judge in yourselves: is it comely that a woman pray unto God uncovered?

14 Doth not even nature itself teach you, that, if a man have long hair, it is a shame unto him?

15 But if a woman have long hair, it is a glory to her: for her hair is given her for a covering.

16 But if any man seem to be contentious, we have no such custom, neither the churches of God.

17 Now in this that I declare unto you I praise you not, that ye come together not for the better, but for the worse.

18 For first of all, when ye come together in the church, I hear that there be divisions among you; and I partly believe it.

19 For there must be also ~~heresies~~ *divisions* among you, that they which are approved may be made manifest among you.

20 When ye come together ~~therefore~~ into one place, ~~this~~ is *it* not to eat the Lord's supper~~.~~ *?*

21 ~~For~~ *But* in eating every one taketh before ~~other~~ his own supper: and one is hungry, and another is drunken.

22 What? have ye not houses to eat and to drink in? or despise ye the church of God, and shame them that have not? What shall I say to you? shall I praise you in this? I praise you not.

23 For I have received of the Lord that which also I delivered unto you, That the Lord Jesus the same night in which he was betrayed took bread:

24 And when he had given thanks, he brake it, and said, Take, eat: this is my body, which is broken for you: this do in remembrance of me.

25 After the same manner also he took the cup, when he had supped, saying, This cup is the new testament in my blood: this do ye, as oft as ye drink it, in remembrance of me.

26 For as often as ye eat this bread, and drink this cup, ye do show the Lord's death till he come.

27 Wherefore whosoever shall eat this bread, and drink this cup of the Lord, unworthily, shall be guilty of the body and blood of the Lord.

28 But let a man examine himself, and so let him eat of that bread, and drink of that cup.

29 For he that eateth and drinketh unworthily, eateth and drinketh ~~damnation~~ *condemnation* to himself, not discerning the Lord's body.

30 For this cause many are weak and sickly among you, and many sleep.

31 For if we would judge ourselves, we should not be judged.

32 But when we are judged, we are chastened of the Lord, that we should not be condemned with the world.

33 Wherefore, my brethren, when ye come

together to eat, tarry one for another.

34 And if any man hunger, let him eat at home; that ye come not together unto condemnation. And the rest will I set in order when I come.

Chapter 12

1 Now concerning spiritual ~~gifts~~ *things*, brethren, I would not have you ignorant.

2 Ye know that ye were Gentiles, carried away unto these dumb idols, even as ye were led.

3 Wherefore I give you to understand, that no man speaking by the Spirit of God calleth Jesus accursed: and that no man can say that Jesus is the Lord, but by the Holy Ghost.

4 Now there are diversities of gifts, but the same Spirit.

5 And there are differences of administrations, but the same Lord.

6 And there are diversities of operations, but it is the same God which worketh all in all.

7 But the manifestation of the Spirit is given to every man to profit withal.

8 For to one is given by the Spirit the word of wisdom; to another the word of knowledge by the same Spirit;

9 To another faith by the same Spirit; to another the gifts of healing by the same Spirit;

10 To another the working of miracles; to another prophecy; to another discerning of spirits; to another divers kinds of tongues; to another the interpretation of tongues:

11 But all these worketh that one and the selfsame Spirit, dividing to every man severally as he will.

12 For as the body is one, and hath many members, and all the members of that one body, being many, are one body: so also is Christ.

13 For by one Spirit are we all baptized into one body, whether we be Jews or Gentiles, whether we be bond or free; and have been all made to drink into one Spirit.

14 For the body is not one member, but many.

15 If the foot shall say, Because I am not the hand, I am not of the body; is it therefore not of the body?

16 And if the ear shall say, Because I am not the eye, I am not of the body; is it therefore not of the body?

17 If the whole body were an eye, where were the hearing? If the whole were hearing, where were the smelling?

18 But now hath God set the members every one of them in the body, as it hath pleased him.

19 And if they were all one member, where were the body?

20 But now are they many members, yet but one body.

21 And the eye cannot say unto the hand, I have no need of thee: nor again the head to the feet, I have no need of you.

22 Nay, much more those members of the body, which seem to be more feeble, are necessary:

23 And those members of the body, which we think to be less honourable, upon these we bestow more abundant honour; and our uncomely parts have more abundant comeliness.

24 For our comely parts have no need: but God hath tempered the body together, having given more abundant honour to that part which lacked:

25 That there should be no schism in the body; but that the members should have the same care one for another.

26 And whether one member suffer, all the members suffer with it; or one member be honoured, all the members rejoice with it.

27 Now ye are the body of Christ, and members in particular.

28 And God hath set some in the church, first apostles, secondarily prophets, thirdly teachers, after that miracles, then gifts of healings, helps, governments, diversities of tongues.

29 Are all apostles? are all prophets? are all teachers? are all workers of miracles?

30 Have all the gifts of healing? do all speak with tongues? do all interpret?

31 *I say unto you, Nay; for I have shown unto you a more excellent way,* ~~But~~ *therefore* covet earnestly the best gifts~~: and yet show I unto you a more excellent way~~.

Chapter 13

1 Though I speak with the tongues of men and of angels, and have not charity, I am become as sounding brass, or a tinkling cymbal.

2 And though I have the gift of prophecy, and understand all mysteries, and all knowledge; and though I have all faith, so that I could remove mountains, and have not charity, I am nothing.

3 And though I bestow all my goods to feed the poor, and though I give my body to be burned, and have not charity, it profiteth me nothing.

4 Charity suffereth long, and is kind; charity envieth not; charity vaunteth not itself, is not puffed up,

5 Doth not behave itself unseemly, seeketh not her own, is not easily provoked, thinketh no evil;

6 Rejoiceth not in iniquity, but rejoiceth in the truth;

7 Beareth all things, believeth all things, hopeth all things, endureth all things.

8 Charity never faileth: but whether there be prophecies, they shall fail; whether there be tongues, they shall cease; whether there be knowledge, it shall vanish away.

9 For we know in part, and we prophesy in part.

10 But when that which is perfect is come, then

that which is in part shall be done away.

11 When I was a child, I spake as a child, I understood as a child, I thought as a child: but when I became a man, I put away childish things.

12 For now we see through a glass, darkly; but then face to face: now I know in part; but then shall I know even as also I am known.

13 And now abideth faith, hope, charity, these three; but the greatest of these is charity.

Chapter 14

1 Follow after charity, and desire spiritual gifts, but rather that ye may prophesy.

2 For he that speaketh in ~~an unknown~~ *another* tongue speaketh not unto men, but unto God: for no man understandeth him; howbeit in the spirit he speaketh mysteries.

3 But he that prophesieth speaketh unto men to edification, and exhortation, and comfort.

4 He that speaketh in ~~an unknown~~ *another* tongue edifieth himself; but he that prophesieth edifieth the church.

5 I would that ye all spake with tongues, but rather that ye prophesied: for greater is he that prophesieth than he that speaketh with tongues, except he interpret, that the church may receive edifying.

6 Now, brethren, if I come unto you speaking with tongues, what shall I profit you, except I shall speak to you either by revelation, or by knowledge, or by prophesying, or by doctrine?

7 And even things without life giving sound, whether pipe or harp, except they give a distinction in the sounds, how shall it be known what is piped or harped?

8 For if the trumpet give an uncertain sound, who shall prepare himself to the battle?

9 So likewise ye, except ye utter by the tongue words easy to be understood, how shall it be known what is spoken? for ye shall speak into the air.

10 There are, it may be, so many kinds of voices in the world, and none of them is without signification.

11 Therefore if I know not the meaning of the voice, I shall be unto him that speaketh a barbarian, and he that speaketh shall be a barbarian unto me.

12 Even so ye, forasmuch as ye are zealous of spiritual gifts, seek that ye may excel to the edifying of the church.

13 Wherefore let him that speaketh in ~~an unknown~~ *another* tongue pray that he may interpret.

14 For if I pray in ~~an unknown~~ *another* tongue, my spirit prayeth, but my understanding is unfruitful.

15 What is it then? I will pray with the spirit, and I will pray with the understanding also: I will sing with the spirit, and I will sing with the understanding also.

16 Else when thou shalt bless with the spirit, how shall he that occupieth the room of the unlearned say Amen at thy giving of thanks, seeing he understandeth not what thou sayest?

17 For thou verily givest thanks well, but the other is not edified.

18 I thank my God, I speak with tongues more than ye all:

19 Yet in the church I had rather speak five words with my understanding, that by my voice I might teach others also, than ten thousand words in ~~an unknown~~ *another* tongue.

20 Brethren, be not children in understanding: howbeit in malice be ye children, but in understanding be men.

21 In the law it is written, With men of other tongues and other lips will I speak unto this people; and yet for all that will they not hear me, saith the Lord.

22 Wherefore tongues are for a sign, not to them that believe, but to them that believe not: but prophesying serveth not for them that believe not, but for them which believe.

23 If therefore the whole church be come together into one place, and all speak with tongues, and there come in those that are unlearned, or unbelievers, will they not say that ye are mad?

24 But if all prophesy, and there come in one that believeth not, or one unlearned, he is convinced of all, he is judged of all:

25 And thus are the secrets of his heart made manifest; and so falling down on his face he will worship God, and report that God is in you of a truth.

26 How is it then, brethren? when ye come together, every one of you hath a psalm, hath a doctrine, hath a tongue, hath a revelation, hath an interpretation. Let all things be done unto edifying.

27 If any man speak in ~~an unknown~~ *another* tongue, let it be by two, or at the most by three, and that by course; and let one interpret.

28 But if there be no interpreter, let him keep silence in the church; and let him speak to himself, and to God.

29 Let the prophets speak two or three, and let the other judge.

30 If any thing be revealed to another that sitteth by, let the first hold his peace.

31 For ye may all prophesy one by one, that all may learn, and all may be comforted.

32 And the spirits of the prophets are subject to the prophets.

33 For God is not the author of confusion, but of peace, as in all churches of the saints.

34 Let your women keep silence in the churches:

for it is not permitted unto them to ~~speak~~ *rule*; but ~~they are commanded~~ to be under obedience, as also saith the law.

35 And if they will learn any thing, let them ask their husbands at home: for it is a shame for women to ~~speak~~ *rule* in the church.

36 What? came the word of God out from you? or came it unto you only?

37 If any man think himself to be a prophet, or spiritual, let him acknowledge that the things that I write unto you are the commandments of the Lord.

38 But if any man be ignorant, let him be ignorant.

39 Wherefore, brethren, covet to prophesy, and forbid not to speak with tongues.

40 Let all things be done decently and in order.

Chapter 15

1 Moreover, brethren, I declare unto you the gospel which I preached unto you, which also ye have received, and wherein ye stand;

2 By which also ye are saved, if ye keep in memory what I preached unto you, unless ye have believed in vain.

3 For I delivered unto you first of all that which I also received, how that Christ died for our sins according to the scriptures;

4 And that he was buried, and that he rose again the third day according to the scriptures:

5 And that he was seen of Cephas, then of the twelve:

6 After that, he was seen of above five hundred brethren at once; of whom the greater part remain unto this present, but some are fallen asleep.

7 After that, he was seen of James; then of all the apostles.

8 And last of all he was seen of me also, as of one born out of due time.

9 For I am the least of the apostles, that am not meet to be called an apostle, because I persecuted the church of God.

10 But by the grace of God I am what I am: and his grace which was bestowed upon me was not in vain; ~~but~~ *for* I ~~laboured~~ *labored* more abundantly than they all: yet not I, but the grace of God which was with me.

11 Therefore whether it were I or they, so we preach, and so ye believed.

12 Now if Christ be preached that he rose from the dead, how say some among you that there is no resurrection of the dead?

13 But if there be no resurrection of the dead, then is Christ not risen:

14 And if Christ be not risen, then is our preaching vain, and your faith is also vain.

15 Yea, and we are found false witnesses of God; because we have testified of God that he raised up Christ: whom he raised not up, if so be that the dead rise not.

16 For if the dead rise not, then is not Christ raised:

17 And if Christ be not raised, your faith is vain; ye are yet in your sins.

18 Then they also which are fallen asleep in Christ are perished.

19 If in this life only we have hope in Christ, we are of all men most miserable.

20 But now is Christ risen from the dead, and become the firstfruits of them that slept.

21 For since by man came death, by man came also the resurrection of the dead.

22 For as in Adam all die, even so in Christ shall all be made alive.

23 But every man in his own order: Christ the firstfruits; afterward they that are Christ's at his coming.

24 ~~Then~~ *Afterward* cometh the end, when he shall have delivered up the kingdom to God, even the Father; when he shall have put down all rule and all authority and power.

25 For he must reign, till he hath put all enemies under his feet.

26 The last enemy, *death,* ~~that~~ shall be destroyed ~~is death~~.

27 ~~For~~ *For he saith, When it is manifest that* he hath put all things under his feet~~. But when he saith~~ *, and that* all things are put under ~~him, it is manifest that he is excepted, which~~ *, he is excepted of the Father who* did put all things under him.

28 And when all things shall be subdued unto him, then shall the Son also himself be subject unto him that put all things under him, that God may be all in all.

29 Else what shall they do which are baptized for the dead, if the dead rise not at all? why are they then baptized for the dead?

30 And why stand we in jeopardy every hour?

31 I protest ~~by your~~ *unto you the resurrection of the dead; and this is my* rejoicing which I have in Christ Jesus our Lord *daily, though* I die ~~daily~~.

32 If after the manner of men I have fought with beasts at Ephesus, what advantageth it me, if the dead rise not? let us eat and drink; for to morrow we die.

33 Be not deceived: evil communications corrupt good manners.

34 Awake to righteousness, and sin not; for some have not the knowledge of God: I speak this to your shame.

35 But some man will say, How are the dead raised up? and with what body do they come?

36 Thou fool, that which thou sowest is not quickened, except it die:

37 And that which thou sowest, thou sowest not that body ~~that~~ *which* shall be, but ~~bare~~ grain, it may ~~chance~~ *be* of wheat, or ~~of~~ some other ~~grain~~:

38 But God giveth it a body as it hath pleased

him, and to every seed his own body.

39 All flesh is not the same flesh: but there is one kind of flesh of men, another flesh of beasts, another of fishes, and another of birds.

40 ~~There are a~~Also celestial bodies, and bodies terrestrial, *and bodies telestial*: but the glory of the celestial ~~is~~ , one, and the ~~glory of the~~ terrestrial ~~is~~ , another; *and the telestial, another*.

41 There is one glory of the sun, and another glory of the moon, and another glory of the stars: for one star differeth from another star in glory.

42 So also is the resurrection of the dead. It is sown in corruption; it is raised in incorruption:

43 It is sown in dishonour; it is raised in glory: it is sown in weakness; it is raised in power:

44 It is sown a natural body; it is raised a spiritual body. There is a natural body, and there is a spiritual body.

45 And so it is written, The first man Adam was made a living soul; the last Adam was made a quickening spirit.

46 Howbeit ~~that was not first which is spiritual, but~~ , that which is natural, *first, and not that which is spiritual*; ~~and~~ *but* afterward*s*, that which is spiritual.

47 The first man is of the earth, earthy: the second man is the Lord from heaven.

48 As is the earthy, such are they also that are earthy: and as is the heavenly, such are they also that are heavenly.

49 And as we have borne the image of the earthy, we shall also bear the image of the heavenly.

50 Now this I say, brethren, that flesh and blood cannot inherit the kingdom of God; neither doth corruption inherit incorruption.

51 Behold, I show you a mystery; We shall not all sleep, but we shall all be changed,

52 In a moment, in the twinkling of an eye, at *the sound of* the last trump: for the trumpet shall sound, and the dead shall be raised incorruptible, and we shall be changed.

53 For this corruptible must put on incorruption, and this mortal must put on immortality.

54 So when this corruptible shall have put on incorruption, and this mortal shall have put on immortality, then shall be brought to pass the saying that is written, Death is swallowed up in victory.

55 O death, where is thy sting? O grave, where is thy victory?

56 The sting of death is sin; and the strength of sin is the law.

57 But thanks be to God, which giveth us the victory through our Lord Jesus Christ.

58 Therefore, my beloved brethren, be ye stedfast, unmoveable, always abounding in the work of the Lord, forasmuch as ye know that your labour is not in vain in the Lord.

Chapter 16

1 Now concerning the collection for the saints, as I have given order to the churches of Galatia, even so do ye.

2 Upon the first day of the week let every one of you lay by him in store, as God hath prospered him, that there be no gatherings when I come.

3 And when I come, whomsoever ye shall approve by your letters, them will I send to bring your liberality unto Jerusalem.

4 And if it be meet that I go also, they shall go with me.

5 Now I will come unto you, when I shall pass through Macedonia: for I do pass through Macedonia.

6 And it may be that I will abide, yea, and winter with you, that ye may bring me on my journey whithersoever I go.

7 For I will not see you now by the way; but I trust to tarry a while with you, if the Lord permit.

8 But I will tarry at Ephesus until Pentecost.

9 For a great door and effectual is opened unto me, and there are many adversaries.

10 Now if Timotheus come, see that he may be with you without fear: for he worketh the work of the Lord, as I also do.

11 Let no man therefore despise him: but conduct him forth in peace, that he may come unto me: for I look for him with the brethren.

12 As touching our brother Apollos, I greatly desired him to come unto you with the brethren: but his will was not at all to come at this time; but he will come when he shall have convenient time.

13 Watch ye, stand fast in the faith, quit you like men, be strong.

14 Let all your things be done with charity.

15 I beseech you, brethren, (ye know the house of Stephanas, that it is the firstfruits of Achaia, and that they have addicted themselves to the ministry of the saints,)

16 That ye submit yourselves unto such, and to every one that helpeth with us, and laboureth.

17 I am glad of the coming of Stephanas and Fortunatus and Achaicus: for that which was lacking on your part they have supplied.

18 For they have refreshed my spirit and yours: therefore acknowledge ye them that are such.

19 The churches of Asia salute you. Aquila and Priscilla salute you much in the Lord, with the church that is in their house.

20 All the brethren greet you. Greet ye one another with a~~n~~ holy ~~kiss~~ *salutation*.

21 The salutation of me Paul with mine own hand.

22 If any man love not the Lord Jesus Christ, let him be Anathema Maranatha.

23 The grace of our Lord Jesus Christ be with you.

24 My love be with you all in Christ Jesus. Amen.

Chapter 1

1 Paul, an apostle of Jesus Christ by the will of God, and Timothy our brother, unto the church of God which is at Corinth, with all the saints which are in all Achaia:

2 Grace be to you and peace from God our Father, and from the Lord Jesus Christ.

3 Blessed be God, even the Father of our Lord Jesus Christ, the Father of mercies, and the God of all comfort;

4 Who comforteth us in all our tribulation, that we may be able to comfort them which are in any trouble, by the comfort wherewith we ourselves are comforted of God.

5 For as the sufferings of Christ abound in us, so our consolation also aboundeth by Christ.

6 And whether we be afflicted, it is for your consolation and salvation, which is effectual in the enduring of the same sufferings which we also suffer: or whether we be comforted, it is for your consolation and salvation.

7 And our hope of you is stedfast, knowing, that as ye are partakers of the sufferings, so shall ye be also of the consolation.

8 For we would not, brethren, have you ignorant of our trouble which came to us in Asia, that we were pressed out of measure, above strength, insomuch that we despaired even of life:

9 But we had the sentence of death in ourselves, that we should not trust in ourselves, but in God which raiseth the dead:

10 Who delivered us from so great a death, and doth deliver: in whom we trust that he will yet deliver us;

11 Ye also helping together by prayer for us, that for the gift bestowed upon us by the means of many persons thanks may be given by many on our behalf.

12 For our rejoicing is this, the testimony of our conscience, that in simplicity and godly sincerity, not with fleshly wisdom, but by the grace of God, we have had our conversation in the world, and more abundantly to you-ward.

13 For we write none other things unto you, than what ye read or acknowledge; and I trust ye shall acknowledge even to the end;

14 As also ye have acknowledged us in part, that we are your rejoicing, even as ye also are ours in the day of the Lord Jesus.

15 And in this confidence I was minded to come unto you before, that ye might have a second benefit;

16 And to pass by you into Macedonia, and to come again out of Macedonia unto you, and of you to be brought on my way toward Judaea.

17 When I therefore was thus minded, did I use lightness? or the things that I purpose, do I purpose according to the flesh, that with me there should *shall* be yea yea, and nay nay?

18 But as God is true, our word toward you was not yea and nay.

19 For the Son of God, Jesus Christ, who was preached among you by us, even by me and Silvanus and Timotheus, was not yea and nay, but in him was yea.

20 For all the promises of God in him are yea, and in him Amen, unto the glory of God by us.

21 Now he which stablisheth us with you in Christ, and hath anointed us, is God;

22 Who hath also sealed us, and given the earnest of the Spirit in our hearts.

23 Moreover I call God for a record upon my soul, that to spare you I came not as yet unto Corinth.

24 Not for that we have dominion over your faith, but are helpers of your joy: for by faith ye stand.

Chapter 2

1 But I determined this with myself, that I would not come again to you in heaviness.

2 For if I make you sorry, who is he then that maketh me glad, but the same which is made sorry by me?

3 And I wrote this same unto you, lest, when I came, I should have sorrow from them of whom I ought to rejoice; having confidence in you all, that my joy is the joy of you all.

4 For out of much affliction and anguish of heart I wrote unto you with many tears; not that ye should be grieved, but that ye might know the love which I have more abundantly unto you.

5 But if any have caused grief, he hath not grieved me, but in part: that I may not overcharge you all.

6 Sufficient to such a man is this punishment, which was inflicted of many.

7 So that contrariwise ye ought rather to forgive him, and comfort him, lest perhaps such a one should be swallowed up with overmuch sorrow.

8 Wherefore I beseech you that ye would confirm your love toward him.

9 For to this end also did I write, that I might know the proof of you, whether ye be obedient in all things.

10 To whom ye forgive any thing, I forgive also: for if I forgave any thing, to whom I forgave it, for your sakes forgave I it in the person of Christ;

11 Lest Satan should get an advantage of us: for we are not ignorant of his devices.

12 Furthermore, when I came to Troas to preach Christ's gospel, and a door was opened unto me of the Lord,

13 I had no rest in my spirit, because I found not Titus my brother: but taking my leave of them, I went from thence into Macedonia.

14 Now thanks be unto God, which always causeth us to triumph in Christ, and maketh manifest the savour of his knowledge by us in every place.

15 For we are unto God a sweet savour of Christ, in them that are saved, and in them that perish:
16 To the one we are the savour of death unto death; and to the other the savour of life unto life. And who is sufficient for these things?
17 For we are not as many, which corrupt the word of God: but as of sincerity, but as of God, in the sight of God speak we in Christ.

Chapter 3

1 Do we begin again to commend ourselves? or need we, as some others, epistles of commendation to you, or letters of commendation from you?
2 Ye are our epistle written in our hearts, known and read of all men:
3 Forasmuch as ye are manifestly declared to be the epistle of Christ ministered by us, written not with ink, but with the Spirit of the living God; not in tables of stone, but in fleshly tables of the heart.
4 And such trust have we through Christ ~~to God-ward:~~ *toward God.*
5 Not that we are sufficient of ourselves to think any thing as of ourselves; but our sufficiency is of God;
6 Who also hath made us able ministers of the new testament; not of the letter, but of the spirit: for the letter killeth, but the spirit giveth life.
7 But if the ministration of death, written and engraven in stones, was glorious, so that the children of Israel could not stedfastly behold the face of Moses for the glory of his countenance; which glory was to be done away:
8 How shall not the ministration of the spirit be rather glorious?
9 For if the ministration of condemnation be glory, much more doth the ministration of righteousness exceed in glory.
10 For even that which was made glorious had no glory in this respect, by reason of the glory that excelleth.
11 For if that which is done away was glorious, much more that which remaineth is glorious.
12 Seeing then that we have such hope, we use great plainness of speech:
13 And not as Moses, which put a veil over his face, that the children of Israel could not stedfastly look to the end of that which is abolished:
14 But their minds were blinded: for until this day remaineth the same veil untaken away in the reading of the old testament; which veil is done away in Christ.
15 But even unto this day, when Moses is read, the veil is upon their heart.
16 Nevertheless when ~~it~~ *their heart* shall turn to the Lord, the veil shall be taken away.
17 Now the Lord is that Spirit: and where the Spirit of the Lord is, there is liberty.
18 But we all, with open face beholding as in a glass the glory of the Lord, are changed into the same image from glory to glory, even as by the Spirit of the Lord.

Chapter 4

1 Therefore seeing we have this ministry, as we have received mercy, we faint not;
2 But have renounced the hidden things of dishonesty, not walking in craftiness, nor handling the word of God deceitfully; but by manifestation of the truth commending ourselves to every man's conscience in the sight of God.
3 But if our gospel be hid, it is hid to them that are lost:
4 In whom the god of this world hath blinded the minds of them which believe not, lest the light of the glorious gospel of Christ, who is the image of God, should shine unto them.
5 For we preach not ourselves, but Christ Jesus the Lord; and ourselves your servants for Jesus' sake.
6 For God, who commanded the light to shine out of darkness, hath shined in our hearts, to give the light of the knowledge of the glory of God in the face of Jesus Christ.
7 But we have this treasure in earthen vessels, that the excellency of the power may be of God, and not of us.
8 We are troubled on every side, yet not distressed; we are perplexed, but not in despair;
9 Persecuted, but not forsaken; cast down, but not destroyed;
10 Always bearing about in the body the dying of the Lord Jesus, that the life also of Jesus might be made manifest in our body.
11 For we which live are alway delivered unto death for Jesus' sake, that the life also of Jesus might be made manifest in our mortal flesh.
12 So then ~~death~~ *it* worketh ~~in~~ *death unto* us, but life ~~in~~ *unto* you.
13 We having the same spirit of faith, according as it is written, I believed, and therefore have I spoken; we also believe, and therefore speak;
14 Knowing that he which raised up the Lord Jesus shall raise up us also by Jesus, and shall present us with you.
15 For *we bear* all things ~~are~~ for your sakes, that the abundant grace might through the thanksgiving of many redound to the glory of God.
16 For which cause we faint not; but though our outward man perish, yet the inward man is renewed day by day.
17 For our light affliction, which is but for a moment, worketh for us a far more exceeding and eternal weight of glory;
18 While we look not at the things which are seen, but at the things which are not seen: for the things which are seen are temporal; but the things which are not seen are eternal.

Chapter 5

1 For we know that if our earthly house of this tabernacle were dissolved, we have a building of God, an house not made with hands, eternal in the heavens.

2 For in this we groan, earnestly desiring to be clothed upon with our house which is from heaven:

3 If so be that being clothed we shall not be found naked.

4 For we that are in this tabernacle do groan, being burdened: not for that we would be unclothed, but clothed upon, that mortality might be swallowed up of life.

5 Now he that hath wrought us for the selfsame thing is God, who also hath given unto us the earnest of the Spirit.

6 Therefore we are always confident, knowing that, whilst we are at home in the body, we are absent from the Lord:

7 (For we walk by faith, not by sight:)

8 We are confident, I say, and willing rather to be absent from the body, and to be present with the Lord.

9 Wherefore we labour, that, whether present or absent, we may be accepted of him.

10 For we must all appear before the judgment seat of Christ; that every one may receive *a reward of* the ~~things~~ *deeds* done in ~~his~~ *the* body, *things* according to ~~that~~ *what* he hath done, whether ~~it be~~ good or bad.

11 Knowing therefore the terror of the Lord, we persuade men; but we are made manifest unto God; and I trust also are made manifest in your consciences.

12 For we commend not ourselves again unto you, but give you occasion to glory on our behalf, that ye may have somewhat to answer them which glory in appearance, and not in heart.

13 For ~~whether~~ *we bear record that* we ~~be~~ *are not* beside ourselves; *for whether we glory*, it is to God: or whether we be sober, it is for your ~~cause~~ *sakes*.

14 For the love of Christ constraineth us; because we thus judge, that if one died for all, then ~~were~~ *are* all dead:

15 And ~~that~~ he died for all, that they which live should not henceforth live unto themselves, but unto him which died for them, and rose again.

16 Wherefore henceforth ~~know we no man~~ *live we no more* after the flesh: yea, though *we once lived after the flesh, yet since* we have known Christ ~~after the flesh, yet~~ now henceforth ~~know we him~~ *live we* no more *after the flesh*.

17 Therefore if any man ~~be~~ *live* in Christ, he is a new creature: old things are passed away; behold, all things are become new.

18 And *receiveth* all *the* things ~~are~~ of God, who hath reconciled us to himself by Jesus Christ, and hath given to us the ministry of reconciliation;

19 To wit, that God ~~was~~ *is* in Christ, reconciling the world unto himself, not imputing their trespasses unto them; and hath committed unto us the word of reconciliation.

20 Now then we are ambassadors for Christ, as though God did beseech you by us: we pray you in Christ's stead, be ye reconciled to God.

21 For he hath made him to be sin for us, who knew no sin; that we might be made the righteousness of God in him.

Chapter 6

1 We then, as workers together with ~~him~~ *Christ*, beseech you also that ye receive not the grace of God in vain.

2 (For he saith, I have heard thee in a time accepted, and in the day of salvation have I succoured thee: behold, now is the accepted time; behold, now is the day of salvation.)

3 Giving no offence in any thing, that the ministry be not blamed:

4 But in all things approving ourselves as the ministers of God, in much patience, in afflictions, in necessities, in distresses,

5 In stripes, in imprisonments, in tumults, in labours, in watchings, in fastings;

6 By pureness, by knowledge, by longsuffering, by kindness, by the Holy Ghost, by love unfeigned,

7 By the word of truth, by the power of God, by the armour of righteousness on the right hand and on the left,

8 By honour and dishonour, by evil report and good report: as deceivers, and yet true;

9 As unknown, and yet well known; as dying, and, behold, we live; as chastened, and not killed;

10 As sorrowful, yet alway rejoicing; as poor, yet making many rich; as having nothing, and yet possessing all things.

11 O ye Corinthians, our mouth is open unto you, our heart is enlarged.

12 Ye are not straitened in us, but ye are straitened in your own bowels.

13 Now for a recompense in the same, (I speak as unto my children,) be ye also enlarged.

14 Be ye not unequally yoked together with unbelievers: for what fellowship hath righteousness with unrighteousness? and what communion hath light with darkness?

15 And what concord hath Christ with Belial? or what part hath he that believeth with an infidel?

16 And what agreement hath the temple of God with idols? for ye are the temple of the living God; as God hath said, I will dwell in them, and walk in them; and I will be their God, and they shall be my people.

17 Wherefore come out from among them, and be ye *the* separate, saith the Lord, and touch not the unclean thing; and I will receive you,

18 And will be a Father unto you, and ye shall

be my sons and daughters, saith the Lord Almighty.

Chapter 7

1 Having therefore these promises, dearly beloved, let us cleanse ourselves from all filthiness of the flesh and spirit, perfecting holiness in the fear of God.

2 Receive us; we have wronged no man, we have corrupted no man, we have defrauded no man.

3 I speak not this to condemn you: for I have said before, that ye are in our hearts to die and live with you.

4 Great is my boldness of speech toward you, great is my glorying of you: I am filled with comfort, I am exceeding joyful in all our tribulation.

5 For, when we were come into Macedonia, our flesh had no rest, but we were troubled on every side; without were fightings, within were fears.

6 Nevertheless God, that comforteth those that are cast down, comforted us by the coming of Titus;

7 And not by his coming only, but by the consolation wherewith he was comforted in you, when he told us your earnest desire, your mourning, your fervent mind toward me; so that I rejoiced the more.

8 For though I made you sorry with a letter, I do not repent, though I did repent: for I perceive that the same epistle hath made you sorry, though it were but for a season.

9 Now I rejoice, not that ye were made sorry, but that ye sorrowed to repentance: for ye were made sorry after a godly manner, that ye might receive damage by us in nothing.

10 For godly sorrow worketh repentance to salvation not to be repented of: but the sorrow of the world worketh death.

11 For behold this selfsame thing, that ye sorrowed after a godly sort, what carefulness it wrought in you, yea, what clearing of yourselves, yea, what indignation, yea, what fear, yea, what vehement desire, yea, what zeal, yea, what revenge! In all things ye have approved yourselves to be clear in this matter.

12 Wherefore, though I wrote unto you, I did it not for his cause that had done the wrong, nor for his cause that suffered wrong, but that our care for you in the sight of God might appear unto you.

13 Therefore we were comforted in your comfort: yea, and exceedingly the more joyed we for the joy of Titus, because his spirit was refreshed by you all.

14 For if I have boasted any thing to him of you, I am not ashamed; but as we spake all things to you in truth, even so our boasting, which I made before Titus, is found a truth.

15 And his inward affection is more abundant toward you, whilst he remembereth the obedience of you all, how with fear and trembling ye received him.

16 I rejoice therefore that I have confidence in you in all things.

Chapter 8

1 Moreover, brethren, we ~~do you to wit~~ *would have you to know* of the grace of God bestowed on the churches of Macedonia;

2 How that in a great trial of affliction the abundance of their joy and their deep poverty abounded unto the riches of their liberality.

3 For to their power, I bear record, yea, and beyond their power they were willing of themselves;

4 Praying us with much entreaty that we would receive the gift, and take upon us the fellowship of the ministering to the saints.

5 And this they did, not as we ~~hoped~~ *required*, but first gave their own selves to the Lord, and unto us by the will of God.

6 Insomuch that we desired Titus, that as he had begun, so he would also finish in you the same grace also.

7 Therefore, as ye abound in every thing, in faith, and utterance, and knowledge, and in all diligence, and in your love to us, see that ye abound in this grace also.

8 I speak not by commandment, but by occasion of the forwardness of others, and to prove the sincerity of your love.

9 For ye know the grace of our Lord Jesus Christ, that, though he was rich, yet for your sakes he became poor, that ye through his poverty might be rich.

10 And herein I give my advice: for this is expedient for you, who have begun before, not only to do, but also to be forward a year ago.

11 Now therefore perform the doing of it; that as there was a readiness to will, so there may be a performance also out of that which ye have.

12 For if there be first a willing mind, it is accepted according to that a man hath, and not according to that he hath not.

13 For I mean not that other men be eased, and ye burdened:

14 But by an equality, that now at this time your abundance may be a supply for their want, that their abundance also may be a supply for your want: that there may be equality:

15 As it is written, He that had gathered much had nothing over; and he that had gathered little had no lack.

16 But thanks be to God, which put the same earnest care into the heart of Titus for you.

17 For indeed he accepted the exhortation; but being more forward, of his own accord he went

unto you.

18 And we have sent with him the brother, whose praise is in the gospel throughout all the churches;
19 And not that only, but who was also chosen of the churches to travel with us with this grace, which is administered by us to the glory of the same Lord, and declaration of your ready mind:
20 Avoiding this, that no man should blame us in this abundance which is administered by us:
21 Providing for honest things, not only in the sight of the Lord, but also in the sight of men.
22 ~~And we have sent with them our brother, whom we have oftentimes proved diligent in many things, but now much more diligent, upon the great confidence which I have in you.~~ *Therefore we send him unto you, in consequence of the great confidence which we have in you, that you will receive the things concerning you, to the glory of Christ;*
23 ~~Whether any do inquire of Titus, he is my partner and fellowhelper concerning you: or our brethren be inquired of, they are the messengers of the churches, and the glory of Christ~~ *whether we send by the hand of Titus, my partner and fellow-laborer, or our brethren, the messengers of the churches.*
24 Wherefore show ye to them, and before the churches, the proof of your love, and of our boasting on your behalf.

Chapter 9

1 For as touching the ministering to the saints, it is superfluous for me to write to you:
2 For I know the forwardness of your mind, for which I boast of you to them of Macedonia, that Achaia was ready a year ago; and your zeal hath provoked very many.
3 Yet have I sent the brethren, lest our boasting of you should be in vain in this behalf; that, as I said, ye may be ready:
4 Lest haply if they of Macedonia come with me, and find you unprepared, we (that we say not, ye) should be ashamed in this same confident boasting.
5 Therefore I thought it necessary to exhort the brethren, that they would go before unto you, and make up before hand your bounty, whereof ye had notice before, that the same might be ready, as a matter of bounty, and not as of covetousness.
6 But this I say, He which soweth sparingly shall reap also sparingly; and he which soweth bountifully shall reap also bountifully.
7 Every man according as he purposeth in his heart, so let him give; not grudgingly, or of necessity: for God loveth a cheerful giver.
8 And God is able to make all grace abound toward you; that ye, always having all sufficiency in all things, may abound to every good work:
9 (As it is written, He hath dispersed abroad; he hath given to the poor: his righteousness remaineth

for ever.
10 Now he that ministereth seed to the sower both minister bread for your food, and multiply your seed sown, and increase the fruits of your righteousness;)
11 Being enriched in every thing to all bountifulness, which causeth through us thanksgiving to God.
12 For the administration of this service not only supplieth the want of the saints, but is abundant also by many thanksgivings unto God;
13 Whiles by the experiment of this ministration they glorify God for your professed subjection unto the gospel of Christ, and for your liberal distribution unto them, and unto all men;
14 And by their prayer for you, which long after you for the exceeding grace of God in you.
15 Thanks be unto God for his unspeakable gift.

Chapter 10

1 Now I Paul myself beseech you by the meekness and gentleness of Christ, who in presence am base among you, but being absent am bold toward you:
2 But I beseech you, that I may not be bold when I am present with that confidence, wherewith I think to be bold against some, which think of us as if we walked according to the flesh.
3 For though we walk in the flesh, we do not war after the flesh:
4 (For the weapons of our warfare are not carnal, but mighty through God to the pulling down of strong holds;)
5 Casting down imaginations, and every high thing that exalteth itself against the knowledge of God, and bringing into captivity every thought to the obedience of Christ;
6 And having in a readiness to revenge all disobedience, when your obedience is fulfilled.
7 Do ye look on things after the outward appearance? If any man trust to himself that he is Christ's, let him of himself think this again, that, as he is Christ's, even so are we Christ's.
8 For though I should boast somewhat more of our authority, which the Lord hath given us for edification, and not for your destruction, I should not be ashamed:
9 That I may not seem as if I would terrify you by letters.
10 For his letters, say they, are weighty and powerful; but his bodily presence is weak, and his speech contemptible.
11 Let such an one think this, that, such as we are in word by letters when we are absent, such will we be also in deed when we are present.
12 For we dare not make ourselves of the number, or compare ourselves with some that commend themselves: but they measuring themselves by themselves, and comparing themselves among

themselves, are not wise.

13 But we will not boast of things without our measure, but according to the measure of the rule which God hath distributed to us, a measure to reach even unto you.

14 For we stretch not ourselves beyond our measure, as though we reached not unto you: for we are come as far as to you also in preaching the gospel of Christ:

15 Not boasting of things without our measure, that is, of other men's labours; but having hope, when your faith is increased, that we shall be enlarged by you according to our rule abundantly,

16 To preach the gospel in the regions beyond you, and not to boast in another man's line of things made ready to our hand.

17 But he that glorieth, let him glory in the Lord.

18 For not he that commendeth himself is approved, but whom the Lord commendeth.

Chapter 11

1 Would to God ye could bear with me a little in my folly: and indeed bear with me.

2 For I am jealous over you with godly jealousy: for I have espoused you to one husband, that I may present you as a chaste virgin to Christ.

3 But I fear, lest by any means, as the serpent beguiled Eve through his subtlety, so your minds should be corrupted from the simplicity that is in Christ.

4 For if he that cometh preacheth another Jesus, whom we have not preached, or if ye receive another spirit, which ye have not received, or another gospel, which ye have not accepted, ye might well bear with ~~him~~ *me*.

5 For I suppose I was not a whit behind the very chiefest apostles.

6 But though I be rude in speech, yet not in knowledge; but we have been thoroughly made manifest among you in all things.

7 Have I committed an offence in abasing myself that ye might be exalted, because I have preached to you the gospel of God freely?

8 I robbed other churches, taking wages of them, to do you service.

9 And when I was present with you, and wanted, I was chargeable to no man: for that which was lacking to me the brethren which came from Macedonia supplied: and in all things I have kept myself from being burdensome unto you, and so will I keep myself.

10 As the truth of Christ is in me, no man shall stop me of this boasting in the regions of Achaia.

11 Wherefore? because I love you not? God knoweth.

12 But what I do, that I will do, that I may cut off occasion from them which desire occasion; that wherein they glory, they may be found even as we.

13 For such are false apostles, deceitful workers, transforming themselves into the apostles of Christ.

14 And no marvel; for Satan himself is transformed into an angel of light.

15 Therefore it is no great thing if his ministers also be transformed as the ministers of righteousness; whose end shall be according to their works.

16 I say again, Let no man think me a fool; if otherwise, yet as a fool receive me, that I may boast myself a little.

17 That which I speak, I speak it not after the Lord, but as it were foolishly, in this confidence of boasting.

18 Seeing that many glory after the flesh, I will glory also.

19 For ye suffer fools gladly, seeing ye yourselves are wise.

20 For ye suffer, if a man bring you into bondage, if a man devour you, if a man take of you, if a man exalt himself, if a man smite you on the face.

21 I speak as concerning reproach, as though we had been weak. Howbeit whereinsoever any is bold, (I speak foolishly,) I am bold also.

22 Are they Hebrews? so am I. Are they Israelites? so am I. Are they the seed of Abraham? so am I.

23 Are they ministers of Christ? (I speak as a fool) ~~I am more~~ *so am I*; in ~~labours~~ *labors* more abundant, in stripes above measure, in prisons more frequent, in deaths oft.

24 Of the Jews five times received I forty stripes save one.

25 Thrice was I beaten with rods, once was I stoned, thrice I suffered shipwreck, a night and a day I have been in the deep;

26 In journeyings often, in perils of waters, in perils of robbers, in perils by mine own countrymen, in perils by the heathen, in perils in the city, in perils in the wilderness, in perils in the sea, in perils among false brethren;

27 In weariness and painfulness, in watchings often, in hunger and thirst, in fastings often, in cold and nakedness.

28 Beside those things that are without, that which cometh upon me daily, the care of all the churches.

29 Who is weak, and I am not weak? who is offended, and I ~~burn~~ *anger* not?

30 If I must needs glory, I will glory of the things which concern mine infirmities.

31 The God and Father of our Lord Jesus Christ, which is blessed for evermore, knoweth that I lie not.

32 In Damascus the governor under Aretas the king kept the city of the Damascenes with a garrison, desirous to apprehend me:

33 And through a window in a basket was I let down by the wall, and escaped his hands.

Chapter 12

1 It is not expedient for me doubtless to glory. I will come to visions and revelations of the Lord.
2 I knew a man in Christ above fourteen years ago, (whether in the body, I cannot tell; or whether out of the body, I cannot tell: God knoweth;) such an one caught up to the third heaven.
3 And I knew such a man, (whether in the body, or out of the body, I cannot tell: God knoweth;)
4 How that he was caught up into paradise, and heard unspeakable words, which it is not lawful for a man to utter.
5 Of such an one will I glory: yet of myself I will not glory, but in mine infirmities.
6 For though I would desire to glory, I shall not be a fool; for I will say the truth: but now I forbear, lest any man should think of me above that which he seeth ~~me to be~~ *of me*, or that he heareth of me.
7 And lest I should be exalted above measure through the abundance of the revelations, there was given to me a thorn in the flesh, the messenger of Satan to buffet me, lest I should be exalted above measure.
8 For this thing I besought the Lord thrice, that it might depart from me.
9 And he said unto me, My grace is sufficient for thee: for my strength is made perfect in weakness. Most gladly therefore will I rather glory in my infirmities, that the power of Christ may rest upon me.
10 Therefore I take pleasure in infirmities, in reproaches, in necessities, in persecutions, in distresses for Christ's sake: for when I am weak, then am I strong.
11 I am become a fool in glorying; ye have compelled me: for I ought to have been commended of you: for in nothing am I behind the very chiefest apostles, though I be nothing.
12 Truly the signs of an apostle were wrought among you in all patience, in signs, and wonders, and mighty deeds.
13 For what is it wherein ye were inferior to other churches, except it be that I myself was not burdensome to you? forgive me this wrong.
14 Behold, the third time I am ready to come to you; and I will not be burdensome to you: for I seek not yours, but you: for the children ought not to lay up for the parents, but the parents for the children.
15 And I will very gladly spend and be spent for you; though the more abundantly I love you, the less I be loved.
16 But be it so, I did not burden you: nevertheless, being crafty, I caught you with guile.
17 Did I make a gain of you by any of them whom I sent unto you?
18 I desired Titus, and with him I sent a brother. Did Titus make a gain of you? walked we not in the same spirit? walked we not in the same steps?
19 Again, think ye that we excuse ourselves unto you? we speak before God in Christ: but we do all things, dearly beloved, for your edifying.
20 For I fear, lest, when I come, I shall not find you such as I would, and that I shall be found unto you such as ye would not: lest there be debates, envyings, wraths, strifes, backbitings, whisperings, swellings, tumults:
21 And lest, when I come again, my God will humble me among you, and that I shall bewail many which have sinned already, and have not repented of the uncleanness and fornication and lasciviousness which they have committed.

Chapter 13

1 This is the third time I am coming to you. In the mouth of two or three witnesses shall every word be established.
2 I told you before, and foretell you, as if I were present, the second time; and being absent now I write to them which heretofore have sinned, and to all other, that, if I come again, I will not spare:
3 Since ye seek a proof of Christ speaking in me, which to you-ward is not weak, but is mighty in you.
4 For though he was crucified through weakness, yet he liveth by the power of God. For we also are weak in him, but we shall live with him by the power of God toward you.
5 Examine yourselves, whether ye be in the faith; prove your own selves. Know ye not your own selves, how that Jesus Christ is in you, except ye be reprobates?
6 But I trust that ye shall know that we are not reprobates.
7 Now I pray to God that ye do no evil; not that we should appear approved, but that ye should do that which is honest, though we be as reprobates.
8 For we can do nothing against the truth, but for the truth.
9 For we are glad, when we are weak, and ye are strong: and this also we wish, even your perfection.
10 Therefore I write these things being absent, lest being present I should use sharpness, according to the power which the Lord hath given me to edification, and not to destruction.
11 Finally, brethren, farewell. Be perfect, be of good comfort, be of one mind, live in peace; and the God of love and peace shall be with you.
12 Greet one another with ~~an~~ holy ~~kiss~~ *salutation*.
13 All the saints salute you.
14 The grace of the Lord Jesus Christ, and the love of God, and the communion of the Holy Ghost, be with you all. Amen.

Chapter 1

1 Paul, an apostle, (not of men, neither by man, but by Jesus Christ, and God the Father, who raised him from the dead;)

2 And all the brethren which are with me, unto the churches of Galatia:

3 Grace be to you and peace from God the Father, and from our Lord Jesus Christ,

4 Who gave himself for our sins, that he might deliver us from this present evil world, according to the will of God and our Father:

5 To whom be glory for ever and ever. Amen.

6 I marvel that ye are so soon removed from him that called you into the grace of Christ unto another gospel:

7 Which is not another; but there be some that trouble you, and would pervert the gospel of Christ

8 But though we, or an angel from heaven, preach any other gospel unto you than that which we have preached unto you, let him be accursed.

9 As we said before, so say I now again, If any man preach any other gospel unto you than that ye have received, let him be accursed.

10 For do I now ~~persuade~~ *please* men, or God? or do I seek to please men? for if I yet pleased men, I should not be the servant of Christ.

11 But I certify you, brethren, that the gospel which was preached of me is not after man.

12 For I neither received it of man, neither was I taught it, but by the revelation of Jesus Christ.

13 For ye have heard of my conversation in time past in the Jews' religion, how that beyond measure I persecuted the church of God, and wasted it:

14 And profited in the Jews' religion above many my equals in mine own nation, being more exceedingly zealous of the traditions of my fathers.

15 But when it pleased God, who separated me from my mother's womb, and called me by his grace,

16 To reveal his Son in me, that I might preach him among the heathen; immediately I conferred not with flesh and blood:

17 Neither went I up to Jerusalem to them which were apostles before me; but I went into Arabia, and returned again unto Damascus.

18 Then after three years I went up to Jerusalem to see Peter, and abode with him fifteen days.

19 But other of the apostles saw I none, save James the Lord's brother.

20 Now the things which I write unto you, behold, before God, I lie not.

21 Afterwards I came into the regions of Syria and Cilicia;

22 And was unknown by face unto the churches of Judaea which were in Christ:

23 But they had heard only, That he which persecuted us in times past now preacheth the faith which once he destroyed.

24 And they glorified God ~~in~~ *on account of* me.

Chapter 2

1 Then fourteen years after I went up again to Jerusalem with Barnabas, and took Titus with me also.

2 And I went up by revelation, and communicated unto them that gospel which I preach among the Gentiles, but privately to them which were of reputation, lest by any means I should run, or had run, in vain.

3 But neither Titus, who was with me, being a Greek, was compelled to be circumcised:

4 ~~And that because of~~ *Notwithstanding, there were some brought in by* false brethren unawares ~~brought in~~ , who came in privily to spy out our liberty which we have in Christ Jesus, that they might bring us into bondage:

5 To whom we gave place by subjection, no, not for an hour; that the truth of the gospel might continue with you.

6 But of these who seemed to be somewhat, (whatsoever they were, it maketh nomatter to me: God accepteth no man's person:) for they who seemed to be somewhat inconference added nothing to me:

7 But contrariwise, when they saw that the gospel of the uncircumcision was committed unto me, as the gospel of the circumcision was unto Peter;

8 (For he that wrought effectually in Peter to the apostleship of the circumcision, the same was mighty in me toward the Gentiles:)

9 And when James, Cephas, and John, who seemed to be pillars, perceived the gracethat was given unto me, they gave to me and Barnabas the right hands of fellowship; that we should go unto the heathen, and they unto the circumcision.

10 Only they would that we should remember the poor; the same which I also was forward to do.

11 But when Peter was come to Antioch, I withstood him to the face, because he wasto be blamed.

12 For before that certain came from James, he did eat with the Gentiles: but when they were come, he withdrew and separated himself, fearing them which were of the circumcision.

13 And the other Jews dissembled likewise with him; insomuch that Barnabas also was carried away with their dissimulation.

14 But when I saw that they walked not uprightly according to the truth of the gospel, I said unto Peter before them all, If thou, being a Jew, livest after the manner of *the* Gentiles, and

not as do the Jews, why compellest thou the Gentiles to live as do the Jews?

15 We who are Jews by nature, and not sinners of the Gentiles,

16 Knowing that a man is not justified by the works of the law, but by the faith of Jesus Christ, even we have believed in Jesus Christ, that we might be justified by the faith of Christ, and not by the works of the law: for by the works of the law shall no flesh be justified.

17 But if, while we seek to be justified by Christ, we ourselves also are found sinners, is therefore Christ the minister of sin? God forbid.

18 For if I build again the things which I destroyed, I make myself a transgressor.

19 For I through the law am dead to the law, that I might live unto God.

20 I am crucified with Christ: nevertheless I live; yet not I, but Christ liveth in me: and the life which I now live in the flesh I live by the faith of the Son of God, who loved me, and gave himself for me.

21 I do not frustrate the grace of God: for if righteousness come by the law, then Christ is dead in vain.

Chapter 3

1 O foolish Galatians, who hath bewitched you, that ye should not obey the truth, before whose eyes Jesus Christ hath been evidently set forth, crucified among you?

2 This only would I learn of you, Received ye the Spirit by the works of the law, or by the hearing of faith?

3 Are ye so foolish? having begun in the Spirit, are ye now made perfect by the flesh?

4 Have ye suffered so many things in vain? if it be yet in vain.

5 He therefore that ministereth to you the Spirit, and worketh miracles among you, doeth he it by the works of the law, or by the hearing of faith?

6 Even as Abraham believed God, and it was accounted to him for righteousness.

7 Know ye therefore that they which are of faith, the same are the children of Abraham.

8 And the scripture, foreseeing that God would justify the heathen through faith, preached before the gospel unto Abraham, saying, In thee shall all nations be blessed.

9 So then they which be of faith are blessed with faithful Abraham.

10 For as many as are of the works of the law are under the curse: for it is written, Cursed is every one that continueth not in all things which are written in the book of the law to do them.

11 But that no man is justified by the law in the sight of God, it is evident: for, The just shall live by faith.

12 And the law is not of faith: but, The man that doeth them shall live in them.

13 Christ hath redeemed us from the curse of the law, being made a curse for us: for it is written, Cursed is every one that hangeth on a tree:

14 That the blessing of Abraham might come on the Gentiles through Jesus Christ; that ~~we~~ *they* might receive the promise of the ~~S~~spirit through faith.

15 Brethren, I speak after the manner of men; Though it be but a man's covenant, yet ~~if~~ *when* it be confirmed, no man disannulleth, or addeth thereto.

16 Now to Abraham and his seed were the promises made. He saith not, And to seeds, as of many; but as of one, And to thy seed, which is Christ.

17 And this I say, that the covenant, that was confirmed before of God in Christ, the law, which was four hundred and thirty years after, cannot disannul, that it should make the promise of none effect.

18 For if the inheritance ~~be~~ *is* of the law, *then* it is no more of promise: but God gave it to Abraham by promise.

19 Wherefore then ~~serveth the law? It~~ *, the law* was added because of transgressions, till the seed should come to whom the promise was made *in the law given to Moses,* ~~; and it~~ *who* was ordained by *the hand of* angels ~~in the hand of~~ *to be* a mediator *of this first covenant, (the law)*.

20 Now ~~a~~ *this* mediator ~~is~~ *was* not a mediator of ~~one, but God is one~~ *the new covenant; but there is one mediator of the new covenant, who is Christ, as it is written in the law concerning the promises made to Abraham and his seed. Now Christ is the mediator of life; for this is the promise which God made unto Abraham*.

21 Is the law then against the promises of God? God forbid: for if there had been a law given which could have given life, verily righteousness should have been by the law.

22 But the scripture hath concluded all under sin, that the promise by faith of Jesus Christ might be given to them that believe.

23 But before faith came, we were kept under the law, shut up unto the faith which should afterwards be revealed.

24 Wherefore the law was our schoolmaster ~~to bring us unto~~ *until* Christ, that we might be justified by faith.

25 But after that faith is come, we are no longer under a schoolmaster.

26 For ye are all the children of God by faith in ~~Christ~~ Jesus *Christ*.

27 For as many of you as have been baptized

into Christ have put on Christ.

28 There is neither Jew nor Greek, there is neither bond nor free, there is neither male nor female: for ye are all one in Christ Jesus.

29 And if ye ~~be~~ *are* Christ's, then are ye Abraham's seed, and heirs according to the promise.

Chapter 4

1 Now I say, That the heir, as long as he is a child, differeth nothing from a servant, though he be lord of all;

2 But is under tutors and governors until the time appointed of the father.

3 Even so we, when we were children, were in bondage under the elements of the world:

4 But when the fulness of the time was come, God sent forth his Son, made of a woman, made under the law,

5 To redeem them that were under the law, that we might receive the adoption of sons.

6 And because ye are sons, God hath sent forth the Spirit of his Son into your hearts, crying, Abba, Father.

7 Wherefore thou art no more a servant, but a son; and if a son, then an heir of God through Christ.

8 Howbeit then, when ye knew not God, ye did service unto them which by nature are no gods.

9 But now, after that ye have known God, or rather are known of God, how turn ye again to the weak and beggarly elements, whereunto ye desire again to be in bondage?

10 Ye observe days, and months, and times, and years.

11 I am afraid of you, lest I have bestowed upon you labour in vain.

12 Brethren, I beseech you, *to* be *perfect* as I am *perfect*; for I am ~~as ye are:~~ *persuaded as ye have a knowledge of me,* ye have not injured me at all *by your sayings*.

13 Ye know how through infirmity of the flesh I preached the gospel unto you at the first.

14 And my temptation which was in my flesh ye despised not, nor rejected; but received me as an angel of God, even as Christ Jesus.

15 Where is then the blessedness ye spake of? for I bear you record, that, if it had been possible, ye would have plucked out your own eyes, and have given them to me.

16 Am I therefore become your enemy, because I tell you the truth?

17 They zealously affect you, but not well; yea, they would exclude you, that ye might affect them.

18 But it is good to be zealously affected always in a good thing, and not only when I am present with you.

19 My little children, of whom I travail in birth again until Christ be formed in you,

20 I desire to be present with you now, and to change my voice; for I stand in doubt of you.

21 Tell me, ye that desire to be under the law, do ye not hear the law?

22 For it is written, that Abraham had two sons, the one by a bondmaid, the other by a freewoman.

23 But he who was of the bondwoman was born after the flesh; but he of the freewoman was by promise.

24 Which things are an allegory: for these are the two covenants; the one from the mount Sinai, which gendereth to bondage, which is Agar.

25 For this Agar is mount Sinai in Arabia, and answereth to Jerusalem which now is, and is in bondage with her children.

26 But Jerusalem which is above is free, which is the mother of us all.

27 For it is written, Rejoice, thou barren that bearest not; break forth and cry, thou that travailest not: for the desolate hath many more children than she which hath an husband.

28 Now we, brethren, as Isaac was, are the children of promise.

29 But as then he that was born after the flesh persecuted him that was born after the Spirit, even so it is now.

30 Nevertheless what saith the scripture? Cast out the bondwoman and her son: for the son of the bondwoman shall not be heir with the son of the freewoman.

31 So then, brethren, we are not children of the bondwoman, but of the free.

Chapter 5

1 Stand fast therefore in the liberty where with Christ hath made us free, and be not entangled again with the yoke of bondage.

2 Behold, I Paul say unto you, that if ye be circumcised, Christ shall profit you nothing.

3 For I testify again to every man that is circumcised, that he is a debtor to do the whole law.

4 Christ is become of no effect unto you, whosoever of you are justified by the law; ye are fallen from grace.

5 For we through the Spirit wait for the hope of righteousness by faith.

6 For in Jesus Christ neither circumcision availeth any thing, nor uncircumcision; but faith which worketh by love.

7 Ye did run well; who did hinder you that ye should not obey the truth?

8 This persuasion cometh not of him that calleth

you.

9 A little leaven leaveneth the whole lump.

10 I have confidence in you through the Lord, that ye will be none otherwise minded: but he that troubleth you shall bear his judgment, whosoever he be.

11 And I, brethren, if I yet preach circumcision, why do I yet suffer persecution? then is the offence of the cross ceased.

12 I would they were even cut off which trouble you.

13 For, brethren, ye have been called unto liberty; only use not liberty for an occasion to the flesh, but by love serve one another.

14 For all the law is fulfilled in one word, even in this; Thou shalt love thy neighbour as thyself.

15 But if ye bite and devour one another, take heed that ye be not consumed one of another.

16 This I say then, Walk in the Spirit, and ye shall not fulfil the lust of the flesh.

17 For the flesh lusteth against the Spirit, and the Spirit against the flesh: and these are contrary the one to the other: so that ye cannot do the things that ye would.

18 But if ye be led of the Spirit, ye are not under the law.

19 Now the works of the flesh are manifest, which are these; Adultery, fornication, uncleanness, lasciviousness,

20 Idolatry, witchcraft, hatred, variance, emulations, wrath, strife, seditions, heresies,

21 Envyings, murders, drunkenness, revellings, and such like: of the which I tell you before, as I have also told you in time past, that they which do such things shall not inherit the kingdom of God.

22 But the fruit of the Spirit is love, joy, peace, longsuffering, gentleness, goodness, faith,

23 Meekness, temperance: against such there is no law.

24 And they that are Christ's have crucified the flesh with the affections and lusts.

25 If we live in the Spirit, let us also walk in the Spirit.

26 Let us not be desirous of vain glory, provoking one another, envying one another.

Chapter 6

1 Brethren, if a man be overtaken in a fault, ye which are spiritual, restore such an one in the spirit of meekness; considering thyself, lest thou also be tempted.

2 Bear ye one another's burdens, and so fulfil the law of Christ.

3 For if a man think himself to be something, when he is nothing, he deceiveth himself.

4 But let every man prove his own work, and then shall he have rejoicing in himself alone, and not in another.

5 For every man shall bear his own burden.

6 Let him that is taught in the word communicate unto him that teacheth in all good things.

7 Be not deceived; God is not mocked: for whatsoever a man soweth, that shall he also reap.

8 For he that soweth to his flesh shall of the flesh reap corruption; but he that soweth to the Spirit shall of the Spirit reap life everlasting.

9 And let us not be weary in well doing: for in due season we shall reap, if we faint not.

10 As we have therefore opportunity, let us do good unto all men, especially unto them who are of the household of faith.

11 Ye see how large a letter I have written unto you with mine own hand.

12 As many as desire to make a fair show in the flesh, they constrain you to be circumcised; only lest they should suffer persecution for the cross of Christ.

13 For neither they themselves who are circumcised keep the law; but desire to have you circumcised, that they may glory in your flesh.

14 But God forbid that I should glory, save in the cross of our Lord Jesus Christ, by whom the world is crucified unto me, and I unto the world.

15 For in Christ Jesus neither circumcision availeth any thing, nor uncircumcision, but a new creature.

16 And as many as walk according to this rule, peace be on them, and mercy, and upon the Israel of God.

17 From henceforth let no man trouble me: for I bear in my body the marks of the Lord Jesus.

18 Brethren, the grace of our Lord Jesus Christ be with your spirit. Amen.

Chapter 1

1 Paul, an apostle of Jesus Christ by the will of God, to the saints which are at Ephesus, and to the faithful in Christ Jesus:

2 Grace be to you, and peace, from God our Father, and from the Lord Jesus Christ.

3 Blessed be the God and Father of our Lord Jesus Christ, who hath blessed us with all spiritual blessings in heavenly places in Christ:

4 According as he hath chosen us in him before the foundation of the world, that we should be holy and without blame before him in love:

5 Having predestinated us unto the adoption of children by Jesus Christ to himself, according to the good pleasure of his will,

6 To the praise of the glory of his grace, wherein he hath made us accepted in the beloved.

7 In whom we have redemption through his blood, the forgiveness of sins, according to the riches of his grace;

8 Wherein he hath abounded toward us in all wisdom and prudence;

9 Having made known unto us the mystery of his will, according to his good pleasure which he hath purposed in himself:

10 That in the dispensation of the fulness of times he might gather together in one all things in Christ, both which are in heaven, and which are on earth; even in him:

11 In whom also we have obtained an inheritance, being predestinated according to the purpose of him who worketh all things after the counsel of his own will:

12 That we should be to the praise of his glory, who first trusted in Christ.

13 In whom ye also trusted, after that ye heard the word of truth, the gospel of your salvation: in whom also after that ye believed, ye were sealed with that holy Spirit of promise,

14 Which is the earnest of our inheritance until the redemption of the purchased possession, unto the praise of his glory.

15 Wherefore I also, after I heard of your faith in the Lord Jesus, and love unto all the saints,

16 Cease not to give thanks for you, making mention of you in my prayers;

17 That the God of our Lord Jesus Christ, the Father of glory, may give unto you the spirit of wisdom and revelation in the knowledge of him:

18 The eyes of your understanding being enlightened; that ye may know what is the hope of his calling, and what the riches of the glory of his inheritance in the saints,

19 And what is the exceeding greatness of his power to us-ward who believe, according to the working of his mighty power,

20 Which he wrought in Christ, when he raised him from the dead, and set him at his own right hand in the heavenly places,

21 Far above all principality, and power, and might, and dominion, and every name that is named, not only in this world, but also in that which is to come:

22 And hath put all things under his feet, and gave him to be the head over all things to the church,

23 Which is his body, the fulness of him that filleth all in all.

Chapter 2

1 And you hath he quickened, who were dead in trespasses and sins:

2 Wherein in time past ye walked according to the course of this world, according to the prince of the power of the air, the spirit that now worketh in the children of disobedience:

3 Among whom also we all had our conversation in times past in the lusts of our flesh, fulfilling the desires of the flesh and of the mind; and were by nature the children of wrath, even as others.

4 But God, who is rich in mercy, for his great love wherewith he loved us,

5 Even when we were dead in sins, hath quickened us together with Christ, (by grace ye are saved;)

6 And hath raised us up together, and made us sit together in heavenly places in Christ Jesus:

7 That in the ages to come he might show the exceeding riches of his grace in his kindness toward us through Christ Jesus.

8 For by grace are ye saved through faith; and that not of yourselves: *but* it is the gift of God:

9 Not of works, lest any man should boast.

10 For we are his workmanship, created in Christ Jesus unto good works, which God hath before ordained that we should walk in them.

11 Wherefore remember, that ye ~~being~~ *were* in time past Gentiles in the flesh, who are called Uncircumcision by that which is called the Circumcision in the flesh made by hands;

12 That at that time ye were without Christ, being aliens from the commonwealth of Israel, and strangers from the covenants of promise, having no hope, and without God in the world:

13 But now in Christ Jesus ye who sometimes were far off are made nigh by the blood of Christ.

14 For he is our peace, who hath made both one, and hath broken down the middle wall of partition between us;

15 Having abolished in his flesh the enmity, even the law of commandments contained in ordinances; for to make in himself of twain one new man, so making peace;

16 And that he might reconcile both unto God in one body by the cross, having slain the enmity thereby:

17 And came and preached peace to you which were afar off, and to them that were nigh.

18 For through him we both have access by one Spirit unto the Father.

19 Now therefore ye are no more strangers and foreigners, but fellowcitizens with the saints, and of the household of God;

20 And are built upon the foundation of the apostles and prophets, Jesus Christ himself being the chief corner stone;

21 In whom all the building fitly framed together groweth unto an holy temple in the Lord:

22 In whom ye also are builded together for an habitation of God through the Spirit.

Chapter 3

1 For this cause I Paul, *am* the prisoner of Jesus Christ ~~for~~ *among* you Gentiles,

2 ~~If ye have heard of~~ *For* the dispensation of the grace of God which is given me to you-ward:

3 ~~How~~ *As ye have heard* that by revelation he made known unto me the mystery *of Christ*; (as I wrote ~~afore~~ *before* in few words,

4 Whereby, when ye read, ye may understand my knowledge in the mystery of Christ)

5 Which in other ages was not made known unto the sons of men, as it is now revealed unto his holy apostles and prophets by the Spirit;

6 That the Gentiles should be fellowheirs, and of the same body, and partakers of his promise in Christ by the gospel:

7 Whereof I was made a minister, according to the gift of the grace of God given unto me by the effectual working of his power.

8 Unto me, who am less than the least of all saints, is this grace given, that I should preach among the Gentiles the unsearchable riches of Christ;

9 And to make all men see what is the fellowship of the mystery, which from the beginning of the world hath been hid in God, who created all things by Jesus Christ:

10 To the intent that now unto the principalities and powers in heavenly places might be known by the church the manifold wisdom of God,

11 According to the eternal purpose which he purposed in Christ Jesus our Lord:

12 In whom we have boldness and access with confidence by the faith of him.

13 Wherefore I desire that ye faint not at my tribulations for you, which is your glory.

14 For this cause I bow my knees unto the Father of our Lord Jesus Christ,

15 Of whom the whole family in heaven and earth is named,

16 That he would grant you, according to the riches of his glory, to be strengthened with might by his Spirit in the inner man;

17 That Christ may dwell in your hearts by faith; that ye, being rooted and grounded in love,

18 May be able to comprehend with all saints what is the breadth, and length, and depth, and height;

19 And to know the love of Christ, which passeth knowledge, that ye might be filled with all the fulness of God.

20 Now unto him that is able to do exceeding abundantly above all that we ask or think, according to the power that worketh in us,

21 Unto him be glory in the church by Christ Jesus throughout all ages, world without end. Amen.

Chapter 4

1 I therefore, the prisoner of the Lord, beseech you that ye walk worthy of the vocation wherewith ye are called,

2 With all lowliness and meekness, with longsuffering, forbearing one another in love;

3 Endeavouring to keep the unity of the Spirit in the bond of peace.

4 ~~There is~~ *In* one body, and one Spirit, even as ye are called in one hope of your calling;

5 One Lord, one faith, one baptism,

6 One God and Father of all, who is above all, and through all, and in you all.

7 But unto every one of us is given grace according to the measure of the gift of Christ.

8 Wherefore he saith, When he ascended up on high, he led captivity captive, and gave gifts unto men.

9 (Now that he ascended, what is it but that he also descended first into the lower parts of the earth?

10 He ~~that~~ *who* descended is the same also ~~that~~ *who* ascended up ~~far above~~ *into heaven, to glorify him who reigneth over* all heavens, that he might fill all things.)

11 And he gave some, apostles; and some, prophets; and some, evangelists; and some, pastors and teachers;

12 For the perfecting of the saints, for the work of the ministry, for the edifying of the body of Christ:

13 Till we, *in the unity of the faith,* all come ~~in the unity of the faith, and of~~ *to* the knowledge of the Son of God, unto a perfect man, unto the measure of the stature of the fulness of Christ:

14 That we henceforth be no more children, tossed to and fro, and carried about with every

wind of doctrine, by the sleight of men, and cunning craftiness, whereby they lie in wait to deceive;

15 But speaking the truth in love, may grow up into him in all things, which is the head, even Christ:

16 From whom the whole body fitly joined together and compacted by that which every joint supplieth, according to the effectual working in the measure of every part, maketh increase of the body unto the edifying of itself in love.

17 This I say therefore, and testify in the Lord, that ye henceforth walk not as other Gentiles walk, in the vanity of their mind,

18 Having the understanding darkened, being alienated from the life of God through the ignorance that is in them, because of the blindness of their heart:

19 Who being past feeling have given themselves over unto lasciviousness, to work all uncleanness with greediness.

20 But ye have not so learned Christ;

21 If so be that ye have ~~heard~~ *learned* him, and have been taught by him, as the truth is in Jesus:

22 ~~That ye put off~~ *And now I speak unto you* concerning the former conversation*, by exhortation, that ye put off* the old man, which is corrupt according to the deceitful lusts;

23 And be renewed in the ~~spirit of your mind~~ *mind of the Spirit*;

24 And that ye put on the new man, which after God is created in righteousness and true holiness.

25 Wherefore putting away lying, speak every man truth with his neighbour: for we are members one of another.

26 ~~Be ye angry, and sin not:~~ *Can ye be angry, and not sin?* let not the sun go down upon your wrath:

27 Neither give place to the devil.

28 Let him that stole steal no more: but rather let him ~~labour~~ *labor*, working with his hands *for* the thing*s* which ~~is~~ *are* good, that he may have to give to him that needeth.

29 Let no corrupt communication proceed out of your mouth, but that which is good to the use of edifying, that it may minister grace unto the hearers.

30 And grieve not the holy Spirit of God, whereby ye are sealed unto the day of redemption.

31 Let all bitterness, and wrath, and anger, and clamour, and evil speaking, be put away from you, with all malice:

32 And be ye kind one to another, tenderhearted, forgiving one another, even as God for Christ's sake hath forgiven you.

Chapter 5

1 Be ye therefore followers of God, as dear children;

2 And walk in love, as Christ also hath loved us, and hath given himself for us an offering and a sacrifice to God for a sweetsmelling savour.

3 But fornication, and all uncleanness, or covetousness, let it not be once named among you, as becometh saints;

4 Neither filthiness, nor foolish talking, nor jesting, which are not convenient: but rather giving of thanks.

5 For this ye know, that no whoremonger, nor unclean person, nor covetous man, who is an idolater, hath any inheritance in the kingdom of Christ and of God.

6 Let no man deceive you with vain words: for because of these things cometh the wrath of God upon the children of disobedience.

7 Be not ye therefore partakers with them.

8 For ye were sometimes darkness, but now are ye light in the Lord: walk as children of light:

9 (For the fruit of the Spirit is in all goodness and righteousness and truth;)

10 Proving what is acceptable unto the Lord.

11 And have no fellowship with the unfruitful works of darkness, but rather reprove them.

12 For it is a shame even to speak of those things which are done of them in secret.

13 But all things that are reproved are made manifest by the light: for whatsoever doth make manifest is light.

14 Wherefore he saith, Awake thou that sleepest, and arise from the dead, and Christ shall give thee light.

15 See then that ye walk circumspectly, not as fools, but as wise,

16 Redeeming the time, because the days are evil.

17 Wherefore be ye not unwise, but understanding what *is* the will of the Lord ~~is~~.

18 And be not drunk with wine, wherein is excess; but be filled with the Spirit;

19 Speaking to yourselves in psalms and hymns and spiritual songs, singing and making melody in your heart to the Lord;

20 Giving thanks always for all things unto God and the Father in the name of our Lord Jesus Christ;

21 Submitting yourselves one to another in the fear of God.

22 Wives, submit yourselves unto your own husbands, as unto the Lord.

23 For the husband is the head of the wife, even as Christ is the head of the church: and he is the saviour of the body.

24 Therefore as the church is subject unto Christ, so let the wives be to their own husbands

in every thing.

25 Husbands, love your wives, even as Christ also loved the church, and gave himself for it;

26 That he might sanctify and cleanse it with the washing of water by the word,

27 That he might present it to himself a glorious church, not having spot, or wrinkle, or any such thing; but that it should be holy and without blemish.

28 So ought men to love their wives as their own bodies. He that loveth his wife loveth himself.

29 For no man ever yet hated his own flesh; but nourisheth and cherisheth it, even as the Lord the church:

30 For we are members of his body, of his flesh, and of his bones.

31 For this cause shall a man leave his father and mother, and shall be joined unto his wife, and they two shall be one flesh.

32 This is a great mystery: but I speak concerning Christ and the church.

33 Nevertheless let every one of you in particular so love his wife even as himself; and the wife see that she reverence her husband.

Chapter 6

1 Children, obey your parents in the Lord: for this is right.

2 Honour thy father and mother; which is the first commandment with promise;

3 That it may be well with thee, and thou mayest live long on the earth.

4 And, ye fathers, provoke not your children to wrath: but bring them up in the nurture and admonition of the Lord.

5 Servants, be obedient to them that are your masters according to the flesh, with fear and trembling, in singleness of your heart, as unto Christ;

6 Not with eyeservice, as menpleasers; but as the servants of Christ, doing the will of God from the heart;

7 With good will doing service, as to the Lord, and not to men:

8 Knowing that whatsoever good thing any man doeth, the same shall he receive of the Lord, whether he be bond or free.

9 And, ye masters, do the same things unto them, forbearing threatening: knowing that your Master also is in heaven; neither is there respect of persons with him.

10 Finally, my brethren, be strong in the Lord, and in the power of his might.

11 Put on the whole armour of God, that ye may be able to stand against the wiles of the devil.

12 For we wrestle not against flesh and blood, but against principalities, against powers, against the rulers of the darkness of this world, against spiritual wickedness in high places.

13 Wherefore take unto you the whole armour of God, that ye may be able to withstand in the evil day, and having done all, to stand.

14 Stand therefore, having your loins girt about with truth, and having on the breastplate of righteousness;

15 And your feet shod with the preparation of the gospel of peace;

16 Above all, taking the shield of faith, wherewith ye shall be able to quench all the fiery darts of the wicked.

17 And take the helmet of salvation, and the sword of the Spirit, which is the word of God:

18 Praying always with all prayer and supplication in the Spirit, and watching thereunto with all perseverance and supplication for all saints;

19 And for me, that utterance may be given unto me, that I may open my mouth boldly, to make known the mystery of the gospel,

20 For which I am an ambassador in bonds: that therein I may speak boldly, as I ought to speak.

21 But that ye also may know my affairs, and how I do, Tychicus, a beloved brother and faithful minister in the Lord, shall make known to you all things:

22 Whom I have sent unto you for the same purpose, that ye might know our affairs, and that he might comfort your hearts.

23 Peace be to the brethren, and love with faith, from God the Father and the Lord Jesus Christ.

24 Grace be with all them that love our Lord Jesus Christ in sincerity. Amen.

Chapter 1

1 Paul and Timotheus, the servants of Jesus Christ, to all the saints in Christ Jesus which are at Philippi, with the bishops and deacons:

2 Grace be unto you, and peace, from God our Father, and from the Lord Jesus Christ.

3 I thank my God upon every remembrance of you,

4 Always in every prayer of mine for *the steadfastness of* you all making request with joy,

5 For your fellowship in the gospel from the first day until now;

6 Being confident of this very thing, that he which hath begun a good work in you will perform it until the day of Jesus Christ:

7 Even as it is meet for me to think this of you all, because I have you in my heart; inasmuch as both in my bonds, and in the defence and confirmation of the gospel, ye all are partakers of my grace.

8 For God is my record, how greatly I long after you all in the bowels of Jesus Christ.

9 And this I pray, that your love may abound yet more and more in knowledge and in all judgment;

10 That ye may approve things that are excellent; that ye may be sincere and without offence till the day of Christ;

11 Being filled with the fruits of righteousness, which are by Jesus Christ, unto the glory and praise of God.

12 But I would ye should understand, brethren, that the things which happened unto me have fallen out rather unto the furtherance of the gospel;

13 So that my bonds in Christ are manifest in all the palace, and in all other places;

14 And many of the brethren in the Lord, waxing confident by my bonds, are much more bold to speak the word without fear.

15 Some indeed preach Christ even of envy and strife; and some also of good will:

16 The one preach Christ of contention, not sincerely, supposing to add affliction to my bonds:

17 But the other of love, knowing that I am set for the defence of the gospel.

18 What then? notwithstanding, every way, whether in pretence, or in truth, Christ is preached; and I therein do rejoice, yea, and will rejoice.

19 For I know that this shall turn to my salvation through your prayer, and the supply of the Spirit of Jesus Christ,

20 According to my earnest expectation and my hope, that in nothing I shall be ashamed, but that with all boldness, as always, so now also Christ shall be magnified in my body, whether it be by life, or by death.

22 But if I live in the flesh, ~~this is~~ *ye are* the fruit of my ~~labour~~ *labor*: yet what I shall choose I ~~wot~~ *know* not.

21 For ~~to~~ me to live is *to do the will of* Christ, and to die is *my* gain. *(verse order of 21 & 22 changed by JST)*

23 ~~For~~ *Now* I am in a strait betwixt two, having a desire to depart, and to be with Christ; which is far better:

24 Nevertheless to abide in the flesh is more needful for you.

25 And having this confidence, I know that I shall abide and continue with you all for your furtherance and joy of faith;

26 That your rejoicing *with me* may be more abundant in Jesus Christ for ~~me by~~ my coming to you again.

27 ~~Only~~ *Therefore* let your conversation be as it becometh the gospel of Christ: that whether I come and see you, or else be absent, I may hear of your affairs, that ye stand fast in one spirit, with one mind striving together for the faith of the gospel;

28 And in nothing terrified by your adversaries; ~~which is to them an evident token of perdition~~, *who reject the gospel, which bringeth on them destruction;* but ~~to you of~~ *you who receive the gospel,* salvation, and that of God.

29 For unto you it is given in the behalf of Christ, not only to believe on him, but also to suffer for his sake;

30 Having the same conflict which ye saw in me, and now ~~hear~~ *know* to be in me.

Chapter 2

1 If there be therefore any consolation in Christ, if any comfort of love, if any fellowship of the Spirit, if any bowels and mercies,

2 Fulfil ye my joy, that ye be likeminded, having the same love, being of one accord, of one mind.

3 Let nothing be done through strife or vainglory; but in lowliness of mind let each esteem other better than themselves.

4 Look not every man on his own things, but every man also on the things of others.

5 Let this mind be in you, which was also in Christ Jesus:

6 Who, being in the form of God, thought it not robbery to be equal with God:

7 But made himself of no reputation, and took upon him the form of a servant, and was made in the likeness of men:

8 And being found in fashion as a man, he humbled himself, and became obedient unto death, even the death of the cross.

9 Wherefore God also hath highly exalted him, and given him a name which is above every name:

10 That at the name of Jesus every knee should bow, of things in heaven, and things in earth, and things under the earth;

11 And that every tongue should confess that Jesus Christ is Lord, to the glory of God the Father.

12 Wherefore, my beloved, as ye have always obeyed, not as in my presence only, but now much more in my absence, work out your own salvation with fear and trembling.

13 For it is God which worketh in you both to will and to do of his good pleasure.

14 Do all things without murmurings and disputings:

15 That ye may be blameless and harmless, the sons of God, without rebuke, in the midst of a crooked and perverse nation, among whom ye shine as lights in the world;

16 Holding forth the word of life; that I may rejoice in the day of Christ, that I have not run in vain, neither laboured in vain.

17 Yea, and if I be offered ~~upon the~~ *a* sacrifice ~~and~~ *upon the* service of your faith, I joy, and rejoice with you all.

18 For the same cause also do ye joy, and rejoice with me.

19 But I trust in the Lord Jesus to send Timotheus shortly unto you, that I also may be of good comfort, when I know your state.

20 For I have no man likeminded, who will naturally care for your state.

21 For all seek their own, not the things which are Jesus Christ's.

22 But ye know the proof of him, that, as a son with the father, he hath served with me in the gospel.

23 Him therefore I hope to send presently, so soon as I shall see how it will go with me.

24 But I trust in the Lord that I also myself shall come shortly.

25 Yet I supposed it necessary to send to you Epaphroditus, my brother, and companion in labour, and fellowsoldier, but your messenger, and he that ministered to my wants.

26 For he longed after you all, and was full of heaviness, because that ye had heard that he had been sick.

27 For indeed he was sick nigh unto death: but God had mercy on him; and not on him only, but on me also, lest I should have sorrow upon sorrow.

28 I sent him therefore the more carefully, that, when ye see him again, ye may rejoice, and that I may be the less sorrowful.

29 Receive him therefore in the Lord with all gladness; and hold such in reputation:

30 Because for the work of Christ he was nigh unto death, not regarding his life, to supply your lack of service toward me.

Chapter 3

1 Finally, my brethren, rejoice in the Lord. To write the same things to you, to me indeed is not grievous, ~~but~~ *and* for you it is safe.

2 Beware of dogs, beware of evil workers, beware of the concision.

3 For we are the circumcision, which worship God in the spirit, and rejoice in Christ Jesus, and have no confidence in the flesh.

4 Though I might also have confidence in the flesh. If any other man thinketh that he hath whereof he might trust in the flesh, I more:

5 Circumcised the eighth day, of the stock of Israel, of the tribe of Benjamin, an Hebrew of the Hebrews; as touching the law, a Pharisee;

6 Concerning zeal, persecuting the church; touching the righteousness which is in the law, blameless.

7 But what things were gain to me, those I counted loss for Christ.

8 Yea doubtless, and I count all things but loss for the excellency of the knowledge of Christ Jesus my Lord: for whom I have suffered the loss of all things, and do count them but dung, that I may win Christ,

9 And be found in him, not having mine own righteousness, which is of the law, but that which is through the faith of Christ, the righteousness which is of God by faith:

10 That I may know him, and the power of his resurrection, and the fellowship of his sufferings, being made conformable unto his death;

11 If by any means I might attain unto the resurrection of the ~~dead~~ *just*.

12 Not as though I had already attained, either were already perfect: but I follow after, if that I may apprehend that for which also I am apprehended of Christ Jesus.

13 Brethren, I count not myself to have apprehended: but this one thing I do, forgetting those things which are behind, and reaching forth unto those things which are before,

14 I press toward the mark for the prize of the high calling of God in Christ Jesus.

15 Let us therefore, as many as be perfect, be thus minded: and if in any thing ye be otherwise minded, God shall reveal even this unto you.

16 Nevertheless, whereto we have already attained, let us walk by the same rule, let us mind the same thing.

17 Brethren, be followers together of me, and mark them which walk so as ye have us for an ensample.

18 (For many walk, of whom I have told you often, and now tell you even weeping, ~~that they are~~ *as* the enemies of the cross of Christ:

19 Whose end is destruction, whose God is their belly, and ~~whose~~ *who* glory ~~is~~ in their shame, who mind earthly things.)

20 For our conversation is in heaven; from whence also we look for the Saviour, the Lord Jesus Christ:

21 Who shall change our vile body, that it may be fashioned like unto his glorious body, according to the working whereby he is able even to subdue all things unto himself.

Chapter 4

1 Therefore, my brethren, dearly beloved and longed for, my joy and crown, so stand fast in the Lord, my dearly beloved.

2 I beseech Euodias, and beseech Syntyche, that they be of the same mind in the Lord.

3 And I entreat thee also, true yokefellow, help those women which laboured with me in the gospel, with Clement also, and with other my fellowlabourers, whose names are in the book of life.

4 Rejoice in the Lord alway: and again I say, Rejoice.

5 Let your moderation be known unto all men. The Lord is at hand.

6 Be ~~careful~~ *afflicted* for nothing; but in every thing by prayer and supplication with thanksgiving let your requests be made known unto God.

7 And the peace of God, which passeth all understanding, shall keep your hearts and minds through Christ Jesus.

8 Finally, brethren, whatsoever things are true, whatsoever things are honest, whatsoever things are just, whatsoever things are pure, whatsoever things are lovely, whatsoever things are of good report; if there be any virtue, and if there be any praise, think on these things.

9 Those things, which ye have both learned, and received, and heard, and seen in me, do: and the God of peace shall be with you.

10 But I rejoiced in the Lord greatly, that now at the last your care of me hath flourished again; wherein ye were also careful, but ye lacked opportunity.

11 Not that I speak in respect of want: for I have learned, in whatsoever state I am, therewith to be content.

12 I know both how to be abased, and I know how to abound: every where and in all things I am instructed both to be full and to be hungry, both to abound and to suffer need.

13 I can do all things through Christ which strengtheneth me.

14 Notwithstanding ye have well done, that ye did communicate with my affliction.

15 Now ye Philippians know also, that in the beginning of the gospel, when I departed from Macedonia, no church communicated with me as concerning giving and receiving, but ye only.

16 For even in Thessalonica ye sent once and again unto my necessity.

17 Not because I desire a gift: but I desire fruit that may abound to your account.

18 But I have all, and abound: I am full, having received of Epaphroditus the things which were sent from you, an odour of a sweet smell, a sacrifice acceptable, wellpleasing to God.

19 But my God shall supply all your need according to his riches in glory by Christ Jesus.

20 Now unto God and our Father be glory for ever and ever. Amen.

21 Salute every saint in Christ Jesus. The brethren which are with me greet you.

22 All the saints salute you, chiefly they that are of Caesar's household.

23 The grace of our Lord Jesus Christ be with you all. Amen.

Chapter 1

1 Paul, an apostle of Jesus Christ by the will of God, and Timotheus our brother,

2 To the saints and faithful brethren in Christ which are at Colosse: Grace be unto you, and peace, from God our Father and the Lord Jesus Christ.

3 We give thanks to God and the Father of our Lord Jesus Christ, praying always for you,

4 Since we heard of your faith in Christ Jesus, and of ~~the~~ *your* love ~~which ye have~~ to all the saints,

5 For the hope which is laid up for you in heaven, whereof ye heard before in the word of the truth of the gospel;

6 Which is come unto you, as ~~it is~~ in all *generations of* the world; and bringeth forth fruit, as it doth also in you, since the day ye heard of it, and knew the grace of God in truth:

7 As ye also learned of Epaphras our dear fellowservant, who is for you a faithful minister of Christ;

8 Who also declared unto us your love in the Spirit.

9 For this cause we also, since the day we heard it, do not cease to pray for you, and to desire that ye might be filled with the knowledge of his will in all wisdom and spiritual understanding;

10 That ye might walk worthy of the Lord unto all pleasing, being fruitful in every good work, and increasing in the knowledge of God;

11 Strengthened with all might, according to his glorious power, unto all patience and longsuffering with joyfulness;

12 Giving thanks unto the Father, which hath made us meet to be partakers of the inheritance of the saints in light:

13 Who hath delivered us from the power of darkness, and hath translated us into the kingdom of his dear Son:

14 In whom we have redemption through his blood, even the forgiveness of sins:

15 Who is the image of the invisible God, the firstborn of every creature:

16 For by him were all things created, that are in heaven, and that are in earth, visible and invisible, whether they be thrones, or dominions, or principalities, or powers: all things were created by him, and for him:

17 And he is before all things, and by him all things consist.

18 And he is the head of the body, the church: who is the beginning, the firstborn from the dead; that in all things he might have the preeminence.

19 For it pleased the Father that in him should all fulness dwell;

20 And, having made peace through the blood of his cross, by him to reconcile all things unto himself; by him, I say, whether they be things in earth, or things in heaven.

21 And you, that were sometime alienated and enemies in your mind by wicked works, yet now hath he reconciled

22 In the body of his flesh through death, to present you holy and unblameable and unreproveable in his sight:

23 If ye continue in the faith grounded and settled, and be not moved away from the hope of the gospel, which ye have heard, and which was preached to every creature which is under heaven; whereof I Paul am made a minister;

24 Who now rejoice in my sufferings for you, and fill up that which is behind of the afflictions of Christ in my flesh for his body's sake, which is the church:

25 Whereof I am made a minister, according to the dispensation of God which is given to me for you, to fulfil the word of God;

26 Even the mystery which hath been hid from ages and from generations, but now is made manifest to his saints:

27 To whom God would make known what is the riches of the glory of this mystery among the Gentiles; which is Christ in you, the hope of glory:

28 Whom we preach, warning every man, and teaching every man in all wisdom; that we may present every man perfect in Christ Jesus:

29 Whereunto I also labour, striving according to his working, which worketh in me mightily.

Chapter 2

1 For I would that ye knew what great conflict I have for you, and for them at Laodicea, and for as many as have not seen my face in the flesh;

2 That their hearts might be comforted, being knit together in love, and unto all riches of the full assurance of understanding, to the acknowledgment of the mystery of God *and of Christ*, ~~and of~~ *who is of God, even* the Father~~, and of Christ~~;

3 In whom are hid all the treasures of wisdom and knowledge.

4 And this I say, lest any man should beguile you with enticing words.

5 For though I be absent in the flesh, yet am I with you in the spirit, joying and beholding your order, and the stedfastness of your faith in Christ.

6 As ye have therefore received Christ Jesus the Lord, so walk ye in him:

7 Rooted and built up in him, and stablished in the faith, as ye have been taught, abounding therein with thanksgiving.

8 Beware lest any man spoil you through philosophy and vain deceit, after the tradition of men, after the rudiments of the world, and not after Christ.

9 For in him dwelleth all the fulness of the Godhead bodily.

10 And ye are complete in him, which is the head of all principality and power:

11 In whom also ye are circumcised with the circumcision made without hands, in putting off the body of the sins of the flesh by the circumcision of Christ:

12 Buried with him in baptism, wherein also ye are risen with him through the faith of the operation of God, who hath raised him from the dead.

13 And you, being dead in your sins and the uncircumcision of your flesh, hath he quickened together with him, having forgiven you all trespasses;

14 Blotting out the handwriting of ordinances that was against us, which was contrary to us, and took it out of the way, nailing it to his cross;

15 And having spoiled principalities and powers, he made a show of them openly, triumphing over them in it.

16 Let no man therefore judge you in meat, or in drink, or in respect of an holyday, or of the new moon, or of the sabbath days:

17 Which are a shadow of things to come; but the body is of Christ.

18 Let no man beguile you of your reward in a voluntary humility and worshipping of angels, intruding into those things which he hath not seen, vainly puffed up by his fleshly mind,

19 And not holding the Head, from which all the body by joints and bands having nourishment ministered, and knit together, increaseth with the increase of God.

20 Wherefore if ye be dead with Christ from the rudiments of the world, why, as though living in the world, are ye subject to ordinances,

21 (*Which are after the doctrines and commandments of men, who teach you to* Touch not; taste not; handle not;

22 *all those things* Which ~~all~~ are to perish with the using~~;) after the commandments and doctrines of men~~?

23 Which things have indeed a ~~shew~~ *show* of wisdom in will-worship, and humility, and neglecting ~~of~~ the body *as to satisfying the flesh*; not in any ~~honour~~ *honor* to ~~the satisfying of the flesh~~ *God*.

Chapter 3

1 If ye then be risen with Christ, seek those things which are above, where Christ sitteth on the right hand of God.

2 Set your affection on things above, not on things on the earth.

3 For ye are dead, and your life is hid with Christ in God.

4 When Christ, who is our life, shall appear, then shall ye also appear with him in glory.

5 Mortify therefore your members which are upon the earth; fornication, uncleanness, inordinate affection, evil concupiscence, and covetousness, which is idolatry:

6 For which things' sake the wrath of God cometh on the children of disobedience:

7 In the which ye also walked some time, when ye lived in them.

8 But now ye also put off all these; anger, wrath, malice, blasphemy, filthy communication out of your mouth.

9 Lie not one to another, seeing that ye have put off the old man with his deeds;

10 And have put on the new man, which is renewed in knowledge after the image of him that created him:

11 Where there is neither Greek nor Jew, circumcision nor uncircumcision, Barbarian, Scythian, bond nor free: but Christ is all, and in all.

12 Put on therefore, as the elect of God, holy and beloved, bowels of mercies, kindness, humbleness of mind, meekness, longsuffering;

13 Forbearing one another, and forgiving one another, if any man have a quarrel against any: even as Christ forgave you, so also do ye.

14 And above all these things put on charity, which is the bond of perfectness.

15 And let the peace of God rule in your hearts, to the which also ye are called in one body; and be ye thankful.

16 Let the word of Christ dwell in you richly in all wisdom; teaching and admonishing one another in psalms and hymns and spiritual songs, singing with grace in your hearts to the Lord.

17 And whatsoever ye do in word or deed, do all in the name of the Lord Jesus, giving thanks to God and the Father by him.

18 Wives, submit yourselves unto your own husbands, as it is fit in the Lord.

19 Husbands, love your wives, and be not bitter against them.

20 Children, obey your parents in all things: for this is well pleasing unto the Lord.

21 Fathers, provoke not your children to anger, lest they be discouraged.

22 Servants, obey in all things your masters according to the flesh; not with eyeservice, as menpleasers; but in singleness of heart, fearing God:

23 And whatsoever ye do, do it heartily, as to

the Lord, and not unto men;

24 Knowing that of the Lord ye shall receive the reward of the inheritance: for ye serve the Lord Christ.

25 But he that doeth wrong shall receive for the wrong which he hath done: and there is no respect of persons.

Chapter 4

1 Masters, give unto your servants that which is just and equal; knowing that ye also have a Master in heaven.

2 Continue in prayer, and watch in the same with thanksgiving;

3 Withal praying also for us, that God would open unto us a door of utterance, to speak the mystery of Christ, for which I am also in bonds:

4 That I may make it manifest, as I ought to speak.

5 Walk in wisdom toward them that are without, redeeming the time.

6 Let your speech be alway with grace, seasoned with salt, that ye may know how ye ought to answer every man.

7 All my state shall Tychicus declare unto you, who is a beloved brother, and a faithful minister and fellowservant in the Lord:

8 Whom I have sent unto you for the same purpose, that he might know your estate, and comfort your hearts;

9 With Onesimus, a faithful and beloved brother, who is one of you. They shall make known unto you all things which are done here.

10 Aristarchus my fellowprisoner saluteth you, and Marcus, sister's son to Barnabas, (touching whom ye received commandments: if he come unto you, receive him;)

11 And Jesus, which is called Justus, who are of the circumcision. These only are my fellowworkers unto the kingdom of God, which have been a comfort unto me.

12 Epaphras, who is one of you, a servant of Christ, saluteth you, always labouring fervently for you in prayers, that ye may stand perfect and complete in all the will of God.

13 For I bear him record, that he hath a great zeal for you, and them that are in Laodicea and them in Hierapolis.

14 Luke, the beloved physician, and Demas, greet you.

15 Salute the brethren which are in Laodicea, and Nymphas, and the church which is in his house.

16 And when this epistle is read among you, cause that it be read also in the church of the Laodiceans; and that ye likewise read the epistle from Laodicea.

17 And say to Archippus, Take heed to the ministry which thou hast received in the Lord, that thou fulfil it.

18 The salutation by the hand of me Paul. Remember my bonds. Grace be with you. Amen.

1st THESSALONIANS

Chapter 1

1 Paul, and Silvanus, and Timotheus, *servants of God the Father and the Lord Jesus Christ,* unto the church of the Thessalonians ~~which is in God the Father and in the Lord Jesus Christ~~: Grace ~~be~~ unto you, and peace, from God our Father, and the Lord Jesus Christ.

2 We give thanks ~~to God~~ always ~~for you all~~, making mention of you *all,* in our prayers *to God for you*;

3 Remembering without ceasing your work of faith, and labour of love, and patience of hope in our Lord Jesus Christ, in the sight of God and our Father;

4 Knowing, brethren beloved, your election of God.

5 For our gospel came not unto you in word only, but also in power, and in the Holy Ghost,

and in much assurance; as ye know what manner of men we were among you for your sake.

6 And ye became followers of us, and of the Lord, having received the word in much affliction, with joy of the Holy Ghost:

7 So that ye were ensamples to all that believe in Macedonia and Achaia.

8 For from you sounded out the word of the Lord not only in Macedonia and Achaia, but also in every place your faith to*ward* God-~~ward~~ is spread abroad; so that we need not to speak any thing.

9 For they themselves show of us what manner of entering in we had unto you, and how ye turned to God from idols to serve the living and true God;

10 And to wait for his Son from heaven, whom he raised from the dead, even Jesus, which delivered us from the wrath to come.

Chapter 2

1 For yourselves, brethren, know our entrance in unto you, that it was not in vain:

2 But even after that we had suffered before, and were shamefully entreated, as ye know, at Philippi, we were bold in our God to speak unto you the gospel of God with much contention.

3 For our exhortation was not of deceit, nor of uncleanness, nor in guile:

4 But as we were allowed of God to be put in trust with the gospel, even so we speak; not as pleasing men, but God, which trieth our hearts.

5 For neither at any time used we flattering words, as ye know, nor a cloak of covetousness; God is witness:

6 Nor of men sought we glory, neither of you, nor yet of others, when we might have been burdensome, as the apostles of Christ.

7 But we were gentle among you, even as a nurse cherisheth her children:

8 So being affectionately desirous of you, we were willing to have imparted unto you, not the gospel of God only, but also our own souls, because ye were dear unto us.

9 For ye remember, brethren, our labour and travail: for labouring night and day, because we would not be chargeable unto any of you, we preached unto you the gospel of God.

10 Ye are witnesses, and God also, how holily and justly and unblameably we behaved ourselves among you that believe:

11 As ye know how we exhorted and comforted and charged every one of you, as a father doth his children,

12 That ye would walk worthy of God, who hath called you unto his kingdom and glory.

13 For this cause also thank we God without ceasing, because, when ye received the word of God which ye heard of us, ye received it not as the word of men, but as it is in truth, the word of God, which effectually worketh also in you that believe.

14 For ye, brethren, became followers of the churches of God which in Judaea are in Christ Jesus: for ye also have suffered like things of your own countrymen, even as they have of the Jews:

15 Who both killed the Lord Jesus, and their own prophets, and have persecuted us; and they please not God, and are contrary to all men:

16 Forbidding us to speak to the Gentiles that they might be saved, to fill up their sins always: for the wrath is ~~come~~ *coming* upon them to the uttermost.

17 But we, brethren, being taken from you for a short time in presence, not in heart, endeavoured the more abundantly to see your face with great desire.

18 Wherefore we would have come unto you, even I Paul, once and again; but Satan hindered us.

19 For what is our hope, or joy, or crown of rejoicing? Are not even ye in the presence of our Lord Jesus Christ at his coming?

20 For ye are our glory and joy.

Chapter 3

1 Wherefore when we could no longer forbear, we thought it good to be left at Athens alone;

2 And sent Timotheus, our brother, and minister of God, and our fellowlabourer in the gospel of Christ, to establish you, and to comfort you concerning your faith:

3 That no man should be moved by these afflictions: for yourselves know that we are appointed thereunto.

4 For verily, when we were with you, we told you before that we should suffer tribulation; even as it came to pass, and ye know.

5 For this cause, when I could no longer forbear, I sent to know your faith, lest by some means the tempter have tempted you, and our labour be in vain.

6 But now when Timotheus came from you unto us, and brought us good tidings of your faith and charity, and that ye have good remembrance of us always, desiring greatly to see us, as we also to see you:

7 Therefore, brethren, we were comforted over you in all our affliction and distress by your faith:

8 For now we live, if ye stand fast in the Lord.

9 For what thanks can we render to God again for you, for all the joy wherewith we joy for your sakes before our God;

10 Night and day praying exceedingly that we might see your face, and might perfect that which is lacking in your faith?

11 Now God himself and our Father, and our Lord Jesus Christ, direct our way unto you.

12 And the Lord make you to increase and abound in love one toward another, and toward all men, even as we do toward you:

13 To the end he may stablish your hearts unblameable in holiness before God, even our Father, at the coming of our Lord Jesus Christ with all his saints.

Chapter 4

1 Furthermore then we beseech you, brethren, and exhort you by the Lord Jesus, that as ye have received of us how ye ought to walk and to please God, so ye would abound more and more.

2 For ye know what commandments we gave you by the Lord Jesus.

3 For this is the will of God, even your sanctification, that ye should abstain from fornication:

4 That every one of you should know how to possess his vessel in sanctification and honour;

5 Not in the lust of concupiscence, even as the Gentiles which know not God:

6 That no man go beyond and defraud his brother in any matter: because that the Lord is the avenger of all such, as we also have forewarned you and testified.

7 For God hath not called us unto uncleanness, but unto holiness.

8 He therefore that despiseth, despiseth not man, but God, who hath also given unto us his holy Spirit.

9 But as touching brotherly love ye need not that I write unto you: for ye yourselves are taught of God to love one another.

10 And indeed ye do it toward all the brethren which are in all Macedonia: but we beseech you, brethren, that ye increase more and more;

11 And that ye study to be quiet, and to do your own business, and to work with your own hands, as we commanded you;

12 That ye may walk honestly toward them that are without, and that ye may have lack of nothing.

13 But I would not have you to be ignorant, brethren, concerning them which are asleep, that ye sorrow not, even as others which have no hope.

14 For if we believe that Jesus died and rose again, even so them also which sleep in Jesus will God bring with him.

15 For this we say unto you by the word of the Lord, that ~~we which~~ *they who are* are alive ~~and remain unto~~ *at* the coming of the Lord shall not prevent them ~~which~~ *who remain unto the coming of the Lord, who* are asleep.

16 For the Lord himself shall descend from heaven with a shout, with the voice of the archangel, and with the trump of God: and the dead in Christ shall rise first:

17 Then ~~we which~~ *they who* are alive ~~and remain~~ shall be caught up together ~~with them in~~ *into* the clouds *with them who remain*, to meet the Lord in the air: and so shall we ~~ever~~ be *ever* with the Lord.

18 Wherefore comfort one another with these words.

Chapter 5

1 But of the times and the seasons, brethren, ye have no need that I write unto you.

2 For yourselves know perfectly that the day of the Lord so cometh as a thief in the night.

3 For when they shall say, Peace and safety; then sudden destruction cometh upon them, as travail upon a woman with child; and they shall not escape.

4 But ye, brethren, are not in darkness, that that day should overtake you as a thief.

5 Ye are all the children of light, and the children of the day: we are not of the night, nor of darkness.

6 Therefore let us not sleep, as do others; but let us watch and be sober.

7 For they that sleep sleep in the night; and they that be drunken are drunken in the night.

8 But let us, who are of the day, be sober, putting on the breastplate of faith and love; and for an helmet, the hope of salvation.

9 For God hath not appointed us to wrath, but to obtain salvation by our Lord Jesus Christ,

10 Who died for us, that, whether we wake or sleep, we should live together with him.

11 Wherefore comfort yourselves together, and edify one another, even as also ye do.

12 And we beseech you, brethren, to know them which labour among you, and are over you in the Lord, and admonish you;

13 And to esteem them very highly in love for their work's sake. And be at peace among yourselves.

14 Now we exhort you, brethren, warn them that are unruly, comfort the feebleminded, support the weak, be patient toward all men.

15 See that none render evil for evil unto any man; but ever follow that which is good, both among yourselves, and to all men.

16 Rejoice evermore.

17 Pray without ceasing.

18 In every thing give thanks: for this is the will of God in Christ Jesus concerning you.

19 Quench not the Spirit.

20 Despise not prophesyings.

21 Prove all things; hold fast that which is good.

22 Abstain from all appearance of evil.

23 And the very God of peace sanctify you wholly; and I pray God your whole spirit and soul and body be preserved blameless unto the coming of our Lord Jesus Christ.

24 Faithful is he that calleth you, who also will do it.

25 Brethren, pray for us.

26 Greet all the brethren with ~~an~~ holy ~~kiss~~ *salutation*.

27 I charge you by the Lord that this epistle be read unto all the holy brethren.

28 The grace of our Lord Jesus Christ be with you. Amen.

Chapter 1

1 Paul, and Silvanus, and Timotheus, *the servants of God the Father and our Lord Jesus Christ,* unto the church of the Thessalonians ~~in God our Father and the Lord Jesus Christ~~:

2 Grace unto you, and peace, from God our Father and the Lord Jesus Christ.

3 We are bound to thank God always for you, brethren, as it is meet, because that your faith groweth exceedingly, and the charity of every one of you all toward each other aboundeth;

4 So that we ourselves glory in you in the churches of God for your patience and faith in all your persecutions and tribulations that ye endure:

5 Which is a manifest token of the righteous judgment of God, that ye may be counted worthy of the kingdom of God, for which ye also suffer:

6 Seeing it is a righteous thing with God to recompense tribulation to them that trouble you;

7 And to you who are troubled rest with us, when the Lord Jesus shall be revealed from heaven with his mighty angels,

8 In flaming fire taking vengeance on them that know not God, and that obey not the gospel of our Lord Jesus Christ:

9 Who shall be punished with ~~everlasting~~ destruction from the presence of the Lord, and from the glory of his *everlasting* power;

10 When he shall come to be glorified in his saints, and to be admired in all them that believe (because our testimony among you was believed) in that day.

11 Wherefore also we pray always for you, that our God would count you worthy of this calling, and fulfil all the good pleasure of his goodness, and the work of faith with power:

12 That the name of our Lord Jesus Christ may be glorified in you, and ye in him, according to the grace of our God and the Lord Jesus Christ.

Chapter 2

1 Now we beseech you, brethren, by the coming of our Lord Jesus Christ, and by our gathering together unto him,

2 That ye be not soon shaken in mind, or be troubled *by letter, except ye receive it from us*, neither by spirit, nor by word, ~~nor by letter as from us,~~ as that the day of Christ is at hand.

3 Let no man deceive you by any means: for ~~that day shall not come, except~~ there *shall* come a falling away first, and that man of sin be revealed, the son of perdition;

4 Who opposeth and exalteth himself above all that is called God, or that is worshipped; so that he as God sitteth in the temple of God, showing himself that he is God.

5 Remember ye not, that, when I was yet with you, I told you these things?

6 And now ye know what withholdeth that he might be revealed in his time.

7 For the mystery of iniquity doth already work, *and he it is who now worketh, and Christ suffereth him to work* : ~~only he who now letteth will let~~ , until *the time is fulfilled that* he *shall* be taken out of the way.

8 And then shall that ~~W~~*w*icked *one* be revealed, whom the Lord shall consume with the spirit of his mouth, and shall destroy with the brightness of his coming:

9 ~~Even him~~ *Yea, the Lord, even Jesus*, whose coming is *not until* after *there cometh a falling away, by* the working of Satan with all power and signs and lying wonders,

10 And with all deceivableness of unrighteousness in them that perish; because they received not the love of the truth, that they might be saved.

11 And for this cause God shall send them strong delusion, that they should believe a lie:

12 That they all might be damned who believed not the truth, but had pleasure in unrighteousness.

13 But we are bound to give thanks alway to God for you, brethren beloved of the Lord, because God hath from the beginning chosen you to salvation through sanctification of the Spirit and belief of the truth:

14 Whereunto he called you by our gospel, to the obtaining of the glory of our Lord Jesus Christ.

15 Therefore, brethren, stand fast, and hold the traditions which ye have been taught, whether by word, or our epistle.

16 Now our Lord Jesus Christ himself, and God, even our Father, which hath loved us, and hath given us everlasting consolation and good hope through grace,

17 Comfort your hearts, and stablish you in every good word and work.

Chapter 3

1 Finally, brethren, pray for us, that the word of the Lord may have free course, and be glorified, even as it is with you:

2 And that we may be delivered from unreasonable and wicked men: for all men have not faith.

3 But the Lord is faithful, who shall stablish you, and keep you from evil.

4 And we have confidence in the Lord touching you, that ye both do and will do the things which

we command you.

5 And the Lord direct your hearts into the love of God, and into the patient waiting for Christ.

6 Now we command you, brethren, in the name of our Lord Jesus Christ, that ye withdraw yourselves from every brother that walketh disorderly, and not after the tradition which he received of us.

7 For yourselves know how ye ought to follow us: for we behaved not ourselves disorderly among you;

8 Neither did we eat any man's bread for nought; but wrought with labour and travail night and day, that we might not be chargeable to any of you:

9 Not because we have not power, but to make ourselves an ensample unto you to follow us.

10 For even when we were with you, this we commanded you, that if any would not work, neither should he eat.

11 For we hear that there are some which walk among you disorderly, working not at all, but are busybodies.

12 Now them that are such we command and exhort by our Lord Jesus Christ, that with quietness they work, and eat their own bread.

13 But ye, brethren, be not weary in well doing.

14 And if any man obey not our word by this epistle, note that man, and have no company with him, that he may be ashamed.

15 Yet count him not as an enemy, but admonish him as a brother.

16 Now the Lord of peace himself give you peace always by all means. The Lord be with you all.

17 The salutation of Paul with mine own hand, which is the token in every epistle: so I write.

18 The grace of our Lord Jesus Christ be with you all. Amen.

1st TIMOTHY

Chapter 1

1 Paul, an apostle of Jesus Christ by the commandment of God ~~our Saviour,~~ and *the* Lord Jesus Christ, *our Savior and* ~~which is~~ our hope;

2 Unto Timothy, my own son in the faith: Grace, mercy, and peace, from God our Father and Jesus Christ our Lord.

3 As I besought thee to abide still at Ephesus, when I went into Macedonia, that thou mightest charge some that they teach no other doctrine,

4 Neither give heed to fables and endless genealogies, which minister questions, rather than godly edifying which is in faith: so do.

5 Now the end of the commandment is charity out of a pure heart, and of a good conscience, and of faith unfeigned:

6 From which some having swerved have turned aside unto vain jangling;

7 Desiring to be teachers of the law; understanding neither what they say, nor whereof they affirm.

8 But we know that the law is good, if a man use it lawfully;

9 Knowing this, that the law is not made for a righteous man, but for the lawless and disobedient, for the ungodly and for sinners, for unholy and profane, for murderers of fathers and murderers of mothers, for manslayers,

10 For whoremongers, for them that defile themselves with mankind, for menstealers, for liars, for perjured persons, and if there be any other thing that is contrary to sound doctrine;

11 According to the glorious gospel of the blessed God, which was committed to my trust.

12 And I thank Christ Jesus our Lord, who hath enabled me, for that he counted me faithful, putting me into the ministry;

13 Who was before a blasphemer, and a persecutor, and injurious: but I obtained mercy, because I did it ignorantly in unbelief.

14 And the grace of our Lord was exceeding abundant with faith and love which is in Christ Jesus.

15 This is a faithful saying, and worthy of all acceptation, that Christ Jesus came into the world to save sinners; of whom I am chief.

16 Howbeit for this cause I obtained mercy, that in me first Jesus Christ might show forth all longsuffering, for a pattern to them which should hereafter believe on him to life everlasting.

17 Now unto the King eternal, immortal, invisible, the only wise God, be honour and glory for ever and ever. Amen.

18 This charge I commit unto thee, son Timothy, according to the prophecies which went before on thee, that thou by them mightest war a good warfare;

19 Holding faith, and a good conscience; which some having put away concerning faith have made

shipwreck:

20 Of whom is Hymenaeus and Alexander; whom I have delivered unto Satan, that they may learn not to blaspheme.

Chapter 2

1 I exhort therefore, that, first of all, supplications, prayers, intercessions, and giving ~~of~~ thanks, be made for all men;

2 For kings, and for all that are in authority; that we may lead a quiet and peaceable life in all godliness and honesty.

3 For this is good and acceptable in the sight of God our Saviour;

4 Who *is* will*ing to* have all men to be saved, and to come unto the knowledge of the truth *which is in Christ Jesus, who is the Only Begotten Son of God, and ordained to be a Mediator between God and man; who is one God, and hath power over all men*.

5 For there is one God, and one mediator between God and men, the man Christ Jesus;

6 Who gave himself a ransom for all, to be testified in due time.

7 Whereunto I am ordained a preacher, and an apostle, (I speak the truth in Christ, and lie not;) a teacher of the Gentiles in faith and verity.

8 I will therefore that men pray every where, lifting up holy hands, without wrath and doubting.

9 In like manner also, that women adorn themselves in modest apparel, with shamefacedness and sobriety; not with ~~broided~~ *braided* hair, or gold, or pearls, or costly array;

10 But (which becometh women professing godliness) with good works.

11 Let the woman learn in silence with all subjection.

12 ~~But~~ *For* I suffer not a woman to teach, nor to usurp authority over the man, but to be in silence.

13 For Adam was first formed, then Eve.

14 And Adam was not deceived, but the woman being deceived was in the transgression.

15 Notwithstanding ~~she~~ *they* shall be saved in childbearing, if they continue in faith and charity and holiness with sobriety.

Chapter 3

1 This is a true saying, If a man desire the office of a bishop, he desireth a good work.

2 A bishop then must be blameless, the husband of one wife, vigilant, sober, of good behaviour, given to hospitality, apt to teach;

3 Not given to wine, no striker, not greedy of filthy lucre; but patient, not a brawler, not covetous;

4 One that ruleth well his own house, having his children in subjection with all gravity;

5 (For if a man know not how to rule his own house, how shall he take care of the church of God?)

6 Not a novice, lest being lifted up with pride he fall into the condemnation of the devil.

7 Moreover he must have a good report of them which are without; lest he fall into reproach and the snare of the devil.

8 Likewise ~~must~~ the deacons *must* be grave, not doubletongued, not given to much wine, not greedy of filthy lucre;

9 Holding the mystery of the faith in a pure conscience.

10 And let these also first be proved; then let them use the office of a deacon, being found blameless.

11 Even so must their wives be grave, not slanderers, sober, faithful in all things.

12 Let the deacons be the husbands of one wife, ruling their children and their own houses well.

13 For they that have used the office of a deacon well purchase to themselves a good degree, and great boldness in the faith which is in Christ Jesus.

14 These things write I unto thee, hoping to come unto thee shortly:

15 But if I tarry long, that thou mayest know how thou oughtest to behave thyself in the house of God, which is the church of the living God~~, the pillar and ground of the truth~~.

16 *The pillar and ground of the truth is, (*And without controversy great is the mystery of godliness ~~:~~ *,)* God was manifest in the flesh, justified in the Spirit, seen of angels, preached unto the Gentiles, believed on in the world, received up into glory.

Chapter 4

1 Now the Spirit speaketh expressly, that in the latter times some shall depart from the faith, giving heed to seducing spirits, and doctrines of devils;

2 Speaking lies in hypocrisy; having their conscience seared *as* with a hot iron;

3 Forbidding to marry, and commanding to abstain from meats, which God hath created to be received with thanksgiving of them which believe and know the truth.

4 For every creature of God is good, and nothing to be refused, if it be received with thanksgiving:

5 For it is sanctified by the word of God and prayer.

6 If thou put the brethren in remembrance of these things, thou shalt be a good minister of Jesus Christ, nourished up in the words of faith and of good doctrine, whereunto thou hast attained.

7 But refuse profane and old wives' fables, and exercise thyself rather unto godliness.

8 For bodily exercise profiteth little: but godliness is profitable unto all things, having promise of the life that now is, and of that which is to come.

9 This is a faithful saying and worthy of all acceptation.

10 For therefore we both labour and suffer reproach, because we trust in the living God, who is the Saviour of all men, specially of those that believe.

11 These things command and teach.

12 Let no man despise thy youth; but be thou an example of the believers, in word, in conversation, in charity, in spirit, in faith, in purity.

13 Till I come, give attendance to reading, to exhortation, to doctrine.

14 Neglect not the gift that is in thee, which was given thee by prophecy, with the laying on of the hands of the presbytery.

15 Meditate upon these things; give thyself wholly to them; that thy profiting may appear to all.

16 Take heed unto thyself, and unto the doctrine; continue in them: for in doing this thou shalt both save thyself, and them that hear thee.

Chapter 5

1 Rebuke not an elder, but entreat him as a father; and the younger men as brethren;

2 The elder women as mothers; the younger as sisters, with all purity.

3 Honour widows that are widows indeed.

4 But if any widow have children or nephews, let them learn first to show piety at home, and to requite their parents: for that is good and acceptable before God.

5 Now she that is a widow indeed, and desolate, trusteth in God, and continueth in supplications and prayers night and day.

6 But she that liveth in pleasure is dead while she liveth.

7 And these things give in charge, that they may be blameless.

8 But if any provide not for his own, and specially for those of his own house, he hath denied the faith, and is worse than an infidel.

9 Let not a widow be taken into the number under threescore years old, having been the wife of one man,

10 Well reported of for good works; if she have brought up children, if she have lodged strangers, if she have washed the saints' ~~feet~~ *clothes*, if she have relieved the afflicted, if she have diligently followed every good work.

11 But the younger widows refuse: for when they have begun to wax wanton against Christ, they will marry;

12 Having damnation, because they have cast off their first faith.

13 And withal they learn to be idle, wandering about from house to house; and not only idle, but tattlers also and busybodies, speaking things which they ought not.

14 I will therefore that the younger women marry, bear children, guide the house, give none occasion to the adversary to speak reproachfully.

15 For some are already turned aside after Satan.

16 If any man or woman that believeth have widows, let them relieve them, and let not the church be charged; that it may relieve them that are widows indeed.

17 Let the elders that rule well be counted worthy of double honour, especially they who labour in the word and doctrine.

18 For the scripture saith, Thou shalt not muzzle the ox that treadeth out the corn. And, The labourer is worthy of his reward.

19 Against an elder receive not an accusation, but before two or three witnesses.

20 Them that sin rebuke before all, that others also may fear.

21 I charge thee before God, and the Lord Jesus Christ, and the elect angels, that thou observe these things without preferring one before another, doing nothing by partiality.

22 Lay hands suddenly on no man, neither be partaker of other men's sins: keep thyself pure.

23 Drink no longer water, but use a little wine for thy stomach's sake and thine often infirmities.

24 Some men's sins are open beforehand, going before to judgment; and some men they follow after.

25 Likewise also the good works of some are manifest beforehand; and they that are otherwise cannot be hid.

Chapter 6

1 Let as many servants as are under the yoke count their own masters worthy of all honour, that the name of God and his doctrine be not blasphemed.

2 And they that have believing masters, let them not despise them, because they are brethren; but

rather do them service, because they are faithful and beloved, partakers of the benefit. These things teach and exhort.

3 If any man teach otherwise, and consent not to wholesome words, even the words of our Lord Jesus Christ, and to the doctrine which is according to godliness;

4 He is proud, knowing nothing, but doting about questions and strifes of words, whereof cometh envy, strife, railings, evil surmisings,

5 Perverse disputings of men of corrupt minds, and destitute of the truth, supposing that gain is godliness: from such withdraw thyself.

6 But godliness with contentment is great gain.

7 For we brought nothing into this world, and it is certain we can carry nothing out.

8 And having food and raiment let us be therewith content.

9 But they that will be rich fall into temptation and a snare, and into many foolish and hurtful lusts, which drown men in destruction and perdition.

10 For the love of money is the root of all evil: which while some coveted after, they have erred from the faith, and pierced themselves through with many sorrows.

11 But thou, O man of God, flee these things; and follow after righteousness, godliness, faith, love, patience, meekness.

12 Fight the good fight of faith, lay hold on eternal life, whereunto thou art also called, and hast professed a good profession before many witnesses.

13 I give thee charge in the sight of God, who quickeneth all things, and before Christ Jesus, who before Pontius Pilate witnessed a good confession;

14 That thou keep this commandment without spot, unrebukeable, until the appearing of our Lord Jesus Christ:

15 Which in his times he shall ~~shew~~ *show*, who is the blessed and only Potentate, the King of kings, and Lord of lords;

16 ~~Who only hath immortality, dwelling in the light which no man can approach unto; whom no man hath seen, nor can see:~~ to whom be ~~honour~~ *honor* and power everlasting. ~~Amen.~~ *Whom no man hath seen, nor can see, unto whom no man can approach, only he who hath the light and the hope of immortality dwelling in him.*

17 Charge them that are rich in this world, that they be not highminded, nor trust in uncertain riches, but in the living God, who giveth us richly all things to enjoy;

18 That they do good, that they be rich in good works, ready to distribute, willing to communicate;

19 Laying up in store for themselves a good foundation against the time to come, that they may lay hold on eternal life.

20 O Timothy, keep that which is committed to thy trust, avoiding profane and vain babblings, and oppositions of science falsely so called:

21 Which some professing have erred concerning the faith. Grace be with thee. Amen.

2nd TIMOTHY

Chapter 1

1 Paul, an apostle of Jesus Christ by the will of God, according to the promise of life which is in Christ Jesus,

2 To Timothy, my dearly beloved son: Grace, mercy, and peace, from God the Father and Christ Jesus our Lord.

3 I thank God, whom I serve from my forefathers with pure conscience, that without ceasing I have remembrance of thee in my prayers night and day;

4 Greatly desiring to see thee, being mindful of thy tears, that I may be filled with joy;

5 When I call to remembrance the unfeigned faith that is in thee, which dwelt first in thy grandmother Lois, and thy mother Eunice; and I

am persuaded that in thee also.

6 Wherefore I put thee in remembrance that thou stir up the gift of God, which is in thee by the putting on of my hands.

7 For God hath not given us the spirit of fe[ar], but of power, and of love, and of a sound [mind].

8 Be not thou therefore ashamed [of the] testimony of our Lord, nor of me his [prisoner:] but be thou partaker of the afflict[ions of the] gospel according to the power of [God;]

9 Who hath saved us, and calle[d us with an holy] calling, not according to our w[orks, but according] to his own purpose and gra[ce, which was given us] in Christ Jesus before th[e world began,]

10 But is now made [manifest by the appearing] of our Saviour Jesu[s Christ, who hath abolished] death, and hath [brought life and immortality]

light through the gospel:

11 Whereunto I am appointed a preacher, and an apostle, and a teacher of the Gentiles.

12 For the which cause I also suffer these things: nevertheless I am not ashamed: for I know whom I have believed, and am persuaded that he is able to keep that which I have committed unto him against that day.

13 Hold fast the form of sound words, which thou hast heard of me, in faith and love which is in Christ Jesus.

14 That good thing which was committed unto thee keep by the Holy Ghost which dwelleth in us.

15 This thou knowest, that all they which are in Asia be turned away from me; of whom are Phygellus and Hermogenes.

16 The Lord give mercy unto the house of Onesiphorus; for he oft refreshed me, and was not ashamed of my chain:

17 But, when he was in Rome, he sought me out very diligently, and found me.

18 The Lord grant unto him that he may find mercy of the Lord in that day: and in how many things he ministered unto me at Ephesus, thou knowest very well.

Chapter 2

1 Thou therefore, my son, be strong in the grace that is in Christ Jesus.

2 And the things that thou hast heard of me among many witnesses, the same commit thou to faithful men, who shall be able to teach others also.

3 Thou therefore endure hardness, as a good soldier of Jesus Christ.

4 No man that warreth entangleth himself with the affairs of this life; that he may please him ~~chosen~~ him to be a soldier.

~~masteries, yet is~~

we deny him, he also will deny us:

13 If we believe not, yet he abideth faithful: he cannot deny himself.

14 Of these things put them in remembrance, charging them before the Lord that they strive not about words to no profit, but to the subverting of the hearers.

15 Study to show thyself approved unto God, a workman that needeth not to be ashamed, rightly dividing the word of truth.

16 But shun profane and vain babblings: for they will increase unto more ungodliness.

17 And their word will eat as doth a canker: of whom is Hymenaeus and Philetus;

18 Who concerning the truth have erred, saying that the resurrection is past already; and overthrow the faith of some.

19 Nevertheless the foundation of God standeth sure, having this seal, The Lord knoweth them that are his. And, Let every one that nameth the name of Christ depart from iniquity.

20 But in a great house there are not only vessels of gold and of silver, but also of wood and of earth; and some to honour, and some to dishonour.

21 If a man therefore purge himself from these, he shall be a vessel unto honour, sanctified, and meet for the master's use, and prepared unto every good work.

22 Flee also youthful lusts: but follow righteousness, faith, charity, peace, with them that call on the Lord out of a pure heart.

23 But foolish and unlearned questions avoid, knowing that they do gender strifes.

24 And the servant of the Lord must not strive; but be gentle unto all men, apt to teach, patient,

25 In meekness instructing those that oppose themselves; if God peradventure will give them repentance to the acknowledging of the truth;

26 And that they may recover themselves out of the snare of the devil, who are taken captive by him at his will.

Chapter 3

1 This know also, that in the last days perilous times shall come.

2 For men shall be lovers of their own selves, covetous, boasters, proud, blasphemers, disobedient to parents, unthankful, unholy,

3 Without natural affection, trucebreakers, false accusers, incontinent, fierce, despisers of those that are good,

4 Traitors, heady, highminded, lovers of pleasures more than lovers of God;

5 Having a form of godliness, but denying the power thereof: from such turn away.

6 For of this sort are they which creep into houses, and lead captive silly women laden with sins, led away with divers lusts,

7 Ever learning, and never able to come to the knowledge of the truth.

8 Now as Jannes and Jambres withstood Moses, so do these also resist the truth: men of corrupt minds, reprobate concerning the faith.

9 But they shall proceed no further: for their folly shall be manifest unto all men, as theirs also was.

10 But thou hast fully known my doctrine, manner of life, purpose, faith, longsuffering, charity, patience,

11 Persecutions, afflictions, which came unto me at Antioch, at Iconium, at Lystra; what persecutions I endured: but out of them all the Lord delivered me.

12 Yea, and all that will live godly in Christ Jesus shall suffer persecution.

13 But *For* evil men and seducers shall wax worse and worse, deceiving, and being deceived.

14 But continue thou in the things which thou hast learned and hast been assured of, knowing of whom thou hast learned them;

15 And that from a child thou hast known the holy scriptures, which are able to make thee wise unto salvation through faith which is in Christ Jesus.

16 *And* All scripture is given by inspiration of God, and is profitable for doctrine, for reproof, for correction, for instruction in righteousness:

17 That the man of God may be perfect, throughly *thoroughly* furnished unto all good works.

Chapter 4

1 I charge thee therefore before God, and the Lord Jesus Christ, who shall judge the quick and the dead at his appearing and *in* his kingdom;

2 Preach the word; be instant in season, *those who are* out of season; reprove, rebuke, exhort with all longsuffering and doctrine.

3 For the time will come when they will not endure sound doctrine; but after their own lusts shall they heap to themselves teachers, having itching ears;

4 And they shall turn away their ears from the truth, and shall be turned unto fables.

5 But watch thou in all things, endure afflictions, do the work of an evangelist, make full proof of thy ministry.

6 For I am now ready to be offered, and the time of my departure is at hand.

7 I have fought a good fight, I have finished my course, I have kept the faith:

8 Henceforth there is laid up for me a crown of righteousness, which the Lord, the righteous judge, shall give me at that day: and not to me only, but unto all them also that love his appearing.

9 Do thy diligence to come shortly unto me:

10 For Demas hath forsaken me, having loved this present world, and is departed unto Thessalonica; Crescens to Galatia, Titus unto Dalmatia.

11 Only Luke is with me. Take Mark, and bring him with thee: for he is profitable to me for the ministry.

12 And Tychicus have I sent to Ephesus.

13 The cloak that I left at Troas with Carpus, when thou comest, bring with thee, and the books, but especially the parchments.

14 Alexander the coppersmith did me much evil: the Lord reward him according to his works:

15 Of whom be thou ware also; for he hath greatly withstood our words.

16 At my first answer no man stood with me, but all men forsook me: I pray God that it may not be laid to their charge.

17 Notwithstanding the Lord stood with me, and strengthened me; that by me the preaching might be fully known, and that all the Gentiles might hear: and I was delivered out of the mouth of the lion.

18 And the Lord shall deliver me from every evil work, and will preserve me unto his heavenly kingdom: to whom be glory for ever and ever. Amen.

19 Salute Prisca and Aquila, and the household of Onesiphorus.

20 Erastus abode at Corinth: but Trophimus have I left at Miletum sick.

21 Do thy diligence to come before winter. Eubulus greeteth thee, and Pudens, and Linus, and Claudia, and all the brethren.

22 The Lord Jesus Christ be with thy spirit. *you, and* Grace be with you *all*. Amen.

Chapter 1

1 Paul, a servant of God, and an apostle of Jesus Christ, according to the faith of God's elect, and the acknowledging of the truth which is after godliness;

2 In hope of eternal life, which God, that cannot lie, promised before the world began;

3 But hath in due times manifested his word through preaching, which is committed unto me according to the commandment of God our Saviour;

4 To Titus, mine own son after the common faith: Grace, mercy, and peace, from God the Father and the Lord Jesus Christ our Saviour.

5 For this cause left I thee in Crete, that thou shouldest set in order the things that are wanting, and ordain elders in every city, as I had appointed thee:

6 If any be blameless, the husband of one wife, having faithful children not accused of riot or unruly.

7 For a bishop must be blameless, as the steward of God; not selfwilled, not soon angry, not given to wine, no striker, not given to filthy lucre;

8 But a lover of hospitality, a lover of good men, sober, just, holy, temperate;

9 Holding fast the faithful word as he hath been taught, that he may be able by sound doctrine both to exhort and to convince the gainsayers.

10 For there are many unruly and vain talkers and deceivers, specially they of the circumcision:

11 Whose mouths must be stopped, who subvert whole houses, teaching things which they ought not, for filthy lucre's sake.

12 One of themselves, even a prophet of their own, said, The Cretians are alway liars, evil beasts, slow bellies.

13 This witness is true. Wherefore rebuke them sharply, that they may be sound in the faith;

14 Not giving heed to Jewish fables, and commandments of men, that turn from the truth.

15 Unto the pure, *let* all things ~~are~~ *be* pure: but unto them ~~that~~ *who* are defiled and unbelieving ~~is~~ nothing *is* pure; but even their mind and conscience is defiled.

16 They profess that they know God; but in works they deny him, being abominable, and disobedient, and unto every good work reprobate.

Chapter 2

1 But speak thou the things which become sound doctrine:

2 That the aged men be sober, grave, temperate, sound in faith, in charity, in patience.

3 The aged women likewise, that they be in behaviour as becometh holiness, not false accusers, not given to much wine, teachers of good things;

4 That they may teach the young women to be sober, to love their husbands, to love their children,

5 To be discreet, chaste, keepers at home, good, obedient to their own husbands, that the word of God be not blasphemed.

6 Young men likewise exhort to be sober minded.

7 In all things showing thyself a pattern of good works: in doctrine showing uncorruptness, gravity, sincerity,

8 Sound speech, that cannot be condemned; that he that is of the contrary part may be ashamed, having no evil thing to say of you.

9 Exhort servants to be obedient unto their own masters, and to please them well in all things; not answering again;

10 Not purloining, but showing all good fidelity; that they may adorn the doctrine of God our Saviour in all things.

11 For the grace of God ~~that~~ *which* bringeth salvation *to all men,* hath appeared ~~to all men,~~ *;*

12 Teaching us that, denying ungodliness and worldly lusts, we should live soberly, righteously, and godly, in this present world;

13 Looking for that blessed hope, and the glorious appearing of the great God and our Saviour Jesus Christ;

14 Who gave himself for us, that he might redeem us from all iniquity, and purify unto himself a peculiar people, zealous of good works.

15 These things speak, and exhort, and rebuke with all authority. Let no man despise thee.

Chapter 3

1 Put them in mind to be subject to principalities and powers, to obey magistrates, to be ready to every good work,

2 To speak evil of no man, to be no brawlers, but gentle, showing all meekness unto all men.

3 For we ourselves also were sometimes foolish, disobedient, deceived, serving divers lusts and pleasures, living in malice and envy, hateful, and hating one another.

4 But after that the kindness and love of God our Saviour toward man appeared,

5 Not by works of righteousness which we have done, but according to his mercy he saved us, by the washing of regeneration, and renewing of the Holy Ghost;

6 Which he shed on us abundantly through Jesus Christ our Saviour;

7 That being justified by his grace, we should be made heirs according to the hope of eternal life.

8 This is a faithful saying, and these things I will that thou affirm constantly, that they which have believed in God might be careful to maintain good works. These things are good and profitable unto men.

9 But avoid foolish questions, and genealogies, and contentions, and strivings about the law; for they are unprofitable and vain.

10 A man that is an heretic after the first and second admonition reject;

11 Knowing that he that is such is subverted, and sinneth, being condemned of himself.

12 When I shall send Artemas unto thee, or Tychicus, be diligent to come unto me to Nicopolis: for I have determined there to winter.

13 Bring Zenas the lawyer and Apollos on their journey diligently, that nothing be wanting unto them.

14 And let ours also learn to maintain good works for necessary uses, that they be not unfruitful.

15 All that are with me salute thee. Greet them that love us in the faith. Grace be with you all. Amen.

PHILEMON

Chapter 1

1 Paul, a prisoner of Jesus Christ, and Timothy our brother, unto Philemon our dearly beloved, and fellow labourer,

2 And to our beloved Apphia, and Archippus our fellowsoldier, and to the church in thy house:

3 Grace to you, and peace, from God our Father and the Lord Jesus Christ.

4 I thank my God, making mention of thee always in my prayers,

5 Hearing of thy love and faith, which thou hast toward the Lord Jesus, and toward all saints;

6 That the communication of thy faith may become effectual by the acknowledging of every good thing which is in you in Christ Jesus.

7 For we have great joy and consolation in thy love, because the bowels of the saints are refreshed by thee, brother.

8 Wherefore, though I might be much bold in Christ to enjoin thee that which is convenient,

9 Yet for love's sake I rather beseech thee, being such an one as Paul the aged, and now also a prisoner of Jesus Christ.

10 I beseech thee for my son Onesimus, whom I have begotten in my bonds:

11 Which in time past was to thee unprofitable, but now profitable to thee and to me:

12 Whom I have sent again: thou therefore receive him, that is, mine own bowels:

13 Whom I would have retained with me, that in thy stead he might have ministered unto me in the bonds of the gospel:

14 But without thy mind would I do nothing; that thy benefit should not be as it were of necessity, but willingly.

15 For perhaps he therefore departed for a season, that thou shouldest receive him for ever;

16 Not now as a servant, but above a servant, a brother beloved, specially to me, but how much more unto thee, both in the flesh, and in the Lord?

17 If thou count me therefore a partner, receive him as myself.

18 If he hath wronged thee, or oweth thee ought, put that on mine account;

19 I Paul have written it with mine own hand, I will repay it: albeit I do not say to thee how thou owest unto me even thine own self besides.

20 Yea, brother, let me have joy of thee in the Lord: refresh my bowels in the Lord.

21 Having confidence in thy obedience I wrote unto thee, knowing that thou wilt also do more than I say.

22 But withal prepare me also a lodging: for I trust that through your prayers I shall be given unto you.

23 There salute thee Epaphras, my fellow prisoner in Christ Jesus;

24 Marcus, Aristarchus, Demas, Lucas, my fellow labourers.

25 The grace of our Lord Jesus Christ be with ~~your spirit~~ *you*. Amen.

Chapter 1

1 God, who at sundry times and in divers maners spake in time past unto the fathers by the prophets,

2 Hath in these last days spoken unto us by his Son, whom he hath appointed heir of all things, by whom also he made the worlds;

3 Who being the brightness of his glory, and the express image of his person, and upholding all things by the word of his power, when he had by himself purged our sins, sat down on the right hand of the Majesty on high;

4 Being made so much better than the angels, as he hath by inheritance obtained a more excellent name than they.

5 For unto which of the angels said he at any time, Thou art my Son, this day have I begotten thee? And again, I will be to him a Father, and he shall be to me a Son?

6 And again, when he bringeth in the first-begotten into the world, he saith, And let all the angels of God worship him, *who maketh his ministers as a flame of fire.*

7 And of the angels he saith, ~~Who maketh his angels spirits, and his ministers a flame of fire.~~ *Angels are ministering spirits.*

8 But unto the Son he saith, Thy throne, O God, is for ever and ever: a sceptre of righteousness is the sceptre of thy kingdom.

9 Thou hast loved righteousness, and hated iniquity; therefore God, even thy God, hath anointed thee with the oil of gladness above thy fellows.

10 And, Thou, Lord, in the beginning hast laid the foundation of the earth; and the heavens are the works of thine hands:

11 They shall perish; but thou remainest; and they all shall wax old as doth a garment;

12 And as a vesture shalt thou fold them up, and they shall be changed: but thou art the same, and thy years shall not fail.

13 But to which of the angels said he at any time, Sit on my right hand, until I make thine enemies thy footstool?

14 Are they not all ministering spirits, sent forth to minister for them who shall be heirs of salvation?

Chapter 2

1 Therefore we ought to give the more earnest heed to the things which we have heard, lest at any time we should let them slip.

2 For if the word spoken by angels was stedfast, and every transgression and disobedience received a just recompense of reward;

3 How shall we escape, if we neglect so great salvation; which at the first began to be spoken by the Lord, and was confirmed unto us by them that heard him;

4 God also bearing them witness, both with signs and wonders, and with divers miracles, and gifts of the Holy Ghost, according to his own will?

5 For unto the angels hath he not put in subjection the world to come, whereof we speak.

6 But one in a certain place testified, saying, What is man, that thou art mindful of him? or the son of man, that thou visitest him?

7 Thou madest him a little lower than the angels; thou crownedst him with glory and honour, and didst set him over the works of thy hands:

8 Thou hast put all things in subjection under his feet. For in that he put all in subjection under him, he left nothing that is not put under him. But now we see not yet all things put under him.

9 But we see Jesus, who was made a little lower than the angels for the suffering of death, crowned with glory and honour; that he by the grace of God should taste death for every man.

10 For it became him, for whom are all things, and by whom are all things, in bringing many sons unto glory, to make the captain of their salvation perfect through sufferings.

11 For both he that sanctifieth and they who are sanctified are all of one: for which cause he is not ashamed to call them brethren,

12 Saying, I will declare thy name unto my brethren, in the midst of the church will I sing praise unto thee.

13 And again, I will put my trust in him. And again, Behold I and the children which God hath given me.

14 Forasmuch then as the children are partakers of flesh and blood, he also himself likewise took part of the same; that through death he might destroy him that had the power of death, that is, the devil;

15 And deliver them who through fear of death were all their lifetime subject to bondage.

16 For verily he took not on him the ~~nature~~ *likeness* of angels; but he took on him the seed of Abraham.

17 Wherefore in all things it behoved him to be made like unto his brethren, that he might be a merciful and faithful high priest in things pertaining to God, to make reconciliation for the sins of the people.

18 For in that he himself hath suffered being tempted, he is able to succour them that are tempted.

Chapter 3

1 Wherefore, holy brethren, partakers of the heavenly calling, consider the Apostle and High

Priest of our profession, Christ Jesus;

2 Who was faithful to him that appointed him, as also Moses was faithful in all his house.

3 For ~~this man~~ *he* was counted worthy of more glory than Moses, inasmuch as he who hath builded the house hath more ~~honour~~ *honor* than the house.

4 For every house is builded by some man; but he that built all things is God.

5 And Moses verily was faithful in all his house, as a servant, for a testimony of those things which were to be spoken after;

6 But Christ as a son over his own house; whose house are we, if we hold fast the confidence and the rejoicing of the hope firm unto the end.

7 Wherefore (as the Holy Ghost saith, To day if ye will hear his voice,

8 Harden not your hearts, as in the provocation, in the day of temptation in the wilderness:

9 When your fathers tempted me, proved me, and saw my works forty years.

10 Wherefore I was grieved with that generation, and said, They do alway err in their heart; and they have not known my ways.

11 So I sware in my wrath, They shall not enter into my rest.)

12 Take heed, brethren, lest there be in any of you an evil heart of unbelief, in departing from the living God.

13 But exhort one another daily, while it is called To day; lest any of you be hardened through the deceitfulness of sin.

14 For we are made partakers of Christ, if we hold the beginning of our confidence stedfast unto the end;

15 While it is said, To day if ye will hear his voice, harden not your hearts, as in the provocation.

16 For some, when they had heard, did provoke: howbeit not all that came out of Egypt by Moses.

17 But with whom was he grieved forty years? was it not with them that had sinned, whose carcases fell in the wilderness?

18 And to whom sware he that they should not enter into his rest, but to them that believed not?

19 So we see that they could not enter in because of unbelief.

Chapter 4

1 Let us therefore fear, lest, a promise being left us of entering into his rest, any of you should seem to come short of it.

2 For unto us was the ~~gospel~~ *rest* preached, as well as unto them: but the word preached did not profit them, not being mixed with faith in them that heard it.

3 For we ~~which~~ *who* have believed do enter into rest, as he said, As I have sworn in my wrath, *iIf* they *harden their hearts they shall not enter into my rest; also, I have sworn, If they will not harden their hearts,* they shall enter into my rest: although the works *of God* were *prepared, (or* finished,*)* from the foundation of the world.

4 For he spake in a certain place of the seventh day on this wise, And God did rest the seventh day from all his works.

5 And in this place again, If *they harden not their hearts* they shall enter into my rest.

6 Seeing therefore it remaineth that some must enter therein, and they to whom it was first preached entered not in because of unbelief:

7 Again, he limiteth a certain day, saying in David, To day, after so long a time; as it is said, To day if ye will hear his voice, harden not your hearts.

8 For if Jesus had given them rest, then would he not afterward have spoken of another day.

9 There remaineth therefore a rest to the people of God.

10 For he that is entered into his rest, he also hath ceased from his own works, as God did from his.

11 Let us labour therefore to enter into that rest, lest any man fall after the same example of unbelief.

12 For the word of God is quick, and powerful, and sharper than any two-edged sword, piercing even to the dividing asunder of ~~soul~~ *body* and spirit, and of the joints and marrow, and is a discerner of the thoughts and intents of the heart.

13 Neither is there any creature that is not manifest in his sight: but all things are naked and opened unto the eyes of him with whom we have to do.

14 Seeing then that we have a great high priest, that is passed into the heavens, Jesus the Son of God, let us hold fast our profession.

15 For we have not an high priest which cannot be touched with the feeling of our infirmities; but was in all points tempted like as we are, yet without sin.

16 Let us therefore come boldly unto the throne of grace, that we may obtain mercy, and find grace to help in time of need.

Chapter 5

1 For every high priest taken from among men is ordained for men in things pertaining to God, that he may offer both gifts and sacrifices for sins:

2 Who can have compassion on the ignorant, and on them that are out of the way; for that he himself also is compassed with infirmity.

3 And by reason hereof he ought, as for the

people, so also for himself, to offer for sins.

4 And no man taketh this honour unto himself, but he that is called of God, as was Aaron.

5 So also Christ glorified not himself to be made an high priest; but he that said unto him, Thou art my Son, to day have I begotten thee.

6 As he saith also in another place, Thou art a priest for ever after the order of Melchisedec.

7 Who in the days of his flesh, when he had offered up prayers and supplications with strong crying and tears unto him that was able to save him from death, and was heard in that he feared;

8 Though he were a Son, yet learned he obedience by the things which he suffered;

9 And being made perfect, he became the author of eternal salvation unto all them that obey him;

10 Called of God an high priest after the order of Melchisedec.

11 Of whom we have many things to say, and hard to be uttered, seeing ye are dull of hearing.

12 For when for the time ye ought to be teachers, ye have need that one teach you again which be the first principles of the oracles of God; and are become such as have need of milk, and not of strong meat.

13 For every one that useth milk is unskilful in the word of righteousness: for he is a babe.

14 But strong meat belongeth to them that are of full age, even those who by reason of use have their senses exercised to discern both good and evil.

Chapter 6

1 Therefore *not* leaving the principles of the doctrine of Christ, let us go on unto perfection; not laying again the foundation of repentance from dead works, and of faith toward God,

2 Of the doctrine of baptisms, ~~and~~ of laying on of hands, and of *the* resurrection of the dead, and of eternal judgment.

3 And ~~this will we do,~~ *we will go on unto perfection* if God permit.

4 For ~~it is~~ *he hath made it* impossible for those who were once enlightened, and have tasted of the heavenly gift, and were made partakers of the Holy Ghost,

5 And have tasted the good word of God, and the powers of the world to come,

6 If they shall fall away, to ~~renew them~~ *be renewed* again unto repentance; seeing they crucify *un*to themselves the Son of God afresh, and put him to an open shame.

7 For the *day cometh that the* earth which drinketh in the rain that cometh oft upon it, and bringeth forth herbs meet for them *who dwelleth thereon,* by whom it is dressed, *who now* receiveth

blessing~~s~~ from God~~:~~ *, shall be cleansed with fire.*

8 ~~But~~ *For* that which beareth thorns and briers is rejected, and is nigh unto cursing; ~~whose~~ *therefore they who bring not forth good fruits, shall be cast into the fire, for their* end is to be burned.

9 But, beloved, we are persuaded *of* better things of you, and things that accompany salvation, though we thus speak.

10 For God is not unrighteous ~~to~~ *, therefore he will not* forget your work and ~~labour~~ *labor* of love, which ye have ~~shewed~~ *showed* toward his name, in that ye have ministered to the saints, and do minister.

11 And we desire that every one of you do show the same diligence to the full assurance of hope unto the end:

12 That ye be not slothful, but followers of them who through faith and patience inherit the promises.

13 For when God made promise to Abraham, because he could swear by no greater, he sware by himself,

14 Saying, Surely blessing I will bless thee, and multiplying I will multiply thee.

15 And so, after he had patiently endured, he obtained the promise.

16 For men verily swear by the greater: and an oath for confirmation is to them an end of all strife.

17 Wherein God, willing more abundantly to show unto the heirs of promise the immutability of his counsel, confirmed it by an oath:

18 That by two immutable things, in which it was impossible for God to lie, we might have a strong consolation, who have fled for refuge to lay hold upon the hope set before us:

19 Which hope we have as an anchor of the soul, both sure and stedfast, and which entereth into that within the veil;

20 Whither the forerunner is for us entered, even Jesus, made an high priest for ever after the order of Melchisedec.

Chapter 7

1 For this Melchisedec, king of Salem, priest of the most high God, who met Abraham returning from the slaughter of the kings, and blessed him;

2 To whom also Abraham gave a tenth part of all; first being by interpretation King of righteousness, and after that also King of Salem, which is, King of peace;

3 *For this Melchizedek was ordained a priest after the order of the Son of God, which order was* ~~W~~*w*ithout father, without mother, without descent, having neither beginning of days, nor end of life; ~~but~~ *And all those who are ordained unto this priesthood are* made like unto the Son of

God; abideth *abiding* a priest continually.

4 Now consider how great this man was, unto whom even the patriarch Abraham gave the tenth of the spoils.

5 And verily they that are of the sons of Levi, who receive the office of the priesthood, have a commandment to take tithes of the people according to the law, that is, of their brethren, though they come out of the loins of Abraham:

6 But he whose descent is not counted from them received tithes of Abraham, and blessed him that had the promises.

7 And without all contradiction the less is blessed of the better.

8 And here men that die receive tithes; but there he receiveth them, of whom it is witnessed that he liveth.

9 And as I may so say, Levi also, who receiveth tithes, payed tithes in Abraham.

10 For he was yet in the loins of his father, when Melchisedec met him.

11 If therefore perfection were by the Levitical priesthood, (for under it the people received the law,) what further need was there that another priest should rise after the order of Melchisedec, and not be called after the order of Aaron?

12 For the priesthood being changed, there is made of necessity a change also of the law.

13 For he of whom these things are spoken pertaineth to another tribe, of which no man gave attendance at the altar.

14 For it is evident that our Lord sprang out of Juda; of which tribe Moses spake nothing concerning priesthood.

15 And it is yet far more evident: for that after the similitude of Melchisedec there ariseth another priest,

16 Who is made, not after the law of a carnal commandment, but after the power of an endless life.

17 For he testifieth, Thou art a priest for ever after the order of Melchisedec.

18 For there is verily a disannulling of the commandment going before for the weakness and unprofitableness thereof.

19 For the law *was administered without an oath and* made nothing perfect, but *was only* the bringing in of a better hope did; by the which we draw nigh unto God.

20 And iInasmuch as *this high priest was* not without an oath , he was made priest:

21 (For those priests were made without an oath; but this with an oath by him that said unto him, The Lord sware and will not repent, Thou art a priest for ever after the order of Melchisedec:)

22 By so much was Jesus made a *the* surety of a better testament.

23 And they truly were many priests, because

they were not suffered to continue by reason of death:

24 But this man, because he continueth ever, hath an unchangeable priesthood.

25 Wherefore he is able also to save them to the uttermost that come unto God by him, seeing he ever liveth to make intercession for them.

26 For such an high priest became us, who is holy, harmless, undefiled, separate from sinners, and made higher than *ruler over* the heavens;

27 Who needeth not daily, *And not* as those high priests, to offer *who offered* up sacrifice *daily*, first for his *their* own sins, and then for the people's: *sins of the people;* for *he needed not to offer sacrifice for his own sins, for he knew no sins; but for the sins of the people. And* this he did once, when he offered up himself.

28 For the law maketh men high priests which have infirmity; but the word of the oath, which was since the law, maketh the Son, who is consecrated for evermore.

Chapter 8

1 Now of the things which we have spoken this is the sum: We have such an high priest, who is set on the right hand of the throne of the Majesty in the heavens;

2 A minister of the sanctuary, and of the true tabernacle, which the Lord pitched, and not man.

3 For every high priest is ordained to offer gifts and sacrifices: wherefore it is of necessity that this man have somewhat also to offer.

4 For if he were *Therefore while he was* on earth, *he offered for a sacrifice his own life for the sins of the people. Now every* he should not be a priest *under the law,* seeing that there are priests that *must needs* offer gifts, *or sacrifices,* according to the law:

5 Who serve unto the example and shadow of heavenly things, as Moses was admonished of God when he was about to make the tabernacle: for, See, saith he, that thou make all things according to the pattern showed to thee in the mount.

6 But now hath he obtained a more excellent ministry, by how much also he is the mediator of a better covenant, which was established upon better promises.

7 For if that first covenant had been faultless, then should no place have been sought for the second.

8 For finding fault with them, he saith, Behold, the days come, saith the Lord, when I will make a new covenant with the house of Israel and with the house of Judah:

9 Not according to the covenant that I made with their fathers in the day when I took them by the hand to lead them out of the land of Egypt;

because they continued not in my covenant, and I regarded them not, saith the Lord.

10 For this is the covenant that I will make with the house of Israel after those days, saith the Lord; I will put my laws into their mind, and write them in their hearts: and I will be to them a God, and they shall be to me a people:

11 And they shall not teach every man his neighbour, and every man his brother, saying, Know the Lord: for all shall know me, from the least to the greatest.

12 For I will be merciful to their unrighteousness, and their sins and their iniquities will I remember no more.

13 In that he saith, A new covenant, he hath made the first old. Now that which decayeth and waxeth old is ready to vanish away.

Chapter 9

1 Then verily the first covenant had also ordinances of divine service, and a worldly sanctuary.

2 For there was a tabernacle made; the first, wherein was the candlestick, and the table, and the showbread; which is called the sanctuary.

3 And after the second veil, the tabernacle which is called the Holiest of all;

4 Which had the golden censer, and the ark of the covenant overlaid round about with gold, wherein was the golden pot that had manna, and Aaron's rod that budded, and the tables of the covenant;

5 And over it the cherubims of glory shadowing the mercyseat; of which we cannot now speak particularly.

6 Now when these things were thus ordained, the priests went always into the first tabernacle, accomplishing the service of God.

7 But into the second went the high priest alone once every year, not without blood, which he offered for himself, and for the errors of the people:

8 The Holy Ghost ~~this~~ signifying *this*, that the way into the holiest of all was not yet made manifest, while as *yet* the first tabernacle was ~~yet~~ standing:

9 Which was a figure for the time then present, in which were offered both gifts and sacrifices, that could not make him that did the service perfect, as pertaining to the conscience;

10 Which ~~stood~~ *consisted* only in meats and drinks, and divers washings, and carnal ordinances, imposed on them until the time of reformation.

11 But Christ being come an high priest of good things to come, by a greater and more perfect tabernacle, not made with hands, that is to say, not of this building;

12 Neither by the blood of goats and calves, but by his own blood he entered in once into the holy place, having obtained eternal redemption for us.

13 For if the blood of bulls and of goats, and the ashes of an heifer sprinkling the unclean, sanctifieth to the purifying of the flesh:

14 How much more shall the blood of Christ, who through the eternal Spirit offered himself without spot to God, purge your conscience from dead works to serve the living God?

15 And for this cause he is the mediator of the new ~~testament~~ *covenant*, that by means of death, for the redemption of the transgressions that were under the first ~~testament~~ *covenant*, they which are called might receive the promise of eternal inheritance.

16 For where a ~~testament~~ *covenant* is, there must also of necessity be the death of the ~~testator~~ *victim*.

17 For a ~~testament~~ *covenant* is of force after ~~men are~~ *the victim is* dead: otherwise it is of no strength at all while the ~~testator~~ *victim* liveth.

18 Whereupon neither the first ~~testament~~ *covenant* was dedicated without blood.

19 For when Moses had spoken every precept to all the people according to the law, he took the blood of calves and of goats, with water, and scarlet wool, and hyssop, and sprinkled both the book, and all the people,

20 Saying, This is the blood of the ~~testament~~ *covenant* which God hath enjoined unto you.

21 Moreover he sprinkled *likewise* with blood both the tabernacle, and all the vessels of the ministry.

22 And almost all things are by the law purged with blood; and without shedding of blood is no remission.

23 It was therefore necessary that the patterns of things in the heavens should be purified with these; but the heavenly things themselves with better sacrifices than these.

24 For Christ is not entered into the holy places made with hands, which are the figures of the true; but into heaven itself, now to appear in the presence of God for us:

25 Nor yet that he should offer himself often, as the high priest entereth into the holy place every year with blood of others;

26 For then must he often have suffered since the foundation of the world: but now once in the ~~end of the world~~ *meridian of time* hath he appeared to put away sin by the sacrifice of himself.

27 And as it is appointed unto men once to die, but after this the judgment:

28 So Christ was once offered to bear the sins of many; and ~~unto them that look for him shall~~ he *shall* appear the second time without sin unto salvation *unto them that look for him.*

Chapter 10

1 For the law having a shadow of good things to come, and not the very image of the things, can never with those sacrifices which they offered *continually* year by year continually make the comers thereunto perfect.

2 For then would they not have ceased to be offered? because that the worshippers once purged should have had no more conscience of sins.

3 But in those sacrifices there is a remembrance again made of sins every year.

4 For it is not possible that the blood of bulls and of goats should take away sins.

5 Wherefore when he cometh into the world, he saith, Sacrifice and offering thou wouldest not, but a body hast thou prepared me:

6 In burnt offerings and sacrifices for sin thou hast had no pleasure.

7 Then said I, Lo, I come (in the volume of the book it is written of me,) to do thy will, O God.

8 Above when he said, Sacrifice and offering and burnt offerings and offering for sin thou wouldest not, neither hadst pleasure therein; which are offered by the law;

9 Then said he, Lo, I come to do thy will, O God. He taketh away the first, that he may establish the second.

10 By the which will we are sanctified through the offering *once* of the body of Jesus Christ once for all.

11 And every priest standeth daily ministering and offering oftentimes the same sacrifices, which can never take away sins:

12 But this man, after he had offered one sacrifice for sins for ever, sat down on the right hand of God;

13 From henceforth expecting till *to reign until* his enemies be made his footstool.

14 For by one offering he hath perfected for ever them that are sanctified.

15 Whereof the Holy Ghost also is a witness to us: for after that he had said before,

16 This is the covenant that I will make with them after those days, saith the Lord, I will put my laws into their hearts, and in their minds will I write them;

17 And their sins and iniquities will I remember no more.

18 Now where remission of these is, there is no more offering for sin.

19 Having therefore, brethren, boldness to enter into the holiest by the blood of Jesus,

20 By a new and living way, which he hath consecrated for us, through the veil, that is to say, his flesh;

21 And having *such* an high priest over the house of God;

22 Let us draw near with a true heart in full assurance of faith, having our hearts sprinkled from an evil conscience, and our bodies washed with pure water.

23 Let us hold fast the profession of our faith without wavering; (for he is faithful that promised;)

24 And let us consider one another to provoke unto love and to good works:

25 Not forsaking the assembling of ourselves together, as the manner of some is; but exhorting one another: and so much the more, as ye see the day approaching.

26 For if we sin wilfully after that we have received the knowledge of the truth, there remaineth no more sacrifice for sins,

27 But a certain fearful looking for of judgment and fiery indignation, which shall devour the adversaries.

28 He that despised Moses' law died without mercy under two or three witnesses:

29 Of how much sorer punishment, suppose ye, shall he be thought worthy, who hath trodden under foot the Son of God, and hath counted the blood of the covenant, wherewith he was sanctified, an unholy thing, and hath done despite unto the Spirit of grace?

30 For we know him that hath said, Vengeance belongeth unto me, I will recompense, saith the Lord. And again, The Lord shall judge his people.

31 It is a fearful thing to fall into the hands of the living God.

32 But call to remembrance the former days, in which, after ye were illuminated, ye endured a great fight of afflictions;

33 Partly, whilst ye were made a gazingstock both by reproaches and afflictions; and partly, whilst ye became companions of them that were so used.

34 For ye had compassion of me in my bonds, and took joyfully the spoiling of your goods, knowing in yourselves that ye have in heaven a better and an enduring substance.

35 Cast not away therefore your confidence, which hath great recompense of reward.

36 For ye have need of patience, that, after ye have done the will of God, ye might receive the promise.

37 For yet a little while, and he that shall come will come, and will not tarry.

38 Now the just shall live by faith: but if any man draw back, my soul shall have no pleasure in him.

39 But we are not of them who draw back unto perdition; but of them that believe to the saving of the soul.

Chapter 11

1 Now faith is the ~~substance~~ *assurance* of things hoped for, the evidence of things not seen.

2 For by it the elders obtained a good report.

3 Through faith we understand that the worlds were framed by the word of God, so that things which are seen were not made of things which do appear.

4 By faith Abel offered unto God a more excellent sacrifice than Cain, by which he obtained witness that he was righteous, God testifying of his gifts: and by it he being dead yet speaketh.

5 By faith Enoch was translated that he should not see death; and was not found, because God had translated him: for before his translation he had this testimony, that he pleased God.

6 But without faith it is impossible to please him: for he that cometh to God must believe that he is, and that he is a rewarder of them that diligently seek him.

7 By faith Noah, being warned of God of things not seen as yet, moved with fear, prepared an ark to the saving of his house; by the which he condemned the world, and became heir of the righteousness which is by faith.

8 By faith Abraham, when he was called to go out into a place which he should after receive for an inheritance, obeyed; and he went out, not knowing whither he went.

9 By faith he sojourned in the land of promise, as in a strange country, dwelling in tabernacles with Isaac and Jacob, the heirs with him of the same promise:

10 For he looked for a city which hath foundations, whose builder and maker is God.

11 Through faith also Sara herself received strength to conceive seed, and was delivered of a child when she was past age, because she judged him faithful who had promised.

12 Therefore sprang there even of one, and him as good as dead, ~~so~~ *as* many as the stars of the sky in multitude, and as the sand which is by the sea-shore innumerable.

13 These all died in faith, not having received the promises, but having seen them afar off, and were persuaded of them, and embraced them, and confessed that they were strangers and pilgrims on the earth.

14 For they that say such things declare plainly that they seek a country.

15 And truly, if they had been mindful of that country from whence they came out, they might have had opportunity to have returned.

16 But now they desire a better country, that is, an heavenly: wherefore God is not ashamed to be called their God: for he hath prepared for them a city.

17 By faith Abraham, when he was tried, offered up Isaac: and he that had received the promises offered up his only begotten son.

18 Of whom it was said, That in Isaac shall thy seed be called:

19 Accounting that God was able to raise him up, even from the dead; from whence also he received him in a figure.

20 By faith Isaac blessed Jacob and Esau concerning things to come.

21 By faith Jacob, when he was a dying, blessed both the sons of Joseph; and worshipped, leaning upon the top of his staff.

22 By faith Joseph, when he died, made mention of the departing of the children of Israel; and gave commandment concerning his bones.

23 By faith Moses, when he was born, was hid three months of his parents, because they saw *that* he was a ~~proper~~ *peculiar* child; and they were not afraid of the king's commandment.

24 By faith Moses, when he was come to years *of discretion*, refused to be called the son of Pharaoh's daughter;

25 Choosing rather to suffer affliction with the people of God, than to enjoy the pleasures of sin for a season;

26 Esteeming the reproach of Christ greater riches than the treasures in Egypt: for he had respect unto the recompense of the reward.

27 By faith he forsook Egypt, not fearing the wrath of the king: for he endured, as seeing him who is invisible.

28 Through faith he kept the passover, and the sprinkling of blood, lest he that destroyed the firstborn should touch them.

29 By faith they passed through the Red sea as by dry land: which the Egyptians assaying to do were drowned.

30 By faith the walls of Jericho fell down, after they were compassed about seven days.

31 By faith the harlot Rahab perished not with them that believed not, when she had received the spies with peace.

32 And what shall I more say? for the time would fail me to tell of Gedeon, and of Barak, and of Samson, and of Jephthae; of David also, and Samuel, and of the prophets:

33 Who through faith subdued kingdoms, wrought righteousness, obtained promises, stopped the mouths of lions,

34 Quenched the violence of fire, escaped the edge of the sword, out of weakness were made strong, waxed valiant in fight, turned to flight the armies of the aliens.

35 Women received their dead raised to life again: and others were tortured, not accepting deliverance; that they might obtain ~~a better~~ *the first* resurrection:

36 And others had trial of cruel mockings and

scourgings, yea, moreover of bonds and imprisonment:

37 They were stoned, they were sawn asunder, were tempted, were slain with the sword: they wandered about in sheepskins and goatskins; being destitute, afflicted, tormented;

38 (Of whom the world was not worthy:) they wandered in deserts, and in mountains, and in dens and caves of the earth.

39 And these all, having obtained a good report through faith, received not the promise:

40 God having provided some better things for ~~us, that they without us should~~ *them through their sufferings, for without sufferings they could* not be made perfect.

Chapter 12

1 Wherefore seeing we also are compassed about with so great a cloud of witnesses, let us lay aside every weight, and the sin which doth so easily beset us, and let us run with patience the race that is set before us,

2 Looking unto Jesus the author and finisher of our faith; who for the joy that was set before him endured the cross, despising the shame, and is set down at the right hand of the throne of God.

3 For consider him that endured such contradiction of sinners against himself, lest ye be wearied and faint in your minds.

4 Ye have not yet resisted unto blood, striving against sin.

5 And ye have forgotten the exhortation which speaketh unto you as unto children, My son, despise not thou the chastening of the Lord, nor faint when thou art rebuked of him:

6 For whom the Lord loveth he chasteneth, and scourgeth every son whom he receiveth.

7 If ye endure chastening, God dealeth with you as with sons; for what son is he whom the father chasteneth not?

8 But if ye be without chastisement, whereof all are partakers, then are ye bastards, and not sons.

9 Furthermore we have had fathers of our flesh which corrected us, and we gave them reverence: shall we not much rather be in subjection unto the Father of spirits, and live?

10 For they verily for a few days chastened us after their own pleasure; but he for our profit, that we might be partakers of his holiness.

11 Now no chastening for the present seemeth to be joyous, but grievous: nevertheless afterward it yieldeth the peaceable fruit of righteousness unto them which are exercised thereby.

12 Wherefore lift up the hands which hang down, and *strengthen* the feeble knees;

13 And make straight paths for your feet, lest that which is lame be turned out of the way; but let it rather be healed.

14 Follow peace with all men, and holiness, without which no man shall see the Lord:

15 Looking diligently lest any man fail of the grace of God; lest any root of bitterness springing up trouble you, and thereby many be defiled;

16 Lest there be any fornicator, or profane person, as Esau, who for one morsel of meat sold his birthright.

17 For ye know how that afterward, when he would have inherited the blessing, he was rejected: for he found no place of repentance, though he sought it carefully with tears.

18 For ye are not come unto the mount that might be touched, and that burned with fire, nor unto blackness, and darkness, and tempest,

19 And the sound of a trumpet, and the voice of words; which voice they that heard entreated that the word should not be spoken to them any more:

20 (For they could not endure that which was commanded, And if so much as a beast touch the mountain, it shall be stoned, or thrust through with a dart:

21 And so terrible was the sight, that Moses said, I exceedingly fear and quake:)

22 But ye are come unto mount Sion, and unto the city of the living God, the heavenly Jerusalem, and to an innumerable company of angels,

23 To the general assembly and church of the firstborn, which are written in heaven, and to God the Judge of all, and to the spirits of just men made perfect,

24 And to Jesus the mediator of the new covenant, and to the blood of sprinkling, that speaketh better things than that of Abel.

25 See that ye refuse not him that speaketh. For if they escaped not who refused him that spake on earth, much more shall not we escape, if we turn away from him that speaketh from heaven:

26 Whose voice then shook the earth: but now he hath promised, saying, Yet once more I shake not the earth only, but also heaven.

27 And this word, Yet once more, signifieth the removing of those things that are shaken, as of things that are made, that those things which cannot be shaken may remain.

28 Wherefore we receiving a kingdom which cannot be moved, ~~let us~~ *should* have grace, whereby we may serve God acceptably with reverence and godly fear:

29 For our God is a consuming fire.

Chapter 13

1 Let brotherly love continue.

2 Be not forgetful to entertain strangers: for

thereby some have entertained angels unawares.

3 Remember them that are in bonds, as bound with them; and them which suffer adversity, as being yourselves also ~~in~~ *of* the body.

4 Marriage is honourable in all, and the bed undefiled: but whoremongers and adulterers God will judge.

5 Let your ~~conversation~~ *consecrations* be without covetousness; and be content with *giving* such things as ye have: for he hath said, I will never leave thee, nor forsake thee.

6 So that we may boldly say, The Lord is my helper, and I will not fear what man shall do unto me.

7 Remember them which have the rule over you, who have spoken unto you the word of God: whose faith follow, considering the end of their conversation.

8 Jesus Christ the same yesterday, and to day, and for ever.

9 Be not carried about with divers and strange doctrines. For it is a good thing that the heart be established with grace; not with meats, which have not profited them that have been occupied therein.

10 We have an altar, whereof they have no right to eat which serve the tabernacle.

11 For the bodies of those beasts, whose blood is brought into the sanctuary by the high priest for sin, are burned without the camp.

12 Wherefore Jesus also, that he might sanctify the people with his own blood, suffered without the gate.

13 Let us go forth therefore unto him without the camp, bearing his reproach.

14 For here have we no continuing city, but we seek one to come.

15 By him therefore let us offer the sacrifice of praise to God continually, that is, the fruit of our lips giving thanks to his name.

16 But to do good and to communicate forget not: for with such sacrifices God is well pleased.

17 Obey them that have the rule over you, and submit yourselves: for they watch for your souls, as they that must give account, that they may do it with joy, and not with grief: for that is unprofitable for you.

18 Pray for us: for we trust we have a good conscience, in all things willing to live honestly.

19 But I beseech you the rather to do this, that I may be restored to you the sooner.

20 Now the God of peace, that brought again from the dead our Lord Jesus, that great shepherd of the sheep, through the blood of the everlasting covenant,

21 Make you perfect in every good work to do his will, working in you that which is wellpleasing in his sight, through Jesus Christ; to whom be glory for ever and ever. Amen.

22 And I beseech you, brethren, suffer the word of exhortation: for I have written a letter unto you in few words.

23 Know ye that our brother Timothy is set at liberty; with whom, if he come shortly, I will see you.

24 Salute all them that have the rule over you, and all the saints. They of Italy salute you.

25 Grace be with you all. Amen.

THE EPISTLE OF JAMES

Chapter 1

1 James, a servant of God and of the Lord Jesus Christ, to the twelve tribes which are scattered abroad, greeting.

2 My brethren, count it all joy when ye fall into ~~divers temptations~~ *many afflictions*;

3 Knowing this, that the trying of your faith worketh patience.

4 But let patience have ~~her~~ *its* perfect work, that ye may be perfect and entire, wanting nothing.

5 If any of you lack wisdom, let him ask of God, that giveth to all men liberally, and upbraideth not; and it shall be given him.

6 But let him ask in faith, nothing wavering. For he that wavereth is like a wave of the sea driven with the wind and tossed.

7 For let not that man think that he shall receive any thing of the Lord.

8 A double minded man is unstable in all his ways.

9 Let the brother of low degree rejoice in that he is exalted:

10 But the rich, in that he is made low: because as the flower of the grass he shall pass away.

11 For the sun is no sooner risen with a burning heat, but it withereth the grass, and the flower thereof falleth, and the grace of the fashion of it perisheth: so also shall the rich man fade away in his ways.

12 Blessed is the man that ~~endureth~~ *resisteth* temptation: for when he is tried, he shall receive the crown of life, which the Lord hath promised to them that love him.

13 Let no man say when he is tempted, I am tempted of God: for God cannot be tempted with evil, neither tempteth he any man:

14 But every man is tempted, when he is drawn away of his own lust, and enticed.

15 Then when lust hath conceived, it bringeth forth sin: and sin, when it is finished, bringeth forth death.

16 Do not err, my beloved brethren.

17 Every good gift and every perfect gift is from above, and cometh down from the Father of lights, with whom is no variableness, neither shadow of turning.

18 Of his own will begat he us with the word of truth, that we should be a kind of firstfruits of his creatures.

19 Wherefore, my beloved brethren, let every man be swift to hear, slow to speak, slow to wrath:

20 For the wrath of man worketh not the righteousness of God.

21 Wherefore lay apart *aside* all filthiness and superfluity of naughtiness, and receive with meekness the engrafted word, which is able to save your souls.

22 But be ye doers of the word, and not hearers only, deceiving your own selves.

23 For if any be a hearer of the word, and not a doer, he is like unto a man beholding his natural face in a glass:

24 For he beholdeth himself, and goeth his way, and straightway forgetteth what manner of man he was.

25 But whoso looketh into the perfect law of liberty, and continueth therein, he being not a forgetful hearer, but a doer of the work, this man shall be blessed in his deed.

26 If any man among you seem to be religious, and bridleth not his tongue, but deceiveth his own heart, this man's religion is vain.

27 Pure religion and undefiled before God and the Father is this, To visit the fatherless and widows in their affliction, and to keep himself unspotted from *the vices of* the world.

Chapter 2

1 My brethren, *ye cannot* have not the faith of our Lord Jesus Christ, the Lord of gGlory, with *and yet have* respect of *to* persons.

2 For *Now* if there come unto your assembly a man with a gold ring, in goodly apparel, and there come in also a poor man in vile raiment;

3 And ye have respect to him that weareth the gay clothing, and say unto him, Sit thou here in a good place; and say to the poor, Stand thou there, or sit here under my footstool:

4 Are ye not then partial in yourselves *partial* judges, and are become judges of evil *in your* thoughts?

5 Hearken, my beloved brethren, Hath not God chosen the poor of this world rich in faith, and heirs of the kingdom which he hath promised to them that love him?

6 But ye have despised the poor. Do not rich men oppress you, and draw you before the judgment seats?

7 Do not they blaspheme that worthy name by the which ye are called?

8 If ye fulfil the royal law according to the scripture, Thou shalt love thy neighbour as thyself, ye do well:

9 But if ye have respect to persons, ye commit sin, and are convinced of the law as transgressors.

10 For whosoever shall, *save in one point,* keep the whole law, and yet offend in one point, he is guilty of all.

11 For he that said, Do not commit adultery, said also, Do not kill. Now if thou commit no adultery, yet if thou kill, thou art become a transgressor of the law.

12 So speak ye, and so do, as they that shall be judged by the law of liberty.

13 For he shall have judgment without mercy, that hath showed no mercy; and mercy rejoiceth against judgment.

14 What doth it profit *is it*, my brethren, though *for* a man *to* say he hath faith, and have *hath* not works? can faith save him?

18 Yea, a man may say, Thou hast faith, and I have works: *I will show thee I have faith without works; but I say,* sShow me thy faith without thy works, and I will shew *show* thee my faith by my works. *(verse order changed by JST)*

15 *For* Iif a brother or sister be naked, and destitute of daily food,

16 And one of you say unto them, Depart in peace, be ye warmed and filled; notwithstanding ye *he* give them not those things which are needful to the body; what doth it profit *is your faith unto such*?

17 Even so faith, if it hath *have* not works, is dead, being alone.

20 But *Therefore* wilt thou know, O vain man, that faith without works is dead *and cannot save you*?

19 Thou believest that there is one God; thou doest well: the devils also believe, and tremble; *thou hast made thyself like unto them, not being justified. (verse order changed by JST)*

21 Was not Abraham our father justified by works, when he had offered Isaac his son upon the altar?

22 Seest thou how faith *works* wrought with his works *faith*, and by works was faith made perfect?

23 And the scripture was fulfilled which saith, Abraham believed God, and it was imputed unto

him for righteousness: and he was called the ~~F~~friend of God.

24 Ye see then ~~how~~ that by works a man is justified, and not by faith only.

25 Likewise also ~~was not~~ Rahab the harlot *was* justified by works, when she had received the messengers, and ~~had~~ sent them out another way~~?~~ .

26 For as the body without the spirit is dead, so faith without works is dead also.

Chapter 3

1 My brethren, ~~be not many masters~~ *strive not for the mastery*, knowing that *in so doing* we shall receive the greater condemnation.

2 For in many things we offend all. If any man offend not in word, the same is a perfect man, and able also to bridle the whole body.

3 Behold, we put bits in the horses' mouths, that they may obey us; and we turn about their whole body.

4 Behold also the ships, which though they be so great, and are driven of fierce winds, yet are they turned about with a very small helm, whithersoever the governor listeth.

5 Even so the tongue is a little member, and boasteth great things. Behold, how great a matter a little fire kindleth!

6 And the tongue is a fire, a world of iniquity: so is the tongue among our members, that it defileth the whole body, and setteth on fire the course of nature; and it is set on fire of hell.

7 For every kind of beasts, and of birds, and of serpents, and of things in the sea, is tamed, and hath been tamed of mankind:

8 But the tongue can no man tame; it is an unruly evil, full of deadly poison.

9 Therewith bless we God, even the Father; and therewith curse we men, which are made after the similitude of God.

10 Out of the same mouth proceedeth blessing and cursing. My brethren, these things ought not so to be.

11 Doth a fountain send forth at the same place sweet water and bitter?

12 Can the fig tree, my brethren, bear olive berries? either a vine, figs? so can no fountain both yield salt water and fresh.

13 Who is a wise man and endued with knowledge among you? let him show out of a good conversation his works with meekness of wisdom.

14 But if ye have bitter envying and strife in your hearts, glory not, and lie not against the truth.

15 This wisdom descendeth not from above, but is earthly, sensual, devilish.

16 For where envying and strife is, there is confusion and every evil work.

17 But the wisdom that is from above is first pure, then peaceable, gentle, and easy to be entreated, full of mercy and good fruits, without partiality, and without hypocrisy.

18 And the fruit of righteousness is sown in peace of them that make peace.

Chapter 4

1 From whence come wars and fightings among you? come they not hence, even of your lusts that war in your members?

2 Ye lust, and have not: ye kill, and desire to have, and cannot obtain: ye fight and war, yet ye have not, because ye ask not.

3 Ye ask, and receive not, because ye ask amiss, that ye may consume it upon your lusts.

4 Ye adulterers and adulteresses, know ye not that the friendship of the world is enmity with God? whosoever therefore will be a friend of the world is the enemy of God.

5 Do ye think that the scripture saith in vain, The spirit that dwelleth in us lusteth to envy?

6 But he giveth more grace. Wherefore he saith, God resisteth the proud, but giveth grace unto the humble.

7 Submit yourselves therefore to God. Resist the devil, and he will flee from you.

8 Draw nigh to God, and he will draw nigh to you. Cleanse your hands, ye sinners; and purify your hearts, ye double minded.

9 Be afflicted, and mourn, and weep: let your laughter be turned to mourning, and your joy to heaviness.

10 Humble yourselves in the sight of the Lord, and he shall lift you up.

11 Speak not evil one of another, brethren. He that speaketh evil of his brother, and judgeth his brother, speaketh evil of the law, and judgeth the law: but if thou judge the law, thou art not a doer of the law, but a judge.

12 There is one lawgiver, who is able to save and to destroy: who art thou that judgest another?

13 Go to now, ye that say, To day or to morrow we will go into such a city, and continue there a year, and buy and sell, and get gain:

14 Whereas ye know not what shall be on the morrow. For what is your life? It is even a vapour, that appeareth for a little time, and then vanisheth away.

15 For that ye ought to say, If the Lord will, we shall live, and do this, or that.

16 But now ye rejoice in your boastings: all such rejoicing is evil.

17 Therefore to him that knoweth to do good, and doeth it not, to him it is sin.

Chapter 5

1 Go to now, ye rich men, weep and howl for your miseries that shall come upon you.

2 Your riches are corrupted, and your garments are motheaten.

3 Your gold and silver is cankered; and the rust of them shall be a witness against you, and shall eat your flesh as it were fire. Ye have heaped treasure together for the last days.

4 Behold, the hire of the labourers who have reaped down your fields, which is of you kept back by fraud, crieth: and the cries of them which have reaped are entered into the ears of the Lord of sabaoth.

5 Ye have lived in pleasure on the earth, and been wanton; ye have nourished your hearts, as in a day of slaughter.

6 Ye have condemned and killed the just; and he doth not resist you.

7 Be patient therefore, brethren, unto the coming of the Lord. Behold, the husbandman waiteth for the precious fruit of the earth, and hath long patience for it, until he receive the early and latter rain.

8 Be ye also patient; stablish your hearts: for the coming of the Lord draweth nigh.

9 Grudge not one against another, brethren, lest ye be condemned: behold, the judge standeth before the door.

10 Take, my brethren, the prophets, who have spoken in the name of the Lord, for an example of suffering affliction, and of patience.

11 Behold, we count them happy which endure. Ye have heard of the patience of Job, and have seen the end of the Lord; that the Lord is very pitiful, and of tender mercy.

12 But above all things, my brethren, swear not, neither by heaven, neither by the earth, neither by any other oath: but let your yea be yea; and your nay, nay; lest ye fall into condemnation.

13 Is any among you afflicted? let him pray. Is any merry? let him sing psalms.

14 Is any sick among you? let him call for the elders of the church; and let them pray over him, anointing him with oil in the name of the Lord:

15 And the prayer of faith shall save the sick, and the Lord shall raise him up; and if he have committed sins, they shall be forgiven him.

16 Confess your faults one to another, and pray one for another, that ye may be healed. The effectual fervent prayer of a righteous man availeth much.

17 Elias was a man subject to like passions as we are, and he prayed earnestly that it might not rain: and it rained not on the earth by the space of three years and six months.

18 And he prayed again, and the heaven gave rain, and the earth brought forth her fruit.

19 Brethren, if any of you do err from the truth, and one convert him;

20 Let him know, that he which converteth the sinner from the error of his way shall save a soul from death, and shall hide a multitude of sins.

1st PETER

Chapter 1

1 Peter, an apostle of Jesus Christ, to the strangers scattered throughout Pontus, Galatia, Cappadocia, Asia, and Bithynia,

2 Elect according to the foreknowledge of God the Father, through sanctification of the Spirit, unto obedience and sprinkling of the blood of Jesus Christ: Grace unto you, and peace, be multiplied.

3 Blessed be the God and Father of our Lord Jesus Christ, which according to his abundant mercy hath begotten us again unto a lively hope by the resurrection of Jesus Christ from the dead,

4 To an inheritance incorruptible, and undefiled, and that fadeth not away, reserved in heaven for you,

5 Who are kept by the power of God through faith unto salvation ready to be revealed in the last time.

6 Wherein ye greatly rejoice, though now for a season, if need be, ye are in heaviness through manifold temptations:

7 That the trial of your faith, being much more precious than of gold that perisheth, though it be tried with fire, might be found unto praise and honour and glory at the appearing of Jesus Christ:

8 Whom having not seen, ye love; in whom, though now ye see him not, yet believing, ye rejoice with joy unspeakable and full of glory:

9 Receiving the ~~end~~ *object* of your faith, even the salvation of your souls.

10 ~~Of~~ *Concerning* which salvation the prophets have inquired and searched diligently, who prophesied of the grace that should come unto you:

11 Searching what *time*, ~~or~~ *and* what manner of

time *salvation* the Spirit of Christ which was in them did signify, when it testified beforehand the sufferings of Christ, and the glory ~~that~~ *which* should follow.

12 Unto whom it was revealed, that not unto themselves, but unto us they did minister the things, which are now reported unto you by them that have preached the gospel unto you with the Holy Ghost sent down from heaven; which things the angels desire to look into.

13 Wherefore gird up the loins of your mind, be sober, and hope to the end for the grace that is to be brought unto you at the revelation of Jesus Christ;

14 As obedient children, not fashioning yourselves according to the former lusts in your ignorance:

15 But as he which hath called you is holy, so be ye holy in all manner of conversation;

16 Because it is written, Be ye holy; for I am holy.

17 And if ye call on the Father, who without respect of persons judgeth according to every man's work, pass the time of your sojourning here in fear:

18 Forasmuch as ye know that ye were not redeemed with corruptible things, as silver and gold, from your vain conversation received by tradition from your fathers;

19 But with the precious blood of Christ, as of a lamb without blemish and without spot:

20 Who verily was foreordained before the foundation of the world, but was manifest in these last times for you,

21 Who by him do believe in God, that raised him up from the dead, and gave him glory; that your faith and hope might be in God.

22 Seeing ye have purified your souls in obeying the truth through the Spirit unto unfeigned love of the brethren, see that ye love one another with a pure heart fervently:

23 Being born again, not of corruptible seed, but of incorruptible, by the word of God, which liveth and abideth for ever.

24 For all flesh is as grass, and all the glory of man as the flower of grass. The grass withereth, and the flower thereof falleth away:

25 But the word of the Lord endureth for ever. And this is the word which by the gospel is preached unto you.

Chapter 2

1 Wherefore laying aside all malice, and all guile, and hypocrisies, and envies, and all evil speakings,

2 As newborn babes, desire the sincere milk of the word, that ye may grow thereby:

3 If so be ye have tasted that the Lord is gracious.

4 To whom coming, as unto a living stone, disallowed indeed of men, but chosen of God, and precious,

5 Ye also, as lively stones, are built up a spiritual house, an holy priesthood, to offer up spiritual sacrifices, acceptable to God by Jesus Christ.

6 Wherefore also it is contained in the scripture, Behold, I lay in Sion a chief corner stone, elect, precious: and he that believeth on him shall not be confounded.

7a Unto you therefore ~~which~~ *who* believe , he is precious: but unto them ~~which be~~ *who are* disobedient, *who stumble at the word, through disobediance, whereunto they were appointed,*

8 ~~And~~ a stone of stumbling, and a rock of offence. ~~, even to them which stumble at the word, being disobedient: whereunto also they were appointed.~~

7b *For* the stone which the builders disallowed, ~~the same is made~~ *is become* the head of the corner, *(verse order of 7b changed by JST)*

9 But ye are a chosen generation, a royal priesthood, ~~an~~ *a* holy nation, a peculiar people; that ye should show forth the praises of him who hath called you out of darkness into his marvellous light:

10 Which in time past were not a people, but are now the people of God: which had not obtained mercy, but now have obtained mercy.

11 Dearly beloved, I beseech you as strangers and pilgrims, abstain from fleshly lusts, which war against the soul;

12 Having your ~~conversation~~ *conduct* honest among the Gentiles: that, whereas they speak against you as evildoers, they may by your good works, which they shall behold, glorify God in the day of visitation.

13 Submit yourselves to every ordinance of man for the Lord's sake: whether it be to the king, as supreme;

14 Or unto governors, as unto them that are sent by him for the punishment of evildoers, and for the praise of them that do well.

15 For so is the will of God, that with well doing ye may put to silence the ignorance of foolish men:

16 As free, and not using your liberty for a cloak of maliciousness, but as the servants of God.

17 Honour all men. Love the brotherhood. Fear God. Honour the king.

18 Servants, be subject to your masters with all fear; not only to the good and gentle, but also to the froward.

19 For this is thankworthy, if a man for conscience toward God endure grief, suffering wrongfully.

20 For what glory is it, if, when ye be buffeted for your faults, ye shall take it patiently? but if, when ye do well, and suffer for it, ye take it patiently, this is acceptable with God.

21 For even hereunto were ye called: because Christ also suffered for us, leaving us an example, that ye should follow his steps:

22 Who did no sin, neither was guile found in his mouth:

23 Who, when he was reviled, reviled not again; when he suffered, he threatened not; but committed himself to him that judgeth righteously:

24 Who his own self bare our sins in his own body on the tree, that we, being dead to sins, should live unto righteousness: by whose stripes ye were healed.

25 For ye were as sheep going astray; but are now returned unto the Shepherd and Bishop of your souls.

Chapter 3

1 Likewise, ye wives, be in subjection to your own husbands; that, if any obey not the word, they also may without the word be won by the ~~conversation~~ *conduct* of the wives;

2 While they behold your chaste ~~conversation~~ *conduct* coupled with fear.

3 *Let your* ~~Whose~~ adorning ~~let it not~~ be *not* that outward adorning of plaiting the hair, and ~~of~~ wearing of gold, or ~~of~~ putting on of apparel;

4 But let it be the hidden man of the heart, in that which is not corruptible, even the ornament of a meek and quiet spirit, which is in the sight of God of great price.

5 For after this manner in the old time the holy women ~~also~~, who trusted in God, adorned themselves, being in subjection unto their own husbands:

6 Even as Sara obeyed Abraham, calling him lord: whose daughters ye are, as long as ye do well, and are not afraid with any amazement.

7 Likewise, ye husbands, dwell with them according to knowledge, giving honour unto the wife, as unto the weaker vessel, and as being heirs together of the grace of life; that your prayers be not hindered.

8 Finally, be ye all of one mind, having compassion one of another, love as brethren, be pitiful, be courteous:

9 Not rendering evil for evil, or railing for railing: but contrariwise blessing; knowing that ye are thereunto called, that ye should inherit a blessing.

10 For he that will love life, and see good days, let him refrain his tongue from evil, and his lips that they speak no guile:

11 Let him eschew evil, and do good; let him seek peace, and ensue it.

12 For the eyes of the Lord are over the righteous, and his ears are open unto their prayers: but the face of the Lord is against them that do evil.

13 And who is he that will harm you, if ye be followers of that which is good?

14 But and if ye suffer for righteousness' sake, happy are ye: and be not afraid of their terror, neither be troubled;

15 But sanctify the Lord God in your hearts: and be ready always to give an answer *with meekness and fear* to every man that asketh *of* you a reason ~~of~~ *for* the hope that is in you ~~with meekness and fear:~~

16 Having a good conscience; that, whereas they speak evil of you, as of evildoers, they may be ashamed that falsely accuse your good ~~conversation~~ in Christ.

17 For it is better, if the will of God be so, that ye suffer for well doing, than for evil doing.

18 For Christ also ~~hath~~ once suffered for sins, the just for the unjust, ~~that he might bring us to God,~~ being put to death in the flesh, but quickened by the Spirit: *that he might bring us to God.*

19 ~~By~~ *For* which *cause* also he went and preached unto the spirits in prison;

20 ~~Which some time~~ *Some of whom* were disobedient *in the days of Noah*, ~~when once~~ *while* the longsuffering of God waited ~~in the days of Noah~~ , while the ark was ~~a~~ preparing, wherein few, that is, eight souls were saved by water.

21 The like figure whereunto even baptism doth also now save us (not the putting away of the filth of the flesh, but the answer of a good conscience toward God,) by the resurrection of Jesus Christ:

22 Who is gone into heaven, and is on the right hand of God; angels and authorities and powers being made subject unto him.

Chapter 4

1 Forasmuch then as Christ hath suffered for us in the flesh, arm yourselves likewise with the same mind: for ~~he~~ *you* ~~that hath~~ *who have* suffered in the flesh ~~hath ceased~~ *should cease* from sin;

2 That ~~he~~ *you* no longer ~~should live~~ the rest of ~~his~~ *your* time in the flesh, *should live* to the lusts of men, but to the will of God.

3 For the time past of ~~our~~ life may suffice ~~us~~ to have wrought the will of the Gentiles, when ~~we~~ *ye* walked in lasciviousness, lusts, excess of wine, revellings, banquetings, and abominable idolatries:

4 Wherein they *speak evil of you,* ~~think~~ *thinking* it strange that ~~ye~~ *you* run not with them to the same excess of riot, ~~speaking evil of you:~~

5 Who shall give account to him that is ready to judge the quick and the dead.

6 ~~For for this cause was~~ , *is* the gospel preached ~~also~~ to them that are dead, that they might be judged according to men in the flesh, but live *in the spirit* according to *the will of* God ~~in the spirit~~.

7 But *to you,* the end of all things is at hand: be ye therefore sober, and watch unto prayer.

8 And above all things have fervent charity among yourselves: for charity ~~shall cover the~~ *preventeth a* multitude of sins.

9 Use hospitality one to another without grudging.

10 As every man hath received the gift, even so minister the same one to another, as good stewards of the manifold grace of God.

11 If any man speak, let him speak as ~~the oracles~~ *an oracle* of God; if any man minister, let him do it as of the ability which God giveth: that God in all things may be glorified through Jesus Christ, to whom be praise and dominion for ever and ever. Amen.

12 Beloved, think it not strange concerning the fiery trial which is to try you, as though some strange thing happened unto you:

13 But rejoice, inasmuch as ye are partakers of Christ's sufferings; that, when his glory shall be revealed, ye may be glad also with exceeding joy.

14 If ye be reproached for the name of Christ, happy are ye; for the spirit of glory and of God resteth upon you: on their part he is evil spoken of, but on your part he is glorified.

15 But let none of you suffer as a murderer, or as a thief, or as an evildoer, or as a busybody in other men's matters.

16 Yet if any man suffer as a Christian, let him not be ashamed; but let him glorify God on this behalf.

17 For the time is come that judgment must begin at the house of God: and if it first begin at us, what shall the end be of them that obey not the gospel of God?

18 And if the righteous scarcely be saved, where shall the ungodly and the sinner appear?

19 Wherefore let them that suffer according to the will of God commit the keeping of their souls to him in well doing, as unto a faithful Creator.

Chapter 5

1 The elders which are among you I exhort, who am also an elder, and a witness of the sufferings of Christ, and also a partaker of the glory that shall be revealed:

2 Feed the flock of God which is among you, taking the oversight thereof, not by constraint, but willingly; not for filthy lucre, but of a ready mind;

3 Neither as being lords over God's heritage, but being ensamples to the flock.

4 And when the chief Shepherd shall appear, ye shall receive a crown of glory that fadeth not away.

5 Likewise, ye younger, submit yourselves unto the elder. Yea, all of you be subject one to another, and be clothed with humility: for God resisteth the proud, and giveth grace to the humble.

6 Humble yourselves therefore under the mighty hand of God, that he may exalt you in due time:

7 Casting all your care upon him; for he careth for you.

8 Be sober, be vigilant; because your adversary the devil, as a roaring lion, walketh about, seeking whom he may devour:

9 Whom resist stedfast in the faith, knowing that the same afflictions are accomplished in your brethren that are in the world.

10 But the God of all grace, who hath called us unto his eternal glory by Christ Jesus, after that ye have suffered a while, make you perfect, stablish, strengthen, settle you.

11 To him be glory and dominion for ever and ever. Amen.

12 By Silvanus, a faithful brother unto you, as I suppose, I have written briefly, exhorting, and testifying that this is the true grace of God wherein ye stand.

13 The church that is at Babylon, elected together with you, saluteth you; and so doth Marcus my son.

14 Greet ye one another with a kiss of charity. Peace be with you all that are in Christ Jesus. Amen.

Chapter 1

1 Simon Peter, a servant and an apostle of Jesus Christ, to them that have obtained like precious faith with us through the righteousness of God and our Saviour Jesus Christ:

2 Grace and peace be multiplied unto you through the knowledge of God, and of Jesus our Lord,

3 According as his divine power hath given unto us all things that pertain unto life and godliness, through the knowledge of him that hath called us to glory and virtue:

4 Whereby are given unto us exceeding great and precious promises: that by these ye might be partakers of the divine nature, having escaped the corruption that is in the world through lust.

5 And beside this, giving all diligence, add to your faith virtue; and to virtue knowledge;

6 And to knowledge temperance; and to temperance patience; and to patience godliness;

7 And to godliness brotherly kindness; and to brotherly kindness charity.

8 For if these things be in you, and abound, they make you that ye shall neither be barren nor unfruitful in the knowledge of our Lord Jesus Christ.

9 But he that lacketh these things is blind, and cannot see afar off, and hath forgotten that he was purged from his old sins.

10 Wherefore the rather, brethren, give diligence to make your calling and election sure: for if ye do these things, ye shall never fall:

11 For so an entrance shall be ministered unto you abundantly into the everlasting kingdom of our Lord and Saviour Jesus Christ.

12 Wherefore I will not be negligent to put you always in remembrance of these things, though ye know them, and be established in the present truth.

13 Yea, I think it meet, as long as I am in this tabernacle, to stir you up by putting you in remembrance;

14 Knowing that shortly I must put off this my tabernacle, even as our Lord Jesus Christ hath showed me.

15 Moreover I will endeavour that ye may be able after my decease to have these things always in remembrance.

16 For we have not followed cunningly devised fables, when we made known unto you the power and coming of our Lord Jesus Christ, but were eyewitnesses of his majesty.

17 For he received from God the Father honour and glory, when there came such a voice to him from the excellent glory, This is my beloved Son, in whom I am well pleased.

18 And this voice which came from heaven we heard, when we were with him in the holy mount.

19 We have ~~also~~ *therefore* a more sure *knowledge of the* word of prophecy; ~~whereunto~~ *to which word of prophesy* ye do well that ye take heed, as unto a light ~~that~~ *which* shineth in a dark place, until the day dawn, and the day star arise in your hearts:

20 Knowing this first, that no prophecy of the scriptures *is given* of any private ~~interpretation~~ *will of man*.

21 For the prophecy came not in old time by the will of man: but holy men of God spake as they were moved by the Holy Ghost.

Chapter 2

1 But there were false prophets also among the people, even as there shall be false teachers among you, who privily shall bring in ~~damnable~~ *abominable* heresies, even denying the Lord that bought them, and bring upon themselves swift destruction.

2 And many shall follow their pernicious ways; by reason of whom the way of truth shall be evil spoken of.

3 And through covetousness shall they with feigned words make merchandise of you: whose judgment now of a long time lingereth not, and their ~~damnation~~ *destruction* slumbereth not.

4 For if God spared not the angels that sinned, but cast them down to hell, and delivered them into chains of darkness, to be reserved unto judgment;

5 And spared not the old world, but saved Noah the eighth person, a preacher of righteousness, bringing in the flood upon the world of the ungodly;

6 And turning the cities of Sodom and Gomorrha into ashes condemned them with an overthrow, making them an ensample unto those that after should live ungodly;

7 And delivered just Lot, vexed with the filthy conversation of the wicked:

8 (For that righteous man dwelling among them, in seeing and hearing, vexed his righteous soul from day to day with their unlawful deeds;)

9 The Lord knoweth how to deliver the godly out of temptations, and to reserve the unjust unto the day of judgment to be punished:

10 But chiefly them that walk after the flesh in the lust of uncleanness, and despise government. Presumptuous are they, selfwilled, they are not afraid to speak evil of dignities.

11 Whereas angels, which are greater in power and might, bring not railing accusation against them before the Lord.

12 But these, as natural brute beasts, made to be taken and destroyed, speak evil of the things that they understand not; and shall utterly perish in their own corruption;

13 And shall receive the reward of unrighteousness, as they that count it pleasure to

riot in the day time. Spots they are and blemishes, sporting themselves with their own deceivings while they feast with you;

14 Having eyes full of adultery, and that cannot cease from sin; beguiling unstable souls: an heart they have exercised with covetous practices; cursed children:

15 Which have forsaken the right way, and are gone astray, following the way of Balaam the son of Bosor, who loved the wages of unrighteousness;

16 But was rebuked for his iniquity: the dumb ass speaking with man's voice forbad the madness of the prophet.

17 These are wells without water, clouds that are carried with a tempest; to whom the mist of darkness is reserved for ever.

18 For when they speak great swelling words of vanity, they allure through the lusts of the flesh, through much wantonness, those that were clean escaped from them who live in error.

19 While they promise them liberty, they themselves are the servants of corruption: for of whom a man is overcome, of the same is he brought in bondage.

20 For if after they have escaped the pollutions of the world through the knowledge of the Lord and Saviour Jesus Christ, they are again entangled therein, and overcome, the latter end is worse with them than the beginning.

21 For it had been better for them not to have known the way of righteousness, than, after they have known it, to turn from the holy commandment delivered unto them.

22 But it is happened unto them according to the true proverb, The dog is turned to his own vomit again; and the sow that was washed to her wallowing in the mire.

Chapter 3

1 This second epistle, beloved, I now write unto you; in ~~both~~ which I stir up your pure minds by way of remembrance:

2 That ye may be mindful of the words which were spoken before by the holy prophets, and of the commandment of us the apostles of the Lord and Saviour:

3 Knowing this first, that *in the last days* there shall come ~~in the last days~~ scoffers, walking after their own lusts,

4 *Denying the Lord Jesus Christ,* ~~A~~and saying, Where is the promise of his coming? for since the fathers fell asleep, all things *must* continue as they ~~were~~ *are, and have continued as they are* from the beginning of the creation.

5 For this they willingly are ignorant of, that ~~by the word of God~~ *of old* the heavens ~~were of old~~ , and the earth standing *in the water and* out of the water ~~and in the water:~~ *, were created by the word*

of God.

6 ~~Whereby~~ *And by the word of God,* the world that then was, being overflowed with water, perished:

7 But the heavens and the earth, which are now, *are kept in store* by the same word ~~are kept in store~~, reserved unto fire against the day of judgment and perdition of ungodly men.

8 But *concerning the coming of the Lord*, beloved, ~~be~~ *I would* not *have you* ignorant of this one thing, that one day is with the Lord as a thousand years, and a thousand years as one day.

9 The Lord is not slack concerning his promise *and coming*, as some men count slackness; but ~~is~~ longsuffering ~~to us-ward~~ *toward us*, not willing that any should perish, but that all should come to repentance.

10 But the day of the Lord will come as a thief in the night; in the which the heavens shall *shake, and the earth also shall tremble, and the mountains shall melt, and* pass away with a great noise, and the elements shall ~~melt~~ *be filled* with fervent heat, the earth also *shall be filled,* and the *corruptible* works ~~that~~ *which* are therein shall be burned up.

11 ~~Seeing~~ *If* then ~~that~~ all these things shall be ~~dissolved~~ *destroyed*, what manner of persons ought ye to be in ~~all~~ holy ~~conversation~~ *conduct* and godliness,

12 Looking *unto, and preparing* for ~~and hasting unto~~ the *day of the* coming of the ~~day of God,~~ *Lord* wherein the *corruptible things of the* heavens being on fire shall be dissolved, and the ~~elements~~ *mountains* shall melt with fervent heat?

13 Nevertheless*, if* we *shall endure, we shall be kept* according to his promise, *And we* look for *a* new heavens and a new earth, wherein dwelleth righteousness.

14 Wherefore, beloved, seeing that ye look for such things, be diligent that ye may be found of him in peace, without spot, and blameless.

15 And account ~~that~~ *, even as our beloved brother Paul also, according to the wisdom given unto him, hath written unto you,* the longsuffering *and waiting* of our Lord ~~is~~ *, for* salvation; ~~even as our beloved brother Paul also according to the wisdom given unto him hath written unto you;~~

16 As also in all his epistles, speaking in them of these things; in which are some things hard to be understood, which ~~they~~ ~~that~~ *who* are unlearned and unstable wrest, as they do also the other ~~s~~*S*criptures, unto their own destruction.

17 Ye therefore, beloved, seeing ye know ~~these things~~ before *the things which are coming*, beware lest ye also, being led away with the error of the wicked, fall from your own ~~stedfastness~~ *steadfastness*.

18 But grow in grace, and ~~in~~ the knowledge of our Lord and ~~Saviour~~ *Savior* Jesus Christ. To him be glory both now and for ever. Amen.

Chapter 1

1 *Brethren, this is the testimony which we give of* ~~T~~that which was from the beginning, which we have heard, which we have seen with our eyes, which we have looked upon, and our hands have handled, of the Word of life;

2 (For the life was manifested, and we have seen it, and bear witness, and show unto you that eternal life, which was with the Father, and was manifested unto us;)

3 That which we have seen and heard declare we unto you, that ye also may have fellowship with us: and truly our fellowship is with the Father, and with his Son Jesus Christ.

4 And these things write we unto you, that your joy may be full.

5 This then is the message which we have heard of him, and declare unto you, that God is light, and in him is no darkness at all.

6 If we say that we have fellowship with him, and walk in darkness, we lie, and do not the truth:

7 But if we walk in the light, as he is in the light, we have fellowship one with another, and the blood of Jesus Christ his Son cleanseth us from all sin.

8 If we say that we have no sin, we deceive ourselves, and the truth is not in us.

9 If we confess our sins, he is faithful and just to forgive us our sins, and to cleanse us from all unrighteousness.

10 If we say that we have not sinned, we make him a liar, and his word is not in us.

Chapter 2

1 My little children, these things write I unto you, that ye sin not. ~~And~~ *But* if any man sin *and repent*, we have an advocate with the Father, Jesus Christ the righteous:

2 And he is the propitiation for our sins: and not for ours only, but also for the sins of the whole world.

3 And hereby we do know that we know him, if we keep his commandments.

4 He that saith, I know him, and keepeth not his commandments, is a liar, and the truth is not in him.

5 But whoso keepeth his word, in him verily is the love of God perfected: hereby know we that we are in him.

6 He that saith he abideth in him ought himself also so to walk, even as he walked.

7 Brethren, I write ~~no~~ *a* new commandment unto you, but ~~an old~~ *it is the same* commandment which ye had from the beginning. The old commandment is the word which ye have heard from the beginning.

8 Again, a new commandment I write unto you, which thing *was of old ordained of God; and* is true in him and in you: because the darkness is past *in you*, and the true light now shineth.

9 He that saith he is in the light, and hateth his brother, is in darkness even until now.

10 He that loveth his brother abideth in the light, and there is none occasion of stumbling in him.

11 But he that hateth his brother is in darkness, and walketh in darkness, and knoweth not whither he goeth, because that darkness hath blinded his eyes.

12 I write unto you, little children, because your sins are forgiven you for his name's sake.

13 I write unto you, fathers, because ye have known him that is from the beginning. I write unto you, young men, because ye have overcome the wicked one. I write unto you, little children, because ye have known the Father.

14 I have written unto you, fathers, because ye have known him that is from the beginning. I have written unto you, young men, because ye are strong, and the word of God abideth in you, and ye have overcome the wicked one.

15 Love not the world, neither the things that are ~~in~~ *of* the world. If any man love the world, the love of the Father is not in him.

16 For all ~~that is~~ in the world, *that is of* the lusts of the flesh, and the lust of the eyes, and the pride of life, is not of the Father, but is of the world.

17 And the world passeth away, and the lust thereof: but he that doeth the will of God abideth for ever.

18 Little children, it is the last time: and as ye have heard that antichrist shall come, even now are there many antichrists; whereby we know that it is the last time.

19 They went out from us, but they were not of us; for if they had been of us, they would no doubt have continued with us: but they went out, that they might be made manifest that they were not all of us.

20 But ye have an unction from the Holy One, and ye know all things.

21 I have not written unto you because ye know not the truth, but because ye know it, and that no lie is of the truth.

22 Who is a liar but he that denieth that Jesus is the Christ? He is antichrist, that denieth the Father and the Son.

23 Whosoever denieth the Son, the same hath not the Father: but he that acknowledgeth the Son hath the Father also.

24 Let that therefore abide in you, which ye have heard from the beginning. If that which ye have heard from the beginning shall remain in you, ye also shall continue in the Son, and *also* in the Father.

25 And this is the promise that he hath promised us, even eternal life.

26 These things have I written unto you concerning them that seduce you.

27 But the anointing which ye have received of him abideth in you, and ye need not that any man teach you: but as the same anointing teacheth you of all things, and is truth, and is no lie, and even as it hath taught you, ye shall abide in him.

28 And now, little children, abide in him; that, when he shall appear, we may have confidence, and not be ashamed before him at his coming.

29 If ye know that he is righteous, ye know that every one that doeth righteousness is born of him.

Chapter 3

1 Behold, what manner of love the Father hath bestowed upon us, that we should be called the sons of God: therefore the world knoweth us not, because it knew him not.

2 Beloved, now are we the sons of God, and it doth not yet appear what we shall be: but we know that, when he shall appear, we shall be like him; for we shall see him as he is.

3 And every man that hath this hope in him purifieth himself, even as he is pure.

4 Whosoever committeth sin transgresseth also the law: for sin is the transgression of the law.

5 And ye know that he was manifested to take away our sins; and in him is no sin.

6 Whosoever abideth in him sinneth not: whosoever ~~sinneth~~ *continueth in sin* hath not seen him, neither known him.

7 Little children, let no man deceive you: he that doeth righteousness is righteous, even as he is righteous.

8 He that ~~committeth~~ *continueth in* sin is of the devil; for the devil sinneth from the beginning. For this purpose the Son of God was manifested, that he might destroy the works of the devil.

9 Whosoever is born of God doth not ~~commit~~ *continueth in* sin; for ~~his seed~~ *the Spirit of God* remaineth in him: and he cannot *continue in* sin, because he is born of God, *having received that holy Spirit of promise*.

10 In this the children of God are manifest, and the children of the devil: whosoever doeth not righteousness is not of God, neither he that loveth not his brother.

11 For this is the message that ye heard from the beginning, that we should love one another.

12 Not as Cain, who was of that wicked one, and slew his brother. And wherefore slew he him? Because his own works were evil, and his brother's righteous.

13 Marvel not, my brethren, if the world hate you.

14 We know that we have passed from death unto life, because we love the brethren. He that loveth not his brother abideth in death.

15 Whosoever hateth his brother is a murderer: and ye know that no murderer hath eternal life abiding in him.

16 Hereby perceive we the love of ~~God~~ *Christ*, because he laid down his life for us: and we ought to lay down our lives for the brethren.

17 But whoso hath this world's good, and seeth his brother have need, and shutteth up his bowels of compassion from him, how dwelleth the love of God in him?

18 My little children, let us not love in word, neither in tongue *only*; but in deed and in truth.

19 And hereby we know that we are of the truth, and shall assure our hearts before him.

20 For if our heart condemn us, God is greater than our heart, and knoweth all things.

21 Beloved, if our heart condemn us not, then have we confidence toward God.

22 And whatsoever we ask, we receive of him, because we keep his commandments, and do those things that are pleasing in his sight.

23 And this is his commandment, That we should believe on the name of his Son Jesus Christ, and love one another, as he gave us commandment.

24 And he that keepeth his commandments dwelleth in him, and he in him. And hereby we know that he abideth in us, by the Spirit which he hath given us.

Chapter 4

1 Beloved, believe not every spirit, but try the spirits whether they are of God: because many false prophets are gone out into the world.

2 Hereby know ye the Spirit of God: Every spirit that confesseth that Jesus Christ is come in the flesh is of God:

3 And every spirit that confesseth not that Jesus Christ is come in the flesh is not of God: and this is that spirit of antichrist, whereof ye have heard that it should come; and even now already ~~is~~ it *is already* in the world.

4 Ye are of God, little children, and have overcome them: because greater is he that is in you, than he that is in the world.

5 They are of the world: therefore speak they of the world, and the world heareth them.

6 We are of God: he that knoweth God heareth us; he that is not of God heareth not us. Hereby know we the spirit of truth, and the spirit of error.

7 Beloved, let us love one another: for love is of God; and every one that loveth is born of God,

and knoweth God.

8 He that loveth not knoweth not God; for God is love.

9 In this was manifested the love of God toward us, because that God sent his only begotten Son into the world, that we might live through him.

10 Herein is love, not that we loved God, but that he loved us, and sent his Son to be the propitiation for our sins.

11 Beloved, if God so loved us, we ought also to love one another.

12 No man hath seen God at any time, *except them who believe*. If we love one another, God dwelleth in us, and his love is perfected in us.

13 Hereby know we that we dwell in him, and he in us, because he hath given us of his Spirit.

14 And we have seen and do testify that the Father sent the Son to be the Saviour of the world.

15 Whosoever shall confess that Jesus is the Son of God, God dwelleth in him, and he in God.

16 And we have known and believed the love that God hath to us. God is love; and he that dwelleth in love dwelleth in God, and God in him.

17 Herein is our love made perfect, that we may have boldness in the day of judgment: because as he is, so are we in this world.

18 There is no fear in love; but perfect love casteth out fear: because fear hath torment. He that feareth is not made perfect in love.

19 We love him, because he first loved us.

20 If a man say, I love God, and hateth his brother, he is a liar: for he that loveth not his brother whom he hath seen, how can he love God whom he hath not seen?

21 And this commandment have we from him, That he who loveth God love his brother also.

Chapter 5

1 Whosoever believeth that Jesus is the Christ is born of God: and every one that loveth him that begat loveth him also that is begotten of him.

2 By this we know that we love the children of God, when we love God, and keep his commandments.

3 For this is the love of God, that we keep his commandments: and his commandments are not grievous.

4 For whatsoever is born of God overcometh the world: and this is the victory that overcometh the world, even our faith.

5 Who is he that overcometh the world, but he that believeth that Jesus is the Son of God?

6 This is he that came by water and blood, even Jesus Christ; not by water only, but by water and blood. And it is the Spirit that beareth witness, because the Spirit is truth.

7 For there are three that bear record in heaven, the Father, the Word, and the Holy Ghost: and these three are one.

8 And there are three that bear witness in earth, the Spirit, and the water, and the blood: and these three agree in one.

9 If we receive the witness of men, the witness of God is greater: for this is the witness of God which he hath testified of his Son.

10 He that believeth on the Son of God hath the witness in himself: he that believeth not God hath made him a liar; because he believeth not the record that God gave of his Son.

11 And this is the record, that God hath given to us eternal life, and this life is in his Son.

12 He that hath the Son hath life; and he that hath not the Son of God hath not life.

13 These things have I written unto you that believe on the name of the Son of God; that ye may know that ye have eternal life, and that ye may *continue to* believe on the name of the Son of God.

14 And this is the confidence that we have in him, that, if we ask any thing according to his will, he heareth us:

15 And if we know that he hear us, whatsoever we ask, we know that we have the petitions that we desired of him.

16 If any man see his brother sin a sin which is not unto death, he shall ask, and he shall give him life for them that sin not unto death. There is a sin unto death: I do not say that he shall pray for it.

17 All unrighteousness is sin: and there is a sin not unto death.

18 We know that whosoever is born of God ~~sinneth~~ *continueth* not *in sin*; but he that is begotten of God *and* keepeth himself, ~~and~~ that wicked one ~~toucheth~~ *overcometh* him not.

19 And we know that we are of God, and the whole world lieth in wickedness.

20 And we know that the Son of God is come, and hath given us an understanding, that we may know him that is true, and we are in him that is true, even in his Son Jesus Christ. This is the true God, and eternal life.

21 Little children, keep yourselves from idols. Amen.

Chapter 1

1 The elder unto the elect lady and her children, whom I love in the truth; and not I only, but also all they that have known the truth;

2 For the truth's sake, which dwelleth in us, and shall be with us for ever.

3 Grace be with you, mercy, [and] peace, from God the Father, and from the Lord Jesus Christ, the Son of the Father, in truth and love.

4 I rejoiced greatly that I found of thy children walking in truth, as we have received a commandment from the Father.

5 And now I beseech thee, lady, not as though I wrote a new commandment unto thee, but that which we had from the beginning, that we love one another.

6 And this is love, that we walk after his commandments. This is the commandment, That, as ye have heard from the beginning, ye should walk in it.

7 For many deceivers are entered into the world, who confess not that Jesus Christ is come in the flesh. This is a deceiver and an antichrist.

8 Look to yourselves, that we lose not those things which we have wrought, but that we receive a full reward.

9 Whosoever transgresseth, and abideth not in the doctrine of Christ, hath not God. He that abideth in the doctrine of Christ, he hath both the Father and the Son.

10 If there come any unto you, and bring not this doctrine, receive him not into [your] house, neither bid him God speed:

11 For he that biddeth him God speed is partaker of his evil deeds.

12 Having many things to write unto you, I would not [write] with paper and ink: but I trust to come unto you, and speak face to face, that our joy may be full.

13 The children of thy elect sister greet thee. Amen.

3rd JOHN

Chapter 1

1 The elder unto the wellbeloved Gaius, whom I love in the truth.

2 Beloved, I wish above all things that thou mayest prosper and be in health, even as thy soul prospereth.

3 For I rejoiced greatly, when the brethren came and testified of the truth that is in thee, even as thou walkest in the truth.

4 I have no greater joy than to hear that my children walk in truth.

5 Beloved, thou doest faithfully whatsoever thou doest to the brethren, and to strangers;

6 Which have borne witness of thy charity before the church: whom if thou bring forward on their journey after a godly sort, thou shalt do well:

7 Because that for his name's sake they went forth, taking nothing of the Gentiles.

8 We therefore ought to receive such, that we might be fellowhelpers to the truth.

9 I wrote unto the church: but Diotrephes, who loveth to have the preeminence among them, receiveth us not.

10 Wherefore, if I come, I will remember his deeds which he doeth, prating against us with malicious words: and not content therewith, neither doth he himself receive the brethren, and forbiddeth them that would, and casteth them out of the church.

11 Beloved, follow not that which is evil, but that which is good. He that doeth good is of God: but he that doeth evil hath not seen God.

12 Demetrius hath good report of all men, and of the truth itself: yea, and we also bear record; and ye know that our record is true.

13 I had many things to write, but I will not with ink and pen write unto thee:

14 But I trust I shall shortly see thee, and we shall speak face to face. Peace be to thee. Our friends salute thee. Greet the friends by name.

Chapter 1

1 Jude, the servant of *God, called of* Jesus Christ, and brother of James, to them ~~that~~ *who* are sanctified ~~by God~~ *of* the Father, and preserved in Jesus Christ~~, and called~~:

2 Mercy unto you, and peace and love, be multiplied.

3 Beloved, when I gave all diligence to write unto you of the common salvation, it was needful for me to write unto you, and exhort you that ye should earnestly contend for the faith which was once delivered unto the saints.

4 For there are certain men crept in unawares, who were before of old ordained to this condemnation, ungodly men, turning the grace of our God into lasciviousness, and denying the only Lord God, and our Lord Jesus Christ.

5 I will therefore put you in remembrance, though ye once knew this, how that the Lord, having saved the people out of the land of Egypt, afterward destroyed them that believed not.

6 And the angels which kept not their first estate, but left their own habitation, he hath reserved in everlasting chains under darkness unto the judgment of the great day.

7 Even as Sodom and Gomorrha, and the cities about them in like manner, giving themselves over to fornication, and going after strange flesh, are set forth for an example, suffering the vengeance of eternal fire.

8 Likewise also these filthy dreamers defile the flesh, despise dominion, and speak evil of dignities.

9 Yet Michael the archangel, when contending with the devil he disputed about the body of Moses, durst not bring against him a railing accusation, but said, The Lord rebuke thee.

10 But these speak evil of those things which they know not: but what they know naturally, as brute beasts, in those things they corrupt themselves.

11 Woe unto them! for they have gone in the way of Cain, and ran greedily after the error of Balaam for reward, and perished in the gainsaying of Core.

12 These are spots in your feasts of charity, when they feast with you, feeding themselves without fear: clouds they are without water, carried about of winds; trees whose fruit withereth, without fruit, twice dead, plucked up by the roots;

13 Raging waves of the sea, foaming out their own shame; wandering stars, to whom is reserved the blackness of darkness for ever.

14 And Enoch also, the seventh from Adam, prophesied of these, saying, Behold, the Lord cometh with ten thousands of his saints,

15 To execute judgment upon all, and to convince all that are ungodly among them of all their ungodly deeds which they have ungodly committed, and of all their hard speeches which ungodly sinners have spoken against him.

16 These are murmurers, complainers, walking after their own lusts; and their mouth speaketh great swelling words, having men's persons in admiration because of advantage.

17 But, beloved, remember ye the words which were spoken before of the apostles of our Lord Jesus Christ;

18 How that they told you there should be mockers in the last time, who should walk after their own ungodly lusts.

19 These be they who separate themselves, sensual, having not the Spirit.

20 But ye, beloved, building up yourselves on your most holy faith, praying in the Holy Ghost,

21 Keep yourselves in the love of God, looking for the mercy of our Lord Jesus Christ unto eternal life.

22 And of some have compassion, making a difference:

23 And others save with fear, pulling them out of the fire; hating even the garment spotted by the flesh.

24 Now unto him that is able to keep you from falling, and to present you faultless before the presence of his glory with exceeding joy,

25 To the only wise God our Saviour, be glory and majesty, dominion and power, both now and for ever. Amen.

Chapter 1

1 The Revelation of ~~Jesus Christ~~ *John, a servant of God*, which ~~God gave~~ *was given* unto him *of Jesus Christ*, to ~~shew~~ *show* unto his servants things which must shortly come to pass; ~~and~~ *that* he sent and signified ~~it~~ by his angel unto his servant John:

2 Who ~~bare~~ *bore* record of the word of God, and of the testimony of Jesus Christ, and of all things that he saw.

3 Blessed ~~is he that~~ *are they who* read~~eth~~, and they ~~that~~ *who* hear *and understand* the words of this prophecy, and keep those things which are written therein: for the time ~~is at hand~~ *of the coming of the Lord draweth nigh*.

4 *Now this is the testimony of* John to the *seven servants who are over the* seven churches ~~which are~~ in Asia: Grace ~~be~~ unto you, and peace, from him ~~which~~ *who* is, and ~~which~~ *who* was, and ~~which who~~ *who* is to come; ~~and from the seven Spirits which are~~ *who hath sent forth his angel from* before his throne ~~;~~ *, to testify unto those who are the seven servants over the seven churches.*

5 ~~And from Jesus Christ, who is~~ *Therefore, I, John,* the faithful witness, ~~and~~ *bear record of the things which were delivered me of the angel, and from Jesus Christ* the first begotten of the dead, and the ~~p~~*P*rince of the kings of the earth. *And* ~~U~~*u*nto him ~~that~~ *who* loved us, *be glory;* ~~and~~ *who* washed us from our sins in his own blood,

6 And hath made us kings and priests unto God ~~and~~ *,* his Father; to him be glory and dominion for ever and ever. Amen.

7 *For* ~~B~~*b*ehold, he cometh ~~with clouds;~~ *in the clouds with ten thousands of his saints in the kingdom, clothed with the glory of his Father.* ~~a~~*A*nd every eye shall see him, and they ~~also which~~ *who* pierced him: and all kindreds of the earth shall wail because of him. Even so, Amen.

8 *For he saith,* I am Alpha and Omega, the beginning and the ending, ~~saith~~ the Lord, ~~which~~ *who* is, and ~~which~~ *who* was, and ~~which~~ *who* is to come, the Almighty.

9 I John, who also am your brother, and companion in tribulation, and in the kingdom and patience of Jesus Christ, was in the isle that is called Patmos, for the word of God, and for the testimony of Jesus Christ.

10 I was in the Spirit on the Lord's day, and heard behind me a great voice, as of a trumpet,

11 Saying, I am Alpha and Omega, the first and the last: and, What thou seest, write in a book, and send it unto the seven churches which are in Asia; unto Ephesus, and unto Smyrna, and unto Pergamos, and unto Thyatira, and unto Sardis, and unto Philadelphia, and unto Laodicea.

12 And I turned to see *from whence* the voice *came* that spake ~~with~~ *to* me. And being turned, I saw seven golden candlesticks;

13 And in the midst of the seven candlesticks one like unto the Son of man, clothed with a garment down to the foot, and girt about the paps with a golden girdle.

14 His head and his hairs were white like wool, as white as snow; and his eyes were as a flame of fire;

15 And his feet like unto fine brass, as if they burned in a furnace; and his voice as the sound of many waters.

16 And he had in his right hand seven stars: and out of his mouth went a sharp ~~twoedged~~ *two-edged* sword: and his countenance was as the sun shineth in his strength.

17 And when I saw him, I fell at his feet as dead. And he laid his right hand upon me, saying unto me, Fear not; I am the first and the last:

18 I am he that liveth, and was dead; and, behold, I am alive for evermore, Amen; and have the keys of hell and of death.

19 Write the things which thou hast seen, and the things which are, and the things which shall be hereafter;

20 *This is* ~~T~~*t*he mystery of the seven stars which thou sawest in my right hand, and the seven golden candlesticks. The seven stars are the ~~angels~~ *servants* of the seven churches: and the seven candlesticks which thou sawest are the seven churches.

Chapter 2

1 Unto the ~~angel~~ *servant* of the church of Ephesus write; These things saith he that holdeth the seven stars in his right hand, who walketh in the midst of the seven golden candlesticks;

2 I know thy works, and thy labour, and thy patience, and how thou canst not bear them which are evil: and thou hast tried them which say they are apostles, and are not, and hast found them liars:

3 And hast borne, and hast patience, and for my name's sake hast laboured, and hast not fainted. 4 Nevertheless I have somewhat against thee, because thou hast left thy first love.

5 Remember therefore from whence thou art fallen, and repent, and do the first works; or else I will come unto thee quickly, and will remove thy candlestick out of his place, except thou repent.

6 But this thou hast, that thou hatest the deeds of the Nicolaitanes, which I also hate.

7 He that hath an ear, let him hear what the Spirit saith unto the churches; To him that overcometh will I give to eat of the tree of life, which is in the midst of the paradise of God.

8 And unto the ~~angel~~ *servant* of the church in Smyrna write; These things saith the first and the last, which was dead, and is alive;

9 I know thy works, and tribulation, and poverty, (but thou art rich) and I know the blasphemy of them which say they are Jews, and are not, but are the synagogue of Satan.

10 Fear none of those things which thou shalt suffer: behold, the devil shall cast some of you into prison, that ye may be tried; and ye shall have tribulation ten days: be thou faithful unto death, and I will give thee a crown of life.

11 He that hath an ear, let him hear what the Spirit saith unto the churches; He that overcometh shall not be hurt of the second death.

12 And to the ~~angel~~ *servant* of the church in Pergamos write; These things saith he which hath the sharp sword with two edges;

13 I know thy works and where thou dwellest, even where Satan's seat is: and thou holdest fast my name, and hast not denied my faith, even in those days wherein Antipas was my faithful martyr, who was slain among you, where Satan dwelleth.

14 But I have a few things against thee, because thou hast there them that hold the doctrine of Balaam, who taught Balac to cast a stumbling-block before the children of Israel, to eat things sacrificed unto idols, and to commit fornication.

15 So hast thou also them that hold the doctrine of the Nicolaitanes, which thing I hate.

16 Repent; or else I will come unto thee quickly, and will fight against them with the sword of my mouth.

17 He that hath an ear, let him hear what the Spirit saith unto the churches; To him that overcometh will I give to eat of the hidden manna, and will give him a white stone, and in the stone a new name written, which no man ~~knoweth~~ *knowest* saving he that receiveth it.

18 And unto the ~~angel~~ *servant* of the church in Thyatira write; These things saith the Son of God, who hath his eyes like unto a flame of fire, and his feet are like fine brass;

19 I know thy works, and charity, and service, and faith, and thy patience, and thy works; and the last to be more than the first.

20 Notwithstanding I have a few things against thee, because thou sufferest that woman Jezebel, which calleth herself a prophetess, to teach and to seduce my servants to commit fornication, and to eat things sacrificed unto idols.

21 And I gave her space to repent of her fornications; and she repented not.

22 Behold, I will cast her into ~~a bed~~ *hell*, and them that commit adultery with her into great tribulation, except they repent of their deeds.

23 And I will kill her children with death; and all the churches shall know that I am he which searcheth the reins and hearts: and I will give unto every one of you according to your works.

24 But unto you I say, and unto the rest in Thyatira, as many as have not this doctrine, and which have not known the depths of Satan, as they speak; I will put upon you none other burden.

25 But that which ye have already hold fast till I come.

26 And ~~he that~~ *to him who* overcometh, and keepeth my ~~works~~ *commandments* unto the end, ~~to him~~ will I give power over ~~the nations~~ *many kingdoms*:

27 And he shall rule them with ~~a rod of iron~~ *the word of God*; *and they shall be in his hands* as the vessels of *clay in the hands of* a potter ~~shall they be broken to shivers:~~ *;and he shall govern them by faith, with equity and justice,* even as I received of my Father.

28 And I will give him the morning star.

29 He that hath an ear, let him hear what the Spirit saith unto the churches.

Chapter 3

1 And unto the ~~angel~~ *servant* of the church in Sardis write; These things saith he ~~that~~ *who* hath ~~the seven Spirits of God, and~~ the seven stars, *which are the seven servants of God*; I know thy works, that thou hast a name that thou livest, and art *not* dead.

2 Be watchful *therefore*, and strengthen ~~the things which~~ *those who* remain, ~~that~~ *who* are ready to die: for I have not found thy works perfect before God.

3 Remember therefore how thou hast received and heard, and hold fast, and repent. If therefore thou shalt not watch, I will come on thee as a thief, and thou shalt not know what hour I will come upon thee.

4 Thou hast a few names even in Sardis which have not defiled their garments; and they shall walk with me in white: for they are worthy.

5 He that overcometh, the same shall be clothed in white raiment; and I will not blot out his name out of the book of life, but I will confess his name before my Father, and before his angels.

6 He that hath an ear, let him hear what the Spirit saith unto the churches.

7 And to the ~~angel~~ *servant* of the church in Philadelphia write; These things saith he that is holy, he that is true, he that hath the key of David, he that openeth, and no man shutteth; and shutteth, and no man openeth;

8 I know thy works: behold, I have set before thee an open door, and no man can shut it: for thou hast a little strength, and hast kept my word, and hast not denied my name.

9 Behold, I will make them of the synagogue of Satan, which say they are Jews, and are not, but do lie; behold, I will make them to come and worship before thy feet, and to know that I have loved thee.

10 Because thou hast kept the word of my patience, I also will keep thee from the hour of temptation, which shall come upon all the world, to try them that dwell upon the earth.

11 Behold, I come quickly: hold that fast which thou hast, that no man take thy crown.

12 Him that overcometh will I make a pillar in the temple of my God, and he shall go no more out: and I will write upon him the name of my God, and the name of the city of my God, ~~which~~ *this* is ~~a~~*N*ew Jerusalem, which cometh down out of heaven from my God: and I will write upon him my new name.

13 He that hath an ear, let him hear what the Spirit saith unto the churches.

14 And unto the ~~angel~~ *servant* of the church of the Laodiceans write; These things saith the Amen, the faithful and true witness, the beginning of the creation of God;

15 I know thy works, that thou art neither cold nor hot: I would thou wert cold or hot.

16 So then because thou art lukewarm, and neither cold nor hot, I will spue thee out of my mouth.

17 Because thou sayest, I am rich, and increased with goods, and have need of nothing; and knowest not that thou art wretched, and miserable, and poor, and blind, and naked:

18 I counsel thee to buy of me gold tried in the fire, that thou mayest be rich; and white raiment, that thou mayest be clothed, and that the shame of thy nakedness do not appear; and anoint thine eyes with eyesalve, that thou mayest see.

19 As many as I love, I rebuke and chasten: be zealous therefore, and repent.

20 Behold, I stand at the door, and knock: if any man hear my voice, and open the door, I will come in to him, and will sup with him, and he with me.

21 To him that overcometh will I grant to sit with me in my throne, even as I also overcame, and am set down with my Father in his throne.

22 He that hath an ear, let him hear what the Spirit saith unto the churches.

Chapter 4

1 After this I looked, and, behold, a door was opened in*to* heaven: and the first voice which I heard was as it were of a trumpet talking with me; which said, Come up hither, and I will ~~shew~~ *show* thee things which must be hereafter.

2 And immediately I was in the spirit; and, behold, a throne was set in heaven, and one sat on the throne.

3 And he that sat *there* was to look upon like a jasper and a sardine stone: and there was a rainbow round about the throne, in sight like unto an emerald.

4 And ~~round about~~ *in the midst of* the throne were four and twenty seats: and upon the seats I saw four and twenty elders sitting, clothed in white raiment; and they had on their heads crowns ~~of~~ *like* gold.

5 And out of the throne proceeded lightnings and thunderings and voices: and there were seven lamps of fire burning before the throne, which are the seven ~~Spirits~~ *servants* of God.

6 And before the throne there was a sea of glass like unto crystal: and in the midst of the throne *were the four and twenty elders*, and round about the throne, were four beasts full of eyes before and behind.

7 And the first beast was like a lion, and the second beast like a calf, and the third beast had a face as a man, and the fourth beast was like a flying eagle.

8 And the four beasts had each of them six wings about him; and they were full of eyes within: and they rest not day and night, saying, Holy, holy, holy, Lord God Almighty, which was, and is, and is to come.

9 And when those beasts give glory and ~~honour~~ *honor* and thanks to him that ~~sat~~ *sits* on the throne, who liveth for ever and ever,

10 The four and twenty elders fall down before him that ~~sat~~ *sits* on the throne, and worship him that liveth for ever and ever, and cast their crowns before the throne, saying,

11 Thou art worthy, O Lord, to receive glory and honour and power: for thou hast created all things, and for thy pleasure they are and were created.

Chapter 5

1 And I saw in the right hand of him that ~~sat~~ *sits* on the throne a book written within and on the backside, sealed with seven seals.

2 And I saw a strong angel, *and heard him* proclaiming with a loud voice, Who is worthy to open the book, and ~~to~~ loose the seals thereof?

3 And no man in heaven, nor in earth, neither under the earth, was able to open the book, neither to look thereon.

4 And I wept much, because no man was found worthy to open and to read the book, neither to look thereon.

5 And one of the elders saith unto me, Weep not: behold, the Lion of the tribe of Juda, the Root of David, hath prevailed to open the book, and to loose the seven seals thereof.

6 And I beheld, and, lo, in the midst of the throne and of the four beasts, and in the midst of the elders, stood a Lamb as it had been slain, having ~~seven~~ *twelve* horns and ~~seven~~ *twelve* eyes, which are the ~~seven Spirits~~ *twelve servants* of God sent forth into all the earth.

7 And he came and took the book out of the right hand of him that sat upon the throne.

8 And when he had taken the book, the four beasts and four and twenty elders fell down before the Lamb, having every one of them harps, and golden vials full of odours, which are the prayers of saints.

9 And they sung a new song, saying, Thou art worthy to take the book, and to open the seals thereof: for thou wast slain, and hast redeemed us to God by thy blood out of every kindred, and tongue, and people, and nation;

10 And hast made us unto our God kings and priests: and we shall reign on the earth.

11 And I beheld, and I heard the voice of many angels round about the throne and the beasts and the elders: and the number of them was ten thousand times ten thousand, and thousands of thousands;

12 Saying with a loud voice, Worthy is the Lamb that was slain to receive power, and riches, and wisdom, and strength, and honour, and glory, and blessing.

13 And every creature which is in heaven, and on the earth, and under the earth, and such as are in the sea, and all that are in them, heard I saying, Blessing, and honour, and glory, and power, be unto him that sitteth upon the throne, and unto the Lamb for ever and ever.

14 And the four beasts said, Amen. And the four and twenty elders fell down and worshipped him that liveth for ever and ever.

Chapter 6

1 And I saw when the Lamb opened one of the seals, *one of the four beasts,* and I heard, as it were the noise of thunder, ~~one of the four beasts~~ saying, Come and see.

2 And I saw, and behold a white horse: and he that sat on him had a bow; and a crown was given unto him: and he went forth conquering, and to conquer.

3 And when he had opened the second seal, I heard the second beast say, Come and see.

4 And there went out another horse that was red: and power was given to him that sat thereon to take peace from the earth, and that they should kill one another: and there was given unto him a great sword.

5 And when he had opened the third seal, I heard the third beast say, Come and see. And I beheld, and lo a black horse; and he that sat on him had a pair of balances in his hand.

6 And I heard a voice in the midst of the four beasts say, A measure of wheat for a penny, and three measures of barley for a penny; and ~~see~~ *hurt not* thou ~~hurt not~~ the oil and the wine.

7 And when he had opened the fourth seal, I heard the voice of the fourth beast say, Come and see.

8 And I looked, and behold a pale horse: and his name that sat on him was Death, and Hell followed with him. And power was given unto them over the fourth part of the earth, to kill with sword, and with hunger, and with death, and with the beasts of the earth.

9 And when he had opened the fifth seal, I saw under the altar the souls of them that were slain for the word of God, and for the testimony which they held:

10 And they cried with a loud voice, saying, How long, O Lord, holy and true, dost thou not judge and avenge our blood on them that dwell on the earth?

11 And white robes were given unto every one of them; and it was said unto them, that they should rest yet for a little season, until their fellowservants also and their brethren, that should be killed as they were, should be fulfilled.

12 And I beheld when he had opened the sixth seal, and, lo, there was a great earthquake; and the sun became black as sackcloth of hair, and the moon became as blood;

13 And the stars of heaven fell unto the earth, even as a fig tree casteth her untimely figs, when she is shaken of a mighty wind.

14 And the heavens ~~departed~~ *opened* as a scroll *is opened* when it is rolled together; and every mountain and island ~~were~~ *was* moved out of ~~their~~ *its* places.

15 And the kings of the earth, and the great men, and the rich men, and the chief captains, and the mighty men, and every bondman, and every free man, hid themselves in the dens and in the rocks of the mountains;

16 And said to the mountains and rocks, Fall on us, and hide us from the face of him that sitteth on the throne, and from the wrath of the Lamb:

17 For the great day of his wrath is come; and who shall be able to stand?

Chapter 7

1 And after these things I saw four angels standing on the four corners of the earth, holding the four winds of the earth, that the wind should not blow on the earth, nor on the sea, nor on any tree.

2 And I saw another angel ascending from the east, having the seal of the living God: and ~~he cried~~ *I heard him cry* with a loud voice to the four angels, to whom it was given to hurt the earth and the sea,

3 Saying, Hurt not the earth, neither the sea, nor the trees, till we have sealed the servants of our God in their foreheads.

4 And ~~I heard~~ the number of them ~~which~~ *who*

were sealed: and there , were sealed an hundred and forty and four thousand of all the tribes of the children of Israel.

5 Of the tribe of Juda were sealed twelve thousand. Of the tribe of Reuben were sealed twelve thousand. Of the tribe of Gad were sealed twelve thousand.

6 Of the tribe of Aser were sealed twelve thousand. Of the tribe of Nephthalim were sealed twelve thousand. Of the tribe of Manasses were sealed twelve thousand.

7 Of the tribe of Simeon were sealed twelve thousand. Of the tribe of Levi were sealed twelve thousand. Of the tribe of Issachar were sealed twelve thousand.

8 Of the tribe of Zabulon were sealed twelve thousand. Of the tribe of Joseph were sealed twelve thousand. Of the tribe of Benjamin were sealed twelve thousand.

9 After this I beheld, and, lo, a great multitude, which no man could number, of all nations, and kindreds, and people, and tongues, stood before the throne, and before the Lamb, clothed with white robes, and palms in their hands;

10 And cried with a loud voice, saying, Salvation to our God which sitteth upon the throne, and unto the Lamb.

11 And all the angels stood round about the throne, and about the elders and the four beasts, and fell before the throne on their faces, and worshipped God,

12 Saying, Amen: Blessing, and glory, and wisdom, and thanksgiving, and honour, and power, and might, be unto our God for ever and ever. Amen.

13 And one of the elders answered, saying unto me, What are these which are arrayed in white robes? and whence came they?

14 And I said unto him, Sir, thou knowest. And he said to me, These are they which came out of great tribulation, and have washed their robes, and made them white in the blood of the Lamb.

15 Therefore are they before the throne of God, and serve him day and night in his temple: and he that sitteth on the throne shall dwell among them.

16 They shall hunger no more, neither thirst any more; neither shall the sun light on them, nor any heat.

17 For the Lamb which is in the midst of the throne shall feed them, and shall lead them unto living fountains of waters: and God shall wipe away all tears from their eyes.

Chapter 8

1 And when he had opened the seventh seal, there was silence in heaven about the space of half an hour.

2 And I saw the seven angels which stood before God; and to them were given seven trumpets.

3 And another angel came and stood at the altar, having a golden censer; and there was given unto him much incense, that he should offer it with the prayers of all saints upon the golden altar which was before the throne.

4 And the smoke of the incense, which came with the prayers of the saints, ascended up before God out of the angel's hand.

5 And the angel took the censer, and filled it with fire of the altar, and cast it into the earth: and there were voices, and thunderings, and lightnings, and an earthquake.

6 And the seven angels which had the seven trumpets prepared themselves to sound.

7 The first angel sounded, and there followed hail and fire mingled with blood, and they were cast upon the earth: and the third part of trees was burnt up, and all green grass was burnt up.

8 And the second angel sounded, and as it were a great mountain burning with fire was cast into the sea: and the third part of the sea became blood;

9 And the third part of the creatures which were in the sea, and had life, died; and the third part of the ships were destroyed.

10 And the third angel sounded, and there fell a great star from heaven, burning as it were a lamp, and it fell upon the third part of the rivers, and upon the fountains of waters;

11 And the name of the star is called Wormwood: and the third part of the waters became wormwood; and many men died of the waters, because they were made bitter.

12 And the fourth angel sounded, and the third part of the sun was smitten, and the third part of the moon, and the third part of the stars; so as *that* the third part of them was darkened, and the day shone not for a third part of it, and the night likewise.

13 And I beheld, and heard an angel flying through the midst of heaven, saying with a loud voice, Woe, woe, woe, to the inhabiters of the earth by reason of the other voices of the trumpet of the three angels, which are yet to sound!

Chapter 9

1 And the fifth angel sounded, and I saw a star fall from heaven unto the earth: and to him *the angel* was given the key of the bottomless pit.

2 And he opened the bottomless pit; and there arose a smoke out of the pit, as the smoke of a great furnace; and the sun and the air were darkened by reason of the smoke of the pit.

3 And there came out of the smoke locusts upon the earth: and unto them was given power, as the

scorpions of the earth have power.

4 And it was commanded them that they should not hurt the grass of the earth, neither any green thing, neither any tree; but only those men which have not the seal of God in their foreheads.

5 And to them it was given that they should not kill them, but that they should be tormented five months: and their torment was as the torment of a scorpion, when he striketh a man.

6 And in those days shall men seek death, and shall not find it; and shall desire to die, and death shall flee from them.

7 And the shapes of the locusts were like unto horses prepared unto battle; and on their heads were as it were crowns like gold, and their faces were as the faces of men.

8 And they had hair as the hair of women, and their teeth were as the teeth of lions.

9 And they had breastplates, as it were breastplates of iron; and the sound of their wings was as the sound of chariots of many horses running to battle.

10 And they had tails like unto scorpions, and there were stings in their tails: and their power was to hurt men five months.

11 And they had a king over them, which is the angel of the bottomless pit, whose name in the Hebrew tongue is Abaddon, but in the Greek tongue hath his name Apollyon.

12 One woe is past; and, behold, there come two woes more hereafter.

13 And the sixth angel sounded, and I heard a voice from the four horns of the golden altar which is before God,

14 Saying to the sixth angel which had the trumpet, Loose the four angels which are bound in the ~~great river Euphrates~~ *bottomless pit*.

15 And the four angels were loosed, which were prepared for an hour, and a day, and a month, and a year, for to slay the third part of men.

16 And the number of the army of the horsemen were two hundred thousand thousand: and I ~~heard~~ *saw* the number of them.

17 And thus I saw the horses in the vision, and them that sat on them, having breastplates of fire, and of jacinth, and brimstone: and the heads of the horses were as the heads of lions; and out of their mouths issued fire and smoke and brimstone.

18 By these three was the third part of men killed, by the fire, and by the smoke, and by the brimstone, which issued out of their mouths.

19 For their power is in their mouth, and in their tails: for their tails were like unto serpents, and had heads, and with them they do hurt.

20 And the rest of the men which were not killed by these plagues yet repented not of the works of their hands, that they should not worship devils, and idols of gold, and silver, and brass, and stone, and of wood: which neither can see, nor hear, nor walk:

21 Neither repented they of their murders, nor of their sorceries, nor of their fornication, nor of their thefts.

Chapter 10

1 And I saw another mighty angel come down from heaven, clothed with a cloud: and a rainbow was upon his head, and his face was as it were the sun, and his feet as pillars of fire:

2 And he had in his hand a little book open: and he set his right foot upon the sea, and his left foot on the earth,

3 And cried with a loud voice, as when a lion roareth: and when he had cried, seven thunders uttered their voices.

4 And when the seven thunders had uttered their voices, I was about to write: and I heard a voice from heaven saying unto me, ~~Seal up t~~*T*hose things *are sealed up* which the seven thunders uttered, and write them not.

5 And the angel which I saw stand upon the sea and upon the earth lifted up his hand to heaven,

6 And sware by him that liveth for ever and ever, who created heaven, and the things that therein are, and the earth, and the things that therein are, and the sea, and the things which are therein, that there should be time no longer:

7 But in the days of the voice of the seventh angel, when he shall begin to sound, the mystery of God should be finished, as he hath declared to his servants the prophets.

8 And the voice which I heard from heaven spake unto me again, and said, Go and take the little book which is open in the hand of the angel which standeth upon the sea and upon the earth.

9 And I went unto the angel, and said unto him, Give me the little book. And he said unto me, Take it, and eat it up; and it shall make thy belly bitter, but it shall be in thy mouth sweet as honey.

10 And I took the little book out of the angel's hand, and ate it up; and it was in my mouth sweet as honey: and as soon as I had eaten it, my belly was bitter.

11 And he said unto me, Thou must prophesy again before many peoples, and nations, and tongues, and kings.

Chapter 11

1 And there was given me a reed like unto a rod: and the angel stood, saying, Rise, and measure the temple of God, and the altar, and them that worship therein.

2 But the court which is without the temple leave out, and measure it not; for it is given unto

the Gentiles: and the holy city shall they tread under foot forty and two months.

3 And I will give power unto my two witnesses, and they shall prophesy a thousand two hundred and threescore days, clothed in sackcloth.

4 These are the two olive trees, and the two candlesticks standing before the God of the earth.

5 And if any man will hurt them, fire proceedeth out of their mouth, and devoureth their enemies: and if any man will hurt them, he must in this manner be killed.

6 These have power to shut heaven, that it rain not in the days of their prophecy: and have power over waters to turn them to blood, and to smite the earth with all plagues, as often as they will.

7 And when they shall have finished their testimony, the beast that ascendeth out of the bottomless pit shall make war against them, and shall overcome them, and kill them.

8 And their dead bodies shall lie in the street of the great city, which spiritually is called Sodom and Egypt, where also our Lord was crucified.

9 And they of the people and kindreds and tongues and nations shall see their dead bodies three days and an half, and shall not suffer their dead bodies to be put in graves.

10 And they that dwell upon the earth shall rejoice over them, and make merry, and shall send gifts one to another; because these two prophets tormented them that dwelt on the earth.

11 And after three days and an half the Spirit of life from God entered into them, and they stood upon their feet; and great fear fell upon them which saw them.

12 And they heard a great voice from heaven saying unto them, Come up hither. And they ascended up to heaven in a cloud; and their enemies beheld them.

13 And the same hour was there a great earthquake, and the tenth part of the city fell, and in the earthquake were slain of men seven thousand: and the remnant were affrighted, and gave glory to the God of heaven.

14 The second woe is past; and, behold, the third woe cometh quickly.

15 And the seventh angel sounded; and there were great voices in heaven, saying, The kingdoms of this world are become the kingdoms of our Lord, and of his Christ; and he shall reign for ever and ever.

16 And the four and twenty elders, which sat before God on their seats, fell upon their faces, and worshipped God,

17 Saying, We give thee thanks, O Lord God Almighty, which art, and wast, and art to come; because thou hast taken to thee thy great power, and hast reigned.

18 And the nations were angry, and thy wrath is come, and the time of the dead, that they should be judged, and that thou shouldest give reward

unto thy servants the prophets, and to the saints, and them that fear thy name, small and great; and shouldest destroy them which destroy the earth.

19 And the temple of God was opened in heaven, and there was seen in his temple the ark of his testament: and there were lightnings, and voices, and thunderings, and an earthquake, and great hail.

Chapter 12

1 And there appeared a great ~~wonder~~ *sign* in heaven *in the likeness of things on the earth*; a woman clothed with the sun, and the moon under her feet, and upon her head a crown of twelve stars:

2 And ~~she~~ *the woman* being with child cried, travailing in birth, and pained to be delivered.

5 And she brought forth a man child, who was to rule all nations with a rod of iron: and her child was caught up unto God, and ~~to~~ his throne. *(verse order change by JST)*

3 And there appeared another ~~wonder~~ *sign* in heaven; and behold a great red dragon, having seven heads and ten horns, and seven crowns upon his heads.

4 And his tail drew the third part of the stars of heaven, and did cast them to the earth: and the dragon stood before the woman which was ~~ready to be~~ delivered, ~~for~~ *ready* to devour her child ~~as soon as~~ *after* it was born.

6 And the woman fled into the wilderness, where she ~~hath~~ *had* a place prepared of God, that they should feed her there a thousand two hundred and threescore ~~days~~ *years*.

7 And there was war in heaven: Michael and his angels fought against the dragon; and the dragon *and his angels* fought ~~and his angels~~ *against Michael*,

8 And *the dragon* prevailed not *against Michael, neither the child, nor the woman which was the church of God, who had been delivered of her pains, and brought forth the kingdom of our God and his Christ* ~~; neither was their place found any more in heaven~~ .

9 ~~And~~ *Neither was there place found in heaven for* the great dragon, *who* was cast out, that old serpent, called the Devil, and *also called* Satan, which deceiveth the whole world: he was cast out into the earth, and his angels were cast out with him.

10 And I heard a loud voice saying in heaven, Now is come salvation, and strength, and the kingdom of our God, and the power of his Christ: for the accuser of our brethren is cast down, which accused them before our God day and night.

11 ~~And~~ *For* they ~~overcame~~ *have overcome* him by

the blood of the Lamb, and by the word of their testimony; ~~and~~ *for* they loved not their *own* lives *but kept the testimony even* unto ~~the~~ death.

12 Therefore rejoice ~~, ye~~ *O* heavens, and ye that dwell in them. *And after these things I heard another voice saying,* Woe to the inhabiters of the earth, *yea,* and *they who dwell upon the islands* of the sea! for the devil is come down unto you, having great wrath, because he knoweth that he hath but a short time.

13 ~~And~~ *For* when the dragon saw that he was cast unto the earth, he persecuted the woman which brought forth the man child.

14 ~~And~~ *Therefore,* to the woman were given two wings of a great eagle, that she might ~~fly~~ *flee* into the wilderness, into her place, where she is nourished for a time, and times, and half a time, from the face of the serpent.

15 And the serpent cast*eth* out of his mouth water as a flood after the woman, that he might cause her to be carried away of the flood.

16 And the earth helped the woman, and the earth opened her mouth, and swallowed up the flood which the dragon cast*eth* out of his mouth.

17 ~~And~~ *Therefore,* the dragon was wroth with the woman, and went to make war with the remnant of her seed, which keep the commandments of God, and have the testimony of Jesus Christ.

Chapter 13

1 And I *saw another sign, in the likeness of the kingdoms of the earth; a beast rise up out of the sea, and he* stood upon the sand of the sea, ~~and saw a beast rise up out of the sea,~~ having seven heads and ten horns, and upon his horns ten crowns, and upon his heads the name of blasphemy.

2 And the beast which I saw was like unto a leopard, and his feet were as the feet of a bear, and his mouth as the mouth of a lion: and the dragon gave him his power, and his seat, and great authority.

3 And I saw one of his heads as it were wounded to death; and his deadly wound was healed: and all the world wondered after the beast.

4 And they worshipped the dragon which gave power unto the beast: and they worshipped the beast, saying, Who is like unto the beast? who is able to make war with him?

5 And there was given unto him a mouth speaking great things and blasphemies; and power was given unto him to continue forty and two months.

6 And he opened his mouth in blasphemy against God, to blaspheme his name, and his tabernacle, and them that dwell in heaven.

7 And it was given unto him to make war with the saints, and to overcome them: and power was given him over all kindreds, and tongues, and nations.

8 And all that dwell upon the earth shall worship him, whose names are not written in the book of life of the Lamb slain from the foundation of the world.

9 If any man have an ear, let him hear.

10 He that leadeth into captivity shall go into captivity: he that killeth with the sword must be killed with the sword. Here is the patience and the faith of the saints.

11 And I beheld another beast coming up out of the earth; and he had two horns like a lamb, and he spake as a dragon.

12 And he exerciseth all the power of the first beast before him, and causeth the earth and them which dwell therein to worship the first beast, whose deadly wound was healed.

13 And he doeth great wonders, so that he maketh fire come down from heaven on the earth in the sight of men,

14 And deceiveth them that dwell on the earth by the means of those miracles which he had power to do in the sight of the beast; saying to them that dwell on the earth, that they should make an image to the beast, which had the wound by a sword, and did live.

15 And he had power to give life unto the image of the beast, that the image of the beast should both speak, and cause that as many as would not worship the image of the beast should be killed.

16 And he causeth all, both small and great, rich and poor, free and bond, to receive a mark in their right hand, or in their foreheads:

17 And that no man might buy or sell, save he that had the mark, or the name of the beast, or the number of his name.

18 Here is wisdom. Let him that hath understanding count the number of the beast: for it is the number of a man; and his number is Six hundred threescore and six.

Chapter 14

1 And I looked, and, lo, a Lamb stood on the mount Sion, and with him ~~an~~ *a* hundred forty and four thousand, having his Father's name written in their foreheads.

2 And I heard a voice from heaven, as the voice of many waters, and as the voice of a great thunder: and I heard the voice of harpers harping with their harps:

3 And they sung as it were a new song before the throne, and before the four beasts, and the elders: and no man could learn that song but the hundred and forty and four thousand, which were redeemed from the earth.

4 These are they which were not defiled with women; for they are virgins. These are they which

follow the Lamb whithersoever he goeth. These were redeemed from among men, being the firstfruits unto God and to the Lamb.

5 And in their mouth was found no guile: for they are without fault before the throne of God.

6 And I saw another angel fly in the midst of heaven, having the everlasting gospel to preach unto them that dwell on the earth, and to every nation, and kindred, and tongue, and people,

7 Saying with a loud voice, Fear God, and give glory to him; for the hour of his judgment is come: and worship him that made heaven, and earth, and the sea, and the fountains of waters.

8 And there followed another angel, saying, Babylon is fallen, is fallen, that great city, because she made all nations drink of the wine of the wrath of her fornication.

9 And the third angel followed them, saying with a loud voice, If any man worship the beast and his image, and receive his mark in his forehead, or in his hand,

10 The same shall drink of the wine of the wrath of God, which is poured out without mixture into the cup of his indignation; and he shall be tormented with fire and brimstone in the presence of the holy angels, and in the presence of the Lamb:

11 And the smoke of their torment ascendeth up for ever and ever: and they have no rest day nor night, who worship the beast and his image, and whosoever receiveth the mark of his name.

12 Here is the patience of the saints: here are they that keep the commandments of God, and the faith of Jesus.

13 And I heard a voice from heaven saying unto me, Write, Blessed are the dead which die in the Lord from henceforth: Yea, saith the Spirit, that they may rest from their labours; and their works do follow them.

14 And I looked, and behold a white cloud, and upon the cloud one sat like unto the Son of man, having on his head a golden crown, and in his hand a sharp sickle.

15 And another angel came out of the temple, crying with a loud voice to him that sat on the cloud, Thrust in thy sickle, and reap: for the time is come for thee to reap; for the harvest of the earth is ripe.

16 And he that sat on the cloud thrust in his sickle on the earth; and the earth was reaped.

17 And another angel came out of the temple which is in heaven, he also having a sharp sickle.

18 And another angel came out from the altar, which had power over fire; and cried with a loud cry to him that had the sharp sickle, saying, Thrust in thy sharp sickle, and gather the clusters of the vine of the earth; for her grapes are fully ripe.

19 And the angel thrust in his sickle into the earth, and gathered the vine of the earth, and cast it into the great winepress of the wrath of God.

20 And the winepress was trodden without the city, and blood came out of the winepress, even unto the horses' bridles, by the space of a thousand and six hundred furlongs.

Chapter 15

1 And I saw another sign in heaven, great and marvellous, seven angels having the seven last plagues; for in them is filled up the wrath of God.

2 And I saw as it were a sea of glass mingled with fire: and them that had gotten the victory over the beast, and over his image, and over his mark, and over the number of his name, stand on the sea of glass, having the harps of God.

3 And they sing the song of Moses the servant of God, and the song of the Lamb, saying, Great and marvellous are thy works, Lord God Almighty; just and true are thy ways, thou King of saints.

4 Who shall not fear thee, O Lord, and glorify thy name? for thou only art holy: for all nations shall come and worship before thee; for thy judgments are made manifest.

5 And after that I looked, and, behold, the temple of the tabernacle of the testimony in heaven was opened:

6 And the seven angels came out of the temple, having the seven plagues, clothed in pure and white linen, and having their breasts girded with golden girdles.

7 And one of the four beasts gave unto the seven angels seven golden vials full of the wrath of God, who liveth for ever and ever.

8 And the temple was filled with smoke from the glory of God, and from his power; and no man was able to enter into the temple, till the seven plagues of the seven angels were fulfilled.

Chapter 16

1 And I heard a great voice out of the temple saying to the seven angels, Go your ways, and pour out the vials of the wrath of God upon the earth.

2 And the first went, and poured out his vial upon the earth; and there fell a noisome and grievous sore upon the men which had the mark of the beast, and upon them which worshipped his image.

3 And the second angel poured out his vial upon the sea; and it became as the blood of a dead man; and every living soul died in the sea.

4 And the third angel poured out his vial upon the rivers and fountains of waters; and they

became blood.

5 And I heard the angel of the waters say, Thou art righteous, O Lord, which art, and wast, and shalt be, because thou hast judged thus.

6 For they have shed the blood of saints and prophets, and thou hast given them blood to drink; for they are worthy.

7 And I heard another *angel who came* out ~~of~~ *from* the altar say*ing*, Even so, Lord God Almighty, true and righteous are thy judgments.

8 And the fourth angel poured out his vial upon the sun; and power was given unto him to scorch men with fire.

9 And men were scorched with great heat, and blasphemed the name of God, which hath power over these plagues: and they repented not to give him glory.

10 And the fifth angel poured out his vial upon the seat of the beast; and his kingdom was full of darkness; and they gnawed their tongues for pain,

11 And blasphemed the God of heaven because of their pains and their sores, and repented not of their deeds.

12 And the sixth angel poured out his vial upon the great river Euphrates; and the water thereof was dried up, that the way of the kings of the east might be prepared.

13 And I saw three unclean spirits like frogs come out of the mouth of the dragon, and out of the mouth of the beast, and out of the mouth of the false prophet.

14 For they are the spirits of devils, working miracles, which go forth unto the kings of the earth and of the whole world, to gather them to the battle of that great day of God Almighty.

15 Behold, I come as a thief. Blessed is he that watcheth, and keepeth his garments, lest he walk naked, and they see his shame.

16 And he gathered them together into a place called in the Hebrew tongue Armageddon.

17 And the seventh angel poured out his vial into the air; and there came a great voice out of the temple of heaven, from the throne, saying, It is done.

18 And there were voices, and thunders, and lightnings; and there was a great earthquake, such as was not since men were upon the earth, so mighty an earthquake, and so great.

19 And the great city was divided into three parts, and the cities of the nations fell: and great Babylon came in remembrance before God, to give unto her the cup of the wine of the fierceness of his wrath.

20 And every island fled away, and the mountains were not found.

21 And there fell upon men a great hail out of heaven, every stone about the weight of a talent: and men blasphemed God because of the plague of the hail; for the plague thereof was exceeding great.

Chapter 17

1 And there came one of the seven angels which had the seven vials, and talked with me, saying unto me, Come hither; I will show unto thee the judgment of the great whore that sitteth upon many waters:

2 With whom the kings of the earth have committed fornication, and the inhabitants of the earth have been made drunk with the wine of her fornication.

3 So he carried me away in the spirit into the wilderness: and I saw a woman sit upon a scarlet coloured beast, full of names of blasphemy, having seven heads and ten horns.

4 And the woman was arrayed in purple and scarlet colour, and decked with gold and precious stones and pearls, having a golden cup in her hand full of abominations and filthiness of her fornication:

5 And upon her forehead was a name written, MYSTERY, BABYLON THE GREAT, THE MOTHER OF HARLOTS AND ABOMINATIONS OF THE EARTH.

6 And I saw the woman drunken with the blood of the saints, and with the blood of the martyrs of Jesus: and when I saw her, I wondered with great admiration.

7 And the angel said unto me, Wherefore didst thou marvel? I will tell thee the mystery of the woman, and of the beast that carrieth her, which hath the seven heads and ten horns.

8 The beast that thou sawest was, and is not; and shall ascend out of the bottomless pit, and go into perdition: and they that dwell on the earth shall wonder, whose names were not written in the book of life from the foundation of the world, when they behold the beast that was, and is not, and yet is.

9 And here is the mind which hath wisdom. The seven heads are seven mountains, on which the woman sitteth.

10 And there are seven kings: five are fallen, and one is, and the other is not yet come; and when he cometh, he must continue a short space.

11 And the beast that was, and is not, even he is the eighth, and is of the seven, and goeth into perdition.

12 And the ten horns which thou sawest are ten kings, which have received no kingdom as yet; but receive power as kings one hour with the beast.

13 These have one mind, and shall give their power and strength unto the beast.

14 These shall make war with the Lamb, and the Lamb shall overcome them: for he is Lord of lords, and King of kings: and they that are with him are called, and chosen, and faithful.

15 And he saith unto me, The waters which thou sawest, where the whore sitteth, are peoples, and multitudes, and nations, and tongues.

16 And the ten horns which thou sawest upon the beast, these shall hate the whore, and shall make her desolate and naked, and shall eat her flesh, and burn her with fire.

17 For God hath put in their hearts to ~~fulfill~~ *fulfil* his will, and to agree, and give their kingdom unto the beast, until the words of God ~~shall be~~ *are* fulfilled.

18 And the woman which thou sawest is that great city, which reigneth over the kings of the earth.

Chapter 18

1 And after these things I saw another angel come down from heaven, having great power; and the earth was lightened with his glory.

2 And he cried mightily with a strong voice, saying, Babylon the great is fallen, is fallen, and is become the habitation of devils, and the hold of every foul spirit, and a cage of every unclean and hateful bird.

3 For all nations have drunk of the wine of the wrath of her fornication, and the kings of the earth have committed fornication with her, and the merchants of the earth are waxed rich through the abundance of her delicacies.

4 And I heard another voice from heaven, saying, Come out of her, my people, that ye be not partakers of her sins, and that ye receive not of her plagues.

5 For her sins have reached unto heaven, and God hath remembered her iniquities.

6 Reward her even as she rewarded you, and double unto her double according to her works: in the cup which she hath filled fill to her double.

7 How much she hath glorified herself, and lived deliciously, so much torment and sorrow give her: for she saith in her heart, I sit a queen, and am no widow, and shall see no sorrow.

8 Therefore shall her plagues come in one day, death, and mourning, and famine; and she shall be utterly burned with fire: for strong is the Lord God who judgeth her.

9 And the kings of the earth, who have committed fornication and lived deliciously with her, shall bewail her, and lament for her, when they shall see the smoke of her burning,

10 Standing afar off for the fear of her torment, saying, Alas, alas that great city Babylon, that mighty city! for in one hour is thy judgment come.

11 And the merchants of the earth shall weep and mourn over her; for no man buyeth their merchandise any more:

12 The merchandise of gold, and silver, and precious stones, and of pearls, and fine linen, and purple, and silk, and scarlet, and all thyine wood, and all manner vessels of ivory, and all manner vessels of most precious wood, and of brass, and iron, and marble,

13 And cinnamon, and odours, and ointments, and frankincense, and wine, and oil, and fine flour, and wheat, and beasts, and sheep, and horses, and chariots, and slaves, and souls of men.

14 And the fruits that thy soul lusted after are departed from thee, and all things which were dainty and goodly are departed from thee, and thou shalt find them no more at all.

15 The merchants of these things, which were made rich by her, shall stand afar off for the fear of her torment, weeping and wailing,

16 And saying, Alas, alas, that great city, that was clothed in fine linen, and purple, and scarlet, and decked with gold, and precious stones, and pearls!

17 For in one hour so great riches is come to nought. And every shipmaster, and all the company in ships, and sailors, and as many as trade by sea, stood afar off,

18 And cried when they saw the smoke of her burning, saying, What city is like unto this great city!

19 And they cast dust on their heads, and cried, weeping and wailing, saying, Alas, alas, that great city, wherein were made rich all that had ships in the sea by reason of her costliness! for in one hour is she made desolate.

20 Rejoice over her, thou heaven, and ye holy apostles and prophets; for God hath avenged you on her.

21 And a mighty angel took up a stone like a great millstone, and cast it into the sea, saying, Thus with violence shall that great city Babylon be thrown down, and shall be found no more at all.

22 And the voice of harpers, and musicians, and of pipers, and trumpeters, shall be heard no more at all in thee; and no craftsman, of whatsoever craft he be, shall be found any more in thee; and the sound of a millstone shall be heard no more at all in thee;

23 And the light of a candle shall shine no more at all in thee; and the voice of the bridegroom and of the bride shall be heard no more at all in thee: for thy merchants were the great men of the earth; for by thy sorceries were all nations deceived.

24 And in her was found the blood of prophets, and of saints, and of all that were slain upon the earth.

Chapter 19

1 And after these things I heard a great voice of much people in heaven, saying, Alleluia; Salvation, and glory, and honour, and power,

unto the Lord our God:

2 For true and righteous are his judgments: for he hath judged the great whore, which did corrupt the earth with her fornication, and hath avenged the blood of his ~~servants~~ *saints* at her hand.

3 And again they said, Alleluia. And her smoke rose up for ever and ever.

4 And the four and twenty elders and the four beasts fell down and worshipped God that sat on the throne, saying, Amen; Alleluia.

5 And a voice came out of the throne, saying, Praise our God, all ye his ~~servants~~ *saints*, and ye that fear him, both small and great.

6 And I heard as it were the voice of a great multitude, and as the voice of many waters, and as the voice of mighty thunderings, saying, Alleluia: for the Lord God omnipotent reigneth.

7 Let us be glad and rejoice, and give honour to him: for the marriage of the Lamb is come, and his wife hath made herself ready.

8 And to her was granted that she should be arrayed in fine linen, clean and white: for the fine linen is the righteousness of saints.

9 And he saith unto me, Write, Blessed are they which are called unto the marriage supper of the Lamb. And he saith unto me, These are the true sayings of God.

10 And I fell at his feet to worship him. And he said unto me, See *that* thou do it not: I am thy fellowservant, and of thy brethren that have the testimony of Jesus: worship God: for the testimony of Jesus is the spirit of prophecy.

11 And I saw heaven opened, and behold a white horse; and he that sat upon him ~~was~~ *is* called Faithful and True, and in righteousness he doth judge and make war.

12 His eyes ~~were~~ as a flame of fire, and *he had* on his head ~~were~~ many crowns; and ~~he had~~ a name written, that no man knew, but ~~he~~ himself.

13 And he ~~was~~ *is* clothed with a vesture dipped in blood: and his name is called The Word of God.

14 And the armies which were in heaven followed him upon white horses, clothed in fine linen, white and clean.

15 And out of his mouth ~~goeth a sharp sword~~ *proceedeth the word of God*, ~~that~~ *and* with it he ~~should~~ *will* smite the nations: and he ~~shall~~ *will* rule them with ~~a rod of iron:~~ *the word of his mouth;* and he treadeth the winepress ~~of~~ *in* the fierceness and wrath of Almighty God.

16 And he hath on ~~his~~ *a* vesture and on his thigh a name written, KING OF KINGS, AND LORD OF LORDS.

17 And I saw an angel standing in the sun; and he cried with a loud voice, saying to all the fowls that fly in the midst of heaven, Come and gather yourselves together unto the supper of the great God;

18 That ye may eat the flesh of kings, and the flesh of captains, and the flesh of mighty men, and the flesh of horses, and of them that sit on them, and the flesh of all ~~men~~ *who fight against the Lamb*, both ~~free and bond~~ *bond and free*, both small and great.

19 And I saw the beast, and the kings of the earth, and their armies, gathered together to make war against him that sat on the horse, and against his army.

20 And the beast was taken, and with him the false prophet that wrought miracles before him, with which he deceived them that had received the mark of the beast, and them that worshipped his image. These both were cast alive into a lake of fire burning with brimstone.

21 And the remnant were slain with the ~~sword~~ *word* of him that sat upon the horse, which ~~sword~~ *word* proceeded out of his mouth: and all the fowls were filled with their flesh.

Chapter 20

1 And I saw an angel come down ~~from~~ *out of* heaven, having the key of the bottomless pit and a great chain in his hand.

2 And he laid hold on the dragon, that old serpent, which is the Devil, and Satan, and bound him a thousand years,

3 And cast him into the bottomless pit, and shut him up, and set a seal upon him, that he should deceive the nations no more, till the thousand years should be fulfilled: and after that he must be loosed a little season.

4 And I saw thrones, and they sat upon them, and judgment was given unto them: and I saw the souls of them that were beheaded for the witness of Jesus, and for the word of God, and which had not worshipped the beast, neither his image, neither had received his mark upon their foreheads, or in their hands; and they lived and reigned with Christ a thousand years.

5 But the rest of the dead lived not again until the thousand years were finished. This is the first resurrection.

6 Blessed and holy ~~is he that hath~~ *are they who have* part in the first resurrection: on such the second death hath no power, but they shall be priests of God and of Christ, and shall reign with him a thousand years.

7 And when the thousand years are expired, Satan shall be loosed out of his prison,

8 And shall go out to deceive the nations which are in the four quarters of the earth, Gog and Magog, to gather them together to battle: the number of whom is as the sand of the sea.

9 And they went up on the breadth of the earth, and compassed the camp of the saints about, and the beloved city: and fire came down from God

out of heaven, and devoured them.

10 And the devil that deceived them was cast into the lake of fire and brimstone, where the beast and the false prophet are, and shall be tormented day and night for ever and ever.

11 And I saw a great white throne, and him that sat on it, from whose face the earth and the heaven fled away; and there was found no place for them.

12 And I saw the dead, small and great, stand before God; and the books were opened: and another book was opened, which is the book of life: and the dead were judged out of those things which were written in the books, according to their works.

13 And the sea gave up the dead which were in it; and death and hell delivered up the dead which were in them: and they were judged every man according to their works.

14 And death and hell were cast into the lake of fire. This is the second death.

15 And whosoever was not found written in the book of life was cast into the lake of fire.

Chapter 21

1 And I saw a new heaven and a new earth: for the first heaven and the first earth were passed away; and there was no more sea.

2 And I John saw the holy city, new Jerusalem, coming down from God out of heaven, prepared as a bride adorned for her husband.

3 And I heard a great voice out of heaven saying, Behold, the tabernacle of God is with men, and he will dwell with them, and they shall be his people, and God himself shall be with them, and be their God.

4 And God shall wipe away all tears from their eyes; and there shall be no more death, neither sorrow, nor crying, neither shall there be any more pain: for the former things are passed away.

5 And he that sat upon the throne said, Behold, I make all things new. And he said unto me, Write: for these words are true and faithful.

6 And he said unto me, It is done. I am Alpha and Omega, the beginning and the end. I will give unto him that is athirst of the fountain of the water of life freely.

7 He that overcometh shall inherit all things; and I will be his God, and he shall be my son.

8 But the fearful, and unbelieving, and the abominable, and murderers, and whoremongers, and sorcerers, and idolaters, and all liars, shall have their part in the lake which burneth with fire and brimstone: which is the second death.

9 And there came unto me one of the seven angels which had the seven vials full of the seven last plagues, and talked with me, saying, Come hither, I will show thee the bride, the Lamb's wife.

10 And he carried me away in the spirit to a great and high mountain, and showed me that great city, the holy Jerusalem, descending out of heaven from God,

11 Having the glory of God: and her light was like unto a stone most precious, even like a jasper stone, clear as crystal;

12 And had a wall great and high, and had twelve gates, and at the gates twelve angels, and names written thereon, which are the names of the twelve tribes of the children of Israel:

13 On the east three gates; on the north three gates; on the south three gates; and on the west three gates.

14 And the wall of the city had twelve foundations, and in them the names of the twelve apostles of the Lamb.

15 And he that talked with me had a golden reed to measure the city, and the gates thereof, and the wall thereof.

16 And the city lieth foursquare, and the length is as large as the breadth: and he measured the city with the reed, twelve thousand furlongs. The length and the breadth and the height of it are equal.

17 And he measured the wall thereof, ~~an~~ *a* hundred and forty and four cubits, according to the measure of a man, that is, of the angel.

18 And the building of the wall of it was of jasper: and the city was pure gold, like unto clear glass.

19 And the foundations of the wall of the city were garnished with all manner of precious stones. The first foundation was jasper; the second, sapphire; the third, a chalcedony; the fourth, an emerald;

20 The fifth, sardonyx; the sixth, sardius; the seventh, chrysolyte; the eighth, beryl; the ninth, a topaz; the tenth, a chrysoprasus; the eleventh, a jacinth; the twelfth, an amethyst.

21 And the twelve gates were twelve pearls: every several gate was of one pearl: and the street of the city was pure gold, as it were transparent glass.

22 And I saw no temple therein: for the Lord God Almighty and the Lamb are the temple of it.

23 And the city had no need of the sun, neither of the moon, to shine in it: for the glory of God did lighten it, and the Lamb is the light thereof.

24 And the nations of them which are saved shall walk in the light of it: and the kings of the earth do bring their glory and honour into it.

25 And the gates of it shall not be shut at all by day: for there shall be no night there.

26 And they shall bring the glory and honour of the nations into it.

27 And there shall in no wise enter into it any thing that defileth, neither whatsoever worketh abomination, or maketh a lie: but they which are written in the Lamb's book of life.

Chapter 22

1 And he showed me a pure river of water of life, clear as crystal, proceeding out of the throne of God and of the Lamb.

2 In the midst of the street of it, and on either side of the river, was there the tree of life, which bare twelve manner of fruits, and yielded her fruit every month: and the leaves of the tree were for the healing of the nations.

3 And there shall be no more curse: but the throne of God and of the Lamb shall be in it; and his servants shall serve him:

4 And they shall see his face; and his name shall be in their foreheads.

5 And there shall be no night there; and they need no candle, neither light of the sun; for the Lord God giveth them light: and they shall reign for ever and ever.

6 And he said unto me, These sayings are faithful and true: and the Lord God of the holy prophets sent his angel to show unto his servants the things which must shortly be done.

7 Behold, I come quickly: blessed is he that keepeth the sayings of the prophecy of this book.

8 And I John saw these things, and heard them. And when I had heard and seen, I fell down to worship before the feet of the angel which showed me these things.

9 Then saith he unto me, See *that* thou do it not: for I am thy fellowservant, and of thy brethren the prophets, and of them which keep the sayings of this book: worship God.

10 And he saith unto me, Seal not the sayings of the prophecy of this book: for the time is at hand.

11 He that is unjust, let him be unjust still: and he which is filthy, let him be filthy still: and he that is righteous, let him be righteous still: and he that is holy, let him be holy still.

12 And, behold, I come quickly; and my reward is with me, to give every man according as his work shall be.

13 I am Alpha and Omega, the beginning and the end, the first and the last.

14 Blessed are they that do his commandments, that they may have right to the tree of life, and may enter in through the gates into the city.

15 For without are dogs, and sorcerers, and whoremongers, and murderers, and idolaters, and whosoever loveth and maketh a lie.

16 I Jesus have sent mine angel to testify unto you these things in the churches. I am the root and the offspring of David, and the bright and morning star.

17 And the Spirit and the bride say, Come. And let him that heareth say, Come. And let him that is athirst come. And whosoever will, let him take the water of life freely.

18 For I testify unto every man that heareth the words of the prophecy of this book, If any man shall add unto these things, God shall add unto him the plagues that are written in this book:

19 And if any man shall take away from the words of the book of this prophecy, God shall take away his part out of the book of life, and out of the holy city, and from the things which are written in this book.

20 He which testifieth these things saith, Surely I come quickly. Amen. Even so, come, Lord Jesus.

21 The grace of our Lord Jesus Christ be with you all. Amen.

CHRONOLOGY
of
Events

Acts to Revelation

The following chronology of events provides a useful way to read and study the New Testament. As these book are presented in their normal order in this text, page numbers have been included here for your quick reference.

References: Anderson, 1983; Brown et al., 1968; Reese, 1980

CHAPTER AND VERSE INDEX

MATTHEW

CHAPTER AND VERSE INDEX

MARK

CHAPTER AND VERSE INDEX

LUKE

CHAPTER AND VERSE INDEX

JOHN

BIBLIOGRAPHY

Anderson, Richard Lloyd. (1983). *Understanding Paul.* Salt Lake City, UT: Deseret Book Company.

Baarda, Tjitze. (1983). *Early Transmission of Words of Jesus: Thomas, Tatian, and the Text of the New Testament: A Collection of Studies.* J. Helderman and S. J. Noorda, ed. Amsterdam: VU Boekhandel/Uitgeverij.

Bible. (1920). Inspired Version, translated and corrected by the spirit of revelation/by Joseph Smith, Jr. The Seer. 20th ed. Lamoni, Iowa: Reorganized Church of Jesus Christ of Latter Day Saints.

Broadus, John A. (1920). *A Harmony of the Gospels in the Revised Version.* A. T. Robertson. Rev. ed. New York: George H. Doran Co.

Brown, Raymond E., Fitzmyer, Joseph A., and Murphy E. Roland (Eds.). (1968). *The Jerome Biblical Commentary.* Englewood Cliffs, NJ: Prentice-Hall, Inc.

Bruce, F. F. (1960). *The New Testament Documents: Are they reliable?* Chicago, Illinois: Intervarsity Press.

Church Educational System. (1979). *The Life and Teachings of Jesus and His Apostles (a course manual).* Salt Lake City, UT: The Church of Jesus Christ of Latter-day Saints.

Clark, J. Reuben, Jr. (1968). *Our Lord of The Gospels.* Salt Lake City, UT: Deseret Book Company.

Coleridge, Henry James. (1890). *The Life of our Life: Introduction, Harmony, and Notes.* London: Burns and Oates.

Edvalson, Fredrick M., Jr. & Smith, William B. (1977). *Inspired Version Study Guide - A Key to the Significant Changes.* Provo, UT: 70's Mission Bookstore.

Matthews, Robert J. (1971). "A Review: Edwards, F. Henry, comp. *Joseph Smith's "New Translation" of the Bible." In Courage: A Journal of History, Thought, and Action.* 1(2).

Matthews, Robert J. (1985). *A Plainer Translation: Joseph Smith's Translation of the Bible. A History and Commentary.* Provo, UT: Brigham Young University Press.

Millet, Robert L. (1985). "Joseph Smith's Translation of the Bible: A Historical Overview" in *The Joseph Smith Translation: The Restoration of Plain and Precious Things.* Salt Lake City, UT: Bookcraft, Inc.

Mumford, Thomas M. (1986). *Horizontal Harmony of the Four Gospels in Parallel Columns.* Salt Lake City, UT: Deseret Book Publishing Company.

Reese, Edward & Klassen, Frank R. (1980). *The Reese Chronological Bible: the Authorized edition of the original work.* Minneapolis, MN: Bethany Fellowship.

Robertson, A. T. (1950). *A Harmony of The Gospels for Students of the Life of Christ (Based on the Broadus Harmony in the Revised Version).* New York, NY: Harper & Row, Publishers.

Smith, Israel A. (1985). *The Inspired Version.* Independence, MO: Price Publishing Co.

The Anchor Bible. (1970). Garden City, NY: Doubleday & Co., Inc.

The Church of Jesus Christ of Latter-day Saints. (1981). "Harmony of The Gospels," in the *Bible Dictionary.* Salt Lake City, UT: The Church of Jesus Christ of Latter-day Saints.

The Holy Bible: King James Version. (1979). Salt Lake City, UT: The Church of Jesus Christ of Latter-day Saints.

The New Layman's Parallel Bible. (1981). Grand Rapids, Michigan: Zondervan Bible Publishers.

The Reorganized Church of Jesus Christ of Latter Day Saints. (1970). *Joseph Smith's "New Translation" of The Bible.* Introduction by F. Henry Edwards. Independence, MO: Herald Publishing House.

ABOUT THE COMPILERS

Steven J. Hite is an Assistant Professor of Educational Leadership at Brigham Young University. He completed his BS and MS degrees at BYU and moved with his wife and young family to Boston where he received his Doctorate in Education from Harvard University. As an Area Coordinator for the LDS Church for 5 years, he taught Institute courses at Harvard, MIT, Boston University, and Wellesley College, while administering the Seminary program in Massachusetts, Connecticut, and Rhode Island. Steve was elected President of the 23-denomination Harvard United Ministry and twice served as the Chair of the Harvard/Radcliffe Martin Luther King, Jr. Memorial Service.

Julie M. Hite is a doctoral candidate in Strategic Management at the University of Utah Eccles School of Business. She received her Master of Organizational Behavior degree from the Brigham Young University Marriott School of Management. She also received her BS degree from Brigham Young University, Magna Cum Laude. During eight years in Boston, Julie successfully developed and managed her own computer services and consultation business with clients throughout New England. The mother of four daughters and one son, she has learned (with focus and determination) to successfully balance the requirements of being a mindful individual, caring spouse, and dedicated mother in our complex, modern world.